Laos

Northern Laos p66

Luang Prabang & Around p34

Vientiane & Around p134

Central Laos p184

Southern Laos p212

THIS EDITION WRITTEN AND RESEARCHED BY

Nick Ray, Greg Bloom, Richard Water

PLAN YOUR TRIP

VIENTIANE P135

MARGIE POLITZER/GETTY IMAGES ©

VANG VIENG P172

ANIA BLAZEJEWSKA/GETTY IMAGES ©

ON THE ROAD

Contents

UNDERSTAND

SURVIVAL GUIDE

OTTO STADLER/GETTY IMAGES ©

LUANG PRABANG P35

Welcome to Laos

Laos, long a forgotten backwater, combines some of the best elements of Southeast Asia in one bite-sized destination.

Land of a Million Elephants

In ancient times, Laos was poetically known as the 'land of a million elephants', but cynical Vietnam War correspondents renamed it the 'land of a million irrelevants'. But four decades after the war, Laos is becoming an increasingly relevant destination for the intrepid traveller. Pockets of pristine environment, a kaleidoscope of diverse cultures and quite possibly the most chilled-out people on earth have earned Laos cult status. Imagine a country where your pulse relaxes, smiles are genuine and the locals are still curious about you.

Refreshingly Simple

Laos still retains much of the tradition that has disappeared in a frenzy of bulldozers and reality TV elsewhere in the region. Village life is refreshingly simple, and even in Vientiane it's hard to believe this sort of languid riverfront life exists in a capital city. Magical Luang Prabang bears witness to hundreds of saffron-robed monks gliding through the streets in search of alms; it's one of the region's iconic images. For many visitors, Luang Prabang is Laos, but more intrepid travellers will discover a country untainted by mass tourism.

Fairytale Landscapes

Away from the cities, it's easy to make a quick detour off the beaten track and end up in a fairytale landscape with jagged limestone cliffs, brooding jungle and the snaking Mekong River as a backdrop. Community-based trekking combines these spectacular natural attractions with the chance to experience the 'real Laos' with a village homestay. The Lao people are wonderfully welcoming hosts and there is no better way to get to know their culture than by sharing their lives.

Something for Everyone

Laos deserves all the accolades it receives. Adrenalin junkies can lose themselves in underground river caves, white-water rapids or jungle ziplines. Wildlife nuts can trek through some of Southeast Asia's most pristine forests, still home to rare creatures. Foodies can experiment with the kaleidoscope of flavours that is Lao cuisine. From thrillseeker to gourmand, every type of traveller finds what they're looking for in Laos, one of the most authentic destinations in Asia.

Why I Love Laos

By Nick Ray, Author

I first came to Laos as a backpacker in 1995, not long after it cautiously opened up to the world, and I quickly succumbed to its natural charms, not to mention ice-cold Beerlao on the banks of the Mekong. Fast forward nearly two decades and innumerable adventures, and Laos still delivers surprises. The Vieng Xai Caves had been a long time coming for this particular history buff and didn't disappoint. Further west, the new Elephant Conservation Center near Sainyabuli is a fantastic experience for a fantastic cause. And, like a vintage wine, Luang Prabang just keeps getting better. From a quiet backwater to today's incarnation, Laos is one of the most beguiling destinations in all of Asia.

For more about our authors, see page 344

Above: Elephant camp (p64), Luang Prabang

Laos

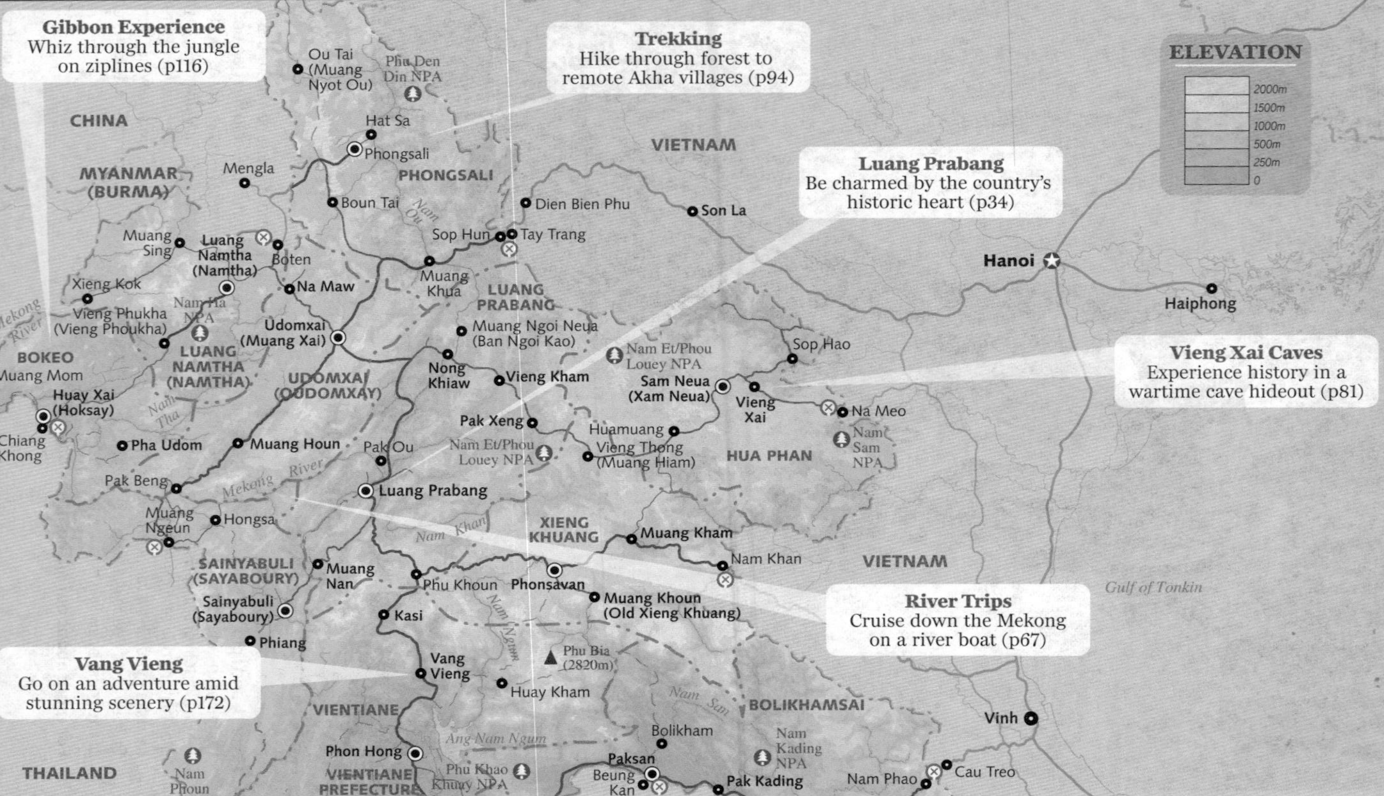

0 100 km
0 60 miles
Gibbon Experience
Whiz through the jungle on ziplines (p116)
Trekking
Hike through forest to remote Akha villages (p94)
Luang Prabang
Be charmed by the country's historic heart (p34)
Vieng Xai Caves
Experience history in a wartime cave hideout (p81)
River Trips
Cruise down the Mekong on a river boat (p67)
Vang Vieng
Go on an adventure amid stunning scenery (p172)
ELEVATION
2000m
1500m
1000m
500m
250m
0
CHINA
MYANMAR (BURMA)
VIETNAM
THAILAND
BOKEO
LUANG NAMTHA (NAMTHA)
PHONGSALI
UDOMXAI (OUDOMXAY)
LUANG PRABANG
HUA PHAN
XIENG KHUANG
SAINYABULI (SAYABOURY)
VIENTIANE
VIENTIANE PREFECTURE
BOLIKHAMSAI
Ou Tai (Muang Nyot Ou)
Phu Den Din NPA
Hat Sa
Phongsali
Mengla
Boun Tai
Nam Ou
Dien Bien Phu
Son La
Sop Hun
Tay Trang
Muang Sing
Luang Namtha (Namtha)
Boten
Na Maw
Muang Khua
Xieng Kok
Vieng Phukha (Vieng Phoukha)
Nam Ha NPA
Mekong River
Udomxai (Muang Xai)
Muang Ngoi Neua (Ban Ngoi Kao)
Nong Khiaw
Vieng Kham
Nam Et/Phou Louey NPA
Sam Neua (Xam Neua)
Sop Hao
Vieng Xai
Na Meo
Nam Sam NPA
Muang Mom
Huay Xai (Hoksay)
Chiang Khong
Nam Tha
Pha Udom
Muang Houn
Pak Ou
Pak Xeng
Huamuang
Vieng Thong (Muang Hiam)
Pak Beng
Luang Prabang
Muang Ngeun
Hongsa
Nam Khan
Muang Kham
Hanoi
Haiphong
Muang Nan
Phu Khoun
Phonsavan
Muang Khoun (Old Xieng Khuang)
Gulf of Tonkin
Sainyabuli (Sayaboury)
Kasi
Phiang
Vang Vieng
Nam Ngum
Phu Bia (2820m)
Huay Kham
Nam Sam
Bolikham
Nam Kading NPA
Vinh
Ang Nam Ngum
Phon Hong
Paksan
Beung Kan
Pak Kading
Nam Phao
Cau Treo
Phu Khao Khuay NPA
Nam Phoun

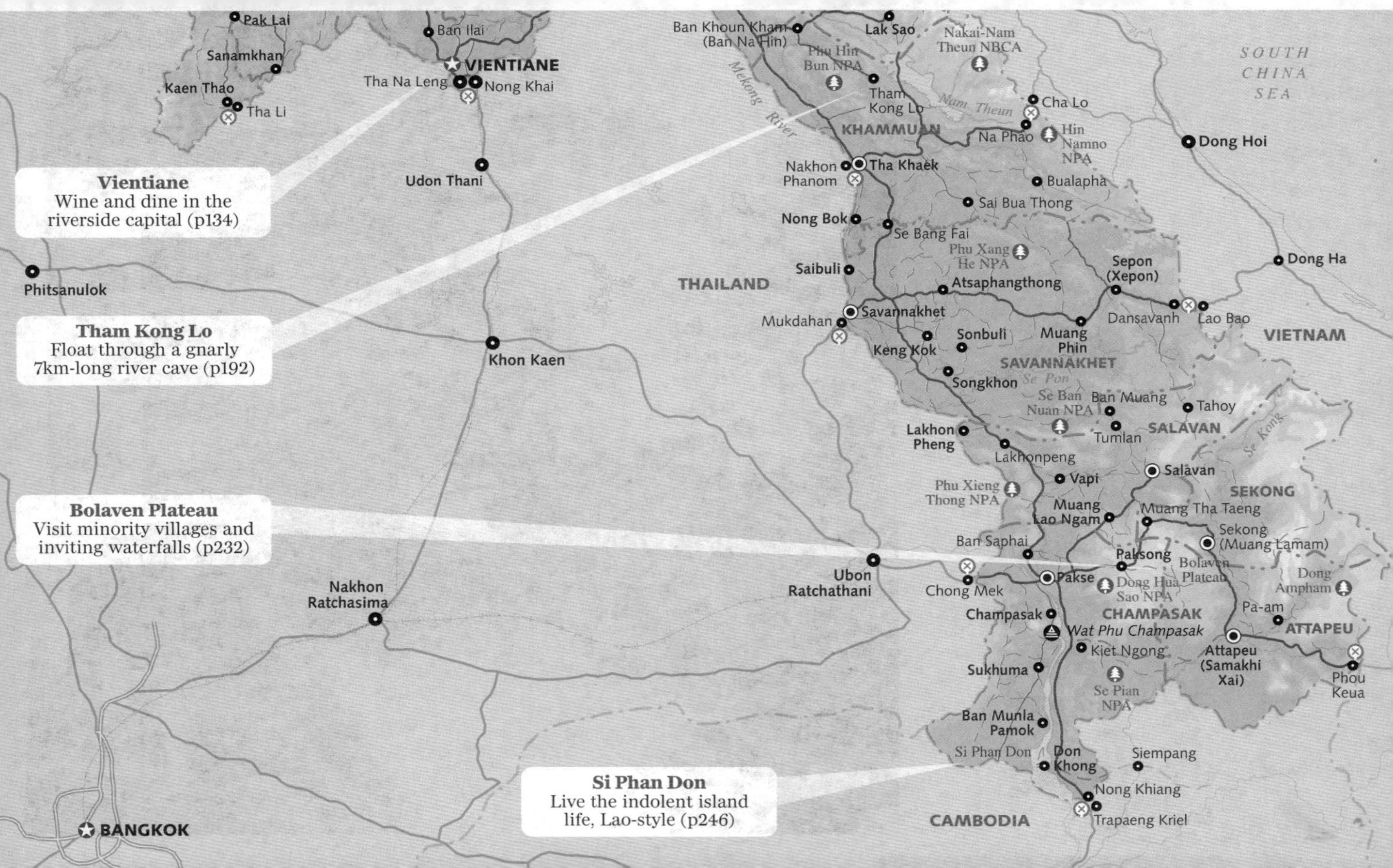
Vientiane
Wine and dine in the riverside capital (p134)
Tham Kong Lo
Float through a gnarly 7km-long river cave (p192)
Bolaven Plateau
Visit minority villages and inviting waterfalls (p232)
Si Phan Don
Live the indolent island life, Lao-style (p246)
Pak Lai
Sanamkhan
Kaen Thao
Tha Li
Ban Ilai
VIENTIANE
Tha Na Leng
Nong Khai
Udon Thani
Phitsanulok
Khon Kaen
Nakhon Ratchasima
BANGKOK
THAILAND
Ban Khoun Kham (Ban Na Hin)
Lak Sao
Nakai-Nam Theun NBCA
Phu Hin Bun NPA
Tham Kong Lo
Mekong River
Nam Theun
Cha Lo
Na Phao
Hin Namno NPA
KHAMMUAN
SOUTH CHINA SEA
Dong Hoi
Nakhon Phanom
Tha Khaek
Bualapha
Sai Bua Thong
Nong Bok
Se Bang Fai
Phu Xang He NPA
Saibuli
Atsaphangthong
Sepon (Xepon)
Dong Ha
Mukdahan
Savannakhet
Dansavanh
Lao Bao
VIETNAM
Keng Kok
Sonbuli
Muang Phin
SAVANNAKHET
Songkhon
Se Pon
Se Ban Nuan NPA
Ban Muang
Tahoy
Lakhon Pheng
Tumlan
SALAVAN
Se Kong
Lakhonpeng
Vapi
Salavan
Phu Xieng Thong NPA
SEKONG
Muang Lao Ngam
Muang Tha Taeng
Ban Saphai
Sekong (Muang Lamam)
Paksong
Bolaven Plateau
Ubon Ratchathani
Chong Mek
Pakse
Dong Hua Sao NPA
Dong Ampham
CHAMPASAK
Champasak
Wat Phu Champasak
Pa-am
ATTAPEU
Kiet Ngong
Attapeu (Samakhi Xai)
Sukhuma
Se Pian NPA
Phou Keua
Ban Munla Pamok
Si Phan Don
Don Khong
Siempang
Nong Khiang
CAMBODIA
Trapaeng Kriel

Laos' Top 10

1

Luang Prabang

1 Hemmed in by the Mekong and Khan rivers, this timeless city (p34) of temples is a travel editor's dream: rich in royal history, saffron-clad monks, stunning river views, world-class French cuisine and the best boutique accommodation in Southeast Asia. Hire a bike and explore the tropical peninsula's backstreets, take a cooking class, go on an elephant trek or just ease back with a restful massage at one of the many affordable spas. Prepare to adjust your timetable and stay a little longer than planned.

Below left: Wat Pa Phai (p41), Luang Prabang

Si Phan Don

2 Legends don't happen by accident. Laos' hammock-flopping mecca (p246) has been catering to weary travellers for years. While these tropical islands bounded by the waters of the Mekong are best-known as a happy haven for catatonic sun worshippers, more active souls are also spoilt for choice. Between tubing and cycling through paddy fields, grab a kayak or fish with the locals, then round off your day with a sunset boat trip to see the rare Irrawaddy dolphin.

Below Right: Don Det (p250)

OTTO STADLER/GETTY IMAGES ©

2

KIMBERLEY COOLE/GETTY IMAGES ©

The Gibbon Experience

3 Whiz hundreds of feet above the forest floor attached to a zipline (p116). These brilliantly engineered cables – some more than 500m long – span forest valleys in the lush Bokeo Nature Reserve (habitat of the black-crested gibbon and Asiatic tiger). Your money goes toward protecting the eponymous endangered primate, and your guides are former poachers turned rangers. Zip into and bed down in vertiginously high treehouses by night, listening to the call of the wild. This is Laos' premier wildlife and adrenalin high.

Vang Vieng

4 The riverine jewel in Laos' karst country, Vang Vieng (p172) sits under soaring cliffs beside the flowing Nam Song and has an easy, outdoorsy vibe. Since the party crowd moved on in 2012, tranquility reigns again with more family-oriented visitors dropping in to soak up such well-organised activities as hot-air ballooning, trekking, caving and climbing. And don't forget the main draw: tubing. As budget guesthouses and fast-food joints wind down, smarter boutique hotels and delicious restaurants are blossoming in their wake. There's never been a better time to visit.

3

AARON GEDDES PHOTOGRAPHY/GETTY IMAGES ©

4

COLIN BRYNN/GETTY IMAGES ©

5

River Trips

5 River trips (p67) are a major feature of travel through Laos. One of the most popular connects Luang Prabang and Huay Xai, the gateway to the Golden Triangle, via Pak Beng. From local boats to luxury cruises, there are options to suit every budget, includes floating through sleepy Si Phan Don in the far south. Beyond the Mekong, many important feeder rivers, such as the Nam Ou and Nam Tha, connect places as diverse as Nong Khiaw and Hat Sa (for Phongsali).

Left: River taxi, Nam Tha (p109)

6

GLEN ALLISON/GETTY IMAGES ©

Trekking & Homestays

6 Laos is famous for its wide range of community-based treks, many of which include a traditional homestay for a night or more. Trekking is possible all over the country, but northern Laos (p94) is one of the most popular areas. Trekking around Phongsali is considered some of the most authentic in Laos and involves the chance to stay with the colourful Akha people. Luang Namtha is the most accessible base for ecotreks in the Nam Ha NPA, one of the best known trekking spots in the Mekong region.

Left: Akha hill-tribe woman

Vieng Xai Caves

7 This is history writ large in stone. An area of outstanding natural beauty, Vieng Xai (p81) was home to the Pathet Lao communist leadership during the US bombing campaign of 1964–73. Beyond the breathtaking beauty of the natural caves, it is the superb audio tour that really brings the experience to life. When the bombers buzz overhead to a soundtrack of Jimi Hendrix, you'll be ducking for cover in the Red Prince's lush garden.

7

KIMBERLEY COOLE/GETTY IMAGES ©

9

AUSTIN BUSH/GETTY IMAGES ©

MATTHEW WAKEM/GETTY IMAGES ©

Bolaven Plateau

8 The air is a little cooler, the waterfalls a little taller and the coffee a little richer on this forest-clad protuberance (p232) rising high above the floodplains of the Mekong. Write your own motorcycle diary along the lonely highways of the plateau, continuing on into the remote southeastern provinces abutting Vietnam. Or chill out for a few days in Tat Lo, a waterfall-studded backpacker hideaway on the plateau's escarpment. Looking for adventure? Trek to distant minority villages or get nose-to-nose with the jungle on ziplines in Dong Hua Sao NPA.

Top left: Tat Lo waterfall (p235)

Tham Kong Lo

9 Imagine your deepest nightmare: the snaggle-toothed mouth of a river cave beneath a towering limestone mountain, the boatman in his rickety longtail taking you into the heart of darkness. Puttering beneath the cathedral-high ceiling of stalactites in this extraordinary 7.5km underworld (p192) in remote Khammuan Province is an awesome experience. You'll be very glad to see the light at the other end!

Vientiane

10 Could this low-slung, Mekong-bound belle (p135) be Southeast Asia's most languid capital? The cracked streets are bordered by tamarind trees and the narrow alleys choke on French villas, Chinese shophouses and glittering wats. The city brews a heady mix of street vendors, monks, fine Gallic cuisine, boutique hotels and a healthy edge that sees visitors taking spas and turning their time to yoga and cycling. It may not have Luang Prabang's good looks, but Vientiane has a vibrant, friendly charm all of its own.

Above: Lao massage, Papaya Spa (p147)

Need to Know

For more information, see Survival Guide (p303)

Currency
Lao kip (K)

Language
Lao

Visas
Tourist visas are readily available at airports and most land borders for between US$30 and US$42 for one month.

Money
ATMs are now widely available in Laos. Credit cards are accepted by some hotels in larger cities.

Mobile Phones
Roaming is possible in Laos but is generally expensive. Local SIM cards and unlocked mobile phones are readily available.

Time
Indochina Time (GMT/UTC plus seven hours)

When to Go

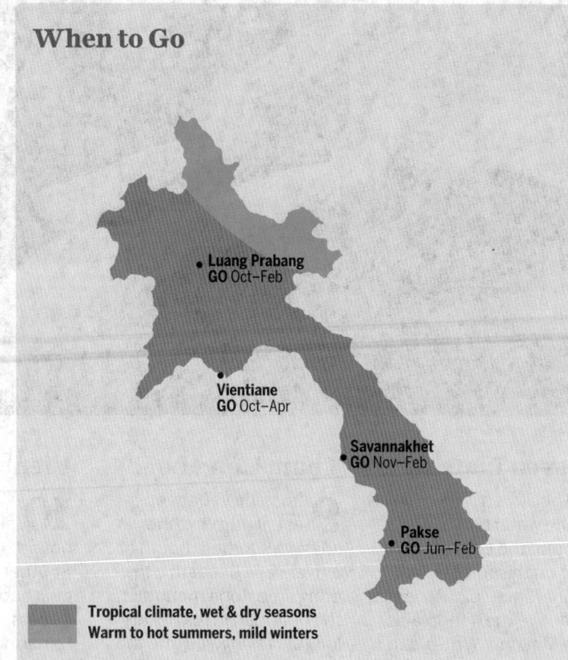

High Season
(Nov–Mar)

- Pleasant temperatures in much of Laos, although cold in the mountains.
- The best all-round time to visit.
- Book accommodation in advance during the peak Christmas and New Year period.

Shoulder Season
(Jul & Aug)

- Wet in most parts of Laos with high humidity, but the landscapes are emerald green.
- Popular time for European tourists to visit from Italy or Spain, plus backpacking students with a long summer break.

Low Season
(Apr–Jun, Sep & Oct)

- April and May brings the hot season to Laos when the thermostat hits 40°C and visitors wilt.
- September and October can be very wet, but there are some incredible cloud formations to accompany the deluge.

Useful Websites

Lonely Planet (www.lonelyplanet.com/laos) Destination information, hotel bookings, traveller forum and more.

Ecotourism Laos (www.ecotourismlaos.com) Information about the Lao environs, focusing on trekking and other ecotourism activities. Recommended.

Lao Bumpkin (www.laobumpkin.blogspot.com) 'Travel, food and other things connected to Laos and the Lao people, or maybe not.'

lao*miao* (www.laomeow.blogspot.com) Up-to-date transportation details, mostly regarding northern Laos.

Lao News Agency (www.kplnet.net) Best source of current news on Laos.

Lao National Tourism Administration (www.tourismlaos.org) Mostly up-to-date travel information from the government. Also has accurate exchange rates.

Important Numbers

To dial listings from outside Laos, dial your international access code, the country code then the number (minus '0', which is used when dialling domestically).

Laos' country code	☎856
International access code	☎00
Ambulance	☎195
Fire	☎190
Police	☎191

Exchange Rates

Prices are quoted in Lao kip (K) or US$, unless otherwise stated. For current exchange rates see www.xe.com.

Australia	A$1	7125K
Canada	C$1	7420K
Euro zone	€1	10,350K
Japan	¥100	7800K
Thailand	10B	2450K
UK	UK£1	12,350K
US	US$1	7650K
Vietnam	10,000d	3600K

Daily Costs

Budget: Less than US$50

➡ Cheap guesthouse room: US$3–10

➡ Local meals and street eats: US$1–2

➡ Local buses: US$2–3 per 100km

Midrange: US$50–US$150

➡ Air-con hotel room: US$15–50

➡ Decent local restaurant meal: US$5–10

➡ Local tour guide per day: US$25

Top End: More than US$150

➡ Boutique hotel or resort: US$50–500

➡ Gastronomic meal with drinks: US$15–50

➡ 4WD rental per day: US$60–120

Opening Hours

Government offices 8am–noon & 1–5pm Monday to Friday

Shops 9am–6pm

Restaurants 10am–10pm

Noodle Shops 7am–1pm

Bars and Clubs 5–11.30pm (later in Vientiane)

Arriving in Laos

Wattay International Airport (Vientiane; p314) Buses and jumbos run to and from the airport. Taxis cost a flat fare of US$10.

Luang Prabang International Airport (p314) Taxis to and from the airport cost a standardised 50,000K.

Savannakhet International Airport (p314) Jumbos cost 70,000K from the airport.

Pakse International Airport (p314) A *săhm-lór* or tuk-tuk to the airport will cost about 50,000K.

Getting Around

Transport in Laos is very good value compared with the developed world, but journeys can take a lot longer than distances on a map might suggest, in part due to long and winding roads and in part due to unexpected delays along the way.

Airplane Laos has an extensive domestic flight network and this can save considerable time on a short visit. The capital Vientiane is the main hub.

Boat Like arteries, rivers are the lifeblood of Laos, and that makes boat journeys an important and enjoyable element of the transport network.

Bus Laos has some smart new buses operating on major routes out of Vientiane, but venture into remote areas and the vehicles are as old as the hills.

Car For those with a more flexible budget, a rented car with driver is the smoothest way to cover a lot of ground in a limited amount of time.

For much more on **getting around**, see p319

If You Like...

Outdoor Activities

For such a laid-back kind of country, Laos is earning a well-deserved reputation as a centre for adrenalin activities.

Bolaven Plateau Impressive waterfalls, elephant treks and the Treetop Explorer zipline adventure (p233).

Luang Namtha Gateway to northwest adventures, Luang Namtha offers trekking, cycling, kayaking and, further down the jungle trail, the Gibbon Experience (p104).

Vang Vieng This area has blossomed as an adventure playground for river tubing, kayaking, caving, climbing and cycling (p172).

Wining & Dining

Lao cuisine may not be as celebrated as that of its neighbours, but there are some superb specialities on offer. Add to this a Gallic gastronomic gene in places like Luang Prabang and Vientiane, and Laos emerges as a diner's delight.

Vientiane Not just the capital, but the culinary capital of the country, Vientiane has Laotian home cooking, Gallic gastronomy and flavours as diverse as Indian and Italian (p154).

Luang Prabang Choose the Mekong side for sunsets or the Nam Khan side for sophisticated set menus (p55).

Luang Namtha Luang Namtha has several excellent restaurants that specialise in interesting ethnic minority cuisine (p104).

River Trips

With the mother Mekong defining the country's contours, it is no surprise that river trips are a major feature. But this mother has many offspring coursing through the country and some of these smaller rivers offer spectacular scenery.

Huay Xai to Luang Prabang One of most accessible river trips in Laos, with an overnight stop at the dramatically situated town of Pak Beng (p118).

Si Phan Don With a name that means 4000 Islands, it's not surprising that boat trips feature strongly in this beautiful southern stretch of the Mekong in Laos (p246).

Tham Kong Lo A river trip with a difference – passing through a 7km cave that is straight out of Greek mythology (p192).

Old Temples

Laos has some of the most beautiful wats in the region, particularly those dotted about the ancient royal capital of Luang Prabang.

Luang Prabang The royal city is home to more than 30 gilded wats, including the soaring roofs of Wat Xieng Thong. Hundreds of monks snake through the streets each morning in search of alms (p37).

Wat Phu Champasak The ancient Khmers once held sway over much of the Mekong region and Wat Phu was one of their hilltop temples (p228).

Vientiane The Lao capital is home to some fine temples, including Pha That Luang, the golden stupa that is the symbol of a nation, and Wat Sisaket, which houses thousands of revered Buddha images (p140).

IF YOU LIKE... ANIMALS

The Gibbon Experience in northern Laos is the premier ecotourism adventure in Southeast Asia. (p116)

JONES/SHIMLOCK-SECRET SEA VISIONS/GETTY IMAGES ©

MARK WATSON/HIGHLUX/GETTY IMAGES ©

(Above) Buddhist temple, Vientiane

(Below) Cyclist, Vang Vieng

Off The Beaten Track

Head further off the trail into some remote corners of the country, exploring extensive protected areas, cave systems and the roads less travelled.

Vieng Xai Caves These underground caves were the Pathet Lao's base during the US bombing campaign. (p81)

Phongsali Province The remote far north is the location for some of the most authentic hill-tribe village treks in the country (p90).

Khammuan Province This rugged central province is peppered with karst limestone peaks and rewards two-wheeled adventurers prepared to head off-piste (p185).

Memorable Markets

Markets in Laos are a step back in time to an earthier Asia, before the advent of the super-sized shopping malls that characterise the region. Dig around for hill-tribe textiles, seek out unusual fruits or simply engage with the friendly stallholders.

Luang Prabang Night markets, day markets, they come in every flavour here, including the night-time handicraft market on main street and an affordable food market. (p60)

Vientiane The Talat Sao (Morning Market) is more like a department store or shopping centre in parts, but it is still one of the best places in Laos to shop for handicrafts and textiles. (p161)

Muang Sing The new market is a blaze of colour and activity in the early morning as ethnic minorities hit the town to trade. (p110)

Month by Month

TOP EVENTS

Pi Mai, April

Makha Busa, February

Bun Bang Fai, May

Bun Awk Phansa, October or November

Bun Nam, October or November

January

Peak season in much of Laos. It's a pleasantly chilled time to be in the main centres and downright cold at higher altitude.

International New Year

A public holiday in sync with embassy and aid workers resident in Laos.

Bun Khun Khao

The annual harvest festival in mid-January sees villagers perform ceremonies offering thanks to the land spirits for their crops.

February

Chinese and Vietnamese New Year often fall in this month which can see some city celebrations in Pakse and Savannakhet.

Makha Busa

Also known as Magha Puja or Bun Khao Chi, this full-moon festival commemorates a speech given by the Buddha to 1250 enlightened monks. Chanting and offerings mark the festival, and celebrations are most fervent in Vientiane and at Wat Phu. (p229)

Vietnamese Tet & Chinese New Year

Celebrated in Vientiane, Pakse and Savannakhet with parties, fireworks and visits to Vietnamese and Chinese temples. Chinese- and Vietnamese-run businesses usually close for several days.

March

Things are starting to warm up and this can be a good time to step up to the higher altitudes of Xieng Khuang and Phongsali.

Bun Pha Wet

This is a temple-centred festival in which the *Jataka* (birth tale) of Prince Vessantara, the Buddha's penultimate life, is recited. This is also a favoured time for Lao males to be ordained into the monkhood.

April

April is the hottest month of the year when the thermometer hits 40°C.

Pi Mai

Lao new year is the most important holiday of the year. Houses are cleaned, people put on new clothes and Buddha images are washed with lustral water. Locals douse one another, and sometimes random tourists, with water, which is an appropriate activity as April is usually the hottest month of the year. This festival is particularly memorable in Luang Prabang, where it includes elephant processions and lots of traditional costuming. There are public holidays on 14, 15 and 16 April, and the vast majority of shops and restaurants are closed. (p50)

May

Events go off with a bang this month, as rockets are fired into the sky. 'Green' (low) season kicks in and prices drop accordingly.

Visakha Busa

Visakha Busa (also known as Visakha Puja) falls on the 15th day of the sixth lunar month, which is considered the day of the Buddha's birth, enlightenment and *parinibbana* (passing away). Activities are centred on the wat, with beautiful candlelit processions by night.

Bun Bang Fai

The Rocket Festival is a pre-Buddhist rain ceremony now celebrated alongside Visakha Busa in Laos and northeastern Thailand. It can be one of the wildest festivals in the country, with music, dance and folk theatre, processions and merrymaking, all culminating in the firing of bamboo rockets. The rockets are supposed to prompt the heavens to initiate the rainy season and bring water to the rice fields.

July

The wet season is winding up with some heavy rains, but it only pours for a short time each day, making this a lush time to explore.

Bun Khao Phansa

Also known as Khao Watsa, this full-moon festival is the beginning of the traditional three-month 'rains retreat', during which Buddhist monks are expected to base themselves in a single monastery. This is also the traditional time of year for men to enter the monkhood temporarily, hence many ordinations take place.

August

Summer holidays in Europe see a mini peak during the off season, which brings French, Italian and Spanish tourists, as well as university students, to the country.

Haw Khao Padap Din

This sombre full-moon festival sees the living pay respect to the dead. Many cremations take place – bones being exhumed for the purpose – and gifts are presented to the Buddhist order (Sangha) so monks will chant on behalf of the deceased.

October

It is all about river action this month. Choose between racing dragon boats in the capital or floating candles across the country.

Bun Awk Phansa

At the end of the three-month rains retreat, monks can leave the monasteries to travel and are presented with robes and alms bowls. The eve of Awk Phansa (Ok Watsa) is celebrated with parties and, near any river, with the release of small banana-leaf boats carrying candles and incense in a ceremony called Van Loi Heua Fai, similar to Loy Krathong in Thailand.

Bun Nam

In many river towns, including Vientiane and Luang Prabang, boat races are held the day after Awk Phansa. In smaller towns the races are often postponed until National Day (2 December) so residents aren't saddled with two costly festivals in two months. Also called Bun Suang Heua. (p148)

November

Peak season begins in earnest and accommodation prices rise once more.

Bun Pha That Luang

The That Luang Festival, centred around Pha That Luang in Vientiane, lasts a week and includes fireworks, music and drinking across the capital. Early on the first morning hundreds of monks receive alms and floral offerings. The festival ends with a fantastic candlelit procession circling That Luang. (p148)

December

Christmas may not be a big Lao festival, but it certainly sees a lot of foreigners arrive in country. Book ahead and be prepared to pay top dollar.

Lao National Day

This public holiday on 2 December celebrates the 1975 victory over the monarchy with parades and speeches. Lao national and Communist hammer-and-sickle flags are flown all over the country.

☆ Luang Prabang Film Festival

This festival in early December sees more than a week of free screenings at several venues around town. The focus is on the blossoming work of Southeast Asian production houses and all films have English subtitles. (www.lpfilmfest.org)

ALDO PAVAN/GETTY IMAGES ©

Plan Your Trip
Itineraries

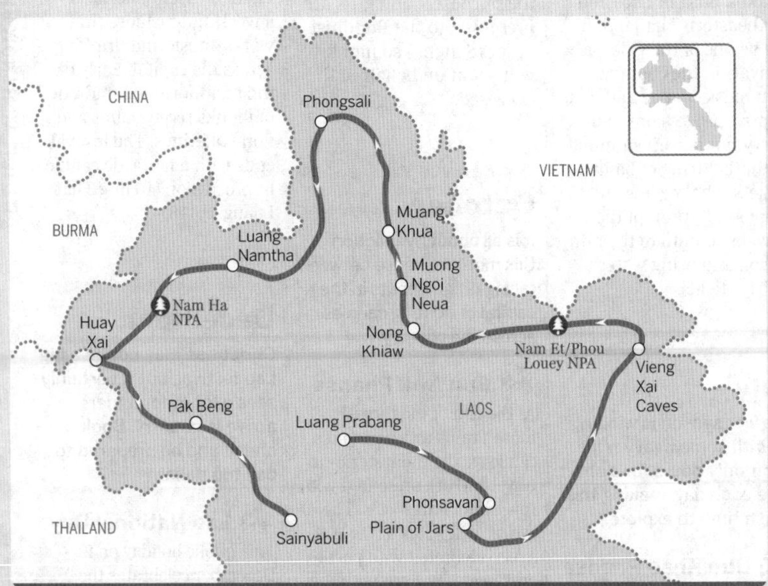

Hit the North

Northern Laos is one of the most popular regions of the country for adrenalin and adventure activities, coupled with an authentic dose of ethnic minority lifestyles. Right at the heart of the region lies Luang Prabang, the perfect place to start or finish a road trip through the remote north.

Lovely **Luang Prabang** is a destination in itself. Spend your time exploring the old town and its myriad temples, traditional buildings and galleries, cafes and shops.

Head southeast from Luang Prabang to **Phonsavan**, gateway to the **Plain of Jars** and its mysterious vessels, one of the most popular destinations in Laos. It is then time to leave the tourist trail and head to the **Vieng Xai Caves**. The setting is spectacular amid the karst caves and the historic audio tour is one of the most compelling experiences in Laos.

Swinging west, it is possible to try a tiger trek in the remote protected area of **Nam Et/Phou Louey NPA**, although a tiger sighting is unlikely. Continue to **Nong Khiaw**, a beautiful village on the banks of

Muang Khua, Phongsali Province (p90)

the Nam Ou (Ou River) with striking limestone crags looming all around. This is the embarkation point for an adventurous boat trip to Phongsali Province via the small villages of **Muong Ngoi Neua** and **Muang Khua**. **Phongsali** is considered the most authentic trekking destination in Laos and it is possible to experience homestays with Akha villagers.

Head on to **Luang Namtha**, a friendly base for some northwesterly adventures. Trek into the **Nam Ha NPA** or try a cycling or kayaking trip in the countryside beyond.

From Luang Namtha head down to **Huay Xai**, a Mekong River border town and gateway to the Golden Triangle. If time is tight, bail out here, but it is better to continue the loop back to Luang Prabang by river. The two-day boat trip from Huay Xai to Luang Prabang via **Pak Beng** is one of the most accessible river trips in the country.

Or take just a one-day boat trip to Pak Beng and then leave the river behind to head to **Sainyabuli** and the superb Elephant Conservation Center on the Nam Tien lake. This can also be visited out of Luang Prabang.

14 DAYS Central and Southern Laos

This classic southern route takes you through the heartland of lowland Lao culture, a world of broad river plains planted with rice and homemade looms shaded by wooden houses on stilts.

Start in **Vientiane**, the country's capital, and soak up the sights, shopping, cuisine and nightlife, as things get quieter from here. Make a side trip to the backpacker mecca of **Vang Vieng**, surrounded by craggy, cave-studded limestone peaks.

Head south to **Tha Khaek**, the archetypal sleepy Mekong riverside town, and go east on Rte 12 to explore the caves of the Khammuan Limestone area or take **the Loop** all the way around, stopping at the incredible cave of **Tham Kong Lo**.

Continue south to **Savannakhet** for a taste of how Vientiane looked before it received a makeover from the Lao PDR government and international aid money.

Roll on southward to **Pakse**, gateway to the southernmost province of Champasak. **Champasak** town is a more relaxed alternative to Pakse and is the base for seeing Laos' most important archaeological site, Wat Phu Champasak, an Angkor-style temple ruin spread across the slopes of sacred Phu Pasak.

A rewarding side trip takes you up onto the **Bolaven Plateau** and to Laos' most impressive waterfall at Tat Fan. This is also the place to try the impressive Treetop Explorer experience, a jungle zipline adventure that is the south's answer to the Gibbon Experience. At the coffee capital of **Paksong**, stop to buy some java before heading to beautiful Tat Lo. This is a great place to hang out and swim in the falls, undertaking gentle treks through local villages or even an elephant ride.

Another option for an elephant ride is from the village of **Kiet Ngong** to the elevated archaeological site of Phu Asa. This is a logical stop on the route south to **Si Phan Don** (Four Thousand Islands), an archipelago of idyllic river islands where the farming and fishing life hasn't changed much for a century or more. Swing in a hammock and relax, before moving on to Cambodia or heading to Thailand via Chong Mek.

TRISTAN SAVATIER/GETTY IMAGES ©

MATTHEW MICAH WRIGHT/GETTY IMAGES ©

Top: Wat Phu Champasak (p227)
Bottom: Mekong River, Si Phan Don (p246)

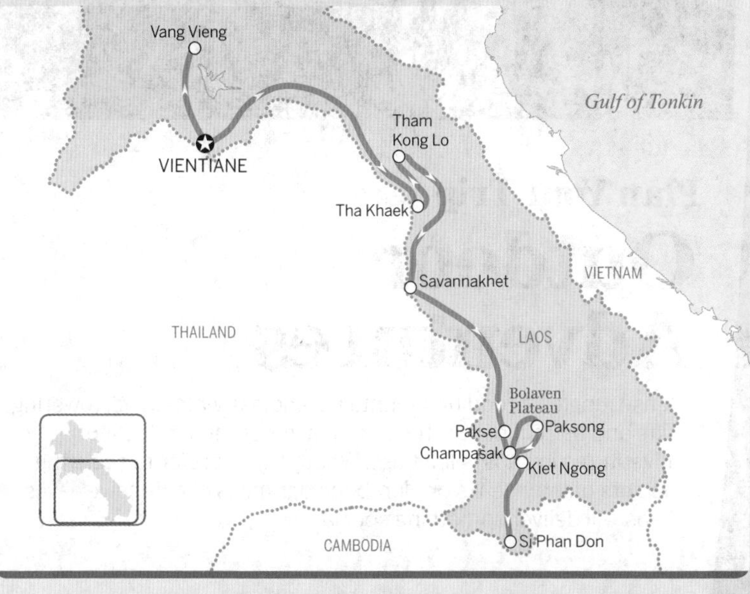
Vang Vieng
Gulf of Tonkin
Tham
Kong Lo
VIENTIANE
Tha Khaek
VIETNAM
Savannakhet
THAILAND
LAOS
Bolaven
Plateau
Pakse
Paksong
Champasak
Kiet Ngong
CAMBODIA
Si Phan Don

Gibbon Experience, Bokeo Nature Reserve (p116)

Plan Your Trip

Outdoor Adventures

Dense jungles, brooding mountains, endless waterways, towering cliffs and hairpin bends: the potential for adrenalin-fuelled adventures in Laos is limitless. Whether you prefer to scale the heights of lofty peaks or plumb the darkness of extensive caves, Laos will deliver something special.

TIM BARKER/GETTY IMAGES ©

When to Go

November to February

This is the cool, dry season and considered the best time for activities like trekking, cycling and motorbiking. Trekking in higher altitude places like Phongsali may be better in spring or autumn, as the winter can be very cold at 1500m.

March to May

Temperatures regularly hit 40°C during the hot season. Common sense dictates that this is a good time to go underground and do some caving or cool off with some kayaking on the Nam Ou.

June to October

The wet season is the time for water-based activities such as rafting or kayaking, as even the smaller rivers have a bit more volume at this time of year.

Boat Trips, Kayaking & Tubing

With the Mekong cutting a swathe through the heart of the country, it is hardly surprising to find that boat trips are a major drawcard here. There are also opportunities to explore small jungled tributaries leading to remote minority villages.

Kayaking has exploded in popularity in Laos in the past few years, particularly around Luang Prabang, Nong Khiaw and Vang Vieng, all popular destinations for a spot of paddling. Kayaking trips start from around US$25 per person and are often combined with cycling.

Tubing down the river has long been a popular activity in Vang Vieng, but the authorities have recently clamped down on riverside bars, rope swings and aerial runways following a spate of alcohol- and drug-related deaths in recent years. Tubing is a lot of fun, but just like driving, it's a safer experience sober.

Where to Go

- **Huay Xai to Luang Prabang** Down the mighty Mekong from the Golden Triangle via Pak Beng to the old royal capital of Laos (p118).
- **Nong Khiaw to Muang Ngoi Neua** A short but very sweet ride passing through a striking landscape of karst limestone (p92).
- **Si Phan Don** A boat is the only way to see the 4000 Islands where the Mekong spreads its girth to almost 13km in the wet season (p246).
- **Tham Kong Lo** The Lao answer to the River Styx – cruise through this other-worldly 7km cave system (p192).

Cycling

Laos is slowly but steadily establishing itself as a cycling destination. For hardcore cyclists, the mountains of northern Laos are the ultimate destination. For those who like a gentler workout, meandering along Mekong villages is memorable, particularly in southern Laos around Si Phan Don.

In most places that see a decent number of tourists, simple single-speed bicycles can be hired for around 20,000K per day. Better mountain bikes will cost from 40,000K to 80,000K per day or US$5 to US$10. Serious tourers should bring their own bicycle. The choice in Laos is fairly limited compared with neighbouring Thailand or Cambodia.

Several tour agencies and guesthouses offer mountain-biking tours, ranging in duration from a few hours to several weeks.

Where to Go

- **Luang Namtha** Cycle through ethnic minority villages (p104).
- **Luang Prabang** Biking is a great way to get around the old town or explore some of the surrounding countryside (p62).

➡ **Udomxai** Three-day cycle challenge to Cham Ong Caves (p98).

➡ **Vientiane** Cycle to surreal Buddha Park (p145).

Motorbiking

For those with a thirst for adventure, motorbike trips into remote areas of Laos are unforgettable. The mobility of two wheels is unrivalled. Motorbikes can traverse trails that even the hardiest 4WD cannot follow. It puts you closer to the countryside – its smells, people and scenery – compared with getting around by car or bus. Just remember to watch the road when the scenery is sublime. Motorbiking is still the mode of transport for many Lao residents, so you'll find repair shops everywhere. If you are not confident riding a motorbike, it's comparatively cheap to hire someone to drive it for you. For those seeking true adventure there is no better way to go.

Where to Go

➡ **The Loop** Tame the back roads of uncharted central Laos in this motorbike circuit out of Tha Khaek (p190).

➡ **Southern Swing** Explore some off-the-beaten-path places in southern Laos with this motorbike adventure up onto the Bolaven Plateau and beyond (p240).

➡ **West Vang Vieng** Delve deep into the limestone karst that peppers the west bank of the Nam Song River with this scenically stunning motorbike ride (p176).

Rock Climbing & Caving

When it comes to organised climbing, Vang Vieng has some of the best climbing in Southeast Asia, along with excellent instructors and safe equipment. Climbing costs in the region start from about US$25 per person for a group of four and rise for more specialised climbs or for instruction.

Real caving of the spelunker variety is not really on offer unless you're mounting a professional expedition. However, there are many extensive cave systems that are open to visitors.

Kayaking on the Mekong, Don Det (p250)

Where to Go

➡ **Vang Vieng** More than 200 rock-climbing routes – many of them bolted – up the limestone cliffs. Most routes are rated between 4a and 8b (p172).

➡ **Vieng Xai Caves** Underground base and wartime capital of the Pathet Lao communists, these caves are set beneath stunning limestone rock formations (p81).

➡ **Tham Kong Lo** This river cave is not for the fainthearted, but offers one of the most memorable underground experiences in Laos (p192).

➡ **Tham Lot Se Bang Fai** The most impressive of Khammuan's cave systems; a river plunges 6.5km through a limestone mountain and can only be explored between January and March (p201).

Trekking

Trekking in Laos is all about exploring the National Protected Areas (NPAs) and visiting the colourful ethnic minority villages – many of which host overnight trekking

Vang Vieng (p172)

ZIPLINING IN LAOS

Ziplining has, well, quite literally taken off in Laos. The Gibbon Experience (p116) in Bokeo Nature Reserve pioneered the use of ziplines to explore the jungle canopy. Visitors hang from a zipline and glide through the forest where the gibbons roam. Stay overnight in treehouses and test drive the Gibbon Spa for a massage in the most memorable of locations.

Ecotourism pioneer Green Discovery (p215) now offers an alternative zipline experience for thrill-seekers in southern Laos. Their Treetop Explorer tour is an exciting network of vertiginous ziplines passing over the semi-evergreen canopy of the south's Dong Hua Sao NPA. Ride so close to a giant waterfall you can taste the spray on your lips. Feel the wind on your face on its longest 450m ride, then flop into bed in your comfortable 20m-high treehouse.

groups. Anything is possible, from half-day hikes to week-long expeditions that include cycling and kayaking. Most treks have both a cultural and an environmental focus, with trekkers sleeping in village homestays and money going directly into some of the poorest communities in the country. There are now a dozen or more areas you can choose from. Less strenuous walks include jungle hikes to pristine waterfalls and village walks in remote areas. The scenery features plunging highland valleys, tiers of rice paddies and soaring limestone mountain,s and is often breathtaking.

Treks are mostly run by small local tour operators and have English-speaking guides. Prices, including all food, guides, transport, accommodation and park fees, start at about US$25 a day for larger groups. For more specialised long treks into remote areas, prices can run into several hundred dollars. In most cases you can trek with as few as two people, with per person costs falling with larger groups.

MARGIE POLITZER/GETTY IMAGES ©

Elephants bathing, Tat Lo (p235)

Where to Go

➡ **Nam Ha NPA** Luang Namtha has developed an award-winning ecotourism project for visits to local ethnic-minority villages in Nam Ha NPA (p106).

➡ **Phongsali Province** Explore fascinating hill-tribe terrain in one of the most authentic trekking destinations in the region. Mountainous and chilly in winter. Multi-day treks include homestays with the colourful Akha people (p90).

➡ **Phu Hin Bun NPA** A karst of thousands (p190).

➡ **Se Pian NPA** Great for elephant treks and general hikes (p232).

➡ **Dong Natad** Treks through beautiful landscapes, organised by Savannakhet's eco-guide unit (p208).

Wildlife Spotting

While wildlife spotting may not be quite as straightforward as on the Serengeti, it is still possible to have some memorable encounters in Laos.

Where to Go

➡ **Gibbon Experience** Take to the trees to live like a gibbon in the jungle canopy at this celebrated ecotourism project. Hang from a zipline and glide through the forest (p116).

➡ **Elephant Conservation Center** Learn about the life of the Laotian elephant at this superb conservation centre near Sainyabuli. Walk with the elephants, learn the art of the mahout and see young jumbos in the nursery (p126).

➡ **Dolphins in Si Phan Don** The freshwater Irrawaddy dolphin is one of the rarest mammals on earth, with fewer than 100 inhabiting stretches of the Mekong. View them in their natural habitat off the shore of Don Khon in southern Laos (p250).

➡ **Nam Et/Phou Louey NPA** The jungle is massive in this incredibly lush national protected area, home to some of the last remaining wild tigers in Laos, although a sighting is highly unlikely (p83).

➡ **Tat Kuang Si Bear Rescue Centre** Tat Kuang Si is a must-visit destination thanks to its iconic menthol-blue waters. There is also a chance to see Asian black bears at the Tat Kuang Si Bear Rescue Centre, home to bears that have been saved from the wildlife trade (p63).

SAFETY GUIDELINES FOR HIKERS

➡ Don't stray from established paths, as there is UXO in many parts of the country.

➡ Guides are worth hiring; they're inexpensive, speak the language and understand indigenous culture.

➡ Dogs can be aggressive; a stout stick can come in handy.

➡ Boots with ankle support are a great investment.

➡ Carry a mosquito net if trekking in malarial zones of the region.

➡ Consider quality socks and repellent to reduce the likelihood of leeches.

➡ Carry water-purification tablets if you have a weak constitution.

➡ Invest in some snack bars or energy snacks to avoid getting riced out on longer treks.

Regions at a Glance

For many short-stay visitors, Luang Prabang is their Laos experience. And a mighty impressive one it is too, thanks to its deserved World Heritage status. Laos' other main city, capital Vientiane, may be bucolic for an Asian city, but it hits home on the charm stakes, with attractive cafes, stylish restaurants and lively bars.

Beyond lies northern Laos, a landscape of towering mountains and dense forests that is home to extensive national parks, rare wildlife and some of the most colourful minorities in the region. Connecting the dots by river boat makes for some of the most iconic journeys in Laos.

The middle of the country is one of the least travelled regions, but also one of the most rewarding. Some of the most dramatic caves systems in Asia are found here, together with spectacular scenery and crumbling colonial-era towns. Head south to live life in the slow lane. The Mekong islands of Si Phan Don suck people in for longer than expected, and there is a real buzz on the Bolaven Plateau – not just from the coffee.

Luang Prabang

Food
Activities
Shopping

Wining & Dining

World-class dining is on the menu in Luang Prabang, with many eateries set in beautifully restored colonial-era properties, complemented by some bohemian little bars.

The Other Luang Prabang

It's not all temples and monks in Luang Prabang, despite the iconic imagery. Just beyond the 'burbs lie action and adventure, including elephant camps, mountain bike trails and more.

Art & Antiquities

The night market on the main drag is lit up with fairy lights and draws visitors to browse its textiles and trinkets. Around town are art galleries and antique shops that reward the curious shopaholic.

p34

Northern Laos

Adventure
Boat Trips
History

Massive Jungle

The jungle really is massive in northern Laos, home to rewarding national parks and the best trekking in the country, not to mention cycling, kayaking and ziplining.

All Aboard

The Mekong meander from the Golden Triangle down to Luang Prabang is one of the most iconic river trips in the region. Smaller rivers reward too, particularly the Nam Ou around Nong Khiaw.

On the Trail of War

The convoluted history of modern Laos comes alive in the Vieng Xai Caves, where the Pathet Lao based their underground government while dodging US bombs, or the Plain of Jars, one of the most contested areas in the country in the 1960s.

p66

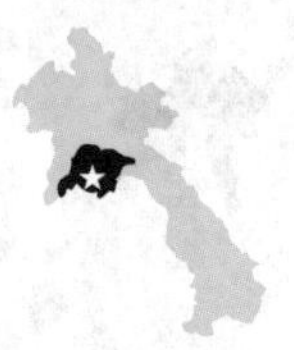

Vientiane & Around

Food
Activities
Shopping

Gastronomic Indulgence

Vientiane's spectrum of global cuisine ranges from Turkish to Japanese and Italian. But perhaps its ace card is its chic French restaurants, so redolent of Indochine they could make the Seine glow green with envy.

Get Your Groove On

Vientiane has great bike tours. There are also frisbee drop-ins, yoga, running clubs, swimming pools and, at 6am daily, free Mao-style mass exercises by the Mekong riverfront.

Textiles to Tintin

Expect locally sourced soap shops and silk boutiques hawking made-to-measure chemises, boho dresses and pashminas. You can still buy lacquer Tintin prints or old Russian watches.

p134

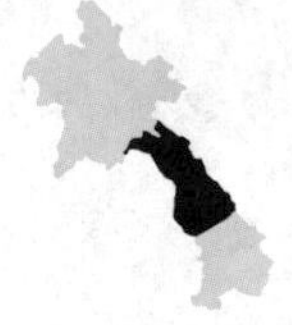

Central Laos

Caves
Architecture
Adventure

Going Underground

Central Laos is honeycombed with caves, from small, Buddha-filled grottoes with swimmable green lagoons, to monstrous river caves, such as Tham Kong Lo, which is cloaked in preternatural darkness.

Colonial-Era Towns

French colonials left not just boules and baguettes here, but also some elegant architecture, still seen today in cities like Tha Khaek and Savannakhet, from beautifully restored to ghostly decrepit.

Two-Wheeled Touring

Hit the road on a motorbike or, if training for the Tour de Laos, bicycle, and experience sublime scenery and destinations a world away from the tourist trail of mainstream Southeast Asia.

p184

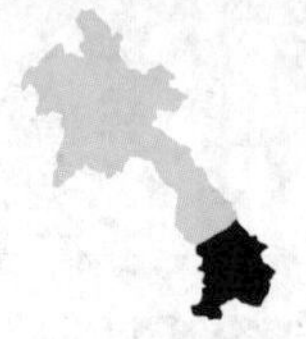

Southern Laos

Rivers
Activities
Remote Travel

Mekong Islands

Zoning out in Si Phan Don is the quintessential southern Laos experience, but do leave your hammock to engage with laid-back locals or kayak around this sublime slice of the Mekong.

Walks & Waterfalls

Jungle walks in a clutch of national parks lead to minority villages, crumbling temples and some of Laos' highest waterfalls. In certain areas elephants can do the leg work for you.

Bike Trips

Southern Laos is ripe for exploration by mountain bike or motorbike. The old Ho Chi Minh Trail serves up rugged rides for seasoned bikers, while anybody can tackle the smooth, scenic highways.

p212

On the Road

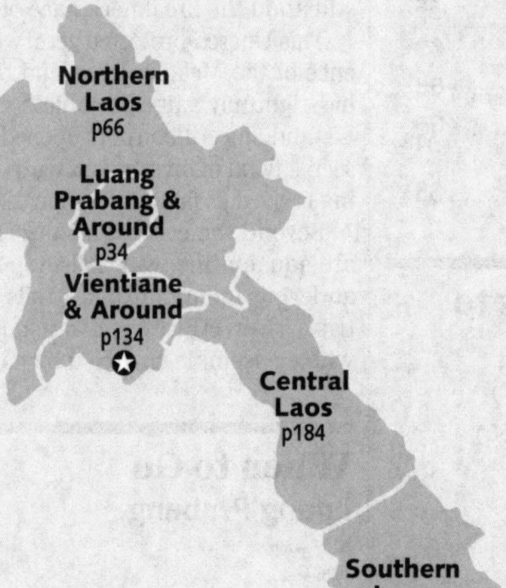

Northern Laos p66

Luang Prabang & Around p34

Vientiane & Around p134

Central Laos p184

Southern Laos p212

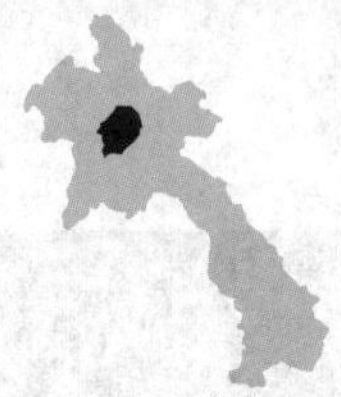

Luang Prabang & Around

Includes ➡

Best Places to Eat

- Dyen Sabai (p57)
- Le Banneton (p56)
- Tamarind (p57)
- Apsara (p57)
- Le Patio (p58)

Best Places to Stay

- La Résidence Phou Vao (p55)
- Le Sen Boutique Hotel (p54)
- Muang Lao Riverside Villa (p53)
- Apsara (p52)
- Xayana Guesthouse (p54)

Why Go?

Languid and lovely Luang Prabang (ຫລວງພະບາງ) is one of the most alluring places in Southeast Asia. Nowhere else can lay claim to the city's old-world romance of 33 gilded wats, saffron-clad monks, faded Indochinese villas and exquisite Gallic cuisine. It's a unique place where time seems to stand still amid the breakneck pace of the surrounding region.

This Unesco-protected gem, which sits at the sacred confluence of the Mekong River and the Nam Khan (Khan River), has rightfully gained mythical status as a travellers' Shangri La, and since its airport opened a decade ago the town has seen a flood of investment, with once-leprous French villas being revived as fabulous – though affordable – boutique hotels.

Beyond the evident history and heritage of the old town are aquamarine waterfalls, top trekking opportunities, meandering mountain bike trails, elephant camps, kayaking trips, river cruises and outstanding natural beauty – the whole ensemble encircled by hazy green mountains.

When to Go

Luang Prabang

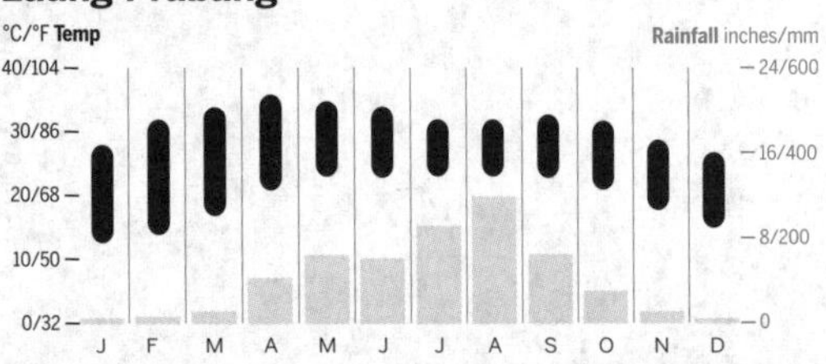

Nov–Feb The ideal season to visit weather-wise, but as this is no secret it's also peak tourist season.

Mar–May Hot season with hazy skies from slash and burn; some like to join in Pi Mai celebrations.

Jun–Oct The Wet season sees numbers and prices, plummet – great if you don't mind the odd downpour.

LUANG PRABANG

☎071 / POP 70,000

History

Legend has it that Luang Prabang's founder was Phunheu Nhanheu, a sexually ambiguous character with a bright red face and a stringy body. His/her ceremonial effigies are kept hidden within Wat Wisunarat, only appearing during Pi Mai (Lao New Year), but models are widely sold as souvenirs.

Known as Muang Sawa (Muang Sua) from 698, then Xiang Dong Xiang Thong (City of Gold) from the 11th century, a city-state here passed between the Nanzhao (Yunnanese), Khmer and greater Mongol empires over several centuries. It flourished at the heart of Lan Xang, following that kingdom's creation in 1353 by Khmer-supported conqueror Fa Ngum. In 1512, Lan Xang's King Visoun accepted the Pha Bang, a celebrated Buddha image, as a gift from the Khmer monarchy.

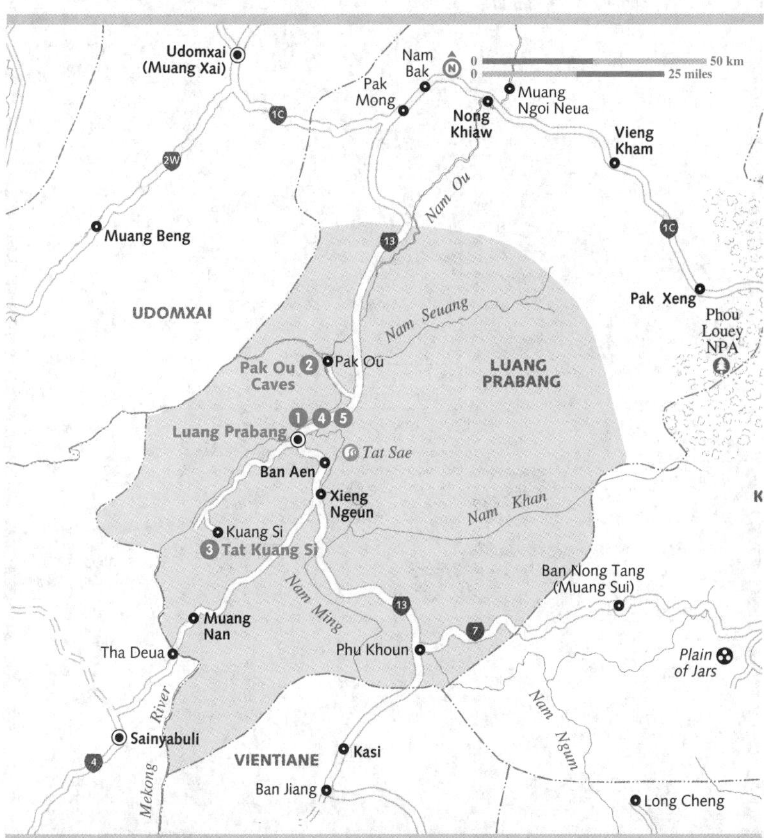

Luang Prabang & Around Highlights

1. Join the dawn call to alms that is the **tak bat** (p45) as locals give their daily offering to the monks of Luang Prabang
2. Cruise up the Mekong River to the **Pak Ou Caves** (p63), a holy sight brimming with Buddha images
3. Plunge into the menthol-blue waters of the falls at **Tat Kuang Si** (p63), some of the most beautiful in all of Laos
4. Marvel at the sweeping roof of **Wat Xieng Thong** (p42), the oldest and most beautiful temple in town
5. Go local on the banks of the Mekong or go gourmet in the old town: **Luang Prabang** is an epicurian delight (p55)

Luang Prabang

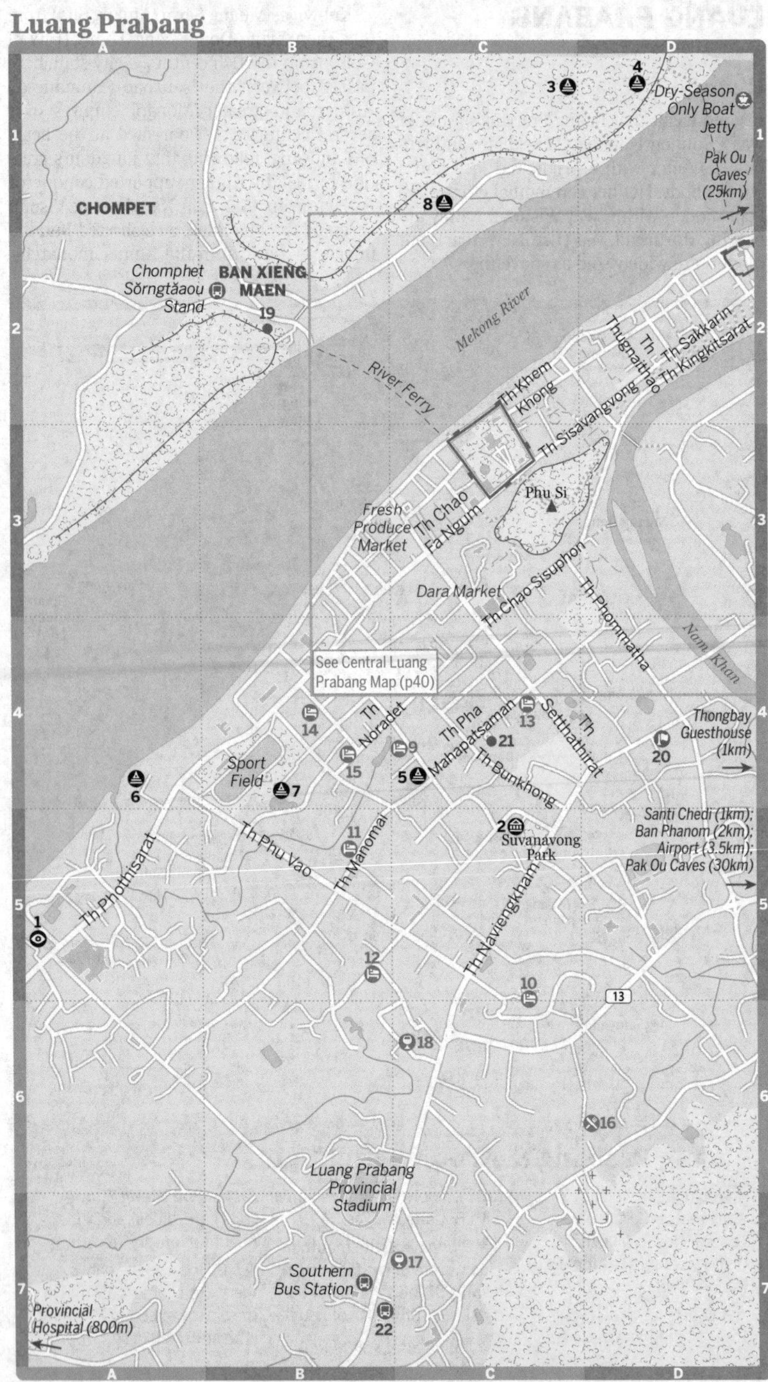

Luang Prabang

Sights
1 OckPopTok Living Crafts Centre A5
2 UXO Laos Information Centre C5
3 Wat Chomphet C1
4 Wat Longkhun D1
5 Wat Manorom C4
6 Wat Phabaht A4
7 Wat That Luang B4
8 Wat Xieng Maen C1

Activities, Courses & Tours
OckPopTok .... (see 1)

Sleeping
9 Ban Lao Hotel C4
10 La Résidence Phou Vao C5
11 Le Sen Boutique Hotel B5
12 Luang Say Residence B5
13 Mano Guest House C4
14 Satri House B4
15 Villa Suan Maak B4

Eating
16 Luang Prabang Secret Pizza D6
Sushi .... (see 13)

Drinking & Nightlife
17 Dao Fah C7
18 La Pistoche C6

Information
19 Jewel Travel Laos B2
20 Vietnamese Consulate D4

Transport
21 Lao Airlines C4
22 Naluang Minibus Station B7
Naluang Rental .... (see 22)

The city was renamed in its honour as Luang (Great/Royal) Prabang (Pha Bang).

Although Viang Chan (Vientiane) became the capital of Lan Xang in 1560, Luang Prabang remained the main source of monarchical power. When Lan Xang broke up following the death of King Suriya Vongsa in 1695, one of Suriya's grandsons set up an independent kingdom in Luang Prabang, which competed with kingdoms in Vientiane and Champasak.

From then on, the Luang Prabang monarchy was so weak that it was forced to pay tribute at various times to the Siamese, Burmese and Vietnamese. The reversal of China's Taiping Rebellion caused several groups of 'Haw' militias to flee southern China and reform as mercenary armies or bandit gangs. The best known of these was the Black Flag Army which devastated Luang Prabang in 1887, destroying and looting virtually every monastery in the city. In the wake of the attack, the Luang Prabang kingdom chose to accept French protection, and a French commissariat was established in the royal capital.

The French allowed Laos to retain the Luang Prabang monarchy. Luang Prabang quickly became a favourite post for French colonials seeking a refuge as far away from Paris as possible. Even during French Indochina's last years, prior to WWII, a river trip from Saigon to Luang Prabang took longer than a steamship voyage from Saigon to France.

The city survived Japanese invasion and remained a royalist stronghold through the Indochina wars, as such avoiding the US bombing that destroyed virtually every other northern Lao city. Through the 1980s, collectivisation of the economy resulted in a major exodus of business people, aristocracy and intelligentsia. With little money for, or interest in, conserving the city's former regal-colonial flavour, Luang Prabang became a ghost of its former self. But after 1989, the return of private enterprise meant that long-closed shops reopened and once-dilapidated villas were converted into hotels and guesthouses. The city received Unesco World Heritage status in 1995, accelerating the process, raising the city's international profile and, in principle, ensuring that any new development in the old city remains true to the architectural spirit of the original. Such has been the city's international popularity in the 21st century that in some quarters, guesthouses, restaurants, boutiques and galleries now outnumber actual homes.

Sights

Royal Palace & Around

★Royal Palace Museum MUSEUM

(ພະຣາຊະວັງຊຽງແກ້ວ, Ho Kham; Map p40; ☎071-212470; Th Sisavangvong; admission 30,000K; ⏲8-11.30am & 1.30-4pm Wed-Mon, last entry 3.30pm) Perfectly framed by an avenue of tall Palmyra palms, the former Royal Palace was built in 1904, blending traditional Lao and French beaux-arts styles. It was the main residence of King Sisavang Vong (r 1905–59) whose statue stands outside. Exhibits are well

LUANG PRABANG IN...

Two Days

Immerse yourself in the **old town** of Luang Prabang with a stroll around the temples and historic buildings. Follow our walking tour for something structured or just amble around at your own pace. Make sure you include the striking temple of **Wat Xieng Thong** and the **Royal Palace Museum**, as well as some of the small alleyways that link the Mekong riverfront and Nam Khan riverfront. Try lunch on the slow-flowing Nam Khan and dinner after sunset on the banks of the mother Mekong. On the second day, rise early to partake in the **tak bat** as the monasteries empty of their monks in search of alms. Continue to the lively **morning market** before taking a boat trip upriver to the **Pak Ou Caves**. If time allows, spend the afternoon trekking and swimming around the lush waterfalls at **Tat Kuang Si**. Round things off with a night on the town at buzzing **Hive Bar** and chilled **Utopia**.

Four Days

Having explored the old town and the headline attractions, it's time for an adrenalin buzz or some cultural immersion. For adrenalin seekers, choose from hiking, biking or kayaking in the surrounding countryside or visit one of the **elephant camps** and learn the skills of the mahout. For more culture than adventure, consider a cooking class at **Tamarind** or **Tum Tum Cheng**, a weaving class at **OckPopTock**, or visit the excellent **Traditional Arts & Ethnology Centre (TAEC)**, also a good stop for lunch thanks to **Le Patio** cafe. Definitely try a gastronomic blowout at one of the classy international restaurants in town. Still want more? Check out **La Pistoche** for the equivalent of a beach experience in town.

labelled in English. Note that you must be 'appropriately dressed' to enter, which means no sleeveless shirts or short shorts.

The main palace building is approached from the south. Italian marble steps lead into an entry hall where the centrepiece is the gilded dais of the former Supreme Patriarch of Lao Buddhism. To the right, the king's reception room has walls covered in light-suffused Gauginesque canvases of Lao life, painted in 1930 by French artist Alix de Fautereau. A line of centuries-old Khamu metal drums leads back to the main throne room whose golden trimmed walls are painted deep red and encrusted with a feast of mosaic-work in Japanese coloured mirror glass. Side galleries here display a collection of small Buddhas, some 16th-century, that were recovered from destroyed or looted stupas.

Behind the throne room are the former royal family's decidedly sober residential quarters, with some rooms preserved much as they were when the king departed in 1975. The children's room, however, displays gamelan-style musical instruments and a series of masks for Ramayana dance-dramas. These were once a classic entertainment for the Lao court and have now been partly revived at the Phrolak-Phralam Theatre (p59), albeit largely for tourist consumption.

Beneath, but entered from the western side, is a series of exhibition halls used for temporary exhibits. Separate outbuildings display the **Floating Buddha collection** of meditation photographs and the five-piece **Royal Palace Car Collection**, including two 1960s Lincoln Continentals, a rare wing-edged 1958 Edsel Citation and a dilapidated Citroën DS.

No single treasure in Laos is more historically resonant than the **Pha Bang** (ພະບາງ), an 83cm-tall gold-alloy Buddha for which the whole city is named. Its arrival here in 1512 spiritually legitimised the Lan Xang royal dynasty as Buddhist rulers. Legend has it that the image was cast around the 1st century AD in Sri Lanka, though it is stylistically Khmer and more likely dates from the 14th century. The Siamese twice carried the Pha Bang off to Thailand (in 1779 and 1827) but it was finally restored to Laos by King Mongkut (Rama IV) in 1867.

Nearing completion in the southeast corner of the palace gardens, **Wat Ho Pha Bang** is a soaring, multi-roofed temple designed to eventually house the **Pha Bang Buddha**. A project planned before the monarchy was abolished in 1975, and construction on this highly ornate pavilion began in 1993. The building's glitzy red-and-gold interior already sports a multilevel 'throne' space for the image and also houses a 16-man gilt palanquin on which the Pha Bang is paraded through town during the classic Pi Mai celebrations.

For now, however, the Pha Bang lives in an easy-to-miss little room surrounded by engraved elephant tusks and three silk screens embroidered by the former queen. To find it, walk east along the palace's exterior south terrace and peep in between the bars at the eastern end. Note that persistent rumours claim that the image on display here is actually a copy and that the original is stored in a vault in Vientiane. The 'real' one supposedly has gold leaf over the eyes and a hole drilled through one ankle.

Footwear cannot be worn inside the museum, no photography is permitted and you must leave bags in a locker room to the left-hand side of the main entrance.

Wat Mai Suwannaphumaham BUDDHIST TEMPLE

(ວັດໃຫມ່ສຸວັນນະພູມອາຮາມ; Map p40; Th Sisavangvong; admission 10,000K; ⌚8am-5pm) Beside the palace, Wat Mai is one of the city's most sumptuous monasteries. Its wooden *sĭm* (ordination hall) has a five-tiered roof in archetypal Luang Prabang style, while the unusually-roofed front verandah features detailed golden reliefs depicting scenes from village life, the Ramayana and Buddha's penultimate birth.

When built in 1821 to replace a 1796 original, this was the *mai* (new) monastery. The name has stuck. It was spared destruction in 1887 by the Haw gangs who reportedly found it too beautiful to harm. Since 1894 it has been home to the Sangharat, the head of Lao Buddhism.

★Phu Si HILL

(ພູສີ; Map p40; admission 20,000K; ⌚8am-6pm) Dominating the old city centre and a favourite with sunset junkies, the abrupt 100m-tall hill of Phu Si is crowned by a 24m gilded stupa called **That Chomsi** (Map p40). Viewed from a distance, especially when floodlit at night, the structure seems to float in the hazy air. From the summit, however, the main attraction is the series of city views. Beside a flagpole on the same summit there's a small remnant anti-aircraft cannon left from the war years.

Ascending Phu Si from the north side (329 steps), stop at the decaying **Wat Pa Huak** (Map p40; admission by donation), one of the few city temples not to have been colourfully (over) renovated. It has a splendid carved wood Buddha riding Airavata, the three-headed elephant from Hindu mythology that featured on Laos' national flag until 1975. The gilded and carved front doors are often locked, but during the day there's usually an attendant nearby who will open the doors for a tip of a few thousand kip. Inside, the original 19th-century murals have excellent colour, considering the lack of any restoration. The murals show historic scenes along the Mekong River, including visits by Chinese diplomats and warriors arriving by river and horse caravans. Three large seated Buddhas and several smaller standing and seated images date from the same time as the murals or possibly earlier

Reaching That Chomsi is also possible from the south and east sides. Two such paths climb through large **Wat Siphoutthabat Thippharam** (Map p40) to a curious miniature shrine that protects a **Buddha Footprint** (Map p40) FREE. If this really is his rocky imprint, then the Buddha must have been the size of a brontosaurus. Directly southwest of here a series of new gilded Buddhas are nestled into rocky clefts and niches around **Wat Thammothayalan** (Map p40). The monastery is free to visit if you don't climb beyond to That Chomsi.

★TAEC MUSEUM

(Traditional Arts & Ethnology Centre; Map p40; ☎071-253364; www.teaclaos.org; admission 20,000K; ⌚9am-6pm Tue-Sun) Visiting this professionally presented three-room museum is a must to learn about northern Laos' various hill-tribe cultures, especially if planning a trek. There's just enough to inform without overloading a beginner. If you want more information, watch the video or ask to leaf through the books of a small library cabinet in the museum's delightful cafe. TAEC is within a former French judge's mansion that was among the city's most opulent buildings of the 1920s.

Xieng Mouane Area

A series of lanes and narrow linking passages run down to the enchanting Mekong riverfront with its shuttered colonial-era house-fronts, river-facing terrace cafes and curio shops.

Central Luang Prabang

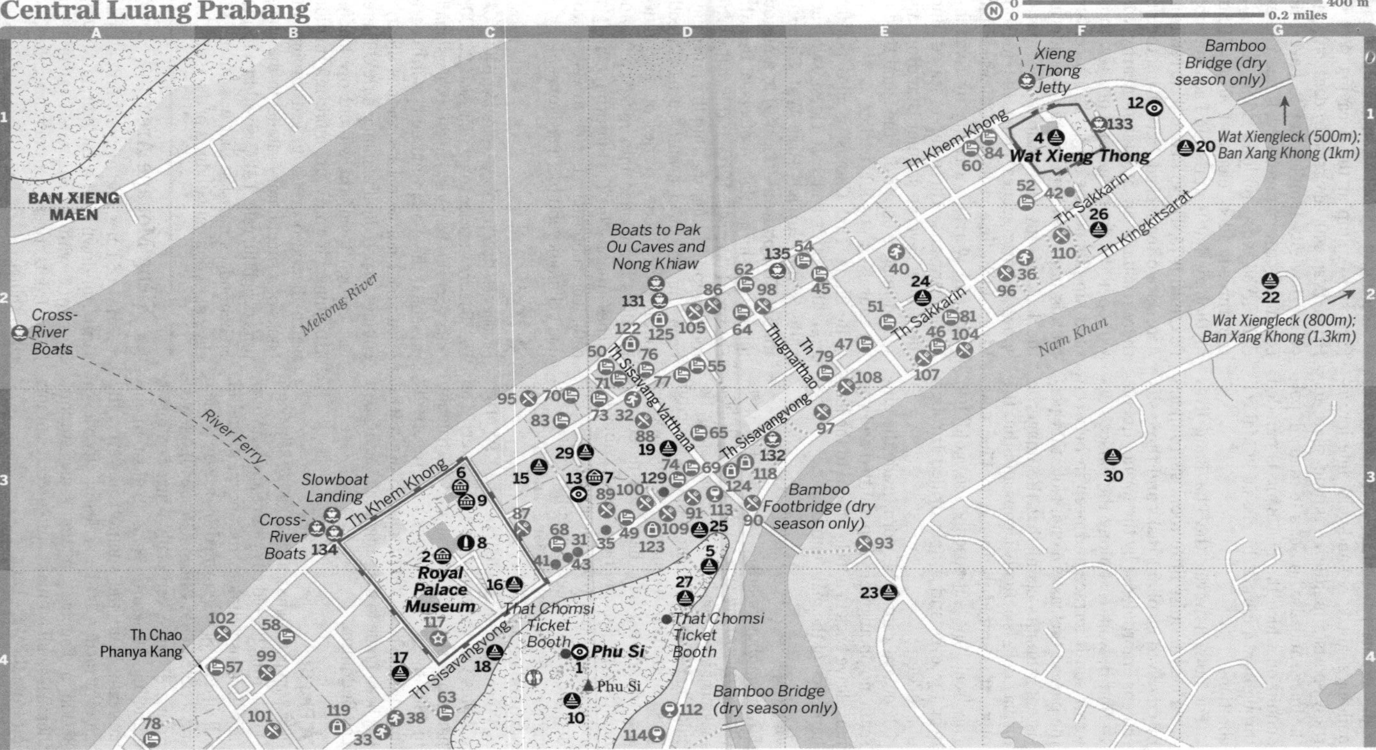

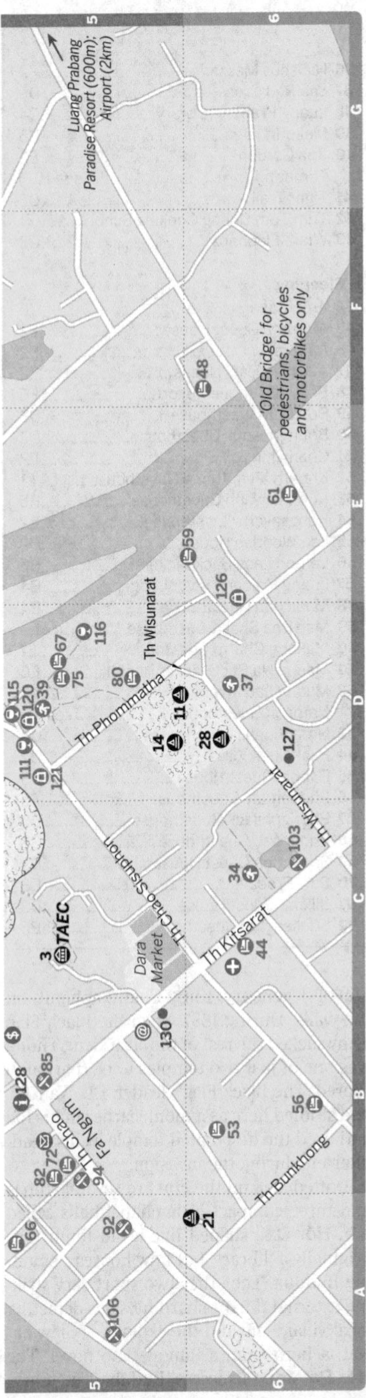

Wat Pa Phai
BUDDHIST TEMPLE

(ວັດປ່າໄຜ່; Map p40; Th Sisavang Vatthana) Over the gilded and carved wooden facade, Wat Pa Phai has a classic Tai–Lao fresco depicting everyday scenes of late 19th-century Lao life.

Villa Xieng Mouane
ARCHITECTURE

(ເຮືອນມໍລະດົກຊຽງມ່ວນ; Map p40) Footpaths lead back from the commercial main drag into a little oasis of palm-shaded calm around the Villa Xieng Mouane, an authentic traditional longhouse on tree-trunk stilts that is now partly used as an occasional exhibition centre.

Heritage House Information Centre
GALLERY

(Map p40) The Heritage House Information Centre has computers on which you can peruse a series of photos and descriptions of the city's numerous Unesco-listed historic buildings.

Wat Xieng Mouane
BUDDHIST TEMPLE

(ວັດຊຽງມ່ວນ; Map p40; ⌚8am-5pm) This large monastery, whose *sĭm* dates back to 1879, runs a training centre which teaches young monks woodcarving, painting, Buddha-casting and other skills necessary to maintain Luang Prabang's temples. Such activities came to a virtual halt after the 1975 revolution and have a fair amount of ground to recover, judging from the unrefined examples sold in their little **showroom** (⌚8.30-10.30am & 1.30-4pm).

Wat Choumkhong
BUDDHIST TEMPLE

(ວັດຈຸມຄ້ອງ; Map p40) The garden around the little Wat Choumkhong is particularly attractive when its poinsettia trees blush red. Built in 1843, the monastery takes its name from a Buddha statue that was originally cast from a melted-down gong.

The Upper Peninsula

The northern tip of the peninsula formed by the Mekong River and the Nam Khan is jam-packed with glittering palm-fronded monasteries. Well before dawn they resonate mysteriously with drum beats and as the morning mists swirl they disgorge a silent procession of saffron-clad monks. The most celebrated monastery is Wat Xieng Thong, but several others are quieter, less touristy, and intriguing in their own right.

A fine viewpoint overlooks the river junction from outside Hotel Mekong Riverside.

Central Luang Prabang

Top Sights

- **1** Phu Si C4
- **2** Royal Palace Museum C3
- **3** TAEC C5
- **4** Wat Xieng Thong F1

Sights

- **5** Buddha Footprint D3
- **6** Floating Buddha Photographs C3
- **7** Heritage House Information Centre D3
- **8** Pha Bang C3
- **9** Royal Palace Car Collection C3
- **10** That Chomsi C4
- **11** That Makmo D5
- **12** Unesco Offices F1
- **13** Villa Xieng Mouane C3
- **14** Wat Aham D5
- **15** Wat Choumkhong C3
- **16** Wat Ho Pha Bang C4
- **17** Wat Mai Suwannaphumaham C4
- **18** Wat Pa Huak C4
- **19** Wat Pa Phai D3
- **20** Wat Pakkhan G1
- **21** Wat Pha Mahathat A6
- **22** Wat Phonsaat G2
- **23** Wat Punluang E4
- **24** Wat Sensoukaram E2
- **25** Wat Siphoutthabat Thippharam D3
- **26** Wat Souvannakhili F2
- **27** Wat Thammothayalan D4
- **28** Wat Wisunarat D6
- **29** Wat Xieng Mouane C3
- **30** Watpakha Xaingaram F3

Activities, Courses & Tours

- **31** All Lao Elephant Camp C3
- **32** Big Brother Mouse D3
- **33** Children's Cultural Centre B4
- **34** Dhammada C6
- **35** Green Discovery D3
- **36** Hibiscus Massage F2
- **37** Lao Red Cross D6
- **38** Luang Prabang Library C4
- **39** Mekong Yoga D5
- **40** Spa Garden E2
- Tamarind .... (see 107)
- **41** Tiger Trail C3
- **42** Tum Tum Cheng Cooking School F1
- **43** White Elephant C3

Sleeping

- **44** Amantaka C6
- **45** Ammata Guest House E2
- **46** Apsara E2
- **47** Auberge les 3 Nagas E2
- **48** BelAir Boutique Resort F6
- **49** Bou Pha Guesthouse D3
- **50** Boungnasouk Guesthouse D2
- **51** Chang Inn E2
- **52** Khoum Xiengthong Guesthouse F1
- **53** Khounsavanh Guesthouse B6
- **54** Kongsavath Guesthouse E2
- **55** Lao Wooden House D2
- **56** Lemon Laos Backpackers B6
- **57** Luang Prabang River Lodge B4
- **58** Manichan Guesthouse B4
- **59** Mao Pha Shak Guesthouse E6
- **60** Mekong Charm Guesthouse E1
- **61** Meune Na Backpacker Hostel E6
- **62** Muang Lao Riverside Villa D2
- Namsok Guesthouse 1 .... (see 71)
- **63** Nora Singh Guesthouse C4
- **64** Pack Luck Villa D2
- **65** Paphai Guest House D3
- **66** Phonemaly Guesthouse A5
- **67** Phongphilack Guesthouse D5
- **68** Phounsab Guesthouse C3
- **69** Sackarinh Guest House D3
- **70** Sala Prabang C3
- **71** Silichit Guest House D2
- **72** Souksavath Guesthouse B5

At the peninsula's far tip, a bamboo bridge (toll 5000K return) that's rebuilt each dry season crosses the Nam Khan, allowing access to a 'beach' and basic sunset-watching bar and offering a shortcut to Ban Xang Khong, 1km northeast.

★ **Wat Xieng Thong** BUDDHIST TEMPLE

(ວັດຊຽງທອງ; Map p40 & 44; off Th Sakkarin; admission 20,000K; 8am-5pm) Luang Prabang's best-known and most visited monastery is centred on a 1560 *sǐm* that's considered a classic of local design. Its roofs sweep low to the ground and there's an idiosyncratic 'tree of life' mosaic set on its west exterior wall. Inside, gold stencil work includes dharma wheels on the ceiling and exploits from the life of legendary King Chanthaphanit on the walls. During 1887 when the Black Flag army sacked the rest of the city, Xieng Thong was one of just two temples to be (partially) spared. The Black Flag's leader, Deo Van Tri, had studied here as a monk earlier in his life and used the desecrated temple as his headquarters during the invasion.

Dotted around the *sǐm* are several stupas and three compact little chapel halls called *hŏr*. **Hŏr Đại**, shaped like a tall tomb, was originally a 'library' but now houses a standing Buddha. The other two sport very striking external mirror-shard mosaics depicting local village life and the exploits of Siaw Sawat, a hero from a famous Lao novel. The **Hŏr Pa Maan** ('success' Buddha sanctuary)

73 Soutikone Guesthouse 1 .... D3
74 Thanaboun Guesthouse D3
75 Vilayvanh Guesthouse D5
76 Villa Champa D2
77 Villa Chitdara D2
78 Villa Pumalin A4
79 Villa Santi E2
80 Villa Sayada D5
81 Villa Senesouk E2
82 Xayana Guesthouse B5
83 Xieng Mouane Guesthouse C3
84 Xiengthong Palace F1

Eating
Apsara .... (see 46)
85 Baguette Stalls B5
86 Big Tree Café D2
87 Blue Lagoon C3
88 Café Toui D3
89 Coconut Garden D3
90 Couleur Cafe D3
91 Dao Fa Bistro D3
92 Delilah's A5
93 Dyen Sabai E3
94 JoMa Bakery Cafe B5
95 Khemkhong View Restaurant C3
96 Le Banneton F2
97 Le Café Ban Vat Sene E3
Le Patio .... (see 3)
98 L'Elephant Restaurant D2
99 Morning Market B4
100 Nazim Indian Food D3
101 Night Food Stalls B4
102 Riverside Barbecue Restaurant B4
103 Roots & Leaves C6
104 Rosella Fusion E2
105 Saffron D2
106 Somchanh Restaurant A5
107 Tamarind E2
108 Tamnak Lao E2
109 Tangor D3
110 Xieng Thong Noodle-Shop F2

Drinking & Nightlife
111 Hive Bar D5
112 House D4
113 Ikon Klub D3
114 Lao Lao Garden D4
115 S Bar D5
116 Utopia D5

Entertainment
117 Phrolak-Phralam Theatre C4

Shopping
118 Caruso Lao Homecraft D3
119 Handicraft Night Market B4
120 Kopnoi D5
121 L'Etranger Books & Tea D5
122 Ma Te Sai D2
Monument Books .... (see 62)
123 Naga Creations D3
124 OckPopTok D3
OckPopTok .... (see 62)
125 Orange Tree D2
126 Pathana Boupha Antique House E6
Wat Xieng Mouane Showroom .... (see 29)

Information
BCEL .... (see 49)
127 Immigration Office D6
128 Provincial Tourism Department B5

Transport
129 Bangkok Airways D3
130 KPTD B5
131 Longboat Office D2
132 Luang Say Cruise D3
133 Mekong River Cruises F1
134 Navigation Office B3
135 Shompoo Cruise D2

remains locked except during the week following Pi Mai. The **Hŏr Đại Pha Sai-nyàat** (reclining Buddha sanctuary) was dubbed La Chapelle Rouge – Red Chapel – by the French. It contains an especially rare reclining Buddha that dates from the construction of the temple. This one-of-a-kind figure has an exquisitely sinuous upper body with a right hand seeming to gesture 'Oh, whatever!' The contrastingly rectilinear feet emerge on die-straight legs from beneath monastic robes that curl upward like rocket fumes.

Fronted in especially lavish gilt work, the **Hóhng Kép Mîen** is a garage for a ceremonial carriage designed to carry the huge golden funeral urns of the Lao royalty. This glittering vehicle is festooned with seven red-tongued *naga* snakes that contrast amusingly with the prosaic Bridgestone tyres of its undercarriage.

Wat Pakkhan BUDDHIST TEMPLE

(ວັດປາກຄານ; Map p40; Th Sakkarin) Dated 1737 but rebuilt a century ago, Wat Pakkhan has a simple, appealingly archaic look with angled support struts holding up the lower of its two superposed roofs. Across the road, the ochre colonial-era villa that now forms **Unesco offices** (Map p40) was once the city's customs office.

Wat Souvannakhili BUDDHIST TEMPLE

(ວັດສຸວັນນະຄີລີ, Wat Khili; Map p40; off Th Sakkarin) The most prominent building of Wat Souvannakhili looks more like a colonial

Wat Xieng Thong

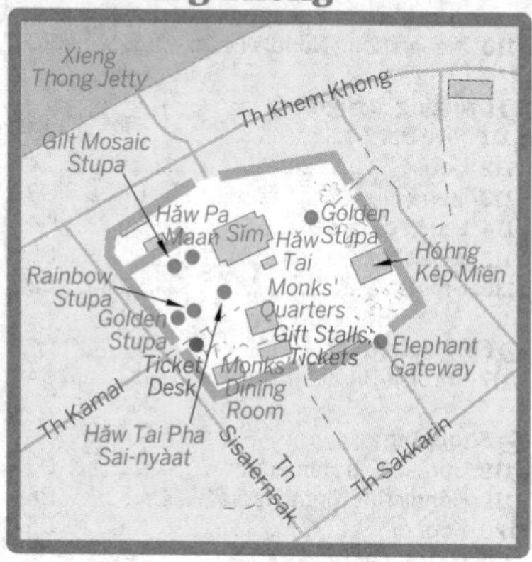

mansion than a monastery, but the small *sĭm* is a classic of now-rare Xieng Khuang style.

Wat Sensoukaram BUDDHIST TEMPLE
(ວັດແສນສຸກອາຣາມ; Map p40; Th Sakkarin) Rich ruby-red walls with intricate gold overlay gives Wat Sensoukaram one of the most dazzling facades of all of Luang Prabang's temples. The name reportedly refers to the initial donation of 100,000K made to build it, a handsome sum back in 1718.

Wat Wisunarat (Wat Visoun) Area

Two of Luang Prabang's most historically important temples lie amid palms in pleasant if traffic-buzzed grounds offering glimpses towards Phu Si.

Wat Wisunarat BUDDHIST TEMPLE
(ວັດວິຊຸນ, Wat Visoun; Map p40; Th Wisunarat; admission 20,000K; ⌚8am-5pm) Facing That Makmo, this wat takes its name from Chao Wisunarat (King Visoun), who founded it in 1513. Though touted as one of Luang Prabang's oldest operating temples it's actually an 1898 reconstruction built following the Black Flag raids. As a rather meagre return for paying the entrance fee you can peruse a sizeable collection of old gilded 'Calling for Rain' Buddhas with long sinuous arms held to each side. These were placed here, along with some medieval ordination stones, for their protection having been rescued from various abandoned or ravaged temples.

Wat Aham BUDDHIST TEMPLE
(ວັດອາຮາມ; Map p40; admission 20,000K; ⌚8am-5pm) This small wat was the residence of the Sangharat (Supreme Patriarch of Lao Buddhism) until superseded by Wat Mai 200 years ago. Colourful, if unsophisticated, murals of Buddhist history and (sometimes gruesome) morality tales cover the interior walls but there are no translations nor interpretations to justify the entrance fee.

That Makmo BUDDHIST SHRINE
(Map p40) This lumpy hemispherical stupa is commonly nicknamed That Makmo, which translates as 'Watermelon Stupa'. Originally constructed in 1503, it was pillaged for hidden treasures during the 1887 destructions and the latest renovation (1932) coated the stupa in drab grey concrete.

South of the Centre

Hop on a bicycle to discover the following sites.

UXO Laos Information Centre MUSEUM
(Map p36; ☎071-252073; www.uxolao.gov.la; admission by donation; ⌚8-11.45am & 2-4pm Mon-Fri) Behind a manicured new park featuring a large clapping statue of the 'Red Prince' lies the sobering UXO Laos Information Centre. Visiting here helps to get a grip on the devastation Laos suffered in the Second Indochina War and how nearly 40 years later, death or injury from unexploded ordnance remains an everyday reality in several provinces. If you miss it here, there's a similar centre in Phonsavan.

Wat Manorom BUDDHIST TEMPLE
(ວັດມະໂນລົມ, Wat Mano, Wat Manolom; Map p36; Th Pha Mahapatsaman) Winding lanes to the west lead to Wat Manorom, set amid frangipani trees just outside what were once the city walls (now invisible). This is possibly the oldest temple site in Luang Prabang and the *sĭm* contains a sitting 6m-tall bronze Buddha originally cast in 1372. During the 1887 devastation the statue was hacked apart but surviving elements were reconstituted in 1919, and in 1971 the missing limbs were replaced with concrete falsies covered in gold leaf.

Wat Pha Mahathat BUDDHIST TEMPLE
(ວັດພະມຫາທາດ, Wat That; Map p40) Wat Pha Mahathat is named for a venerable Lanna-style stupa erected in 1548. The 1910 *sĭm* in front has carved wooden windows and por-

tico, rosette-gilded pillars and exterior reliefs retelling tales of the Buddha's past lives.

Wat That Luang BUDDHIST TEMPLE

(ວັດທາດຫຼວງ; Map p36; admission 10,000K; ⊙8am-6pm) Traditionally the cremation site for Lao royalty, legend has it that Wat That Luang was originally established by Ashokan missionaries in the 3rd century BC. However, the current large *sĭm* is a 1818 rebuild whose leafy column-capitals look more Corinthian than Indian. The *sĭm* is bracketed by two stupas, the larger of which is plated with an armour of corroded old brass plates. It reputedly contains the ashes of King Sisavang Vong, even though it was built in 1910, 50 years before his death.

Wat Phabaht BUDDHIST TEMPLE

(ວັດພະບາດ; Map p36; Th Phothisarat; admission 10,000K) The modern Vietnamese–Lao temple of Wat Phabaht is fronted by a distinctive if kitschy array of spires. Behind is a shady Mekong-front terrace from which steps lead down to another gigantic holy footprint hidden beneath a turquoise shelter.

OckPopTok Living Crafts Centre ARTS CENTRE

(Map p36; ☎071-212597; www.ockpoptok.com; ⊙9am-5pm) FREE Just beyond the extensive Talat Market, a tiny lane leads about 200m towards the Mekong, emerging at the excellent OckPopTok Living Crafts Centre, a beautifully laid-out traditionally styled workshop where weavers, spinners and batik makers produce top-quality fabrics. Free tours of the centre start roughly half-hourly and give a superb insight into silk production and dye-making.

If you're waiting for a tour, there's plenty of information to peruse along with a great river-view cafe serving drinks and excellent Lao food. Or try a cup of the surprisingly pleasant worm-poo tea – yes, a unique infusion made from silk-worm

TAK BAT – THE MONKS' CALL TO ALMS

Daily at dawn, saffron-clad monks pad barefoot through the streets while pious townsfolk place tiny balls of sticky rice in their begging bowls. It's a quiet, meditative ceremony through which monks demonstrate their vows of poverty and humility while lay Buddhists gain spiritual merit by the act of respectful giving.

Although such processions occur all over Laos, old Luang Prabang's peaceful atmosphere and extraordinary concentration of mist-shrouded temples means that the morning's perambulations along Th Sakkarin and Th Kamal create an especially romantic scene. Sadly, as a result, tourists are progressively coming to outnumber participants. Despite constant campaigns begging visitors not to poke cameras in the monks' faces, the amateur paparazzi seem incapable of keeping a decent distance. Sensitive, non-participating observers should follow these guidelines:

- Stand across the road from the procession or better still watch inconspicuously from the window of your hotel (where possible).
- Refrain from taking photos or at best do so from a considerable distance with a long zoom. Never use flash.
- Maintain the silence (arrive by bicycle or on foot; don't chatter).

If it's genuinely meaningful to you, you may take part in the ceremony – meaningful in this case implies not wanting to be photographed in the process. Joining in takes some preparation and knowledge to avoid causing unspoken offence. Don't be pushed into half-hearted participation by sales-folk along the route. Such vendors contribute to the procession's commercialisation and many sell overpriced, low-grade rice that is worse than giving nothing at all. Instead, organise some *kao kai noi* (the best grade sticky rice) to be cooked to order by your guesthouse. Or buy it fresh-cooked from the morning market before the procession. Carry it in a decent rice-basket, not a plastic bag. Before arriving, dress respectfully as you would for a temple (covered upper arms and chest, skirts for women, long trousers for men). Wash your hands and don't use perfumes or lotions that might flavour the rice as you're handing it out.

Once in situ, remove your shoes and put a sash or scarf across your left shoulder. Women should kneel with their feet folded behind them (don't sit) while men may stand. Avoid making eye contact with the monks.

droppings. Weaving and dyeing courses are possible here and accommodation is available.

Across the Mekong River

For a very different 'village' atmosphere, cross the Mekong to Muang Chomphet. To get there, take a cross-river boat (local/foreigner 2000/5000K) from the navigation office (p61) behind the Royal Palace. Boats depart once they have a handful of passengers. Alternatively, boatmen at various other points on the Luang Prabang waterfront will run you across to virtually any point on the north bank for around 20,000K per boat. If water levels allow, a good excursion idea is to hire such a boat to the Wat Longkhun jetty then walk back via Ban Xieng Maen to the main crossing point. However, reaching Wat Longkhun by boat isn't always practicable due to seasonally changing sandbanks.

Above the ferry landing on the other side, a branch of **Jewel Travel Laos** (Map p36; www.jeweltravellaos.com; ⏲8am-4pm) sells district sketch maps (4000K) and rents mountain bikes (per day 50,000K). However, you'll need neither bike nor map to visit the series of attractive monasteries that are scattered east along the riverbank from the traffic-free village of Ban Xieng Maen.

Wat Xieng Maen BUDDHIST TEMPLE

(ວັດຊຽງແມນ; Map p36; admission 10,000K) First founded in 1592, Wat Xieng Maen gained a hallowed air in 1867 by housing the Pha Bang for seven nights while on its way back to Luang Prabang after 40 years in Thai hands. The monastery's current, colourful *sĭm* contains an attractive 'family' of Buddhas and has stencilled columns conspicuously inscribed with the names of US donors who paid for their renovation.

Wat Chomphet BUDDHIST TEMPLE

(ວັດຈອມເພັດ; Map p36; ⏲8am-5pm) Ban Xieng Maen's long, narrow, brick-edged 'street' slowly degrades into a rough track, eventually becoming little more than a rocky footpath. At about this point, climb an obvious 123-step stairway to find the 1888 Wat Chomphet fronted by greying twin pagodas. The hilltop temple is little more than a shell but the site offers undisturbed views of the town and river.

Wat Longkhun BUDDHIST TEMPLE

(ວັດລ່ອງຄຸນ; Map p36; admission 10,000K; ⏲8am-5pm) The enchanting Wat Longkhun is set amid bougainvillea and starburst Palmyra palms. When the coronation of a Luang Prabang king was pending, it was customary for him to spend three days in retreat at Wat Longkhun before ascending the throne. Today various monastic outbuildings retain a cohesive rustic style, while the central *sĭm* features old murals with a curious sense of perspective. One scene depicts giant fish attacking shipwrecked sailors.

If you ask at the ticket desk they should give you the key and torches (flashlights) required to visit **Tham Sakkalin** (admission incl with Wat Longkhun ticket). It's three minutes' walk further east then up a few stairs beneath some overhanging bougainvillea. Flicking the switch to the right of the door only partially illuminates this slippery, 100m-long limestone cave. A few Buddha fragments are kept in a niche to the right as you descend but the only really remarkable feature here is the inexplicable heat that the cave seems to produce.

Wat Had Siaw BUDDHIST TEMPLE

FREE Around 20 minutes' walk further east is the operational, if rather decrepit, little Wat Had Siaw – take the unpromising right fork about halfway along just after the main path turns inland. You'll pass a lonely hut and cross a one-plank stream-bridge before arriving.

Beyond Wat Had Siaw a path climbs a wooded hill that's buzzing with birdsong and is topped with a new gilt Buddha sat on a seven-headed snake (15 minutes' walk).

WORTH A TRIP

LIVING LAND FARM

Living Land Farm (www.livinglandlao.com) is a community enterprise that strives to benefit the Lao people. At this organic farm, located in Ban Phong Van, about 5km outside Luang Prabang on the road to Tat Kuang Si, you can learn about the life of the Lao farmer. Visitors can get a really hands-on experience by planting or harvesting rice, depending on the season, as well as dehusking and winnowing the rice. It's an educational experience, although at 300,000K per person, it's way beyond the budget of the average Lao farmer and even the more frugal backpacker.

LUANG PRABANG FOR CHILDREN

While wats and museums may not seem a recipe for excited children, there are now plenty of attractions in and around Luang Prabang that will get their attention. Children of all ages will love Tat Kuang Si (p63) and Tat Sae (p65) for the natural swimming pools. Kuang Si offers a fascinating glimpse of Asian black bears in their impressive enclosure, while Tat Sae has informal elephant rides. Boat trips on the Mekong are also relaxing and destinations include the Pak Ou Caves (p63), a nice diversion for budding explorers.

Older children will enjoy the activities on offer around town like cycling or kayaking. The younger ones can always spend some time at the **ABC School** (per child 20,000K; 3-9pm Mon-Fri, 9am-9pm Sat & Sun) with its extensive playground, located on the other side of the Nam Khan not far from Dyen Sabai. There are plenty of family-friendly cafes around town, but if it's a swimming pool they crave, then it's probably better to consider accommodation beyond the historic old town or make for the chilled out La Pistoche (p59).

Across the Nam Khan

In the dry season, once water levels have dropped significantly, a pair of bamboo footbridges (2000K) are constructed, making for easy access to the Nam Khan's east bank and its semi-rural neighbourhoods. When the river is high (June to November), the bridges disappear and access takes longer via the 'Old Bridge' by bicycle or motorbike, or via the northern bus station by car.

Crossing the southern bamboo bridge, climb steps past the highly recommended garden cafe, Dyen Sabai (p57), emerging beside **Wat Punluang** (Map p40). The dusty unpaved road to the left leads 2km to the interesting craft village of Ban Xang Khong, passing **Watpakha Xaingaram** (Map p40) with its ruined shell of a temple, peaceful riverside **Wat Phonsaat** (Map p40), and **Wat Xiengleck**, which sports a wobbly old brick stupa in an Angkorian-style state of atmospheric dilapidation. Half a kilometre beyond, Ban Xang Khonghas a 400m-strip of old houses and craft boutiques where you can watch weavers and papermakers at work, buy examples of their work and sometimes organise practical courses to learn the skills. The most visually striking gallery-workshop is **Artisans du Mekong** (071-254981; 8.30am-4pm), an ensemble of buildings in temple-archaic style behind a giant 'tusk' gateway. The raised floor-seat cafe serves tea and coffee and a selection of snacks.

Activities

Some of the most popular activities in Luang Prabang are based in the countryside beyond, including trekking, cycling and kayaking tours. Another popular activity is visiting one of the elephant camps beyond town and learning the art of the mahout for a day or more.

Yoga

Luang Prabang has emerged as something of a hotspot for yoga classes. Check out the website www.luangprabangyoga.org for more on classes around town or head to Utopia (p59) at 7.30am for their morning session (50,000K) overlooking the Nam Khan river. Some days also see sunset sessions and a couple of evening classes at the OckPopTok Living Crafts Centre (p45).

Mekong Yoga YOGA
(Map p40; Wat Aphay; per class 80,000K) Newcomer Mekong Yoga offers classes in a traditional Lao-style house within Wat Aphay temple in the shadow of Phu Si. Look out for the sign within the grounds.

Massage & Sauna

Options are abundant for herbal saunas and Lao, Khamu or Swedish massage. The cheapest places (including a trio on Th Khem Khong and several on central Th Sisavangvong) charge from 40,000K per hour for body or foot massage and 60,000K with oils.

Some of the top-end hotels have sumptuous spas that are open to non-guests.

Dhammada MASSAGE
(Map p40; 071-212642; www.dhammada.com; Namneua Lane; per hour foot/oriental/aromatherapy massage 100,000/100,000/160,000K; 11am-11pm) One of the best in town. A stylish rustic place beside a meditative lotus pond.

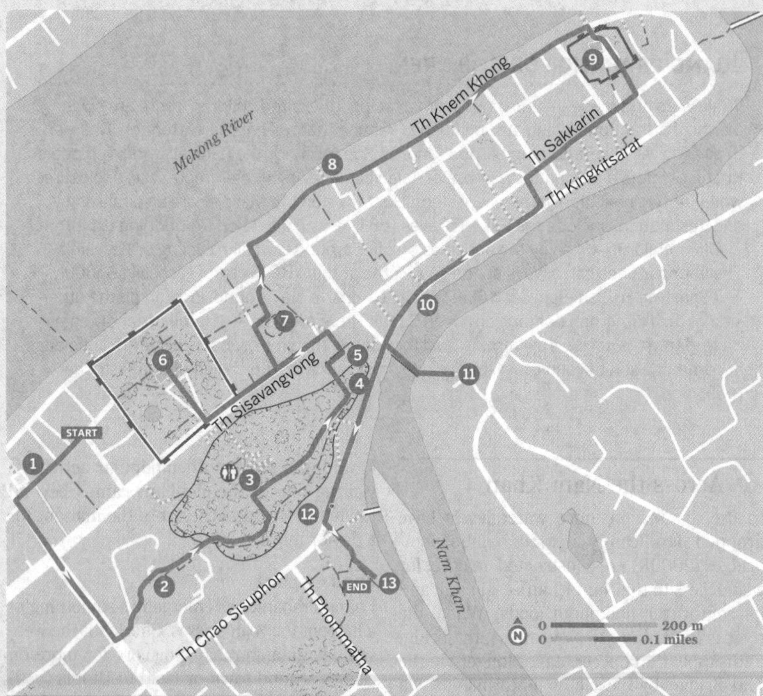

City Walk
Old Luang Prabang

START MORNING MARKET
END UTOPIA OR DYEN SABAI
LENGTH 4.5KM; FOUR TO FIVE HOURS

This walk meanders through the heart of the historic city in a leisurely half day, assuming plenty of stops. We suggest starting bright and early to miss the afternoon heat on Phu Si, and avoiding Tuesday to fit in with museum opening times. But if you accept that it's the overall atmosphere and cafe scene that makes Luang Prabang special rather than any particular sights, the walk can work any time.

After an early stroll through the 1 **Morning Market** (p56) and a local breakfast in a cafe, arrive at 2 **TAEC** (p39). Peruse the excellent little exhibition on northern Laos' ethnic mosaic or simply enjoy great coffee or fruit shakes at attached Le Patio. Suitably fuelled, try to weave your way through the untouristed little maze of residential homes to reach the southern flank of Phu Si. Climb to 3 **That Chomsi** (p39) before the day gets too hot. Or, if the air looks too hazy for views, continue instead around the hill via Buddha's oversized 4 **footprint** (p39) and descend to the main commercial street through 5 **Wat Siphoutthabat Thippharam** (p39). If you can arrive by 11am, visit the 6 **Royal Palace Museum** (p37) to see how Lao royalty lived until 1975. Then meander through the palm-shaded footpaths of 7 **Xieng Mouane area** to reach the 8 **Mekong waterfront** with its inviting cafe terraces and Lao-French colonial houses. If you didn't already explore them at dawn after the monks' alms procession, dip into a selection of atmospheric wats as you wander up the spine of the peninsula. Don't miss the most famous monastery of all, 9 **Wat Xieng Thong** (p42). Stroll back, taking in a stretch of the lovely 10 **Nam Khan waterfront** and, in the dry season, cross the bamboo bridge for a well-deserved lunch at delightful 11 **Dyen Sabai** (p57). If the bridge isn't there (June to November), or you are walking in the afternoon, unwind in 12 **Lao Lao Garden** (p59), or seek the winding path to 13 **Utopia** (p59).

Hibiscus Massage MASSAGE
(Map p40; ☎030-923 5079; Th Sakkarin; traditional massage from 60,000K; ⊙10am-10pm) Set in a former gallery in an old French building, Hibiscus wafts chilled tunes through its silk-draped walls while you get pummelled to perfection.

Lao Red Cross MASSAGE, SPA
(Map p40; ☎071-253448; Th Wisunarat; massage 10,000-50,000K; ⊙7am-10.30pm) In traditional (basic!) surroundings of wood rafters, cool fans and stone floors, sample a range of head and body massages, steams, reflexology and aromatherapy. Donations go directly to improving the lives of the poorest villages in Laos.

Spa Garden MASSAGE, SPA
(Map p40; ☎071-212325; massage 60,000-350,000K, sauna/manicure 30,000/60,000K) Attractive property set amid a flourishing garden, with various relaxation and detox packages.

Courses

Cooking

Tamarind COOKING
(Map p40; ☎020-7777 0484; www.tamarindlaos.com; Ban Wat Nong; 1-day course 270,000K; ⊙9am-3pm Mon-Sat) Join Tamarind at its lakeside pavilion for a day's tuition in the art of Lao cuisine, meeting first at its restaurant before heading to the market for ingredients for classic dishes such as *mok pa* (steamed fish in banana leaves). Evening classes are available from 4pm for 200,000K, but no market visit is included.

Tum Tum Cheng Cooking School COOKING
(Map p40; ☎071-253388; 29/2 Th Sakkarin; 1-day course incl cookbook 250,000K) Celebrated chef Chandra teaches you the secrets of his alchemy. Includes a visit to the market to select your vegetables. The day usually starts at the school on the peninsula at 8.30am and finishes at 2pm.

Massage

Dhammada MASSAGE
(☎071-212642; Namneua Lane; 1-/5-day course US$50/350) Offers one- to five-day massage courses.

Weaving

Some weavers in Ban Xang Khong offer informal courses on request.

OckPopTok COURSE
(Map p36; ☎071-212597; www.ockpoptok.com; 1-day course US$72; ⊙8.45am-4pm Mon-Sat) Learn to weave your own scarf and textiles with OckPopTok's classes, as well as its half-day bamboo weaving (US$18). Teachers are master craftspeople, you get to keep your handiwork and lunch is included. Situated 2km past Phousy market; a free tuk-tuk will pick you up and bring you back.

Tours

Luang Prabang has an abundance of travel agents vying for your patronage for half- to multiday tours. Tours to waterfalls and the Pak Ou Caves are particularly popular and prices are generally competitive, but it still pays to shop around. Many agencies, notably those lining Th Sisavangvong, also book flights, rent bicycles, change money and arrange visas (but note that Vietnamese visas and Lao visa extensions are easy and cheaper to arrange yourself).

The following agencies aren't necessarily the cheapest but have a wider range of offerings including regional trekking, kayaking and biking trips, are well organised and/or stand out for their ecotourism projects and community involvement.

Green Discovery OUTDOORS
(Map p40; ☎071-212093; www.greendiscoverylaos.com; 44/3 Th Sisavangvong) The daddy of ecotourism in Laos. They offer kayaking, trekking, mountain biking, motorcycling and multiday trips north, including motorcycle tours.

Tiger Trail HIKING
(Map p40; ☎071-252655; www.laos-adventures.com; Th Sisavangvong; ⊙8.30am-9pm) Focusing on socially responsible fair treks benefitting local people, Tiger Trail offers hikes through Hmong and Khamu villages. All tours can be tailored to include kayaking, elephant riding, rafting or mountain biking.

White Elephant HIKING
(Map p40; ☎071-254481; www.white-elephant-adventures-laos.com; Th Sisavangvong) White Elephant is hailed for its relationships with remote Hmong and Khamu villages, allowing a deeper insight into ethnic life. You can do this on a trek or by cycle in solid two- and three-day tours. Look out for the BMW motorbike and communist flag.

Festivals & Events

Pi Mai CULTURAL

(Lao New Year) Large numbers of visitors converge on Luang Prabang for the 'water throwing' festival Pi Mai in April, so advance bookings are wise at such times.

Bun Awk Phansa CULTURAL

(End of the Rains Retreat) Bun Awk Phansa sees boat races on the Nam Khan in September or October.

Sleeping

Accommodation costs are considerably higher in Luang Prabang than elsewhere in Laos. Rates given here are for the high season (October to March). Prices briefly climb higher for Pi Mai (mid-April) and Christmas, but will typically fall at least 25% from May. The choice is bewildering, with hundreds of existing options and new guesthouses opening every month. Old town peninsular accommodation generally comes at a hefty premium.

PI MAI (LAO NEW YEAR)

In the middle of April when the dry season reaches its hottest peak, Lao New Year (Pi Mai) marks the sun's passage from the zodiac sign of Pisces into Aries. The old year's spirit departs and the new one arrives amid a series of celebrations and a frenzy of good-hearted water throwing. Festivities are especially colourful in Luang Prabang where many people dress in traditional clothes for major events, which stretch over seven days.

Transport can be hard to find at this time and hotel occupancy (and prices) will be at a peak, especially in Luang Prabang.

Traditional Ceremonies

Day 1 The old spirit departs, people give their homes a thorough cleaning and at Hat Muang Khoun, a Mekong River island beach near Ban Xieng Maen, locals gather to build and decorate miniature sand stupas for good luck.

Day 2 Civic groups mount a colourful, costumed parade down Luang Prabang's main avenue from Wat Pha Mahathat to Wat Xieng Thong.

Day 3 A 'rest day' without parades when the devout take time to wash Buddha images at their local wat.

Day 4 In the early morning people climb Phu Si to make offerings of sticky rice at the summit stupa. Then in the afternoon they participate in *baci* (*bąasĭi;* sacred string-tying ceremonies) with family and friends.

Day 5 In a solemn procession, the Pha Bang leaves the Royal Palace Museum and is taken to a temporary pavilion erected in front of Wat Mai Suwannaphumaham.

Day 6 The new spirit arrives. This day is considered especially crucial, and cleansing rituals extend to the bathing of Buddhist holy images – particularly the Pha Bang, temporarily at Wat Mai – by pouring water onto them through wooden sluice pipes shaped like *naga* (mythical water serpents). Senior monks receive a similar treatment, and younger Lao will also pour water over the hands (palms held together) of their elderly relatives in a gesture of respect.

Day 7 A colourful final procession carries the Pha Bang from Wat Mai back to the museum.

Water Throwing

Overlaying all the traditional ceremonies, Pi Mai is nowadays mainly a festival of fun and water throwing. This being the height of the hot season, being anointed with a cup or two of cold water can indeed be refreshing. However, bucket-loads hurled into passing tuk-tuks are less amusing, especially if you haven't thought to bag up your valuables. Remember that foreigners are not exempt from the soaking and indeed some are guilty of egging on locals to use high-powered water guns that are far removed from the original spirit of the event.

Many walk-in rates are intimidating, but booking well ahead through websites like www.agoda.com might save up to 50% from the listed price. Rates for most top-end places attract an additional 10% tax and 10% service charge.

There are also some impressive ecolodges and resorts in the lush countryside beyond Luang Prabang.

Th Sisavangvong & Around

Paphai Guest House GUESTHOUSE $
(Map p40; ☎071-212752; Th Sisavang Vatthana; r without bathroom 50,000-60,000K;) This place is as cheap and basic as it gets in the old town. Rooms are set in a traditional wooden house near the heart of Th Sisavangvong. Rooms are fan-cooled, rattan-walled and have padlocks on the doors.

Bou Pha Guesthouse GUESTHOUSE $
(Map p40; ☎071-252405; Th Sisavangvong; r 60,000-100,000K;) This takes us back to 1990s Luang Prabang – an old house in the heart of the city with rooms for less than a tenner. Run by a lovely older couple, the cheapest rooms have shared bathroom. Upstairs rooms at 100,000K have street view.

Silichit Guest House GUESTHOUSE $
(Map p40; ☎071-212758; Th Sisavang Vatthana; r 80,000-120,000K;) A popular place with boxy, basic rooms finished in traditional Lao style. It's the location that wins you over as it is in the heart of the old town near the Mekong. Try for rooms 4 and 6 upstairs.

Namsok Guesthouse 1 GUESTHOUSE $
(Map p40; ☎071-212251; www.namsok-hotel.com; Th Sisavang Vatthana; r 100,000-200,000K;) The friendly and helpful Namsok is one of a trio of family-run guesthouses in the old town. Rooms are spread over two buildings with cheaper fan digs in the old building. The new building includes mod-cons like air-con, TV and a fridge.

Sackarinh Guest House GUESTHOUSE $
(Map p40; ☎071-254412; Th Sisavangvong; r 120,000-150,000K;) Hidden down a side-street choking on flowers, this is a colourful and central option while you get your bearings. Right in the centre of town. Rooms are basic but spacious.

Nora Singh Guesthouse GUESTHOUSE $
(Map p40; ☎071-212033; Th Sisavangvong; r 130,000K;) Tucked away in the lower reaches of Phu Si, this is a likeable little wooden home with just seven guest rooms, which include air-con, hot water and free wi-fi. It feels quite secluded when compared to the main drag, but is just a stumble away.

Thanaboun Guesthouse GUESTHOUSE $$
(Map p40; ☎071-260606; Th Sisavangvong; r 160,000-280,000K; @) In the heart of town, Thanaboun excels with clean, tastefully finished rooms. Those backing on to the temple grounds are quieter. There's also an internet cafe.

Phounsab Guesthouse GUESTHOUSE $$
(Map p40; ☎071-212975; www.phoun-thavy-sab.jimdo.com; Th Sisavangvong; r US$25-45;) Slap-bang in the heart of the old-city's commercial centre, the Phounsab's newer rooms are set back off a narrow courtyard and the great-value front ones are big and breezy with wooden trim and polished board floors.

Villa Senesouk HOTEL $$
(Map p40; ☎071-212074; senesouk@laohotel.com; Th Sakkarin; r US$30-50;) The morning monks' procession passes right outside the cheaper rooms. The upper ones are brighter and share a wat-view balcony. Tucked away across a garden courtyard, the 'new' block is designed to look like a traditional family home. Wood-panelled rooms here have full mod-cons, with the US$50 options offering additional space.

Xieng Mouane Guesthouse GUESTHOUSE $$
(Map p40; ☎071-252152; xiengmouane@yahoo.com; 86/6 Ban Xieng Mouane; r US$35-45;) This white two-storey colonial house has snug rooms with local fabric wall-hangings, sparkling floors and slightly dated bathrooms. The palm-shaded courtyard garden creates an oasis of calm.

Pack Luck Villa GUESTHOUSE $$
(Map p40; ☎071-253373; www.packluck.com; Th Thugnaithao; r US$35-55;) This imaginatively upgraded colonial-era building looks enchanting at night when soft light picks out the flecks of gold leaf on its colourful walls. Rooms are a little tight but the three with upper balconies overlook the monks' morning meander. All have striking fabrics and paper lanterns. Downstairs is the popular Pack Luck Liquor wine bar.

★Khoum Xiengthong Guesthouse GUESTHOUSE $$
(Map p40; ☎071-212906; www.khoumxiengthong.com; Th Sisalernsak; r US$50-70;) Bedecked

in tea lights by night, by day this delightful guesthouse with a strong whiff of Indochic nestles around a pretty garden. Stone-floored, white-walled rooms enjoy golden tapestries and chrome fans: rooms 2 (lower floor) and 5 (upper floor) are vast and include four-poster beds.

Chang Inn BOUTIQUE HOTEL **$$**
(Map p40; ☎071-253553; www.burasariheritage.com; Th Sakkarin; r from US$65; ❄📶) The lounge foyer of this enticing place sports a melange of dark woods, Chinese vases, mother-of-pearl inlay furniture and old clocks. Wooden mock-deer trophies lead down a short corridor to petite rooms with sepia photos and polished rosewood floors. A leafy brick-floored garden lies behind.

Villa Santi HISTORIC HOTEL **$$$**
(Map p40; ☎071-252157; www.villasantihotel.com; Th Sakkarin; r US$128-288; ❄📶🏊) This striking old royal building has three very different personalities. The original 19th-century villa, once home to King Sisavang Vong's wife, has just six vast 'royal' suites, plus an upstairs breakfast room with an enviable road-view terrace. Many 'deluxe' (ie standard) rooms are in a central annexe behind, while the majority are actually in a well-appointed 'resort' 5km south of town.

★ **Auberge les 3 Nagas** BOUTIQUE HOTEL **$$$**
(Map p40; ☎071-253888; www.3-nagas.com; Th Sakkarin; r from US$200; ❄@📶) Luang Prabang style was minted at this boutique hotel, bookended by mango trees and a burgundy 1950s Mercedes. The 100-year-old Lao-style building brims with old-world atmosphere and across the road another wing is an architectural gem. Palatial suites sport sink-to-sleep four-poster beds, tanned-wood bathrooms and a modern Asian design fusing colonial French roots.

Nam Khan Riverfront

Meune Na Backpacker Hostel HOSTEL **$**
(Map p40; ☎071-260851; Th Phetsarath; dm 30,000K, r from 60,000K; 📶) A real budget crashpad close the old Nam Khan bridge, the dorms here only have five beds to a room, making it a little less crowded than some of the other backpacker hostels around town. There's a traditional costume place next door if you fancy a souvenir photo decked out in Lao wedding clothes.

Mao Pha Shak Guesthouse GUESHOUSE **$**
(Map p40; ☎071-212513; Ban Visoun; r 80,000-130,000K; ❄📶) Set down a quiet side alley close to the Nam Khan, this is a friendly, family-run guesthouse. The two rooms offering oblique river views are the most expensive.

Luang Prabang Paradise Resort HOTEL **$$**
(☎071-213103; www.luangprabangparadiseresort.com; r US$38-75; 🏊) Near the Nam Khan, but a long way out of town over the new bridge, this is a relaxing place to stay for those who want to get away from it all. The all-wood bungalows surround the generous swimming pool.

BelAir Boutique Resort RESORT **$$**
(Map p40; ☎071-254699; www.lebelairhotels.com; r from US$60; ❄📶) BelAir's thatched cottages might look rustic from the outside, but inside all is modern and well chosen, including curtained display-baths and sunset-facing private balconies. Standard rooms are large and similarly stylish in a complex that's widely spaced amid palm trees and beautifully manicured lawns.

★ **Apsara** BOUTIQUE HOTEL **$$$**
(Map p40; ☎071-212420; www.theapsara.com; Th Kingkitsarat; r incl breakfast US$70-130; ❄📶) Apsara commands fine views of the sleepy Nam Khan. Its Indochinese lobby is peppered with silk lanterns and the bar springs from an old classic film, while each of the open-plan rooms is individually designed. From its turquoise walls to its coloured glass Buddhas, everything about this place screams style.

Mekong Riverfront & Around

Boungnasouk Guesthouse GUESTHOUSE **$**
(Map p40; ☎071-212749; 1/3 Th Khem Kong; r US$10; 📶) This cheap and cheerful family-run guesthouse has an enticing location down on the Mekong riverfront. There are just six rooms here, three twins and three doubles, but no river views, as the family have bagged those. Just across the road, the family also operate a restaurant with a view of the Mekong, which is a fine place for a light lunch or cheap dinner.

Soutikone Guesthouse 1 GUESTHOUSE **$**
(Map p40; ☎071-253990; r 100,000-180,000K; ❄📶) The interiors aren't luxurious but are almost totally panelled in varnished wood, giving the vague impression of 1920s ocean-

liner cabins. Rooms vary considerably and some have oddities such as doorways to nowhere, missing windows or unfinished bathrooms. A small, shared balcony gives oblique Mekong glimpses.

★ **Muang Lao Riverside Villa** HOTEL $$
(Map p40; ☎071-252219; www.xandriahotels.com; Th Khem Khong; r US$25-45;) Set in a charming wooden property overlooking the Mekong, the small rooms here are very good value for the location. All include such touches as flat-screen TVs and rain showers, plus some offer balcony views over the river.

Kongsavath Guesthouse GUESTHOUSE $$
(Map p40; ☎071-212994; www.khongsavath.com; Th Khem Khong; r US$30-60;) This lovely, vine-choked villa has wood-panelled rooms reminiscent of a captain's bunk in an old schooner. Boasting a great Mekong-front location, the family suite overlooking the river is the best.

Ammata Guest House GUESTHOUSE $$
(Map p40; ☎071-212175; pphilasouk@yahoo.com; Ban Wat Nong; r $30-40;) Friendly and family-run, this small, popular guesthouse has a low-key ambience, spotless and spacious rooms with polished wood interiors, and renovated bathrooms. Most rooms are upstairs, running off a shared and shaded balcony.

Mekong Charm Guesthouse GUESTHOUSE $$
(Map p40; ☎071-213086; www.mekongcharm.com; Th Khem Khong; r US$35-45;) Located at the top end of the peninsular near Wat Xieng Thong, this riverside place has plenty of Mekong charm. Scrupulously clean rooms include number 2 with a flat-screen TV and bathtub. Several others have balconies.

Lao Wooden House GUESTHOUSE $$
(Map p40; ☎071-260283; www.laowoodenhouse.com; Th Khounswa; r incl breakfast US$45-55;) This friendly, well-appointed half-timbered guesthouse-hotel is typical of the neat, pleasant pseudo-traditional new buildings that have popped up in this part of the old quarter.

Villa Champa GUESTHOUSE $$
(Map p40; ☎071-253555; www.villachampa.com; Th Sisavang Vatthana; r US$40-65;) This tastefully renovated traditional house has a prime location between the Mekong River and the old temple district. The nine rooms include all mod-cons like air-con, TV and minibar, plus some more traditional Laotian textiles to complete the picture.

Luang Prabang River Lodge HOTEL $$
(Map p40; ☎071-253314; www.luang-prabang-river-lodge.com; Th Khem Khong; r US$40-60;) This shuttered colonial corner house has an alluring patio draped in floral vines and framed by a lychgate and old bomb casings. Interiors have clean lines and restrained decor. A few rooms offer Mekong views.

Villa Chitdara GUESTHOUSE $$
(Map p40; ☎071-254949; www.villachitdara.com; r from US$55;) Set amid a spacious verdant garden in the heart of the old town, Villa Chitdara is a charming base to explore. Rooms include TVs, hot water and safes. The friendly owners speak eloquent French.

Sala Prabang HOTEL $$$
(Map p40; ☎071-252460; www.salalao.com; 102/6 Th Khem Khong; r incl breakfast US$80-90;) Housed in an old French villa, Sala's rooms have limewashed walls, guacamole-coloured linen and hardwood floors, and are separated from the bathrooms by Japanese-style screens. Opt for a quieter room at the back.

Xiengthong Palace HISTORIC HOTEL $$$
(Map p40; ☎071-213200; www.xiengthongpalace.com; Th Khem Khong; r US$200-500;) This former royal residence has a striking setting overlooking the Mekong River next to Wat Xieng Thong. The 26 rooms are luxuriously appointed and include open-plan Mekong suites with grandstand views and two-storey suites with their own private plunge pools and lounges.

Ban Hoxieng

Compact, pretty and generally good value, Ban Hoxieng is a delightful little network of formerly residential lanes tucked behind the main post office, with a great concentration of relatively central choices.

Lemon Laos Backpackers HOSTEL $
(Map p40; ☎071-212500; www.spicylaosbackpacker.com; Th Noradet; dm 30,000K;) Formerly Spicy Laos Backpackers, the Lao owners have renamed it Lemon Laos. One of the cheapest crashpads in town, travellers aren't really here for the beds, but to avoid going to bed, as it rumbles on into the early hours. BBQs and cheap shots add up to a carnival atmosphere, but the smarter neighbours are not that happy.

★**Xayana Guesthouse** GUESTHOUSE $
(Map p40; ☎071-260680; www.mylaohome.com; Th Hoxieng; dm 40,000K, r from 80,000K; 📶) Also known as the X3 Capsule Hotel, this budget pad has immaculately clean dorms, which are considerably more spacious than 'capsule' would suggest, including three bathrooms to every eight beds. There's an inviting courtyard out front to hang out in, drink coffee and meet other travellers.

Phonemaly Guesthouse GUESTHOUSE $
(Map p40; ☎071-253504; Th Hoxieng; r from 100,000K; ❄📶) This pair of traditionally styled wooden houses has very much the feel of a real home yet all the conveniences of a well-run guesthouse. The best timber-clad rooms are upstairs. Obliging family owners ensure a free supply of bananas and coffee.

Souksavath Guesthouse GUESTHOUSE $
(Map p40; ☎071-212043; Th Hoxieng; r 120,000-200,000K; ❄📶) Souksavath has house-proud rooms with fresh paint, bureaus and wall-mounted flat-screen TVs. Good value.

Manichan Guesthouse GUESTHOUSE $$
(Map p40; ☎020-5692 0137; www.manichanguest house.com; r 150,000-360,000K; ❄📶) The upper rooms come with bright, two-coloured walls and share a bathroom that's worthy of a boutique hotel, plus a wide terrace with Phu Si views. The ground-floor rooms come with paintings and en suite bathrooms with screened showers. Low season rates are 80,000K to 200,000K.

Villa Suan Maak GUESTHOUSE $$
(Map p36; ☎071-252775; www.villa-suan-maak-laos.com; Th Noradet; r incl breakfast downstairs/upstairs US$22/40; ❄📶) The centrepiece here is a homely little colonial villa where two shuttered upper rooms feature local fabrics, columns and views across the quiet patch of garden. Newer downstairs rooms are tacked around the old house and are well appointed. It's popular with long-term volunteers staying in Luang Prabang, so has a real community vibe.

Villa Pumalin BOUTIQUE HOTEL $$
(Map p40; ☎071-212777; www.villapumalin.com; Th Hoxieng; r incl breakfast US$55-75; ❄📶) Rosewood steps lead across a tiny carp pool on the way up to this hotel, which has superbly finished rooms that combine stylish bathroom fittings with semi-traditional woodwork interiors, top quality linens and free wi-fi. The best room (201) has a private balcony with glimpses of the Mekong.

Ban Lao Hotel HOTEL $$
(Map p36; ☎071-252078; www.banlaohotel.com; Th Thammamikalath; r incl breakfast US$25-75; ❄@📶) Tastefully comfortable rooms are set behind a late-colonial-era mansion that's 'hollowed out' so that you can see the garden's palms and jackfruit trees while checking in. Deluxe rooms come on sturdy stilts over fountain walls and swing seats. Breakfast is served in a large pavilion perched over a pond. It's peaceful and good value.

Maison Dalabua BOUTIQUE HOTEL $$$
(☎071-255588; www.maison-dalabua.com; Th Phothisarath ; US$75-100; ❄📶) Set in spacious grounds that include a vast pond dotted with water lillies, Maison Dalabua is a real hideaway. The 15 rooms are in an attractive building and include flat-screen TVs and generously proportioned beds. More expensive rooms include a bathtub.

★**Le Sen Boutique Hotel** BOUTIQUE HOTEL $$$
(Map p36; ☎071-261661; www.lesenhotel.com; 113 Th Manomai; r US$95-160; ❄@📶🏊) This stylish boutique hotel is exceptional value when compared with some of the heritage hotels crammed into the old quarter. Rooms are well-appointed with modish bathrooms and flat-screen TVs, and all face the inviting central swimming pool. Extra touches include a well-equipped gym and free use of bicycles.

Satri House HISTORIC HOTEL $$$
(Map p36; ☎071-253491; www.satrihouse.com; 57 Th Phothisarath; r US$192-384; ❄📶🏊) Built at the turn of the last century as a royal villa, Satri House has grown in size and stature to become one of Luang Prabang's leading heritage hotels. Rooms are tastefully decorated with Asian textiles and antiquities, including some quirky touches here and there. The hotel includes two pools and a spectacular spa.

Amantaka LUXURY HOTEL $$$
(Map p40; ☎071-860333; www.amanresorts.com; Th Kitsarat; ste US$800-1700; ❄📶🏊) Set in a meticulously renovated former French colonial-era hospital, Amantaka is the most opulent resort in Luang Prabang. The Khan pool suites are the best all-round lodgings, but they still attract a compulsary board charge of US$135 per person per day on top of the room charge.

South of Phu Si

A selection of budget and lower-midrange places south of Phu Si are generally less atmospheric but there's a cluster of good bars nearby. Bigger hotels, some aimed at package tours and Thai/Chinese groups, are mostly further south, notably along Th Phu Vao. Few are original enough to warrant the out-of-centre location.

Khounsavanh Guesthouse GUESTHOUSE **$**
(Map p40; ☎071-212297; Ban Thongchaleum; r without bathroom 60,000K, with bathroom 80,000-140,000K; ❄📶) Khounsavanh is the most appealing of several budget guesthouses strung along a quiet lane near Dara Market. The air-con en suite rooms share a wide open terrace with views of Phu Si's summit temple spire.

Mano Guest House GUESTHOUSE **$**
(Map p36; ☎071-253112; manosotsay@hotmail.com; Th Pha Mahapatsaman; r 80,000-120,000K; ❄📶) We first stayed in this spacious and homey place more than a decade ago. The all-wood rooms include large TVs, tiled bathrooms, iris-stemmed lights and wall hangings.

Vilayvanh Guesthouse GUESTHOUSE
(Map p40; ☎071-252757; r 100,000K; ❄@) This sparkling clean guesthouse is excellent value and quietly tucked down a pretty residential alley. Plug-in internet, coffee, drinking water and bananas are all free for guests.

Phongphilack Guesthouse GUESTHOUSE **$**
(Map p40; ☎071-252189; phongphilack@hotmail.com; Ban Aphay; r 100,000-120,000K; ❄📶) Hidden away in the alleys of Ban Aphay, this guesthouse was recently renovated, making for a good deal. Rooms include hot water, air-con and ceiling fans. The friendly family speak English and it's walking distance to the main bar strip.

Villa Sayada HOTEL **$**
(Map p40; ☎071-254872; www.villa-shayada-laos.com; Th Phommatha; r 120,000-200,000K; ❄📶) Opposite Wat Visoun. The sign says Sayada, the website Shayada, but either way this welcoming nine-room mini-hotel has generously sized rooms, hung fabrics, handmade lamps and decent hot showers.

Thongbay Guesthouse GUESTHOUSE **$$**
(☎071-253234; www.thongbay-guesthouses.com; r US$34-75; ❄📶) Subtle lighting and immaculately managed foliage intersperse the Thongbay's close-packed wood-and-thatch bungalows, most of which overlook the Nam Khan. Facilities include balconies, minibars and good tiled bathrooms with step-in showers. The downside is an isolated location on an unpaved backstreet.

Luang Say Residence LUXURY HOTEL **$$$**
(Map p36; ☎071-260891; www.luangsayresidence.com; Ban Phonepheng; ste US$255-520; ❄@📶🏊) Conjuring up the colonial heyday of Luang Prabang, this sophisticated all-suite hotel consists of six French-accented buildings set amid verdant gardens. Furnishings are sumptuous and there is an inviting swimming pool. The Belle Epoque Restaurant is considered one of the top dining destinations in town.

★**La Résidence Phou Vao** LUXURY HOTEL **$$$**
(Map p36; ☎071-212530; www.residencephouvao.com; r US$485-540; ❄@📶🏊) There's no better high-end choice in Luang Prabang than La Résidence Phou Vao, with seamless, proactive service and impeccably stylish rooms. The infinity pool reflects distant Phu Si hill and is flanked by a top-notch Franco-Lao restaurant. The Mekong Spa is spectacular and has won several awards.

Eating

Several enchanting restaurants are dotted along the main strip with many more along the riverbanks. We recommend the Mekong riverfront at sunset, when a glowing orange ball casts its reflection on the rippled waters. The Nam Khan riverfront is generally quieter and offers glimpses of rural life within the city.

Luang Prabang has a unique cuisine all of its own. Archetypal dishes include ubiquitous local sausages and a soup-stew called *orlam (ǎw lám)* made with meat, mushrooms and eggplant with special bitter-spicy wood chips added for flavouring (don't swallow them!). A great local snack is *kai Ƀâan* (Mekong riverweed). Reminiscent of nori seaweed, it is formed into squares, briefly fried in seasoned oil, topped with sesame seeds and ideally served with *jąaou borng*, a sweet-spicy jam-like condiment made with chillies and dried buffalo skin.

A variety of well-filled French-bread sandwiches are available at makeshift **baguette stalls** (Map p40; ⏲7am-10pm) facing the tourist office. Fresh fruit shakes are also a favourite here.

GIVING SOMETHING BACK

There are several ways in which travellers can give back to the local community in Luang Prabang.

➡ Travellers can buy books to distribute to local children from **Big Brother Mouse** (BBM; Map p40; ☎071-254937; www.bigbrothermouse.com; Th Sothikuman). As well as promoting literacy, the idea is that it's more beneficial for visitors to hand out books than candy.

➡ **Luang Prabang Library** (Map p40; ☎071-254813; www.communitylearninginternational.org; Th Sisavangvong; ⏲8am-5pm Tue-Sun) collects donations to provide local books for a 'book-boat' library that sails to remote villages.

➡ The **Children's Cultural Centre** (Map p40; ☎071-253732; cccLuangPrabang@gmail.com; Th Sisavangvong; ⏲4-5pm Tue-Fri, 8-11.30am & 2-4pm Sat) seeks donations of virtually anything recyclable or resalable to provide after-school activities for kids.

➡ At the **Lao Red Cross** (☎071-253448; Th Wisunarat; ⏲7am-10.30pm) travellers can donate used, washed clothing or even give blood (9am to 4pm, days vary), a precious commodity in Laos as anywhere.

Many unexotic shop-stalls serve strong Lao coffee at around 5000K a cup. However, if you're seeking out European pastries and espresso-style coffee there's a growing selection of cafes to tempt you.

Food markets are great for fresh fruit, vegetables and 'meat' in more versions than you can imagine. Self-caterers should check out the **Morning Market** (Map p40; ⏲5.30am-4pm Sat-Mon), a colourful street market in Ban Pakam that's at its liveliest in the early morning when locals stock up on leafy greens, eggs, dried shrimp and live frogs.

Th Sisavangvong & Around

★Le Banneton BAKERY $
(Map p40; Th Sakkarin; meals 20,000-40,000K; ⏲6.30am-6pm; 📶) Offering the best croissants in Laos, this peaceful peninsula cafe is celebrated by pastry buffs for the quality of its flour. It has a sweet-toothed menu of *pain au chocolat,* fruit shakes, sandwiches, quiches and homemade sorbets.

Café Toui FUSION $
(Map p40; Th Sisavang Vatthana; mains 30,000-80,000K; ⏲7am-10pm; 📶🌿) Candlelit tunes harmonise with gold-stencilled oxblood walls at this chichi little eatery. The menu is vegetarian-friendly and Asian fusion with standout dishes such as tofu *láhp,* plus an inviting sampler menu.

Le Café Ban Vat Sene FRENCH $
(Map p40; Th Sakkarin; mains 30,000K; ⏲7.30am-10pm; 📶) Retro fans whir over an Indochinese scene of flower-shaded lights and stylish refinement. This is the place to work, sip an afternoon pastis and read a paper. French wine, salads, quiche, pasta and pizza ...*parfait!*

Xieng Thong Noodle-Shop LAOTIAN $
(Map p40; Th Sakkarin; noodle soup 15,000K; ⏲from 6.30am) The best *kòw Ђęeak sèn* (round rice noodles served in a broth with pieces of chicken or deep-fried crispy pork belly) in town is served from an entirely unexotic shopfront well up the peninsula. Stocks are usually finished by 2pm.

Nazim Indian Food INDIAN $
(Map p40; Th Sisavangvong; mains 15,000-40,000K; ⏲11am-11pm) The biriyanis might be as flaky as the decor but the crispy dosai are tasty and the kitchen keeps cooking until nearly 11pm, unusually late for Luang Prabang.

★Coconut Garden LAOTIAN, INTERNATIONAL $$
(Map p40; ☎071-260436; Th Sisavangvong; meals 35,000-150,000K; ⏲8am-11pm; 📶🌿) An excellent 100,000K vegetarian set meal provides five top-quality Lao dishes, which allows a single diner to create the subtle palate of flavours that you'd normally only get from a multiperson feast. Coconut Garden has front and rear yards, and is a great spot for lunch or dinner. International favourites are also available.

Dao Fa Bistro INTERNATIONAL $$
(Map p40; Th Sisavangvong; mains 30,000-75,000K; ⏲11am-10pm or later; 📶) One of the first international restaurants to open on

the central strip, this is still one of the best places in town for pizzas, pastas and a selection of home comfort food. It's also a great spot for creative cocktails and post-dinner drinks.

Tangor FUSION $$
(Map p40; ☎071-260761; www.letangor.com; Th Sisavangvong; mains 40,000-80,000K; ⏰11am-10pm; 📶) A gastronomic addition to the Luang Prabang dining scene, Tangor serves beautifully crafted fusion food, blending the best of seasonal Lao produce with French flair.

Tamnak Lao LAOTIAN $$
(Map p40; ☎071-252525; www.tamnaklao.net; Th Sakkarin; mains 35,000-75,000K; ⏰9am-4pm & 6-10pm) Plenty of Lao and Luang Prabang options served in an archetypal half-timbered house with sturdy arched balconies overlooking the street. Service is obliging but it often fills up with international tour groups. Cooking classes (US$30) available by day.

Nam Khan Riverfront & Around

★**Rosella Fusion** FUSION $
(Map p40; Th Kingkitsarat; mains 15,000-35,000K) Established by a former Amantaka bartender, this riverside restaurant offers an innovative selection of affordable fusion flavours. The owner is particularly proud of his bargain cocktails, so consider dropping by for a sundowner before dinner.

★**Tamarind** LAOTIAN $
(Map p40; ☎071-213128; www.tamarindlaos.com; Th Kingkitsarat; mains 25,000-60,000K, set dinners 100,000-150,000K; ⏰11am-10pm; 📶) On the banks of the Nam Khan next to Apsara hotel, chic Tamarind has created its very own strain of 'Mod Lao' cuisine. The à la carte menu boasts delicious sampling platters with bamboo dip, stuffed lemongrass and *meuyang* (DIY parcels of noodles, herbs, fish and chilli pastes, and vegetables).

★**Dyen Sabai** LAOTIAN, INTERNATIONAL $
(Map p40; ☎020-5510 4817; Ban Phan Luang; mains 20,000-35,000K; ⏰8am-11pm; 📶) One of Luang Prabang's top destinations for fabulous Lao food. The eggplant dip and the fried Mekong riverweed here are as good as anywhere. Most seating is on recliner cushions in rustic open-sided pavilions. It's a short stroll across the Nam Khan bamboo bridge in the dry season or a free boat ride at other times. Two-for-one cocktails between noon and 7pm.

Apsara FUSION $$
(Map p40; ☎071-254670; www.theapsara.com; Th Kingkitsarat; mains 60,000-110,000K; ⏰7am-10pm; 📶) This chic eatery fronting the Nam Khan offers fusion cuisine blending east and west. Choose from buffalo steak, stuffed panin fish to share or braised pork belly for a main. Save some space for the divine desserts such as poached nashi pear in lime and ginger syrup served with coconut ice cream and a Lao poppadom.

Couleur Cafe INTERNATIONAL $$
(Map p40; ☎071-254694; Th Kingkirsarat; mains 40,000-100,000K; ⏰11am-10pm; 📶) Always well-regarded by long-term residents, Couleur Cafe relocated to the Nam Khan side of the peninsula but continues to serve stylish French-accented and creatively presented Laotian cuisine. Menu highlights include chicken casserole with ginger and lemongrass, and duck breast with honey and mango chutney.

Mekong Riverfront & Around

Riverside Barbecue Restaurant BARBECUE $
(Map p40; Th Khem Khong; set meal small/large 30,000/60,000K; ⏰5-11pm) Tabletop barbecues *(sìn daat)* are pretty popular in Luang Prabang and this Mekong riverfront restaurant may just be the most popular of all. If you don't finish the larger set meal, you'll be charged extra to avoid wastage.

Khemkhong View Restaurant LAOTIAN $
(Map p40; Th Khem Khong; meals 15,000-35,000K; ⏰7am-9pm) One of the many riverside restaurants lining the Mekong, the split-level Khemkhong View has an extensive menu with choices such as spicy prawn and coconut soup, squid *láhp* (or intestine *láhp* for the more adventurous) and steamed, fermented fish.

Saffron CAFE $
(Map p40; Th Khem Khong; mains 20,000-35,000K; ⏰7am-9pm; 📶) The perfect riverside stop for breakfast, this stylish cafe hung with lush black-and-white photography turns out great pasta dishes, serves excellent coffee and has warm service. There's also a choice of interior and al fresco dining.

Big Tree Café KOREAN, INTERNATIONAL $
(Map p40; www.bigtreecafe.com; Th Khem Khong; mains 25,000-50,000K; ⏰9am-9pm; 📶) Korean

food made by a genuine Korean in Luang Prabang. Eat in the cafe – which is full of Adri Berger's alluring Lao photography – or outside on the sun terrace overlooking the Mekong. There's also a choice of Western and Japanese dishes.

L'Elephant Restaurant FRENCH **$$$**
(Map p40; www.elephant-restau.com; Ban Wat Nong; mains 80,000-250,000K; ⌚11.30am-10pm) L'Elephant serves arguably the most sophisticated cuisine in the city in a renovated villa with wooden floors, stucco pillars, stencilled ochre walls and bags of atmosphere. The Menu du Chasseur (240,000K) includes terrines, soups, duck breast and other Gallic specialities. The buffalo steak tartare is amazing.

Royal Palace Museum & Ban Hoxieng

Night Food Stalls LAOTIAN **$**
(Map p40; ⌚6-10pm; 🌿) Food stalls emerge at dusk on a narrow street behind the tourist office with illuminated communal tables so you don't have to eat on the hoof. There's no better place to taste a wide variety of cheap yet well-cooked local food. There are plenty of vegetarian stalls offering a range of dishes for just 10,000K. Whole roast fish stuffed with lemongrass is a bargain at around 20,000K.

JoMa Bakery Cafe BAKERY **$**
(Map p40; Th Chao Fa Ngum; mains 10,000-35,000K; ⌚7am-9pm; 📶) This haven of cool with comfy chairs and a contemporary vibe is one of the city's busiest bakeries. It offers delectable comfort food in the form of soups, salads, bagels, creatives coffees and wholesome shakes.

Somchanh Restaurant VEGETARIAN **$**
(Map p40; Th Suvannabanlang; mains 15,000-30,000K; ⌚7am-7pm; 🌿) This simple outdoor eatery near the cluster of guesthouses in Ban Wat That serves a large selection of Lao and Luang Prabang dishes, including the best choice of vegetarian Lao food in town. Opt for seating across the road on the riverbank.

Delilah's INTERNATIONAL **$**
(Map p40; Th Chao Fa Ngum; mains 20,000-50,000K; 📶) Just beyond the main strip, but convenient for the Ban Hoxieng guesthouses, Delilah's serves up healthy breakfasts and a wide range of home comfort food such as sandwiches, wraps and pastas. Tasty Laotian specialities are also available.

Blue Lagoon INTERNATIONAL **$$**
(Map p40; www.blue-lagoon-restaurant.com; mains 45,000-140,000K; ⌚10am-10pm; 📶) A favourite with expats for its lantern-festooned walls, leafy patio and jazz-infused atmosphere. The menu features Luang Prabang sausage, pasta, salads and very tasty *làhp*.

South of Phu Si

★ **Le Patio** LAOTIAN, INTERNATIONAL **$**
(Map p40; ☎071-253364; TAEC; sandwiches 30,000K; ⌚9am-5.45pm Tue-Sun; 📶) Sip Phongsali smoked teas or Lao Arabica espressos and nibble delicious feta-olive baguette sandwiches on a shaded terrace with attractive mountain views. Ethnic minority dishes, such as Akha meatballs and Hmong pork belly, are also available.

Roots & Leaves LAOTIAN **$$**
(Map p40; ☎071-254870; www.rootsinlaos.com; mains 30,000-60,000K, set dinner US$25; ⌚7.30am-10pm) The outdoor setting sees tables ranged beneath palms around a lotus pond, where an artificial 'island' forms a stage for performances by local musicians. Various dinner shows are performed here, generally 7pm to 9pm Monday to Saturday, but there are seasonal variations. Bring some mosquito repellent.

Luang Prabang Secret Pizza ITALIAN **$$**
(Map p36; mains 50,000-60,000K; ⌚from 6.30pm Tue & Fri) Alright, so the secret is out, but it's well worth sharing. Long the preserve of Luang Prabang residents, host Andrea prepares wood-fired pizzas, classic lasagne and homemade gnocchi in the garden of his lovely home. Profiteroles round things off nicely, plus a fine bottle of Italian wine. Signposted from the main road.

Sushi JAPANESE **$$**
(Map p36; ☎020-7751 8300; Th Pha Mahapatsaman; set meals 50,000-80,000K, sushi 30,000-150,000K; ⌚10am-10.30pm; 📶) If the fresh fish isn't delivered there might not be much sushi on the menu. However, a delicious range of other Japanese favourites include *gyoza*, *katsudon* and *katsukare*. Sets come with miso soup, daikon pickles and rice.

Drinking & Nightlife

The main stretch of Th Sisavangvong northeast of the palace has plenty of drinking places, including some appealing wine bars. The main hub for drinkers is just south of Phu Si on Th Kingkitsarat around Hive Bar (p59) and Lao Lao Garden (p59). Legal closing time is 11.30pm and this is fairly strictly enforced. The local Chinese-run superbowl, out in the suburbs near the southern bus terminal, is the one exception and is an amusing place to partake (or just watch) drunken bowling. Mind your toes!

La Pistoche BAR

(Map p36; Ban Phong Pheng; entry 20,000K; ⏲10am-11pm; 📶) The perfect medicine for landlocked Laos, La Pistoche offers two swimming pools set amid a spacious garden in the suburbs south of town. Entry includes games of pétanque and water volleyball if you're feeling active. Generous happy hours from noon to 7pm mean there's a bit of a hippy trippy vibe by day, but full moon parties are on the cards.

Utopia BAR

(Map p40; 📶) This vernal oasis with a Khmer twist has celestial views of the Nam Khan. Utopia is all recliner cushions, low-slung tables and hookah pipes. It sounds wrong but works perfectly. Chill over a fruit shake, play a board game or volleyball, or lose yourself in a sea of candles come sunset. Yoga by day, bar snacks by night, this place pulls in the backpacker crowd. Take the turn-off at the top of Th Phommatha.

Lao Lao Garden BAR

(Map p40; Th Kingkitsarat; 📶) Lit up like a jungle Vegas, this garden bar on the skirts of Phu Si calls you to chill by candlelight, listen to easy sounds and warm your cockles by the firepit. There's happy hour all day for Bloody Mary and mojito enthusiasts. Also good for a wide range of foods, including *orlam* and buffalo stew, plus cook-it-yourself Lao hotpot-barbecue *(sìn daat)*.

Hive Bar BAR

(Map p40; Th Kingkitsarat; 📶) The buzz is back at this stylish den of hidden coves. Out back in the garden there's a dance floor, projector wall and more tables. Check out the excellent ethnic fashion show every night at 7pm, which also features a hip-hop crew. Tapas, happy hour and cocktails.

S Bar BAR

(Map p40; Th Kingsarat) A popular watering hole for resident foreigners living in Luang Prabang, S Bar has a pool table and the ever-popular *bebe-foot* (table football). Fills up with the after-dinner crowd from about 9pm.

Ikon Klub BAR

(Map p40; Th Sisavang Vatthana; ⏲5pm-late) Less a club and more of a boudoir, there's something deliciously subversive about this boho bar; the lights are low and the decor is tinged with elements of the 1930s. Tom Waits croaking through the speakers finishes it off perfectly.

House BAR

(Map p40; Th Kingkitsarat; 📶) Fairy-lit House is a tempting stop for a Belgian beer, including Chimay and Duvel. The gardens are pretty, and the snacks and breakfasts are delicious, including *stoofvlees* (beef stew).

Dao Fah CLUB

(Map p36; ⏲9-11.30pm) A young Lao crowd packs this cavernous club, located off the road to the southern bus terminal. Live bands playing Lao and Thai pop alternate with DJs who spin rap and hip hop.

☆ Entertainment

The Luang Prabang Film Festival runs every year in early December at several venues around town.

Phrolak-Phralam Theatre TRADITIONAL DANCE

(Map p40; Royal Palace Grounds; tickets 70,000-170,000K; ⏲shows 6pm or 6.30pm Mon, Wed, Fri & Sat) The misleadingly named Royal Lao Ballet puts on slow-moving traditional dances accompanied by a 10-piece Lao 'orchestra'. Performances last about 1¼ hours and include a Ramayana-based scene. It's well worth reading the typewritten notes provided at the entrance to have an idea of what's going on. Be aware that despite the nominal 'royal' connections, the theatre has all the glamour of a 1970s school hall. If all the seats are full (rare), guests who bought the very cheapest tickets could end up standing.

Shopping

The best areas for shopping are Th Sisavangvong and the Mekong waterfront, where characterful boutiques selling local art, gilded Buddhas, handmade paper products and all manner of tempting souvenirs abound.

Silver shops are attached to several houses in Ban Ho Xieng, the traditional royal silversmiths' district.

DON'T MISS

HANDICRAFT NIGHT MARKET

Every evening this tourist-oriented but highly appealing **market** (Map p40; Th Sisavangvong; ⏲5.30-10pm) fills the main road from the Royal Palace Museum to Th Kitsarat. Low-lit and quiet, it is devoid of hard selling and is possibly the most tranquil market in Asia. Tens of dozens of traders sell silk scarves, wall hangings, Hmong appliqué blankets, T-shirts, clothing, shoes, paper, silver, bags, ceramics, bamboo lamps and more. Prices are remarkably fair but cheaper 'local' creations sometimes originate from China, Thailand or Vietnam.

OckPopTok HANDICRAFTS, CLOTHING
(Map p40; ☎071-254761; www.ockpoptok.com; 73/5 Ban Wat Nong; ⏲8am-9pm) OckPopTok works with a wide range of different tribes to preserve their handicraft traditions. Fine silk and cotton scarves, chemises, dresses, wall hangings and cushion covers make perfect presents. Also has a branch on **Th Sisavangvong** (Map p40; ☎071-254406; Th Sisavangvong; ⏲8am-9pm).

Ma Te Sai HANDICRAFTS
(Map p40; www.matesai.com; Th Khem Khong) The name means 'where is it from' in Lao, and all the silk, paper and gift items in this attractive boutique come from villages around Luang Prabang.

Kopnoi HANDICRAFTS
(Map p40; Th Vatmou-Enna) This shop targets the discerning shopper with east-meets-west clothing in natural fabrics and dyes, designer jewellery, homewares and handicrafts, books on Lao cuisine, architecture and crafts, packaged spices and teas, and local art.

Naga Creations JEWELLERY
(Map p40; Th Sisavangvong) Specialising in jewellery, Naga Creations produces individual masterpieces using a variety of semi-precious stones and silver. All items are handcrafted and you can see the jewellers at work in the store.

Pathana Boupha Antique House ANTIQUES
(Map p40; Th Phommatha) Follow the sweeping stairs in the garden of this impressive old French mansion to discover an Aladdin's cave of antique Buddhas, golden *naga,* silver betel-nut pots, Akha-style bracelets and Hmong necklaces. Also sells fine silk scarves from Sam Neua.

Orange Tree ANTIQUES
(Map p40; Th Khem Khong) This riverfront antiques shop is a testament to its owners' magpie wanderings, with Hong Kong tea tins, Chinese retro alarm clocks, Mao revolutionary crockery, Bakelite inkwells, Vietnamese clocks and Burmese Buddhist statuary. Curio heaven!

Caruso Lao Homecraft HOMEWARES
(Map p40; ☎071-254574; Th Sakkarin) Caruso houses a gallery of beautiful homewares, photo frames, linen and silk.

L'Etranger Books & Tea BOOKS
(Map p40; Th Kingkitsarat; ⏲8am-10pm Mon-Sat, 10am-10pm Sun) The cheapest spot for secondhand travel books and thrillers. Upstairs there's a comfy lounge-lizard cafe in which to read them. Films shown nightly.

Monument Books BOOKS
(Map p40; www.monument-books.com; Ban Wat Nong; ⏲9am-9pm Mon-Fri, to 6pm Sat & Sun) Part of a regional chain, this shop stocks guidebooks, maps, novels, magazines and books on Lao history.

ℹ Orientation

The historic centre occupies the peninsula formed between the Mekong River and the Nam Khan and surveyed by the stupa-topped hill whose name, Phu Si (Pu-si, Phousy), raises many a cheap guffaw from native English speakers.

Traditionally the town is divided into minuscule 'villages' (ban), often named for the local wat. Many official addresses use that system rather than street names, which have changed at least three times in the last 20 years. So don't be surprised to find widely varying addresses on maps and visit-cards. The main street heading northeast up the peninsula is currently called Th Phothisarat (Phothisalat) southwest of the palace, Th Sisavangvong in its middle reach and Th Sakkarin (Sakkaline Rd) at the northeastern end. The road that runs along the Mekong waterfront is variously known as Souvannakhamphong, Oun Kham and Suvannabanlang, although most locals call it Th Khem Khong (Mekong Riverside Rd). Understandably for directions, most locals use landmarks rather than street names.

Various commercial city maps are available, but by far the most accurate and comprehensive is the regularly updated **Hobo Maps Luang Prabang** (www.hobomaps.com; 25,000K) which marks virtually every business and around 200 guesthouses with a very useful series of indexes.

Information

IMMIGRATION

Immigration Office (Map p40; ☎071-212 435; Th Wisunarat; ⏰8.30am-4.30pm Mon-Fri) Apply before it has expired and it's usually possible to extend a Lao visa for up to 30 extra days (US$2 per day).

INTERNET ACCESS

It's increasingly common to find wi-fi in guesthouses, hotels and cafes but you'll need your own laptop or mobile device. Most guesthouses and hotels also now include a desktop computer in the lobby area for the use of guests. There are numerous internet cafes, many within travel agencies. Most charge around 100K per minute, with a 20-minute minimum. Beware that many such computers are riddled with viruses. If your laptop is playing up or your camera's flash memory has been zapped by viruses, **DSCom** (Map p40; ☎071-253 905; ⏰9.30am-noon & 1-6pm Mon-Sat) might be able to save the day and the owner speaks good English.

MEDICAL SERVICES

Provincial Hospital (Map p40; ☎071-254025; Ban Naxang; doctor's consultation 100,000K) OK for minor problems but for any serious illnesses consider flying to Bangkok or returning to Vientiane and neighbouring hospitals across the Thai border. Note that the hospital in Luang Prabang charges double for consultations at weekends or anytime after 4pm.

MONEY

There are lots of ATMs in town. Several tour companies on Th Sisavangvong offer cash advances on Visa or MasterCard for around 3% commission. They'll change money too but rates tend to be poor.

BCEL (Map p40; Th Sisavangvong; ⏰8.30am-3.30pm Mon-Sat) Changes major currencies in cash or travellers cheques, has a 24-hour ATM and offers cash advances against Visa and MasterCard.

Minipost Booth (Map p40; Th Sisavangvong; ⏰7.45am-8.30pm, cash advances 9am-3pm) Changes most major currencies at fair rates and is open daily. After 6pm it's easy to miss, hidden behind market stalls.

POST

Post Office (Map p40; Th Chao Fa Ngum; ⏰8.30am-3.30pm Mon-Fri, to noon Sat) Phone calls and Western Union facilities.

TELEPHONE

Most internet cafes in town have Skype and MSN Messenger and can offer international calls at 2000K per minute or less.

The Minipost Booth sells mobile phone SIM cards.

TOURIST INFORMATION

Provincial Tourism Department (Map p40; www.tourismlaos.com; Th Sisavangvong; ⏰8am-4pm Mon-Fri) General information stop on festivals and ethnic groups. Also offers some maps and leaflets, plus information on buses and boats. Unfortunately staff speak limited English.

Getting There & Away

AIR

Around 4km from the city centre, **Luang Prabang International Airport** (☎071-212173) is decidedly modest, though big expansion plans are afoot. For Bangkok (from US$190, 100 minutes), **Bangkok Airways** (Map p40; www.bangkokair.com) and **Lao Airlines** (Map p36; ☎071-212172; www.laoairlines.com; Th Pha Mahapatsaman) both fly twice daily. Lao Airlines also serves Vientiane (US$101, several daily), Pakse (US$182, daily), Chiang Mai (US$150, daily), Hanoi (US$155, daily) and Siem Reap (US$195, daily). **Vietnam Airlines** (☎071-213049; www.vietnamairlines.com) flies to both Siem Reap (codeshare with Lao Airlines) and Hanoi daily.

BOAT

For slowboats to Pak Beng (110,000K, nine hours, 8am), buy tickets from the **navigation office** (Map p40; ⏰8-11am & 2-4pm) behind the Royal Palace. Through-tickets to Huay Xai (220,000K, two days) are also available but you'll have to sleep in Pak Beng; curiously it's slightly cheaper to pay the fare to Pak Beng, then buy the onward section there. This also allows you to stay a little longer in Pak Beng should you like the place. The main slowboat landing is directly behind the navigation office but departure points can vary according to river levels.

The more upscale **Luang Say Cruise** (Mekong Cruises; Map p40; ☎071-254768; www.luangsay.com; 50/4 Th Sakkarin; cruise US$362-491 depending on the season, single supplement from US$67; ⏰9.30am-9.30pm) departs on two-day rides to Huay Xai from the Xieng Thong jetty opposite Wat Xieng Thong. Rates include an overnight stay at the Luang Say Lodge in Pak Beng. A cheaper alternative is **Shompoo Cruise** (Map p40; ☎071-213190; www.shompoocruise.com; Th Khem Khong; cruise incl breakfast & 2 lunches US$110), a two-day cruise aboard a smart boutique boat. Accommodation in Pak Beng is not included.

Fast but uncomfortable and seriously hazardous six-person speedboats can shoot you up the Mekong to Pak Beng (250,000K, three hours) and Huay Xai (400,000K, seven hours). However, there are no fixed departure times and prices assume a full boat so unless you organise things through an agency, it's worth heading up to the speedboat station the day before to make enquiries. It's around 5km north of town: turn west off Rte 13 beside the Km 390 post then head 300m down an unpaved road that becomes an unlikely dirt track once you cross the only crossroads en route.

River levels permitting, **Mekong River Cruises** (Map p40; www.cruisemekong.com) makes lazy seven-day trips from Luang Prabang to Thailand's Golden Triangle on innovative new two-storey German-Lao riverboats with a sun deck and sixteen cabins in which you sleep as well as travel (departs Thursdays).

Numerous boats for the Pak Ou Caves depart between 8.30am and lunchtime. A single boat to Nong Khiaw (110,000K, six hours) departs around 8.30am assuming enough people have signed up. Buy tickets at the easily missed little **longboat office** (Map p40; Th Khem Khong).

Banana Boat Laos (☎071-260654; www.bananaboatlaos.com; Ma Te Sai, Th Sisavangvong) offer better organised boat trips for those who aren't worried about every last kip. Boats leave from behind the Royal Palace Museum.

BUS & MINIBUS

Predictably enough, the **northern bus station** (☎071-252729; Rte 13, 700m beyond Km 387) and **southern bus station** (Bannaluang Bus Station; Map p36; ☎071-252066; Rte 13, Km 383) are at opposite ends of town. Several popular bus routes are duplicated by minibuses/minivans from the **Naluang minibus station** (Map p36; ☎071-212979; souknasing@hotmail.com; Rte 13, 800m past Km 382), diagonally opposite the latter. Booking through agencies or guesthouses you'll generally pay around 25,000K extra. That includes a transfer to the relevant station but getting your own tuk-tuk is often quicker and slightly cheaper.

For less than double the bus fare, a great option is to gather your own group and rent a comfortable six-seater minivan. Prices include photo stops and you'll avoid the farcical petrol-stop and driver-buys-lunch shenanigans that typify many a public departure. Directly booked through the minibus station, prices are about 1,000,000K to Phonsavan or Vang Vieng and 500,000K to Nong Khiaw, including pick-up from the guesthouse.

Vientiane & Vang Vieng

From the southern bus station there are up to 10 daily Vientiane services (express/VIP 130,000/150,000K, nine to 12 hours) via Vang Vieng between 6.30am and 7.30pm. VIP buses leave at 9am. A plethora of morning minibuses to Vang Vieng (105,000K, seven hours) depart from the Naluang minibus station. The scenery en route is consistently splendid.

Sainyabuli & Hongsa

Buses to Sainyabuli (60,000K, three hours) depart the southern bus station at 9am and 2pm. The new Tha Deua bridge over the Mekong River is now open and has reduced the journey time to Sainyabuli to two hours or so by private vehicle . There is also a new minibus service to Elephant Conservation Center in Sainyabuli, operated by Sakura Tour (p127). For Hongsa, the new bridge means it is easiest to travel to Sainyabuli and connect from there.

Phonsavan

For Phonsavan (10 hours) there's an 8.30am minibus (95,000K) from Naluang minibus station and an 8am bus (ordinary/express 85,000/105,000K, 10 hours) from the southern bus station.

Nong Khiaw & Sam Neua

For Nong Khiaw (40,000K, four hours), 9am minibuses start from Naluang minibus station. Alternatively, from the northern bus station use *sŏrngtăaou* (40,000K) at 9am, 11am and 1pm or the 8.30am bus that continues to Sam Neua (140,000K, 17 hours) via Vieng Thong (110,000K, 10 hours). Another Sam Neua–bound bus (from Vientiane) should pull in sometime around 5.30pm.

Northwestern Laos & China

The sleeper bus to Kunming, China (450,000K, 24 hours) departs from the southern bus station at 7am, sometimes earlier. Pre-booking, and checking the departure location, is wise. From the northern bus station buses run to Udomxai (55,000K, five hours) at 9am, noon and 4pm, Luang Namtha (90,000K, nine hours) at 9am and Huay Xai (Borkeo, 120,000K, 15 hours) at 5.30pm and a VIP service at 7pm (145,000K).

ℹ Getting Around

Luang Prabang has no motorbike taxis, only tuk-tuks, plus the odd taxi-van from the airport charging a standardised 50,000K into town. These will cost more if more than three people share the ride. From town back to the airport you might pay marginally less.

Around town locals often pay just 5000K for short tuk-tuk rides but foreigners are charged a flat 20,000K per hop. To the speedboat landing reckon on 50,000K for the vehicle.

A much more satisfying way to get around is by bicycle. They're rented by numerous shops and some guesthouses for 15,000K to 30,000K per day. Motorcycle rental typically costs US$15 a day or US$20 for 24 hours. However, almost all agencies actually subcontract for **Naluang Rental** (Map p36; ☎071-212979; Naluang Minibus Station) who charge US$15 for 24 hours if you book directly with them. **KPTD** (Map p40; ☎071-253447; Th Kitsarat) has a wide range of bikes available including Honda Waves

(100,000K semi-automatic), Honda Scoopy (160,000K, automatic) and a thoroughly mean Honda CRF (US$65) for motocross riders only.

Be careful to lock bicycles and motorbikes securely and don't leave them on the roadside overnight. Note that the peninsula's outer road is one-way anticlockwise: signs are easy to miss and although you'll see locals flouting the rule (and riding without helmets), police will occasionally fine foreigners.

AROUND LUANG PRABANG

Adrenalin activities abound around Luang Prabang, including trekking, cycling, kayaking, rafting and elephant riding. Many tour operators in Luang Prabang can arrange activities in this area.

For those with limited time in Luang Prabang, agents vie to sell one day 'tours' combining the Pak Ou Caves and Tat Kuang Si (prices from 120,000K). It's an odd combination, given that the sites are in opposite directions, but the advantage is that the vehicle to the Kuang Si waterfalls should be waiting when you return to the agency office from your boat trip. Note that tour prices don't include entry fees.

Pak Ou Caves ຖ້ຳປາກອູ

The Nam Ou (Ou River) joins the Mekong beneath a dramat ic karst formation that, from some distance south, looks like a vast green eagle taking off. Facing it is the village of Ban Pak Ou, where a handful of riverfront restaurants gaze out across the Mekong. On the other side (there's no bridge) are two famous **caves** (Tham Ting; admission 20,000K) cut into the limestone cliff. Both are crammed with Buddha images of various styles and sizes. A few steps from the river, the lower 'cave' is actually more of an overhang. A group of Buddhas pose perfectly as silhouettes against the grand riverine backdrop. To reach the upper cave, follow stairs to the left and climb for five sweaty minutes. This one is 50m-deep behind an old carved-wooden portal. If you didn't bring a torch (flashlight), you can borrow one for a suitable donation from a desk at the front.

Appealing as the scene may be, the caves themselves are less of an attraction for many visitors than the Mekong boat trip from Luang Prabang to get here. Be aware that you'll see the exact same stretch of river should you do a Luang Prabang–Pak Beng or Luang Prabang–Nong Khiaw boat trip. Between January and April, villagers along the Mekong sandbanks en route pan for gold using large wooden platters.

Whether by road or by boat, most visitors en route to Pak Ou stop at the 'Lao Lao Village' **Ban Xang Hay** where the narrow paths behind the very attractive (if mostly new) wat are full of weavers' looms, colourful fabric stalls and a few stills producing the wide range of liquors sold.

Luang Prabang's longboat office sells return boat tickets to Pak Ou (per person/boat 60,000/400,000K return) taking two hours upstream, 1¼ hours back and allowing around an hour at the caves plus 20 minutes at Ban Xang Hay. Departures are most numerous around 8.30am but generally continue all morning. Travel agencies and guesthouses sell the same tickets for a little more, often including a tuk-tuk transfer.

An alternative is to go by road to Ban Pak Ou (30km, around 150,000K return for a tuk-tuk) then take a motor-canoe across the river (20,000K return). Ban Pak Ou is 10km down a decent unpaved road that turns off Rte 13 near Km 405.

Tat Kuang Si ຕາດກວາງຊີ

Bikinis, bears and beautiful mature trees make curious bedfellows in this appealing if busy jungle **park** (admission 20,000K; ⏲7.30am-5.30pm) 30km southwest of town. The park is centred on a many-tiered waterfall that is one of Laos' most impressive, especially in the dry season. A five-minute forest walk from the restaurant-ringed carpark brings you to the first of several cascades. These tumble into azure-blue pools that are popular for swimming or rope-swings and there are even a few changing booths (bring togs and towels). Five minutes further is the main waterfall, a powerful beauty whose longest leap is around 25m. The best views are from the footbridge at its base but you can climb to the top via steep footpaths on either side (around 15 minutes up). The one to the right is a slippery scramble while the one on the left is better maintained with sections of steps. Unless water is very high you can easily wade through the top pools to link the two routes.

Upon entering the park, one of the first attractions is the **Tat Kuang Si Bear Rescue Centre** (www.freethebears.org.au) FREE. The residents here have been confiscated

ELEPHANT CAMPS & BOUTIQUE LODGES

Dotted about the beautiful countryside around Luang Prabang are several elephant camps and boutique lodges. While many prefer to stay in the heart of the old town on their first visit, these striking properties can be a good option for repeat visitors or those with a focus on a nature-based experience or on learning more about the lives of Lao elephants. For the ultimate elephant experience, consider a trip to Sainyabuli Province and the excellent Elephant Conservation Center (p126). For more on how to select an elephant experience around Luang Prabang, check out the *Read Before You Ride: How to Choose a Quality Elephant Camp in the Land of a Million Elephants*, available to download from ElefantAsia (www.elefantasia.org). Click on What We Do, then Public Awareness.

Near the village of Ban Noun Savath is the **All Lao Elephant Camp** (071-253522; www.alllaoservice.com; elephant ride per person US$30, 1-/2-day mahout course US$85/150; 8am-3pm). Elephant rides lasting around 90 minutes start at 8am, 9.30am, 11.30am and 1.30pm with elephant bathing at 2.30pm. For longer mahout courses with an overnight at their **Mahout Lodge** (www.mahoutlodge.com; bungalow US$40-80) and riding-kayaking combination trips (there are dozens of possibilities), contact the **Luang Prabang office** (Map p40; 071-253522; Th Sisavangvong). Originally squarely aimed at backpackers, prices have recently risen significantly.

Around 5km beyond, the German-run **Elephant Village** (071-252417; www.elephantvillage-laos.com; mahout course per day US$86) offers a more exclusive elephant experience and is worth visiting just to enjoy the riverside setting facing a splendid karst ridge. Rides, mahout courses and multiday experiences are available here and they have their own **Elephant Camp** (www.elephantvillage-laos.com; per night US$120-140) on site. Elephant Village is down the spur road that dead-ends after 2km in Ban Xieng Lom village. Close by Elephant Village, there is some very impressive accommodation on offer in the shape of **Lao Spirit Resort** (030-514 0111; www.lao-spirit.com; r US$125-160 Oct-Apr, from US$100 May-Sep) and the more upscale **Shangri-Lao Explorer Camp** (mahout course 1-day US$139, 2-day including overnight at camp US$330). Lao Spirit is on the banks of the river and has a convivial collection of thatched cottages on sturdy brick stilts. Shangri-Lao is arguably the most luxurious tented camp in Laos boasting two locations, one on the river by Elephant Village and another in the primary forest of Huay Khot Valley. The Shangri-Lao packages are pretty good value given the exceptional colonial grandeur of the camp.

Higher up the same hill, Canadian-owned **Zen Namkhan** (030-514 2411; www.zennamkhanresort.com; r US$170-200;) takes the exclusive boutique hotel approach. Expansive, stylishly minimalist bungalows enjoy wide-view balconies and inside-outside showers. Service is highly attentive. The spring-fed swimming pool is ecofriendly.

In an alternative direction out towards the Tat Kuang Si, **Hillside Resort** (030-571 7342; www.hillsidelaos.com; r US$59-75;) is a newcomer in 2012. There are eight bungalows and a family unit, and plenty of activities on tap, including board games, volleyball, *petang* and a swimming pool. Top set-up and exceptional value at these prices.

from poachers and are kept here in preference to releasing them to the same certain fate. Souvenirs are sold to fund their feeding, including t-shirts and water bottles. It is possible to see the bears being fed daily.

Many cheap eateries line the entrance car park at the top end of the Khamu village of Ban Thapene.

Tuk-tuks from Luang Prabang typically charge 200,000K for one person, from 300,000K for several. Some folks manage to cobble together an impromptu group by meeting fellow travellers beside the baguette sellers' area near the tourist office. Or pay 50,000K per person and let an agency organise a shared vehicle.

Visiting Kuang Si by hired motorcycle is very pleasant now that the road is decently paved and allows stops in villages along the way. By bicycle, be prepared for two long, steady hills to climb.

An appealing alternative is to charter a boat down the Mekong to Ban Ou (one hour downstream), from where the remaining 5km to the falls should be easy to hitch: Rte 2501 to the falls turns 90 degrees away from the river directly behind Ban Ou's wat. Some boatmen, however, have been known to drop passengers at different villages from which there's no choice but to charter a 'friend's' tuk-tuk.

Tat Sae ນ້ຳຕົກຕາດແສ້

The wide, multi-level cascade pools of this **waterfall** (admission 15,000K, elephant rides per person 150,000K; ⏲ 8am-5pm, elephant rides 8am-3.30pm) are a particularly memorable sight from August to November. They dry up almost completely by February and, unlike Tat Kuang Si, there's no single long-drop centrepiece. But several year-round gimmicks keep visitors coming, notably elephant rides and a loop of 14 **ziplines** (☎ 020-5429 0848; www.flightofthenature.com; per person 300,000K) that allow you to 'fly' around and across the falls. Only two of those lines are more than 100m long, so don't imagine a serious competitor to the Gibbon Experience (p116).

Part of the attraction of a visit is getting there on a very pleasant seven-minute boat ride (20,000K per person return, 40,000K minimum) that starts from Ban Aen, a peaceful Lao village that's just 1km east of Rte 13 (turn east at Km 371.5). By tuk-tuk, the 30-minute ride south of Luang Prabang costs up to 150,000K return, including a couple of hours' wait.

Ban Phanom & Beyond
ບ້ານພະນົມ/ສຸສານຫມູຫິດ

If you climbed Phu Si you'll surely have spied a large octagonal stupa near the 'New Bridge' painted a dazzling golden hue. This is the 1988 **Santi Chedi** (Peacefulness Pagoda; donation expected; ⏲ 8-10am & 1.30-4.30pm Mon-Fri), whose five interior levels are painted with all manner of Buddhist stories and moral admonitions. It's on a gentle rise, 1km off Rte 13 beside the road to **Ban Phanom**, a prosperous weaving and handicrafts village less than 1km further east. A mostly unpaved road initially follows the Nam Khan east and south, looping round eventually after 14km to **Ban Kok Gniew**, the 'pineapple village' at Km372 on Rte 13, just 500m short of the turning to Tat Sae waterfall.

The road is dusty and gently hilly but quiet and scenic with some attractive karst scenery and several points of interest. Around 4.5km from Ban Phanom, a steep signed track descends in around 300m to the whitewashed **tomb of Henri Mouhot**. Mouhot was a French explorer best known for 'discovering' Angkor Wat. He died of malaria in Luang Prabang in 1861, scrawling in his diary 'Have pity on me, O my God' before expiring. His heavily bearded statue at the site looks altogether more cheerful and in the drier months the riverside 'beach' beneath becomes a popular picnic and swimming spot.

Less than 2km further along the road are the mural-daubed old wat and gilded stupa of **Ban Noun Savath**. The scene is especially photogenic in afternoon light with a large karst-hump mountain forming a perfect backdrop.

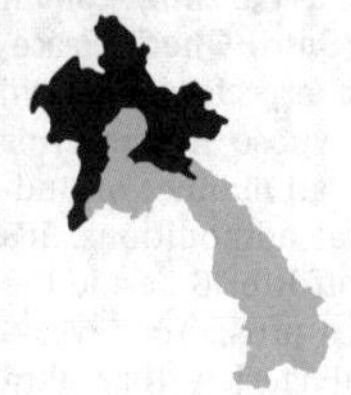

Northern Laos

Includes ➡

Best Places to Eat

- Bamboozle Restaurant & Bar (p74)
- Bar How (p117)
- Coco Home Bar & Restaurant (p87)
- Forest Retreat Gourmet Cafe (p107)
- Riverside Restaurant (p89)

Best Places to Stay

- Daauw Homestay (p115)
- Luang Say Lodge (p121)
- Muang La Resort (p103)
- Nong Kiau Riverside (p86)
- Phou Iu III Guesthouse (p105)

Why Go?

Whether it's trekking, cycling, kayaking, ziplining, riding an elephant or staying in a family homestay, a visit to northern Laos is for many the highlight of their trip. Dotted about are unfettered, dense forests still home to tigers, gibbons and a cornucopia of other wildlife, with a well-established ecotourism infrastructure to take you into their very heart.

Here the Land of a Million Elephants morphs into the land of a million hellish bends and travel is not for the faint-hearted, as the roads twist and turn endlessly through towering mountain ranges and serpentine river valleys. By contrast, most northern towns are functional places, rebuilt after wholesale bombing during the 20th-century Indochina wars.

But visitors aren't in northern Laos for the towns. It's all about the rural life. River trips also offer a wonderful way to discover the bucolic scenery as well as a practical alternative to tortuous bus rides.

When to Go

Luang Prabang

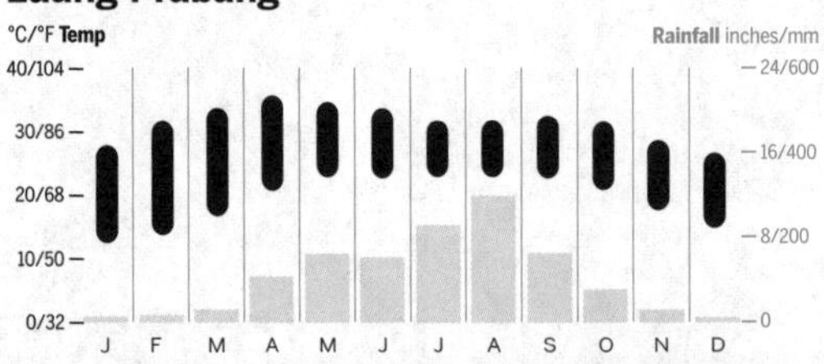

Nov–Feb The ideal season to visit, with little rain and clear skies; chilly at higher altitudes.

Mar–May This time of year is cooking at lower altitudes; lots of haze around from slash and burn.

Jun–Oct Wet season but not as wet as name suggests; good for greenery and cheaper rooms.

Climate

The best time of year is November to February, when days typically range from warm to hot once the sun burns through the chilly morning mists. A decent jacket is useful to deal with colder night-time temperatures in higher mountainous areas, particularly Luang Namtha, Phongsali, Xieng Khuang and Hua Phan provinces. Wrap up warmly if travelling by boat or motorbike before 10am. As the dry season continues, river levels drop and by February some sections of the Nam Tha might be too low for navigation. March is a bad time to visit the whole region as the air becomes choked with smoke and visibility is severely reduced thanks to the widespread fires of slash-and-burn agriculture. In April the searing heat of the Mekong Valley is tempered by a week of good-humoured water throwing during the Pi Mai festival, a time when transport gets particularly crowded. Rain is likely after Pi Mai in the far north, although the rainy season typically peaks between June and September. Rains are not constant, and in between showers the sky clears and the rice paddies glow emerald green. But unpaved roads can become impassably muddy, trekking paths can get slippery, leeches may appear in the grass and river fords become awkward to cross.

WHICH RIVER TRIP?

Until the 1990s, riverboats were an essential form of inter-city passenger transport in Laos. Today villagers in roadless hamlets still travel by river, while several longer distance water routes remain possible thanks in significant part to tourist interest. In each case the journey is an attraction in itself.

Mekong Slowboats

Huay Xai–Pak Beng or Pak Beng–Luang Prabang (one day; p118) Both sectors are very pleasant one-day rides. Boats are designed for 70 passengers but are sometimes seriously overcrowded. The seats are usually very hard, but you can get up and walk around. There's a toilet on board and usually a stall selling snacks and overpriced beer.

Huay Xai–Luang Prabang (two days; p118) Travel in relative luxury with Luang Say Cruise or Shompoo Cruise. Both run boats that are similar in size to other Mekong slowboats but carry a maximum of 40 passengers. The Luang Say Cruise is not for the budget traveller, but includes meals, sightseeing stops and excellent overnight accommodation at the Luang Say Lodge.

Mekong Speedboats

Huay Xai–Luang Prabang (one day; p119) Scarily fast, potentially dangerous and excruciatingly uncomfortable if you're not small and supple.

Xieng Kok–Muang Mom (three hours; p120) There are similar speedboat dangers and problems, but it's virtually the only way to see this attractive stretch of the Mekong.

Nam Tha Boats

Luang Namtha–Huay Xai or Na Lae–Huay Xai longboat (two days; p108) Escape the tourist trail on an open boat with a maximum capacity of around six. One night is spent in the boatman's village. Scenery is attractive but only gets at all dramatic for a one-hour section around Ban Phaeng. When the river levels are low there's lots of rapids-shooting. Trying to organise this one can be expensive or time-consuming.

Hat Sa–Muang Khua, Muang Khua–Nong Khiaw and Nong Khiaw–Luang Prabang riverboats (one day each; p92) A traveller favourite: covered boats usually depart daily on each sector. Boats typically hold up to 20 people in sometimes cramped conditions. Bring your own snacks. Arguably the most scenically dramatic sections of any navigable river in Laos are within an hour or two's ride in either direction from Nong Khiaw. Much of that you can see from the twice-daily boat between Nong Khiaw and Muang Ngoi Neua (90 minutes upstream, 70 minutes downstream).

Northern Laos Highlights

1. Soar through the jungle canopy on ziplines to remote treehouses at the **Gibbon Experience** (p116) near Huay Xai

2. Karst away on a boat ride or kayak trip down the **Nam Ou** (p67) between Muang Ngoi Neua and Nong Khiaw

3. Learn about the local lifestyle in homestays on a tribal trek in remote **Phongsali** (p92)

4. Discover the history of the incredible limestone landscape where the Pathet Lao hid from US aerial assault in the **Vieng Xai Caves** (p81)

5. Explore Xieng Khuang's mysterious **Plain of Jars** (p76)

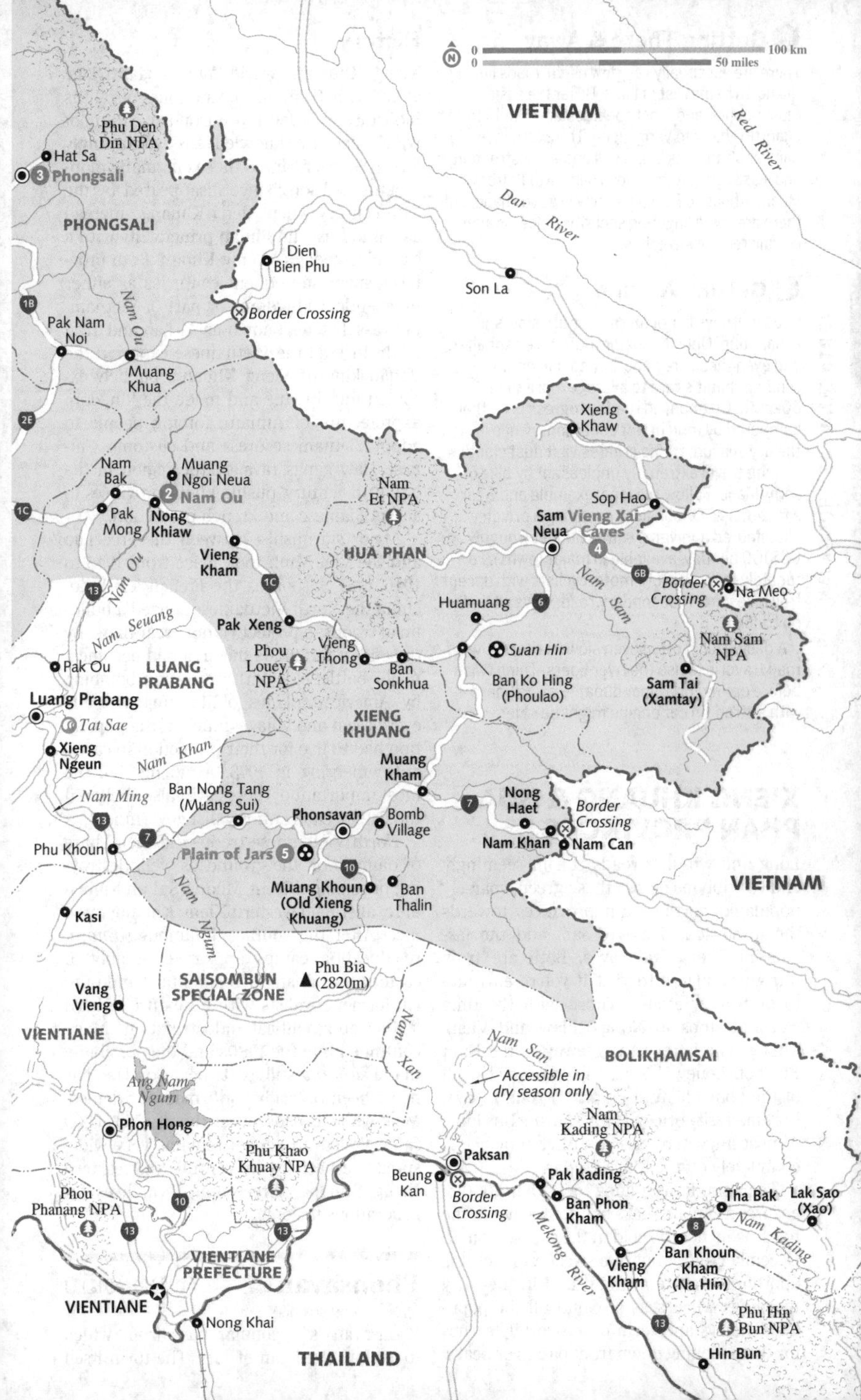

0
100 km
0
50 miles
VIETNAM
Red River
Dar River
Phu Den Din NPA
Hat Sa
3 Phongsali
PHONGSALI
Dien Bien Phu
Son La
Border Crossing
Nam Ou
Pak Nam Noi
Muang Khua
Xieng Khaw
Nam Bak
Muang Ngoi Neua
2 Nam Ou
Nam Et NPA
Sop Hao
Pak Mong
Nong Khiaw
Sam Neua
Vieng Xai Caves
4
Vieng Kham
HUA PHAN
Nam Sam
Border Crossing
Na Meo
Huamuang
Nam Seuang
Pak Xeng
Nam Sam NPA
Vieng Thong
Suan Hin
Pak Ou
LUANG PRABANG
Phou Louey NPA
Ban Sonkhua
Ban Ko Hing (Phoulao)
Sam Tai (Xamtay)
Luang Prabang
Tat Sae
XIENG KHUANG
Xieng Ngeun
Nam Khan
Muang Kham
Nam Ming
Ban Nong Tang (Muang Sui)
Nong Haet
Border Crossing
Phonsavan
Bomb Village
Phu Khoun
Nam Khan
Nam Can
Plain of Jars 5
VIETNAM
Nam Ngum
Muang Khoun (Old Xieng Khuang)
Ban Thalin
Kasi
Phu Bia (2820m)
SAISOMBUN SPECIAL ZONE
Vang Vieng
Nam Xan
VIENTIANE
Nam San
BOLIKHAMSAI
Accessible in dry season only
Ang Nam Ngum
Phon Hong
Nam Kading NPA
Phu Khao Khuay NPA
Paksan
Beung Kan
Border Crossing
Pak Kading
Phou Phanang NPA
Ban Phon Kham
Tha Bak
Lak Sao (Xao)
Mekong River
Nam Kading
VIENTIANE PREFECTURE
Vieng Kham
Ban Khoun Kham (Na Hin)
VIENTIANE
Nong Khai
Phu Hin Bun NPA
THAILAND
Hin Bun

Getting There & Away

There are essentially very few useful roads linking the north to the rest of Laos. By far the easiest, most popular and most spectacular is Rte 13 from Luang Prabang to Vang Vieng. The alternative, via Sainyabuli and Pak Lai, is still under construction and less scenic. A third possibility, Rte 10 from Muang Khoun to Paksan, is now in good shape, but there are some lingering security concerns along certain remote stretches.

Getting Around

Road journeys in northern Laos are slow and exhausting. Only the major routes are asphalted and even these are generally so narrow and winding that it's rare to average more than 30km/h. On unpaved roads progress is further hampered by mud in wet conditions, while in the dry season, traffic creates vast dust clouds making travel extremely unpleasant by bike or *sŏrngtăaou*. Follow the local example and wear a face-mask. Or consider engaging a private chauffeured minivan if within budget (roughly US$100 per day, available in major towns). Fortunately for adventure motorcyclists with decent trail bikes, many secondary roads have virtually no traffic.

A delightful, if often even slower, alternative to road travel is to use the river boats. Think twice before opting for a 'speedboat' – a surfboard with a strap-on car engine might be safer.

XIENG KHUANG & HUA PHAN PROVINCES

Long and winding roads run in seemingly endless ribbons across these green, sparsely populated northeastern provinces towards the mysterious Plain of Jars and the fascinating Vieng Xai caves. Both are truly intriguing places to visit if you're en route to or from Vietnam. Those with the time can add stops in Nong Khiaw and Vieng Thong. The latter is a gateway to the Nam Et/Phou Louey NPA and its 'tiger treks'. All of the above feature on **Stray Asia's** (www.straytravel.asia) pricey *Long Thaang* bus loop. Almost anywhere else in either province is completely off the tourist radar.

The altitude, averaging more than 1000m, ensures a climate that's neither too hot in the hot season, nor too cold in the cool season. In December and January, a sweater or jacket is appropriate attire at night and in the early mornings when seas of cloud fill the populated valleys and form other-worldly scenes for those looking down from passes or peaks.

History

Xieng Khuang's world-famous giant 'jars' along with Hintang's mysterious megaliths indicate a well-developed iron-age culture of which historical knowledge is astonishingly hazy. Whoever carved those enigmatic monuments had long since disappeared by the 13th century when Xieng Khuang emerged as a Buddhist, Tai Phuan principality with a capital at today's Muang Khoun. Both provinces spent subsequent centuries as either independent kingdoms or part of Vietnamese vassal states known as Ai Lao and Tran Ninh. In 1832 the Vietnamese captured the Phuan king of Xieng Khuang, publicly executed him in Hué and made the kingdom a prefecture of Annam, forcing people to adopt Vietnamese dress and customs. Chinese Haw gangs ravaged the region in the late 19th century, pushing both provinces to accept Siamese and French protection.

Major skirmishes between the Free Lao and the Viet Minh took place from 1945 to 1946, and as soon as the French left Indochina the North Vietnamese started a build-up of troops to protect Hanoi's rear flank. By the end of the 1960s the area had become a major battlefield. With saturation bombing by American planes obliterating virtually every town and village, much of the population had to live for their protection in caves, only emerging in 1973. At Vieng Xai, the most important of these caves also sheltered the Pathet Lao's anti-royalist government.

North Vietnamese troops did their share of damage on the ground as well, destroying once-magnificent Muang Sui and much of royalist-held western Xieng Khuang province. After the conflict, infamous *samana* re-education camps appeared, notably in eastern Hua Phan, to 'rehabilitate' and punish former royalists with a mixture of hard labour and political indoctrination. Many continued into the 1980s and the possibility that a *samana* still exists near Sop Hao has never been officially confirmed nor denied. Meanwhile, decades after the conflict, UXO (unexploded ordnance) remains very widespread, especially in central and eastern Xieng Khuang, threatening local lives for generations to come.

Phonsavan ໂພນສະຫວັນ

☎061 / POP 60,000

Phonsavan is a popular base from which to explore the Plain of Jars. The town itself

UXO & WAR JUNK

During the Indochina wars, Laos earned the dubious distinction of becoming the most heavily bombed nation per capita in world history. Xieng Khuang Province was especially hard hit and even today, innumerable scraps of combat debris remain. Much of it is potentially deadly UXO (unexploded ordnance), including mortar shells, white phosphorous canisters (used to mark bomb targets) and assorted bombs. Some of the most problematic UXO comes from cluster bombs, 1.5m-long torpedo-shaped packages of evil whose outer metal casing was designed to split open lengthwise in mid-air, scattering 670 tennis-ball-sized bomblets ('bombies') over a 5000-sq-metre area. Once disturbed, a bombie would explode, projecting around 30 steel pellets like bullets killing anyone within a 20m radius. Nearly 40 years after bombing ceased, almost one person a day is still injured or killed by UXO in Laos, 40% of them children. Tens of millions of bombies remain embedded in the land, causing an ever-present danger to builders, farmers and especially young children, who fatally mistake them for toys. And for impoverished villagers, the economic temptation to collect UXO to sell as scrap metal has caused numerous fatalities. Despite valiant ongoing clearance efforts, at current rates it would take an estimated 150 years to deal with the problem.

Cluster-bomb casings, which were not themselves explosive, have meanwhile found a wide range of more positive new uses. In some places you can see them reused as architectural features, feeding troughs, pots for growing spring onions or simply as ornaments around houses or hotels.

If you find any war debris, don't be tempted to touch it. Even if it appears to be an exhibit in a collection, beware that some hotels display war junk that's never been properly defused and might remain explosive. Even if it isn't live and dangerous, the Lao legal code makes it illegal to trade in war leftovers of any kind. Purchase, sale or theft of any old weaponry can result in a prison term of between six months and five years.

has an unfinished feel and is very spread out with its two parallel main boulevards stretching for about 3km east–west. Fortunately a very handy concentration of hotels, restaurants and tour agents is crammed into a short if architecturally uninspired central 'strip'. More shops, markets and facilities straggle along Rte 7. But the town is best appreciated from the surrounding hills, several of which are pine-clad and topped with small resorts.

The region has long been a centre of Phuan language and culture (part of the Tai-Kadai family). There's also a strong Vietnamese presence.

Sights

UXO Information Centre INFORMATION CENTRE
(061-252004; www.maginternational.org/laopdr; 8am-8pm) FREE Decades after America's 'secret' war on Laos, unexploded bombs and mines remain a devastating problem throughout this region. To understand just how bad things are, visit the thought-provoking UXO Information Centre run by British organisation MAG (Mines Advisory Group) that has been helping to clear Laos' unexploded ordnance since 1994. The centre's photos, slide shows and map software underline the enormity of the bomb drops and there are examples of (defused) UXO to ponder. Late-afternoon screenings show the powerful documentaries *Bomb Harvest* (4.30pm; www.bombharvest.com), *Surviving the Peace* (5.50pm) and *Bombies* (6.30pm; www.itvs.org/bombies/film.html). Donations are encouraged: US$12 pays for the clearing of around 10 sq m and qualifies the giver for a commemorative T-shirt.

Xieng Khouang UXO-Survivors' Information Centre INFORMATION CENTRE
(www.laos.worlded.org; 8am-8pm) This is an insightful information centre displays prosthetic limbs, wheelchairs and bomb parts and gives harrowing insight into the UXO problem.

Mulberries SILK FARM
(ປໍສາ; 061-561271; www.mulberries.org; 8am-4pm Mon-Sat) This is a fair-trade silk farm that offers interesting free visits including a complete introduction to the silk-weaving process from cocoon to colourful scarves. It's off Rte 7 just west of the main bus station.

Phonsavan

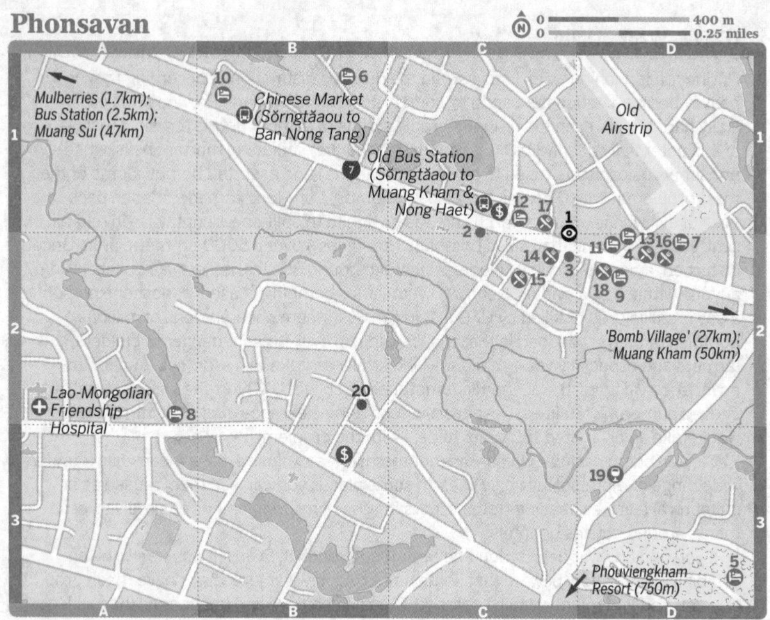

Phonsavan

Sights
1 UXO Information Centre........................C1
Xieng Khouang UXO-Survivors' Information Centre..................... (see 1)

Activities, Courses & Tours
2 Amazing Lao Travel..............................C1
3 Sousath Travel....................................C2

Sleeping
4 Anoulack Khen Lao Hotel D2
5 Auberge de La Plaine des Jarres..........D3
6 Hillside Residence................................B1
7 Kong Keo Guesthouse D2
8 Maly Hotel...A2
9 Nice Guesthouse..................................D2
10 Vansana Plain of Jars Hotel..................B1
11 White Orchid Guesthouse....................D2
12 Xieng Khouang Hotel............................C1

Eating
13 Bamboozle Restaurant & Bar...............D2
14 Craters Bar & Restaurant......................C2
15 Fresh Food Market...............................C2
16 Nisha Restaurant..................................D2
17 Sanga Restaurant................................. C1
18 Simmaly Restaurant.............................D2

Drinking & Nightlife
19 Barview D3

Information
Internet Shop.................................(see 1)
Provincial Tourist Office...............(see 4)

Transport
20 Lao Airlines...B2
Lao-Falang Restaurant.................(see 4)

Tours

Several agents on the main drag and virtually every guesthouse is ready to slot you into a one-day Plain of Jars tour visiting the three main sites. The going rate is 150,000K including a noodle-soup lunch and entry fees. This prices is contingent on there being at least seven fellow passengers.

Other advertised tours include trips to places such as Muang Khoun, Muang Sui or Tham Piu, but these rarely garner enough customers for prices to be competitive. Try gathering your own group.

Amazing Lao Travel HIKING
(☎020-2234 0005; www.amazinglao.com; Rte 7) Runs treks to the jar sites and two-day treks

in the mountain,s including a homestay in a Hmong village. As ever, the more the merrier, with prices falling for larger groups.

Sousath Travel GUIDED TOUR

(☎061-312031; Rte 7) Run by a pair of well-informed brothers, Sousath offers reliable tours to the Plain of Jars and the Ho Chi Minh Trail as well as homestays in Hmong villages. They also rent motorbikes (100,000K per day). Films are shown nightly at their little office-cum-cafe.

Sleeping

Central Strip

Kong Keo Guesthouse GUESTHOUSE $

(☎061-211354; www.kongkeojar.com; r 50,000-80,000K;) This is the most backpacker-friendly spot in town, offering cabins with en suites, as well as a newer block of more comfortable rooms. There is a small bar-restaurant with an open-pit barbecue and occasional guitar strum-alongs. Charismatic owner Mr Keo runs excellent tours to the jars, as well as specialised trips.

Nice Guesthouse GUESTHOUSE $

(☎061-312454; vuemany@hotmail.com; r 80,000-110,000K;) With fresh and fragrant rooms, clean bathrooms and firm beds, Nice shows no signs of ageing just yet. Chinese lanterns cast a ruby glow into the chilled night and upstairs rooms include a bathtub.

White Orchid Guesthouse GUESTHOUSE $

(☎061-312403; r incl breakfast 80,000-200,000K;) The menthol-green walls include clean en suite bathrooms and welcome blankets. The higher you ascend, the higher the price and better the views. The price includes a pick-up from the airport or bus station.

Anoulack Khen Lao Hotel HOTEL $$

(☎061-213599; www.anoulackkhenlaohotel.com; r 200,000-300,000K;) This modern five-storey tower offers a striking jump in quality over all nearby competitors. Bright, clean and ample-sized 200,000K rooms are the best value with white linens, kettles, fridges, shower booths and breakfast included. Has a lift and, more importantly, a generator to power it.

Xieng Khouang Hotel HOTEL $$

(☎061-213567; xiengkhouanghotel@gmail.com; r US$20-100;) Finished in baby blue, this Vietnamese-style hulk of a building offers a range of clean but soulless rooms. Popular with visiting Lao government delegations. Prices include free wi-fi.

Around Town

There are several smarter lodge-style hotels spread around town, including some imperiously perched atop pine-clad hills.

Hillside Residence HOTEL $$

(☎061-213300; www.thehillsideresidence.com; Ban Tai; r incl breakfast US$30;) Set in a lush little garden, this replica half-timbered mansion looks like it belongs in a colonial-era hill town. Rooms are petite but attractive with all the trimmings. There's a shared upper sitting terrace and some upstairs rooms have their own balconies. Free wi-fi.

Maly Hotel HOTEL $$

(☎061-312031; www.malyhotel.com; r incl breakfast US$25-60; @) In a barren accommodation landscape in this part of town, Maly excels with wood beams and candlelit ambience. Rooms include en suites, TVs, hot water and Lao textiles. Room 8 is a spacious corner suite at the top of the range.

★ **Auberge de la Plaine des Jarres** CABIN $$

(☎030-517 0282; www.plainedesjarres.com; r US$50-60; @) Hillside elevation, Scotch pines and Swiss-style wooden interiors give these inviting all-wood cabins an incongruously alpine feel. There's a great French and Lao restaurant with a nightly fire and some panoramic vistas over the town. Rooms show signs of age, but there is oodles of charm. It's a 10-minute drive from town.

Vansana Plain of Jars Hotel HOTEL $$

(☎061-213170; www.vansanahotel-group.com; r 400,000-500,000K) Opulent by Phonsavan standards, this grand hotel occupies its own small summit above town. The comfortable rooms have plush carpeting, large TVs, minibars, tasteful decor and big tubs in the bathroom. Each also has a small balcony with great views over town. The VIP rooms are huge, making this place popular with tour groups.

Phouviengkham Resort HOTEL $$

(☎061-213417; phouviengkham@live.com; r US$65-85) Probably the smartest place in Phonsavan, Phouviengkham sits panoramically above the town on an isolated hilltop. Rooms are spacious and stylish (at least for this part of Laos), with Lao cotton bedspreads and

GETTING TO VIETNAM: PHONSAVAN TO VINH

Getting to the Border

Direct buses to Vinh from Phonsavan (four weekly) and Luang Prabang (twice weekly) cross the lonely **Nong Haet (Laos)/Nam Can (Vietnam) border crossing** (8am-noon & 1.30-5pm) around 240km northwest of Vinh. The nearest town on the Lao side is Nong Haet, 13km west, with up to four daily bus services to Phonsavan (35,000K, four hours) and a *sŏrngtăaou* to the border leaving around noon (20,000K).

At the Border

This crossing doesn't see a whole lot of travellers. Laos visas are available on arrival for the standard prices, although additional charges are sometimes levied for 'overtime'. Vietnamese visas are not available at the border, so arrange one in advance in Luang Prabang or Vientiane.

Moving On

From the Vietnam side, 21km of hairpins wind down to the first small town, Mu'òng Xén. There's no public transport from the border but paid hitching or motorbike taxis are a possibility. Mu'òng Xén has a basic hotel and a bus to Vinh departing around 4pm. However, due to the very realistic likelihood of overcharging for local transport on either side of the border, it is easier to take the international bus service between Phonsavan and Vinh.

bamboo furnishings. Curiously a mountain view costs US$20 less per night than the rather predictable city view. Mountain it is then!

Eating & Drinking

Wild matsutake mushrooms (*hét wâi*) and fermented swallows (*nok ạen dạwng*) are local specialities – try the **fresh food market** (6am-5pm). If you want to avoid an unpleasant surprise, note that several Vietnamese restaurants serve dog (*thit chó*).

★Bamboozle Restaurant & Bar INTERNATIONAL $
(Rte 7; meals 15,000-52,000K; 7-10.30am & 3.30-11pm; wi-fi) The liveliest spot in town after dark, Bamboozle offers a decent range of comfort food, including pizzas, as well as the best of Lao cuisine. A percentage of profits go towards the **Lone Buffalo Foundation** (LBP; www.facebook.com/lonebuffalo), which supports the town's youth.

Nisha Restaurant INDIAN $
(Rte 7; meals 10,000-30,000K; 7am-10pm; menu) It doesn't look like much from the outside, but inside Nisha turns out to be one of the best Indian restaurants in northern Laos. The menu includes a wide range of vegetarian options. There's also delicious dosa (flat bread), tikka masala and rogan josh, as well as great lassi.

Simmaly Restaurant LAOTIAN $
(Rte 7; meals 15,000-30,000K; 6am-9pm) Dishes up a tasty line of rice dishes, noodles and spicy meats, including steaming *fĕr*. The pork with ginger is lovely.

Sanga Restaurant LAOTIAN $
(mains 15,000-30,000K; 11am-10pm) The venue is a bland box of a front room but the meals are unexpectedly accomplished for such sensible prices. The chicken *làhp* is especially tasty and the steak and chips is a popular bargain at 30,000K.

Craters Bar & Restaurant INTERNATIONAL $
(Rte 7; meals 20,000-50,000K; 7am-10pm; wi-fi) An old-timer establishment popular with NGOs and travellers, Craters has CNN on the tube as you munch through its toasties, soups, burgers, fried chicken, steaks and pizzas.

Barview BAR
(8am-11pm) Try this simple shack for sunset beers over the rice-paddy fields. Locals gather here to play guitars and munch on barbecued meat.

Information

Currency exchange is available at **Lao Development Bank** (061-312188), at **BCEL** (061-213291; Rte 7) and from several travel agents. There are two ATMs along Rte 7.

Don't underestimate the dangers of UXO (unexploded ordnance) in this most heavily bombed of provinces.

Internet Shop (per min 200K; ⌚7am-10pm) Beside Simmaly Restaurant, with excellent connection speeds.

Lao-Mongolian Friendship Hospital (☎061-312166) Might be able to assist with minor health concerns.

Provincial Tourist Office (☎061-312217) The oddly located tourist office has a series of information scrolls to peruse and has developed some regional treks. Free maps and leaflets for Phonsavan and Xieng Khuang are also available. The yard is crammed full of war junk.

Getting There & Away

Airline and bus timetables usually call Phonsavan 'Xieng Khuang', even though that was originally the name for Muang Khoun.

AIR

Lao Airlines (☎061-212027) has daily flights to/from Vientiane (US$101). Sometimes a weekly flight to/from Luang Prabang operates in peak season.

BUS

International & Long Distance

Longer-distance bus tickets presold by travel agencies typically cost around 40,000K more than standard fares but include a transfer to the bus station, around 4km west of the centre. From here Vietnam-bound buses depart to Vinh (180,000K, 11 hours) at 6.30am on Tuesday, Thursday, Friday and Sunday, continuing seasonally on Mondays to Hanoi (320,000K). For Vientiane (140,000K, 11 hours) there are air-con buses at 7am, 8am, 10.30am, 4.30pm, 6.30pm and a VIP bus (160,000K) at 8pm. These all pass through Vang Vieng, to where there's an additional 7.30am departure (95,000K). For Luang Prabang (10 hours) both minivans (95,000K) and VIP buses (120,000K) depart at 8.30am. There's an 8am bus to Sam Neua (110,000K, eight to 10 hours) plus two Vientiane–Sam Neua buses passing through. A 7.30am bus is timetabled to Paksan (130,000K) on the new road.

Local Services

Local buses and *sŏrngtăaou* use the Chinese market and destinations include Muang Khoun (15,000K, hourly), Muang Kham (20,000K, two hours, hourly) and Nong Haet (35,000K, four hours, four daily).

Getting Around

Tuk-tuks, if and when you can find them, cost from 10,000K for a short hop to about 20,000K to the airport. **Lao-Falang Restaurant** (☎020-2221 2456; Rte 7; ⌚8am-6pm) rents bicycles (40,000K per day) and 100cc motorbikes (100,000K), ideal for reaching a selection of jar sites. They also have some Chinese quad bikes (160,000K) if you're feeling brave.

Chauffeured six-seater vans or 4WDs can be chartered through most guesthouses and hotels. You're looking at US$150 to Sam Neua or US$120 to Luang Prabang.

Around Phonsavan

Plain Of Jars ທົ່ງໄຫຫີນ

Giant stone jars of unknown ancient origin are scattered over hundreds of square kilometres around Phonsavan, giving the area the misleading name of Plain of Jars. In fact it's no more of a plain than the rice-bowl valleys at Muang Sing or Luang Namtha, and indeed most of the curious jar sites are on hills. But what is more fascinating than the jars themselves is the mystery of which civilisation created them. Remarkably, nobody knows. But that doesn't stop guides guessing, often amusingly randomly. Meanwhile, a fanciful legend claims that they were made to brew vast quantities of rice wine to celebrate the local people's 6th-century liberation from cruel overlords by the Tai-Lao hero Khun Jeuam. In some versions of this story, the jars were 'cast' from

Plain of Jars

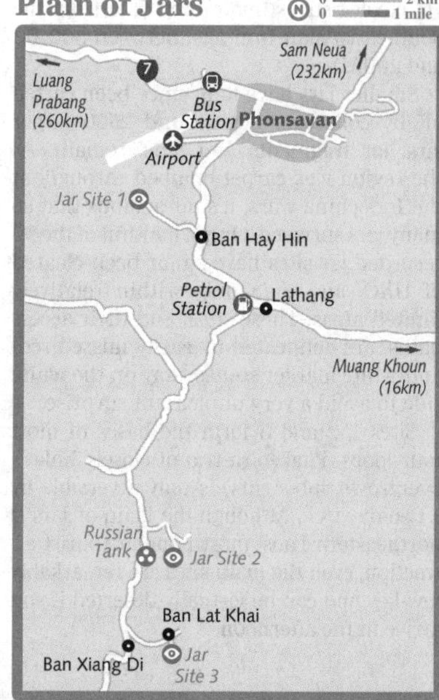

PHAKEO TREK

Organised through Phonsavan agencies, this excellent two-day trek combines many essential elements of the Xieng Khuang experience. On the long first day, hike across secondary forested mountain ridges to a three-part jar site with about 400 ancient jars and jar fragments, many moss-encrusted and shaded by foliage. The trek then descends into the roadless Hmong village of Ban Phakeo, whose shingle-roofed mud-floor homes huddle around a central rocky knoll. A purpose-built Hmong-style guest-shack provides a basic sleeping platform with space for eight hikers. There's no electricity. The next day, the hike descends into attractive semi-agricultural valleys then climbs up the cascades of a multi-terraced waterfall to arrive in the famous 'Bomb Village', that no longer has many bombs after extensive clearance work.

a type of cement made from buffalo skin, sand, water and sugar cane, then fired in 'kilns'. Some even claim that the cave beside Jar Site 1 housed one such kiln. In fact, the jars were fashioned from solid stone and archaeologists estimate they date from the Southeast Asian iron age, between 500 BC and 200AD.

Smaller jars have long since been carted off by collectors but around 2500 larger jars, jar fragments and 'lids' remain. As the region was carpet-bombed throughout the Indochina wars, it's miraculous that so many jars survived. Only a handful of the 90 recorded jar sites have so far been cleared of UXO, and then only within relatively limited areas. These sites, and their access paths, are delineated by easily missed red-and-white marker stones: stay on the white side to avoid a very unpleasant surprise.

Sites 1, 2 and 3 form the bases of most tour loops. Phakeo (a trio of closely linked, overgrown sub-sights) is only accessible by a two-day trek. Although the Plain of Jars is northeastern Laos' most popular tourist attraction, even the main sites are remarkably low-key and can be virtually deserted if you arrive in the afternoon.

Sights

While the jars at Sites 2 and 3 aren't as large nor as plentiful as at Site 1, they have their own charm. Set in very different locations, the journey to reach them offers glimpses of some typical local villages.

Jar Site 1 ARCHAEOLOGICAL SITE

(Thong Hai Hin; admission 10,000K) The biggest collection and most easily accessible, Site 1 features 334 jars or jar fragments relatively close-packed on a pair of hilly slopes pocked with bomb craters. The biggest, **Hai Jeuam**, weighs around 6 tonnes, stands more than 2.5m high and is said to have been the mythical victory cup of Khun Jeuam. The bare, hilly landscape is appealing, although in one direction the views of Phonsavan airport seem discordant. There is a small cafe, gift shop and toilets near the entrance.

Jar Site 2 ARCHAEOLOGICAL SITE

(Hai Hin Phu Salato; admission 10,000K) Site 2 is a pair of hillocks divided by a shallow gully that forms the access lane. This rises 700m from the ticket desk in what becomes a muddy slither in wet conditions. To the left in thin woodlands, look for a cracked stone urn through which a tree has managed to grow. To the right another set of jars sits on a grassy knoll with panoramas of layered hills, paddies and cow-fields. It is very atmospheric and there are now some basic cold drinks available at the ticket booth.

Jar Site 3 ARCHAEOLOGICAL SITE

(Hai Hin Lat Khai; admission 10,000K) The 150-jar Site 3 sits on a scenic hillside in pretty woodland near Ban Lat Khai village. The access road to Lat Khai leads east beside a tiny motorbike repair hut just before Ban Xiang Di (Ban Siang Dii). The ticket booth is beside a simple local restaurant that offers somewhat overpriced *fĕr* (30,000K). The jars are reached by a little wooden footbridge and an attractive 10-minute walk across rice fields.

Getting There & Away

All three main sites can be visited by rented motorbike from Phonsavan in around five hours, while Site 1 is within bicycle range. Site 1 is just 8km southwest of central Phonsavan, 2.3km west of the Muang Khoun road: turn at the signed junction in Ban Hay Hin. For Sites 2 and 3, turn west of the Muang Khoun road just past Km 8. Follow the unpaved road for 10km/14km to find the turnings for Sites 2/3, then follow muddy tracks for 1.5/1.8km respectively.

Alternatively, sign up the night before to join one of several regular guided minibus tours. Most throw in a noodle-soup lunch at Site 3 and a quick stop to see the lumpy rusting remnant of an armoured vehicle in a roadside copse at Ban Nakho: its nickname, the 'Russian Tank', exaggerates the appeal.

Muang Khoun (Old Xieng Khuang) ຊຽງຂວາງເກົ່າ (ເມືອງຄູນ)

POP 4000

The region's ancient capital, Muang Khoun was ravaged in the 19th century by Chinese and Vietnamese invaders, then so heavily bombarded during the Second Indochina War that by 1975 it was almost completely abandoned. However, a handful of aged monuments survived as ruins and the town slowly redeveloped, although it is very much a village by comparison with the new capital Phonsavan. It's certainly not a 'must-see' but might be worth the detour for those staying a few days in the region.

A good asphalt road from Phonsavan (30km) passes through some attractive rice-terrace villages, several sporting Phuan-style houses built of sturdy timbers. Buying the Muang Khoun Visitor's Ticket (10,000K) at any of the following sights supports ongoing maintenance efforts.

Sights

The main historic sights are a trio of historic stupas, all walking distance from the Khoun Guesthouse. One is directly behind in the grounds of the colourfully rebuilt active monastery, **Wat Si Phoum**. The other two are on a facing ridge, accessed via the brick-and-mud lane that climbs opposite the guesthouse, petering out into a narrow footpath. The 1576 **That Foun** (also called That Chomsi) is around 25m tall and built in the Lan Xang/Lanna style. It now has a distinct lean to its spire and you can climb right through a hole that was made by 19th-century Chinese Haw marauders, who tunnelled in to loot the priceless Buddha relics enshrined within. A five-minute walk around the easy ridge track brings you to the stubbier remnants of the Cham-built 16th-century stupa **That Chom Phet**.

The main road continuing east swerves south just before Km 30 after **Wat Phia Wat**. Of Wat Phia Wat's original 1582 building just the base platform and a few brick columns survived a devastating 1966 bombing raid. But these columns photogenically frame an age-greyed, shell-shocked Buddha with a whiplash smile.

The unpaved road continuing east passes the small, very degraded **Jar Site 16** after about 5km. This road becomes increasingly difficult and finally dead-ends some 12km beyond at **Ban Thalin**, an interesting village without any commercial facilities that's used as the starting point for the Phakeo trek.

Sleeping & Eating

Khoun Guesthouse & Restaurant GUESTHOUSE $
(☎061-212464; Rte 10, Km 29; r 40,000-80,000K) This is the town's sole accommodation option. The 40,000K rooms are cell-like at best but the 80,000K rooms include TV and hot water. The restaurant includes an English-language menu of Lao staples and some tour groups stop here for lunch.

Getting There & Away

Buses to Phonsavan (15,000K, 45 minutes) depart throughout the day. By motorbike it's possible to visit Muang Khoun plus the three main jar sites in one long day.

Muang Kham & Around ເມືອງຄຳ

Central Muang Kham is little more than a highway trading post with a market and a couple of guesthouses. Located 700m past Km 185 (2.5km west of central Muang Kham), **Kham District Handicrafts Group** (☎030-517 0185) weave some high quality, fair-priced fabrics and have a small display on natural dyestuffs.

Sights

Tham Piu CAVE
(ຖ້ຳພິວ; admission 5000K; ⏲7am-4pm) North of Muang Kham rises an imposing wall of abrupt wooded ridges and exposed limestone rock-faces. Carved into one such cliffside is Tham Piu, a cave where villagers sought protection from American bombers during the Indochina war. Hundreds died here in November 1968 when a US fighter plane fired a rocket into the cave and the site still holds major emotional resonance for the Laotian people. Today the setting is pretty but the small museum in the car park adds little information to give meaning to a visit and its collection of photos and bomb fragments aren't directly related to the Tham Piu incident. The cave, ten minutes'

climb via an obvious stairway, still shows signs of smoke damage while the floor is littered by small, unsophisticated memorial cairns. The cave mouth is wide enough to allow natural light into the main cavern but a torch (flashlight) would be useful to venture a little deeper.

The site is 2.6km up a degraded asphalt lane that heads west from the main road at a turning signed 'Tham Piew', around 4km north of Muang Kham.

Sam Neua (Xam Neua) ຊຳເຫນືອ

064 / POP 16,000

Behind a shallow disguise of well-spaced concrete modernity, Sam Neua offers eye-widening produce markets and a colourful ethnic diversity. The town is a logical transit point for visiting nearby Vieng Xai or catching the daily bus to Vietnam and remains one of Laos' least-visited provincial capitals. At an altitude of roughly 1200m, some warm clothes are advisable in the dry winter period, at least by night and until the thick morning fog burns off. From April to October the lush landscapes are contrastingly warm and wet.

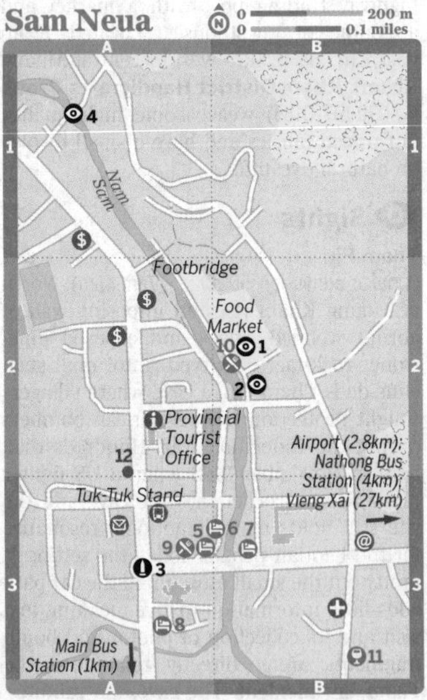

Sights

Apart from two modest old stupas that somehow survived the wartime bombs, the main road seems brash and modern. However, just metres away, enchanting river scenes are visible from the bike-and-pedestrian **suspension bridge**.

Suan Keo Lak Meung Monument MONUMENT

(ສວນແກ້ວຫຼັກເມືອງ) At the town's central junction stands the bizarre Suan Keo Lak Meung Monument. Four hooked concrete pincers hold aloft a glittery disco-ball that is intended to celebrate Sam Neua's folk-song image as an 'indestructible jewel'. However, the effect is unintentionally comic with its backing of half-hearted fountains and a frieze full of communist triumphalist soldiers.

Main Market MARKET

The main market is predominantly stocked with Chinese and Vietnamese consumer goods. However, some fabric stalls here stock regional textiles, and jewellers sell antique coins and silverware used for tribal headgear.

Food Market MARKET

The fascinating food market is well stocked with fresh vegetables and meats, some rather startling. Field rats are displayed cut

Sam Neua

0 — 200 m
0 — 0.1 miles

Sam Neua

Sights
1 Food Market B2
2 Main Market B2
3 Suan Keo Lak Meung Monument A3
4 Suspension Bridge A1

Sleeping
5 Bounhome Guest House A3
6 Phonchalern Hotel B3
7 Sam Neua Hotel B3
8 Xayphasouk Hotel A3

Eating
Chittavanh Restaurant .... (see 6)
9 Dan Nao Muang Xam Restaurant A3
10 Food Stalls B2

Drinking & Nightlife
11 Nang Nok Bar B3

Information
Foreign Exchange .... (see 2)

Transport
12 Motorcycle Shop A2

open to show the freshness of their entrails. Banana leaves might be stuffed with squirming insects. And there's plenty of dead furry wildlife that you'd probably prefer to see alive in the forests.

Sleeping

There are plenty of guesthouses in town, with many budget options just across the river from the market.

Bounhome Guest House GUESTHOUSE $
(064-312223; r 60,000-100,000K;) Plenty of sunlight fills the fine little rooms upstairs in this guesthouse. Their neat interiors have firm, low-set beds, are fan-cooled and include hot-water showers.

Phonchalern Hotel HOTEL $
(064-312192; www.phonechalernhotel.com; r 100,000-120,000K;) The first place in Sam Neua to install a lift, this hotel is a real deal for such a clean and comfortable place to stay, with rooms including a TV and fridge. Try to bag a front-facing room with a balcony overlooking the river.

Sam Neua Hotel HOTEL $
(064-314777; snhotel_08@yahoo.com; r 100,000-200,000K;) Located over the bridge on the same side as the main market, this well-maintained hotel has 17 rooms complete with fresh linen, pine furniture, satellite TV and ensuite bathrooms with hot water.

★ **Xayphasouk Hotel** HOTEL $
(064-312033; xayphasoukhotel@gmail.com; r 150,000-200,000K;) The smartest hotel in Sam Neua. The huge lobby-restaurant is woefully underused, but the rooms are very comfortable for such a remote region of Laos. All include piping hot showers, flat-screen TVs, tasteful furnishings and crisp linen. Plus free wi-fi.

Eating & Drinking

Cheap *fĕr* and many harder-to-identify local morsels are sold from **food stalls** (dawn-dusk) around the main market.

Dan Nao Muang Xam Restaurant LAOTIAN $
(mains 15,000-50,000K; 7am-9.30pm) This hole-in-the-wall spot is hardly brimming with atmosphere, but it has the most foreigner-friendly menu in town in concise English. Breakfast includes cornflakes and a delicious *fĕr*. Dinner includes some excellent rice and soup combinations, plus a steak with al dente vegetables arranged star-like around the plate.

Chittavanh Restaurant LAOTIAN $
(mains 20,000-40,000K; 7am-9.30pm) Savouring a delicious Chinese fried tofu dish makes it worth braving the reverberant clatter of this cavernous hotel restaurant where vinyl tablecloths have been nailed into place. Locals like to eat here as well – always a good sign.

Nang Nok Bar BAR
Sam Neua is not going to win any awards for its nightlife, but Nang Nok might be one of the only contenders. It's a thatched pavilion on the edge of town where young locals come to down big bottles of Beerlao.

Information

Many hotels and guesthouses have wi-fi these days.

Agricultural Promotion Bank (8am-noon & 1.30-4pm Mon-Fri) Exchanges Thai baht and US dollars at fair rates.

BCEL (8am-3.30pm Mon-Fri) Has a couple of ATMs dispensing kip, plus can exchange most major currencies.

Foreign Exchange (to 5pm) Changing money is generally quickest through one of the fabric stalls in the main market: they exchange Vietnamese dong and are open at weekends.

Lao Development Bank (064-312171; 8am-4pm Mon-Fri) On the main road 400m north of the bus station on the left; exchanges cash and travellers cheques.

Provincial Tourist Office (064-312567; 8am-noon & 1.30-4pm Mon-Fri) An excellent tourist office with English-speaking staff eager to help.

Tam.com Internet Service (per min 150K; 8am-10pm) A relatively reliable internet cafe.

Getting There & Around

AIR

Sam Neua's little **Nathong Airfield** is 3km east of the centre towards Vieng Xai. **Lao Air** (www.lao-air.com) offers connections to Vientiane (915,000K) on Monday, Wednesday and Friday. All too frequently the flights get cancelled just before departure. Phonsavan/Xieng Khuang airport is more reliable.

BUS

Sam Neua has two bus stations. Schedules change frequently so double check and certainly don't rely on timetables printed on tourist maps and notice boards.

GETTING TO VIETNAM: SAM NEUA TO THANH HOA

Getting to the Border

If crossing the **Nam Soi (Laos)/Na Meo (Vietnam) border** (Km 175; ⏲7.30-11.30am, 1.30-4.30pm), the easiest transport option is to take the daily direct bus (sometimes minibus) between Sam Neua and Thanh Hoa which passes close to Vieng Xai but doesn't enter town. It departs daily at 8am (180,000K, 11 hours). Prepurchase your ticket at the main bus station to avoid overcharging. 'Through tickets' to Hanoi still go via Thanh Hoa with a change of bus.

It's quite possible to reach the border by the 8am Na Meo *sǒrngtăaou* from Sam Neua (three hours). However, organising onward transport from the Vietnamese side is complicated by unscrupulous operators who seem intent on overcharging.

At the Border

Westbound, note that the Lao border post (Nam Soi) isn't a town. There are a few simple restaurant shacks but no accommodation and no waiting transport apart from the 11.30am *sǒrngtăaou* to Sam Neua.

Laos visas are available on arrival at this border but Vietnamese visas are not, so plan ahead if heading east.

Moving On

Once in Thanh Hoa, there's a night train to Hanoi departing at 11.30pm and arriving very early around 4am. Returning from Thanh Hoa (8am), tickets should cost 200,000 dong but foreigners are often asked for significantly more.

Main Bus Station

The main station is on a hilltop 1.2km south of the central monument, just off the Vieng Thong road. From here buses leave to Vientiane (170,000K, 22 hours) via Phonsavan (80,000K, 10 hours) at 9am, noon and 2pm. An additional 8am Vientiane bus goes via Vieng Thong (40,000K, six hours), Luang Prabang (140,000K, 17 hours) and Vang Vieng. There are also daily minibuses to Vieng Thong and Luang Prabang.

Nathong Bus Station

The Nathong bus station is 1km beyond the airport on the Vieng Xai road at the easternmost edge of town. *Sǒrngtăaou* to Vieng Xai (15,000K) leave five times daily, currently at 8am, 10am, 11am, 2.30pm and 4pm. Other services include 'Nameo' (actually the Nam Soi border post) at 8am (30,000K, three hours) and Sam Tai (Xamtay) at 9.30am (50,000K, five hours).

CAR & MOTORCYCLE

A central **motorcycle shop** (⏲7am-6pm) rents out low-quality motorbikes at 60,000K per day.

Around Sam Neua

It doesn't take much effort to get into some timeless rural villages around Sam Neua. For random motorcycle trips you might try heading south from the hospital for a few kilometres or heading north up the unpaved lane directly to the right-hand side of Wat Phoxaysanalam. The latter winds its way after 11km to **Ban Tham**, just before which there's an inconsequential **Buddha cave** (to the left around 100m before the school and shop). But more appealing are rice terrace valleys around 4km out of Sam Neua where two picturesque villages across the river each sport spindly old greying stupas. With a decent motorbike it is easy to make a day trip to Vieng Xai or a longer side trip to Hintang via Tat Saloei.

Vieng Xai ວຽງໄຊ

☎064 / POP 10,000

Vieng Xai's thought-provoking 'bomb-shelter caves' are set amid dramatic karst outcrops and offer a truly inspirational opportunity to learn about northern Laos' painful 20th-century history. Imagine Vang Vieng, but with a compelling historical twist instead of happy tubing. Or think of it as Ho Chi Minh City's Cu Chi Tunnels cast in stone.

History

For centuries the minuscule hamlet of Long Ko sat peacefully here, lost amid deep ancient forests and towering karst outcrops. But in 1963, political repression and a spate of assassinations in Vientiane led the Pathet

Lao leadership to retreat deep into the Hua Phan hinterland, eventually taking up residence in the area's caves. As the US Secret War gathered momentum, surrounding villages were mercilessly bombarded. Horrified and bemused, locals initially had no idea of who was attacking them, nor why. For safety, they retreated into the vastly expanded cave systems, more than 450 of which eventually came to shelter up to 23,000 people. As the war dragged on, cave sites came to host printing works, hospitals, markets and even a metalwork factory. After almost a decade in the caves, the 1973 ceasefire allowed the refugees to tentatively emerge and construct a small town here. Indeed, until December 1975, it was the de facto capital of the Pathet Lao's Liberated Territories. The town was named Vieng Xai as that had been the secret codename of future president Kaysone Phomvihane while has was in hiding here. Decades later, many of Vieng Xai's cave sites still retain visible signs of their wartime roles, making the complex one of the world's most complete revolutionary bases to have survived from the cold war period.

Sights

★**Vieng Xai Caves** CAVE
(ຖ້ຳວຽງໄຊ; www.visit-viengxay.com; admission incl audio tour 60,000K) Joining a truly fascinating 18-point tour is the only way to see Vieng Xai's seven most important war-shelter cave complexes, along with several 1970s postwar buildings associated with major liberation heroes. All are set in beautiful yet very natural gardens and backed by fabulous karst scenery. A local guide unlocks each site and can answer basic questions. Meanwhile, an audioguide gives a wealth of first-hand background information and historical context, offering a moving, balanced and uniquely fascinating glimpse of how people struggled on through the war years. Compared to anything else you're likely to encounter in Laos, the sheer professionalism is mind-boggling. The production incorporates original interviews from local survivors and is enlivened with sound effects and accompanying music: the Hendrixesque soundtrack to the Air America piece is particularly memorable and you may find yourself ducking for cover when the jet fighters screech overhead.

Most caves have minor elements of original furnishings. Some have 'emergency rooms' – air-locked concrete caves-within-caves designed to protect top politburo members from possible chemical or gas attacks. No such attacks occurred but the emergency room of the **Kaysone Phomvihane Cave** still has its air-circulation pump in working order. Enjoy bamboo-framed views of town from the ledge of the **Nouhak Phoumsavan Cave** and look for two rocket-impact holes in the karst outcrop above the **Souphanouvong Cave**, once the hideout of Laos' famous 'Red Prince'. Almost all the main cave sites are well illuminated but bring a torch (flashlight) if you want to traverse the unadorned **hospital cave** (occasionally flooded).

Steps lead down from the hand-dug **Khamtay Siphandone Cave** to the **Barracks Caves**, extensive natural caverns that would have housed hundreds of conscripted liberation soldiers. Above is the **Artillery Cave** from whose open ledge spotters would watch for incoming American planes. The tour culminates in the **Xanglot Cave**, a wide double-ended cavern that was used as a wedding hall, cinema and even as a theatre. Incredibly, performers from Russia, China and Vietnam all managed to mount productions here during the war. Fans of Colin Cotterill's Dr Siri series of novels should note that *Disco for the Departed* is set in and around the Vieng Xai caves.

DON'T MISS

THAM NOK ANN

Tham Nok Ann (Nok Ann Cave, ຖ້ຳນົກແອນ; admission 10,000K, twin kayak 30,000K; 8am-5pm) is a newly opened cave complex that includes a gentle kayaking trip along an underwater stream that flows through the mountain. This is a mini Tham Kong Lo experience for those that don't have the time to explore central Laos and is well worth the detour. The caves are well lit and include some huge jellyfish-like rock formations. The cave complex includes a Vietnamese military hospital. There are no life jackets included with the kayaks and you do need to stay alert for low-hanging stalactites.

Look for a signpost on the main road about 5km before Vieng Xai and follow the small track around to the right until it dead ends at an entrance booth and small suspension bridge.

Tours start at 9am and 1pm from the caves office. By arrangement private visits are also possible at other times (costing an extra 50,000K per group), depending on guide availability. Seeing all 18 sites in the three hours available is possible without feeling unduly rushed, assuming you rent a bicycle (available for 10,000/20,000K per tour/day from the caves office) and that you listen to the longer audio tracks while travelling between the sites rather than waiting to arrive before pressing play.

Sleeping & Eating

There is only a handful of guesthouses in Vieng Xai, making Sam Neua the better option for those seeking a little more comfort.

There is not a great selection of eating establishments in Vieng Xai and many have run out of food by 8pm. By 9pm the town is in hibernation. Several *fĕr* shops in the market serve rice and cheap noodle dishes until around 5pm.

Naxay Guesthouse GUESTHOUSE $
(☎064-314330; r 60,000-80,000K) Opposite the caves office, Vieng Xai's most comfortable option offers bamboo-lined bungalows or concrete cubicles set around a patch of greenery backed by an impressive split-toothed crag. Beds are comfy, hot water flows and the attached beach-style cafe pavilion occasionally serves up food.

Orientation

Twin roads run 1km south off Rte 3 to the busy market area. Beyond, the town retains the quiet, wide avenues and well-spaced houses of Kaysone's 1973 'capital' interspersed with man-made lakes, trees, flowers and several karst outcrops.

Information

Vieng Xai Cave Tourist Office (☎064-314321; www.visit-viengxay.com; ⊙8-11.30am & 1-4.30pm) Around 1km south of the market, the caves office organises all cave visits, rents bicycles and has maps, a small book exchange and a useful information board. There's even a display case full of old Lenin busts and assorted socialist iconograpy.

Getting There & Away

Sŏrngtăaou to Sam Neua (15,000K, 50 minutes) leave at approximately 7am, 10am, 1pm, 2.30pm and 4pm from the market. Buses between Sam Neua and Sam Tai, Nam Soi or Thanh Hoa (one bus daily to each) bypass Vieng Xai 1km to the north but will usually stop on request. Visiting Vieng Xai by rented tuk-tuk from Sam Neua costs around 250,000K return per vehicle.

Sam Neua to Vietnam

The scenic route via fascinating Vieng Xai is open to foreigners, Vietnamese visas permitting. It's narrow but paved and offers a feast of varied views. The best incorporate giant teeth of tree-dappled karst outcrops backing bucolic valleys layered with rice terraces. Several villages en route, including **Ban Piang Ban** (Km 144.5), specialise in basket-making and bamboo crafts. Across the river at Km 169 is a **'steel cave'** where knives and agricultural tools were made on an almost industrial scale during the Second Indochina War.

Turn south at Km 164 for the recently asphalted spur road to **Sam Tai** (Xamtay), famous for producing magnificent textiles. It has a couple of guesthouses should you feel like getting well off the beaten track to investigate. Public access to the remote **Nam Sam NPA** beyond is not currently permitted.

Sam Neua to Nong Khiaw

From Sam Neua, Rte 6 runs along winding mountain ridges passing Hintang Archaeological Park and meeting Phonsavan-bound Rte 1 at minuscule Phoulao (Ban Kho Hing), 92km west of Sam Neua, where kilometre markings reset. West of Phoulao the green mountains become much more heavily deforested until reaching the boundary of the Nam Et/Phou Louey NPA, which is best visited from Vieng Thong, also a convenient place to break the long journey. The descent towards Nong Khiaw lasts many kilometres and offers some glimpses of superb scenery.

Sights

Tat Saloei WATERFALL
(Phonesai Waterfall) This impressive series of cascades forms a combined drop of almost 100m. It's briefly visible from eastbound Rte 6 roughly 1km after Km 55 (ie 36km from Sam Neua), but easy to miss westbound. There are some small local cafes and restaurants on the roadside here, plus what looks like a ticket booth, although no-one was charging for entry during our visit.

Hintang Archaeological Park ARCHAEOLOGICAL SITE

(Suan Hin, ສວນຫີນ) Almost as mysterious as Xieng Khuang's more famous jars, this unique, unfenced collection of **standing stones** is thought to be at least 1500 years old. Spindly stones up to 3m tall are interspersed with **disks** that formerly covered funerary sites. Some are over a metre in diameter. It is more Avebury stone circle than Stonehenge, but the 'families' of stones do have a certain magic and it is now a Unesco World Heritage site. Local mythology claims that the stones were originally cut using a magic axe wielded by a giant called Ba Hat whose plans to build a great city here were thwarted by the cunning of the Luang Prabang king.

Access is up a rough, rutted track that cuts south from Rte 6 at **Ban Phao** (Km 35.3), 57km from Sam Neua. This track can be impracticably muddy for vehicles after any rain. The main site is right beside the track after 6km, around 800m beyond the obvious radio mast summit. Some 2km back towards the main road, an orange sign points to the **Keohintang Trail**, which allows more intrepid visitors to seek out lesser-known megalith groups hidden along a partially marked two-hour hiking trail. Take the narrow rising path, not the bigger track that descends towards Ban Nakham. If you don't get lost, the trail should emerge back onto Rte 6 at **Ban Tao Hin** (Km 31.5), a tiny village without any facilities.

Chartered tuk-tuks from Sam Neua want around 500,000K return. When driving between Sam Neua and either Phonsavan or Nong Khiaw, allow two hours extra for the very slow detour to the main site. Using public transport it is necessary to walk to and from Rte 6. Practicalities work out best if visiting between Sam Neua and Phonsavan: starting with the Vieng Thong–bound minibus, there is around six hours for the walk before the last Phonsavan/Vientiane-bound bus rumbles past.

Vieng Thong (Muang Hiam) ວຽງທອງ (ເມືອງຫ້ຽມ)

☎064 / POP 4000

If you're travelling between Nong Khiaw and Sam Neua, stopping here for at least one night makes the long journey altogether more enjoyable. US bombing destroyed the town's once-grand monastery but its surviving stupa, **That Hiam**, is on the rise beside the district administration buildings. The dazzling green rice fields around town are photogenic and short walks or bicycle rides can take you to pretty Tai Daeng, Hmong and Khamu villages.

Many locals still refer to Vieng Thong by its original name Muang Hiam. Coming

NAM ET/PHOU LOUEY NPA

In the vast Nam Et/Phou Louey NPA (ປ່າສະຫງວນແຫ່ງຊາດນ້ຳແອດພູເລີຍ), rare civets, Asian golden cats, river otters, white-cheeked crested gibbons and the utterly unique Laotian warty newt *(Paramesotriton laoensis)* share 4200 sq km of relatively pristine forests with around a dozen tigers. Approximately half is an inaccessible core zone. The remainder includes 98 ethnic-minority hamlets. Two-day wildlife-watching excursions have been pioneered to the park's remote Nam Nern field station, a roadless former village site where a campsite and surrounding walking trails have been professionally cleared of UXO. Highlights of the trip include a nighttime boat ride 'spotlighting' for animals and daytime guided hikes learning about wildlife tracking. Actually seeing a live tiger is unlikely but there's more hope of spotting sambar and barking deer and for each significant sighting, nearby villages receive a small payment. This is a cleverly thought-out scheme that encourages the local population to work actively against poachers.

Trips are organised through the NPA office (p84) in Vieng Thong but contacting them well in advance is advisable since there's a limit of two departures per week. Tour costs (US$80/100 per person in groups of five/two people) and include guides, cooks, food and camping equipment, with a significant proportion of the fee going into village development funds. The price also includes the 90-minute boat ride from Ban Sonkhua, around 50km east of Vieng Thong on Rte 1. Getting to Ban Sonkhua (not included) is possible on the morning public minibus from Vieng Thong or Phonsavan but be sure to discuss travel arrangements with the organisers.

from a Tai Daeng word meaning 'watch out', that was highly suitable back when dangerous tigers roamed the surrounding forests. These days barely a dozen still survive, deep in the enormous Nam Et/Phou Louey NPA, but Vieng Thong is the main starting point to look for them on newly initiated **'tiger treks'**. These are organised through the **Nam Et/Phou Louey NPA office** (064-810008; www.namet.org; 8am-noon & 1-4.30pm Mon-Fri), housed in the Vieng Thong visitors' centre. Drop in here to learn more about the park's imaginative wildlife protection programs and to peruse remarkable animal photos snapped by ingenious camera-traps dotted around the park. The office is at the northwestern edge of town, 700m beyond the market area: cross the river (Nam Khao) on Rte 1, turn immediately right at Km 197 taking the unsurfaced Muang Pur (Meuagper) road, then swing immediately left up the 200m access lane.

Ten minutes walk further towards Muang Pur is a little **hot spring area**. Now somewhat developed, entry is 10,000K per person, but the bathing facilities are very poorly presented. The springs bubble up from the ground a few hundred metres upstream amid a pretty wood, but the water is scalding hot here. Further downstream is a scum-ridden pond that really should be cleaned up and turned into a giant hot tub. Instead the water is piped out for locals to do their washing and eventually turns into shower taps next to the car park where locals take a bath. There are three small 'hot tubs' for bathing, but two were only ankle-deep and the other full of cold water. So much potential, but it's hard to really recommend the place in its current state.

Sleeping & Eating

A handful of restaurant stands at the bus station offer varied delicacies such as frog-on-a-stick to passing travellers.

Dork Khoun Thong Guesthouse GUESTHOUSE $
(064-810017; r 50,000-80,000K) The most appealing of Vieng Thong's limited options, this guesthouse is located right in the centre of the small town. Very clean, decent-sized rooms have hot showers, netted windows and comfortable new beds with love-message sheets and teddy-bear towels. There's a pleasant first-floor sitting area and attractive views across riverside fields from the rear terrace.

Dokchampa Guesthouse GUESHOUSE $
(064-810005; r without/with bathroom 30,000/50,000K) This small guesthouse has basic rooms with mosquito nets, hot-water showers and squat toilets. The owners offer a few traveller-friendly services such as bicycles for rent (30,000K per day), free wi-fi and a small attached internet cafe (5000K per hour).

Tontavanh Restaurant LAOTIAN $
(mains 10,000-20,000K) This typical-looking local eatery serves unexpectedly appetising food and even has a menu in concise English.

Getting There & Away

Westbound buses arrive from Sam Neua around noon, continuing after lunch to Nong Khiaw (60,000K, five hours), Pak Mong and Luang Prabang (130,000K, nine hours). Eastbound, the best choice for Sam Neua is the 7am minibus (40,000K, six hours) as the two Sam Neua through-services (from Luang Prabang/Vientiane) both travel the road largely by night.

The bus station is 300m along Rte 6 from the market at the eastern edge of town.

MUANG NGOI DISTRICT

Tracts of green mountains are attractive wherever you go in northern Laos. But at Nong Khiaw and tiny, roadless Muang Ngoi Neua, the contours do something altogether more dramatic. At both places, vast karst peaks and towering cliffs rear dramatically out of the Nam Ou, creating jaw-droppingly beautiful scenes. Both villages make convenient rural getaways from Luang Prabang and are accessible by riverboat from Muang Khua. Nong Khiaw also makes an excellent rural rest stop between Luang Prabang and Vieng Thong or Sam Neua.

Nong Khiaw ໜອງຂຽວ

071 / POP 3500

Location, location, location: Nong Khiaw certainly has it. This sleepy little village is a pair of quiet streets on the west bank of the languid Nam Ou. On the river's scenic east bank (officially called Ban Sop Houn) is a selection of guesthouses and restaurants catering to travellers. Linking the two, a high concrete bridge built in 1973 offers particularly mesmerising views of soaring limestone crags and haphazard chunks of mountain.

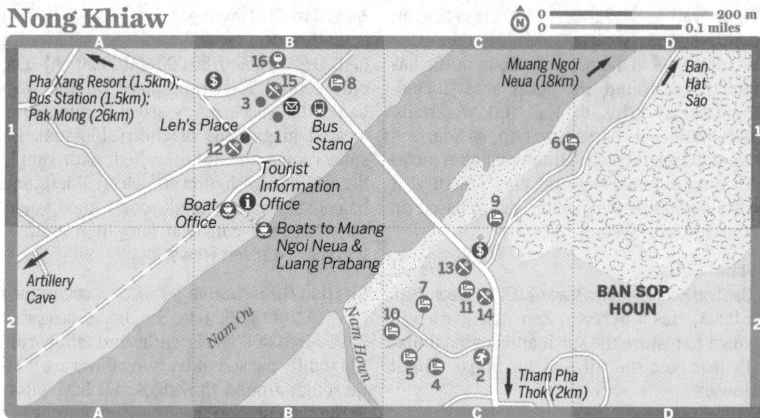

Be aware that Nong Khiaw is alternatively known as Muang Ngoi (the name of the surrounding district), creating obvious confusion with Muang Ngoi Neua, a 75-minute boat ride further north.

Sights

It's hard to beat just standing on the bridge and gazing at the river. And do return to the bridge at dusk when fabulous star shows turn the deep indigo sky into a pointillist canvas that subtly outlines the riverside massifs.

Tham Pha Thok CAVE

(ຖ້ຳຜາທອກ; admission 5000K; ⌚7.30am-6.30pm) Around 2km east along remarkably quiet Rte 1C, the horizon's array of towering karst formations reaches a brief but particularly impressive climax. Just beyond, Tham Pha Thok is a series of caves in an abrupt limestone cliff. This is where villagers and much of the Pathet Lao's Luang Prabang provincial government lived during the Second Indochina War to avoid American bombing. The first and most obvious cave is around 30m above ground level, accessed by a lichen-crusted wooden stairway. Much smaller but more exciting to visit (unless you're claustrophobic) is a second cave 300m around the cliff. Home to the region's main bank between 1968 and 1974, it's accessed through a narrow, twisting former siphon passage. It's pitch black inside the caves so bring a head-torch or rent one for 5000K at the ticket booth.

Activities

There are several ecotourism outfits in Nong Khiaw that offer trekking, cycling and kayaking around the area.

Nong Khiaw

Activities, Courses & Tours

1 Green Discovery ... B1
2 Sabai Sabai ... C2
3 Tiger Trail ... B1

Sleeping

4 Amphai Guesthouse ... C2
5 Namhoun Guesthouse ... C2
6 Nong Kiau Riverside ... C1
7 Paradise Bamboo Guesthouse ... C2
8 Sengdao Chittavong Guesthouse ... B1
9 Sunrise Guesthouse ... C1
10 Sunset Guest House ... C2
11 Vongmany Guesthouse ... C2

Eating

12 Coco Home Bar & Restaurant ... B1
13 CT Restaurant and Bakery ... C2
14 Deen ... C2
15 Delilah's Place ... B1

Drinking & Nightlife

16 Hive Bar ... B1

Green Discovery HIKING, CYCLING

(☎071-810018; www.greendiscoverylaos.com) This well-established company organises several treks and various kayaking options, including a three-day paddle-camping expedition to Luang Prabang (from 1,330,000K per person). A one-day trip starting with a longboat ride to Muang Ngoi Neua then paddling back costs 350,000 per person, assuming four participants in two-person kayaks. Experienced staff can also organise longer treks or expeditions towards Muang Khua and in the Nam Et/Phou Louey NPA, where night safaris are organised.

Tiger Trail HIKING, CYCLING

(☎071-252655; www.laos-adventures.com; Delilah's Place) This eco-conscious outfit has fair treks around the local area, including one-day trips to the '100 waterfalls' (350,000K per person, group of four). A two-day trek through Hmong villages incorporating a homestay and clay school visit costs 500,000K per person, again based on at least four travellers.

Sabai Sabai MASSAGE

(Ban Sop Houn; body massage 40,000K, steam bath 15,000K) Has a peaceful Zen-style garden in which to restore the spirit and aching limbs. It's just past the turn-off for Sunset Guest House.

Sleeping

In the low season, prices are definitely negotiable. Look out for the new Mandala Ou Resort, opened in the second half of 2013.

Namhoun Guesthouse GUESTHOUSE $

(☎071-810039; bungalows 50,000-100,000K; wi-fi) Cheaper bungalows are set around a small garden behind the family house. Better are the riverside bungalows facing the Nam Ou, but they come at a premium 100,000K. All rooms have mosquito nets and balconies with the compulsory hammock.

Amphai Guesthouse GUESTHOUSE $

(☎020-5577 3637; Ban Sop Houn; r 60,000K; wi-fi) It lacks the riverfront location of some competitors, but the prices more than reflect this. Rooms are spacious and cool, with clean bathrooms and hot water. A new Indian restaurant has just opened in the downstairs courtyard.

Paradise Bamboo Guesthouse GUESTHOUSE $

(☎020-5554 5286; Ban Sop Houn; r 60,000-100,000K; wi-fi) Choose between the modern peach-coloured block for comfort and hot water or the rickety bungalows, which are more rustic but offer better views. They also have a two-storey wooden house with rooms that are somewhere between the other two options in terms of comfort.

Vongmany Guesthouse GUESTHOUSE $

(☎030-923 0639; Ban Sop Houn; wi-fi) Explore behind the restaurant to discover a smart two-storey structure with views to the river. Rooms are spacious and clean, and have hot water. Rooms 12 and 14 come with the grandstand views and cost 100,000K.

Sengdao Chittavong Guesthouse GUESTHOUSE $

(☎030-923 7089; r 80,000-100,000K; wi-fi) The only central riverfront place on the west bank, this place offers sizeable bungalows located in gardens of cherry blossom. En suite rooms are rattan-walled, with simple decoration, fresh flowers, clean linen, and balconies, making it all-round good value. There's also a convivial fairy-lit restaurant with river-garden views.

Sunrise Guesthouse GUESTHOUSE $

(☎020-2247 8799; Ban Sop Houn; bungalows 70,000-150,000K; wi-fi) Friendly and family-run, the tightly packed older bungalows are a little rough around the edges, but have views to the river and bridge. There are four newer bungalows that include swish bathrooms, polished wood and even tea- and coffee-making facilities.

Sunset Guest House GUESTHOUSE $

(☎071-810033; sunsetgh2@hotmail.com; Ban Sop Houn; r 150,000-200,000K; wi-fi) The ever-evolving Sunset has an lively new roof cafe and two pretty bungalows isolated in a little meadow. However, the pricing is a little ambitious compared with the cheaper guesthouses around town and you are effectively paying a big premium for the river view.

★**Nong Kiau Riverside** GUESTHOUSE $$

(☎020-5570 5000; www.nongkiau.com; Ban Sop Houn; s/d incl breakfast 310,000/350,000K; @wi-fi) In a class of its own, Riverside's elegant bungalows are romantically finished with mosquito nets, ambient lighting, wooden floors and woven bedspreads. Each includes an attractively finished bathroom and a balcony for blissful river views of the looming karsts. The views get better the further you venture from the striking reception area and restaurant, so ask for a higher-numbered room. The restaurant is surprisingly affordable and has breathtaking views.

Pha Xang Resort HOTEL $$

(☎071-810014; wi-fi) Pha Xang offers an upscale collection of bungalows in a quiet part of town near the bus station. The views across to the gnarly peaks are specatacular. Bungalows are finished in wood and rattan, and include a spacious bathroom.

Eating & Drinking

A few traveller-oriented eateries line Rte 1C on the east bank. A couple of unnamed stilt cafes are perched above the main jetty but think twice before ordering food less than an hour before a boat departure, as cooking can take forever.

★Coco Home Bar & Restaurant LAOTIAN, INTERNATIONAL $
(mains 15,000-45,000K;) Located on the main drag on the west bank, this is the liveliest all-rounder in town, offering dining in an attractive garden setting above the boat dock. The menu includes Lao, Thai and international favourites, plus the drinks continue to flow into the night. Movies are screened upstairs nightly, but this doesn't distract the diners below.

Deen INDIAN $
(Ban Sop Houn; mains 20,000-35,000K; 8.30am-10pm;) A superb little Indian eatery with wood-fired naan bread, moreish tandoori dishes, zesty curries and a comfortable atmosphere, Deen is always packed. There's also a bank of computers (internet 15,000K per hour; wi-fi is free).

Delilah's Place INTERNATIONAL, LAOTIAN $
(mains 15,000-35,000K; 7am-10pm;) Strung with creeper vines, this tasteful eatery offers an eclectic selection ranging from delicious pancakes, bagels, salads, spring rolls and Lao green curries to hamburgers and Western breakfasts. There is even a proper latte available here.

CT Restaurant and Bakery INTERNATIONAL, LAOTIAN $
(Ban Sop Houn; mains 15,000-30,000K; 7am-10pm) Located in a commanding position at the end of the bridge, CT has a Western-friendly menu of pancakes, breakfasts, sandwiches and staple Lao dishes. It also offers takeaway sandwiches for trekking.

Hive Bar BAR
(5pm-late) It may not have quite the buzz of the more famous Hive Bar in Luang Prabang, but it is one of the only late-night spots in town, offering a free *lòw-lów* (Lao whisky) shot to first-timers.

Information

Wi-fi is now available pretty much everywhere and Deen (p87) offers internet access.

BCEL Has an ATM at the end of the bridge on the Ban Sop Houn side.

Post Office (8.30am-5pm) The tiny post office exchanges baht and US dollars at slightly unfavourable rates.

Tourist Information Office Above the boat landing. Rarely open.

Getting There & Away

BOAT

River-boat rides are a highlight of visiting Nong Khiaw. For Luang Prabang (110,000K, five to eight hours, 11am), sign up one day before departure at the **boat office**. A charter costs 1,500,000K per boat. Sometimes when water levels are very low, there are sections of the trip where it is necessary to push the boat through shallows and/or take a 10km tuk-tuk ride around them. Plan ahead with suitable footwear.

Boats to Muang Ngoi Neua (25,000K, 1¼ hours) leave at 11am and 2pm. It's a lovely ride and in high season extra departures are possible. The 11am boat continues all the way to Muang Khua (120,000K, seven hours) for connections to Phongsali or Dien Bien Phu in Vietnam.

BUS & SŎRNGTĂAOU

The journey to Luang Prabang is possible in three hours but in reality usually takes at least four. Minibuses or *sŏrngtăaou* (40,000K) start at around 9am and 11am, plus there's a minivan (50,000K) at 1pm. Tickets are sold at the bus stand but the 11am service actually starts at the boat office, filling up with folks arriving off the boat(s) from Muang Ngoi. When a boat arrives from Muang Khua there'll usually be additional Luang Prabang minivans departing at around 3pm from the boat office.

For Udomxai a direct minibus (50,000K, three hours) leaves at 11am. Alternatively take any westbound transport and change at Pak Mong (25,000K, 50 minutes).

Originating in Luang Prabang, the minibus to Sam Neua (130,000K, 12 hours) via Vieng Thong (100,000K, five hours) makes a quick lunch stop in Nong Khiaw around 11.30am. Another Sam Neua bus (arriving from Vientiane) passes through at night.

Getting Around

Bicycle rental makes sense to explore local villages or reach the caves. Town bicycles cost 20,000K per day and mountain bikes cost 30,000K, both available from unsigned **Leh's Place** on the main drag.

Muang Ngoi Neua (Ban Ngoi Kao) ເມືອງງອຍເໜືອ (ບ້ານງອຍເກົ່າ)

POP 1000

Flanked in all directions by sculpted layers of majestic karst mountain and cliff, this almost roadless village enjoys one of northern Laos' prettiest riverside settings. The one 500m-long 'street' fires itself dead straight from the main monastery towards a dramatic pyramidal tooth of forest-dappled limestone. Short unaided hikes take you into timeless neighbouring villages while kayaking trips are a great way to savour the memorable Nam Ou, which has its most scenically spectacular stretches either side of the village.

Need to choose between Nong Khiaw and Muong Ngoi Neua? It's a tough call, but generally Nong Khiaw has better accommodation and dining, while Muong Ngoi Neua is more rural and timeless with nearby trekking opportunities.

History

Muang Ngoi was once a regional centre but it was pulverised during the Second Indochina War, with bombs destroying all three of its once-celebrated historic monasteries. Such was the devastation that a 'new' postwar Muang Ngoi (ie Nong Khiaw) took over as the district headquarters, a potential confusion that still sometimes causes mix-ups. The rebuilt village was 'discovered' by travellers in the late 1990s when its beauty and laissez-faire atmosphere gained it a major pre-Twitter-era buzz, despite not featuring in any guidebooks. By 2002 virtually every guesthouse hosted dollar-a-night *falang,* some of whom stayed for months in a chilled-out opiate haze, but Laos' clamp down on drugs changed the atmosphere radically. Most of the very cheapest guesthouses closed or improved their facilities to cater for a (slightly) more demanding new generation of travellers who still enjoy the enchanting boat journeys from Nong Khiaw but are now more interested in hiking, kayaking and simply enjoying the riverscape. If you want a super-cheap homestay, that's still possible in nearby Huay Bo.

Sights & Activities

Such is the grandeur of the riverside views that you could happily linger all day just lazing on your balcony or sitting at one of the better-placed restaurant shacks. A little after dawn it's interesting to watch locals delivering alms to monks at the rebuilt monastery, **Wat Okadsayaram**.

Numerous freelance guides offer a wide range of walks to Lao, Hmong and Khamu villages and to regional waterfalls. Prices are remarkably reasonable and some visits, such as to the **That Mok** falls, involve boat rides. Others are easy hikes that you could do perfectly well unguided, possibly staying the night in one of three pretty outlying villages.

Kayaking is a great way to appreciate the fabulous riverine scenery that stretches both ways along the Nam Ou. **Lao Youth Travel** (☎030-514 0046; www.laoyouthtravel.com; ⏲7.30-10.30am & 1.30-6pm) has its own kayaks and is handily located where the boat-landing path passes the two-storey Rainbow House.

Sleeping

Uniquely for such a tiny place, budget accommodation abounds and English is widely spoken so you get the experience of a remote village without the inconvenience. The only drawback is that the accommodation is showing its age compared with up and coming Nong Khiaw just down the river.

Most of the basic guesthouses have inspiring views over the Nam Ou and its multilayered karst massifs. Savouring such views from your bungalow is one of Muang Ngoi's great attractions, so think twice before choosing an inland guesthouse just to save 10,000K.

★ **Ning Ning Guest House** GUESTHOUSE $
(☎020-3386 3306; r incl breakfast US$17-20) Nestled around a peaceful garden, Ning Ning is the smartest place in the village, offering immaculate wooden bungalows. The trim includes mosquito nets, verandahs, en suite bathroom and bed linen, plus the walls are draped with ethnic tapestries. There's a nice restaurant with riverfront views.

Phetdavanh Guesthouse GUESTHOUSE $
(dm/r from 30,000/40,000K, bungalows from 80,000K) No views and no hammocks in the main house but its 24-hour power and a range of cheap rooms, including various dormitory-style affairs, keep the travellers coming. Riverfront bungalows are a worthy investment for those wanting to chill out.

Nicksa's Place GUESTHOUSE $
(r 50,000K) This friendly place is named after the owner's daughter and includes seven bungalows spread along a pretty riverfront garden. Each has a balcony and obligatory hammock to take in the impressive vista. Cold-water showers only.

Rainbow Guest House GUESTHOUSE $
(☎020-2295 7880; r 60,000K) Close to the boat ramp, this newly constructed house has

clean if charmless rooms. Fragrant linen, large en suites, a communal verandah and a sunset-facing cafe.

Bungalows Ecolodge GUESTHOUSE $
(r 80,000K) Decent-sized new bungalows hidden down a side street, with sliding shutters that allow you to lie in bed and watch the sky turn amber over the karsts. Tasteful linen, solar-heated showers, mosquito nets and locally sourced food elevate it above the crowd.

Aloune Mai Guesthouse GUESTHOUSE $
(r 70,000K) Not to be confused with rickety Aloune Mai by the river, this hidden gem, found down a dirt track and over a bridge, sits beside a meadow and has 10 fresh rooms in a handsome rattan building with heated showers. There's a little restaurant and stunning views of the cliffs on the other side, but no river views.

Lattanavongsa Guesthouse GUESTHOUSE $
(☎030-514 0770; r from 100,000K) In a palm-filled garden, Lattanavongsa's sun-terraced bungalows enjoy views of the karst formations. Inside rooms are tasteful with house-proud flourishes, including gas-fired showers and upscale linen. There are four rattan bungalows near the river and 12 bungalows above the boat landing.

Veranda GUESTHOUSE $
(☎020-2386 2021; r 100,000K) The five bamboo-weave bungalows form an arc around a panoramic river view. All have hammocks, embroidered bedspreads, good beds and solar-heated showers. It was under partial renovation during our visit which may see it re-emerge as a basic boutique resort with higher prices.

Eating & Drinking

Several guesthouses cook a range of local food and traveller fare.

★**Riverside Restaurant** LAOTIAN $
(meals 15,000-35,000K; ⏲7.30am-10pm) Shaded by a mature mango tree festooned with lanterns, this lively haunt has lovely views of the Nam Ou. The menu encompasses noodles, fried dishes and *làhp*. A real traveller magnet, it deserves all the attention it receives.

Nang Phone Keo Restaurant LAOTIAN $
(mains 10,000-20,000K; ⏲7.30am-9pm) On the deck of this Main St house-restaurant you can get Muang Ngoi's most exotic dessert, a flaming plate of fried bananas flambéed in *lòw-lów*. Also imaginative is the *falang* roll with peanut butter, banana, sticky rice and honey.

Phetdavanh Street Buffet LAOTIAN $
(per person 20,000K; ⏲7pm) Phetdavanh runs an affordable nightly buffet that draws in locals and travellers alike. It sets up on the street around 7pm, serving barbecued pork, chicken, fish, sticky rice and vegetables.

Bee Tree BARBECUE $
(mains 15,000-35,000K; ⏲11.30am-11.30pm) Located at the end of the main drag, this barbecue restaurant-cum-beer-garden has a relaxed ambience. Choose from Lao dishes and some comfort food or stroll along here for happy hour cocktails between 5pm and 8pm.

Information

There is now mains electricity in Muang Ngoi, which also translates to internet access and wi-fi. In emergencies you could exchange US dollars at a few of the guesthouses but rates are, not surprisingly, poor.

Thefts from Muang Ngoi Neua's cheaper guesthouses tend to occur when over-relaxed guests leave flimsy doors and shutters unsecured or place valuables within easy reach of long-armed pincers – most windows here have no glass.

Getting There & Away

Boats to Nong Khiaw (25,000K, one hour) leave around 9am, with tickets on sale from 8am at the boat office beside Ning Ning Guest House. Boats from Muang Khua pick up in Muang Ngoi Neua for Nong Khiaw around 1.30pm. Going to Muang Khua (120,000K, six hours), a boat leaves at 9.30am if enough people sign up the day before on the list at the boat office. The first hour of the ride cuts through particularly spectacular scenery.

A new road is under construction that will connect Muang Ngoi Neua to Nong Khiaw. This may change the atmosphere considerably as modern Laos intrudes.

Around Muang Ngoi Neua

Muang Ngoi Neua is a great place for making short hikes through clouds of white and orange butterflies into beautiful karst-edged countryside. Reaching the three closest villages is easy without a guide or map. Start by heading east away from the river along the continuation of the boat-landing access track. Around 25 minutes' walk further is a small tollbooth that charges foreigners 10,000K to continue. Your toll also allows access to the adjacent **Tham Kang**, a modest limestone cave set between poinsettia bushes and trumpet lilies. Inside you might spot a few bats and there's the eerie sight of a stream emerging through what at first glance look like giant stone jaws. For refreshments, cross a little bamboo bridge over the crystal clear Nam Ngoi river to the simple little **Cave View Restaurant** (mains 10,000-30,000K; ⏲8am-6pm).

Continuing for 15 minutes, cross a stream (wading is safer than risking the slippery stepping stones) and reach a large area of rice fields. Keep left just as you first enter the rice fields. Then at the next junction (three minutes later) bear left for Huay Sen (45 minutes) or right for Ban Na (15 minutes) and Huay Bo (40 minutes). Sticking to the convoluted but well-worn main path is wise as there are little hand-painted signposts at each of the few possible confusion points. All three villages offer very basic, ultra-cheap accommodation with shared outdoor squat toilets and associated restaurant shacks that are open if and when anyone happens to be around to cook.

For stilt-house architecture, **Huay Sen** has the most authentic vibe of the three villages. The sole **guesthouse** (r 10,000K) is a sorry set of minuscule bamboo-boxes, but the enthusiastic owner speaks some English, can rustle up a decent fried rice and stocks an unusually flavoursome bamboo-macerated *lòw-lów*. He also offers guided two-hour walks to neighbouring Hmong villages.

The houses of **Ban Na** look less rustic but you can observe local weavers at work and both village guesthouses overlook a sea of rice fields with a jutting karst horizon. **OB Bungalows** (☎020-3386 3225; r 10,000K) at the farthest end of the village has the better view and its new, relatively sizeable bamboo huts are particularly good value. **Chantanohm Guesthouse** (r 10,000K) has a pretty setting and features a *petang* track and bomb casings.

The walk to **Huay Bo** is very attractive but requires fording one intermediate river. You'll pass a particularly sharp limestone spike and follow beneath a high ridge. The village comprises mostly stilt and bamboo-weave houses albeit with a less serene atmosphere than in Huay Sen. Three simple side-by-side guesthouses all charge 5000K, possibly the cheapest anywhere in Laos.

PHONGSALI PROVINCE

No longer Laos, not yet China, Phongsali is a visual feast and is home to some of the nation's most traditional hill tribes. Trekkers might feel that they've walked onto the pages of *National Geographic*. For travellers, the province's most visited settlement is Muang Khua, a useful transit point linked by river to Nong Khiaw and by road to Dien Bien Phu in Vietnam. Further north the province is kept well off the standard tourist trail by arduous journeys on snaking roads that twist and turn endlessly. The only asphalt links Muang Khua to Udomxai, Phongsali and on to Mengla in China. Inconveniently foreigners can't cross the Chinese border anywhere in the province. The road to Dien Bien Phu is now in great shape on the Lao side, not so great shape on the Vietnamese side.

Plans to make Boun Neua the new provincial capital have yet to be realised though it's already home to misnamed 'Phongsali' Airport.

Muang Khua ເມືອງຂວາ

☎088 / POP 4000

Pretty little Muang Khua is an inevitable stop when transiting between Laos and Dien Bien Phu in Vietnam or taking the Nam Ou river route between Hat Sa (Phongsali) and Nong Khiaw. While not as spectacular as the latter, Muang Khua has oodles of small-town charm set amid starburst palms where the Nam Ou and Nam Phak rivers meet. If you are arriving from Dien Bien Phu, please relax. This is Laos, and unlike in neighbouring Vietnam, hard bargaining is neither required nor appropriate.

Sights & Activities

A short walk leads to the rustic Khamu quarter across a high, creaky **suspension bridge** (bike/pedestrian only) over the Nam Phak river. An even easier stroll passes the colourful little **wat** and heads into another palm-dappled village area where the road peters out. The **ethnic handicrafts shop** at Chaleunsuk Guesthouse sells a small but appealing range of local crafts. Photo-

Muang Khua

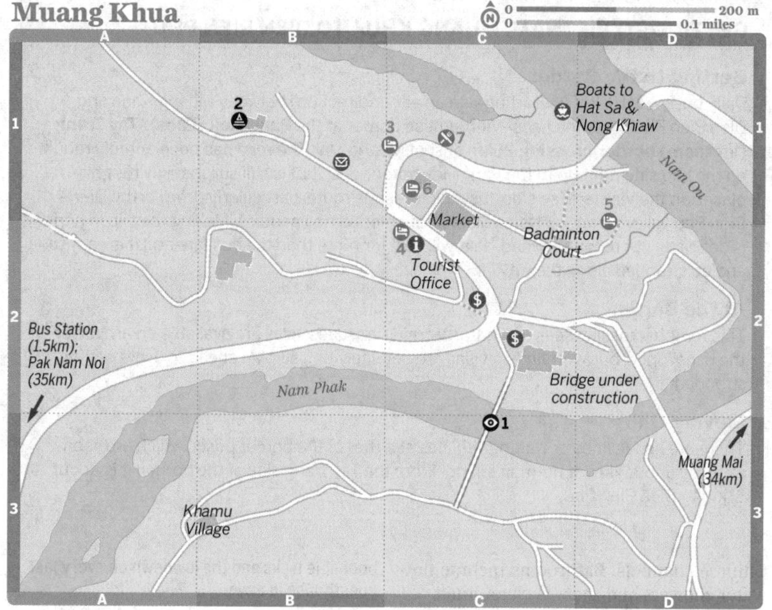

Muang Khua

Sights

1 Suspension Bridge C3
2 Wat B1

Sleeping

3 Chaleunsuk Guesthouse C1
4 Manhchai Guesthouse C2
5 Nam Ou Guesthouse D1
6 Sernalli Hotel C1

Eating

7 Sayfon C1

Shopping

Ethnic Handicrafts Shop .... (see 3)

explanation boards show their production and introduce the villages that your purchases support.

The tourist office organises several trekking options, including a rewarding one-day trek to **Ban Bakha**, an Akha Pala village high on the heavily deforested ridges above Pak Nam Noi. The population only moved here in 1990 and many of the women still wear the traditional gaudy-coloured Pala aprons and metal-beaded top-knots.

Luang Prabang–based Tiger Trail (p49) offers six-day Akha Village 'voluntourism' experiences for longer, experience-based stays in such villages, costing US$399.

Sleeping & Eating

Nam Ou Guesthouse GUESTHOUSE $
(088-210844; r without/with bathroom 40,000/50,000K) This rambling guesthouse overlooking the Nam Ou has a hodgepodge of rooms. The best have a hot shower and shared terrace but the cheaper ones are very basic bamboo boxes. Perched on stilts, the traveller-friendly restaurant serves tasty, if wafer-thin, 'steak' and chips, plus a selection of stir-fries. Duck features prominently on the menu.

Chaleunsuk Guesthouse GUESTHOUSE $
(088-210847; r 60,000K; @) Above the boat dock, the clean, generously sized rooms have large comfy beds and hot showers. Most also come with a desk and a ceiling patterned with stars and plastic planets. Free tea is available in the ample communal sitting terrace.

Manhchai Guesthouse GUESTHOUSE $
(088-210841; r 100,000K) Above a family shop beside the tourist office, the Manhchai has been given a facelift, including flat-screen TVs in the rooms, which still only pump out Lao, Thai, Vietnamese and

GETTING TO VIETNAM: MUANG KHUA TO DIEN BIEN PHU

Getting to the Border

Daily buses (50,000K, departing 6am in either direction) between Muang Khua and Dien Bien Phu cross the Laos–Vietnamese border at the **Pang Hok (Laos)/Tay Trang (Vietnam) border crossing** 26km east of Muang Mai. The road has been entirely rebuilt on the Lao side right up to the Pang Hok border post, but is still surprisingly rough in places on the Vietnamese side. It's a picturesque route, particularly down in the Dien Bien Phu valley which is often a blanket of emerald rice paddies. Making the trip in hops is definitely not recommended, as it will cost far more than the bus fare and it is easy to end up stranded along the way.

At the Border

This remote crossing sees a handful of travellers. Laos visas are available on arrival for the usual price, but Vietnamese visas are definitely not, so plan ahead to avoid getting stranded.

Moving On

There are no facilities or waiting vehicles at either of the border posts, which are separated by about 4km of no-man's-land. From the Tay Trang side of the border, it is about 31km to Dien Bien Phu.

Chinese channels. Bathrooms include hot-water showers and there is clean linen.

Sernalli Hotel HOTEL $$
(☎088-212445; r 200,000K) Muang Khua's top address, the Sernalli has a facade that suggests a certain neo-colonial elegance and the small lobby is full of carved hardwood furniture. The rooms are clean and comfortable enough, including wooden furnishings and reliable hot water. Extra touches include aircon and large flat-screen TVs.

Sayfon LAOTIAN $
(mains 15,000-30,000K) Set high above the river with views through the palm trees, the Sayfon has a wide English-language menu, some of which is usually available. The mushrooms in ginger are particularly good.

Information

There are now two ATMs in town. Both **BCEL** and **Lao Development Bank** can change major currencies such as US dollars (clean new notes only), euros, Vietnamese dong and Thai baht. Internet access is available at the Chaleunsuk Guesthouse for 10,000K per hour, including headphones and camera for Skype access.

The helpful **tourist office** (☎020-2284 8020; ⊙8.30-11.30am & 1.30-4.30pm Mon-Fri) opposite the Sernalli Hotel can answer questions and arrange treks. If you want to book a trek out of office hours, call **Keo** (☎020-284 8020) to arrange a meeting. Otherwise check out www.muangkhua.com, with some bookable treks and the lowdown on every last guesthouse in town.

Getting There & Away

The bus to Dien Bien Phu in Vietnam (50,000K) departs from outside the BCEL branch. Bus departures are currently around 6am in both directions and take about six hours, including the border crossing. However, it is not guaranteed to leave daily if there are not enough passengers.

Muang Khua's inconvenient **bus station** (Rte 2E, 900m past Km 97) is nearly 2km west of the river towards Udomxai. Very rare tuk-tuks (5000K per person) head out there once full from outside BCEL. Buses to Udomxai (35,000K, three hours) depart at 8.30am, noon and 3pm. For Phongsali take the 8am *sŏrngtăaou* to Pak Nam Noi (15,000K, one hour) and await the Udomxai–Phongsali bus there. It usually arrives around 10am.

Boat travel on the Nam Ou is a very attractive alternative, as long as there's no hurry. Upriver to Hat Sa (105,000K, seven hours, 10am), boats sometimes arrive too late to connect with the last bus to Phongsali, so the trip might take longer than anticipated. Downriver boats run to Muang Ngoi Neua (100,000K, five hours, 9am) and Nong Khiaw (120,000K, six hours).

Phongsali ຜົ້ງສາລີ

☎088 / POP 15,000 / ELEV 1400M

Quite unlike any other Lao provincial capital, Phongsali sits high on a small ridgetop plateau above which the peak of Phu Fa

('Sky Mountain'; 1625m) rises steeply. The location gives the town panoramic views and a refreshing climate that can swing from pleasantly warm to downright cold in a matter of hours. Bring a jacket and waterproofs just in case, even in April. The town's population is a mix of Phu Noi and Haw/Yunnanese, both long-term residents and more recent immigrants. That said, no-one comes to Phongsali to experience the town; it's all about the trekking in the surrounding hill country.

History

According to tradition the Phu Noi were originally a warlike tribe who had migrated from Burma to Luang Prabang. Seeing danger and opportunity in equal measure, the Lan Xang king granted them land in the far north of his domains, today's Phongsali, where they maintained the borderlands against incursions from the Tai Lü kingdom of Sipsong Panna.

Sights

Old Town
HISTORIC AREA

The town's modest but distinctive old-town area includes a three-block grid of rough, stone-flagged alleys and a winding street mostly lined with traditional **Yunnanese shophouses** whose wooden frontages recall the architecture of old Kunming. Tiny, new and functional, the **Chinese Temple** overlooks a pond, behind which **Wat Keo** is more memorable for its *petang*-playing monks than its architecture.

Phu Fa
HILL

(ພູຟ້າ) For great views across town climb to the stupa-topped peak of Phu Fa, a punishing, tree-shaded climb up over 400 stone steps or a very bumpy, steep road that's just passable by motorbike in first gear. A 4000K toll is payable on the last section of the ascent from a picnic area. A new alternative descent returns to the Hat Sa road near a tea factory 2km east of town.

Phongsali

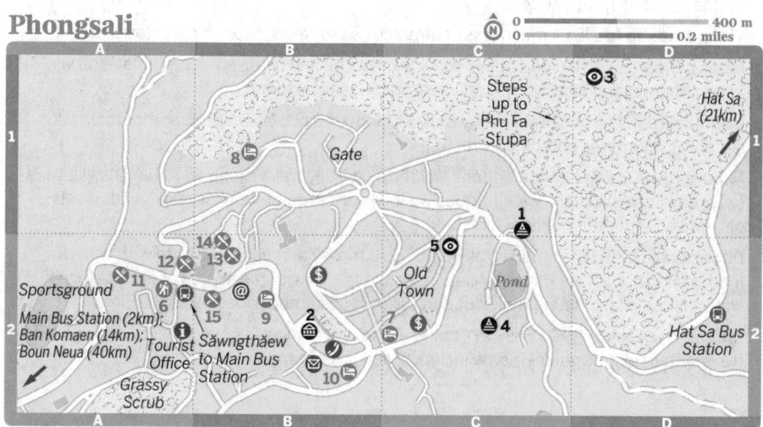

Phongsali

Sights
- 1 Chinese Temple C1
- 2 Museum of Tribes B2
- 3 Phu Fa D1
- 4 Wat Keo C2
- 5 Yunnanese Shophouses C2

Activities, Courses & Tours
- 6 Amazing Lao Travel A2

Sleeping
- 7 Phongsali Hotel C2
- 8 Phou Fa Hotel B1
- 9 Sengsaly Guesthouse B2
- 10 Viphaphone Hotel B2

Eating
- 11 Laojerm Restaurant A2
- 12 Laoper Restaurant A2
- 13 Market B2
- 14 Noodle Stands B2
- 15 Yeehua Guesthouse B2

Transport
- Lao Air .... (see 10)

TREKKING IN NORTHERN LAOS

Northern Laos has won prizes for its 'ecotrekking' system, pioneered in Luang Namtha and Nam Ha NPA. Registered agencies pledge to return a significant (and stated) percentage of profits to the villages visited and to abide by sensible, ecologically friendly guidelines. Visiting remote off-road villages without a guide is of dubious legality. Fortunately, guides and any necessary trekking permits can usually be arranged very quickly by local agencies, often the evening before departure. Costs excluding transport are typically around US$50 to US$75 per person per day for one, falling to US$25 per person for a larger group. Agencies don't generally compete directly so comparing product is more relevant than comparing prices. Employing freelance guides might be cheaper but is discouraged as they'll rarely make contributions to village development funds. Visit the excellent website www.ecotourismlaos.com for more information. The following list is a generalised overview of what differentiates the various trekking centres.

Phongsali (p92) Nowhere is better for striking out into truly timeless villages where traditional costumes and arcane animist beliefs are still commonplace, particularly in the remote Akha communities. Many homes retain picture-book thatched roofs, at least for now. Virgin-forest treks are also possible near Boun Neua.

Luang Namtha (p104)Treks are very well organised and have numerous options, some combining trekking with other activities such as biking and kayaking. Forest hikes to Nam Ha NPA 'jungle camps' are especially popular. To reduce pressure on any single host village, most agents have unique routes. However, this inadvertently adds to the complexity of deciding just what you actually want to see and where you'll find it. Not all routes are equally inspiring.

Vieng Phukha (p108) A much less commercial starting point for Nam Ha forest treks.

Muang Sing (p109) Guided or DIY visits to colourful and relatively accessible Akha villages (where many local women still wear traditional costumes).

Udomxai (p98) A specialist agency makes Udomxai a popular centre for mountain biking, some itineraries combined with treks.

Muang Khua (p90) Limited options include a one-day trek visiting an Akha Pala village (where some local ladies wear curiously gaudy semi-traditional costumes), with plenty of views en route but minimal forest.

Phonsavan (p70) One unique trek combines a mossy archaeological site with accommodation in a roadless Hmong village, and culminates with the ascent of a multistage waterfall. It's a fascinating walk, but don't expect costumed tribesfolk in this area.

Muang Ngoi Neua (p87) Easy DIY day walks to pretty villages or very inexpensive group treks with freelance guides, some including scenic boat trips.

Museum of Tribes MUSEUM
(admission 5000K; ⏲8am-11.30am & 1.30-4.30pm Mon-Fri) Just ten minutes is ample to see this museum displaying the local costumes of the province's diverse cultures. If the door is locked, ask for the key from the post office across the road.

Activities

Hill-tribe treks in Phongsali Province are among the most authentic and rewarding in all of Laos. Tours have a heavy emphasis on ecological and cultural sensitivity, with a sizeable chunk of the fee going into development funds for the host villages. Carefully thought-out treks are offered through the well-organised tourist office. Most treks can be organised for next-day departure, especially if you phone ahead. A popular option is the **Jungle Trek** (two short days starting from Boun Neua), visiting an Akha Phixo village as well as crossing a rare surviving stand of primary forest. Various multi-day treks include boat rides up the Nam Ou from Hat Sa and visiting unforgettable Akha Nuqui villages linked by high ridgetop paths. One-way treks like the three-day **Nam Lan Trek** to Boun Tai can be organised to include delivery of your backpack to the destination so that you don't have to backtrack. This trek passes through Yang, Laobit, Akha Djepia and Akha Nuqui villages. However, with more than 30 stream and river crossings, it should only be attempted later in the dry season. To organise guides, phone well ahead to Phongsali's tourist office or get in touch with Amazing Lao Travel.

Prices per person per day range from 165,000K as part of a larger group to about 365,000K if going it alone. This includes the guide's fee, food and ultra-basic homestays in real village homes. Add to this transport costs, which are very variable according to whether using public transport or charter vehicles. 'Experience tours' allow you to spend more time with village folk including, perhaps, guided foraging trips to collect the ingredients for the local family dinner.

Amazing Lao Travel HIKING
(Northern Travelling Center; ☎088-210594; www.explorephongsalylaos.com; ⏲8am-5pm or later) The main independent trekking operator in Phongsali, which offers its own selection of treks. Many travellers have written to us praising their level of service.

Sleeping

All of the following have hot water, a blessing in the cold winter, but electricity is sometimes limited to a few hours a day.

Phou Fa Hotel HOTEL $
(☎088-210031; r 100,000-200,000; ❄📶) Western toilets, room heaters and golden bed covers give the Phou Fa a marginal edge as Phongsali's top choice. More expensive rooms are almost suites and include a carpet. This compound housed the Chinese consulate until 1975. This was the only place with wi-fi at the time of writing, which makes the soulless restaurant worth considering for a drink or snack.

Sengsaly Guesthouse GUESTHOUSE $
(☎088-210165; r 60,000-80,000K) The best of three cheapies on the main drag, the Sengsaly has 60,000K rooms with ageing bedding but basic private bathrooms. Better rooms are newly built and comfy, if overly colourful, and come with hot showers.

Viphaphone Hotel HOTEL $
(☎088-210111; r 100,000-150,000K) Not much of a looker from the outside, but rooms are somewhat better than first impressions. The rooms are spacious and include a desk, wardrobe and TV.

Phongsali Hotel HOTEL $
(☎088-210042; r 100,000K) The Chinese-built Phongsali Hotel, in a centrally located four-storey building, has austere but bright rooms owing to large windows. Most rooms have three beds and the most expensive have hot water. The staff are fairly indifferent, however.

Eating

Flavoursome *kòw sóy* (noodle soup with minced pork and tomato) is available from **noodle stands** (noodles 10,000K; ⏲6.30am-5pm) hidden away in the northwest corner of the **market**, which is at its most interesting at dawn. None of the town's eateries make any attempt at decoration and restaurant food is predominantly Chinese. *Đôm Ɓąh* (fondue-style fish soup) is a local speciality, notably served at simple places along the Hat Sa road (Km 2 and Km 4).

Yeehua Guesthouse LAOTIAN $
(mains 15,000-30,000K; ⏲7am-10pm) Beneath Phongsali's cheapest (but not recommended) guesthouse, the Yeehua's functional restaurant serves inexpensive traveller fare, French wines, Chinese beer and thick Lao coffee. The menu is in English and there is internet access.

Laojerm Restaurant LAOTIAN $
(mains 20,000-35,000K; ⏲11am-10.30pm) The well-prepared food here comes in decent-sized portions and the menu's approximate English includes inscrutable offerings such as 'High-handed Pig's liver' and 'Palace Protects the Meat Cubelets'.

Laoper Restaurant LAOTIAN $
(mains 15,000-30,000K; ⏲5-10pm) Considered by locals to serve the best food in town, Laoper has no menu, just a display box of the possible ingredients. Point to a selection and see what turns up. It's good for groups sharing a mixture of dishes but not ideal for single diners.

Drinking

Phongsali region, especially Ban Komaen, is famous for Chinese-style green tea. The tourist office sells samples along with excellent local *lòw-lów*. The pale green tint comes from having been passed over raspberry leaves after fermentation.

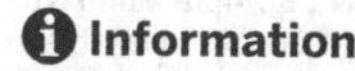

Information

BCEL Includes an ATM across the road.

SENSITIVE TREKKING

When visiting tribal villages it is important to learn slightly different etiquette according to each local culture. The following notes focus particularly on the Akha, as Akha women's coin-encrusted indigo costumes make their villages popular trekking targets while their animist beliefs are also some of the most unexpected.

Shoes & Feet Entering an ethnic Lao home it would be rude not to remove shoes, but in mud-floored dwellings of Hmong, Akha and some other tribal peoples, it is fine to keep them on. However, still avoid pointing feet at anyone.

Toilets If there's a village toilet, use it. When in the forest be sure to dump away from watercourses. But in remote villages with no toilets at all, check with the guide as to the local custom: although trekking etiquette usually dictates burying faeces, in some villages the deposit will be gobbled up greedily by the local pigs, so shouldn't be wasted! Nonetheless, please do carry out used toilet paper, tampons etc, however unpleasant that might seem.

Photos While many hill-tribe boys are delighted to be photographed, most village women run squealing from a camera. Asking permission to snap a passing stranger often results in straight refusal, which should be respected. However, a great advantage of staying in a village homestay is that you become 'friends' with a family. Try snapping digital photos of babies and men, show those casually to your host ladies and eventually it's quite likely that they will want to see themselves on camera. Never force the issue, however, as a few really might believe the crusty old superstition that photographers are soul-stealers.

Gifts If you want to give gifts, consider fruit and vegetable seeds or saplings that continue to give after you've left. Always ask the guide first if it's appropriate to give anything and, if so, only give directly to friends or to the village chief. Giving gifts to children can encourage begging, which undermines societies that have always been self-sufficient.

Beds In trekking villages it is common to sleep in the house of the village chief. In traditional Akha homes all the men-folk sleep on one raised, curtained platform, most of the women on another (which it is absolutely taboo to visit) and the daughter-in-law gets a curtained box-space poignantly befitting her almost slave-like status. To make space for visitors, most men-folk move out for the night to sleep in other houses, leaving the guide, trekkers and maybe a village elder or two to snuggle up in a line in the male section. Bringing a sleeping bag gives a greater semblance of privacy. Note that female trekkers count as 'honorary men'.

Spirits The spirit world is every bit as lively in hill-tribe cultures as it is in other Lao cultures and it would be exceedingly bad form for a visitor to touch a village totem (Tai Lü villages), a spirit gate (Akha) or any other taboo item. Ask the guide to explain and don't even think of dangling yourself on an Akha swing (*hacheu*).

Breasts & Babies Akha women who display their bare breasts are neither being careless nor offering a sexual come-on; they're simply following a belief that young mothers who cover both breasts will attract harm to their newborn offspring. Eating stones while pregnant is an odder custom, while the brutal Akha attitude to twins is quite unpalatable.

Lao Development Bank (8.30am-3.30pm Mon-Fri) Can change multiple currencies to kip and cashes US-dollar travellers cheques without commission. Includes an ATM and represents Western Union.

Lao Telecom International calls possible.

Tourist Office (088-210 098; www.phongsaly.net; 8am-11.30am & 1.30-4pm Mon-Fri) Helpful maps and brochures are also available online and free from most guesthouses. If you need emergency help or want to book a tour out of hours, call 020-2257 2373 or the mobile phone number of duty staff posted on the front door.

Wang Electronics Shop (7am-10pm) Internet access and a regular power supply.

Getting There & Away

Phongsali's airport is actually at Boun Neua but air tickets with **Lao Air** (088-210999; www.

lao-air.com) to Vientiane (990,000K) are sold at the Viphaphone Hotel. The ticket price includes a minibus shuttle from the airport to Phongsali. Travelling back to Boun Neua, the shuttle costs 30,000K.

Boats to/from Muang Khua depart/arrive at Hat Sa, to which buses (15,000K) leave daily at 8am and 1.30pm from the Hat Sa bus station, 10 minutes' walk east of town.

Phongsali's main bus station is at Km 3, west of town. A *sŏrngtăaou* shuttle runs there from the market area (5000K) at 6.30am but only very infrequently after that, so leave plenty of time. The daily bus to Vientiane (190,000K, more than 20 hours) leaves at 8.20am, passing through Luang Prabang (130,000K), and the bus to Udomxai (75,000K, seven hours) leaves at 8am. As foreigners can't cross the Chinese border at Ban Pakha, the buses to Mengla (7am and 1.30pm) are only useful for reaching Boun Neua (15,000K).

Amazing Lao Travel rents out small motorbikes from 100,000K per day.

Around Phongsali

Ban Komaen ບ້ານກໍແມນ

088 / POP 400

Phongsali's famous tea village is a very attractive place commanding stupendous valley views. These sweep nearly 360° when you stand on the promontory behind the school. A fair percentage of authentic Phu Noi homes are set on stone-pile platforms. Arriving from Phongsali (15km), the drive passes plenty of tea bushes, but those beside the main road through the village centre are reputedly more than 400 years old and are said to be the world's oldest.

Ban Komaen makes a very pleasant motorbike excursion. Take the Boun Neua road, turn left directly opposite the inspirationally named Km4 Nightclub (not the asphalt road just before) then curve steadily around on the main unpaved road, keeping left at most junctions but avoiding any turn that descends into the valley.

Hat Sa ຫາດສາ

088 / POP 500

Hat Sa is a tiny river 'port' village climbing the steep wooded bank of the Nam Ou. It's 21km east of Phongsali by unsealed road. There's a handful of noodle stalls and a market on the 15th and 30th of each month, which is liveliest from dawn and mainly sells Chinese goods to hill-tribe folk. That's directly above the river landing from where boats leave to Muang Khua (105,000K), around 30 minutes after the arrival of the first bus from Phongsali, assuming sufficient clientele and decent water levels. Finding the right boat is easy enough and an official adds up passenger numbers to calculate whether it is necessary to pay a supplement. When water levels are low departures can drop to a couple a week and prices will be higher.

There's no guesthouse but if you're stuck in Hat Sa (quite possible if the boat arrives late from Muang Khua), it is possible to sleep in one of three unfurnished bamboo-walled crash-pad rooms above **Wanna Ngyai Shop** (per person 30,000K), the first two-storey shack to the right above the boat landing. Mosquito nets and thin floor mats are available but it's preferable to bring your own sleeping bag. Wash in the river.

Buses to Phongsali (15,000K) depart at around 9am and 2pm from the market, taking up to 1½ hours westbound due to the steep climb. An additional *sŏrngtăaou* will generally depart to Phongsali after the boat arrives from Muang Khua, charging 20,000K per person assuming the driver can make 100,000K minimum.

Phu Den Din NPA ປ່າສະຫງວນແຫ່ງຊາດພູແດນດິນ

This vast area of partly unexplored, relatively pristine forest is layered across inaccessible mountains that climax at almost 2000m near the Vietnamese border. At present the only legal way to get a glimpse of its grandeur is on irregular boating or kayaking trips down the Nam Ou river between Ban Tha and Hat Sa, which requires a lot of planning and organisation. You'll also need to carry your own camping necessities, as there's a lengthy section without any habitation. Some tourists have made ill-considered attempts to drive into the park from Hat Sa. While there is a French-built suspension bridge and rough unpaved road leading there, it passes through rather monotonous slash-and-burn landscapes. Then, after slogging for 70km, you reach an army checkpoint that prevents any access to the NPA anyway. Sneaking past that is very unwise as you risk being shot as a suspected poacher.

NORTHWESTERN LAOS

Northern Udomxai and Luang Namtha provinces form a mountainous tapestry of rivers, forests and traditional villages that are home to almost 40 classified ethnicities. Luang Namtha is the most developed of several traveller-friendly towns ranged around the 2224-sq-km Nam Ha NPA with hiking, biking, kayaking and boating adventures all easily arranged at short notice. Udomxai is the regional transport hub, while Boten is the one China–Laos border open to international visitors.

Udomxai (Oudomsay, Muang Xai) ອຸດົມໄຊ (ເມືອງໄຊ)

081 / POP 25,000

Booming Udomxai is a Laos–China trade centre and handy crossroads city that's about as metropolitan a place as you'll find in northern Laos. The brash main street and lack of a traveller vibe puts off many short-term visitors, but it takes minimal effort to find the real Laos nearby. The well-organised tourist office has many ideas to tempt you to stay longer.

Around 25% of Udomxai's population is Chinese, with the Yunnanese dialect as common as Lao in some businesses and hotels.

Sights

Stairways lead up from the main road to two facing hills each offering excellent views. One is topped by the pretty little **Phu That Stupa**, a historic structure that was totally rebuilt after wartime destruction. Full-moon days see religious ceremonies here; there's attractive little **Wat Phu That** and a brand new standing Buddha. The other hill hosts a disappointing **museum** (8-11am & 2-4pm) FREE in a grand, new two-storey mansion featuring colonial style shutters and oriental gables.

Banjeng Temple BUDDHIST TEMPLE
(Wat Santiphab; dawn-dusk) Udomxai's foremost monastery is Banjeng Temple, which is modest but very attractively set on a riverside knoll. The most notable feature here is an imaginative concrete 'tree of life'. Tinkling in the breeze, its metal leaves hide a menagerie of naively crafted animal and bird statues that illustrate a local Buddha myth.

PMC ARTS CENTRE
(Productivity & Marketing Center of Oudomxay; 081-212803; www.pmc.oudomxay.org; 8am-noon & 2-5pm) This is a small exhibition room and shop introducing local fibres and selling handmade paper products, bags and local essences. If you're wondering why it's part-funded by the UN Office on Drugs and Crime, that's because these crafts are an attempt to find non-narcotic-based commerce for former poppy-growing communities. Hence its ironic nickname, the 'opium shop'.

Activities

The tourist office (p100) offers one-day tours around Udomxai, a city walk, two- and three-day visits to the Chom Ong Caves, plus two possible trekking routes with Khamu village homestays. To find potential fellow trekkers arrive at 4pm for a 'rendezvous meeting' the day before departure.

Samlaan Cycling CYCLING
(020-5560 9790; www.samlaancycling.com) Organises excellent one-day cycling tours and multiday combination cycling/trekking adventures. Call ahead as their 'office' is frequently closed when staff are busy.

Lao Red Cross MASSAGE
(081-312391; steam bath 20,000K, massage per ½hr 30,000K; 3-7.30pm) On a hillock overlooking a beautiful river bend, the Lao Red Cross offers Lao Swedish-style massage and herbal steam baths in a modest bamboo-matted structure.

Courses

The tourist office (p100) organises an interesting series of papermaking workshops (from 100,000K depending on group size) that include gathering the raw materials. Their cooking courses (from 100,000K per person with minimum four, 200,000K per person for a couple) include shopping for ingredients, but the teacher speaks better French than English.

Sleeping

Udomxai has an abundance of accommodation, including several soulless Chinese hotels in the 100,000K range. For an interesting rural alternative, you might also consider staying 28km north in pretty Muang La, which hosts the region's most exclusive boutique resort as well as some guesthouses.

Udomxai

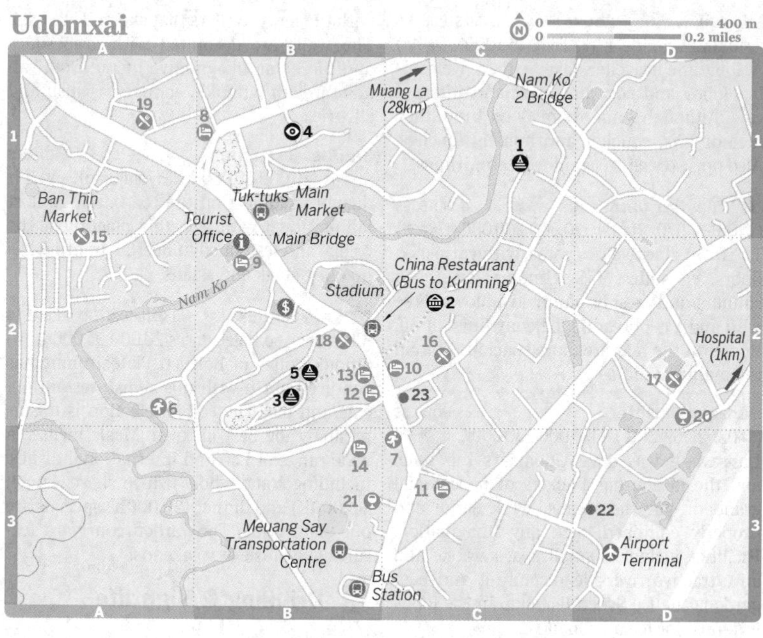

Udomxai

Sights

1	Banjeng Temple	C1
2	Museum	C2
3	Phu That Stupa	B2
4	PMC	B1
5	Wat Phu That	B2

Activities, Courses & Tours

6	Lao Red Cross	A2
7	Samlaan Cycling	C3

Sleeping

8	Charming Lao Hotel	B1
9	Dansavanh Hotel	B2
10	Lithavixay Guesthouse	C2
11	Saylomen Guesthouse	C3
12	Vilavong Guesthouse	B2
13	Villa Keoseumsack	B2
14	Xayxana Guest House	B3

Eating

15	Ban Thin Market	A2
	Cafe Sinouk	(see 8)
16	Meuang Neua Restaurant	C2
17	Nonmengda Market	D2
18	Sinphet Restaurant	B2
19	Souphailin Restaurant	A1

Drinking & Nightlife

20	Ming Khouan	D2
21	Phonemali Nightclub	B3

Transport

22	Lao Airlines	D3
23	Xai-Ya	C2

Vilavong Guesthouse GUESTHOUSE $
(☎081-212503; Rte 1; r 50,000-60,000K; 📶) Upstairs 60,000K, downstairs 50,000K, although there aren't any views to write home about. The owners are helpful and prices are fair for such a central location.

Saylomen Guesthouse GUESTHOUSE $
(☎081-211377; r with fan/air-con 60,000/100,000K; ❄) Simple, fair-sized fan rooms with hot water, top sheets and technicolored coat stands are better value than the average guesthouse around town. Air-con is a good investment in the hot season.

Xayxana Guest House GUESTHOUSE $
(☎020-5578 0429; off Rte 1; r 70,000-100,000K; ❄📶) Set in a sprawling compound, Xayxana is cool and spacious, with immaculate white rooms, tiled floors and very comfy beds. All rooms come with en suite bathrooms.

Lithavixay Guesthouse GUESTHOUSE $
(☎081-212175; Rte 1; r 70,000-150,000K; ❄📶) A longtime traveller fave with a welcoming lobby and cosy breakfast and internet cafe. Although some rooms look tired, they include TVs, couches and homely touches. Also operates as an agent for Lao Airlines.

★**Villa Keoseumsack** HOTEL $$
(☎081-312170; Rte 1; r 120,000-200,000K; ❄📶) The town's best-value rooms, with varnished floors, en suites, TVs, Hmong-woven bed runners and freshly plumped pillows. Free wi-fi and a cool reading balcony finish it off. Rooms at the rear are more spacious than in the main building.

Dansavanh Hotel HOTEL $$
(☎081-212698; Rte 1; r 120,000-250,000K; ❄@📶) Dansavanh was once Udomxai's top hotel and the facade has buckets of neocolonial grandeur but the rooms, while large and properly equipped, lack any imagination. Facilities include a small spa, karaoke and an attractive riverside restaurant and beer garden. The De Syuen tea shop in the lobby is a must for tea aficionados.

Charming Lao Hotel BOUTIQUE HOTEL $$
(☎081-212881; www.charminglaohotel.com; d/tw incl breakfast 405,000/485,000K, ste incl breakfast from 687,000K; ❄@📶) A most unexpected treat for Udomxai, this boutique hotel does offer a certain charm once you're happily ensconced in the tastefully furnished rooms. Extra touches include large flat-screen TVs and contemporary bathrooms. The complex includes a spa and an inviting northern branch of Pakse's Cafe Sinouk (p100).

Eating

The **Ban Thin** and **Nonmengda markets** peddle vegetables, fruit and meat including some live and dead exotica (particularly at weekends).

Souphailin Restaurant LAOTIAN $
(mains 20,000-40,000K; ⏲7am-10pm) Souphailin creates culinary magic with authentic, northern Lao food like *mok bah* (a banana-leaf fish dish) plus imaginative creations of her own. Her small, backstreet restaurant is a traditional bamboo-weave house whose decor is just the pots hung on the wall. If other guests are dining, you might need to be very patient.

Meuang Neua Restaurant LAOTIAN $
(mains 20,000-40,000K; ⏲7am-10pm) Relocated to the main strip, this place is popular with the few travellers that stay in Udomxai. The walls are decorated with arabesques and there's an imaginative menu, from salads through pumpkin soup, curry, fish and stir-fries.

Sinphet Restaurant LAOTIAN $
(mains 20,000-30,000K; ⏲7am-9pm) A bit dusty (it's almost on the road), and almost falling down with age, this place near the bridge and festooned in Beerlao bunting has noodles, steak and salads.

★**Cafe Sinouk** LAOTIAN, INTERNATIONAL $$
(Charming Lao Hotel; mains 20,000-95,000K; 📶) Sinouk Coffee of Bolaven Plateau fame has ventured north with this stylish restaurant, cafe and bar. The coffee selection is unsurprisingly the best in town. Meals include a wide range of Lao and international dishes, including some whole fish to share. Lunch (15,000K) and dinner (20,000K) specials are one-plate value. The garden courtyard features live music at weekends.

Drinking & Nightlife

Ming Khouan BAR
(⏲11am-11pm) Ming Khouan is where it's at in Udomxai. The lively wooden and bamboo beer garden draws a young crowd to quaff Beerlao by the crate. The central fountain is a bit of a diversion, but good Lao food is available, including barbecued skewers. Near the airport.

Phonemali Nightclub CLUB
(⏲8-11.30pm) FREE This is the quintessential provincial Lao nightclub where a typical evening's floor fillers start with Lao line dancing and progress through Thai disco to a few international dance anthems. Yes, that does include 'Gangnam Style'.

Information

Most guesthouses and hotels now offer free wi-fi to guests.

BCEL (☎211260; Rte 1) Has an ATM, changes several major currencies and accepts some travellers cheques (2% commission).

Tourist Office (Provincial Tourism Department of Oudomxay; ☎081-211797; www.oudomxay.info; ⏲7.30-11.30am & 1.30-6pm Mon-Fri Apr-Sep, 8am-noon & 1.30-4pm Mon-Fri Oct-Mar) The tourist office has masses of information about onward travel, accommodation and local sights. Its professional flyers and excellent free town maps can also be found in many guesthouses and on the bus station noticeboard. The office organises a selection of treks and tours

BUSES FROM UDOMXAI

DESTINATION	PRICE (K)	DEPARTURES	DURATION (HR)
Boten	40,000	8am	2
Luang Prabang	55,000	9am, noon, 3pm	6
Luang Namtha	40,000	8.30am, 11.30am, 3.30pm	3
Muang Houn	30,000	noon, 2pm, 4pm	2
Muang Khua	35,000	8.30am, 11.30am, 3pm	3
Nong Khiaw	45,000	9am	4
Pak Beng	40,000	8.30am, 10am	4
Pak Mong	35,000	2pm, 4pm	3
Phongsali	75,000	8.30am & around 2am	7
Vientiane	150,000	11am	18
Vientiane (VIP)	190,000	4pm, 6pm	16

and sells the GT-Rider Laos maps. The office sometimes opens on weekends, but the hours are irregular.

Getting There & Away

AIR

Lao Airlines (081-312047) flies to/from Vientiane (895,000K) daily at the time of writing. Specials are sometimes offered from 645,000K. Tickets are also available from Lithavixay Guesthouse (p100).

BUS & SŎRNGTĂAOU

Long Distance

The **bus station** is southwest of the centre.

Regional

Sŏrngtăaou to Muang La (10,000K) depart when full at around 8.30am and 11.30am from the **Meuang Say Transportation Centre**.

To China

An 8am minibus to Mengla leaves from the bus station. The Kunming-bound bed-bus from Luang Prabang bypasses the bus station but makes a short snack break at the **China Restaurant** around 11.30am. Booking isn't possible but they'll take extra passengers if space allows.

Getting Around

Xai-Ya (081-212753; 9am-10pm) rents out 100cc motorbikes (old/new 50,000/100,000K per day if returned by 5pm, 80,000/150,000K per 24 hours). New ones are well worth the extra kip. Lithavixay Guesthouse rents decent bicycles (per half-/full-day 20,000/40,000K) and Samlaan Cycling rents high-quality mountain bikes (per day US$10). Xai-Ya, Lithavixay and the tourist office can all help arrange chauffeured minivans from US$100 per day.

Tuk-tuks cost 10,000K per person per hop within city limits, if you can find one.

Around Udomxai

Hop on a decent motorbike and head out in any direction and you'll quickly find attractive scenery and plenty of rural interest. A rewarding target is **Nam Kat Waterfall**, a picnic site around 23km from the centre of town. Turn right in Ban Fan, continue to the parking area then walk the last half hour or so through protected forests.

Chom Ong Caves & Ban Chom Ong ຖ້ຳຈອມອອງ/ບ້ານຈອມອອງ

Udomxai's top tourist attraction, the extensive cave system of **Chom Ong Caves**, burrows more than 15km beneath a forested karst ridge near the Khamu village Ban Chom Ong, 48km from Udomxai. Often as high as 40m within, it's a veritable cathedral of a place whose first 450m have been lit with solar-powered lamps. Over millions of years the time-worn stalactites have been coated with curious crusts of minerals and sometimes studded with gravel from later wash-throughs. To gain access you'll need to borrow the gate-key and engage a guide (40,000K) in **Ban Chom Ong**, from which the cave entrance is an hour's walk. The village commands a wide, attractive valley. Tall sentinel trees add character to the surrounding expanse of rice terraces backed by patches of mature woodland and bamboo-covered hills. It's a great place to observe weaving, spinning, milling, girls fetching water in

THE PRA SINGKHAM BUDDHA

You've got exams to pass? Want to get rich? Afraid you might be infertile? Don't worry. Whatever your concern, just ask the Pra Singkham Buddha and your wish will be granted...providing, of course, that you are pure of heart. And that when it all pans out, you pop back and leave the gift you promised him. It's a story common to a great many temples, but Muang La's Pra Singkham Buddha is considered to be especially potent.

Inlaid with precious stones, the 200kg gold-and-bronze statue has an interesting history. Legend claims it was cast in Sri Lanka just a few generations after the historical Buddha's death, and reached Laos in AD 868 via Ayodhya in India. In 1355 it was reputedly one of five great Buddhist masterpieces sent out by Lan Xang founder Fa Ngum to inspire the faithful at the far reaches of his new kingdom. However, the boat carrying the statue was sunk in a battle. Later found by a fisherman, Pra Singkham was dragged out of the water amid considerable tribulations and thereupon became the subject of a contest between residents of Muang La and Muang Khua regions. The sneaky folks from Muang Khua, downriver, suggested that the Buddha choose for himself and set the statue on a raft to 'decide'. However, the seemingly hopeless contest went Muang La's way when the raft magically floated upstream against the current, 'proving' it belonged in La. Kept initially in the Singkham Cave, by 1457 it had found a home in a specially built temple around which today's town of Muang La is now ranged. Like almost everything else in rural Laos, the temple was bombed to oblivion during the 20th-century Indochina wars. However, the statue had been rehidden in the Singkham Cave. By the time a new temple was consecrated in 1987, the Buddha had turned a black-green colour 'with sadness at the destruction'. But today he's once again a gleaming gold.

The Singkham Cave, where the famous Buddha statue once rested, is 3.7km west of Ban Samakisai, around halfway between Udomxai and Muang La. In Samakisai ask 'Khor kajeh tham noy' (may I have the cave key please) at the second hut south of the bridge. Then cross the bridge and take the second rough track west, which is just about passable by tuk-tuk or motorbike. This terminates at a collection of huts from which it's just three minutes' walk to the cave, climbing a shallow staircase at the end. The cave isn't huge and obviously the statue inside is a modern replica but the setting is attractive, with a woodland thicket opening into a fan of steep dry-rice valley slopes.

hollow bamboos and red-toothed old ladies chewing betel. The village's simple, unmarked 'guesthouse' is a purpose-built local-style longhouse with roll-out bedding and the relative luxury of a tap and porcelain squat in the outside shared toilets. Note that the village has no electricity and that very little English is spoken. As there are no restaurants or shops, organising food as well as the guide and key will require some spoken Lao, Khamu or plenty of gesticulation. A bigger problem is that the uncomfortable access 'roads' are almost entirely unpaved, impassably muddy after rain and improbably steep and rutted in places.

ℹ Getting There & Away

Two- and three-day tours, including meals, an English-speaking guide and ample time to observe typical village scenes can be organised through the Udomxai tourist office but transport is by excruciatingly uncomfortable jeep-*sŏrngtăaou*. Samlaan Cycling runs inclusive three-day guided loop-trips by mountain bike (US$65/155 per person in groups of seven/three, or US$195 for one person only). The Udomxai tourist office can arrange two-day/one-night trips from 595,000K per person with minimum eight people or 1,270,000K per person for a couple.

Muang La ເມືອງຫລາ

Scenic Muang La, just 28km from Udomxai towards Phongsali, offers a charming rural alternative to the 'big city'. This Tai Lü village sits at the confluence of the Nam La and Nam Phak rivers, attractively awash with palm trees. Its central feature is a classically styled temple that hosts one of northern Laos' most revered Buddha statues, the Pra Singkham Buddha. Wander down to the river to discover Muang La's modest **hot spring** that bubbles into the river when water levels are high.

Dr Houmpheng Guesthouse (☎020-5428 0029; r without/with bathroom 50,000/60,000K) is

Muang La's most conspicuous accommodation, an orange-and-turquoise house with a small shared terrace amid palms. The toilets are bucket-flush squats.

Just behind here nestled on the banks of the river is the **Lhakham Hotel** (☎020-5555 5930; lhakhamhotel@gmail.com; r 100,000K), which offers some of the best-value rooms in northern Laos. Furnishings are tasteful, the bathrooms include a rain shower and the river views are pretty, adding up to a steal. If only the exterior were more sympathetic, it would blend with its surroundings. There is also a riverside restaurant here.

The memorable **Muang La Resort** (☎020-2284 1264; www.muangla.com; 3-night package per person from US$691) hides an elegant rustic refinement behind tall, whitewashed walls. It accepts neither walk-in guests nor visitors, so you'll need to prebook a two-nights or more package to enjoy the stylishly appointed *colombage* guestrooms, sauna, and creatively raised open-air hot tub, all set between palms.

When river levels are low, a flimsy bamboo suspension bridge allows access from the hot springs to an area where salt is produced by a mud-leeching process.

Buses to Phongsali and Muang Khua pass through Muang La around an hour after departing Udomxai. The last bus returning to Udomxai usually rolls through around 5pm. There's no bus station – just wave the bus down. Additional *sŏrngtăaou* to Udomxai (10,000K) depart at around 7am and 11am if there's sufficient custom.

Boten ບໍ່ເຕນ

This frontier town on the Chinese border is a spectacular case of boom to bust. Carved out of a tiny hamlet over the past 15 years, it boasts hotels, casinos, malls and karaoke parlours. The population hit 10,000 at the height of its fame in 2010. However, the Royal Jinlun Hotel and Casino and other gambling and karaoke dens were closed down in 2011 following high-profile kidnaps of Chinese gamblers. China banned its citizens from gambling in Boten and encouraged the Lao government to clamp down on illicit activities. The end result is that Boten Golden City is more like Boten Ghost Town these days.

Boten is the only Laos–China border open to foreigners and makes an easy short excursion while en route from Udomxai to Luang Namtha. At the top (north) end of the market on the main street the **Lao Development Bank** (⌚8.30am-3.30pm Mon-Fri) changes major currencies, but for effortless yuan–kip exchange at fair rates use the supermarket across the road.

ℹ Getting There & Away

Although Boten taxi drivers try to persuade travellers otherwise, there are regular buses to/from Luang Namtha (40,000K, two hours) plus assorted China–Laos through-buses. Chartered taxi-vans charge about 160,000K to Luang Namtha and around 80,000K to Ban Na Theuy.

GETTING TO CHINA: BOTEN TO MENGLA

Getting to the Border

The Lao immigration post at the **Boten (Laos)/Móhān (China) border crossing** (⌚7.30am-4.30pm Laos time, 8.30am-5.30pm China time) is a few minutes' walk north of Boten market. Tuk-tuks shuttle across no-man's land to the Chinese immigration post in Móhān (Bohan) or it's an easy 10-minute walk.

Alternatively, take one of the growing number of handy Laos–China through-bus connections such as Udomxai–Mengla, Luang Namtha–Jinghong and Luang Prabang–Kunming.

At the Border

Northbound it is necessary to have a Chinese visa in advance.

Moving On

From the Chinese immigration post it's a 15-minute walk up Mohan's main street to the stand where little buses depart for Mengla (RMB16, one hour) every 20 minutes or so till mid-afternoon. These arrive at Mengla's bus station No 2. Nip across that city to the northern bus station for Jinghong (RMB42, two hours, frequent till 6pm) or Kunming (mornings only).

Luang Namtha (Namtha) ຫຼວງນ້ຳທາ

086 / POP 21,000

Luang Namtha's grid-pattern centre offers all the facilities you need to head straight off into the wide surrounding rice-bowl valley, where mountain ridges form layered silhouettes in the golden glow of sunset. Nowhere in Laos offers a better range of outdoor activities or organised 'ecotreks' to get you into the region's forests and ethnically diverse villages.

Sights

Renting a bicycle or motorbike saves a lot of sweat even within the main centre, and without wheels, getting much further will be a major pain. Tuk-tuks can be few and far between, and virtually disappear after dark.

Luang Nam Tha Museum MUSEUM
(ພິພິດທະພັນຫຼວງນ້ຳທາ; admission 5000K; ⌚8.30-11.30am & 1.30-3.30pm Mon-Thu, 8.30-11.30am Fri) The Luang Nam Tha Museum contains a collection of local anthropological artefacts, such as ethnic clothing, Khamu bronze drums and ceramics. There are also a number of Buddha images and the usual display chronicling the Revolution.

Luang Namtha

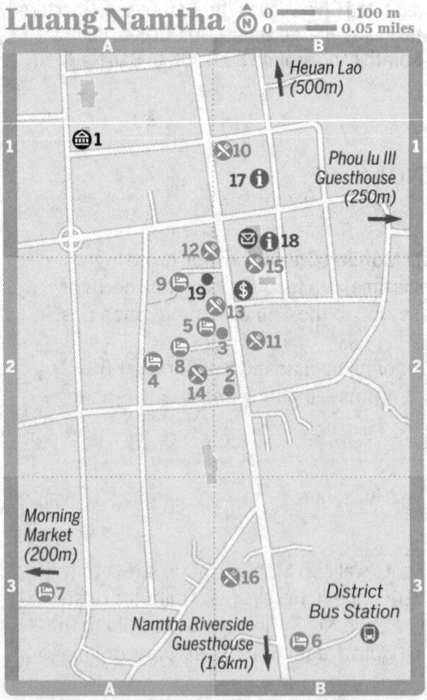

0 — 100 m
0 — 0.05 miles

Heuan Lao (500m)
Phou Iu III Guesthouse (250m)
Morning Market (200m)
District Bus Station
Namtha Riverside Guesthouse (1.6km)

Ban Nam Di VILLAGE
(Nam Dy; parking fee bicycle/motorcycle/car 1000/2000/3000K) Although barely 3km out of Luang Namtha, this hamlet is populated by Lao Huay (Lenten) people whose womenfolk still wear traditional indigo tunics with purple sash-belts and silver-hoop necklaces. They specialise in turning bamboo pulp into rustic paper, using cotton screens that you'll spot along the scenic riverbanks. At the eastern edge of the village, a three-minute stroll leads from a small carpark to a 6m-high **waterfall** (admission 2000K). You'll find it's more of a picnic site than a scenic wonder but a visit helps put a little money into village coffers. Unless the water level is really high there's no need to struggle up and over the hillside steps so ignore that sign and walk along the pretty stream.

Golden Stupa BUDDHIST TEMPLE
(admission 5000K) By far Namtha's most striking landmark, the large golden stupa sits on a steep ridge directly northwest of town. It

Luang Namtha

Sights
1 Luang Nam Tha Museum A1

Activities, Courses & Tours
Forest Retreat Laos .... (see 11)
2 Green Discovery B2
3 Jungle Eco-Guide Services B2
Nam Ha Ecoguide Service .... (see 18)
Namtha River Experience .... (see 14)

Sleeping
4 Adounsiri Guest House A2
5 Khamking Guesthouse A2
6 Lao Style Guesthouse B3
7 Royal Hotel A3
8 Thoulasith Guesthouse A2
9 Zuela Guesthouse A2

Eating
10 Aysha Restaurant B1
11 Forest Retreat Gourmet Cafe B2
12 Manikong Bakery Cafe A1
13 Manychan Guesthouse & Restaurant B2
14 Minority Restaurant A2
15 Night Market B2
16 Panda Restaurant B3

Information
17 Nam Ha Ecotourism Project B1
18 Provincial Tourism Office B1

Transport
19 Bicycle Shops A2

gleams majestically when viewed from afar. Up close, the effect is a bit more bling, but the views over town are impressive

That Phum Phuk BUDDHIST TEMPLE

(admission 5000K) The red-gold stupa you see when first approaching the small and historic That Phum Phuk is a 2003 replica. Right beside it lies the brick and stucco rubble of an earlier version, blown over by the force of a US bombing raid during the Second Indochina War. Judging by the ferro-concrete protrusions, that wasn't the 1628 original either. The site is a hillock 3km northwest of the oddly isolated Phouvan Guesthouse, on a stony laterite road that initially parallels the airfield. An obvious set of *naga* stairs lead up to the stupa from a road junction in front.

Activities

Luang Namtha is a major starting point for trekking, rafting, mountain biking and kayaking trips in the Nam Ha NPA. Many of the tours stop for at least a night in a minority village. Most photogenic for their costumes are those of the Lao Huay and Akha peoples but all are fascinating for genuine glimpses of village life.

Treks all follow carefully considered sustainability guidelines but they vary in duration and difficulty. In the wet season, leeches are a minor nuisance.

Namtha agents display boards listing their tour options and how many punters have already signed up, which is very helpful if you're trying to join a group to make things cheaper (maximum eight people). If you don't want others to join you, some agents will accept a 'private surcharge' of around US$50.

Around a dozen agencies operate, each with its own specialities.

Nam Ha Ecoguide Service ECOTOUR

(086-211534; 8am-noon & 1.30-8pm) A wing of the provincial tourism office. Retains the rights to some of the best trekking routes.

Green Discovery ECOTOUR

(086-211484; www.greendiscoverylaos.com; 8am-9pm) The granddaddy of ecotourism in Laos, Green Discovery offers different tours from those offered by the tourism office in order to eliminate direct competition and increase the spread of proceeds.

Jungle Eco-Guide Services ECOTOUR

(086-212025; www.thejungle-ecotour.com; 8am-9pm) Offers many trips ranging from one-day treks in Nam Ha NPA to Khamu homestays. It also runs three-day treks (staying at jungle camps) that take visitors deeper into the interior.

Forest Retreat Laos ECOTOUR

(020-5568 0031; www.forestretreatlaos.com; 7am-11.30pm) Based at the Forest Retreat cafe, this ecotourism outfit offers a mix of jungle adventures, river trips and two-wheeled exhilaration. They also offer one- to six-day multi-activity adventures and recruit staff and guides from ethnic minority backgrounds where possible.

Namtha River Experience KAYAKING, RAFTING

(086-212047; www.namtha-river-experience-laos.com; 8am-9pm) Specialises in kayaking and rafting trips through Khamu and Lenten villages. Also facilitates homestays.

Sleeping

Popular places fill up fast, especially during the November to February high season.

Central

Most lodging in Luang Namtha is in the architecturally bland northern part of town around the traveller restaurants.

★ **Phou Iu III Guesthouse** GUESTHOUSE $

(030-571 0422; www.luangnamtha-oasis-resort.com; r from 100,000K) Part of the same family as the Phou Iu II in Muang Sing, this place is cracking value. Bungalows are spacious and nicely fitted out with lumber-wood beds, fireplaces and inviting terraces. The garden is a work in progress, but at this price it's a steal. It's well-signposted from the centre of town.

Zuela Guesthouse GUESTHOUSE $

(020-5588 6694; www.zuela-laos.com; r 60,000-120,000K;) Located in a leafy courtyard, Zuela just keeps on expanding. New additions include a house built from wood and exposed brick, and a great restaurant serving 'power breakfasts', pancakes, shakes, salads and chilli-based Akha dishes. Rooms have wooden floors, fans and fresh linen. It also rents out scooters and operates an air-con minivan service to Huay Xai.

NAM HA NPA

Within easy reach of Luang Namtha, Muang Sing and Vieng Phukha, the 2224-sq-km Nam Ha NPA is one of Laos' most accessible natural preserves. That accessibility is a blessing and a curse. Both around and within the mountainous park, woodlands have to compete with pressure from villages of various ethnicities, including Lao Huay, Akha and Khamu. But the inhabitants of these villages are also learning the economic benefits of ecotourism. Since 1999, the prize-winning **Nam Ha Ecotourism Project** (www.unescobkk.org/culture/our-projects/sustainable-cultural-tourism-and-ecotourism/namha-ecotourism-project) has tried to ensure that tour operators and villagers work together to provide a genuine experience for trekkers while ensuring minimum impact to local communities and the environment. Tours are limited to small groups, each agent has its own routes and, in principle, each village receives visitors no more than twice a week. Authorities don't dictate what villagers can and can't do, but by providing information on sustainable forestry and fishing practices it's hoped that forest protection will become a self-chosen priority for the communities.

Adounsiri Guest House GUESTHOUSE **$**
(020-2299 1898; adounsiri@yahoo.com; r 60,000-100,000K; wi-fi) Located down a quiet street, this homely Lao villa has scrupulously clean rooms with white walls draped in handicrafts, fresh bed linen and tiled floors. TVs in every room, plus free wi-fi, tea and coffee.

Thoulasith Guesthouse GUESTHOUSE **$**
(086-212166; www.thoulasith-guesthouse.com; r 70,000-100,000K; air-con wi-fi) This traveller-friendly spot on the main strip offers spotless rooms with bedside lamps, art on the walls and comfortable wi-fi-enabled balconies. It's set back from the road and is a peaceful spot to wind down before or after a trek.

Khamking Guesthouse GUESTHOUSE **$**
(086-312238; r 70,000-100,000K) Fresh and colourful Khamking is good value, with interior flourishes such as bedside lights and attractive curtains and bedcovers. Be warned though – you're in the chicken zone with a coop just behind you, so earplugs are essential!

Lao Style Guesthouse GUESTHOUSE **$**
(030-921 1319; r 80,000-100,000K; air-con) Set in a striking wooden building near the district bus station, Lao Style almost resembles a wat or temple. Inside, the decoration is signature Laos and the extras include fan or air-con, satellite TV and hot water.

Royal Hotel HOTEL **$$**
(086-212151; d/ste 250,000/350,000K) The Royal is Namtha's glitziest hotel. Standard rooms have excellent beds, walk-in showers and elements of modernistic style. The suites come with carpeting and luxurious bathrobes. Staff speak Chinese but not English.

Further Afield

Chaleunsuk Homestays HOMESTAY **$**
(020-5555 7768; Rte 3, 500m past Km 45; per person 80,000K) Beside the main Rte 3 highway, around 20km from central Luang Namtha, four rustic homes in Chaleunsuk village offer a real Khamu homestay experience without the need to trek. The fee includes breakfast, dinner and a contribution to the village development fund with a guided forest walk added for 20,000K more. It all sounds great in principle but as very little English is spoken, coming alone without language skills can feel awkward. Ask at the Luang Namtha tourist office for more information.

Namtha Riverside Guesthouse GUESTHOUSE **$$**
(086-212025; namthariverside@gmail.com; r 60,000-200,000K) This relaxed resort offers a tranquil Nam Tha setting. Riverfront bungalows are spacious and include tribal motifs and solar-powered hot water. *Petang* is available and there are lounger-cushions on the balconies. It's 2km south of the centre. Good value.

Boat Landing Guest House & Restaurant RESORT **$$**
(086-312398; www.theboatlanding.com; r incl breakfast US$40-60) One of the country's original ecolodges, the Boat Landing has riverside acacia groves hugging tastefully finished wooden bungalows with solar-heated showers. It's rustic in places, but the atmos-

phere more than makes up for the lack of sophistication. It's located 7km south of the new town and about 150m off the main road.

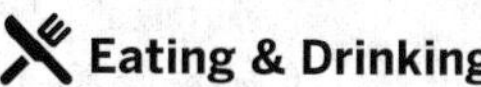

Eating & Drinking

The lively **night market** (7-10pm) is a good place for snack grazing. Find noodle stands galore in the **morning market**.

Minority Restaurant LAOTIAN $
(mains 15,000-35,000K; 7am-10.30pm) This inviting, wood-beamed restaurant hidden down a little side alley offers the chance to sample typical ethnic dishes from the Khamu, Tai Dam and Akha tribes. If the likes of rattan shoots and banana-flower soup doesn't appeal, there's also a range of stir-fries.

★ **Forest Retreat Gourmet Cafe** INTERNATIONAL $
(www.forestretreatlaos.com; mains 20,000-50,000K, pizzas 50,000-90,000K) Famous beyond Luang Namtha for the sheer variety of the menu, Forest Retreat is a home away from home. DIY sandwiches, pastas, wood-fired pizzas, vegetarian risottos and homemade pancakes – it's time to indulge before or after a trek, which they also conveniently organise. Doubles as Bamboo Bar by night with cocktails aplenty.

Manychan Guesthouse & Restaurant LAOTIAN, INTERNATIONAL $
(mains 15,000-40,000K; 6.30am-10.30pm;) An inviting all-wood interior spilling out onto a fairy-lit street terrace keeps this place among the most popular *falang* venues in town. Wi-fi is free and the menu covers the gamut of possibilities. Beers arrive in coolers and the coffee has a kick.

Manikong Bakery Cafe BAKERY $
(mains 10,000-50,000K; 6.30am-10pm) A hole-in-the-wall cafe serving tasty salads, bagels, sandwiches and homemade cakes. Sample shakes and coffees by day or cocktails by night, with a happy hour from 5pm to 7pm.

Panda Restaurant INTERNATIONAL, LAOTIAN $
(mains 15,000-35,000K; 6.30am-9.30pm;) Overlooking a pond, paddy fields and distant mountains, Panda has wood beams that are interestingly strung with bees' nests (minus the bees) and buffalo horns. The menu is equally random, with dishes such as fish and chips and spaghetti carbonara as well as Lao and Thai soups and some vegetarian options.

Aysha Restaurant INDIAN $
(mains 30,000K; 7am-10pm;) This little eatery has delicious Madras cuisine, dished up with flair and spice. Homemade naan bread, veggie options galore and chicken korma that could make you weep for joy after a day in the boonies.

Heuan Lao LAOTIAN, THAI $
(mains 20,000-50,000K; 8am-10pm;) This attractive upstairs corner restaurant has a timber and bamboo-panelled interior and a shady wraparound terrace. The menu of Thai and Lao dishes is only partly translated into English.

Boat Landing Restaurant LAOTIAN $$
(meals 20,000-150,000K; 7am-8.30pm) The relaxing riverside setting complements some of the most authentic northern Lao cuisine on offer. From five-dish menus for two or three people to one-plate meals, the flavour combinations are divine. If you're baffled by the choice try snacking on a selection of *jąaou* used as dipping sauces for balls of sticky rice.

Orientation

Virtually flat, Namtha is in fact a 10km-long collection of villages coalescing in an administrative hub at the northern end. Built since 1976, the administrative hub is a well-spaced grid within which there's a two-block traveller enclave dotted with guesthouses, internet cafes and tour agencies. A smaller, prettier second centre is 7km further south near the airport. This used to be Namtha's commercial heart before it was bombed to bits in the Second Indochina War. Today it's a mostly residential area called Meuang Luang Namtha or simply Ban Luang. The new long-distance bus station is 3km further south on the Rte 3 bypass, an improbable 10km out of the main centre.

Information

There are several internet cafes on the main strip but most guesthouses and hotels offer free wi-fi these days.

BCEL (8.30am-3.30pm Mon-Fri) Changes major currencies (commission-free) and travellers cheques (2% commission, minimum US$3) and has a 24-hour ATM.

Provincial Tourism Office (086-211534; 8am-noon & 2-5pm) Doubles as Nam Ha Ecoguide Service.

BUSES FROM LUANG NAMTHA

DESTINATION	COST (K)	DURATION (HR)	STATION	DEPARTURES
Boten	35,000	2	district	6 daily 8am-3.30pm
Huay Xai ('Borkeo')	60,000	4	long distance	9am, 1.30pm bus, 8.30am minibus
Jinghong (China)	90,000	6	long distance	8.30am
Luang Prabang	90,000-100,000	8	long distance	9am bus, 8am minibus
Mengla (China)	50,000	3½	long distance	8am
Muang Long	60,000	4	district	8.30am
Luang Sing	30,000	2	district	6 daily 8am-3.30pm
Na Lae	40,000	3	district	9.30am, noon
Udomxai	40,000	4	long distance	8.30am, noon, 2.30pm
Vieng Phukha	35,000	1½	long distance	9.30am, noon
Vientiane	180,000-200,000	21-24	long distance	8.30am, 2.30pm

Getting There & Away

AIR

Lao Airlines (086-312180; www.laoairlines.com) flies to Vientiane (895,000K) daily and specials are sometimes available for 645,000K.

BOAT

An inspiring, alternative way to reach Huay Xai is on a two-day longboat odyssey down the Nam Tha, sleeping en route at a roadless village. But hurry – this option might be lost forever if a proposed dam project near Ban Phaeng moves forward. For the ride, Luang Namtha agencies charge around US$120 to US$300 per person depending on exact numbers, including accommodation, meals and a tour guide throughout. You might get a slightly better deal from the **boat station** (086-312014) right beside the Boat Landing Guest House. When river levels are low (typically January to June), the boat station closes and departures start from Na Lae, with agencies providing tuk-tuk transfers and pre-arranging a boat.

BUS & SŎRNGTĂAOU

There are two bus stations. The district bus station is walking distance from the traveller strip. The main long distance bus station is 10km south of town. In either case, prebooking a ticket doesn't guarantee a seat – arrive early and claim one in person.

For Nong Khiaw take a Vientiane or Luang Prabang bus and change at Pak Mong.

Getting Around

Chartered tuk-tuks charge 10,000K per person (minimum 40,000K) between the bus station or airport and the town centre. Most agencies and guesthouses sell ticket packages for long-distance buses that include a transfer from the guesthouse and cost around 20,000K above the usual fare.

Cycling is the ideal way to explore the wats, waterfalls, bans (villages) and landscape surrounding Luang Namtha. There are a couple of **bicycle shops** (bicycle per day 10,000-25,000K, motorcycle per day 30,000-50,000K; 9am-6.30pm) in front of the Zuela Guesthouse. Choose from a bicycle or motorcycle depending on how energetic you are feeling.

Around Luang Namtha

Vieng Phukha (Vieng Phoukha) ວຽງພູຄາ

Sleepy Vieng Phukha is an alternative trekking base for visiting the western limits of the Nam Ha NPA, notably on three-day Akha trail hikes. Such trails see fewer visitors than many from Luang Namtha and the partly forested landscapes can be magnificent, though many hills in Vieng Phukha's direct vicinity have been completely deforested. The tiny town centre consists of just three parallel streets. Within a few hundred metres you'll find a handful of guesthouses and eco-tourism outfits, including **Nam Ha Ecoguide Service Vieng Phoukha** (020-5598 5289; www.namha-npa.org; 8am-noon & 1.30-5pm) and **Nam Ha Hilltribe Ecotrek** (020-9944 0084; www.trekviengphoukha.com; 8am-noon & 1-6pm).

Sleeping & Eating

Virtually all Vieng Phukha accommodation is in simple thatched bungalows with cold showers.

Phuet Mung Khun Guesthouse GUESTHOUSE $
(020-5588 6089; r 50,000K) Located on the banks of the river, the friendly Phuet Mung Khun Guesthouse has neat little bungalows, plus a small restaurant. The owner speaks rudimentary English.

Samlangchai Guesthouse GUESTHOUSE $
(020-5588 6089; r/bungalow 40,000/50,000K) On the hilltop, up a steep 300m access lane, Samlangchai Guesthouse has bungalows with comfy beds and balconies, although it's starting to show its age and the garden features a rusty bulldozer as an incongruous 'sculpture'.

Thongmyxai Guesthouse GUESTHOUSE $
(020-2239 0351; r 60,000-80,000K) Just about the smartest accommodation in town is the Thongmyxai Guesthouse, set in an attractive garden and offering somewhat solid bungalows.

Mein Restaurant LAOTIAN $
(020-5408 0110; Rte 3; mains 10,000-30,000K; 7am-9pm) On the southern edge town, Mein Restaurant has an English menu though little on it is actually available.

Getting There & Away

Sŏrngtăaou for Luang Namtha (30,000K, 1½ hours) depart at around 9am and 1pm from the middle of town. Or wave down a Huay Xai–Namtha through service (three daily).

Down the Nam Tha

For some 35km south of Luang Namtha, the pea-green Nam Tha flows across a series of pretty rapids tumbling between high-sided banks that are attractively shaggy with bamboo-choked forests. Luang Namtha tour agencies can organise one-day supported **kayaking** trips here, possibly combined with Nam Ha jungle treks. By bicycle or motorbike, the passably well-graded dirt road that runs along the river's eastern bank offers a quiet if potentially dusty way to enjoy some pretty views and see some interesting minority villages without the need for hiking.

Muang Sing ເມືອງສິງ

081 / POP 10,000

Bordering Myanmar and almost within grasp of the green hills of China, this is the heart of the Golden Triangle. Rural Muang Sing has a backwater feel that transports you to a less complicated time. Formerly on the once infamous opium trail, it's a sleepy town of wilting, Tai Lü–style houses, and trekking has overtaken smuggling contraband. Hmong, Tai Lü, Akha and Tai Dam are all seen here in traditional dress at the morning market (get there for dawn), giving the town a frontier feel.

Back in the late '90s, this was one of the must-visit destinations in Laos, but in the past decade, with the end of fast boat services and the clampdown on the opium trade, it has somewhat dropped off the traveller radar, eclipsed by other adventure centres like Nong Khiaw or Vang Vieng. There is an air of torpor about the town, but the real draw is the countryside beyond. Visitors with time to explore are rewarded with some of the

WORTH A TRIP

KAO RAO CAVES

Well signed beside Rte 3, 1.5km east of Nam Eng village, is this extensive, accessible **cave system** (ຖ້ຳເກົາເລົາ; admission 10,000K), of which a 700m section is open to visitors. The main limestone formations include old stalactites encrusted with crystal deposits. Curious corrugations in the floor that now look like great old tree roots once formed the lips of carbonate pools like those at Turkey's Pamukkale. Local guides accompany visitors through the cave, but speak no English and have feeble torches. Extensive lighting is already wired up, but there are often power cuts, meaning a torch (flashlight) is a handy accessory. Allow around 45 minutes for the visit.

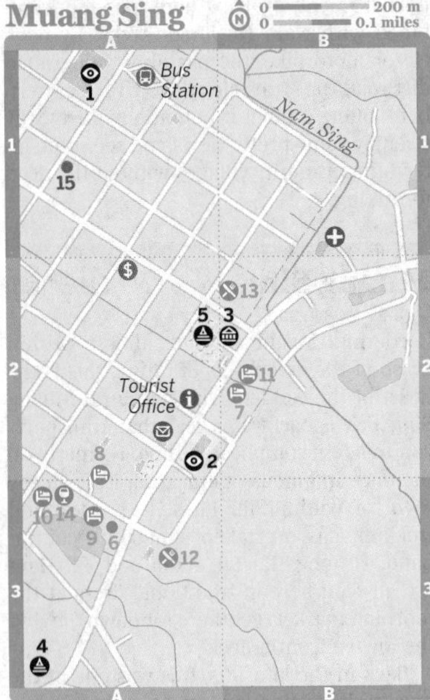

Muang Sing

Sights
- 1 New Market A1
- 2 Old Market A2
- 3 Tribal Museum B2
- 4 Wat Namkeo Luang A3
- 5 Wat Xieng Jai A2

Activities, Courses & Tours
- 6 Phou Iu Travel A3

Sleeping
- 7 Dan Neau 2 Guesthouse B2
- 8 Phou Iu 2 Guesthouse A2
- 9 Sing Cha Lern Hotel A3
- 10 Singduangdao Bungalows A3
- 11 Thai Lü Guest House B2

Eating
- 12 Muang Sing View Restaurant A3
- 13 Phunnar Restaurant B2

Drinking & Nightlife
- 14 Singsavanh Nightclub A3

Transport
- 15 Kalao Motorcycle A1

most scenic responsible trekking opportunities in the Nam Ha NPA.

History

In the late 18th century, a dowager of the Chiang Khaen principality founded the square, grid-plan citadel of Wiang Fa Ya (today's Muang Sing) along with the That Xieng Tung stupa. In 1803 this area became vassal to Nan (now in Thailand) and was largely abandoned following the deportations of 1805 and 1813. But the Chiang Khaen princes returned, moving their capital here in 1884 from Xiang Khaeng on the Mekong. This kicked off a 20-year tug of war between France, Britain and Siam, causing the principality to be split in two, with the western sector (including Muang Sing) being absorbed into French Indochina. Muang Sing rapidly became the biggest opium market in the Golden Triangle, a function officially sanctioned by the French. In 1946, parts of town were devastated by Kuomintang troops who continued to operate here well into the 1950s after losing the Chinese civil war. In 1958 the famous American 'jungle doctor' Tom Dooley set up his hospital in Muang Sing, which became the setting for a series of international intrigues.

Sights

Sprinkled along the town's main street are a few classic Lao-French hybrid mansion-houses. These mostly 1920s structures have ground-floor walls of brick and stucco topped with a wooden upper storey featuring a wraparound roofed verandah. Classic examples house the tourist office and the Thai Lü Guesthouse.

The **old market**, built in 1954, was under reconstruction at the time of writing. The bustling **new market** is near the bus station and is very colourful first thing in the morning.

Tribal Museum MUSEUM

(admission 5000K; 8.30am-4.30pm Mon-Fri, 8-11am Sat) The most distinctive of the old Lao-French buildings is now home to the two-room Tribal Museum, which boasts costume displays downstairs and six cases of cultural artefacts upstairs. Watching a 40-minute video on the Akha people costs 5000K extra.

Wat Xieng Jai & Wat Namkeo Luang BUDDHIST TEMPLE

In local wats, look for typical Tai Lü details such as silver-stencilled patterning on red pillars and ceilings, and the use of long vertical prayer flags. The most visually striking monastic buildings are at **Wat Xieng Jai** and **Wat Namkeo Luang** (ວັດນ້ຳແກ້ວຫລວງ). The latter features an entry porch adorned with red-tongued golden naga and an unusually tall and ornate gilded stupa. Some villagers still draw water from *shaduf*-style lever wells in the slowly gentrifying *bâan* opposite. Nearby you can also find a modest Lak Bâan spirit-totem, but touching it would cause serious offence.

That Xieng Tung BUDDHIST TEMPLE
(ທາດຊຽງຕຶງ) Around 6km southeast of Muang Sing, That Xieng Tung is the famous stupa built by Muang Sing's founder dowager-queen in 1792. Shorter and less embellished than that at Wat Namkeo Luang, the octagonal layout is reminiscent of similar structures in Xishuangbanna, across the Chinese border. It's on a grassy plateau dotted with 'sacred trees', 1km up a very rough access track that branches south off the Luang Namtha road 200m after Km 52. This place really comes alive at festival time (full moon of the 12th lunar month, between late October and mid-November) when hordes of merit-makers offer candles, flowers and incense around the base of the stupa, monks from around the province gather to collect alms and traditional dance performances add to a general carnival atmosphere that spills over into town.

Activities

The main reason visitors come to Muang Sing is to venture into the minority villages that dot the valley of rice paddies and sugar cane fields surrounding town. To do it yourself by bicycle or motorbike, start by purchasing Wolfgang Korn's helpful *Muang Sing Cultural Guide Book* from the tourist office. The map shows major roads and labels the ethnicities of the valley's villages. To make the village-visiting experience somewhat less voyeuristic you can engage a guide for as little as 100,000K from one of Muang Sing's ecotour agencies, which also offer a gamut of longer treks and homestay experiences.

Phou Iu Travel ADVENTURE TOUR
(☎081-400012; www.muangsingtravel.com; ⏰7am-7pm) The leading tour operator in Muang Sing, run out of the Phou Iu II Guesthouse, offers well-organised treks around Muang Sing. They also offer treks to the more remote Xieng Khaeng district towards Burma, but check www.adventure-trek-laos.com for details.

Sleeping

Central Muang Sing

Thai Lü Guest House GUESTHOUSE $
(☎086-400375; r 30,000-40,000K) Looking like a backdrop in an old Bruce Lee flick, this creaky wooden building has a certain charm, even if the rattan-walled, squat-loo rooms are uninspiring. The restaurant downstairs (meals 10,000K to 25,000K) serves Thai, Laotian and Western dishes.

Sing Cha Lern Hotel HOTEL $
(☎086-400020; r 60,000-120,000; ❄📶) This ochre two-storey building offers 22 clean and neat, if characterless, rooms with hot water and fans. A breezy communal area has two lounge chairs, plus ageing mock-leather sofas and a television blaring out Asian soap operas. Also accepts payment in yuan.

Dan Neau 2 Guesthouse GUESTHOUSE $
(☎020-2239 3398; r from 60,000K) The entrance from the main road isn't particularly promising, but walk around the side to find an altogether larger annexe with presentable rooms, including satellite TV, hot water and fan.

MYSTERIOUS TOM DOOLEY

Saint or shameless self-promoter? Humanitarian or CIA pawn? Fifty years after his early death, opinions are still divided over the 'jungle doctor' who set up his famous benevolent hospital in Muang Sing in 1958. Passionately Catholic yet dismissed from the US Navy for his sexual orientation, this complex character was cited by President Kennedy as an inspiration for the Peace Corps (founded in 1961, the year Dooley succumbed to cancer). However, his anti-communist books helped encourage the US political slide towards war in Indochina and rumours abound that the flights that brought in medical supplies to his Muang Sing base would return laden with opium. For much more read James Fisher's flawed but detailed Dooley biography *Dr America*.

Singduangdao Bungalows GUESTHOUSE $
(☎020-2200 4565; r from 70,000K) Set in a verdant garden, Singduangdao offers appealing bungalows hidden away behind the truck weighbridge. All have hot showers. English is also spoken.

Phou Iu 2 Guesthouse GUESTHOUSE $$
(☎086-400012; www.muangsingtravel.com; bungalow small/medium/large 100,000/200,000/400,000K) Set around an expansive garden, the biggest bungalows have fun outdoor rock-clad shower spaces. All rooms have comfortable beds, mosquito nets, fans and small verandahs, plus there's an on-site herbal sauna (10,000K) and massage (50,000K per hour). There is also a small restaurant here.

Outside Muang Sing

★**Adima Guesthouse** GUESTHOUSE $
(☎020-2239 3398; r 100,000K) The big selling point of Adima is that you're on the edge of exactly the kind of classic Akha village that most people come to the region to see – the popular yet still authentic village of Nam Dath is only 700m up the trail. Many other minority villages are within easy walking distance. Adima's sturdy brick-and-thatch bungalows include hot showers and bucket-flush toilets. Their appealing rustic restaurant overlooks fishponds. From Muang Sing take the Pang Hai road to the far edge of Ban Udomsin (500m after Km 7), turn right and Adima is 600m south. A tuk-tuk from town costs about 20,000K.

Eating & Drinking

There is not a huge range of eateries in Muang Sing. It's fair to say visitors aren't drawn here for the dining.

Phunnar Restaurant LAOTIAN $
(Panna Restaurant; mains 15000-30,000K; ⏲7.30am-8pm) Located in a quiet backstreet, the Phunnar is an open-air place providing inexpensive fried rice, noodles, *làhp* and soups.

Muang Sing View Restaurant LAOTIAN $
(mains 15,000-30,000K; ⏲8am-7pm) This simple bamboo-floored stilt pavilion overlooks a seemingly endless sea of rice paddies, making it very much the most attractive place in town to eat. The menu is wide-ranging but much of it is not actually available. It's a good spot for a sundowner.

Singsavanh Nightclub CLUB
(⏲7pm-11.30pm) Most of Muang Sing is dead asleep by 9pm except at the Singsavanh where the locals get down to live Lao and Chinese pop. It might look permanently closed down by day, but somehow it picks itself up at night.

Information

Lao Development Bank (⏲8am-noon & 2-3.30pm Mon-Fri) Exchanges US dollars, Thai baht and Chinese yuan but at less than favourable rates.

Post Office (⏲8am-4pm Mon-Fri) As tiny as the *petang* rectangle next to it.

Tourist Office (⏲8am-4pm Mon-Fri) Displays of fact scrolls are useful but the staff aren't likely to win the Lao National Tourism Authority's employee of the month award.

Getting There & Away

From the bus station in the northwest corner of town, *sǒrngtǎaou* depart for Muang Long (40,000K, 1½ hours) at 8am, 11am and 1.30pm. To Luang Namtha (50,000K, two hours, 58km) minibuses leave at 8am, 9am, 11am, 12.30pm, 2pm and 3pm.

Getting Around

Kalao Motorcycle (per day 80,000K; ⏲8am-5pm), on the road to the main market, rents motorbikes, but bring a good phrasebook as nobody here speaks English. Bicycle rental (per day 30,000K) is available from several main-street agencies and guesthouses.

Xieng Kok ຊຽງກົກ

On market days (the 14th and 28th of every month) Xieng Kok attracts hill-tribe folks and traders from surrounding countries. Otherwise, despite its reputation as a smuggling route, it's a sleepy, attractive little place surveying a deep slice of Mekong Valley and the Burmese banks behind. In autumn, when river levels are high, Chinese barges call in at the river port and Xieng Kok attracts a trickle of travellers who come to find a boat along one of Laos' more attractive stretches of the Mekong. The area between here and Muang Mom is roadless and a speedboat should cost around 900/3500B per person/boat. Consider paying 1200/4500B and continuing to Tonpheung, from which onward *sǒrngtǎaou* to Huay Xai are easier to find. A daily 9am speedboat departure is touted by the

Muang Long tourist office, but if there are no fellow passengers it is necessary to charter a boat. From late January to June the water levels are usually too low to make the river trip at all.

Arriving in Xieng Kok by boat you climb the steep riverbank to a loop of asphalt road that fronts the immigration booth. Veer left for the **Xieng Kok Resort** (☎030-511 0696; r from 60,000K), a line of 11 simple timber bungalows overlooking the Mekong, each with balcony, private squat toilet and cold shower.

The two roads converge again within 300m where the minibus to Muang Long (20,000K, 35 minutes) leaves at 6am, 8am and 2pm from outside the town's little pharmacy. Finding any other vehicle can be hard here, even if you're prepared to charter.

THE MIDDLE MEKONG

The mighty Mekong threads together the provinces of Bokeo and Sainyabuli, along with Pak Beng in southern Udomxai. For many tourists the region is seen merely in passing between Thailand and Luang Prabang – typically on the two-day slowboat route from Huay Xai via Pak Beng – but there's plenty to interest the more adventurous traveller. Bokeo, meaning 'Gem Mine', takes its name from the sapphire deposits in Huay Xai district, and the province is home to 34 ethnicities despite a particularly sparse population. Sainyabuli Province is synonymous with working elephants and there is an excellent new Elephant Conservation Center (p126) just outside the eponymous capital. Other than in Huay Xai and Pak Beng you'll need a decent phrasebook wherever you go. Western Sainyabuli remains particularly far off the traveller radar but if you want to be way ahead of the crowds, places like dramatic Khop district are 'last frontiers' with a complex ethnic mix and reputedly high proportion of still-pristine forests.

Huay Xai (Hoksay)

ຫ້ວຍຊາຍ

☎084 / POP 20,000

Allegedly home to a US heroin-processing plant during the Secret War, these days the only things trafficked through Huay Xai are travellers en route to Luang Prabang. Separated from Thailand by the mother river that is the Mekong, for many travellers Huay Xai is their first impression of Laos: don't worry, it does get better. By night its central drag dons its fairy lights and fires up roadside food vendors, and there are some welcoming traveller guesthouses and tasty cafes. Huay Xai is also the HQ of the now-fabled Gibbon Experience, the most talked-about environmentally responsible jungle adventure in the country.

Sights

Huay Xai's modest tourist attractions include the Mekong views from several colourful wats.

Wat Jom Khao Manilat BUDDHIST TEMPLE
(ວັດຈອມເຂົາມະນີລັດ) *Naga* stairs, ascending opposite the ferry access lane, emerge at this hilltop wat, originally constructed in 1880.

Wat Thadsuvanna Phakham BUDDHIST TEMPLE
(ວັດທາດສວັນນະຜ້າຄຳ) Commanding the rise directly above the speedboat landing, 3km south of the central area, Wat Thadsuvanna Phakham is a colourful new temple featuring a row of eight gilded Buddhas demonstrating the main meditation postures and disdaining Mekong views beneath the foliage.

Wat Khonekeo Xaiyaram BUDDHIST TEMPLE
(ວັດໂຄນແກ້ວ) Wat Khonekeo Xaiyaram, in Ban Khonekeo, has a lavish frontage with dazzling red, gold and green pillars and doors.

Wat Keophone Savanthanaram BUDDHIST TEMPLE
Wat Keophone Savanthanaram features murals of gruesome torture scenes on the *sĭm*'s north wall while on the slope above, a long Buddha reclines behind chicken wire.

Fort Carnot FORT
The very dilapidated shell of French-built Fort Carnot sits on the hilltop behind the Bokeo Governor's Office. Two towers are still standing, one straddling the gateway, but the tiles are falling off the old barrack room roofs and the whole sparse site is hardly a highlight of Huay Xai. Tucked in the valley behind is Huay Xai's vibrant **main market**.

Activities

Most hill-tribe treks advertised by Huay Xai agencies actually start from Vieng Phukha so you'll generally do better to book them

Huay Xai

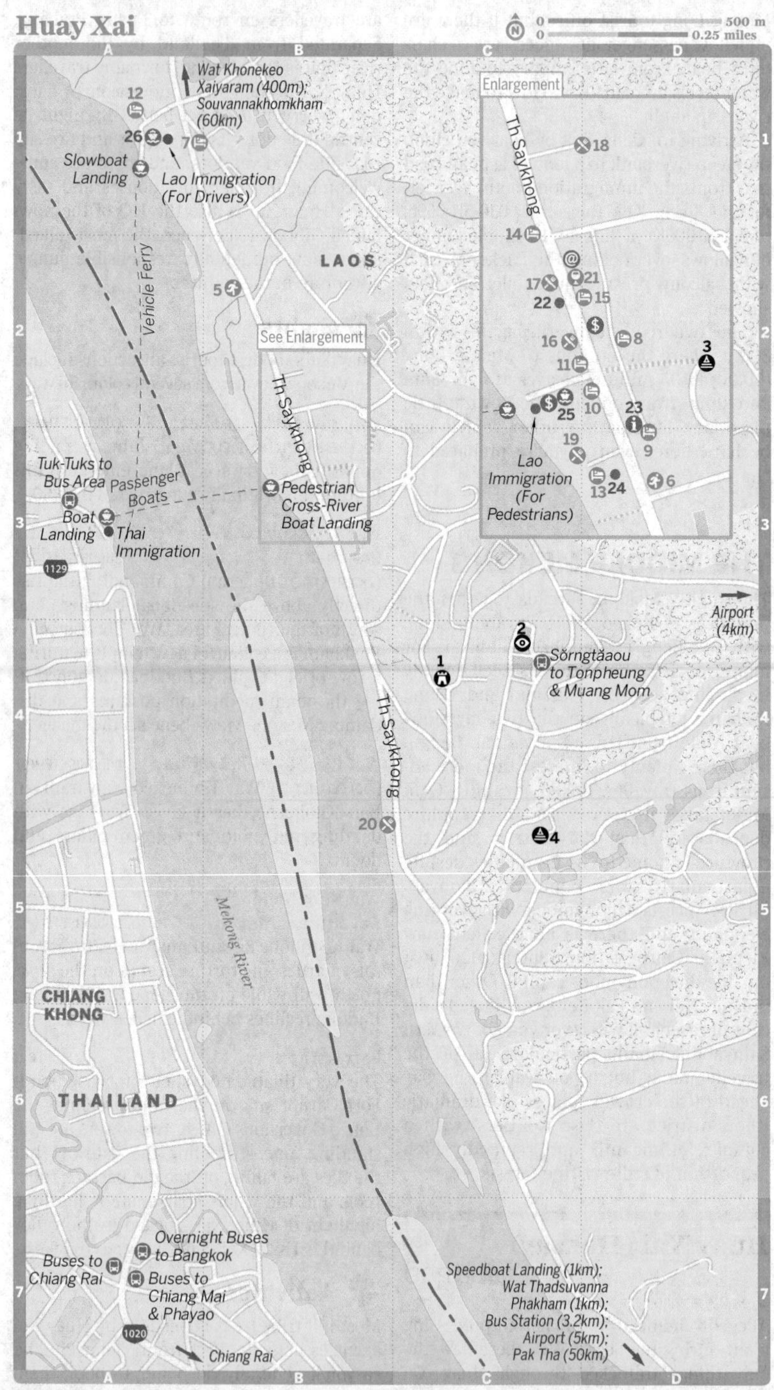

0 500 m
0 0.25 miles
Wat Khonekeo Xaiyaram (400m); Souvannakhomkham (60km)
Enlargement
Th Saykhong
18
12
26
7
Slowboat Landing
Lao Immigration (For Drivers)
14
@
17
21
22
15
LAOS
5
Vehicle Ferry
$
16
8
3
See Enlargement
11
25
10
23
Th Saykhong
9
19
Lao Immigration (For Pedestrians)
13
24
6
Tuk-Tuks to Bus Area
Passenger Boats
Pedestrian Cross-River Boat Landing
Boat Landing
Thai Immigration
1129
Airport (4km)
2
1
Sŏrngtăaou to Tonpheung & Muang Mom
Th Saykhong
20
4
Mekong River
CHIANG KHONG
THAILAND
Overnight Buses to Bangkok
Buses to Chiang Rai
Buses to Chiang Mai & Phayao
Speedboat Landing (1km); Wat Thadsuvanna Phakham (1km); Bus Station (3.2km); Airport (5km); Pak Tha (50km)
1020
Chiang Rai

Huay Xai

Sights

1 Fort Carnot C4
2 Main Market C4
3 Wat Jom Khao Manilat D2
4 Wat Keophone Savanthanaram C5

Activities, Courses & Tours

5 Lao Red Cross B2
6 Wangview Tour D3

Sleeping

7 Arimid Guest House A1
8 Daauw Homestay D2
9 Friendship Guesthouse D3
10 Gateway Villa Hotel D2
11 Phonetip Guesthouse C2
12 Phonevichith Guesthouse & Restaurant A1
13 Riverside Houayxay Hotel D3
14 Sabaydee Guest House C1
15 Thaveesinh Hotel D2

Eating

16 BAP Guesthouse C2
Daauw .... (see 8)
17 Maung Ner Cafe C2
18 Nut Pop Restaurant D1
19 Riverside Restaurant C3
20 Tavendeng Restaurant B5

Drinking & Nightlife

21 Bar How C2

Information

22 Gibbon Experience Office C2
23 Tourist Information Office D2

Transport

24 Lao Airlines D3
25 Luang Say Cruise C2
26 Slowboat Ticket Booth A1

there. One-day tours to Souvannakhomkham, including a boat ride around the Golden Triangle, are also offered but there are rarely enough travellers signing up to make the prices viable. A DIY trip by motorbike is easier to arrange.

Lao Red Cross MASSAGE
(☎084-211935; massage per hour from 35,000K, herbal sauna 15,000K; ⊙1.30-9pm Mon-Fri, 10.30am-9pm Sat & Sun) Lao Red Cross offers Swedish-Lao massage and a traditional herbal sauna (from 4pm) in a stately old mansion beside the Mekong.

Sleeping

The central drag is packed with guesthouses and many more are dotted around the edge of town.

Phonetip Guesthouse GUESTHOUSE $
(☎084-211084; Th Saykhong; r 50,000-120,000K; ❄📶) Simple, central and clean by budget standards. The cheapest options are just beds in boxes but there's a pleasant road-facing communal area to sit in upstairs if you can grab a seat.

★**Daauw Homestay** HOMESTAY $
(☎030-904 1296; www.projectkajsiablaos.org; r 60,000-80,000K) Run by grassroots organisation Project Kajsiab, the Daauw Homestay is a way to contribute something to women's empowerment and minority rights with an overnight stay in a bungalow. As well as accommodation, there is a restaurant-bar, plus a small handicrafts shop. One-week to one-month volunteering positions are available for 850,000K per week, including board and lodging. It's located just off the stairs to Wat Jom Khao Manilat, halfway up on the right-hand side.

Friendship Guesthouse GUESTHOUSE $
(☎084-211219; s/d/tr/q from 70,000/80,000/160,000/200,000K; 📶) Rooms have the usual aged patches and beds can be creaky but the selling point here is the open roof with great views and three simple tables at which to enjoy them.

Thaveesinh Hotel HOTEL $
(☎084-211502; thaveesinh.info@gmail.com; Th Saykhong; s/d with fan 70,000/90,000K, with air-con 100,000/130,000K; ❄📶) Rooms in this very central hotel are fair-sized and clean if chintzy thanks to the pink curtains. Heavy wooden furniture and ornaments decorate common areas and there's a rooftop breakfast room.

Gateway Villa Hotel GUESTHOUSE $
(☎084-212180; gatewayconsult@hotmail.com; Th Saykhong; r with fan/air-con from 81,000/127,000K; ❄📶) Close to the boat landing, Gateway Villa has tastefully furnished rooms with hardwood floors, wicker chairs, TVs and contemporary-looking linen. Some rooms are more prettified than others. The owners operate three more properties dotted about town.

DON'T MISS

THE GIBBON EXPERIENCE

Adrenalin meets conservation in this ecofriendly adventure in the 106,000 hectares of the Bokeo Nature Reserve wilderness. The **Gibbon Experience** (☎084-212021; www.gibbonexperience.org; express 2-day US$190, 3-day classic or waterfall US$290) is essentially a series of navigable 'ziplines' criss-crossing the canopy of some of Laos' most pristine forest, home to tigers, clouded leopards, black bears and the black-crested gibbon.

Seven years ago poaching was threatening the existence of the black-crested gibbon, but thanks to Animo, a conservation-based tour group, the hunters of Bokeo were convinced to become the forest's guardians. As guides they now make more for their families than in their old predatory days.

The benchmark for sustainable monkey business, this three-day experience is one of Laos' most unforgettable adventures. Essentially this is an extended chance to play Tarzan; living two nights in soaring tree-houses within thickly forested hills and swinging high across valleys on incredible ziplines, some more than 500m long. It's a heart-stopping, superhero experience. Should it rain, remember you need more time to slow down with your humble brake. The guides are helpful, though make sure you're personally vigilant with the knots in your harness.

For those on the classic experience there's a good chance of hearing the gibbons' incredible calls. Actually seeing gibbons is much rarer but some lucky groups do catch a fleeting glimpse. Unless making a pre-dawn trek to tree-house 3, participants on the waterfall trek are far less likely to hear gibbons. More recently a faster two-day express trip has been added to the roster for those with less time to spare in the forest canopy. The days also involve a serious amount of trekking. Bring a pair of hiking boots and long socks to deter the ever-persistent leeches.

Accommodation is located in unique thatched tree-houses that are spaced sufficiently far from each other so that each feels entirely alone in the jungle. Often around 40m above the ground and set in natural amphitheatres with spectacular views, most of the tree-houses sleep eight people with bedding laid out beneath large cloth nets, although some tree-houses sleep just two people. Large spiders on the walls and rats rustling in the ceilings will be your companions too, but this is the jungle after all. Well-cooked meals consisting of rice and four accompaniments are ziplined in from one of three rustic kitchens while coffee, tea, hot chocolate and various additional snacks are available in each tree-house. Keeping anything edible in the provided strong box is essential to avoid the forest rats being attracted.

More recently added for sybarites who need a little more comfort, the gibbon spa incorporates the best of the classic with gourmet food, improved lodgings and massages. Whichever you choose – book weeks in advance – this is one funky gibbon you'll never forget.

Pre-payment online through Paypal works well but do be patient as communication isn't always immediate. One day before departure, check in at the Huay Xai **Gibbon Experience office** (Th Saykhong). Gloves (essential for using the ziplines) are sold next door. It's also advisable to bring a torch (flashlight), water bottle and earplugs to deflect the sound of a million crickets, but otherwise leave most of your baggage in the office storeroom. Everything you bring you must carry on your back over some steep hikes and on the ziplines. As there'll be no electricity, don't forget to pre-charge camera batteries.

Sabaydee Guest House GUESTHOUSE $
(☎084-212252; Th Saykhong; r incl breakfast 90,000-130,000K; ❄@📶) Sabaydee has unfailingly clean rooms with comfy beds, TVs, fans and en suites. Decked in bright colours and pleasant furnishings, some rooms overlook the river. There's also a nice communal area with internet access.

Arimid Guest House GUESTHOUSE $$
(☎084-211040; Ban Huay Xai Neua; s/d 80,000/180,000K; ❄) Armid has rustic cabanas with pleasant balconies set in manicured gardens peppered with statues. Some of them are ageing more than others so definitely ask to see a selection.

Riverside Houayxay Hotel HOTEL $$
(☎084-211064; riverside_houayxay_laos@hotmail.com; deluxe/riverview r 600/900B) Located just off the main strip and overlooking the mighty Mekong, this is the most upmarket hotel in the centre of town. Rooms are spacious and spotlessly clean. Hot water is on tap, plus there is satellite TV and a minibar.

Phonevichith Guesthouse & Restaurant GUESTHOUSE $$
(☎084-211765; houayxairiverside.com; Ban Khonekeo; r 600-1000B;) Colourful fabrics, fans and kitschy lamps add a little character to the smart rooms, which come with piping-hot showers and air-con. A new wing offers the smartest beds in town, which are verging on the boutique hotel. The main attraction is the Mekong perch and handy proximity to the slowboat landing.

Eating & Drinking

Of three *falang*-style restaurants near the slowboat pier, that at Phonevichith Guesthouse has the best river views.

BAP Guesthouse LAOTIAN $
(Th Saykhong; mains 15,000-35,000K;) Run by English-speaking Mrs Changpeng, this wayfarer's fave has an inviting restaurant dishing up snacks, vegetarian dishes and Lao staples. It's close to Lao immigration.

Nut Pop Restaurant LAOTIAN $
(Th Saykhong; meals 20,000-40,000K; 4.30-10pm) Reached via a bridge and by night alluringly lit with ropes of golden light, this tree-house-style restaurant makes for a romantic dinner. It serves up tasty Laotian and Vietnamese food.

Daauw LAOTIAN $
(mains 20,000-50,000K;) There is something of a Thai island vibe to this place with its chill-out terrace, low cushions and open pit fire. Choose from freshly prepared organic Hmong food, plenty of vegetarian options or whole barbecued Mekong fish or chicken. Linger for *laojitos* if there's a crowd, a mojito made with *lòw-lów*.

Riverside Restaurant LAOTIAN, THAI $
(Th Saykhong; mains 20,000-60,000K; 7am-11pm) The Mekong terrace here offers a great vantage point from which to watch the boats shuttling to and fro to Thailand. The menu has a wide range of Thai and Lao food, plus Western breakfasts. It's a good spot for sunset if you can tolerate theMuzak.

Maung Ner Cafe LAOTIAN, INTERNATIONAL $
(Gecko Bar; Th Saykhong; meals 20,000-40,000K; 6.30am-11pm) With its worn turquoise walls adorned in animal horns, Muang Ner remains a popular choice. Mouthwatering *làhp,* Western breakfasts and wood-fired pizzas all complement the welcoming vibe.

Tavendeng Restaurant LAOTIAN $
(mains 25,000-80,000K; 7am-11pm) Predominantly aimed at Thai tourists, this large wooden dining complex features live music and exotic foods such as frog and fried crocodile.

Bar How BAR
(Th Saykhong; meals 20,000-40,000K; 6.30am-11pm;) The funkiest little bar-restaurant on Huay Xai's main strip, Bar How is a little hole in the wall that serves food by day and plenty of drinks by night. The bar is laden with homemade *lòw-lów* or rice wine, infused with everything from blueberry to tamarind. Try them all if you dare...we did.

Information

BCEL (Th Saykhong; 8.30am-4.30pm Mon-Fri) 24-hour ATM, exchange facility and Western Union.

Lao Development Bank Exchange Booth (8am-5pm) Handy booth right beside the pedestrian immigration window. Most major currencies exchanged into kip. US-dollar bills must be dated 2006 or later.

Tourist Information Office (☎084-211162; Th Saykhong; 8am-4.30pm Mon-Fri) Has free tourist maps of the town and some suggestions for excursions around the province.

Yon Computer Internet Cafe (Th Saykhong; per hour 10,000K; 9am-9pm) Decent connection with Skype. Also fixes laptops.

Getting There & Away

For years, streams of Luang Prabang–bound travellers have piled into Huay Xai and jumped straight aboard a boat for the memorable descent of the Mekong. Today, improving roads mean that an ever-increasing proportion opt instead for the overnight bus. But although slightly cheaper than the slowboat, the bus is far less social, less attractive and leaves most travellers exhausted on arrival so it isn't necessarily a great time-saver either.

AIR

Huay Xai's airport is oddly perched on a hillside off the city bypass, 1.5km northwest of the bus station. **Lao Airlines** (☎084-211026; www.laoairlines.com) flies daily to/from Vientiane

GETTING TO THAILAND: HUAY XAI TO CHIANG KHONG

Getting to the Border

Crossing the **Lao–Thai border** (⏲8am-6pm) here is by Mekong riverboat, although a much-delayed bridge is planned eventually. Even if you're planning to head straight for Luang Prabang, don't let sneaky Thai-side signs like 'last chips', 'last drinks' etc mislead you into thinking that you won't find snacks for sale on the Lao side.

Pedestrians cross by longboat (three minutes), costing per person/big bag 30/10B from the Thai side, 10,000/3000K from the Lao side. Boats leave within a few minutes, even with only two or three passengers.

A vehicle ferry crosses a few times daily (except Sunday) between the main Thai immigration point and the slowboat landing in Huay Xai, costing 500B for motorcycles, 1000B for cars (or 1500B on the 5pm sailing).

At the Border

As usual the Lao immigration post offers thirty-day tourist visas on arrival (most nationalities US$30 to US$42 plus a US$1 surcharge at weekends or after 4pm). If you don't have a passport-style mugshot they'll charge 40B extra. An exchange booth right beside Lao immigration (open till 5pm) converts currencies at a fair rate. Arriving on the Thai side you'll need 30B to pay the port charge (or 60B after 4.30pm) and another 30B for the tuk-tuk to the bus station. The nearest Thai-side ATM is nearly 2km south.

Moving On

On the Thai side, buses leave from assorted offices around 2.5km south of Chiang Khong's Thai immigration post. Tuk-tuks wait just above the immigration post and beside a market close to the bus offices. Pay 30B between the two points.

To Chiang Rai (65B, 2¼ hours) local services leave hourly on the hour from 6am to 5pm in either direction. **Greenbus** (☎0066 5365 5732; www.greenbusthailand.com) has services to Chiang Mai at 6am, 9am and 11.40am. Several overnight buses leave for Bangkok (500B to 750B, 10 hours) from nearby at 3pm and 3.30pm.

for 895,000K, although seasonal specials for 645,000K are sometimes available.

BOAT

Slowboats to Pak Beng & Luang Prabang

Slowboats currently depart from Huay Xai at 11am daily. Purchase tickets at the **slowboat ticket booth** (☎084-211659) to Pak Beng (100,000K, one day) or Luang Prabang (200,000K not including accommodation, two days). Sales start at 8am on the day of travel. Buying a ticket from a travel agent (500B to Pak Beng) simply means you get an overpriced tuk-tuk transfer to the pier and then have to sit around awaiting departure.

'Seats' are typically uncomfortable wooden benches for which you'll value the expenditure of 10,000K for a cushion (sold at many an agency in town). Some boats also have a number of more comfy airliner-style seats. If the boat operators try to cram on too many passengers (over 70 or so), a tactic that really works is for later arrivals to simply refuse to get aboard until a second boat is provided.

Other scams we have heard about include pretending the boat will take four or five days to reach Luang Prabang due to high water and concealed rocks, but this is usually just a low-season ruse to shift people on to the bus and save money on operating the boat.

'Luxury' Slowboats

To do the two-day river journey to Luang Prabang in more comfort, a popular alternative is the stylish 40-seat **Luang Say Cruise** (☎020-5509 0718; www.luangsay.com; per person US$362-491, single supplement from US$67; ⏲8am-3pm). Packages include meals, guides, visits en route and a night's accommodation at the lovely Luang Say Lodge in Pak Beng. Departures are three or four times weekly in peak season, with prices varying according to season. There's no service at all in June or when the Mekong is too low.

Another more affordable option is the newer **Shompoo Cruise** (☎020-5930 5555; www.shompoocruise.com; per person from US$110). This is a tastefully upgraded boat which heads downstream Monday, Wednesday and Friday and upstream on Tuesday, Thursday and Sunday. It includes two lunches and a dinner in Pak Beng, but no accommodation, leaving travellers free to select their own place to stay.

With some patience a small group could charter their own slowboat, starting from around US$750 (highly negotiable).

Speedboats & Longboats

The **speedboat landing** (☎084-211457; Rte 3, 200m beyond Km 202) is directly beneath Wat Thadsuvanna Phakham, 3km south of town. Six-passenger speedboats (*héua wái*) zip thrillingly but dangerously and with great physical discomfort to Pak Beng (160,000/960,000K per person/boat, three hours) and Luang Prabang (360,000/2,040,000K, seven hours including lunch stop) typically departing around 8am. For speedboats to Xieng Kok it's cheaper to start from Muang Mom.

For the two-day longboat trip to Luang Namtha (or to Na Lae in the dry season), charters cost around 6000B/US$200 if organised by agencies, about 1,300,000K when discussed directly with a boatman (something that's tough without spoken Lao). It's sometimes possible to find a longboat bound for Ban Khon Kham leaving after dawn from the speedboat landing, in which case boatmen charge just 150,000K per person – from Ban Khon Kham you'll need to organise onward boats to Na Lae.

BUS & SŎRNGTĂAOU

Note that Huay Xai–bound buses are usually marked 'Borkeo'. The bus station is 5km east of town. Buses to Luang Prabang (120,000K, 14 to 17 hours) via Luang Namtha and Udomxai depart at 9am, 11.30am, 1pm and 5pm. The 11.30am continues to Vientiane (230,000K, 25 hours). The 5pm Luang Prabang bus is a VIP service (135,000K) that includes blankets and seats that recline a little but certainly aren't ideal for sleeping. For Udomxai (85,000K, nine hours) there's also an 8.30am service. For Luang Namtha (60,000K, four hours) an additional bus departs at 9am.

Travel-agency minibuses to Luang Namtha leave from central Huay Xai at around 9am (100,000K) but still arrive at Namtha's inconveniently out-of-town bus station.

Sŏrngtăaou to Tonpheung (35,000K) leave when full from beside the main market, very occasionally continuing to Muang Mom.

ℹ Getting Around

Wangview Tour (☎084-211 055; www.wangviewtour.net; ⏲8am-noon & 1.30-5pm) rents small, relatively new motorcycles (150/250B per half/full day). Bicycles (30,000K per day) and older motorbikes are available from the Thaveesinh Hotel (p115).

Tuk-tuks line up on the main road just 50m beyond Lao immigration, charging 20,000K per person to the speedboat or slowboat landings and 30,000K to the airport or bus station. The road here is one way so don't panic if they seem to head off in the 'wrong' direction.

Around Huay Xai

Souvannakhomkham

In a wide bend of the Mekong are the scattered ruins of Souvannakhomkham, an ancient city site re-founded in the 1560s by Lan Xang king Sai Setthathirat. Today all you'll see are a few brick-piles that were once stupas plus a couple of crumbling Buddha statues all dotted widely about an expanse of almost-flat maize fields. The greatest concentration of sites lies 900m off the lane between Ban Don That and Ban Hanjin. Get there by heading 8km southwest from Tonpheung, turning right when you spot the '900' on an otherwise all-Lao script sign. Fork left just before arriving at the 7.2m-high seated **brick Buddha**, a very eroded figure that's the site's best-known icon. The setting amid towering flame trees is quietly magical. And distantly visible across the Mekong on the Thai side shimmers a larger golden Buddha. Sadly, Souvannakhomkham's access roads are infuriatingly rutted, dusty when dry and appalling muddy when wet.

Golden Triangle ສາມຫຼ່ຽມຄຳ

Around 5km north of Tonpheung, small Rte 3 abruptly undergoes an astonishing transformation. Suddenly you're gliding along a two-coloured paved avenue, lined with palm trees and immaculately swept by teams of cleaners. Golden domes and pseudo-classical charioteers rear beside you. No, you haven't ingested a happy pizza. This is the Golden Triangle's very own Laos Vegas, a casino and entertainment project still a work in progress, but planned to eventually cover almost 100 sq km. After 2.5km this surreal strip turns left and dead-ends after 600m at the Mekong beside another Disneyesque fantasy dome and a mini Big Ben. The huge casino here is open to all, but most of the games are aimed at Chinese or Thai gamblers and may not be familiar. Electronic roulette tables are the most accessible of the games on offer.

This area of riverfront is part of the famous Golden Triangle, where Thailand and Laos face off, with Myanmar sticking a long-nosed sand bank between the two. Boat cruises potter past from the Thai side. On the Lao bank speedboats await but foreigners can't cross the border without prearranged authorisation.

Muang Mom ເມືອງມອມ

Rte 3's fairytale avenue turns back into a bumpy pumpkin before Ban Siboun (Km 58), a conspicuously wealthy village with a colourful new wat. The road ends at Muang Mom (Km 68), which is of interest mainly for those wishing to take a speedboat (900/3500K per person/boat) up the Mekong to Xieng Kok. There's no certain schedule and the route is impossible when river levels are low, typically January to May. Muang Mom's inconspicuous speedboat jetty is tucked behind the main wat.

Pak Beng ປາກແບ່ງ

☎084 / POP 20,000

This winding, one-street strip town is perched on the vertiginous slopes of the riverbank and to call it listless is going overboard, as barely a chicken stirs. The numerous pretty river views are particularly striking when dry-season water levels drop to reveal jagged waterside rocks. However, the town makes little of its tourist potential and most travellers simply stop one night here when en route to Huay Xai or Luang Prabang by slowboat, or take a break here for lunch on Huay Xai–Luang Prabang speedboats.

Sights & Activities

The tourist office can suggest a typical selection of local caves and waterfalls in the district and there are villages to explore if you can find a motorbike for rent – try asking at your guesthouse (individuals around the market ask a steep 40,000K per hour).

Even if you don't plan to visit the Elephant Camp, a pleasant excursion is to cross the river (motor canoe 5000K) then walk for about ten minutes diagonally right away from the river to a tiny, authentic Hmong hamlet.

Wat Sin Jong Jaeng BUDDHIST TEMPLE

(ວັດສິນຈົງແຈ້ງ) Overlooking the Mekong, archaic little Wat Sin Jong Jaeng dates back to the early colonial period. Although its eaves have been entirely repainted, an old, very faded mural remains on the *sĭm*'s eastern exterior. Look carefully and you'll spot a moustachioed figure with hat, umbrella and big nose, presumably representing an early European visitor.

Mekong Elephant Camp ELEPHANT CAMP

(☎071-254130) Across the river is the Mekong Elephant Camp, operated in conjunction with the Pak Beng Lodge. This camp offers rides on former working elephants and bath-time fun. There are several visits available ranging from a half day to a full day and prices run from US$40 to US$82, several including dinner at the lodge.

Sleeping

Prices are high by rural Lao standards. Pushy and not entirely honest touts meet

Pak Beng

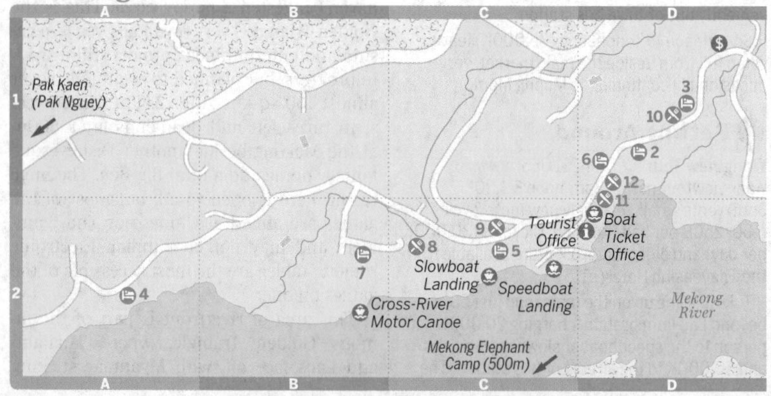

boats, offering cheap digs from around 150B, generally tiny rooms with hard mattresses and shared facilities. 300B will secure a decent room with hot water. Prices quoted here are low season and will pretty much double during the November to March high season. With almost 20 relatively similar options within five minutes' walk it's worth shopping around. Generally prices seem to drop the further up the hill the guesthouse is located.

Donevilasak Guesthouse GUESTHOUSE $
(084-212315; old building s/d/tr 30,000/40,000/50,000K, new building s/d 70,000/80,000K;) The last guesthouse on the strip has several sprawling buildings. One is a dowdy old timber house with very basic box rooms sharing a bathroom (hot water). The others are generously proportioned and have private bathrooms with hot water.

Villa Santisouk GUESTHOUSE $
(020-5578 1797; r in low season 100-400B;) This uber-friendly place is a welcoming place to stay. The new building includes rooms with stylishly presented towels on comfy new beds and sash curtains. Rooms in the old building are contrastingly basic with hard beds and hardboard ceilings. A simple terrace restaurant allows guests to contemplate the Mekong.

Dockhoun Guesthouse GUESTHOUSE $
(084-212540; dockhoun@hotmail.com; r from 300B;) Located at the top of the strip, the Dockhoun has inviting rooms with fresh linen and hot-water showers. There is also an attractive balcony cafe with homemade cakes – perfect to take in the Mekong views.

Monsavan Guesthouse GUESTHOUSE $
(084-212619; r from 100,000K;) This big guesthouse on the main strip has an alabaster front and polished wood doors, but the rooms inside are a simpler affair with bamboo walls and shared bathrooms. It's clean and tidy with a good location, plus they operate a river-view cafe just across the street with free wi-fi.

★**Mekong Riverside Lodge** BOUTIQUE HOTEL $$
(020-5517 1068; www.mekongriversidelodge.com; r from US$40;) This is a great option for those on a midrange budget who can't quite stretch to the full Luang Say experience. The bungalows are very similar in style with highly polished floors, stylish bathrooms and a terrace with river views. Some rooms with an adjoining door can be combined for families. Breakfast is included opposite at Khopchaideu.

Luang Say Lodge LODGE $$
(084-212296; www.luangsay.com; r from 700,000K) This impressive lodge is principally for the use of passengers cruising between Huay Xai and Luang Prabang aboard the Luang Say Cruise. Built in tasteful traditional Lao style of hardwoods and rattan, the lodge has stylish bungalows overlooking a dramatic stretch of river, all with a spacious layout, fans and private hot-water showers. A terrace restaurant overlooks the Mekong.

Pak Beng Lodge BOUTIQUE HOTEL $$$
(084-212304; www.pakbenglodge.com; r US$84-184;) Pak Beng Lodge has elegantly

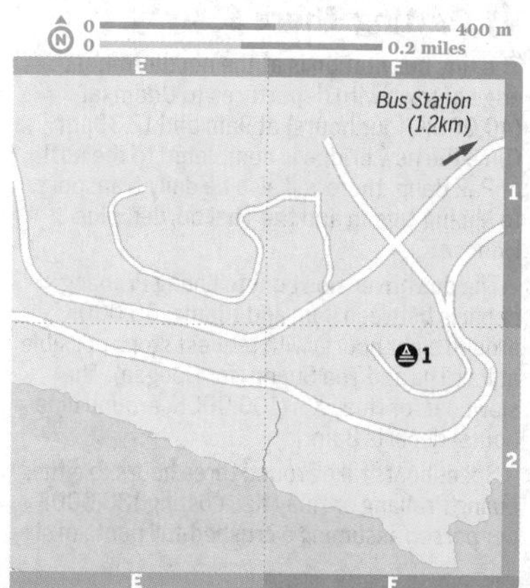

Pak Beng

Sights
1 Wat Sin Jong Jaeng F2

Sleeping
2 Dockhoun Guesthouse D1
3 Donevilasak Guesthouse D1
4 Luang Say Lodge A2
5 Mekong Riverside Lodge C2
6 Monsavan Guesthouse D1
7 Pak Beng Lodge B2

Eating
8 Bounmee Guesthouse C2
Hashan .... (see 12)
9 Khopchaideu C2
10 Ounhoan D1
11 Sarika D2
12 Sivilai D1

LAND OF A MILLION ELEPHANTS

Laos was originally known as Lan Xang, the land of a million elephants, yet curiously no recent statistics accurately record how many remain. Especially in Sainyabuli Province, working elephants have long been a mainstay of the logging industry, allowing tree trunks to be dragged out selectively without the clear-felling required for tractor access. Elephants are trained and worked by a mahout (handler) whose relationship with the animal is akin to a marriage and can last a lifetime. Elephants are generally owned by a consortium of villagers who share profits, costs and risks. To ensure a profit, owners need their animals to keep working but as a result, few working elephants have the energy for romance nor the time for a two-year maternity leave. With Lao elephants dying 10 times more often than they're born, the domestic elephant is likely to become extinct within 50 years at 2010 rates, according to **ElefantAsia** (www.elefantasia.org), which is behind the highly impressive Elephant Conservation Center (p126) outside town. It also helped to found the popular **Elephant Festival** (http://festival.elefantasia.org; mid-Feb) FREE, a vast two-day jamboree featuring music, theatre and many a beer tent as well as elephant parades and skills demonstrations. In past years the venue has rotated annually between Pak Lai and Ban Viengkeo (near Hongsa), but it has finally settled here in Sainyabuli. Meanwhile, numerous retired or 'unemployed' elephants have found alternative employment in tourism, notably around Luang Prabang and Pak Beng. ElefantAsia's website offers various 'read before you ride' tips to help tourists choose well-managed elephant camps, as not all are equal.

presented rooms with pretty interiors, Western-style bathrooms and minibars, all offering panoramic views. The bar-restaurant is a stylish spot for a sundown drink or a meal and traditional Lao massage is also available. Part of the profit goes towards funding a healthcare initiative called Les Medicins du Pakbeng.

Eating & Drinking

There's a string of eateries almost as long as the guesthouse strip. Most places have long menus and all charge approximately the same prices (mains 15,000K to 35,000K) for standard Lao, Thai and Western fare. By day, pick one with a good Mekong view like the **Bounmee Guesthouse**, **Sarika** or **Sivilai**. The latter offers a 6pm happy hour. By night, colourful lanterns make **Ounhoan** a favourite. Indian restaurant **Hashan** also has appealing lighting and decor with good river views. **Khopchaideu** is one of the best all-rounders despite the lack of a riverview. Most eateries open around 7am and make sandwiches to sell as takeaway boat lunches. Most kitchens stop cooking around 9pm and by 10pm it might be a struggle just to find a beer.

The Luang Say Lodge's (p121) impressive bar-restaurant is ideal for enjoying Mekong views with a sundowner such as a gin and tonic or a glass of wine. Ethnic dance shows are regularly held here for guests on the Luang Say Cruise.

Information

Guesthouses can change money at unimpressive rates. Thai baht are also widely used here. Most guesthouses now offer free wi-fi as part of the package.

Lao Development Bank Has an ATM in town near the redeveloped market. It has been known to run out of money at busy times.

Tourist Office (www.oudomxay.info; 7am-noon & 2-9pm) Can arrange guides and has maps of the town.

Getting There & Away

The tiny bus station is at the northernmost edge of town with departures to Udomxai (40,000K, four hours) at 9am and 12.30pm. Once the new bridge is completed to the north of Pak Beng, there will also be daily transport to Muang Ngeun and the Thai border, plus Hongsa.

The downriver slowboat to Luang Prabang departs between 9am and 10am (100,000K, around eight hours) with request stops possible at Pak Tha and Tha Suang (for Hongsa). The slowboat for Huay Xai (100,000K, around nine hours) departs 8am.

Speedboats take around three hours to either Luang Prabang or Huay Xai, costing 180,000K per person assuming a crushed-full quota of six passengers (dangerous and highly uncomfortable, but cheaper than a 1.3 million kip charter). Arriving by speedboat, local boys will generally offer to carry your bags for about 5000K (after some bargaining). If your bags are unwieldy this can prove money well spent, as when river levels are low you'll need to cross two planks and climb a steep sandbank to reach the road into town.

Tha Suang

POP 40

This scattering of homes is simply the Mekong jetty for Hongsa. Slowboats are met by Hongsa-bound *sŏrngtăaou* (25,000K, 70 minutes). However, this may all change with the new Mekong bridge under construction to the north of Pakbeng, as regular buses will then ply the route from Pak Beng to Muang Ngeun and Hongsa. Tha Suang may fall off the map once this happens.

Hongsa ຫົງສາ

☎074 / POP 10,000

Hongsa is famous for its elephants and many visitors pass through to ride a working elephant, although the new Elephant Conservation Center (p126) near Sainyabuli is a more complete experience. Hongsa is the site of a massive new power station constructed by Thai investors and unfortunately this is a major blight on the horizon. Still, it has been good for employment in the town and there is a mini-boom going on in Hongsa.

Hongsa is a logical break between Luang Prabang and Nan (Thailand, via Muang Ngeun). The centre is a grid of newer constructions but the town's stream-ribboned edges (away from the power station) are backed by beautiful layered rice fields. Both **BCEL** and **Lao Development Bank** have ATMs and can exchange baht, US dollars and euros.

Sights

Wat Simungkhun BUDDHIST TEMPLE

(ວັດສີມຸງຄຸນ, Wat Nya) The most characterful of Hongsa's several monasteries is Wat Simungkhun. Its initiation pavilion (*hang song pa*) is fashioned in attractive naive style while the archaic, muralled *sĭm* sits on an oddly raised stone platform that allegedly covers a large hole 'leading to the end of the world'. It's 1km west of the centre towards Muang Ngeun then 100m north after the first river bridge.

Ban Viengkeo VILLAGE

(ບ້ານວຽງແກ້ວ) Given a day's notice, Jumbo Guesthouse can organise 5km elephant rides across a wide valley of rice paddies and watermelon fields to Ban Viengkeo. Many of Viengkeo's log-and-timber Tai Lü homes

GETTING TO THAILAND: HONGSA TO PHRAE

Getting to the Border

The **Muang Ngeun (Laos)/Huay Kon (Thailand) border crossing** (⏰8am-5pm) is around 2.5km west of Muang Ngeun junction. Several *sŏrngtăaou* make the run from Hongsa (40,000K, 1½ hours) to Muang Ngeun. Once the new bridge north of Pakbeng is open, there will also be a bus service.

Coming back from Thailand, there's no restaurant nor any waiting transport on the Lao side but if you can persuade the immigration officer to call for you, the afternoon *sŏrngtăaou* to Hongsa should be prepared to collect you for a small fee.

At the Border

Lao visas are available on arrival at this border, payable in US dollars or Thai baht, albeit at a unfavourable exchange rate. Most nationalities crossing into Thailand do not require a visa.

Moving On

From the Thai side, if you don't want to walk your bags across the 1km of no-man's-land you can pay 100B for a motorbike with luggage-carrying sidecar. The Thai border post, Huay Kon, is not quite a village but does have simple noodle shops. The only public transport is a luxurious minibus (☎083-024 3675) to Phrae (160B, five hours) via Nan (100B, three hours) departing from the border post at 11.45am. Northbound it leaves the bus stations in Phrae at 6am, and Nan at 8am.

have weavers' looms beneath the high stilted floors and the village is the area's major centre for working elephants.

Sleeping & Eating

A block west of Jumbo Guesthouse, **Nong Bua Daeng (Lotus) Café** (Lotus Café; mains 15,000-35,000K; ⏲8am-9pm) and **Saylomyen Restaurant** (mains 15,000-35,000K) are attractive thatched pavilions perched between fishponds but neither have written menus and there's minimal spoken English.

Jumbo Guesthouse GUESTHOUSE $
(☎020-5685 6488; www.lotuselephant.com; r 100,000-120,000K; @) Brazil-born German anthropologist Monica invites travellers into a family-style home where bathrooms are shared but the six rooms are tidy and inviting. A community feeling is fostered by group dinners but do check prices for meals, breakfast and imported coffee. It's the best place in town for comprehensive local information and elephant rides are available, including a day with a working elephant in Ban Viengkeo and two-day or even four-day immersions in the countryside.

Getting There & Away

The transport **ticket office** (☎020-5558 711) beside the market opens around 7.30am with vehicles departing for Sainyabuli (70,000K, three hours) and Muang Ngeun (40,000K, 1¼ hours) as soon as a decent quota of guests has piled aboard (usually before 9am).

Muang Ngeun ເມືອງເງິນ

This very quiet border 'town' is in fact a diffuse collection of predominantly Tai Lü villages interspersed by patches of rice paddy. Around 2.5km east of the border post, head 1km north of the Hongsa–Nan road to find the sparse centre around a small, new market where traders can organise baht–kip exchange.

Phouxay Guesthouse (☎020-2214 2826; r 60,000K) is a row of reasonable bungalows sat on a slight rise with commanding views, 800m west of the main junction towards Thailand.

From a tiny **passenger car station** (☎020-244 4130, 020-245 0145) beside the market, *sŏrngtăaou* run to Hongsa (40,000K, 1½ hours), departing between 2pm and 4pm. Once the new bridge north of Pakbeng is open, there will also be daily transport heading there.

Sainyabuli (Sayaboury) ໄຊຍະບູລີ

☎074 / POP 20,000

One of Laos' 'elephant capitals', Sainyabuli (variously spelt Xaignabouri, Xayaboury, Sayabouli and Sayabouri) is a prosperous town backed to the east by an attractive range of high forested ridges. Making a self-conscious attempt to look urban, central Sainyabuli consists of overspaced avenues and showy new administrative buildings that are surprising for their scale but hardly an attraction. Starting around the tourist office and continuing south you'll find an increasing proportion of attractive wooden or part-timber structures, some with languid settings among arching palm trees. Overall it's a friendly and entirely untouristed place, but numbers are unlikely to increase dramatically with new roads, as most visitors will be heading directly to the Elephant Conservation Center (p126).

Sights

Many spots along the riverside are rendered especially idyllic thanks to the dramatic ridge of **Pak Kimin** reflected in the waters of the Nam Heung.

Wat Sibounheuang BUDDHIST TEMPLE
(ວັດສີບູນເຮືອງ) Wat Sibounheuang, the town's most evocative monastery, sports a lopsided gilded stupa and reclining Buddha in a delightful garden setting where the bare-brick ruins of the tiny original *sĭm* are reckoned to be from the early 14th century. The 'new' *sĭm* is covered in murals, including anti-adultery scenes in a style reminiscent of Matisse. This building covers a mysterious 'hole' traditionally associated with sinkhone spirit-ghosts who are placated in the **Phaveth Festival** (the 13th to the 15th day of the third Lao month) leading up to the February full moon.

Nam Tien LAKE
(ນ້ຳຕຽນ) To fully appreciate the charm of Sainyabuli's setting, drive 9km southwest to the Nam Tien reservoir-lake, access point for the Elephant Conservation Center (p126). A restaurant here is perched above the dam, offering views across emerald rice paddies

Sainyabuli (Sayaboury)

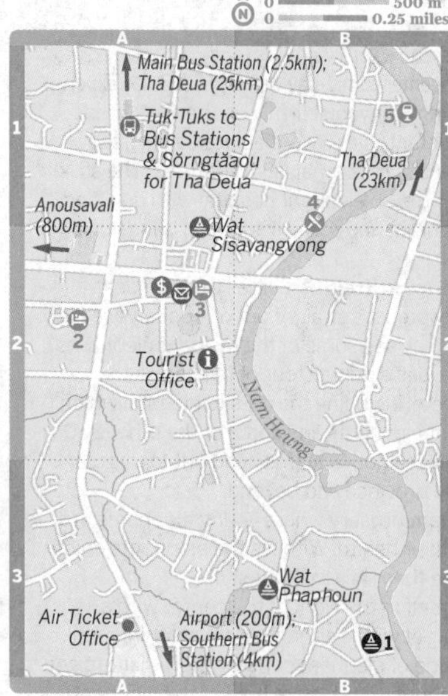

and wooded slopes towards a western horizon where Pak Kimin and Pak Xang ridges overlap.

The 3km asphalt spur road to Nam Tien branches west off the Pak Lai road around 500m before the south bus station, just before a bridge (6.5km from central Sainyabuli).

Sleeping

Alooncheer Hotel GUESTHOUSE $
(074-213136; r with fan 50,000-70,000K, r with air-con 80,000-120,000K;) This sizeable Hmong-owned complex is quiet yet central. Its polished wood-panelled lobby is decorated with traditional instruments and most rooms have high ceilings, twee lamps and minibars. Good value, but beware that the very cheapest rooms are a significant step down in quality.

Sayananh Hotel HOTEL $
(074-211116; r without/with TV 100,000/120,000K, ste 200,000K;) Conspicuous and central, this three-storey hotel has a grand-looking, wood-filled entrance that belies the fairly standard rooms off corridors that could have featured in *The Shining*. The water is piping hot at least.

Sainyabuli (Sayaboury)

Sights
1 Wat Sibounheuang B3

Sleeping
2 Alooncheer Hotel A2
3 Sayananh Hotel A2

Eating
4 Sainamhoung Restaurant B1

Drinking & Nightlife
5 Beer Gardens B1

Eating & Drinking

A **night market** (6-10pm) near the central roundabout has food stalls for noodle soup, Lao grills, fresh fruits and *khànŏm* (traditional sweets).

Sainamhoung Restaurant LAOTIAN $
(074-211171; mains 25,000-70,000K; 7am-10pm) Contemplate the bamboo-banked river and the looming Pak Kimin massif as you dine on tasty Lao food. Dishes include delectable steamed fish, grilled meats and varied exotica such as fried crickets, fried wasps and bamboo worms.

Nam Tiene Restaurant LAOTIAN $
(mains 25,000-60,000K, fish by weight; 6.30am-11pm) Well-made, professionally presented food along with lovely reservoir views amply reward the excursion out to the Nam Tien dam. Locals descend here at weekends and rent kooky avian-inspired pedalos.

Beer Gardens BEER GARDEN
There is some life beyond the dodgy and dark nightclubs in Sainyabuli and it comes in the form of a pair of lively beer gardens on the banks of the Nam Heung. They draw a young crowd with a thirst for Beerlao.

Information

BCEL (8.30am-3.30pm Mon-Fri) Changes money and has an ATM.

Post Office (8-11am & 1-5pm Mon-Fri)

Tourist Office (030-518 0095; Sayaboury_ptd@tourismlaos.org; 8.30-11am & 2-4pm Mon-Fri) Good free city maps, English-speaking staff and rental of bikes and motorcycles.

Getting There & Away

The airport is beside the main Pak Lai road, around 3km south of the town centre.

DON'T MISS

ELEPHANT CONSERVATION CENTER

Set on the shores of the stunning Nam Tien lake, the **Elephant Conservation Center** (ECC; ☎020-2302 5210; www.elephantconservationcenter.com; 1-day visit US$60, 3-day experience US$175, 6-day ecoexperience US$399) is putting Sainyabuli firmly on the visitor map. Established in partnership with elephant NGO ElefantAsia (www.elefantasia.org), the centre offers visitors a unique insight into the lives of these majestic creatures. The strikingly set complex includes a mahout training centre, an elephant hospital with qualified international vets, an information centre, a restaurant and some traditional bungalows and dormitory rooms for overnight guests.

Arriving at the centre is a memorable experience in itself, as a small wooden boat glides through the green weeds that carpet the water. It's straight out of *Apocalypse Now* and as the boat approaches the centre, visitors may see some of the resident elephants enjoying their morning bath. A one-day visit includes a guided tour of the centre to learn more about the conservation work done here, including the on-site hospital which does work to safeguard the health of the resident elephants and some of the other 360 registered elephants working in Sainyabuli Province. Mobile teams head out for regular check-ups on the health of elephants around the province and beyond.

On another part of the lakeshore is the elephant nursery where young elephants are reared safely isolated from possible threats to their health. Witness the elephants enjoying a hearty breakfast and then learn how to ride them in a mahout style.

If time allows, it's rewarding to immerse yourself in the work of the centre with a three-day stay. This includes the chance to interact with elephants from morning until evening. As well as learning about the serious side of elephant conservation, visitors get to have some real fun learning the art of the mahout. Classes are held at the elephant yard and Laotian guides teach visitors simple commands such as 'stop' and 'go', 'left' and 'right'. Getting the pronunciation right can be tricky, but it is well worth mastering 'haow' (stop) when commandeering one of nature's living, breathing tractors. Feeding, grooming and washing the elephants are all part of this longer experience. It also includes the opportunity to follow the elephants to their night resting place.

For those with a jumbo-sized interest in elephants, it is possible to volunteer for six days or more, offering an even greater insight into the lives of the elephants and their mahouts, as well as the work of the centre. Those on the longer volunteer stay live in the dormitory accommodation and take meals with the project staff, offering a fascinating insight into the Lao lifestyle.

Accommodation at the center is in basic thatched bungalows that include some electricity after dark to power LED lights for reading. They include a mosquito net and a small verandah to relax on during the heat of the day. Bathroom facilities are shared but scrupulously clean. Eventually, smarter bungalows are planned in a second location as the centre reaches out to tour operators based out of Vientiane and Luang Prabang.

All meals and transportation from and to Sainyabuli are included in all packages. The ECC has also teamed up with Sakura Tour to run minibuses from Luang Prabang to Sainyabuli. Meals are enjoyed at the welcoming restaurant that offers a panoramic view of the lake and centre. The food is tasty Laotian cuisine and a range of snacks and drinks are available on demand. However, this is a long way from Vientiane, so should you be craving something special or have special dietary requirements, then plan ahead.

The Elephant Conservation Center is not your typical tourist elephant camp. It is run by people with a passion for the animals and the proceeds generated from your visit go towards funding the centre and other elephant conservation projects around the country.

Lao Air (☎074-213152; www.laocapricornair.net; ⏲8am-noon & 2-4pm Mon-Fri) flies from/to Vientiane on Monday, Wednesday and Friday at 9.30am/10.30am. Air tickets (715,000K) are sold from the tiny ticket office 800m further north.

From the **main bus station** 2.5km north of the town centre, an 11am *sŏrngtăaou* runs to Hongsa (70,000K, three hours), continuing some days to Muang Ngeun (90,000K).

Vientiane is served via Luang Prabang and Pak Lai, both costing 110,000K. Services via Luang

Prabang depart at 1pm and 4pm. The service via Pak Lai departs at 9.30am and currently in the dry season only. Given the appallingly dusty road, this bus is a much better way to reach Pak Lai (80,000K, four hours) than taking a *sŏrngtăaou*, which depart around 9am and noon from the **southern bus station**, a tiny stand 4km southwest of the airport.

The new Tha Deua bridge over the Mekong River is now open and this slashes journey times to Luang Prabang to just two to three hours by minibus or private vehicle. Slower buses (60,000K, three hours) depart at 9am and 2pm. **Sakura Tour** (☎074-212112) has teamed up with the Elephant Conservation Center (p126) to run a daily shuttle bus between Sainyabuli and Luang Prabang (90,000K, 2½ hours), departing at 8.30am in both directions. Contact Sakura or the Elephant Conservation Center for more details on this new service.

Tuk-tuks to the bus stations (main/south 10,000/15,000K per person) depart from the main market.

Pak Lai ປາກລາຍ

☎074 / POP 12,000

This bustling Mekong river port is an almost unavoidable stop on the off-beat route between Sainyabuli and Loei in Thailand. The town follows a 5km curl of Rte 4 paralleled a block further east by a shorter riverside road that's sparsely dotted with historic structures in both Lao and French-colonial styles. Exploring north to south, start at **Wat Sisavang** (Wat Sisavangvong), which sports some older monks' quarters as well as a gaudily ornate new bell tower and gateway. Within the next 500m you'll pass the main guesthouses, the river port and **BCEL** (ATM and exchange available) before crossing a little old wooden bridge into an attractive village-like area of local homes beyond a small market.

Sleeping & Eating

Conveniently central, **Jenny Guesthouse** (☎020-2236 5971; r with fan/air-con 60,000/100,000K; ❄) has hot showers and Mekong views from some rooms. The odd cobweb is forgivable. Newer and just marginally fresher is the all air-con **Sengchaleurn Guesthouse** (☎020-2206 8888; r 120,000K; ❄) a block north. Next door within an older wooden building, the **Kemkhong Restaurant** (mains 20,000-40,000K; ⏲6am-10.30pm) is good for a quiet beer with river views. **Saykhong** (mains 20,000-40,000K) beside Jenny Guesthouse is livelier and also overlooks the river.

Getting There & Away

Bring a facemask and disposable clothes if you attempt the Pak Lai–Sainyabuli journey by *sŏrngtăaou* (80,000K, four hours). These depart in both directions between 7.30am and 9.30am and once again around noon. Mud-crusted victims arrive at Pak Lai's little Sainyabuli bus station, 3km north of the centre. From there, tuk-tuks charge 10,000K per person to the guesthouses or 15,000K to the southern bus terminal. This terminal has a 9am bus to Vientiane (100,000K, around six hours).

GETTING TO THAILAND: PAK LAI TO LOEI

Getting to the Border

The quiet rural **Kaen Thao (Laos)/Tha Li (Thailand) border crossing** (⏲8am to 6pm) is the home of yet another (small) Friendship Bridge, this time over the Nam Heuang. From Pak Lai, there are *sŏrngtăaou* to the border post at Kaen Thao at around 10am and noon (40,000K, 1¾ hours).

At the Border

Lao visas are available on arrival at this border – one passport-sized photo is required. Most nationalities crossing into Thailand do not require a visa.

Moving On

After walking across the bridge you'll have to take a short *sŏrngtăaou* ride (30B) 8km to Tha Li before transferring to another *sŏrngtăaou* (40B) the remaining 46km to Loei, from where there are regular connections to Bangkok and elsewhere.

1

BARTOSZ HADYNIAK/GETTY IMAGES ©

2

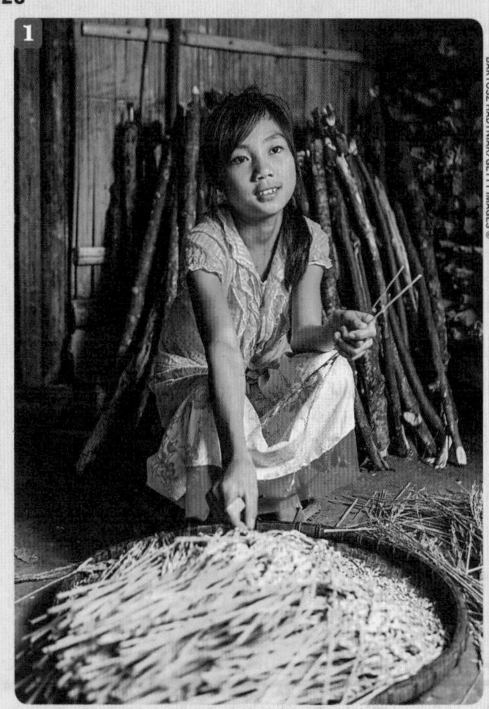

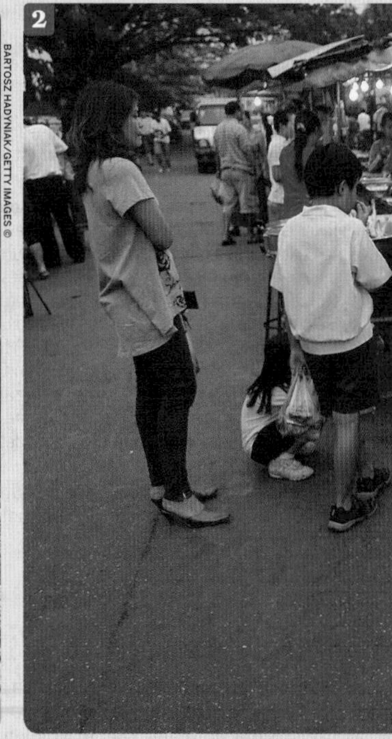

4

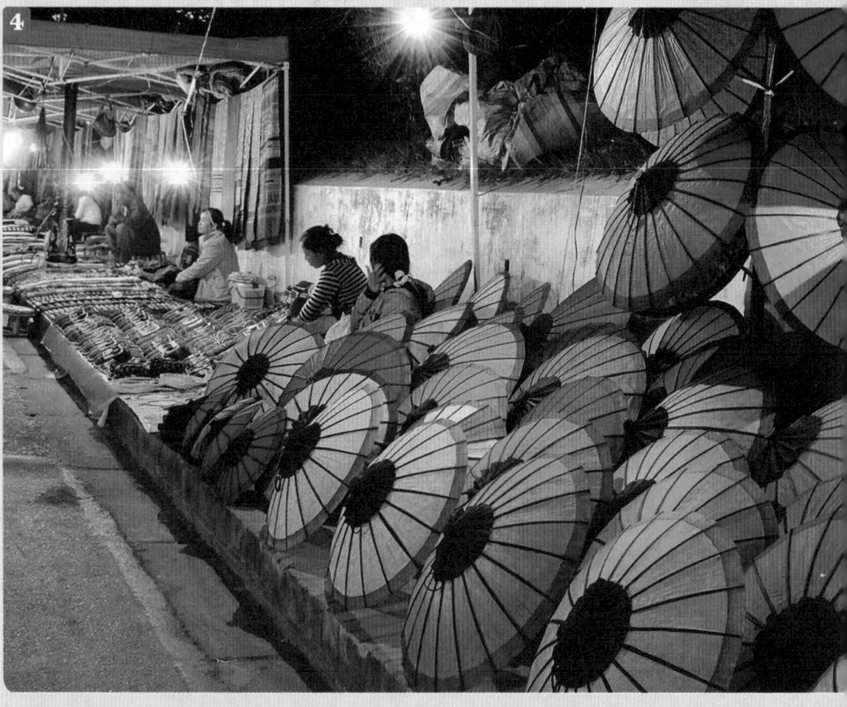

AUSTIN BUSH/GETTY IMAGES ©

GRANT DIXON/GETTY IMAGES ©

3

FLASH PARKER/GETTY IMAGES ©

1. Village life, Luang Namtha (p104)
A young girl harvests rice in a hill-tribe village near Luang Namtha.

2. Night Market, Vientiane (p158)
A vendor prepares Laos street-food dishes at a night market in Vientiane.

3. Street food (p307)
Traditional Lao barbecue of pork, beef and vegetables served on a banana leaf.

4. Night Market (p60), Luang Prabang
Paper umbrellas on display at Luang Prabang's colourful evening handicraft market.

1

2

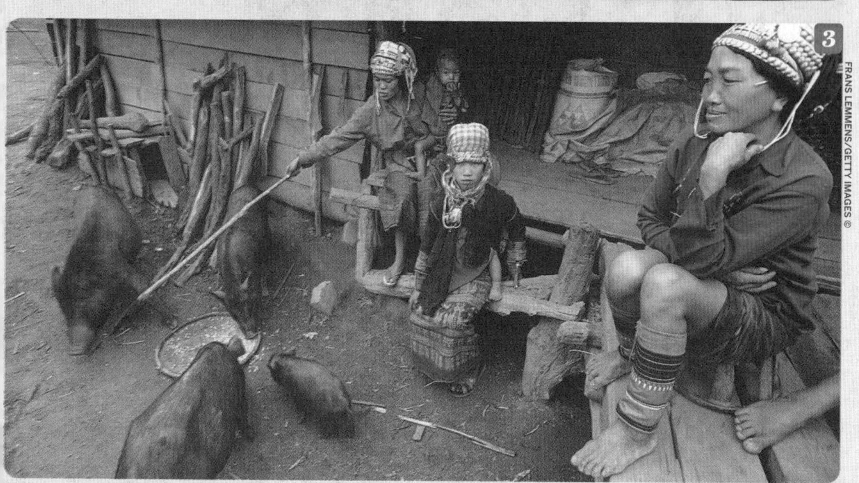

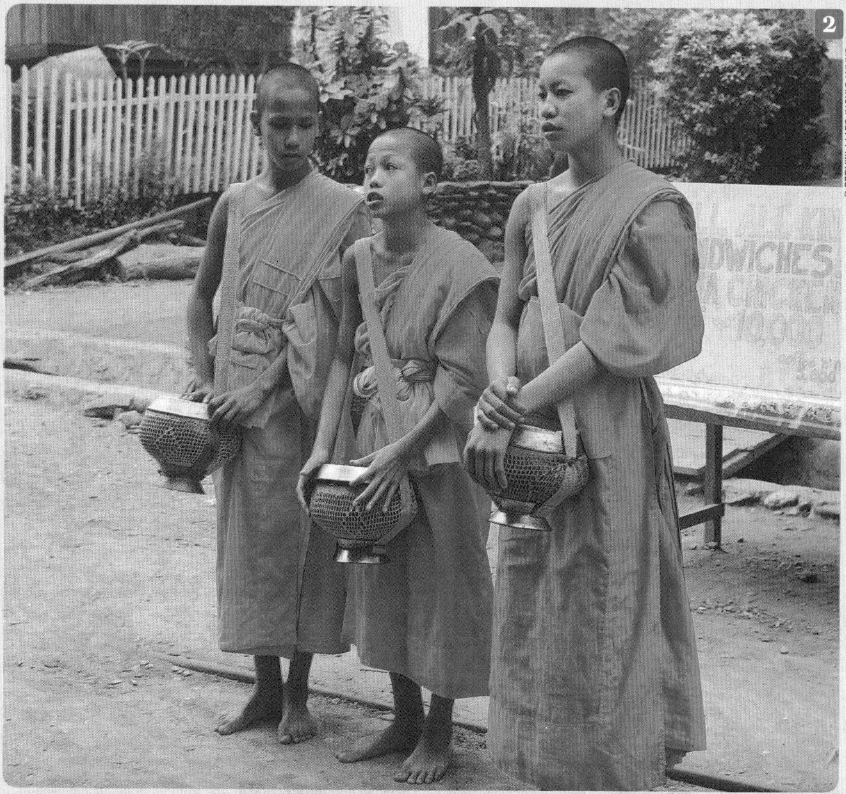

GRANT DIXON/GETTY IMAGES ©

3

FRANS LEMMENS/GETTY IMAGES ©

1. Muang Sing (p109)
A Yao woman embroiders clothes near Muang Sing, Luang Namtha Province, northern Laos.

2. Muang Ngoi Neua (p87)
Monks collecting alms, Muang Ngoi Neua, northern Laos.

3. Luang Namtha (p104)
Akha hill-tribe village, northern Laos.

River Life

The Mekong River is the lifeblood of Laos. It's like an artery cutting through the heart of the country, while other important rivers are the veins, breathing life into the landscape and providing transport links between remote landlocked communities. For many Laotians, the river is not just part of their life, it is their life.

1

GRANT DIXON/GETTY IMAGES ©

2

MATTHEW MICAH WRIGHT/GETTY IMAGES ©

3

ALEXANDERCLAYTON/GETTY IMAGES ©

1. Nam Ou, Muang Ngoi Neua (p87)
A longtail boat 'taxi' carries passengers on the Nam Ou.

2. Mekong River, Vientiane (p134)
Working on the river, near Vientiane.

3. Tha Khaek (p194)
Traditional net fishing on the Mekong River.

4. Don Det (p250) Travellers leap into the Mekong River on the island of Don Det.

4

MATTHEW MICAH WRIGHT/GETTY IMAGES ©

Vientiane & Around

Includes ➡

Best Places to Eat

- La Signature (p158)
- Le Silapa (p156)
- Lao Kitchen (p156)
- Makphet (p154)

Best Places to Stay

- Mandala Boutique Hotel (p154)
- Hotel Khamvongsa (p150)
- Ansara Hôtel (p154)
- Settha Palace Hotel (p152)

Why Go?

From its sleepy tuk-tuk drivers to its cafe society and affordable spas, this former French trading post is languid to say the least. Eminently walkable, the historic old quarter of Vientiane beguiles with tree-lined boulevards crowded with frangipani and tamarind, glittering temples, wandering Buddhist monks and lunging *naga* (dragon) statues.

For the well-heeled traveller and backpacker, the city acquits itself equally well, be it low-cost digs and street markets, or upscale, jaw-droppingly pretty boutique hotels and French restaurants with reputable Parisian chefs. There are even more cafes and bakeries here than in Luang Prabang, and such a global spectrum of cuisine. It may add another notch to your belt!

From lounging with a book in an old-fashioned bakery to shopping in silk shops, swigging Beerlao and drinking up the fiery sunset over the Mekong, you might find you'll miss this place more than you ever expected.

When to Go

Vientiane

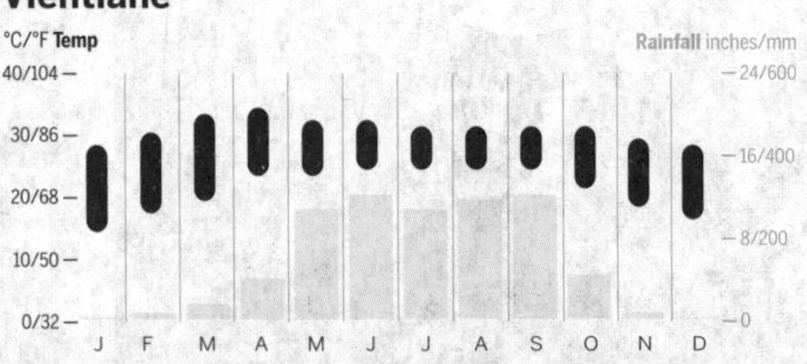

Nov–Feb A great time to visit, with the magical Bun Pha That Luang (Full Moon Festival) in November.

Mar–May Heat and humidity climb, but hotel prices fall; many places have air-conditioning!

Jun–Nov Monsoon brings fresh air and a raft of river festivals like Bun Awk Phansa and Bun Nam.

VIENTIANE

021 / POP 254,500

History

Set on a bend in the Mekong River, Vientiane (ວຽງຈັນ) was first settled around the 9th century AD and formed part of one of the early Lao valley *meuang* (city-states) that were consolidated around the 10th century. The Lao who settled here did so because the surrounding alluvial plains were so fertile, and initially the Vientiane *meuang* prospered and enjoyed a fragile sovereignty.

In the ensuing 10 or so centuries of its history, Vientiane's fortunes have been mixed. At various times it has been a major regional centre; at other times it has been controlled by the Vietnamese, Burmese and Siamese.

The height of Vientiane's success was probably in the years after it became the Lan Xang capital in the mid-16th century. (King Setthathirat moved the capital of the Lan Xang kingdom from the city now known as Luang Prabang.) Several of Vientiane's wats were built following this shift and the city became a major centre of Buddhist learning.

It didn't last. Periodic invasions by the Burmese, Siamese and Chinese, and the eventual division of the Lan Xang kingdom, took their toll on the city.

It wasn't until the Siamese installed Chao Anou (a Lao prince who had been educated in Bangkok) on the throne in 1805 that the city received an overdue makeover. Chao Anou's public works included Wat Si Saket, built between 1818 and 1824.

Unfortunately, Chao Anou's attempts to assert Lao independence over the Siamese resulted in the most violent and destructive episode in Vientiane's history.

In 1828 the Siamese defeated Chao Anou's armies and wasted no time in razing the city and carting off much of the population. Wat Si Saket was the only major building to survive, and the city was abandoned.

In 1867, French explorers arrived but it wasn't until late in the century, after Vientiane had been made capital of the French protectorate, that serious reconstruction began. A simple grid plan was laid out for the city and a sprinkling of colonial-style mansions and administrative buildings emerged. However, Vientiane was always low in the French order of Indochinese priorities, as the modest building program testifies.

In 1928 the 'city' was home to just 9000 inhabitants – many of them Vietnamese administrators brought in by the French – and it wasn't until the end of WWII that Vientiane's population began to grow with any vigour. It was a growth fed primarily by Cold War dollars, with first French and later American advisors arriving in a variety of guises.

VIENTIANE IN...

Two Days

Start with a coffee and croissant at **Le Banneton** bakery before embarking on the **Monument to Mekong cycling tour**. This will take you through most of Vientiane's main sights, including **Wat Si Saket**, **Haw Pha Kaeo** and **Talat Sao**. Top off your day with riverside cocktails at **Spirit House**. On day two consider getting some motorised wheels and leaving the city centre to check out the myriad concrete Buddhas and Hindu deities at **Xieng Khuan**. On the way back stop at **Pha That Luang** for great afternoon photos. Enjoy a fine French meal at **La Signature**.

Four Days

Depending on what time you crawl out of bed on day three, make **PVO**, arguably the home of Vientiane's best baguettes and fruit shakes, your lunch destination. From here it's just a short walk to the **COPE Visitor Centre**, where you could easily spend a couple of hours checking out excellent exhibits and watching the powerful documentaries. After a light Lao dinner at **Khambang Lao Food Restaurant**, head around the corner to the **Herbal Sauna** for a good healthy Lao-style sweat. Rehydrate with draught Beerlao at **Bor Pennyang** before calling it a night. Day four can be spent studying in a Lao cooking course at **Villa Lao**, or shopping at the handicraft and textile shops of Th Nokèokoummane, rummaging for communist wristwatches and glass Buddhas at **Indochina Handicrafts**, or sniffing and waxing lyrical about the handmade soaps and oils at **T'Shop Lai Gallery**.

Vientiane & Around Highlights

1 Explore mercifully flat Vientiane on two wheels, with a **Vientiane By Cycle** (p148) tour

2 Treat yourself to a traditional sauna and massage at **Wat Sok Pa Luang** (p146) or **The Spa** (p146)

3 Enjoy golden-brown croissants at **Le Banneton** (p154) or Gallic cuisine at achingly cool restaurants such as **La Signature** (p157)

4 Tube, climb, kayak, cycle, motorbike or walk through the rivers and stunning karst terrain around **Vang Vieng** (p172)

5 Discover the emerging ecotourism area of Nam Lik basin by staying at the **Nam Lik Eco-Village** (p172) and zipping 40m above the jungle at **Nam Lik Jungle Fly** (p171)

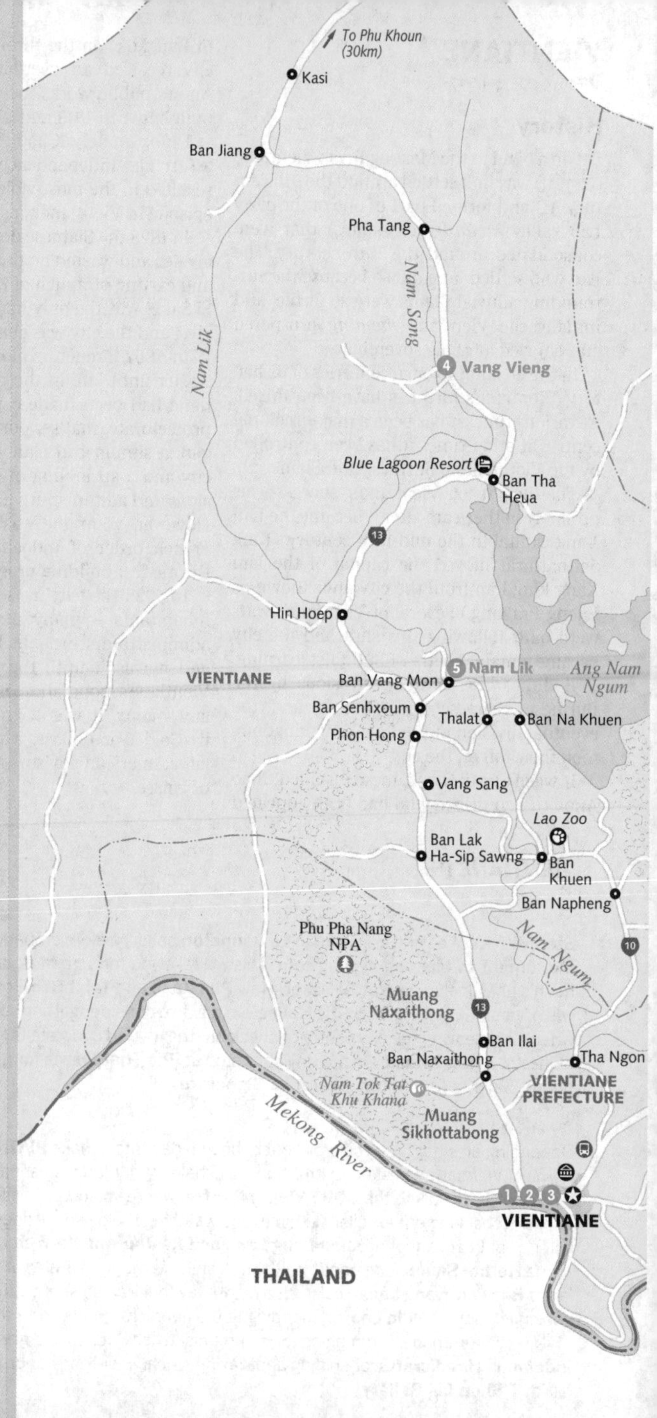

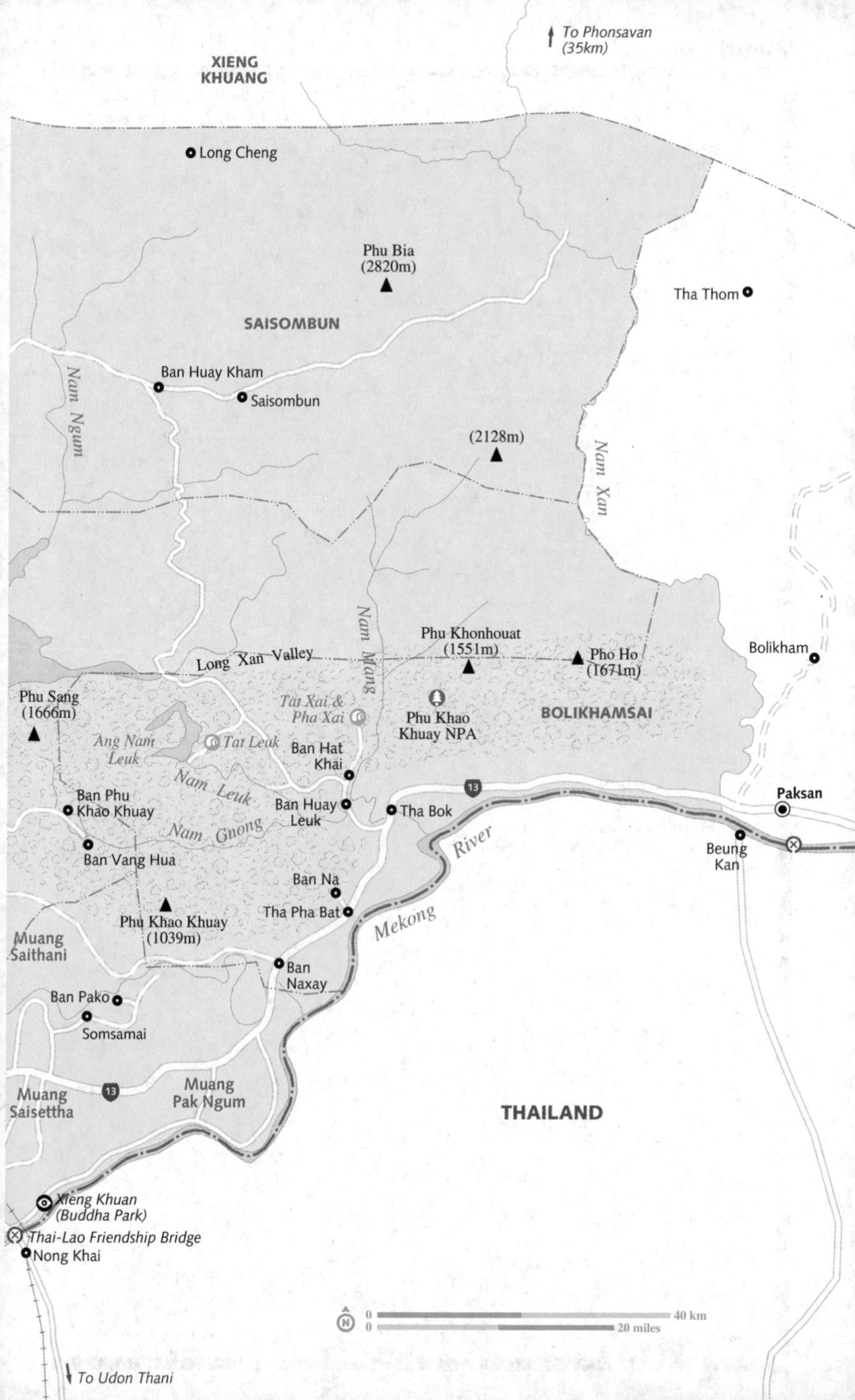

To Phonsavan (35km)
XIENG KHUANG
Long Cheng
Phu Bia (2820m)
Tha Thom
SAISOMBUN
Ban Huay Kham
Saisombun
Nam Ngum
(2128m)
Nam Xan
Nam Mang
Phu Khonhouat (1551m)
Pho Ho (1671m)
Bolikham
Long Xan Valley
Phu Sang (1666m)
Tat Xai & Pha Xai
Phu Khao Khuay NPA
BOLIKHAMSAI
Ang Nam Leuk
Tat Leuk
Ban Hat Khai
Nam Leuk
Paksan
Ban Phu Khao Khuay
Ban Huay Leuk
Tha Bok
Nam Gnong
River
Beung Kan
Ban Vang Hua
Ban Na
Tha Pha Bat
Phu Khao Khuay (1039m)
Mekong
Muang Saithani
Ban Naxay
Ban Pako
Somsamai
Muang Saisettha
Muang Pak Ngum
THAILAND
Xieng Khuan (Buddha Park)
Thai-Lao Friendship Bridge
Nong Khai
0 40 km
0 20 miles
To Udon Thani

Vientiane

A B C D

MUANG SIKHOTTABONG

MUANG CHANTHABULI

Th T2

Th Nong Douang

29

Alliance International Medical Center

Rte 13 North

Wat Tai

Th Luang Prabang

13

17

22

28

23

16

21

Th Phagna Sy

5

15

12

Th Sibouaban

Th Sithane

Mekong River

THAILAND

1 2 3 4 5 6 7

A B C D

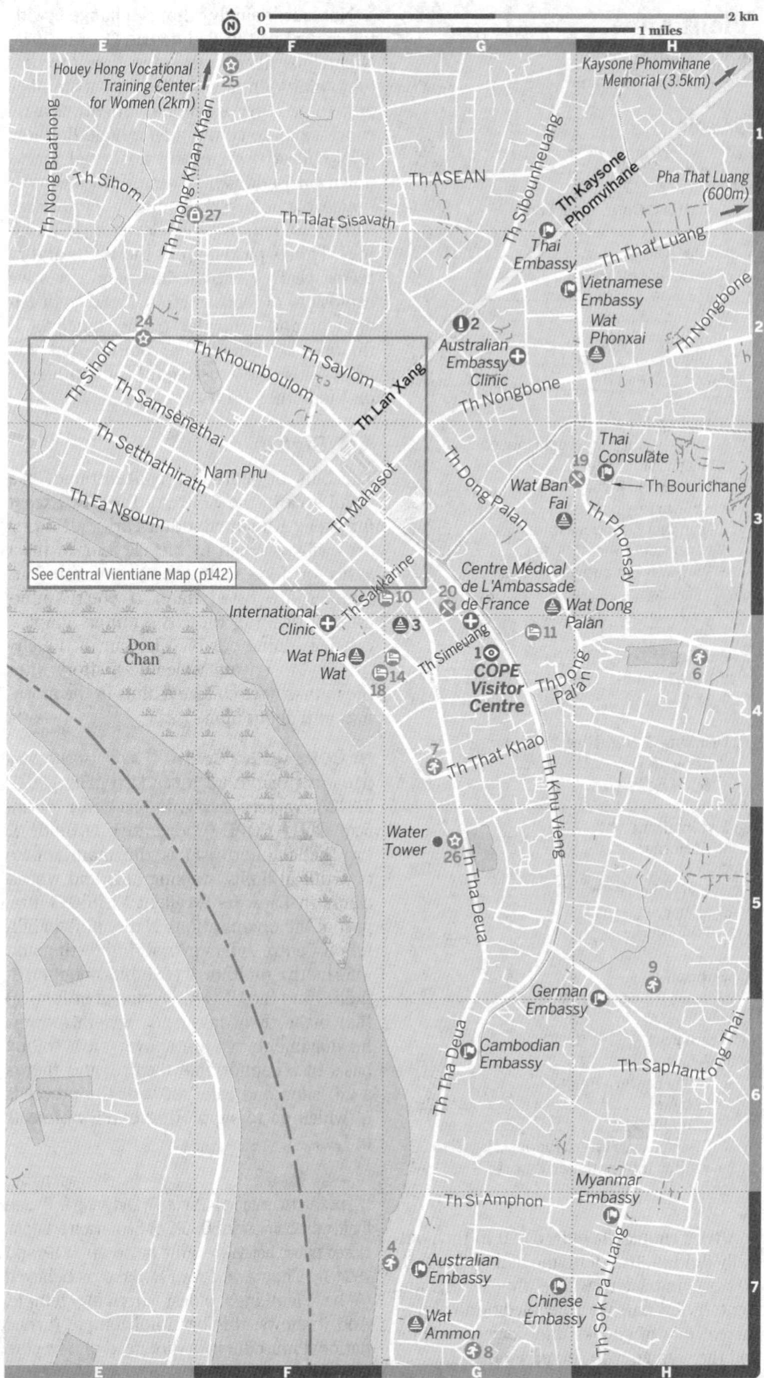
0
2 km
0
1 miles
E
F
G
H
1
2
3
4
5
6
7
Houey Hong Vocational Training Center for Women (2km)
25
Kaysone Phomvihane Memorial (3.5km)
Th Nong Buathong
Th Sihom
Th Thong Khan Khan
Th ASEAN
Th Sibounheuang
Th Kaysone Phomvihane
Pha That Luang (600m)
27
Th Talat Sisavath
Thai Embassy
Th That Luang
Vietnamese Embassy
Wat Phonxai
Th Nongbone
2
24
Australian Embassy Clinic
Th Sihom
Th Khounboulom
Th Saylom
Th Lan Xang
Th Nongbone
Th Samsenethai
Th Setthathirath
Nam Phu
Th Mahasot
Th Dong Palan
Thai Consulate
19
Wat Ban Fai
Th Bourichane
Th Phonsay
Th Fa Ngoum
See Central Vientiane Map (p142)
Centre Médical de L'Ambassade de France
20
Wat Dong Palan
10
Th Sakkarine
International Clinic
3
11
Don Chan
Wat Phia Wat
14
18
Th Simeuang
1
COPE Visitor Centre
Th Dong Palan
6
7
Th That Khao
Th Khu Vieng
Water Tower
26
Th Tha Deua
9
German Embassy
Th Tha Deua
Cambodian Embassy
Th Saphantong Thai
Myanmar Embassy
Th Si Amphon
4
Australian Embassy
Chinese Embassy
Th Sok Pa Luang
Wat Ammon
8

Vientiane

Top Sights

1 COPE Visitor Centre ... G4

Sights

2 Patuxai ... G2
3 Wat Si Muang ... G4

Activities, Courses & Tours

4 Bee Bee Fitness ... G7
5 Papaya Spa ... D2
6 Sengdara Fitness ... H4
7 The Spa ... G4
8 Ultimate Frisbee ... G7
Vientiane By Cycle ... (see 21)
Villa Lao ... (see 17)
9 Wat Sok Pa Luang ... H5

Sleeping

10 Dorkket Garden Guest House ... G3
11 Green Park Hotel ... G4
12 Hotel Beau Rivage Mekong ... D3
13 Khunta Residence ... C2
14 Mandala Boutique Hotel ... G4
15 Nalinthone Guesthouse ... D2
16 Parkview Executive Suites ... D2
17 Villa Lao ... D2
18 Villa Manoly ... F4

Eating

19 Cafe Nomad ... H3
20 PVO ... G3

Drinking & Nightlife

21 Kong View ... B2
Spirit House ... (see 15)

Entertainment

22 At Home ... C2
23 Echo ... D2
24 Lao National Opera Theatre ... E2
25 National Circus ... F1
26 Peurk-may ... G5

Shopping

27 Talat Thong Khan Kham ... E1

Transport

Air Asia ... (see 29)
China Eastern Airlines ... (see 28)
Lao Air ... (see 29)
Lao Airlines ... (see 29)
28 Thai Airways International ... C2
29 Wattay International Airport ... A1

After a couple of coups d'état in the politically fluid 1960s, Vientiane had by the early '70s become a city where almost anything went. Its few bars were peopled by an almost surreal mix of spooks and correspondents, and the women who served them.

Not surprisingly, things changed with the arrival of the Pathet Lao (PL) in 1975. Nightclubs filled with spies were the first to go and Vientiane settled into a slumber punctuated by occasional unenthusiastic concessions to communism, including low level collectivisation and an initial crackdown on Buddhism. These days the most noticeable leftovers from the period are some less-than-inspired Soviet-style buildings. Things picked up in the 1990s and in recent years Vientiane has seen a relative explosion of construction, road redevelopment and vehicular traffic, much of it financed by China, the country that will likely have the most significant influence on Vientiane's future.

Sights

The bulk of sights are concentrated in a small area in the centre of the city. Except for Xieng Khuan (Buddha Park), all sights are easily reached by bicycle and, in most cases, on foot. Only the more prestigious temples are listed here; if you're interested in visiting the city's minor temples, consider doing our bicycle tour of the city (p148). Most wats welcome visitors after the monks have collected alms in the morning until about 6pm.

★ **COPE Visitor Centre** INFORMATION CENTRE

(ສູນຟື້ນຟູຄົນພິການແຫ່ງຊາດ; Map p138; ☎021-218427; www.copelaos.org; Th Khu Vieng; ⏰9am-6pm) FREE COPE (Cooperative Orthotic & Prosthetic Enterprise) is the main source of artificial limbs, walking aids and wheelchairs in Laos. Its excellent Visitor Centre, part of the organisation's National Rehabilitation Centre, offers myriad interesting and informative multimedia exhibits about prosthetics and the UXO (unexploded ordnance) that make them necessary. Several powerful documentaries are shown on a rolling basis in a comfortable theatre, and there's a gift shop and cafe, 100% of the proceeds of which go to supporting COPE's projects in Laos.

Wat Si Saket BUDDHIST TEMPLE

(ວັດສີສະເກດ; Map p142; cnr Th Lan Xang & Th Setthathirath; admission 5000K; ⏰8am-noon & 1-4pm, closed public holidays) Built between 1819 and 1824 by Chao Anou, Wat Si Saket is believed to be Vientiane's oldest surviving temple. And it shows; this beautiful temple turned national museum is in dire need of a facelift.

Haw Pha Kaeo MUSEUM

(ຫໍພະແກ້ວ; Map p142; Th Setthathirath; admission 5000K; ⏲8am-noon & 1-4pm) Once a royal temple built specifically to house the famed Emerald Buddha, Haw Pha Kaeo is today a national museum of religious art. It is about 100m southeast of Wat Si Saket.

Patuxai MONUMENT

(ປະຕູໄຊ, Victory Monument; Map p138; Th Lan Xang; admission 5000K; ⏲8am-5pm) Vientiane's Arc de Triomphe replica is a slightly incongruous sight, dominating the commercial district around Th Lan Xang. Officially called 'Victory Monument' *and* commemorating the Lao who died in prerevolutionary wars, it was built in 1969 with cement donated by the USA intended for the construction of a new airport; hence expats refer to it as 'the vertical runway'. Climb to the summit for panoramic views over Vientiane.

Lao National Museum MUSEUM

(ພິພິດທະພັນປະຫວັດສາດແຫ່ງຊາດລາວ; Map p142; ☎021-212461; Th Samsènethai; admission 10,000K; ⏲8am-noon & 1-4pm) Sadly this charming French-era building, flanked by cherry blossom and magnolia trees, is due to be knocked down and moved to newer premises. Formerly known as the Lao Revolutionary Museum, much of its collection retains an unshakeable revolutionary zeal. Downstairs has a potted account of Khmer culture in the south, accompanied by tools and Buddha statuary; upstairs has ponderous displays that tell the story of the Pathet Lao, peppered with busts of Lenin and Ho Chi Minh.

Wat Si Muang BUDDHIST TEMPLE

(ວັດສີເມືອງ; Map p138; cnr Th Setthathirath, Th Samsènethai & Th Tha Deua; ⏲6am-7pm daily, until 10pm on special days) The most frequently used grounds in Vientiane are those of Wat Si Muang, the site of the *lák méuang* (city pillar), which is considered the home of the guardian spirit of Vientiane.

The large *sǐm* (ordination hall; destroyed in 1828 and rebuilt in 1915) was constructed around the *lák méuang,* and consists of two halls. The large entry hall features a copy of the Pha Kaeo (Emerald Buddha), and a much smaller, rather melted-looking seated stone Buddha that allegedly survived the 1828 inferno. Locals believe it has the power to grant wishes or answer troubling questions, and the practice is to lift it off the pillow three times while mentally phrasing a question or request. If your request is granted, then you are supposed to return later with an offering of bananas, green coconuts, flowers, incense and candles (usually two of each).

The pillar itself is located in the rear hall, and is believed to date from the Khmer period, indicating the site has been used for religious purposes for more than 1000 years. Today it is wrapped in sacred cloth, and in front of it is a carved wooden stele with a seated Buddha in relief.

Behind the *sǐm* is a crumbling laterite *jęhdii* (stupa), almost certainly of Khmer origin. Devotees deposit broken deity images and pottery around the stupa's base so the spirits of the stupa will 'heal' the bad luck created by the breaking of these items. In

NO SACRIFICE TOO GREAT

Legend has it that a group of sages selected the site for Wat Si Muang in 1563, when King Setthathirat moved his capital to Vientiane. Once the spot was chosen, a large hole was dug to receive the heavy stone pillar (probably taken from an ancient Khmer site nearby) that would become the *lák méuang* (city pillar). When the pillar arrived it was suspended over the hole with ropes. Drums and gongs were sounded to summon the townspeople to the area and everyone waited for a volunteer to jump into the hole as a sacrifice to the spirit.

Depending on who's relating it, the legend has several conclusions. What is common to all of them is that a pregnant woman named Sao Si leaped in and the ropes were released, killing her and in the process establishing the town guardianship. Variations include her leaping in upon a horse, and/or with a diminutive monk.

However, Lao scholars think that if there is any truth to this story it is likely to have occurred much earlier than Setthathirat's time, in the pre-Buddhist Mon or Khmer periods when human sacrifice was ritually practised...and that Sao Si's legendary leap might not have been her choice at all.

Central Vientiane

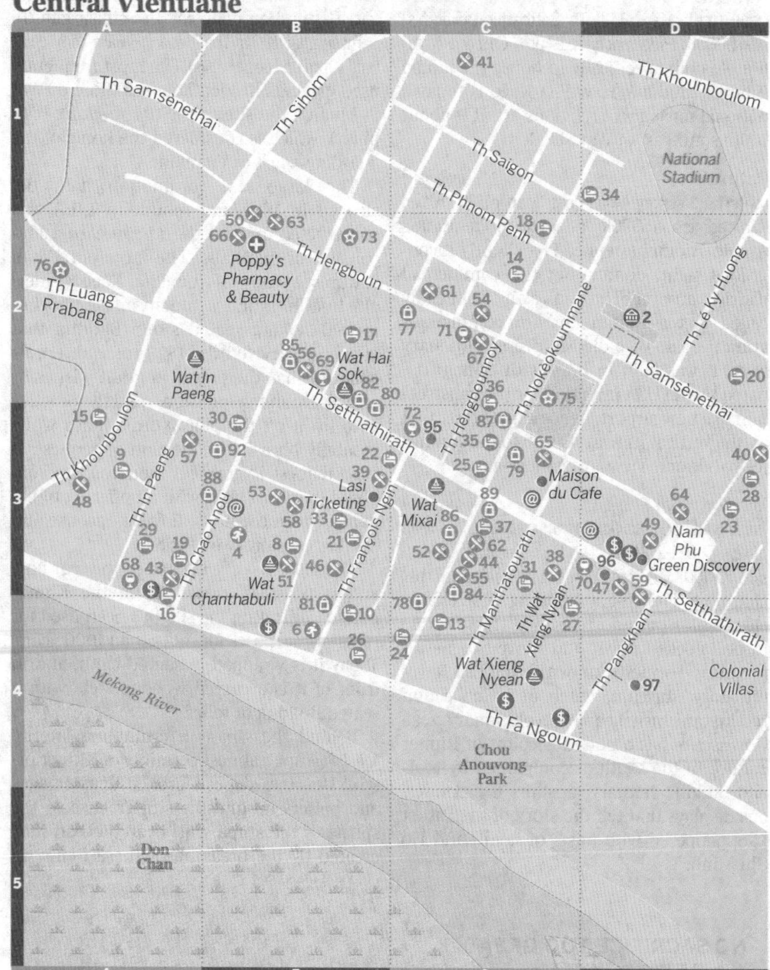

front of the *sĭm* is a little public park with a statue of King Sisavang Vong (1904–59).

Kaysone Phomvihane Memorial MUSEUM
(ຫໍພິພິດທະພັນແລະອະນຸສາວລີໄກສອນພົມວິຫານ; admission museum/house 5000/5000K; ⏲museum 8am-noon & 1-4pm Tue-Sun, house 8am-4pm Tue-Sun) Opened in 1995 to celebrate the late president's 75th birthday, the Kaysone Phomvihane Memorial near Km 6 on Rte 13 south serves as a tribute to Indochina's most pragmatic communist leader. Kaysone's former house is a model of modesty, while in contrast, the museum is a vast Vietnamese-style celebration of the cult of Kaysone (a cult he never encouraged).

It's possible to cycle here or take any transport on Rte 13 south. Kaysone's house is a bit trickier to find, so it's easiest to backtrack; after visiting the museum, return south, the way you came. Upon reaching the first stop light, turn right and continue 1km until you see the sign on your right that says 'Mémorial du Président Kaysone Phomvihane'. Alternatively, a tuk-tuk will cost around 40,000K from the centre.

The museum is impossible to miss, with its mega-sized bronze statue of Kaysone

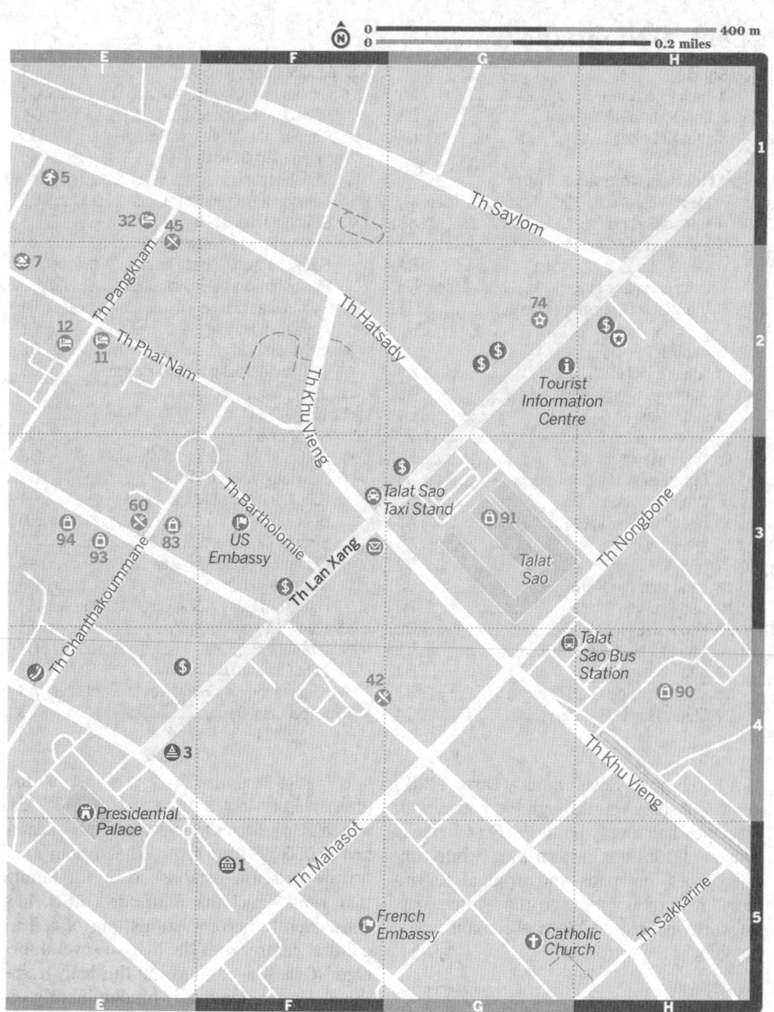

out front flanked by large sculptures in the Heroes of Socialism style, complete with members of various ethnic groups and a sportsman looking like a super-serious Superman. The building is a stark contrast, too, and is filled with a remarkably complete collection of memorabilia of both Kaysone and the Party. These include a mock-up of Kaysone's childhood home in Savannakhet, his desk from the French school he attended at Ban Tai, and a model of a portion of 'Kaysone Cave' in Hua Phan Province, complete with revolver, binoculars, radio and other personal effects.

In contrast, Kaysone's house is a remarkably modest affair, yet fascinating both because of its history and that it remains virtually untouched since the great man died in 1992. The house is inside the former USAID/CIA compound, a self-contained headquarters known as 'Six Klicks City' because of its location 6km from central Vientiane. It once featured bars, restaurants, tennis courts, swimming pools, a commissary and assorted offices from where the Secret War was orchestrated. During the 1975 takeover of Vientiane, Pathet Lao forces ejected the Americans and occupied the compound. Kaysone lived here until his death.

Central Vientiane

Sights

1 Haw Pha Kaeo F5
2 Lao National Museum D2
3 Wat Si Saket E4

Activities, Courses & Tours

Best Western .... (see 10)
4 Herbal Sauna B3
5 Lao Bowling Centre E1
6 Oasis B4
Settha Palace Hotel .... (see 32)
7 Vientiane Swimming Pool E2

Sleeping

8 Ansara Hôtel B3
9 Auberge Sala Inpeng A3
10 Best Western B4
11 City Inn E2
12 Day Inn Hotel E2
13 Douang Deuane Hotel C4
14 Dragon Lodge C2
15 Hotel Khamvongsa A3
16 Intercity Hotel A3
17 Lani's House B2
18 Lao Heritage Hotel C2
19 Lao Orchid Hotel A3
20 Lao Plaza Hotel D2
21 Lao Silk Hotel B3
22 Lao Youth Inn B3
23 Mali Namphu Guest House D3
24 Mixay Guest House C4
25 Mixok Guest House C3
26 Orchid Guesthouse B4
27 Phasouk Residence C4
28 Phonepaseuth Guest House D3
29 Phonethip Guesthouse A3
RD Guesthouse .... (see 24)
30 Salana Boutique Hotel B3
31 Saysouly Guest House C3
32 Settha Palace Hotel E1
Soukchaleun Guest House .... (see 25)
33 Souphaphone Guesthouse B3
34 Syri 1 Guest House D1
35 Vayakorn House C3
36 Vayakorn Inn C2
37 Vientiane Backpackers Hostel C3

Eating

38 Amphone C3
39 Aria B3
40 Baguette & Páté Vendor D3
41 Ban Anou Night Market C1
Benoni Café .... (see 59)
42 Bistrot 22 .... F4
43 Common Ground Café A3
44 Croissant d'Or C3
Han Sam Euay Nong .... (see 19)
45 Han Ton Phai E1
46 Istanbul B3
47 JoMa Bakery Café D3
48 Khambang Lao Food Restaurant A3
49 Khop Chai Deu D3

A Lao People's Revolutionary Party (LPRP) guide will show you through the house, with Kaysone's half-empty bottles of Scotch, tacky souvenirs from the Eastern Bloc, white running shoes, notepads and original Kelvinator air-conditioners. Even the winter coats he wore on visits to Moscow remain neatly hanging in the wardrobe.

Pha That Luang BUDDHIST STUPA

(ພະທາດຫລວງ, Great Sacred Reliquary, Great Stupa; Th That Luang; admission 5000K; ⏲8am-noon & 1-4pm Tue-Sun) Svelte and golden Pha That Luang is the most important national monument in Laos, a symbol of Buddhist religion and Lao sovereignty. Legend has it that Ashokan missionaries from India erected a *tâht* (stupa) here to enclose a piece of Buddha's breastbone as early as the 3rd century BC.

A high-walled cloister with tiny windows surrounds the 45m-high stupa. The cloister measures 85m on each side and contains various Buddha images. Pha That Luang is about 4km northeast of the city centre at the end of Th That Luang.

Lao Textile Museum MUSEUM

(ພິພິດທະພັນຜ້າໄໝບູຮານລາວ; ☎030-572 7423; www.ibiss.co.jp/laomuseum/access.html; admission 30,000K; ⏲10am-4pm) What began as a private museum, established by the family that runs Kanchana Boutique (p161), has subsequently become something of a Lao cultural centre, with the help of several foreign NGOs. The emphasis at this leafy traditional Lao compound is predominantly on textiles, and in addition to a wooden house filled with looms and antique Lao textiles representing several ethnic groups, there are courses in weaving and dyeing, and a shop.

The museum also offers Lao cooking classes, although these didn't yet appear to be up and running during our visit, and on Saturdays, lessons on traditional Lao music, although the latter are only for those with experience playing Lao instruments and who are fluent in the Lao language. For both of these we'd advise calling the museum or Kanchana Boutique in advance.

The museum is located about 3km northeast of the National Circus (Hong Kanyasin); Kanchana Boutique can provide a map.

50 Korean Restaurant ... B2
51 La Signature ... B3
52 La Terrasse ... C3
53 L'Adresse de Tinay ... B3
54 Lao Kitchen ... C2
55 Le Banneton ... C3
56 Le Silapa ... B2
57 Le Vendôme ... A3
58 Makphet ... B3
Paradlce ... (see 74)
59 Phimphone Market ... D3
60 PhimPhone Market 2 ... E3
61 Pho Dung ... C2
62 Pimentón ... C3
63 Rice Noodle – Lao Porridge ... B2
64 Scandinavian Bakery ... D3
65 Taj Mahal Restaurant ... C3
66 Vieng Sawan ... B2
67 YuLaLa Cafe ... C2

Drinking & Nightlife
68 Bor Pennyang ... A3
69 iBeam ... B2
70 Jazzy Brick ... D3
Khop Chai Deu ... (see 49)
71 Noy's Fruit Heaven ... C2
72 Samlo Pub ... C3

Entertainment
73 Anou Cabaret ... B2
74 Institut Français ... G2
75 Lao National Culture Hall ... C2
76 Wind West ... A2

Shopping
77 Book Café ... C2
78 Camacrafts ... C4
79 Carol Cassidy Lao Textiles ... C3
80 Carterie du Laos ... B3
81 Couleur d'Asie ... B4
82 Indochina Handicrafts ... B2
83 Kanchana Boutique ... E3
84 Khampan Lao Handicraft ... C3
85 KPP Handicraft Promotion Enterprise of Sekong Province ... B2
86 Mixay Boutique ... C3
87 Monument Books ... C3
88 Oriental Bookshop ... B3
89 Satri Lao ... C3
90 Talat Khua Din ... H4
91 Talat Sao ... G3
Treasures of Asia ... (see 72)
True Colour ... (see 25)
92 T'Shop Lai Gallery ... B3
93 VanSom ... E3
94 Vins de France ... E3

Transport
95 Europcar ... C3
96 Jules' Classic Rental ... D3
97 Lao Airlines ... D4
Vietnam Airlines ... (see 20)

Xieng Khuan MUSEUM
(ຊຽງຂວັນ, Suan Phut, Buddha Park; admission 5000K, camera 3000K; 8am-4.30pm) About 25km southeast of Vientiane, eccentric Xieng Khuan thrills with other-worldly Buddhist and Hindu sculptures, and was designed and built in 1958 by Luang Pu, a yogi-priest-shaman who merged Hindu and Buddhist philosophy, mythology and iconography into a cryptic whole.

Bus 14 (8000K, one hour) leaves from the Talat Sao bus station every 15 or 20 minutes throughout the day and goes all the way to Xieng Khuan. Alternatively, charter a tuk-tuk (200,000K return).

Activities

Frisbee

Ultimate Frisbee FRISBEE
(Map p138; American soccer pitch; 12,000K; 6.15pm Mon) Every Monday evening aerial wizards meet at the American soccer pitch to play Ultimate Frisbee (two teams of seven players). Check out the Facebook page (Vientiane Ultimate Frisbee) for more info and to arrange a lift with a regular. Mixed boys and girls, Lao and expats. A great way to meet local people if you're staying a few days or a while.

Bowling

Lao Bowling Centre BOWLING
(Map p142; 021-218661; Th Khun Bulom; per game with shoe hire 16,000K; 9am-midnight) Bright lights, Beerlao and boisterous bowlers are what you'll find here.

Gyms & Yoga

Bee Bee Fitness HEALTH & FITNESS
(Map p138; 021-315 877; 1-day membership 40,000K.; 6am-9pm Mon-Fri, 7am-9pm Sat & Sun) This terrific gym opposite the Australian embassy overlooks the Mekong so you can run on the treadmill while watching passing boats. Loads of room to enjoy the decent equipment: rowing machines, spinning bikes and weightlifting apparatus. There's also a pool being built, and regular zumba and pilates classes too.

VIEWING PHA THAT LUANG

Each level of Pha That Luang (p144) has different architectural features in which Buddhist doctrine is encoded; visitors are supposed to contemplate the meaning of these features as they walk around. The first level is an approximately square base measuring 68m by 69m that supports 323 *sěe máh* (ordination stones). It represents the material world, and also features four arched *hŏr wái* (prayer halls), one on each side, with short stairways leading to them and beyond to the second level.

The second level is 48m by 48m and is surrounded by 120 lotus petals. There are 288 *sěe máh* on this level, as well as 30 small stupas symbolising the 30 Buddhist perfections *(báhlamée săhm-síp tat)*, beginning with alms-giving and ending with equanimity.

Arched gates again lead to the next level, a 30m by 30m square. The tall central stupa, which has a brick core that has been stuccoed over, is supported here by a bowl-shaped base reminiscent of India's first Buddhist stupa at Sanchi. At the top of this mound the superstructure, surrounded by lotus petals, begins.

The curvilinear, four-sided spire resembles an elongated lotus bud and is said to symbolise the growth of a lotus from a seed in a muddy lake bottom to a bloom over the lake's surface, a metaphor for human advancement from ignorance to enlightenment in Buddhism. The entire *tâht* (stupa) was regilded in 1995 to celebrate the 20th anniversary of the Lao People's Democratic Republic (PDR), and is crowned by a stylised banana flower and parasol. From ground to pinnacle, Pha That Luang is 45m tall.

Sengdara Fitness HEALTH & FITNESS
(Map p138; ☎021-452159; 5/77 Th Dong Palan; ⊙6am-10pm) Sengdara has decent facilities and plenty of running machines, as well as sauna, pool, massage (one hour 60,000K), aerobics and yoga classes. Visitors can buy a 45,000K day pass, which includes use of everything. Also has evening tae kwon do classes.

Best Western HEALTH & FITNESS
(Map p142; ☎021-216906; 22/3 Th François Ngin; per visit 80,000K) Small fitness room and sauna as well as a dinky pool; central location.

Lemongrass Yoga YOGA
(☎020-5887 2027; www.lemongrassyoga.com; per class 70,000K; ⊙6.30-8pm Thu, noon-1.30pm Sun) The city's best yoga instructor is based at her own traditional wooden Lao house. Shelley has been practising for 15 years and teaches hatha yoga one-to-one, or in small groups. The yoga house (No 6) is located in the middle of a *soi* (lane) just off of Th Boulichanh in Dongphalan Thong Village. The nearest landmark is Vieng Vang tower: a six-storey business tower which marks the entrance to the *soi*, and is between the Thai consulate and Ton Lam restaurant on Th Boulichanh.

Massage/Sauna

★ **The Spa** MASSAGE
(Map p138; ☎021-285113; www.the-spa-laos.com; Th That Khao; ⊙10am-10pm; 📶) A few minutes by tuk-tuk from town, this restful oasis is the best spa in town, with glacially cool surroundings and a litany of heavenly treatments including head massage (98,000K), oil massage (185,000K) and herbal steam and sauna (110,000K). Two cuboid-faced Persian cats finish off the voluptuous aesthetic.

Oasis MASSAGE
(Map p142; Th François Ngin; ⊙9am-9pm) Cool, clean and professional, this is an excellent central place to enjoy foot massage (50,000K), Lao-style body massage (60,000K) or a peppermint body scrub (200,000K), to name a few.

Wat Sok Pa Luang MASSAGE, SPA
(Map p138; Th Sok Pa Luang; ⊙1-7pm) Forget air-con and glitz, this is healthy herbal sauna Lao style, in the leafy grounds of Wat Sok Pa Luang. A witch's broth of eucalyptus, lemongrass, basil and lime is stirred in a giant cauldron, the fumes of which are then fed into the sauna (20,000K). Traditional massage (40,000K) and meditation class (free) are also available. It's 3km from the city centre. Avoid rush hour between 3pm and 6pm.

Herbal Sauna MASSAGE
(Map p142; ☎020-5504 4655; off Th Chao Anou; ⊙1-9pm) Located near the river, this no-frills outfit offers Lao-style herbal saunas (15,000K) in separate rooms for men and women. In addition to the sauna it also of-

fers a variety of massage, including Lao (per hour 40,000K), oil (per hour 80,000K) and foot (per hour 40,000K). The fee includes a cloth (for men) and towel; women must pay an additional 2000K for the rental of a sarong.

Papaya Spa SPA
(Map p138; ☎020-5561 0565; www.papayaspa.com; Th Phagna Sy; ⏰9am-7pm) Part boho lounge, part opium den, this faded villa is the perfect spot to unwind. Massages start at 110,000K, herbal saunas 30,000K; Swedish massage or coconut or papaya body scrubs cost 210,000K. The owner is lovely but recent reports suggest quality oscillates wildly from sublime to adequate.

White Lotus Yoga & Massage MASSAGE
(☎021-217492; Th Pangkham; ⏰9am-9pm) Just north of Nam Phu, this central one-stop shop for weary feet and muscles also offers facials and waxes (110,000K). The walls need a lick of paint and the Lao-style massages (50,000K) are forgettable, but sit back in one of the retro chairs and enjoy a foot massage (55,000K). Yoga classes are also offered on a regular basis.

Running

Vientiane Hash House Harriers RUNNING
(www.hashlaos.com) The Vientiane Hash House Harriers welcome runners to their two weekly hashes. The Saturday hash is the more challenging run and starts at 3.45pm from Nam Phu. It's followed by food and no shortage of Beerlao. Monday's easier run starts at 5pm from varying locations – look for maps at the Scandinavian Bakery or Asia Vehicle Rentals, where owner **Joe Rumble** (☎020-5551 1293) is more than happy to help you out.

Swimming

There are several places in Vientiane where you can work on your stroke or simply take a cooling dip. You could try Sengdara Fitness, where a day pass costs 45,000K. Several hotels welcome non-guests, including the beautiful **Settha Palace Hotel** (Map p142; 6 Th Pangkham; ⏰7am-8pm) with its decadent pool and surrounding bar, as well as the Lao Plaza Hotel (p152) which is a fair size and also has plenty of loungers (but will set you back 120,000K).

Vientiane Swimming Pool SWIMMING
(Map p142; ☎020-5552 1002; Th Ki Huang; admission 15,000K; ⏰8am-7pm) The Vientiane Swimming Pool is quiet, central and clean and is usually fine for swimming laps. Hire or bring goggles though – there's enough chlorine in there to strip barnacles off a shipwreck.

 Courses

Villa Lao COOKING
(Map p138; ☎021-242292; www.villa-lao-guesthouse.com; off Th Nong Douang; half-day class 150,000K) As well as being a great place to stay, Villa Lao offers cooking courses at 9am and 2pm by appointment, involving a trip to the market, preparation of three dishes of your choice and sampling your creations. The price is per class, so the more people involved the cheaper it will be per person, but to give you an idea it should cost around 150,000K each.

Houey Hong Vocational Training Center for Women WEAVING
(☎021-560006; www.houeyhongcentre.com; Ban Houey Hong; ⏰8.30am-4.30pm Mon-Sat) You can learn how to dye textiles using natural pigments and then weave them on a traditional loom at this NGO group, run by a Lao-Japanese woman. It was established north of Vientiane to train disadvantaged rural women in the dying art of natural dyeing and traditional silk-weaving practices. Visitors can look for free or partake in the dyeing process (120,000K, two hours, two scarves) or weaving (200,000K, whole day). You keep the fruits of your labour. Transportation to and from the centre is provided for an additional 33,000K. The centre's contact point and commercial venture in Vientiane is True Colour (p161).

Lao Textile Museum WEAVING
(☎030-525 8293; www.ibiss.co.jp/laomuseum/access.html; lessons US$50; ⏰10am-4pm) Classes in weaving and dyeing are available at this museum, run by Kanchana Boutique. Lessons must be arranged in advance, and some English is spoken, although those truly interested should probably bring a translator. It is 5km out of town.

Vipassana Meditation

Wat Sok Pa Luang MEDITATION
(☎021-2311938; Th Sok Pa Luang) Every Saturday from 4pm to 5.30pm, monks lead a session of sitting and walking meditation. Both Lao and foreigners are welcome and there's no charge. There's usually a

translator for the question period held after the meditation.

Tours

Vientiane By Cycle CYCLING TOUR

(Map p138; ☎020-5581 2337; www.vientianebycycle.com; half/full day 350,000/450,000K) Run by energetic and likeable former guide Aline, this tour affords you the chance to experience another side of Vientiane as you meander along its riverfront, through affluent and poor suburbs, and past schools and temples. To contact or book a tour visit website or call. Starts 8am at Kong View on the Mekong.

Festivals & Events

You can rest assured that whatever the festival, celebrations in Vientiane will be as vigorous as anywhere in the country. Whatever you do *don't* drive or ride about in the city during festivals; drunk driving is the norm and accidents myriad.

Bun Pha That Luang CULTURE

(That Luang Festival; Nov) Bun Pha That Luang, usually in early November, is the largest temple fair in Laos. Apart from the religious fervour, the festival features a trade show and a number of carnival games. The festivities begin with a *wéean téean* (circumambulation) around Wat Si Muang, followed by a procession to Pha That Luang, which is illuminated all night for a week. The festival climaxes on the morning of the full moon with the *đák bàht* ceremony, in which several thousand monks from across the country receive alms food. That evening there's a final *wéean téean* around Pha That Luang, with devotees carrying *ƀạhsàht* (miniature temples made from banana stems and decorated with flowers and other offerings). Fireworks cap off the evening and everyone makes merit or merry until dawn.

Bun Nam BOAT RACE

(Bun Suang Héua; Oct) Another huge annual event is Bun Nam at the end of *pansăh* (the Buddhist rains retreat) in October, during which boat races are held on the Mekong River. Rowing teams from all over the country, as well as from Thailand, China and Myanmar, compete; the riverbank is lined with food stalls, temporary discos, carnival games and beer gardens for three days and nights. Vientiane is jam-packed during Bun Nam, and given how far away the

Cycling Tour
Monument to Mekong

START LE BANNETON
END SPIRIT HOUSE
LENGTH 5KM; FOUR TO SIX HOURS

Vientiane is a great city to explore on bicycle. We suggest starting in the cool hours of the morning and have included breakfast and lunch stops; if you're doing the tour later you could regard these as lunch and dinner stops. Some attractions, such as Talat Khua Din, are best visited early in the day.

Begin your day with coffee and a crispy croissant at one of Th Nokèokoummane's excellent French bakeries such as 1 **Le Banneton** (p154). There's a bike rental place virtually next door, and a few more on adjacent Th François Ngin; most open at 7am and charge about 10,000K per day.

Hop on your bike, turn on to one-way Th Setthathirath and passing 2 **Nam Phu**, Vientiane's underwhelming fountain, continue about 1km to the stoplight. On your right is the 3 **Presidential Palace**, a vast *beaux arts*-style chateau built to house the French colonial governor.

Directly opposite is 4 **Wat Si Saket** (p140), with its thousands of Buddha figures, and just up the road, 5 **Haw Pha Kaeo** (p141), the national museum for religious objects. By arriving in the morning you'll beat most of the crowds.

Continuing along Th Setthathirath, cross Th Mahasot and turn left down Th Gallieni. You'll know you're in the right place by the white walls of the 6 **French Embassy** on your left and the towering 7 **Catholic Church** on your right. Continue northwest along this street until you reach the T-intersection; on the opposite side is the barely noticeable entrance to 8 **Talat Khua Din** (p161), one of Vientiane's largest fresh food markets.

Continuing northwest along Th Khu Vieng, turn right onto Th Lan Xang, a street sometimes (very) generously described as the 'Champs-Élysées of the East'. At this point you're directly in front of Vientiane's biggest market, 9 **Talat Sao** (p161), a great place for textiles.

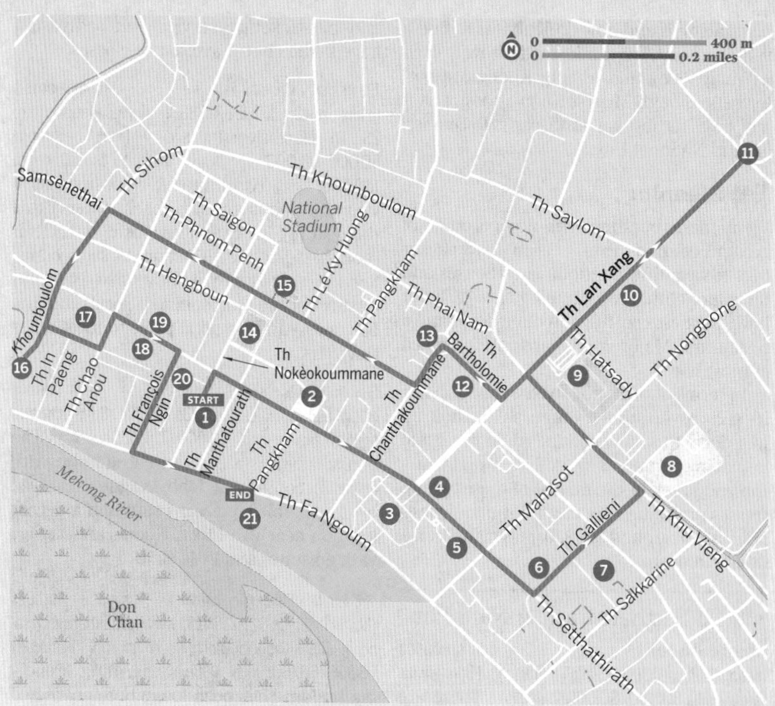

Continuing northeast along Th Lan Xang, you'll pass by the 10 **Tourist Information Centre** (p163). At this point you're also only 500m from 11 **Patuxai** (p141), which is worth climbing for unbeatable views of the city and surrounds.

Circle around Patuxai and continue southwest along Th Lan Xang. Turn right into quiet Th Bartholomie. Buzz past the walls of the 12 **US Embassy** and continue to 13 **That Dam**. The gold that covered this stupa was allegedly carted off by the Siamese during their pillaging of 1828. If you can pass here without being swallowed by the giant *naga* that purportedly lurks beneath, continue southwest and turn right onto Th Samsènethai.

Continue for two blocks until, on your left-hand side, you see the gaudy Chinese-funded 14 **Lao National Culture Hall**. Directly opposite is the 15 **Lao National Museum** (p141), worth a stop to gain some insight into ancient and modern Laos.

Continue another 500m along one-way Th Samsènethai until you reach the stoplight. Turn left and head southwest along Th Sihom, continuing straight through the next stoplight, after which the road turns into Th Khounboulom. Continue about 250m southwest until you reach 16 **Khambang Lao Food Restaurant** (p158). This family-run place is central Vientiane's best Lao restaurant and your lunch destination.

Backtrack a block northeast along Th Khounboulom until you reach 17 **Wat In Paeng**, famed for the artistry displayed in the stucco relief of the *sĭm* (ordination hall). Weaving to Th Setthathirath via Th Chao Anou, park your bike at 18 **Wat Ong Teu Mahawihan** and visit the temple's namesake, a 16th-century bronze Buddha measuring 5.8m tall and weighing several tonnes. The *sĭm* that houses the Buddha is famous for the wooden facade over its front terrace, a masterpiece of Lao carving. Take a break at shady and little-visited 19 **Wat Hai Sok** before your final temple stop, 20 **Wat Mixai**, with its Bangkok-style *sĭm* and heavy gates, flanked by two *nyak* (guardian giants). From here it's a short ride to return your bike.

Walk southeast towards the Mekong, find a seat at the 21 **Spirit House** (p159), and rest your legs with a Bloody Mary as the sky turns a burnt peach.

boat racing is and how difficult it is to find a vantage point, we think smaller towns such as Vang Vieng and Muang Khong are better bets, though Muang Khong doesn't usually hold its festival until early December, around National Day.

Sleeping

Vientiane is bursting with a wide range of accommodation from cheap backpacker digs to beautiful boutique guesthouses and huge monolithic corporate hotels. The latter have business centres, and often pools and a restaurant. Major credit cards are accepted at most hotels.

In terms of price, for shoestring travellers it's still easy to stretch your cash and hole up in a dorm for a few dollars, while you could be paying hundreds of dollars a night in a top-end hotel. In the middle of these two extremes are some very clean, intimate guesthouses for around US$20 per night (for a double room).

Th Setthathirath & Nam Phu

Lao Youth Inn GUESTHOUSE $
(Map p142; ☎021-241352; Th François Ngin; r with fan/air-con 60,000/80,000K; ❄ wi-fi) There are a couple of mint-green Lao Youth Inns on Th François Ngin, the best one being at the top of the street nearest Th Setthathirath. Rooms are a little boxy but fragrant, with en suites and polished tiled floors, and what the place lacks in refinement it makes up for in amenities, including ticketing services, bike (10,000K) and scooter (60,000K) rental, and friendly staff.

Vientiane Backpackers Hostel HOSTEL $
(Map p142; ☎020-9544 4147; www.vientianebackpackerhostel.com; Th Nokèokoummane; @ wi-fi) Great new hostel with three large fan-cooled dorms. There's a cafe, free vodka after 9pm, laundry services, free wi-fi and bike (10,000K) and scooter (70,000K) rental. Bathrooms and showers are modern and clean, while self-catering facilities are more than adequate. Free breakfast, ticketing and visa services, plus friendly European management, make this a worthy option.

Mixok Guest House GUESTHOUSE $
(Map p142; ☎021-251606; Th Setthathirath; r inc breakfast 130,000K; ❄ @ wi-fi) Rooms here all enjoy air-con, TV and wi-fi. There's also an attached internet cafe (6000K per hour) and bus-ticketing service, but sadly staff have taken charm-avoidance classes.

Saysouly Guest House GUESTHOUSE $
(Map p142; ☎021-218383; www.saysouly.com; 23 Th Manthatourath; s/d without bathroom 50,000/90,000K, r with air-con & bathroom 130,000K; ❄) Two minutes' walk from Nam Phu and popular with backpackers, this three-storey place offers basic but clean rooms, some with shared bathrooms. Service can't exactly be described as enthusiastic, but the atmosphere is social, and the balconies can be a good place to meet other travellers.

Soukchaleun Guest House GUESTHOUSE $
(Map p142; ☎021-218723; 121 Th Setthathirath; r with fan/air-con 80,000/110,000K; ❄) The Soukchaleun is a basic, tired old joint with a small communal lobby vaguely cheered by a myna bird, pleasant staff and a decent location near Wat Mixai. Rooms are average with en suites and little élan.

★ **Hotel Khamvongsa** HOTEL $$
(Map p142; ☎021-218415; www.hotelkhamvongsa.com; Th Khounboulom; s/d/tr incl breakfast US$35/50/60; ❄ wi-fi) This charming French-era building has been lovingly reincarnated as a divinely homey boutique hotel, with belle-époque touches such as glass tear lightshades, checkered tile floors, and exquisitely simple rooms, softly lit with wood floors and Indo-chic decor. Rooms on the 3rd and 4th floors have masterful views. There's also a tranquil courtyard and restaurant.

Lani's House GUESTHOUSE $$
(Map p142; ☎021-215639; www.lanishouse.com; Th Setthathirath; s/d US$50/60; P ❄) This chandeliered, art-deco–accented place hides down a quiet, leafy lane beside a temple. Peppered with antiques and Lao handicraft, it feels like an authentic slice of Indochina; rooms are cool and cozy with wood-blade fans, romantic desks to write long *par avion* letters, shabby-chic armoires, cable TV, fridges, wall hangings, mosquito nets and bamboo-framed beds. Its atmospheric lobby is adorned with handicrafts and stuffed animals.

Vayakorn Inn HOTEL $$
(Map p142; ☎021-215348; www.vayakorn.biz; 19 Th Hèngbounnoy; r US$35; ❄ @ wi-fi) On a quiet street just off increasingly hectic Th Setthathirath, this tasteful, peaceful hotel is great value given its chandeliered lobby

festooned with handicrafts, bijou cafe and hardwood floors. Generously sized rooms are impeccably clean with super-fresh linen, choice art, flat-screen TVs, desks and modern en suites. The rooms on the upper floors have excellent city views.

Vayakorn House HOTEL $$
(Map p142; ☎021-241911; www.vayakorn.biz; 91 Th Nokèokoummane; s/d/tr 140,000/200,000/260,000K; ❄📶) Vayakorn Inn's older, more inexpensive sister, this is a calm, clean and great-value spot to rest up. There's a welcoming lobby, with a pleasant breakfast area plus a chillsome verandah outside to watch life go by on the busy street. There are 21 pristine and stylishly spartan rooms with fresh linen, en suites, TV and air-con. Accepts credit cards.

Phonepaseuth Guest House GUESTHOUSE $$
(Map p142; ☎021-212263; www.laoguesthouse.com; 97 Th Pangkham; r with fan/air-con US$22/25; ❄@📶) This old trusty just yards away from the Scandinavian Bakery is still going strong thanks to fresh walls, cool, spacious rooms, clean en suites, cable TV, wi-fi and crisp linen. Opt for rooms facing the road if you want your own little balcony. Nice interior touches include Hmong bed-runners and wall-mounted shell lampshades.

Mali Namphu Guest House GUESTHOUSE $$
(Map p142; ☎021-215093; www.malinamphu.com; 114 Th Pangkham; s/d/tr incl breakfast 210,000/260,000/350,000K; ❄@📶) On the tailor's street, this old stalwart shows no signs of fatigue, with bright rooms wrapped around a leafy courtyard where you also take breakfast. Fragrant rooms, decked in Lao handicrafts, have desks, impeccably clean bathrooms and air-con. There's also cable TV.

Souphaphone Guesthouse GUESTHOUSE $$
(Map p142; ☎021-261468; www.souphaphone.net; off Th François Ngin; r US$20; ❄@📶) Very tidy with house-proud owners, this guesthouse has 22 rooms, some with windows but all with fresh linen, cool tiled floors and pristine walls. Rooms also enjoy en suite, fridge, wi-fi and TV. Understandably, given the price, it's often booked up.

Salana Boutique Hotel BOUTIQUE HOTEL $$$
(Map p142; ☎021-254254; www.salanaboutique.com; Th Chao Anou; r standard/deluxe US$135/145; ⊖❄📶) Highly polished, wood-flavoured Salana fuses Lao and contemporary styles to produce a sleek addition to Vientiane's accommodation. Rooms have wood floors, ethnically inspired bed runners, soft lighting, flat-screen TVs, safety deposit boxes, rain showers and nice little touches including frangipani flowers scattered around. Some rooms have fantastic temple views. There's also a bar on the 4th floor with great city views to drink up over a cocktail.

Th Samsenthai & Around

Syri 1 Guest House GUESTHOUSE $
(Map p142; ☎021-212682; Th Saigon; r 50,000-150,000K; ❄@📶) Flame-muralled, shabby-chic Syri sits on a quiet street and is run by the gentle-natured Air and his family. It's been a traveller fave for many years and with good reason: generously sized rooms (air-con and fan, en suite and shared bathroom), recesses to chill, a DVD lounge, bikes for rent, and tailored bike tours of the city. And 100% friendly.

★**Lao Heritage Hotel** GUESTHOUSE $$
(Map p142; ☎021-265093; Th Phnom Penh; r US$20-25; ❄@📶) Like a slice of home, this quirky old Lao house hidden in plants and vines is as friendly as it is chic. Not far off being a boutique hotel, it's undergoing a steady makeover under new management,

APARTMENTS

If you're going to be here for a while check out these luxury apartment complexes: **Parkview Executive Suites** (Map p138; ☎021-250888; www.parkviewexecutive.com; Th Luang Prabang; ❄@📶🏊) and the French-run **Khunta Residence** (Map p138; ☎021-251199; www.khuntaresidence.com; off Th Luang Prabang; ❄📶🏊). Monthly rates start from US$1300 for a studio and US$1700 for a one-bedroom apartment.

Many of Vientiane's newish small hotels such as **City Inn** (Map p142; ☎021-281333; www.cityinnvientiane.com; Th Pangkham; r incl breakfast 550,000K, ste incl breakfast 810,000-900,000K; ❄📶) and **Phasouk Residence** (Map p142; ☎021-243415; www.phasoukresidence.com; 57/4 Th Wat Xieng Nyean; r/ste US$55/75; ❄@📶) also operate equally well as serviced apartments for those with generous housing allowances.

with a great new tapas restaurant. Rooms have wood floors, bed runners, TVs, somewhat tired en suites, and fridges. Delightful staff and management. There are plenty of nooks to chill out in, as well as in-room wi-fi. Rooms 1 and 2 are our favourites.

Day Inn Hotel HOTEL $$

(Map p142; ☎021-222985; dayinn@laopdr.com; 59/3 Th Pangkham; s/d/tr incl breakfast 450,000/650,000/850,000K;) This efficiently run hotel is something of a business-traveller's choice, and from its vanilla exterior to its fresh green restaurant serving up Asian fusion cuisine, we can see why. It has 32 rooms, some old, some new, with large beds, bureaus, flat-screen TVs, air-con and no-nonsense international-style decor. En suites have bath-tubs. Ask for a room away from the road though. There's also free airport pick-up. Good value.

Dragon Lodge GUESTHOUSE $$

(Map p142; ☎021-250114; dragonlodge2002@yahoo.com; Th Samsènethai; r 130,000-180,000K;) Contemporary-looking Dragon has terracotta-coloured walls, a swish bar and restaurant festooned with lanterns, and 40 pastel-shaded, scrupulously clean rooms with air-con, TV and en suite. Check out its useful noticeboard. Friendly staff, visa and ticketing service, and a convenient location close to Chinatown's Tha Hengboun Street.

★ **Settha Palace Hotel** HOTEL $$$

(Map p142; ☎021-217581; www.setthapalace.com; 6 Th Pangkham; r standard/deluxe US$152/234;) This stately building, set in grounds ablaze with flowers, is as graceful as it is relaxing. Fans whirr over marble floors so polished you can see your champagne glass in them, while service is impeccable. Rooms are equally enchanting with four-posters, desks and wood floors – particularly the larger deluxe ones (ask for a garden view). The belle-époque restaurant is smart and formal; indeed Settha, like a defiant outpost of Indochine, recalls a bygone era. Check out the kidney-shaped pool.

Lao Plaza Hotel HOTEL $$$

(Map p142; ☎021-218800; www.laoplazahotel.com; 63 Th Samsènethai; s/d/ste incl breakfast US$190/215/380;) A strong choice for business travellers, this blandly designed marbled edifice boasts a vast international style lobby and comfy rooms. Expect wi-fi, fridges, cable TV, bath-tubs and silk bedheads. That said, the corridors are in definite need of new carpets. There's also a great pool (120,000K if you're not a resident) perfect for sunbathing and escaping the heat. Finally you'll find Bangkok Airways and Vietnam Airlines here, as well as three restaurants.

Mekong Riverfront & Around

Phonethip Guesthouse GUESTHOUSE $

(Map p142; ☎021-217239; 72 Th In Paeng; r with fan/air-con US$10/15;) With its babbling water feature and shaded courtyard peppered with swing chairs and spots to relax, this place feels like an escape from the heat and crowds. There's a range of rooms, some with fridges and TVs, and better than others, so look at a few. Friendly owner.

Douang Deuane Hotel HOTEL $

(Map p142; ☎021-222301; DD_hotel@hotmail.com; Th Nokèokoummane; s/tw/tr incl breakfast 120,000/170,000/220,000K;) Soviet-grey and forbidding from its exterior and shadowy lobby, but things are better inside the rooms themselves, with fridges, hardwood floors, cable TV, armoires, and retro battleship-grey chairs. Some rooms have balconies looking out over colourful Th Nokèokoummane. Also rents scooters for 60,000K per day.

RD Guesthouse GUESTHOUSE $

(Map p142; ☎021-262112; www.rdlao.com; 37-01 Th Nokèokoummane; dm US$6, r US$12-17;) The rooms at RD (Relax & Dream away) hardly deserve the moniker, but they're clean enough, and enjoy TV, air-con and en suite. The basic six-bed dorm is cramped but has an en suite too. Conveniently located near the riverfront, RD also has a small library and communal kitchen.

Mixay Guest House GUESTHOUSE $

(Map p142; ☎021-262210; 39 Th Nokèokoummane; dm 50,000K, s/d without bathroom 80,000/90,000K, r with air-con & bathroom 120,000K;) A remnant of Vientiane's old-school cheap digs, but nothing to get excited about, Mixay has fan-cooled and air-con rooms. Some have hot-water bathrooms, while others are bereft of windows. Also a left-luggage facility and ticketing service.

Orchid Guesthouse GUESTHOUSE $

(Map p142; ☎021-252825; Th Fa Ngoum; r 90,000-160,000K;) Teetering into the sky like some lantern-festooned Jenga tower, Chinese-owned Orchid is short on charm, but its maze of 43 paint-thirsty rooms, many of which are windowless, at least have en suites, optional air-con and TV. There's also a sundown terrace overlooking the Mekong. Opt for a newer double room. Wi-fi extends only as far as the 1st floor.

Villa Manoly GUESTHOUSE **$$**
(Map p138; manoly20@hotmail.com; off Th Fa Ngoum; r incl breakfast US$35-45; ❄🏊) This beautifully antiquated house, in a garden swimming in mature plants and frangipani flowers, feels like the sort of place Le Carré might ensconce himself to write a novel (witness its collection of vintage telephones and typewriters). Nicely furnished rooms with wood floors, air-con, en suites and bedside lamps look onto a delightful pool.

Best Western HOTEL **$$**
(Map p142; ☎021-216909; www.bestwesternvientiane.com; 2-12 Th François Ngin; s/d/deluxe incl breakfast US$70/80/89; 🚭❄@📶🏊) This gleaming hotel is a welcoming spot if you're looking for a cool, plush lobby, a calm outside garden with a pool, a gym and a general level of upscale style. There's also a tempting Asian fusion restaurant attached. Rooms, of which there are 44, are equally swanky with wood floors, snow-white linen and quality fittings. Add to this cable TVs, fridges and spotless en suites and you have a winner.

Hotel Beau Rivage Mekong GUESTHOUSE **$$**
(Map p138; ☎021-243375; www.hbrm.com; Th Fa Ngoum; r without/with view incl breakfast US$55/67; 🚭❄@📶) A little less romantic from the outside since the dirt track running parallel with the river was paved and denuded of trees, this flamingo-pink boutique hotel still packs a punch with superb rooms decked in bamboo screens, waffled bedspreads, high ceilings, and a pleasant garden out back. Desirable for couples.

Lao Silk Hotel GUESTHOUSE **$$**
(Map p142; ☎021-213976; www.laosilkhotel.com; Th François Ngin; r US$25-35; ❄📶) All 20 rooms in this sleek hotel are fragrantly fresh and well attired in stylish decor and bijou en suites. While rooms might be a little small for a professional wrestler, the wi-fi, cable TV, air-con and general plushness make this one a winner. Downstairs is a relaxing cafe-bar to work or read in.

Dorkket Garden Guest House GUESTHOUSE **$$**
(Map p138; ☎020-5571 2288; www.dorkketgarden.com; Th Sakkarine; r US$30-40; ❄📶) Beautifully finished rooms with parquet floors, air-con, huge beds, finely carved wardrobes, wicker chairs, wall-hangings and clean en suites. Other comforts in this old house dripping in plants and ambience include fridges, TV and pleasant gardens. Worth the short journey out of the centre (about five minutes from Nam Phu in a tuk-tuk). Prepare to be very relaxed.

Lao Orchid Hotel HOTEL **$$**
(Map p142; ☎021-264134; www.lao-orchid-hotel.com; Th Chao Anou; d/ste incl breakfast US$65/95; ❄📶) Attractive, modern hotel with a swish lobby and chilled verandah cafe with a great view of the road; there are 32 welcoming rooms here with varnished wood floors, mint-fresh linen, desks, balconies, fridges and Indochinese-style furniture. Ask for a room at the front to take in the Mekong views. Good value.

Auberge Sala Inpeng GUESTHOUSE **$$**
(Map p142; ☎021-242021; www.salalao.com; Th In Paeng; r incl breakfast US$25-40; ❄📶) Thoroughly individual and unlike anything else in the city, this pretty complex of wood cabanas and a handsome traditional Laotian house is set in gardens spilling over with tamarind and champa (frangipani) flowers. The grander rooms have a whiff of rustic chic, with en suites and air-con. And although the cheaper cabanas are small, they're bursting with atmosphere. Meanwhile staff are as welcoming as a slice of home.

Intercity Hotel HOTEL **$$**
(Map p142; ☎021-242843; www.laointercity.com; 24-25 Th Fa Ngoum; s/d/ste incl breakfast US$40/60/80; ❄@📶) Unprepossessing and dust ridden from its river-facing exterior. Within its wine-dark walls, however, is a world woven of mosaic floors and 47 rooms boasting trad art and fine handicraft. The deluxe rooms are *far* superior, with romantic Mekong views, while the standard rooms, in comparison, are forgettable. Downstairs, the lobby is choking on quirky Buddhist statuary, Khmer friezes and marauding vegetation.

Nalinthone Guesthouse GUESTHOUSE **$$**
(Map p138; ☎021-243659; namrinnvte@yahoo.com; Th Fa Ngoum; r US$25-30; P❄@📶) This family-run, modern place on the river lacks a little in atmosphere, but the clean and comfortable rooms are great value considering the position – the doubles with river views (US$30) are the pick. As a further boon it's a few yards down from the lovely Spirit House (p159).

★ **Ansara Hôtel** BOUTIQUE HOTEL $$$

(Map p142; ☎021-213514; www.ansarahotel.com; off Th Fa Ngum; incl breakfast r US$123-133, ste US$198-250;) Achingly beautiful Ansara is housed in a recently built French villa with heavy whiffs of Indochina. Its alfresco dining terrace is as refined as its Gallic cuisine. There are 16 rooms in the house and manicured garden, all of which are lovely with wood floor, balcony, flat-screen, bath and exquisite handicrafts.

Around Vientiane

Villa Lao GUESTHOUSE $$

(Map p138; ☎021-242292; www.villa-lao-guesthouse.com; off Th Nong Douang; r 100,000-180,000K;) A garden oasis about 1.5km west of town, Villa Lao sprawls with ferns and palms, and has 23 delightful, rustic rooms bursting with character – think wood stilts, white walls, mosquito nets and a charming communal balcony and lounge. The cheapest rooms are bare, fan-cooled and have shared bathrooms, however, all rooms are large and cool with low-lying beds. The English-speaking owners are passionate about Lao food and run a great morning cooking course (150,000K). Bikes can also be hired.

★ **Mandala Boutique Hotel** BOUTIQUE HOTEL $$$

(Map p138; ☎021-214493; www.mandalahotel.asia; off Th Fa Ngoum; r incl breakfast US$80-100;) This new, super-chic hotel offers the city's brightest, coolest accommodation (we're talking 'Wallpaper' rather than The Fonz). An old French villa built in the 1960s is its setting, and flashes of vivid colour and chichi flourishes such as lacquered granite floors, flat-screen TVs and dark-wood furniture blend perfectly with the aesthetic of its art-deco lines. The four-poster beds are possibly the most comfortable in Laos. There's also a very natty Asian fusion restaurant in the gardens, the menu of which was being finalised when we visited.

Green Park Hotel BOUTIQUE HOTEL $$$

(Map p138; ☎021-264097; www.greenparkvientiane.com; 248 Th Khu Vieng; r incl breakfast US$145-450;) A real urban oasis, this charming boutique hotel exudes calm and escape the moment you enter its dark-wood lobby and step into its centrepiece garden abuzz with flowers and a sparkling pool, and shaded by sugar palms and frangipani trees. Rooms are super-chic and feature hardwood floors, capacious bathrooms, couches, safety deposit boxes and step-in mosquito nets. The staff are friendly, the breakfast and dinner fantastic; they alone merit the journey.

Eating

Few places in Southeast Asia boast such a dizzying array of global cuisine; be it felafel at an authentic Turkish restaurant, or upscale Japanese and Korean barbecue. The streets that radiate off Th Setthathirath are vivid with smells and steam as old-school restaurants serve up fine Italian and French fare in the choicest of surroundings. Lao food has enjoyed a real contemporary makeover in recent years with well-executed traditional dishes given a modern twist in 21st-century-style restaurants. And finally, if it's comfort food you seek, look no further than the bakeries left by the French footprint, for the city is famous for its fresh-baked baguettes and crispy croissants, with full-bodied coffee that could make the Seine glow green with envy.

For all its Gallic refinement, Vientiane is equally informal; cheap food on the hop can be grabbed from pâté vendors dotted around the old quarter, and the impromptu braziers that fire up grilled chicken and Mekong fish on skewers. And don't miss the chance to wander through the redolent witch's broth that is Chinatown on Th Hengboun.

Th Setthathirath & Nam Phu

★ **Makphet** LAOTIAN $

(Map p142; Th Setthathirath; mains 40,000K; 11am-9pm Mon, Wed, Thu, Fri & Sat, 6-9pm Tue;) Managed by Friends International (www.friends-international.org), Makphet helps disadvantaged kids build a future as chefs and waiters, while reviving the country's traditional cuisine. Guacamole-green walls and hardwood furnishings add style to delicious dishes such as spicy green papaya salad. It's located opposite Wat Ong Teu off Th Setthathirath.

★ **Le Banneton** BAKERY $

(Map p142; Th Nokèokoummane; breakfast 45,000K; 7am-9pm;) Hands-down the country's best croissants, though to get them at their best and before the supply runs out, get yourself here first thing in the morning. Le Banneton's Doisneau-spattered interior makes for a nice place to read a paper over a tart, salad, panini or tasty omelette, or you can sit outside on the small terrace.

Aria ITALIAN $
(Map p142; ☎021-222589; www.aria.org.com; 8 Th François Ngin; mains 60,000K; ⏰11am-2.30pm & 5.30-11pm) This ice-cool Italian haunt pipes classical music across its tangerine interior hung with Lao tapestries, and serves a range of soup, pasta, risotto, pizza and steak dishes with aplomb. If there's a better pie in town, we haven't found it.

Taj Mahal Restaurant INDIAN $
(Map p142; off Th Setthathirath; meals 25,000K; ⏰10am-10.30pm Mon-Sat, 4-10.30pm Sun; ✎) Hidden down a side street opposite the back of the Culture Hall, this unpretentious earthy joint dishes up fresh and lively curries and melt-in-your mouth naan. Portions are generous and you can sit semi-alfresco. Good veggie selection too (20 dishes). Tasty chicken masala.

Scandinavian Bakery BAKERY $
(Map p142; www.scandinavianbakerylaos.com; Nam Phu; mains 10,000-30,000K; ⏰7am-9pm; ❄📶👪) Its wilting wood facade might look as if it's shipwrecked, but this Vientiane institution is the original bakery to get your carb fix, with a treasure trove of fresh subs, breakfasts, brownies, muffins, bagels and delicious coffees. And when you're done with your main course get stuck into their sweets counter of eclairs, cheesecake and doughnuts. Loads of comfy couches and alfresco tables upstairs and down.

JoMa Bakery Café BAKERY $
(Map p142; Th Setthathirath; mains 29,000K; ⏰7am-9pm Mon-Sat; ❄📶👪) Packed to the gills with hungry travellers and expats, this mocha-hued cafe is Vientiane's busiest, most stylish bakery thanks to its soothingly cool atmosphere and cornucopia of lush salads (25,000K) and bespoke bagels - choose from salami, ham, salmon, turkey, cheese and salad fillings. It also serves tacos, breakfast and soup. Comfy couches, free wi-fi, unfailing cleanliness and a central location will keep you coming back for more.

Croissant d'Or BAKERY $
(Map p142; ☎021-223741; 96/1 Th Nokèokoummane; ⏰6.30am-9pm; ❄📶) This simple bakery has a modest interior of umbrella-shaded lights and a cold-selection counter of ham, salami, cheeses and salads. The coffee packs a punch and the baguettes are light and fluffy.

Phimphone Market SELF-CATERING $
(Map p142; 94/6 Th Setthathirath; ⏰7am-9pm Mon-Sat; 📶) This self-catering oasis stocks everything from gleaming fresh veg, Western magazines, ice cream, imported French and German salami, bread, biscuits and chocolate, as well as Western toiletries. Don't miss its cafe serving great coffees, juices and tasty baguette sandwiches. Also stocks Hobo maps of the city.

L'Adresse de Tinay FRENCH $$
(Map p142; ☎020-5691 3434; off Th Setthathirath; mains 130,000K; ⏰6-11pm; ❄📶) Alchemising an eclectic gastro landscape of snails

OODLES OF NOODLES

Noodles of all kinds are popular in Laos, and Vientiane has the country's greatest variety. The most popular noodle of all is undoubtedly *fĕr*, the local version of Vietnamese *pho*, served with beef or pork and accompanied, Lao-style, by a huge plate of fresh herbs and vegetables and a ridiculous amount of condiments. Central Vientiane's most popular *fĕr* joint is Pho Dung (p157). Also popular are *kòw ƀûn*, the thin rice noodles known as *kànŏm jeen* in Thailand, taken in Laos with a spicy curry-like broth as is done at Amphone (p156), or sometimes in a clear pork broth *(kòw ƀûn nâm jąaou)*, as available at Han Sam Euay Nong (p158). There's also *kòw ƀęeak sèn*, thick rice- and tapioca-flour noodles served in a slightly viscous broth with crispy deep-fried pork belly or chicken. A good place to sample this dish is **Rice Noodle – Lao Porridge** (Map p142; ☎020-5541 4455; Th Hengboun; mains 8000K; ⏰4pm-1am).

Other popular noodles include *mii* (traditional Chinese egg noodle), particularly prevalent in the unofficial Chinatown area bounded by Th Hengboun, Th Chao Anou, Th Khounboulom and the western end of Th Samsènethai, and *băn kŭan*, Lao for *bánh cuôn*, a freshly steamed rice noodle filled with minced pork, mushrooms and carrots, a Vietnamese speciality that is popular in Laos. Look for it in the mornings near the intersection of Th Chao Anou and Th Hengboun.

and scrambled eggs, sea bream fillet, beef tenderloin, rack of lamb and rosemary, and a to-die-for crème brûleé perfumed with Madagascan vanilla, Chef Tinay is one of the city's top chefs. Great place to dress up, and in a new location right next to Makphet.

Khop Chai Deu ASIAN FUSION **$$**
(KCD; Map p142; 021-251564; 54 Th Setthathirath; mains 25,000-60,000K; 8am-midnight;) In a remodelled colonial-era villa near Nam Phu, Khop Chai Deu has been a travellers' favourite for years because of its range of well-prepared Lao, Thai, Indian and assorted European fare. You can pick your live fish from the kitchen and see it a few minutes later on your plate. KCD has plenty of fun activities, such as speed-dating on every 11th of the month, women's arm wrestling and free beauty makeovers on arrival. Upstairs is a new low-lit bar with slick urban swagger.

Benoni Café ASIAN FUSION **$$**
(Map p142; 021-213334; Th Setthathirath; mains 40,000-50,000K; 10am-6pm Mon-Sat) A stylish addition to Th Setthathirath, Benoni is only open till early evening which seems to be making it even *more* popular. Come lunchtime, its contemporary interior (upstairs above Phimphone Market) is packed with NGOs and Lao urbanites, and has a menu that boasts Asian fusion meets Italian cuisine. Super-fresh snacks, salads and pasta dishes. The carbonara is excellent.

Le Vendôme FRENCH **$$**
(Map p142; 39 Th In Paeng; mains 50,000K; 5-10pm Tue-Sun) Hidden behind a cascade of ivy, it's almost as if this vintage French restaurant is in hiding. The menu comprises very reasonably priced soufflés, pâtés, salads, wood-fired pizzas, terrines and steaks. The candle-lit interior, peppered with vintage bull-fighting posters, is perfect for a romantic evening.

Amphone LAOTIAN **$$**
(Map p142; 10/3 Th Wat Xieng Nyean; mains 45,000K; 11am-2pm & 5.30-10pm;) Featured on celebrity chef Anthony Bourdain's *Discovery* TV series, this upscale oasis of wood floors and salmon-coloured walls is refined and cool. Aside of an encyclopaedic wine list, Amphone's menu replicates traditional Laotian dishes based on owner Mook's grandmother's creations. 'Luang Prabang sausage' and 'fish citronella' are but a few. Try the snake bean salad or tom yum soup.

La Terrasse FRENCH **$$**
(Map p142; Th Nokèokoummane; mains 40,000-100,000K; 11am-2pm & 6-10pm Mon-Sat;) With its old-fashioned French ambience of white-topped tables and custard-cream interior, this is a real gem for well-executed Gallic cuisine. Plenty of choice from *steak au frites, steak Provencal,* pan-fried fish, quiche, soup and *boeuf bourguignon,* as well as thin-crust pizza. It's also popular with French expats for its tempting wine list.

★ **Le Silapa** FRENCH **$$$**
(Map p142; 021-219689; 88 Th Setthathirat Rd; mains US$20; 11am-11pm;) Recently relocated Le Silapa is beautiful in its chichi whiteness complemented by wood floors, raftered ceiling and bird-cage lights. Vientiane's finest Gallic restaurant features favourites from foie gras to salads, steaks to brain casserole. It's upstairs at the excellent iBeam bar. Magnifique!

Pimentón SPANISH **$$$**
(Map p142; 021-215506; www.pimentonrestaurant-vte.com; Th Nokèokoummane; mains 80,000-170,000K; lunch & dinner;) Industrial-chic Pimentón exudes style and heavenly aromas from imported meats sizzling on its open range. This is Vientiane's new mecca for steaks: Chateaubriand, rib-eye, tenderloin or ribs, plus other delights such as flame-grilled chicken or chorizo. With Spanish owners, this is also the place to savour authentic tapas including empanadas (with beef, green olives and raisins), *calamares* and charcuterie of cured meats.

Th Samsènethai & Around

★ **Lao Kitchen** LAOTIAN **$**
(Map p142; 021-254332; www.lao-kitchen.com; Th Hengboun; mains 30,000-40,000K; 11am-10pm;) This superb new Lao restaurant is contemporary, fresh and unfailingly creative in its execution of trad-Lao dishes. Colourful walls dotted with superior photography, indie tunes and decent service complement a menu spanning stews to Luang Prabang sausage (full of vim), variations on *láhp* (spicy Lao-style salad of minced meat, poultry or fish), stir-fried Morning Glory, and various palate-friendly sorbets. Prepare to return again and again.

YuLaLa Cafe ASIAN FUSION **$**
(Map p142; Th Hengboun; mains 50,000K; 11.30am-2pm & 6-9.30pm Tue-Sun;) This

impeccably clean, restful gem pipes classical music across its wood-floored space and travellers sit cross-legged on cushions (leave yer shoes outside!). Look out for favourites such as tofu dumplings, stewed eggplant and sautéed salt pork. A little bit of zen to take you from the bustle of the city.

PVO VIETNAMESE **$**

(Map p138; ☎021-454663; off Th Simeuang; mains 18,000K; ⏰6am-7pm Mon-Sat, 6am-2pm Sun;) This fresh, no-frills Vietnamese-run eatery is one of the better places in town to grab lunch; in addition to several tasty Vietnamese spring roll–based dishes (16,000K), PVO does some of the best *kòw jee ƀá-đê* (half/whole baguettes 8000K) in town.

Pho Dung LAOTIAN **$**

(Map p142; ☎021-213775; 158 Th Hengboun; noodle soup 12,000-15,000K; ⏰6am-2pm) This excellent *fĕr* (rice-noodle soup) diner is a packed melting pot of locals and travellers. Choose from pork, beef or chicken noodle soup. The friendly Vietnamese family who run this place serve up gargantuan bowls Lao-style – that is, with heaps of optional seasonings and immense plates of fresh veggies and herbs.

Vieng Sawan VIETNAMESE **$**

(Map p142; ☎021-213990; Th Hengboun; mains 16,000-46,000K; ⏰11am-10pm) In the middle of Chinatown, Vieng Sawan is a bustling open-sided restaurant that offers a fun eating experience. It specialises in *nǎam néuang* (Vietnamese barbecued pork meatballs) and many varieties of *yór* (spring rolls), usually sold in 'sets' *(sut)* with *kòw ƀûn,* fresh lettuce leaves, mint, basil, various sauces for dipping, sliced starfruit and green banana.

Han Ton Phai LAOTIAN **$**

(Map p142; ☎021-252542; Th Pangkham; mains 10,000-20,000K; ⏰9am-10pm) An escape from carb-heavy bakeries, this Lao mainstay is earthy and authentic, its menu spanning pork *láhp* (minced pork in a chilli-spiced mint salad) to *kôy pạa* (a chunky salad of freshwater fish and fresh herbs; 10,000K to 20,000K). There's no English sign, so keep an eye open for the billboard that says 'traditional food'.

Korean Restaurant KOREAN **$**

(Map p142; ☎020-208 7080; Th Hengboun; mains 30,000-180,00K; ⏰9am-11pm) Lacklustre name aside, this Korean-run place is great for sampling what is currently the most popular cuisine in Southeast Asia. Most locals go directly for the Korean barbecue (80,000K), but we liked the kimchi stew (30,000K), served Korean-style with heaps of side dishes.

Noy's Fruit Heaven JUICE BAR **$**

(Map p142; Th Hengboun; fruit shakes 8000K; ⏰7am-9pm;) Homely, colourful juice bar with Chinese paper lanterns hanging from the ceiling. Stop in to pick up a few of your *five a day* or decimate your hangover with one of their dragonfruit, coconut, mango, or tomato juice shakes. They also turn out super-fresh fruit salads and burgers, and rent bikes (10,000K).

Baguette & Pâté Vendor STREET VENDOR **$**

(Map p142; Th Samsènethai; half/whole baguette 11,000/22,000K; ⏰6am-8pm) Great *kòw jịi pâtê* (baguettes with liver pâté, veg and cream cheese, dripping with sweet chilli sauce). There's no English-language sign here, but the stall is directly on the corner of Th Pangkham and Th Samsènethai.

Phimphone Market 2 SELF-CATERING **$**

(Map p142; ☎021-214609; cnr Th Samsènethai & Th Chanthakoummane; ⏰8.30am-8.30pm) This smaller branch of the Phimphone market stocks fresh baguettes, biscuits, crisps, toiletries, cereals, fresh milk, salami and hams, and also includes a small wine cellar.

★Bistrot 22 FRENCH **$$**

(Map p142; ☎020-5552 7286; Th Samsènethai; mains 65,000-250,000K; ⏰11.30am-2pm & 6-10pm;) Moved a little further out of the centre to a less bubbly locale, Bistrot 22 is, however, enjoying great reviews for Chef Philippe's lustrous cuisine and dishes such as pear salad, deep-fried apple and camembert salad, tender steaks and cauliflower soup. This intimate little restaurant is the gastro highlight of many people's visit to Laos.

Mekong Riverfront & Around

Istanbul TURKISH **$**

(Map p142; ☎020-7797 8190; Th François Ngin; mains 20,000-90,000K; ⏰9.30am-10.30pm;) An authentic slice of Istanbul, this welcoming, family-run joint is lively, with a funky interior and a few tables out front. An equally colourful menu of doner and shish kebabs as well as favourites such as meatballs, hummus and felafel. Try the Iskender kebab – grilled beef with pepper sauce, yoghurt and green chilli. All meats are fully marinated and the super-charged Turkish coffee will put a spring in your step.

Common Ground Café MEXICAN $
(Map p142; 020-7872 7183; Th Chao Anou; mains 29,000K; 7am-8pm Mon-Sat;) It's air-con cool in this family-friendly Mexican cafe. Sofas to read on, a cold-selection counter boasting wraps, quesadillas, felafel, salads and homemade cookies. Best of all though if you've got kids, is the enclosed shaded play area out back with a slide and climbing frame. Finally, a place you can relax while your kids are within view.

Khambang Lao Food Restaurant LAOTIAN $
(Map p142; 021-217198; 97/2 Th Khounboulom; mains 10,000-70,000K; 11.30am-2.30pm & 5.30-9pm) The Lao food in this powder-blue joint, a little up from the river, is worth the wait. Expect fresh grub so spicy it leaves a zingy footprint on your palate. Delicious *láhp* (spicy pork salad), roasted Mekong fish, fried frogs' legs; *áw lám*, described on the menu as 'spicy beef stew', and tasty Luang Prabang–style sausage. Yum!

Han Sam Euay Nong LAO $
(Map p142; Th Chao Anou; mains 8000-20,000K; 8am-7pm) Cheap, tidy and tasty, this busy family-run restaurant features must-have dishes such as *năam kòw,* crispy balls of deep-fried rice and sour pork sausage shredded into a saladlike dish, and the delicious *kòw Ђûn nâm jąaou,* thin rice noodles served in a pork broth with pork, bamboo and herbs. This unmarked restaurant is located directly adjacent to the Lao Orchid Hotel.

★ **La Signature** FRENCH $$
(Map p142; 021-213523; www.ansarahotel.com; Ansara Hotel;) With Billie Holiday drifting onto the fan-cooled terrace of glass-topped wicker tables (and upstairs in the ochre-hued restaurant), La Signature is perfect for throwing on your smarts and taking a romantic supper. Pan-fried salmon with blue cheese, lobster, roast lamb and thyme... a few of the delights awaiting you in this beautiful French villa.

Around Vientiane

Cafe Nomad CAFE $
(Map p138; Th Phonsay; mains 29,000K; 8am-7pm Mon-Fri, 8am-6pm Sat & Sun;) Right near the Thai embassy, this hidden treasure has original artwork on the mustard-coloured walls, whirring fans, various delicious paninis and allegedly the best brownies in town. Flavoursome coffee and friendly staff. A great place to work, tellingly it's popular with expats.

ParadIce FRENCH $
(Map p142; 021-312836; Th Lan Xang; mains 35,000-45,000K; 11am-7pm Mon-Sat;) In the grounds of the Institut Français this airy, comfortable cafe is a real oasis to sit and read accompanied by a coffee (and quick wi-fi). There's French news on the tube and a range of sandwiches and cakes to keep you quiet. Don't miss the delicious ice creams and chocolates.

Ban Anou Night Market LAOTIAN $
(Map p142; meals 10,000-15,000K; 5-10pm) Setting up on a small street off the north end of Th Chao Anou every evening, this atmospheric open-air market dishes up Lao cuisine, from grilled meats to chilli-based dips with vegetables and sticky rice.

Drinking & Nightlife

Vientiane is no longer the illicit pleasure palace it was when Paul Theroux described it in his 1975 book *The Great Railway Bazaar,* as a place in which 'the brothels are cleaner than the hotels, marijuana is cheaper than pipe tobacco and opium easier to find than a cold glass of beer'. Nowadays, brothels are strictly prohibited, Talat Sao's marijuana stands have been removed from prominent display, and cold Beerlao has definitely replaced opium as the nightly drug of choice. Most of the bars, restaurants and discos close by 11.30pm or midnight.

DJs have only recently caught on in Vientiane and a visit to one of a clutch of Lao nightclubs may drive you to the nearest pharmacy to seek a pair of earplugs. Insanely noisy, the vibe is a bit confused, with Lao youth who haven't quite got their heads around rave music; one particular club looked like the audience was playing freeze-frame. Karaoke is also popular here, as is live music playing Western songs.

Conveniently, two of the better clubs are within walking distance of each other on the way to the airport. **Echo** (Map p138; 021-213570; Th Samsènethai; 8pm-1am), at the Mercure Hotel, is pretty cool by Western standards and is popular with Vientiane's beautiful people. Just up the road, **At Home** (Map p138; Th Luang Prabang; 8pm-midnight) thumps with trance and house.

★Khop Chai Deu BAR

(KCD; Map p142; ☎021-251564; www.inthira.com; Th Setthathirath) KCD is the city's original watering hole and these days has massively finessed its nocturnal offerings – think low-lit interiors and a sophisticated drinks list, plus more activities than any other bar, such as speed dating and women's arm wrestling. Upstairs on the 3rd floor a new bar has opened; more South Beach Miami than Vientiane, it's slick urban, and very cool.

★iBeam BAR

(Map p142; ☎021-254528; Th Setthathirath; ⊙11am-11pm;) The classiest new joint in town, with its glass panel walls and beautiful interior, iBeam invites you to sit back and gaze at the old *New Yorker* prints and beautiful people, while snacking on tapas and working your way through an extensive wine list. Wednesday is ladies' night and nets you 50% off. Sorry chaps.

Spirit House COCKTAIL BAR

(Map p138; ☎021-262530; Th Fa Ngoum; cocktails 40,000K; ⊙7am-11pm;) This traditional Lao house facing the Mekong has a well-stocked bar with enough cocktails on the menu to keep a *roué* smiling. Chillsome tunes complement the dark woods and comfy couches of its stylish interior.

Bor Pennyang BAR

(Map p142; ☎020-7873 965; Th Fa Ngoum; ⊙10am-midnight) Way up in the gods overlooking mother Mekong, a cast of locals, expats, bar girls and travellers assemble at this tin-roofed, wood-raftered watering hole. From balcony seats you can gaze out at nearby Thailand over a sunset Beerlao. There are easy-on-the-ear Western tunes, pool tables and a huge bar to drape yourself over, as well as sports on TV.

Samlo Pub BAR

(Map p142; ☎021-222308; Th Setthathirath; ⊙7pm-late) Just as sleazy and dimly lit as ever, this joint feels like the lovechild of an East End Kray's pub that married a Patpong good-time bar. Perfect for an atmospheric drink, the person next to you could be a rogue, hooker, ladyboy, criminal, or your own reflection. Duck in for a quickie (drink) but don't hang around!

Kong View BAR

(Map p138; ☎021-520522; off Th Luang Prabang; dishes 25,000-70,000K; ⊙11am-midnight) This stylish balcony, suspended over a quiet section of the Mekong, functions equally well as a beer garden or dinner destination.

Jazzy Brick BAR

(Map p142; ☎020-244 9307; Th Setthathirath; ⊙7pm-late;) With its stylish, exposed-brick interior adorned in old jazz posters, and Coltrane sliding through the low-lit atmosphere, this is perfect for an upscale evening on the tiles. Occasional live Latin and bossa nova, and enough cocktails on the menu to keep a hellraiser busy (great mojitos).

☆ Entertainment

Like everything else, Vientiane's entertainment scene is picking up as money and politics allows, though the range remains fairly limited. By law, entertainment venues must close by 11.30pm, though most push it to about midnight.

Cinema

Lao cinemas died out in the video-shop tidal wave of the 1990s, though there is a cinema due to be built next to the Green Park Hotel at the upcoming World Trade Shopping Centre.

Institut Français CINEMA

(French Cultural Centre; Map p142; ☎021-215764; www.ambafrance-laos.org/centre; Th Lan Xang; admission free; ⊙9.30am-6.30pm Mon-Fri, to noon Sat) Dance, art exhibitions, literary discussions and live music all take place in this Gallic hive of cultural activity. As well as cult French films (shown Saturday at 7.30pm), the centre also offers French and Lao language lessons.

Circus

National Circus PERFORMING ARTS

(Hong Kanyasin; Map p138; Th Thong Khan Kham;) The old 'Russian Circus' established in the 1980s is now known as Hong Kanyasin. It performs from time to time in the National Circus venue, in the north of town. Check for dates in the *Vientiane Times*.

Live Music

Anou Cabaret LIVE MUSIC

(Map p142; ☎021-213630; cnr Th Hengboun & Th Chao Anou; ⊙8pm-midnight) On the ground floor of the Anou Paradise Hotel, the cabaret has been swinging along for years. It's a funny place, with old crooners and a palpable 1960s feel.

Wind West LIVE MUSIC

(Map p142; ☎020-200 0777; Th Luang Prabang; ⊙5pm-1am) A US roadhouse-style bar and restaurant, Wind West (yes, Wind, that's not a typo) has live Lao and Western rock music most nights – the music usually starts about 9pm and finishes around 1am. Depending on the night it can be heaving, or completely dead but the interior, hung with 10-gallon hats, antlers, and wooden Native American statues, lends the place a folksy atmosphere.

Peurk-may LIVE MUSIC
(Map p138; ☎021-315536; Th Tha Deua; ⏲6pm-midnight) The name means 'tree bark', a design theme that dominates this self-designated 'Acoustic Guitar Bar'. Thai folk and pop dominates, and even if you're not a fan of the genre, the conversation-level volume and the enticing Thai-Lao menu (mains 16,000K to 65,000K) make Peurk-may a good low-key destination.

Traditional Music & Dancing

Six types of traditional Lao dance can be seen nightly from 7.30pm to 11pm in the Lane Xang Hotel. The **Lao National Culture Hall** (Map p142; Th Samsènethai) also hosts similar performances on occasions, but with no publicly available schedule of events you'll need to keep a close eye on the *Vientiane Times* for an announcement.

Lao National Opera Theatre THEATRE
(Map p138; ☎021-260300; Th Khounboulom; admission 70,000K; ⏲7-8.30pm Tue, Thu & Sat) This state-sponsored performance venue features a smorgasbord of Lao entertainment ranging from self-proclaimed 'Lao oldies' to Lao boxing and traditional performances of *Pha Lak Pha Lam*, the Lao version of the Indian epic the Ramayana.

Shopping

Just about anything made in Laos is available for purchase in Vientiane, including hill-tribe crafts, jewellery, traditional textiles and carvings. The main shopping area in town is along Th Setthathirath and the streets radiating from it.

Bookshops

Book Café BOOKS
(Map p142; Th Hengboun; ⏲8am-8pm Mon-Fri) Vientiane's best stocked secondhand bookshop is owned by anthropologist and author Dr Robert Cooper, and sells loads of travel guides, thrillers and informative books on Laos' culture and history.

Monument Books BOOKS
(Map p142; 124 Th Nokèokoummane; ⏲9am-8pm Mon-Fri, to 6pm Sat & Sun) Great one-stop shop for glossy magazines and a tasteful range of modern classic novels, plus travel guides, thrillers, lush pictorials on Laos, as well as a few toys and books for kids.

Oriental Bookshop BOOKS
(Map p142; ☎021-215352; 121 Th Chao Anou; ⏲10am-8pm) Mr Ngo stocks a decent selection of secondhand novels, postcards and stamps, and also a comprehensive range of books on Laos ethnicity. Coffee and internet (per hour 5000K) are also available.

Handicrafts, Antiques & Art

Several shops along Th Samsènethai, Th Pangkham and Th Setthathirath sell Lao and Thai tribal and hill-tribe crafts. The Lao goods are increasingly complemented by products from Vietnam and Thailand, such as lacquer work and Buddha images. Many of the places listed in the Textiles & Clothing section also carry handicrafts and antiques.

★**T'Shop Lai Gallery** BEAUTY, HOMEWARES
(Map p142; www.laococo.com/tshoplai.htm; off Th In Paeng; ⏲8am-8pm Mon-Sat, 10-6pm Sun) Easily Vientiane's finest shopping experience – step into this palace of the senses and the first thing you notice is the melange of aromas: coconut, aloe vera, honey, frangipani and magnolia; all of them emanate from the body oils, soaps, sprays, perfumes and lip balms that are made and beautifully packaged by self-taught *parfumier*, Michel 'Mimi' Saada. Next check out the tortoiseshell–inlaid furniture – a hint of Bauhaus fused with traditional Lao – and the old apothecary units beguilingly stocked with illuminated antique bottles. Cards, bangles, prints, fountain pens...these wonderful objets d'art and products are all made with sustainable, locally sourced products, and by disadvantaged women who make up the Les Artisans Lao cooperative. Inspired.

Carterie du Laos GIFTS
(Map p142; ☎021-241401; 118/2 Th Setthathirath; ⏲9am-5pm) This shop has a wide range of postcards, cards, posters and books, and a few small souvenirs.

Indochina Handicrafts HANDICRAFTS
(Map p142; ☎021-223528; Th Setthathirath; ⏲10am-7pm) Laos' version of the Old Curiosity Shop, this enchanting den of Buddha statuary, antique Ho Chi Minh and Mao busts, Russian wristwatches and communist memorabilia, Matchbox cars, medals,

snuff boxes and vintage serving trays, is a stop that shouldn't be missed. Next to Carterie Du Laos; look for the plant-crowded exterior.

Satri Lao SOUVENIRS
(Map p142; ☎021-244384; Th Setthathirath; ⊙9am-8pm Mon-Sat, 10am-7pm Sun) Set across three polished, fragrant floors, this Aladdin's cave of an emporium hawks high-quality jewellery, Hmong handbags, pillowcases, Oriental-style chemises, Tintin lacquer paintings, Buddha statuary, and a whole lot more. Expensive, but perfect for a last-minute keepsake.

Treasures of Asia ART
(Map p142; ☎021-222236; 86/7 Th Setthathirath; ⊙noon-7pm Mon-Fri) This tiny gallery holds the original works of established Lao artists, many of whom are featured in the book *Lao Contemporary Art,* also available here.

Markets

Talat Sao MARKET
(Morning Market; Map p142; Th Lan Xang; ⊙7am-5pm) A once-memorable Vientiane shopping experience, Talat Sao has sadly undergone a facelift; two-thirds of its weave-world of stalls selling opium pipes, jewellery and traditional antiques have been ripped down and replaced with a eunuch of a modern mall. The remaining building's fabric merchants are hanging by a thread.

Talat Khua Din MARKET
(Map p142; Th Khu Vieng; ⊙5am-1pm) East of Talat Sao and beyond the bus terminal, this rather muddy market offers fresh produce and meats, as well as flowers, tobacco and other assorted goods.

Talat Thong Khan Kham MARKET
(Map p138; cnr Th Thong Khan Kham & Th Dong Miang; ⊙5am-3pm) This market north of the centre in Ban Khan Kham is open all day, but is best in the morning. It's one of the biggest in Vientiane and has virtually everything, from food to tools. Nearby are basket and pottery vendors.

Textiles & Clothing

Downtown Vientiane is littered with stores selling textiles. Th Nokèokoummane is the epicentre; Talat Sao is also a good place to buy fabrics. You'll find antiques as well as modern fabrics, plus utilitarian items such as shoulder bags (some artfully constructed around squares of antique fabric), cushions and pillows.

To see Lao weaving in action, seek out the weaving district of Ban Nong Buathong, northeast of the town centre in Muang Chanthabuli. About 20 families (many originally from Sam Neua in Hua Phan Province) live and work here, including a couple of households that sell textiles directly to the public.

Carol Cassidy Lao Textiles HANDICRAFTS
(Map p142; ☎021-212123; www.laotextiles.com; 84-86 Th Nokèokoummane; ⊙8am-noon & 2-5pm Mon-Fri, 8am-noon Sat, or by appointment) Lao Textiles sells high-end contemporary, original-design fabrics inspired by older Lao weaving patterns, motifs and techniques. The American designer, Carol Cassidy, employs Lao weavers who work out the back of the attractive old French-Lao house. Internationally known, with prices to match.

Couleur d'Asie FASHION
(Map p142; ☎021-223008; www.couleurdasie.net; 201 Th François Ngin; ⊙9am-5pm Mon-Sat) Colourful as an artist's palette, this delightful boutique owned by a French-Vietnamese dress designer has a vivid range of ladies' dresses, men's linen shirts and boho chemises. It also sells lovely jewellery, bed runners, and silk shawls. Upstairs you can see the dresses being made and have one fitted to order.

Kanchana Boutique HANDICRAFTS
(Map p142; ☎021-213467; 102 Th Chanthakoummane; ⊙8am-9pm Mon-Sat) This shop carries what is possibly the most upscale selection of Lao silk in town (the most expensive designs, some of which sell for several thousand US dollars, are kept in an adjacent room), and the friendly owners can arrange a visit to their Lao Textile Museum, or even lessons in weaving and dyeing.

KPP Handicraft Promotion Enterprise of Sekong Province HANDICRAFTS
(Map p142; ☎021-241421; cnr Th Setthathirath & Th Chao Anou; ⊙9am-8pm) This modest-looking place sells fair-trade textiles from the Bolaven Plateau province of Sekong.

True Colour HANDICRAFTS
(Map p142; ☎021-214410; Th Setthathirath; ⊙9am-8pm Mon-Sat) This store sells a wide spectrum of hand-spun silk shawls and wall hangings, as well as vividly coloured Hmong handbags and pin cushions. All made in the Houey Hong Vocational Training Center for Women (p147).

Khampan Lao Handicraft HANDICRAFTS
(Map p142; ☎021-222000; Th Nokèokoummane; ⊙8am-9pm) Sells textiles from the Sam Neua area at very reasonable prices.

Mixay Boutique HANDICRAFTS
(Map p142; ☎021-216592; Th Nokèokoummane; ⊙9am-8pm) Upmarket Mixay deals in locally made silks.

Camacrafts HANDICRAFTS
(Map p142; www.camacrafts.org; Th Nokèokoummane; ⊙10am-6pm Mon-Sat) Stocks silk clothes and weavings from Xieng Khuang Province, plus some bed and cushion covers in striking Hmong-inspired designs.

Wine

Vins de France WINE
(Map p142; ☎021-217700; 354 Th Samsènethai; ⊙8am-8pm) Vins de France (the sign says 'baràvin') is one of the best French wine cellars in Southeast Asia. Even if you don't like wine, it's worth popping in for a look at a place so completely out of character with its surrounds. If you do like wine, the US$3 degustation (*avec saucissons*!) might be a wise investment.

VanSom WINE
(Map p142; ☎021-212196; 110/01 Th Samsènethai; ⊙8am-8pm Mon-Sat) Another well-stocked and equally slick wine cellar.

Orientation

Vientiane curves along the Mekong River following a meandering northwest–southeast axis, with the central district of Muang Chanthabuli at the centre of the bend. Most of the government offices, hotels, restaurants and historic temples are located in Chanthabuli, near the river. Some old French colonial buildings and Vietnamese-Chinese shophouses remain, set alongside newer structures built according to the rather boxy social realist school of architecture.

Wattay International Airport is around 4km northwest of the centre. The Northern bus station, where long-distance services to points north begin and end, is about 2km northwest of the centre. The Southern bus station deals with most services heading south and is 9km northeast of the centre on Rte 13. The border with Thailand at the Thai-Lao Friendship Bridge is 19km southeast of the city.

Street signs are limited to major roads and the central, more touristy part of town. Where they do exist, the English and French designations vary (eg route, *rue*, road and avenue) but the Lao script always reads *tanŏn* (Th). Therefore, when asking directions it's always best to just use *tanŏn*.

The parallel Th Setthathirath (which is home to several famous temples) and Th Samsènethai are the main streets in central Vientiane. Heading northwest they both eventually lead to Th Luang Prabang and Rte 13 north. In the other direction they run perpendicular to and eventually cross Th Lan Xang, a major boulevard leading from the presidential palace past Talat Sao (Morning Market) to Patuxai (Victory Monument) and, after turning into Th Phon Kheng, to Rte 13 south and the Southern Bus Station.

The *meuang* of Vientiane are broken up into *bâan* (Ban), which are neighbourhoods or villages associated with local wats. Wattay International Airport, for example, is in Ban Wat Tai – the area in which Wat Tai is located.

MAPS

Hobo Maps (www.hobomaps.com; US$2) Has probably the best generally available map of the city; get it at bookshops and Phimphone Markets.

Information

DANGERS & ANNOYANCES

By international standards Vientiane has a very low crime rate, but readers' reports and local anecdotes suggest there's an increasing risk of getting mugged. Be especially careful around the BCEL Bank on the riverfront, where bag-snatchers, usually a two-man team with a motorbike, have been known to strike; common sense should be an adequate defence. Violent crime against visitors is extremely rare.

Also stay off the city's roads during festivals, particularly **Pi Mai** (⊙Apr), when drunk-driving–related accidents skyrocket. Pickpocketing also occurs more frequently then.

EMERGENCY

Ambulance (☎195)

Fire (☎190)

Police (☎191)

Tourist Police (Map p142; ☎021-251128; Th Lan Xang)

INTERNET ACCESS

There's a row of internet cafes on the north side of Th Setthathirath between Nam Phu (the fountain) and Th Manthatourath, open from 9am to 11pm and charging 6000K an hour. Wi-fi, often for free, is also available at many of Vientiane's cafes.

Oriental Bookshop (Map p142; ☎021-215352; 121 Th Chao Anou; per hr 5000K; ⊙8.30am-10pm) This bookshop also offers several computers with internet access.

True Coffee Internet (Map p142; Th Setthathirath; per hr 8000K; ⊙9am-9pm) The coolest, most stylish spot to catch up on your emails, this great cafe also sells Apple

Mac accesories and has brownies, yoghurt and fresh juices. Enjoy a latte as you Skype, or use the free wi-fi on your own laptop.

MEDIA

Laos' only English-language newspaper is the government-run *Vientiane Times*; hopelessly state censored, it does, however, feature stories on Laos' commercial relations with China and other foreign countries, detailing mining and hydro power developments. French-speakers should look for *Le Rénovateur*. Also worth keeping an eye out for listings of upcoming happenings is the Facebook page of Pasai.

MEDICAL SERVICES

Vientiane's medical facilities can leave a lot to be desired, so for anything serious make a break for the border and the much more sophisticated hospitals in Thailand. **Aek Udon International Hospital** (☎042-342555; Th Phosri) can dispatch an ambulance to take you to Udon Thani. Less serious ailments can be dealt with in Vientiane.

Alliance International Medical Center (Map p138; ☎021-513095; Th Luang Prabang) This brand new hospital is fresh, clean and treats basic ailments such as broken bones and dispenses antibiotics. It's behind the Honda Showroom near Wattay International Airport.

Australian Embassy Clinic (Map p138; ☎021-353840; ⏲8.30am-5pm Mon-Fri) For nationals of Australia, Britain, Canada, Papua New Guinea and New Zealand only. This clinic's Australian doctor treats minor problems by appointment; it doesn't have emergency facilities. Accepts cash or credit cards. A block southeast of Patuxai.

Centre Médical de L'Ambassade de France (French Embassy Medical Centre; Map p138; ☎021-214150; cnr Th Khu Vieng & Th Simeuang; ⏲8.30am-noon & 4.30-7pm Mon, Tue, Thu & Fri, 1.30-5pm Wed, 9am-noon Sat) Open to all, but visits outside regular hours are by appointment only.

International Clinic (Map p138; ☎021-214021/2; Th Fa Ngoum; ⏲24hr) Part of the Mahasot Hospital; probably the best place for not-too-complex emergencies. Some English-speaking doctors. Take ID and cash.

Setthathirat Hospital (☎021-351156) Thanks to a recent overhaul by the Japanese, this hospital 6.5km northeast of the city centre is another option for minor ailments.

Poppy's Pharmacy & Beauty (Map p142; ☎030-981 0108; Th Hengboun; ⏲8am-10pm) Bright and clean, this modern, well-stocked pharmacy is great for toiletries, cosmetics, sun cream, malaria pills (not Larium) and sleeping tablets for long bus journeys.

MONEY

Licensed money-changing booths can be found in much of central Vientiane, particularly along Th Setthathirath between Th François Ngin and Th Pangkham. You can also change cash at various shops, hotels or markets for no commission but at poor rates.

Banks listed here change cash and travellers cheques and issue cash advances (mostly in kip, but occasionally in US dollars and Thai baht) against Visa and/or MasterCard. Many now have ATMs that work with foreign cards, but it's often cheaper to get a cash advance manually. All are open 8.30am to 3.30pm Monday to Friday.

ANZ (☎021-222700; 33 Th Lan Xang) Main branch has two ATMs and can provide cash advances on Visa or MasterCard for a flat fee of 45,000K. Additional ATMs can be found on Th Setthathirath and Th Fa Ngoum.

Bank of Ayudhya (Map p142; ☎021-214575; 79/6 Th Lan Xang) Cash advances on Visa cards here carry a 1.5% commission.

Banque pour le Commerce Extérieur Lao (BCEL; Map p142; cnr Th Pangkham & Th Fa Ngoum; ⏲8.30am-7pm Mon-Fri, to 3pm Sat & Sun) Best rates; longest hours. Exchange booth on Th Fa Ngoum and three ATMs attached to the main building.

Joint Development Bank (Map p142; 75/1-5 Th Lan Xang) Usually charges the lowest commission on cash advances. Also has an ATM.

Krung Thai Bank (Map p142; ☎021-213480; Th Lan Xang) Also has an exchange booth on Th Fa Ngoum.

Siam Commercial Bank (Map p142; 117 Th Lan Xang) ATM and cash advances on Visa.

POST

Post, Telephone & Telegraph (PTT; Map p142; cnr Th Lan Xang & Th Khu Vieng; ⏲8am-5pm Mon-Fri, to noon Sat & Sun) Come here for poste restante and stamps.

TELEPHONE

International calls can be made from most internet cafes for about 5000K per minute, though it's better if you can Skype. Local calls can be made from any hotel lobby, often for free.

Lao Telecom Numphu Centre (Map p142; Th Setthathirath; ⏲9am-7pm) Has fax and international-call facilities for 2000K a minute (1000K a minute for domestic calls).

TOURIST INFORMATION

Tourist Information Centre (NTAL; Map p142; www.ecotourismlaos.com; Th Lan Xang; ⏲8.30am-noon & 1.30-4pm) Between Talat Sao and Patuxai, the ground-floor office of the government's tourist information centre is worth a visit. Based in an attractive, easy-to-use room it has descriptions of each province and what you'll find there. When we visited, staff spoke decent English and were able to answer most of our questions. You can pick up brochures and some regional maps, and staff can provide detailed information on visiting Phu Khao Khuay NPA.

TRAVEL AGENCIES

Central Vientiane has plenty of agencies that can book air tickets, Thai train tickets and organise visas for Myanmar and Vietnam.

Green Discovery (Map p142; ☎021-264528; www.greendiscoverylaos.com; Th Setthathirath) Deservedly the country's most respected adventure tours specialist; as well as kayaking, cycling, ziplining and trekking trips, they can also help with travel arrangements.

Lasi Ticketing (Map p142; ☎021-222851; www.lasiglobal.com; Th François Ngin; ⏰8am-5pm Mon-Fri, 8.30am-noon Sat) With helpful English-speaking staff, Lasi sells air, VIP bus and train tickets, as well as arranging visas for Cambodia and Vietnam. Speak to Miss Pha.

Maison du Cafe (Map p142; ☎021-219743, 020-780 4842; 119 Th Manthatourath; ⏰8am-10pm) This shop offers ticketing and visa

BUSES FROM VIENTIANE

DESTINATION	DEPARTURE POINT	PRICE (K)	DISTANCE (KM)	DURATION (HR)	DEPARTURES
Attapeu (fan)	southern bus station	140,000	812	22-24	9.30am, 5.30pm
Attapeu (VIP)	southern bus station	200,000	812	14-16	8.30pm
Don Khong (fan)	southern bus station	150,000	788	16-19	10.30am
Huay Xai (air-con)	northern bus station	230,000	869	24	5.30pm
Khon Kaen (air-con)	Talat Sao bus station	52,000	197	4	8.15am, 2.45pm
Lak Sao (fan)	southern bus station	85,000	334	6-8	5am, 6am, 7am, 8.30pm
Luang Namtha	northern bus station	180,000	676	24	8.30pm (fan)
Luang Prabang	northern bus station	110,000	384	10-11	6.30am, 7.30am, 9am, 11am, 1.30pm, 4pm, 6pm, 7.30pm (air-con)
Luang Prabang (VIP)	northern bus station	150,000	384	9-12	7.30pm, 8pm
Nakhon Ratchasima (air-con)	Talat Sao bus station	82,000	387	7	7.30am
Nong Khai (air-con)	Talat Sao bus station	17,000	25	1½	7.30am, 9.30am, 12.40pm, 2.30pm, 3.30pm, 6pm
Nong Khiang (fan)	southern bus station	130,000	818	16-20	11am
Paksan	southern bus station	40,000-50,000	143	3-4	7am-3pm (tuk-tuk); take any bus going south
Pakse (fan)	southern bus station	140,000	677	16-18	hourly from 7am to 8pm
Pakse (VIP)	southern bus station	180,000	677	8-10	9pm
Phongsali	northern bus station	190,000	811	25-28	6.45am (fan)

services, and has a few computers for internet use (6000K per hour).

Getting There & Away

AIR

Departures from Vientiane's **Wattay International Airport** (Map p138; ☎021-512165) are perfectly straightforward. The domestic terminal is in the older, white building east of the more impressive international terminal. There is an (often unstaffed) information counter in the arrivals hall, and food can be found upstairs in the international terminal.

Air Asia (Map p138; www.airasia.com; Wattay Airport International Terminal) Vientiane to Kuala Lumpur several times per week.

China Eastern Airlines (Map p138; www.ce-air.com; Th Luang Prabang) Flies daily to Kunming and Nanning.

Lao Air (Map p138; ☎021-513022; www.lao-air.com; Wattay Airport Domestic Terminal; ⏲8am-

DESTINATION	DEPARTURE POINT	PRICE (K)	DISTANCE (KM)	DURATION (HR)	DEPARTURES
Phonsavan	northern bus station	110,000	374	10-11	6.30am, 8am, 9.30am, 11am, 4pm, 6.40pm (air-con) 8pm
Phonsavan (VIP)	northern bus station	150,000	374	10-11	8.30pm
Sainyabuli (fan)	northern bus station	110,000	485	14-16	9am, 4pm, 6.30pm
Salavan (fan)	southern bus station	120,000	774	15-20	4.30pm, 7.30pm
Salavan (air-con)	southern bus station	150,000	774	16	7.30pm
Salavan (VIP)	southern bus station	180,000	774	13	8pm
Sam Neua (fan)	northern bus station	170,000	612	22-24	7am, 9am, noon
Sam Neua (air-con)	northern bus station	190,000	612	22-24	2pm
Savannakhet (fan)	southern bus station	75,000	457	8-11	5.30am, 6am, 7am, 8am, 9am, or any bus to Pakse
Savannakhet (VIP)	southern bus station	120,000	457	8-10	8.30pm
Tha Khaek (fan)	southern bus station	60,000	332	6	4am, 5am, 6am, or any bus to Savannakhet or Pakse
Tha Khaek (VIP)	southern bus station	80,000	332	5	noon, 1pm
Udomxai	northern bus station	170,000	578	16-19	6.45am, 1.45pm (fan)
Udomxai (VIP)	northern bus station	190,000	578	15-17	4pm
Udon Thani (air-con)	Talat Sao bus station	22,000	82	2½	8am, 10.30am, 11.30am, 2pm, 4pm, 6pm
Vang Vieng (fan)	Talat Sao bus station	30,000	157	3-4	7am, 9.30am, 1pm, 3pm

GETTING TO THAILAND: VIENTIANE TO NONG KHAI

Getting to the Border

At the **Nong Khai (Thailand)/Tha Na Leng (Laos) border** (6am-10pm), the Thai-Lao Friendship Bridge (Saphan Mittaphap Thai-Lao) spans the Mekong River. The Laos border is approximately 20km southeast of Vientiane, and the easiest and cheapest way to the bridge is to cross on the Thai-Lao International Bus. It conducts daily departures for the Thai cities of Khon Kaen, Nakhon Ratchasima, Nong Khai and Udon Thani. Alternative means of transport between Vientiane and the bridge include taxi (300B), tuk-tuk (shared/charter 5000K/250B), jumbo (250B to 300B) or the number 14 Tha Deua bus from Talat Sao bus station (15,000K) between 6am and 6.30pm.

To cross from Thailand, tuk-tuks are available from Nong Khai's train station (20B) and bus station (55B) to the Thai border post at the bridge. You can also hop on the Thai-Lao International Bus from Nong Khai bus station (55B, 1½ hours) or Udon Thani bus station (80B, two hours), both of which terminate at Vientiane's Talat Sao bus station. If flying into Udon Thani, a tuk-tuk from the airport to the city's bus station should cost about 120B.

Since 2009, it's also possible to cross the bridge by train, as tracks have been extended from Nong Khai's train station 3.5km into Laos, terminating at Dongphasy Station, about 13km from central Vientiane. From Nong Khai there are two daily departures (9.30am and 4pm, fan/air-con 20/50B, 15 minutes) and border formalities are taken care of at the respective train stations.

At the Border

At the border, 30-day Lao visas are available for US$20 to US$42, depending on your nationality. If you don't have a photo you'll be charged an extra US$1, and be aware that an additional US$1 'overtime fee' is charged from 6am to 8am and 6pm to 10pm on weekdays, as well as on weekends and holidays. You'll also need to pay a US$1 entry fee. Don't be tempted to use a tuk-tuk driver to get your Lao visa, no matter what they tell you – it will take far longer than doing it yourself, and you'll have to pay for the 'service'. Insist they take you straight to the bridge.

Travellers from most countries can travel visa-free to Thailand.

Moving On

The train from Nong Khai to Bangkok leaves at 6.20pm and costs US$23/37 for a 2nd-class/sleeper ticket.

If crossing from Thailand, you can choose between minivan (100B), tuk-tuk (250B) or taxi (300B) for the remaining 19km from the border to Vientiane. The number 14 local bus to Talat Sao is the cheapest at around 15,000K or 20B, and runs until 6.30pm.

5pm) Operates flights thrice weekly to Sam Neua (US$116) and Sainyabuli (US$90), and twice a week to Phongsali (US$126).

Lao Airlines (Map p142; 021-212051; www.laoairlines.com; Th Pangkham; 8am-noon & 1-4pm Mon-Sat, to noon Sun) Conducts domestic flights between Vientiane and Huay Xai (US$115, thrice weekly), Luang Prabang (US$90, 40 minutes, five daily), Luang Namtha (US$115, four weekly), Pakse (US$134, four weekly) and Phonsavan (US$90, daily), Savannakhet (US$115, four weekly), Udomxai (US$115, four weekly), and daily international flights between Vientiane and Bangkok (US$170), Chiang Mai (US$165), Hanoi (US$165), Kunming (US$265), Phnom Penh (US$185), Siem Reap (US$185), Ho Chi Minh City (US$205) and Guangzhou (US$360). Also has an office at the **airport** (Map p138; 021-512028; Wattay Airport International Terminal; 4am-8pm).

Thai Airways International (Map p138; www.thaiairways.com; Th Luang Prabang) Vientiane to Bangkok connections twice daily.

Vietnam Airlines (Map p142; www.vietnamairlines.com; Lao Plaza Hotel, 63 Th Samsènethai; 9am-5pm) Connects Vientiane with Ho Chi Minh City, Hanoi and Phnom Penh, plus Luang Prabang with Hanoi and Siem Reap.

BOAT

Passenger boat services between Vientiane and Luang Prabang have become almost extinct as most people now take the bus, which is both faster and cheaper.

A regular slow boat makes the trip from Vientiane to Pak Lai, 115km away. Boats leave Monday, Wednesday and Saturday at 8am (120,000K, about eight hours).

BUS

Buses use three stations in Vientiane, with some English-speaking staff, and food and drink stands.

Northern bus station (Th Asiane) About 2km northwest of the centre, serves all points north of Vang Vieng, including China. Destinations and the latest ticket prices are listed in English.

Southern bus station (Rte 13 South) Commonly known as Dong Dok bus station or just *kéw lot lák ków* (9km bus station), is 9km out of town and serves everywhere south. Buses to Vietnam depart from here.

Talat Sao bus station (Map p142; ☎021-216507; Th Khu Vieng),The final departure point is the from where desperately slow local buses run to destinations within Vientiane Province, including Vang Vieng, and some more distant destinations, though for the latter you're better going to the northern or southern stations. The Thai-Lao International Bus also uses this station for its trips to Khon Kaen, Nakhon Ratchasima, Nong Khai and Udon Thani.

In Laos, roads are poor and buses break down, so it might take longer than advertised. In addition to domestic departures, there are now several buses to various Thai cities from the Talat Sao bus station. For buses to China (terminating in Kunming), contact the Tong Li Bus Company at the northern bus station. For Vietnam, buses leave the southern bus station daily at 7pm for Hanoi (220,000K, 24 hours) via Vinh (180,000K, 16 hours), and for Danang (230,000K) via Hue (200,000K, 19 hours). On Mondays, Thursdays and Sundays they leave at 6pm. For Ho Chi Minh City change at Danang; contact SPT for details.

TRAIN

In March 2009 tracks were extended from Nong Khai's train station across the Thai-Lao Friendship Bridge to Dongphasy in Laos, effectively forming Laos' first railway line. At research time the government announced plans to extend the tracks an additional 9km, part of a plan that will see the commencement of a national railway grid sometime in the next five years, but for now Laos boasts a total of 3.5km of rolling track.

ℹ Getting Around

Central Vientiane is entirely accessible on foot. For exploring neighbouring districts, however, you'll need transport.

TO/FROM THE AIRPORT

Wattay International Airport is about 4km northwest of the city centre, which makes the US$10 flat fare for a taxi more than a little steep. The fare is set by the government, and the US$10 takes you anywhere in Vientiane (though to the Thai-Lao Friendship Bridge is only US$13). Only official taxis can pick up at the airport.

If you're on a budget and don't have a lot of luggage, simply walk 500m to the airport gate and cross Th Luang Prabang and hail a shared jumbo (20,000K per person). Official tuk-tuk tariffs from the city centre list the airport as a

AN IDIOT'S GUIDE TO TUK-TUKS & JUMBOS

Two different types of tuk-tuk/jumbo operate in Vientiane and if you know the difference it can save you money and a lot of argument.

Tourist Tuk-Tuks

You'll find these loitering in queues outside popular tourist spots, such as at Nam Phu. In theory, chartering a tuk-tuk should be no more than 20,000K for distances of 1km or less, but these guys will usually show you a laminated card with a list of fares at least double what a Lao person would pay. Bargaining is essentially fruitless because there is an agreement within the queue that tuk-tuks won't budge from the agreed tariff.

Wandering Tuk-Tuks

These tuk-tuks will pick you up anywhere and negotiate a fare to anywhere – prices are lower than tourist tuk-tuks and rise as you head further away from main roads. If you're going somewhere within the centre of town, you can probably get away with handing the driver 15,000K to 20,000K and telling him where you want to go.

Fixed-Route Share Jumbos

The cheapest tuk-tuks are more like buses, starting at tuk-tuk stations and operating along set routes for fixed fares. The biggest station is near Talat Sao and one very useful route runs to the Friendship Bridge (5000K, compared with about 200B for a charter). Just turn up and tell them where you want to go.

60,000K ride. Prices on shared transport will rise if you're going further than the centre.

The number 30 Tha Pa and the number 49 Nong Taeng buses from Talat Sao bus station make the journey for 10,000K.

BICYCLE

Cycling is a cheap, easy and recommended way of getting around mostly flat Vientiane. Loads of guesthouses and several shops hire out bikes for about 10,000K per day; you won't need a map to find them.

BUS

There is a city bus system, but it's oriented more towards the distant suburbs than the central Chanthabuli district. Most buses leave from Talat Sao bus station; the number 14 Tha Deua bus to the Thai-Lao Friendship Bridge runs every two hours from 6am to 6.30pm and costs 15,000K.

CAR & MOTORCYCLE

Scooters are a popular means of getting around Vientiane and can be hired throughout the centre of town. In particular, there are a couple of places on the west side of Th Nokèokoummane near the Douang Deuane Hotel (p152). The place directly in front of the hotel is the cheapest and rents 110cc bikes for 70,000K per day.

Jules' Classic Rental (Map p142; ☎020-9728 2636; www.bike-rental-laos.com; Th Setthathirath; per day US$35, minimum rental one week) Friendly outfit with a range of regularly serviced scooters and, for the intrepid, new, heavy-duty 250cc and 450cc motocross bikes. Owner Thierry can even send your luggage on to your destination (for a charge), or if you're headed far afield and don't want to double back (say, to Luang Prabang), you can also leave the bike there for US$50. In case of emergency you can call them and they'll either sort you with a nearby mechanic (if they know one) or come and get you. Look out for the vintage bikes out front. Excellent quality.

Europcar (Map p142; ☎021-223867; www.europcarlaos.com; Th Setthathirath; ⏲8.30am-6.30pm Mon-Fri, 8.30am-1pm Sat & Sun) Hires quality cars from small sedans (US$55 per day) to sturdy 4WDs (US$77 per day). You can also hire a driver for US$10 per day, but if you want to drive outside Vientiane it costs US$20 to cover the driver's keep. You can even leave the car at your destination for a charge. Third-party insurance as standard.

MOTORCYCLE TOURS

Motorbike activities have been on the slow burn in Laos for some time, but 2013 was the year it all came together in a perfect storm of freshly laid tarmac, tyres and well organised bike-rental outfits. Now it's possible to travel on sturdy, well-maintained motocross bikes, connected by Laos' competent mobile-phone service for back-up with base, and handheld GPS devices to always keep you on track. And with drop-off and luggage-forwarding facilities to your destination available, it's now possible to tackle a slice of your holiday on two wheels (preferable, we think, to duking it out on soggy, overcrowded buses). Hire a bike from Jules' Classic Rental for the week to take in the north or central Laos, riding through the mountains to Vang Vieng for a few days, before moving on to Luang Prabang and the rest of the north before leaving your bike in Luang Prabang.

Alternatively you can bus it towards Vang Vieng and take a trip with **Uncle Tom's Trail Bike Tour** (☎020-2995 8903; uncletomstrails@hotmail.com; Blue Lagoon Resort, Ban Theua, Ang Nam Ngum; 2-night trip per person US$110) based at the Blue Lagoon resort on the nearby Ang Nam Ngum. It is a great new outfit run by a Tom Jones–lookalike Welshman who can teach you riding skills (beginners too), before taking you on a tailored one-day tour.

And if you're thinking of doing Khammuan Province's 'Loop', forget skidding off the road on a wobbly scooter, for Mad Monkey Motorbike (p199) has just opened and rents new 250cc Honda dirt bikes from Tha Khaek, an excellent base to do the Loop and mythic Kong Lo Cave. Better still the owner, DC, can come and get you if you run into trouble in the boonies.

And finally, thanks to the mysteriously monikered **Midnight Mapper** (☎020-5865 6994; espritdemer@hotmail.com) spending the last 10 years tirelessly mapping Laos, you can buy his satellite map off his website and plug it into your GPS gadget (costs US$50, and he mails you the sim card), or he'll rent you one of his Garmin handheld GPS devices for US$10 per day and plug in your coordinates so you never get lost. He can also take you into unchartered, off-the-beaten-track territory around Attapeu Province and the old Ho Chi Minh Trail.

JUMBO & TUK-TUK

Drivers of jumbos and tuk-tuks will take passengers on journeys as short as 500m or as far as 20km. Understanding the various types of tuk-tuk is important if you don't want to be overcharged (see p167). Tourist tuk-tuks are the most expensive; share jumbos that run regular routes around town (eg Th Luang Prabang to Th Setthathirath or Th Lan Xang to That Luang) are much cheaper – usually about 20,000K per person.

TAXI

Car taxis of varying shapes, sizes and vintages can often be found stationed in front of the larger hotels or at the airport. Bargaining is the rule for all, the exception being **Meter Taxi Service** (☎ 021-454168). Drivers from this company often wait for fares on Th Pangkham, roughly across from the Day Inn Hotel. Another useful new company is **Taxi Vientiane Capital Lao Group** (☎ 021-454168; ⌚ 24hr).

The **Talat Sao taxi stand** (Map p142; ⌚ 7am-6pm) at the corner of Th Lan Xang and Th Khu Vieng, across from Talat Sao, is where you'll find taxis to the Friendship Bridge (300B).

A car and driver costs about US$50 per day as long as the vehicle doesn't leave town. If you want to go further afield, such as to Ang Nam Ngum or Vang Vieng, expect to pay more.

AROUND VIENTIANE

There are several places worth seeing that are an easy trip from Vientiane. Some make good day trips while others could detain you for much longer.

Phu Khao Khuay NPA ສວນອຸດທິຍານແຫ່ງຊາດພູເຂົາຄວາຍ

Covering more than 2000 sq km of mountains and rivers to the east of Vientiane, the underrated **Phu Khao Khuay NPA** (www.trekkingcentrallaos.com) is the most easily accessed protected area in Laos. Treks ranging in duration from a couple of hours to three days have been developed in close consultation with two villages on the edge of the NPA, Ban Na and Ban Hat Khai.

Phu Khao Khuay *(poo cow kwai)* means 'Buffalo Horn Mountain', a name derived from local legend, and is home to three major rivers that flow off a sandstone mountain range and into the Ang Nam Leuk Reservoir. It boasts an extraordinary array of endangered wildlife, including wild elephant, gibbon, Asiatic black bear, clouded leopard, Siamese fireback pheasant and green peafowl. About 88% of the NPA is forested, though only 32% has been classified as dense, mature forest. Depending on elevation, visitors may encounter dry evergreen dipterocarp (a Southeast Asian tree with two-winged fruit), mixed deciduous forest, conifer forest or grassy uplands. Several impressive waterfalls are accessible as day trips from Vientiane.

But while all of this is undoubtedly impressive, by far the greatest attraction at Phu Khao Khuay has been its herd of wild elephants. Sadly, thanks to a series of tragic events over the last few years, the chances of seeing these animals are ever slimmer.

Detailed information on trekking, accommodation and getting to and from Phu Khao Khuay can be found at the Tourist Information Centre in Vientiane (p163). Trekking in Phu Khao Khuay costs 160,000K per person per day, and you must also purchase a permit to enter the NPA (50,000K) and contribute to the village fund (50,000K). If trekking from Ban Hat Khai you'll also have to pay for boat transport (70,000K per boat; up to five passengers).

ℹ Getting There & Away

Buses from Vientiane's southern bus station leave regularly for Ban Tha Bok and Paksan. For Wat Pha Baht Phonsan and Ban Na get off at Tha Pha Bat near the Km 81 stone; the shrine is right on Rte 13 and Ban Na is about 2km north – follow the signs.

For Ban Hat Khai, keep on the bus until a turn-off left (north) at Km 92, just before Ban Tha Bok. If you have your own transport, continue 8km along the smooth laterite road until you cross the new bridge. Turn right at the Y-intersection and it's 1km to Ban Hat Khai and another 9km to Tat Xai; turn left, continue another 6km and Tat Leuk is accessible via a rough 4km road. Alternatively, villagers in Ban Hat Khai can arrange motorcyle pick-up from Ban Tha Bok for 15,000K one-way if you call ahead.

Note that as you come from Vientiane there are three signed entrances to Phu Khao Khuay; the second leads to Ban Na and the third to Ban Hat Khai and the waterfalls.

Ban Na ບ້ານນາ

The lowland farming village of Ban Na, 82km northeast of Vientiane, is home to about 600 people. The village is typical Lao, with women weaving baskets from bamboo (skills they will happily impart for a small fee) and men tending the fields. But it's the local herd of elephants that has historically been most interesting to visitors.

The farmers of Ban Na grow rice and vegetables, but a few years ago they began planting sugar cane. What they didn't count on was the collective sweet tooth of the elephants in the nearby mountains. It wasn't long before these jumbos sniffed out the delights in the field below and were happily eating the sugar cane, pineapples and bananas planted around Ban Na. Not surprisingly, the farmers weren't happy. They decided the only way to get rid of the elephants was to rip up the sugar cane and go back to planting boring (and less lucrative) vegetables.

It was hoped the 30-odd elephants would take the hint and return to the mountains. Instead, they made the lowland forests, bamboo belt and fields around Ban Na their home, causing significant destruction to the environment and finances of Ban Na. The only way the villagers could continue to live with the elephants (ie not shoot them) was by making them pay their way. The result was elephant ecotourism.

The truth is that today the elephants have vanished. In 2007 there was an estimated 25-strong herd in Phu Khao Khuay. In 2009, five were killed – stripped of their tusks and hind legs, which suggests that they were murdered by poachers rather than vengeful villagers. In 2010 a further two were recorded dead; according to the Lao Army, they had been electrocuted by lightning. There should still be 18 elephants from the 2007 tally of 25, but their whereabouts are unknown.

Village guides lead one-, two- and three-day treks from Ban Na to Keng Khani (three to four hours one-way), through deep forest to the waterfall of **Tat Fa** (four to five hours) and to the elephant observation tower at **Pung Xay** (4km). The one-hour trek to this tower is easy, passing by plantations and through the skirts of the jungle itself. The tower overlooks a salt lick, which the elephants *used* to visit regularly. Trekkers sleep in the tower (100,000K per person) beneath a mosquito net on a mattress, and guides cook a tasty local dinner. Even minus the elephants, it still makes for a fun adventure.

Homestay-style accommodation is also available for 30,000K per person per night, with an additional 30,000K per person for food. The prices do not include transport from Vientiane and are not negotiable. All monies go to the village and NPA. To contact Ban Na directly, call Lao-speaking **Mr Bounthanom** (☎ 020-220 8286).

En route to Ban Na it's worth stopping briefly at **Wat Pha Baht Phonsan**, which sits on a rocky outcrop at Tha Pha Baht, beside Rte 13 about 2km south of Ban Na. The wat is revered for its large *pa bàht* (Buddha footprint) shrine, monastery and substantial reclining Buddha figure. You'll know it by the large and well-ornamented 1933-vintage stupa.

Ban Hat Khai ບ້ານຫາດໄຂ່

Along with Ban Na, the village of Ban Hat Khai is a launch point for treks into Phu Khao Khuay NPA. Destinations include the huge cliff, views and beautiful landscape of **Pha Luang** (three to four hours one-way), and the forested areas around **Huay Khi Ling** (two to three hours one-way). A trek taking in both these areas takes two or three days, depending on the season, and involves sleeping in the forest (guides cost 160,00K per day, a permit costs 50,000K, plus you need to contribute 50,000K to the village fund). Boats can be arranged here (70,000K per person; up to five people) to take you upriver to **Pha Xai**.

Homestay-style accommodation is also available in Ban Hat Khai for 30,000K per person, per night, with an additional 30,000K per person for food. The prices do not include transport from Vientiane and are not negotiable. All monies go to the village and NPA. Call Lao-speaking **Mr Khammuan** (☎ 020-224 0343).

Tat Xai, Pha Xai & Tat Leuk

Phu Khao Khuay's three most impressive waterfalls are accessed from the road running north from Rte 13, just before Ban Tha Bok. **Tat Xai** cascades down seven steps, and 800m downstream **Pha Xai** plunges over a 40m-high cataract. There's a pool that's good for swimming, though it can get dangerous during the wet season.

Tat Leuk is much smaller but makes a beautiful place to camp for the night. You can swim above the falls if the water isn't flowing too fast, and the visitor centre has some information about the area, including a detailed guide to the 1.5km-long **Huay Bon Nature Trail**. The guy who looks after the visitor centre can arrange local treks for 160,000K, and rents quality four-person tents for 30,000K, plus hammocks, mattresses, mosquito nets and sleeping bags for 10,000K each. There's a very basic restaurant, best supplemented with food you bring from outside, and small library of wildlife books and a pair of binoculars.

Vientiane to Vang Vieng

On the way to Vang Vieng are a few interesting stopover possibilities. The **Nam Tok Tat Khu Khana** waterfall (also called Hin Khana) is easy to reach via a 10km dirt road, leading west from Rte 13 near the village of Ban Naxaithong, near Km 17.

At **Vang Sang**, 65km north of Vientiane via Rte 13, a cluster of 10 high-relief Buddha sculptures on cliffs is thought to date from the 16th century. Two of the Buddhas are more than 3m tall. The name means 'Elephant Palace', a reference to an elephant graveyard once found nearby. To reach Vang Sang, follow the sign to the Vang Xang Resort, near the Km 62 marker, then take the laterite road around a small lake, up the hill and right until you reach the shaded forest at the end.

A bit further north is the prosperous town of Phon Hong, the turn-off for Thalat and **Ang Nam Ngum**, a vast artificial lake created when the Nam Ngum was dammed in 1971. The highest peaks of the former river valley became forested islands after the valley was inundated, and following the 1975 PL conquest of Vientiane, an estimated 3000 prostitutes, petty criminals and drug addicts were rounded up from the capital and banished to two of these islands; one each for men and women. Today the Nam Ngum hydroelectric plant generates most of the electricity used in the Vientiane area and sells power to Thailand. Ang Nam Ngum is dotted with picturesque little islands and it is well worth arranging a cruise. Boats can be hired from Ban Na Khuen, which is also home to the area's best accommodation and restaurants, for 150,000K for a half-day or 300,000K for a full day.

At the village of Ban Senhxoum, just past Km 80, turn right and continue about 7km along the smooth laterite road and you'll reach a quiet but emerging ecodestination revolving around the banks of **Nam Lik**. In addition to being a great place to stay, the Nam Lik Eco-Village (p172), a riverside resort located on the west bank of the Nam Lik, is a good base for outdoor activities such as orchid walks, kayaking in the river or mountain biking. It's also a good jumping-off point for the area's flashest attraction, the **Nam Lik Jungle Fly** (☎020-5662 2001; www.laosjunglefly.com). Opened in early 2010, the jungle fly consists of a series of 10 ziplines and rope bridges spanning a total of 2km. It also offers comfortable tent accommodation on a hilltop overlooking the Nam Lik. Bookings and price enquiries can be made at **Green Discovery** (☎021-264528; www.greendiscoverylaos.com) offices in Vientiane and Vang Vieng, the most likely jumping-off points for the attraction. To give you a rough idea though, a group of four people would pay US$177 per person for overnight camping, ziplining and kayaking. Visits can be approached as a day trip or combined with camping. Getting there involves a 10-minute boat ride up the Nam Lik.

North of Hin Hoep, at the market village of Ban Tha Heua, you'll reach the turn-off to the **(Former) Saisombun Special Zone**. After 30 years as a no-go zone, due to an armed insurgency by Hmong rebels that has persisted since 1975, the Saisombun Special Zone is no longer required, according to the Lao government. The zone was actually a 4506-sq-km area of rugged mountains and plateaus at the northeast corner of Vientiane Province, stretching into Xieng Khuang Province. It was established because the area is home to a large population of Hmong, and was the home of **Long Cheng**, the 'secret city' from where the Hmong and CIA operated during the Second Indochina War.

War buffs may be interested in visiting Long Cheng, but what remains of the former base (now a Lao military base) is still very much off limits – especially since an engineer working on the Chinese-run Phu Bia (Laos' highest mountain) mine was recently shot by a suspected Hmong insurgent.

Sleeping & Eating

Basic accommodation is available intermittently along the entire stretch of Rte 13 from Vientiane to Vang Vieng.

Vang Xang Resort GUESTHOUSE $
(☎021-211526; r 60,000K) If you're cycling from Vientiane, a good initial stop is Vang Xang Resort, located about 65km north of Vientiane.

Blue Lagoon Resort CABIN $$
(020-5489 4272; www.blue-lagoon-resort-laos.com; Ban Theua; cabanas US$20-45; P ❄ ☎) Blue Lagoon has great new bungalows on the shores of the reservoir. Rooms vary from basic to deluxe with air-con. Great for families looking to wakeboard, jet-ski and take a motorcycle class and tour with Uncle Tom's Trail Bike Tour (p168).

Salapa Fisherman's Haven CABIN $$
(030-526 6026; www.salapafishermans.com; Ban Na Khuen; bungalows incl breakfast US$30; ❄) Around Ang Nam Ngum, Ban Na Khuen, a short distance from the dam, is the best place in the area to sleep and eat. Salapa Fisherman's Haven offers attractive bungalows looking over the reservoir. The owner, a Lao who lived in France for 30 years, is a fishing enthusiast and can provide equipment and advice.

Nam Lik Eco-Village CABIN $$
(020-202 6817, 020-5550 8719; www.namlik.org/eco; bungalows US$15-50) Located on the west bank of the Nam Lik just outside Ban Vang Mon, the highly recommended Nam Lik Eco-Village plays hosts to a variety of visiting scientists, entomologists and orchid nerds, in addition to those simply looking for a rural escape. The resort consists of 12 spacious en-suite bungalows and a good restaurant, and the emphasis on activities – kayaking, fishing and mountain biking – in the surrounding forest and involvement of locals, thoroughly justify the 'Eco' label. Also a collection of fish and reptiles.

Nam Ngeum LAOTIAN $
(020-5551 3521; Ban Na Khuen; mains 15,000-50,000K) One of a handful of restaurants at Ban Na Khuen, Nam Ngeum gets good reviews for its tasty *gôy Ƀąh* (tart and spicy fish salad), *gąang Ƀąh* (fish soup) and *neung Ƀąh* (steamed fish with fresh herbs).

Getting There & Away

From Vientiane's Talat Sao bus station buses leave every hour from 6.30am to 5.30pm bound for Thalat (15,000K, 2½ hours, 87km), the largest city near Ang Nam Ngum; from Thalat you can take a *sŏrngtăaou* to Ban Na Khuen (15,000K), or Salapa Fisherman's Haven can pick you up if you're staying at the resort. Taxis in Vientiane usually charge around US$50 return to the lake. Ask the driver to take the more scenic Rte 10 through Ban Khuen for the return trip.

Both Nam Lik Eco-Village and Nam Lik Jungle Fly provide transport if booked in advance. Otherwise, from Vientiane, you can hop on any bus bound for Vang Vieng and get off at Ban Senhxoum (25,000K, about three hours), calling in at Nam Lik Eco-Village or hitching a ride the remaining 7km to Ban Vang Mon.

Vang Vieng ວັງວຽງ

023 / POP 33,612

Like a rural scene from an Oriental silk painting, Vang Vieng crouches low over the Nam Song (Song River) with a backdrop of serene cliffs and a tapestry of vivid green paddy fields. Thanks to the iron fist of the Lao government finally making its presence felt in 2012 (when the river rave bars were finally closed down), the increasingly toxic party scene has been banished and the community is recalibrating itself as an outdoor paradise home with some achingly lovely boutique hotels and a raft of adrenalin-inducing and nature-based activities.

For the first time in years Western families and a more mature crowd are visiting (many en route to fabled Luang Prabang), stopping to kayak the Nam Song, go caving and climb the karsts. Relief pretty much describes the current feeling of Vang Vieng's inhabitants. It is mixed with a dose of anxiety as to how they are going to fill their empty guesthouses, for at its height 170,000 footfalls swept through the town on a yearly basis. Still, locals are glad that Vang Vieng is now untroubled by thumping music, disrespectful teens and the misconception that anything goes.

Spend a few days here – rent a scooter, take a motorcycle tour, go tubing, trekking – and prepare to manually close your jaw as you gape at one of Laos' most stunningly picturesque spots.

Sights & Activities

Vang Vieng has evolved into Laos' number-one adventure destination, with kayaking, rafting, caving, mountain biking and world-class rock climbing all available. These activities tend to be more popular than the sights, which are mainly monasteries dating from the 16th and 17th centuries. Among these, **Wat Si Vieng Song** (Wat That), **Wat Kang** and **Wat Si Suman** are the most notable. Over the river are a couple of villages to which Hmong have been relocated, which are accessible by bicycle or motorbike.

Caves

Following, we've described several of the most accessible *tàm* (caves). Most are signed in English as well as Lao, and an admission fee is collected at the entrance to each cave. A guide (often a young village boy) will lead you through the cave for a small fee; bring water and a torch (flashlight), and be *sure* your batteries aren't about to die – in fact, bearing in mind some of the 'lost in the darkness' horror stories that circulate, it's vital to have a spare.

The caves around Vang Vieng are spectacular, but being caves they come with certain hazards – they're dark, slippery and disorienting. It's easy to get lost, especially if your torch batteries die. It's well worth hiring a guide at the cave, and always carry two torches lest one runs out.

For more extensive multicave tours, most guesthouses can arrange a guide. Trips including river tubing and cave tours cost around US$15/25 for a half-/full day.

Tham Jang CAVE

(ຖ້ຳຈັງ; admission 17,000K) The most famous of the caves, Tham Jang, was used as a bunker in defence against marauding *jęen hôr* (Yunnanese Chinese) in the early 19th century (*jąng* means 'steadfast'). Stairs lead up to the main cavern entrance.

Tham Phu Kham CAVE

(ຖ້ຳພູຄຳ, Blue Lagoon; admission 10,000K) The vast Tham Phu Kham is considered sacred by Lao and is popular largely due to the lagoon in the cave. The beautiful green-blue waters are perfect for a dip after the stiff climb. The main cave chamber contains a Thai bronze reclining Buddha, and from here deeper galleries branch off into the mountain. To get here, come along a scenic but unpaved road to the village of Ban Na Thong. From Ban Na Thong follow the signs towards the cliff and climb a steep 200m through scrub forest.

Tham Sang Triangle CAVE

A popular half-day trip that's easy to do on your own takes in Tham Sang plus three other caves within a short walk. Begin this caving odyssey by riding a motorcycle or taking a jumbo 13km north along Rte 13, turning left a few hundred metres beyond the barely readable Km 169 stone. A rough road leads to the river, where you cross a toll bridge (5000K), or during the wet season, a boatman will ferry you across to Ban Tham Sang (20,000K return). Tham Sang itself is right here, as is a small restaurant.

Tham Sang (admission 5000K), meaning 'Elephant Cave', is a small cavern containing a few Buddha images and a Buddha 'foot-

LOCAL KNOWLEDGE

SANGTHONG (ADAM) NIESELT, ROCK CLIMBER

Santhong (Adam) Nieselt, who started Adam's Rock Climbing School (p175), fills us in on the rock-climbing scene in Vang Vieng.

Who were the first people to climb at Vang Vieng? The first rock climbing was in 2002 by a half-French half-Lao guy called David. The first place he bolted was at Pha Daeng, 2km west of Vang Vieng by the Nam Song.

And you? When and where did you learn how to climb? I would say that I am the first Lao rock climber ever! I started rock climbing in 1997 in the south of Thailand. After six years in Krabi as a rock-climbing instructor, and after 3½ years of climbing in Germany and France, I came to Vang Vieng and started my rock-climbing business in 2005.

How would you describe the climbing at Vang Vieng compared to other places in the world? I think Vang Vieng is the number-one rock-climbing place in Asia. There is so much limestone from Vang Vieng all the way up to China, and most of it forms high cliffs, over 200m.

Is Vang Vieng only for expert climbers, or it is a good place for beginners to learn how to climb too? This is the right place to learn how to rock climb for beginners. Mostly we put beginners on 4a and 5a only, not any harder than that. The bungalows and guesthouses in Vang Vieng are very cheap and near the river, and the food is tasty.

Has the government clean-up operation helped in Vang Vieng? It's better now because the river is cleaner for local fishermen, and more people are doing adventure activities like climbing again...not to mention more families are coming.

Vang Vieng

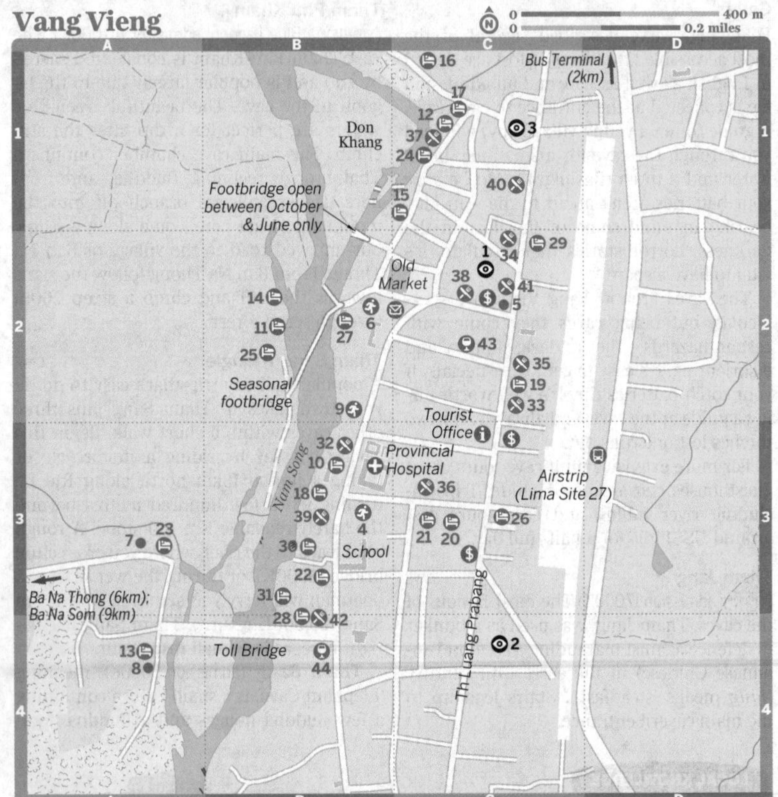

print', plus the (vaguely) elephant-shaped stalactite that gives the cave its name. It's best visited in the morning when light enters the cave.

From Tham Sang a path takes you about 1km northwest through rice fields to the entrances of **Tham Hoi** and **Tham Loup** (combined admission 10,000K). The path isn't entirely clear, but the local kids are happy to show you the way for a small fee. The entrance to Tham Hoi is guarded by a large Buddha figure; reportedly the cave continues about 3km into the limestone and an underground lake. Tham Loup is a large and delightfully untouched cavern with some impressive stalactites.

About 400m south of Tham Hoi, along a well-used path, is the highlight of this trip, **Tham Nam** (admission 5000K). The cave is about 500m long, and a tributary of the Nam Song flows out of its low entrance. In the dry season you can wade into the cave, but when the water is higher you need to take a tube from the friendly woman near the entrance; the tube and headlamp are included in the entrance fee. Dragging yourself through the tunnel on the fixed rope is fun.

If you've still got the energy, a path leads about 2km south from Tham Nam along a stream to **Tham Pha Thao**, a cave said to be a couple of kilometres long with a pool in the middle. Otherwise, it's an easy 1km walk back to Ban Tham Sang. This loop is usually included in the kayaking/trekking/tubing combo trip run by most Vang Vieng tour operators.

Kayaking

Kayaking is almost as popular as tubing, and trips typically combine with either visits to caves and villages, optional climbing, cycling and the traverse of a few rapids, the danger of which depends on the speed of the water. There are loads of operators and prices are

Vang Vieng

Sights

1	Wat Kang	C2
2	Wat Si Suman	C4
3	Wat Si Vieng Song	C1

Activities, Courses & Tours

4	Adam's Rock Climbing School	B3
5	Green Discovery	C2
6	Tubing Operators	B2
7	Uncle Tom's Trail Bike Tours	A3
8	Vang Vieng Jeep Tour	A4
9	VLT	B2

Sleeping

10	Ban Sabai Bungalows	B3
11	Banana Bungalows	B2
12	Champa Lao	C1
13	Chez Mango	A4
14	Cliff View Bungalows	B2
15	Domon Guesthouse	C1
16	D-Rose Resort	C1
17	Easy Go Hostel	C1
18	Elephant Crossing	B3
19	Inthira Hotel	C2
20	Khamphone Guest House	C3
21	Kianethong Guest House	C3
22	Le Jardin Organique	B3
23	Maylyn Guest House	A3
24	Nam Song Garden	C1
25	Other Side	B2
26	Pan's Place	C3
27	Phoubane Guest House	B2
28	Riverside Boutique Resort	B4
29	Seng Aloun Guesthouse	C2
30	Thavonsouk Resort	B3
31	Villa Nam Song	B3

Eating

32	Ban Sabai Restaurant	B3
33	Breakfast Vendors	C2
34	Grilled-Meat Vendor	C2
35	Kitchen	C2
36	Le Café De Paris	C3
37	Living Room	C1
38	Luang Prabang Bakery	C2
39	Mama Sababa	B3
40	Mitthaphap Fusion	C1
	Nam Song Garden	(see 24)
41	Nazim	C2
42	Restaurant Du Crabe D'Or	B4

Drinking & Nightlife

43	Gary's Irish Bar	C2
44	Kangaroo Sunset Bar	B4

about US$15 per person per day. Kayaking trips to Vientiane along the Nam Lik are conducted by the excellent Green Discovery (p176), which also runs kayaking adventures on the Nam Song, and involve a lot of paddling. This is only possible post-monsoon, when the water is sufficiently high.

Another useful tour operator for kayaking is VLT (p178).

Rock Climbing

In just a few years the limestone walls around Vang Vieng have gained a reputation as some of the best climbing in Southeast Asia. More than 200 routes have been identified and most have been bolted. The routes are rated between 4a and 8b, with the majority being in or near a cave. The most popular climbing spots are at **Tham Non** (Sleeping Cave), with more than 20 routes, and the tougher **Sleeping Wall** nearby, where some routes have difficult overhangs.

The climbing season usually runs between October and May, with most routes too wet at other times. However, there are some rock-shaded overhangs on Phadeng Mountain that have recently been bolted down (23 routes), and can still be used in the wet season. **Adam's Rock Climbing School** (☎020-5501 0832; www.laos-climbing.com; half-/full day climbing 180,000/260,000K, 2-day course US$100;) Opposite the hospital, Adam's offers fully outfitted courses ranging in skill from beginner to advanced. Adam himself is one of the most experienced climbers in the area (see p173), his multilingual guides get good reports and equipment rental is also available (350,000K). Green Discovery (p176) conducts climbing courses (half-/full day around US$27/36) and when available, can provide a handy climbing guide to the area.

Tubing

Virtually every younger traveller who comes to Vang Vieng goes tubing down the Nam Song in an inflated tractor-tyre tube. The tubing drop-off point is 3.5km north of town, and depending on the speed and level of the river it can be a soporific crawl beneath the jungle-vined karsts or a speedy glide downstream back to Vang Vieng. Since the river bars shut in 2012 there's less chance of getting plastered and losing your balance in dangerous currents, but always wear a life jacket when the river runs fast (even if you're not floating in an alternative universe) – the many stories of travellers who have drowned in this seemingly peaceful river don't make for pleasant reading. Whether tubing or kayaking down the Nam Song, rivers can be dangerous. When tubing, it's worth asking how long the trip should take (durations vary depending on the time of year) so you can allow plenty of time to get back to Vang Vieng before dark – it's black by about 6pm in winter. Finally, don't forget that while tubing the Nam Song might be more fun when you're stoned, it's also more dangerous.

The **tubing operators** (8.30am-7pm) have formed a cartel so all tubing is organised from a small building across from where the old market once was. It costs 55,000K to rent a tube plus a 60,000K refundable deposit. Life jackets are available and you can rent a dry bag for 20,000K. The fee includes transport to the tubing drop-off point, but keep in mind that you must return the tube before 6pm, otherwise you'll have to pay a 20,000K late fee. If you lose your tube, you have to pay 60,000K.

The other thing you should remember, girls, is to take something – a sarong, perhaps – to put on when you finish the trip and have to walk through town. The locals don't appreciate people walking around in bikinis or Speedos. In times of high water, rapids along the Nam Song can be quite daunting.

Tours

Several companies operate adventure tours out of Vang Vieng. Prices vary according to the size of your group (more heads equal cheaper prices) and standards also vary, though the following have good reputations.

★**Green Discovery** ADVENTURE TOUR

(023-511230; www.greendiscoverylaos.com; Th Luang Prabang; 1-day cycling tour per person US$37, half-/full day rock climbing US$27/36, kayaking to Vientiane per person US$53) Green Discovery is Vang Vieng's biggest and most reliable operator offering trekking, kayaking, rafting, rock climbing and caving. From here you can also head out with them to Nam Lik Jungle Fly (p171). Equipment is up to date, plus it has a solid reputation to protect, so safety comes first.

★**Vang Vieng Jeep Tour** ADVENTURE TOUR

(020-5443 5747; noedouine@yahoo.fr; Chez Mango; minimum group of 4, per person 120,000K;) Based at Chez Mango (p180), VV Jeep Tour takes in the best of the countryside in friendly Noé's jeep; first he'll take you to a

Motorcycle Tour
West Vang Vieng Loop

START MAYLYN GUEST HOUSE
END MAYLYN GUEST HOUSE
LENGTH 26KM; SIX HOURS

To get right into the heart of the limestone karsts rising out of the rice paddies opposite Vang Vieng, consider this loop by motorbike or mountain bike. We reckon it's best approached as a day trip, with stops at the various caves, viewpoints and swimming holes. It's best done on a trail bike, though possible on smaller motos or mountain bikes. The latter half of the loop involves a few dry-season toll-bridge crossings, the lack of which would make doing the entire loop difficult, if not impossible, during the wet season. Other than Joe at Maylyn Guest House, the best guide to the area is the Hobo Maps *Vang Vieng* (www.hobomaps.com; US$2) map, which includes heaps of helpful details including handy references to the numbered power poles that run along part of the road.

Heading west from 1 **Maylyn Guest House** you'll see hand-painted signs to various caves along the first couple of kilometres of the path, only some of which are visit-worthy, and all of which charge 10,000K for admission and/or guiding. Worth considering are 2 **Tham Pha Daeng**, the turn-off to which is located after pole 16. There's a cave pool and the area is allegedly the best place to watch the bats stream from their caves every evening. The 2km walk to 3 **Tham Khan**, approached via a 1.5km side road after pole 24, is probably more worthwhile than the long but claustrophobic cave.

At the Hmong village of Ban Phone Ngeun about 3km from Maylyn Guest House, turn right just after pole 42, opposite two basic shops. A flagged road leads past the local school to a desk where the local kids will collect a fee of 10,000K to take you on the steep 45-minute hike to the top of 4 **Pha Ngeun**, a rocky cliff where the locals have built a few basic observation decks offering arguably the most dramatic views of the area.

Returning to the main road, keep right at the next intersection where you'll pass

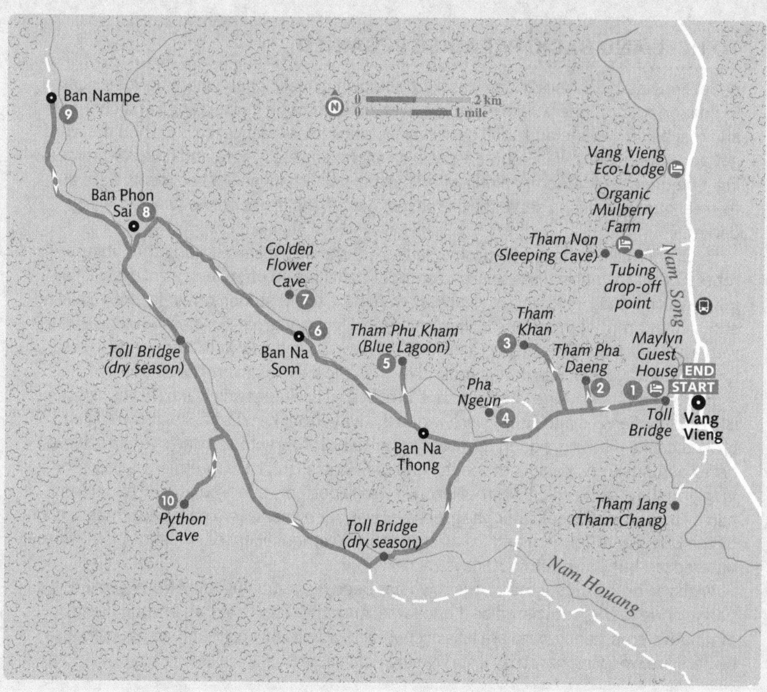

through the Lao Loum village of Ban Na Thong. After 2km you'll come to another fork and a sign pointing right to 5 **Tham Phu Kham** (p173), about 700m along a track. Don't confuse this with nearby Tham Phu Thong, as both are referred to by locals as the Blue Lagoon, but Tham Phu Thong is more like a muddy pond. The natural pool at Tham Phu Kham is a great place to stop for a refreshing swim, particularly if you scaled Pha Ngeun, and equally refreshing organic fruit shakes are sold at the entrance to the cave.

Back on the main track, continue west and you'll soon be in 6 **Ban Na Som**, a village of Hmong who have been resettled here. Around here the vegetation on the karsts is scarred by slash-and-burn farming. Just beyond Na Som are signs to 7 **Golden Flower Cave**. Reaching it involves walking through rice fields, climbing a fence and following two white arrows for a few minutes. The cave is about 50m up the hill – look into the undergrowth for the vague stairs, but it's barely worth the effort.

Continuing west a beautiful stretch of track hugs the edge of the karsts and crosses a couple of streams that could be difficult in the wet, and eventually comes to 8 **Ban Phon Sai**. Here the track joins with a better dirt road, but first you need to cross the Nam Houang (Houang River), which is tricky in the wet season.

You have a choice now: continue 5km west through more dramatic scenery to 9 **Ban Nampe**, a pretty village but nothing more, or start heading back east along the southern route. About 6km southeast of Ban Phon Sai, over another couple of creeks, signs point across a small bridge to a track to 10 **Python Cave**, about 800m away. Once you've seen this, it's plain sailing back to Vang Vieng. Keep along the road, then go left at the junction (follow the power poles), immediately cross a stream and soon you'll be back on the main track, loop complete.

TO HELL AND BACK: PARADISE REGAINED

As recently as 1999, Vang Vieng was a little-known, bucolic affair where travellers came to float on tractor inner tubes down the river, cycle through its stunning karst country and maybe smoke the odd spliff between exploring its fantastical caves. Then the word got out – Vang Vieng was Southeast Asia's next hedonistic mecca and ravers were marking it on their party itinerary along with Thailand's Ko Phangan. As Lao locals were quick to erect guesthouses to serve the increased footfall, the drugs got heavier, the party darker.

By 2009 makeshift rave platforms had established themselves along the tubing route. Forget the natural scenery and outdoor activities on offer such as climbing, biking, kayaking and trekking; gap-year kids were here to get stoned on reefer, Red Bull and shots, methamphetamine and opium cocktails. Ugly, but great business – some bars were making UK£1700 per day (a fortune in Laos). Drug busts were frequent, as were half-naked travellers, wandering around town like lost extras from *The Beach*.

But behind the revelry was a darker truth; by 2011 a staggering 20 to 25 young tourists (mainly Aussies and Brits) were variously dying from heart attacks, drowning and broken necks – having ridden the 'deathslide' (a hastily erected zipline over an often-times perilously low river). Around the end of August 2012, Laos' premier visited Vang Vieng on the eve of an ASEAN meeting. He was reportedly shocked at how bad things had become, and a week later Vang Vieng's river bar owners were called to a meeting by the Ministry of Tourism and Culture, and those without licenses (most of them) were ordered to shut down within 10 days.

With the drugs off the menu, the town has been repositioning itself from a soiled party venue to the rural paradise it once was. And while local doctors in Vang Vieng's diminutive emergency ward are less overworked, admittedly a great many guesthouse owners are worrying how they'll survive the next season.

nearby mountain which you'll gently ascend for an amazing view, then on a walk in the paddy fields followed by a swim in the blue lagoon at Tham Phou Kam, before taking a closer look in the cave itself.

VLT ADVENTURE TOUR

(☎020-5520 8283, 023-511369; www.vangviengtour.com) Run by Vone, VLT is well established and charges US$13 for one-day's kayaking, US$22 for one-day mountain-bike trips, and US$33 for one-day treks. Also runs hot-air balloon flights (US$80) at 6.30am, 4pm and 4.30pm every day, lasting 40 minutes. It is a lovely way to see the cliffs, tapestry of paddy fields and snaking river below.

Sleeping

Since the 24-hour party was officially extinguished in 2012, there's now too many guesthouses (130) for the reduced footfall. And while many of the midrange and top-end hotels are enjoying good business with the wealthier demographic, it's the backpacker joints that are languishing. Increasingly boutique hotels are moving in as VV ditches its dreads in favour of a stylish coiffure.

Vang Vieng Town

Champa Lao GUESTHOUSE $

(☎020-5823 4612; r without/with bathroom 70,000/100,000K, tr 130,000K; @ wi-fi) This heavily wooded traditional stilted Lao house has basic fan rooms with mosquito nets. The garden is a delight and you can swing like a metronome on a hammock while taking in the sunset and karst from its aerial balcony. The ambient-lit garden restaurant casts off heavenly aromas, while there are also bungalows down the bank by the river.

Khamphone Guest House GUESTHOUSE $

(☎023-511062; r 80,000-120,000K; air-con) Peach-coloured Khamphone's three buildings on the southern edge of town offer good-value en-suite rooms; the 120,000K options with TV, air-con and fridge are best. Check out the newer building as there's more room here.

Pan's Place GUESTHOUSE $

(☎023-511484; Th Luang Prabang; r 30,000-70,000K, cabanas s/d 30,000/40,000K; @ wi-fi) This old trusty smacks of backpacker charm and has basic but cosy fan rooms with tiled floors and en suites. Out back are cabanas in a leafy garden, plus a communal chilling area. There's also a natty little cafe (crepes, fruit salads) and a cinema room upstairs with hundreds of DVDs to choose from.

Le Jardin Organique GUESTHOUSE $
(023-511420; r 100,000K, tr 150,000K; P ❄ @ 📶) Hidden by Villa Nam Song, these are spotlessly clean if admittedly characterless rooms. TV, air-con, en suites and bedside lamps. Only five of the rooms have sufficient elevation to catch the jawdropping views, so make sure you ask for one. There's also a little cafe that serves breakfast and Lao fare.

Seng Aloun Guesthouse GUESTHOUSE $
(023-511203, 020-5512 1052; r with fan/air-con 80,000/100,000K, tr 150,000K; P ❄ 📶) Quiet, clean and friendly, this family-run guesthouse has 20 triple and double cream rooms with firm wood beds, cupboards and TV. Pretty ordinary but peaceful given its central location.

Nam Song Garden GUESTHOUSE $
(023-511544; bungalows 50,000-70,000K, 4-bed dm 120,000K; 📶) At the north end of the town this higgledy-piggledy hillside affair enjoys one of the best views in town from its leafy garden. There's a large room which sleeps four, and various bungalows with and without bathrooms and fine views. Food is available (mains 40,000K).

Kianethong Guest House GUESTHOUSE $
(023-511069; www.kanaeng.com/kianethong.html; r 60,000-100,000K; P ❄ 📶) The 40-plus rooms here are reminiscent of a US-style motel, and likewise are cheap, tidy and reliable. Expect desks, TV and, in some cases, a view of a garden. Functional.

Domon Guesthouse GUESTHOUSE $
(023-511210, 020-9989 8678; r with fan & without view/with air-con & view 100,000/150,000K; ❄ 📶) Run by a charming Vietnamese lady, rooms here, on the banks of the Nam Song north of the old market, are large and clean, with powder-blue walls, quality furniture, TV, en suite and oodles of space. A sun deck and restaurant will have been built by the time you read this.

Easy Go Hostel HOSTEL $
(020-5536 6679; www.easygohostel.com; dm/d without bathroom 25,000/40,000K) This dimly lit backpacker haunt is crafted from bamboo and rattan, and with its wooden walkways and maze of five cramped dorms, it smacks a little of *The Beach*. While not special, rooms are clean, and the friendly owners are proactive with organising activities.

★**Ban Sabai Bungalows** GUESTHOUSE $$
(Xayoh Riverside Bungalows; 023-511088; www.ban-sabai-bungalows.com; r US$42-54; P ⊖ ❄ @ 📶) This hidden boutique hotel has beautifully finished cabanas on a hill overlooking panoramic views of the river and karsts. Imagine manicured lawns bursting with flowers, and cosy rooms with huge beds, chichi decor and slick modern en suites. There's a pool, a verandah to take in the view, and an elevated, peaceful restaurant. By night, candles flicker and lanterns glow. Perfectly romantic.

Inthira Hotel BOUTIQUE HOTEL $$
(023-511070; www.inthirahotel.com; Th Luang Prabang; standard/superior/deluxe incl breakfast US$32/43/54; ⊖ ❄ @ 📶) On the main drag, this boutique hotel is an oasis of oxblood rooms with views of the karsts and the old CIA runway (Lima Site 27). With the usual style you'd expect from the Inthira Group, it has hardwood floors, upscale furniture, elegant art, bedside lamps and modern, spotless en suites. The restaurant is cool and leafy, and staff are professional.

Elephant Crossing HOTEL $$
(023-511232; www.theelephantcrossinghotel.com; r 350,000-650,000K; P ❄ @ 📶) Set in leafy gardens peppered with swing chairs and an attractive terrace to take breakfast by the river, Elephant has 36 tasteful rooms with glass panel walls, spotless en suites and the whitest walls imaginable outside of Heaven. Hmong bed runners, wood floors, air-con, TV and fridge complete the bargain. Make sure you ask for a river view, though!

Thavonsouk Resort HOTEL $$
(023-511096; www.thavonsouk.com; r incl breakfast 250,000-450,000K; P ❄ @ 📶) Beautiful wood-accented rooms bursting with light and enjoying full frontal views of the karsts and lush gardens. Waffle quilts, antique beds, the scent of freshly applied beeswax and a high level of spec make this a winner. In the garden are swing chairs and romantic nooks. There's a tempting restaurant, too.

Cliff View Bungalows CABINS $$
(020-5555 7780; r with fan/air-con 150,000/250,000K; ❄ 📶) Next to Banana Bungalows, this solid addition to Vang Vieng's bungalow scene has upmarket cabanas with

new beds, fresh linen, balconies, en suites and marvellous views of the karsts.

D-Rose Resort HOTEL **$$**
(023-511035; www.drosehotelvientiane.com; basic cabanas incl breakfast 120,000K, deluxe bungalows 250,000-320,000K;) Set beside the river in large, well-tended grounds, these are basic cabanas with fan and shared bathroom, or classier bungalows with cream rattan walls, mosquito net, en suite, verandah, wi-fi and TV. There's also a pool to escape the heat.

Phoubane Guest House BUNGALOW **$$**
(023-511306; r/tr with fan 50,000/70,000K, s/d with air-con & river view 200,000/250,000K, bungalows s/d 160,000/200,000K;) Phoubane has cool, river-facing bungalows with tiled floors and clean bathrooms with hot water. Its original wooden bungalows are basic, fan-cooled affairs and a 10th of the price of the new ones. There's a decent communal sundowner verandah, however, the noise from a nearby bar ruins the peace.

★Riverside Boutique Resort BOUTIQUE HOTEL **$$$**
(023-511 726; www.riversidevangvieng.com; r US$123-150;) Sugar-white and uber-stylish, this beautiful boutique belle is run by the folk who manage Green Park Hotel and exudes equal flair with generously spaced rooms wrapped around a citrus green pool and a verdant garden looking out onto the karsts. Rooms themselves are gorgeous with balconies, crisp white sheets, and chic decor straight from the pages of *Wallpaper*. Enjoy a cocktail in the restaurant watching people trundling over the nearby bridge – if you can tear yourself from the sparkling pool.

Villa Nam Song GUESTHOUSE **$$$**
(023-511015; www.villanamsong.com; r US$100-130;) With serene views of the cliffs, this fine hotel sits in grounds choking on mango, palm, orchid and bougainvillea. The pink adobe bungalows are fragrant and parquet-floored with cream walls and high-end furniture. There's also a semi-alfresco restaurant featuring Lao, Thai, Japanese and Vietnamese dishes, and a wind-chimed breeze that sweaps through. Try the duck in honey sauce (60,000K)

Out of Town

If Vang Vieng town isn't your bag, head out of town for a quieter location.

★Organic Mulberry Farm GUESTHOUSE **$**
(023-511220; www.laofarm.org; dm 30,000K, r 40,000-150,000K, deluxe cliff-facing bungalows 200,000K;) Known locally as Phoudindaeng Mulberry Farm, this organic farm a few kilometres out of town sits by the Nam Song in an idyllically quiet spot. Great for families, the smartest accommodation (bungalows) look out onto either mulberry fields or the soaring cliffs above. The rooms themselves are sparklingly clean with mosquito nets, en suites and verandahs. Up the hill are three eight-bed dorms in fan-cooled, spotless buildings. There's also a great restaurant – try the mulberry pancakes or mulberry mojitos! Ask about volunteering for the permaculture program. There are art classes for local kids at the weekend and stone painting if you want to lend a hand. Cooking classes cost US$30.

Chez Mango GUESTHOUSE **$**
(020-5443 5747; www.chezmango.com; r 50,000-70,000K;) Located over the bridge, Mango is friendly and scrupulously clean with seven basic but colourful cabanas (some with bathrooms) in its flowery gardens. Run by Frenchman, Noé, it makes for a soporific and restful spot. Breakfast is available. He also runs Vang Vieng Jeep Tours (p176) from here. Recommended.

Maylyn Guest House GUESTHOUSE **$**
(020-5560 4095; jophus_foley@hotmail.com; r 50,000-80,000K;) Over the bridge, Maylyn is a stalwart of peace and old Vang Vieng. Run by gregarious Jo, Maylyn's cosy, well-spaced cabanas are set in lush gardens bursting with butterflies and lantana flowers, affording possibly the most dramatic views of the karsts. There's a new building with immaculate en-suite rooms, a maze of nooks for kids to play in, plus a pond and a cafe.

Vang Vieng Eco-Lodge CABIN **$**
(020-224 7323; r US$25;) We're not convinced about the green credentials, however, this delightful accommodation, opposite Tham Jang, sits in a peaceful spot by the river. The only sound you're likely to hear is the babbling water and the odd rooster. Bungalows are cool and traditional with wood floors, four-posters and desks. Rural paradise.

Other Side BUNGALOW **$**
(020-5512 6288; bungalows 70,000K) These stilted, mint-green bungalows with balconies, en suites and fan may be uber-basic, but

they enjoy exquisite, uninterrupted views of the cliffs. Thanks to recent changes in nocturnal wildlife it's more peaceful too. Climb into that hammock and relax.

Banana Bungalows BUNGALOW $
(☎023-941 5999; r with bathroom & air-con 100,000K, with fan & shared bathroom 70,000K; ❄) Banana Bungalows has decrepit, tired cabanas on stilts. Rooms are extremely basic but on the upside it's cheap, there are hammocks and balconies, and these days it's quiet.

Eating

Vang Vieng isn't exactly Luang Prabang, but a couple of decent restaurants have recently opened. You'll also find quality restaurants at the top-end hotels.

For Lao food, a string of **breakfast vendors** (Th Luang Prabang; mains 5000-7000K; ⏰6-9am) set up shop every morning across from the Organic Mulberry Farm Cafe, serving basic but tasty Lao dishes. In the evenings, hit the strip of Th Luang Prabang directly north of Chillao guesthouse, where popular **Mitthaphap Fusion** (☎020-225 4515; Th Luang Prabang; set barbecue 45,000K; ⏰5-10pm) serves *seen dàat,* do-it-yourself Korean-style barbecue, and a **grilled-meat vendor** (Th Luang Prabang; mains 15,000K; ⏰1-9pm) does *Ъêeng mŏo* (grilled pork) and delicious *năam kòw* (balls of cooked rice mixed with sour pork sausage), both of which are served with platters of fresh leaves and herbs; there's no English sign.

★Kitchen INTERNATIONAL $
(www.inthira.com; Inthira Hotel, Th Luang Prabang; mains 30,000K; ⏰7am-10pm; 📶🖉) Somewhere between a Lao kitchen and smart restaurant this place strikes a fine balance between informality and style. It's often packed to the gills and once you've netted the coconut shrimp, pad thai, spare ribs and steamed fish, you'll understand why. Also serves pizza and pasta dishes.

Ban Sabai Restaurant INTERNATIONAL $
(Ban Sabai Bungalows; mains 30,000K; ⏰7am-10pm; 📶🖉👪) In a prime location by the Nam Ou, you can tuck into English breakfasts or fruit salads come morning. By night it's enchanting, the garden aglow with lanterns as the kitchen alchemises an Asian-fusion menu of zesty *lâhp* salads, tom yum (tamarind and lemongrass) soup, and various seafood dishes. Decent steaks and well-executed pasta dishes too.

Living Room ASIAN $
(☎020-5491 9169; ⏰3-11pm) Classy new custard-coloured cafe with a funky sundowner terrace enjoying amazing karst views, a reggae soundtrack and a Lao – wait for it – Austrian fusion menu. Fresh juices, shakes (10,000K), soups, tofu, pork schnitzel and really inventive dishes such as spaghetti Vang Vieng – a kind of bolognese meets spicy *lâhp* salad. Delicious and fresh. It's next to Champa Lao Guesthouse

Le Café de Paris FRENCH $
(mains 20,000-30,000K; ⏰5.30-11.30pm) When it opened, this simple Gallic haunt quickly developed a following for its steak tartare, *boeuf bourgignon* and hot dog Parisien. A number of red and white wines on the menu, along with the homely decor and friendly, low-lit ambience make this a worthwhile haunt.

Nazim INDIAN $
(☎023-511214; Th Luang Prabang; mains 30,000K; 🖉) Nazim, a countrywide chain, is pretty consistent at delivering Malay and southern Indian cuisine in clean, if basic, spaces. This Vang Vieng branch is no different, with faves including chicken tikka, lamb masala and vegetable *jalfrezi.*

Nam Song Garden ASIAN FUSION $
(☎023-511544; ⏰7am-11pm; 📶) This alfresco restaurant perches at elevation above Don Khang, and makes for a romantic stop to gaze at the jagged karsts bathed in dusky light. The menu is pretty varied, spanning barbecued fish, chicken and meat dishes, breakfasts, *lâhp* variations and sweet and sour dishes. At the very least pop in here for a sunset cocktail (mojitos 30,000K).

Mama Sababa JEWISH $
(mains 15,000-40,000K; ⏰7am-10pm) Sababa ('Cool' in Hebrew) is allegedly run by a Lao Jew, boasts a Hebrew-language menu, and not surprisingly, is the best place in town to find your inner felafel. The chicken schnitzel also gets good reviews, as does the tofu, salads and steak.

Luang Prabang Bakery BAKERY $
(☎023-511145; mains 25,000-60,000K; ⏰7am-10.30pm; 📶) Never so chic, the LPB has upgraded its decor to wood lanterns and wicker chairs and tables. The real ace though is the treasure chest of choccy brownies, cookies, doughnuts, gateaux and Danish – a treat for the munchies.

★Restaurant du Crabe d'Or INTERNATIONAL $$

(☎023-511726; www.riversidevangvieng.com; Riverside Boutique Resort; ⊙7-10am & noon-10pm;) Set in the tasteful gardens of the Riverside Boutique Resort, this fine restaurant exudes high-end decor with a Lao flavour, and affords amazing views of the cliffs. The menu will please most palates with grilled salmon steak, pork cutlet with honey and lime sauce, as well as a raft of trad-Asian dishes. All delivered with panache. The best spot in town to enjoy the sunset over a glass of chilled Tattinger.

Drinking & Nightlife

The new, improved Vang Vieng has ditched all-night parties in favour of chilling.

Gary's Irish Bar IRISH PUB

(☎020-5825 5774; mains 35,000K; ⊙9am-midnight) Run by a friendly Irish guy, this is a cool, easy joint to while away a pleasant evening listening to indie tunes, playing a spot of pool or watching the latest sports on the box. Great full breakfasts, homemade pies and happy hour from 6pm to 10pm. There are also burgers (25,000K), snacks and Lao food.

Kangaroo Sunset Bar BAR

(☎020-7714291; mains 35,000K; ⊙8am-11.30pm;) Newly revamped and under fresh management, a Vang Vieng legend is reborn. Colourful lanterns and chilled rock and jazz music complement a decent menu of Lao and Western cuisine – Beerlao patty, veggie wraps, chicken club sandwich, pasta and salads. It's also well placed for meditative sunset beers by the river. Welcome back.

Fluid Bar BAR

(☎020-5929 5840;) Run by gregarious hipster Greg, this river bar survived the infamous 2012 cull. And we're glad about that, for within its denim-blue walls are original trippy art, mosaics, a relaxing balcony bar, pool table, cool tunes, crazy golf course and a vibrant garden with sun loungers and hammocks. There is also a menu boasting Thai dishes, veggie numbers, various cocktails and snacks. Creative and friendly. It is opposite Tham Lom Cave; take the second left turn after the bus station.

DRUGS

Since the 2012 clean-up, drugs are not so widespread in Vang Vieng; certainly the likes of *yaba* (methamphetamine) is no longer available. But dope is still around and local police are particularly adept at sniffing out spliffs, especially late at night. If you're caught with a stash of marijuana (or anything else) it can be expensive. The normal practice is for police to take your passport and fine you US$500. Don't expect a receipt, and don't bother calling your embassy.

If you must use opium, don't mix it with too much else and certainly not with lime juice. Several Vang Vieng residents told us that at least one traveller has died after using opium and having an innocuous-sounding glass of lime juice. According to local folklore, this mix has long been used by hill-tribe women who suicide as an ultimate act of protest against a bad husband.

Information

Internet cafes are scattered all over town, most charging around 300K per minute. A useful website detailing up-to-date events is www.vangviengbiz.com.

Most visitors leave Vang Vieng with nothing more serious than a hangover, but this tranquil setting is also the most dangerous place in Laos for travellers. Visitors die every year from river accidents, and while caving. Theft can also be a problem, with fellow travellers often the culprits. Take the usual precautions and don't leave valuables outside caves.

Agricultural Promotion Bank (Th Luang Prabang) Exchanges cash only.

BCEL (☎023-511434; Th Luang Prabang; ⊙8.30am-3.30pm) Exchanges cash and travellers cheques, and handles cash advances on Visa, MasterCard and JCB. Has two ATMs in town including at its other branch by the old market.

Post Office (☎023-511009) Beside the old market.

Provincial Hospital (☎023-511604) This modest hospital has X-ray facilities and is fine for broken bones, cuts and malaria. When we visited, the doctor spoke reasonable English.

Tourist Office (☎023-511707; Th Luang Prabang; ⊙8am-noon & 2-4pm) The staff's English might be minimal, however, this is a useful port of call to pick up various leaflets on local things to do in the area.

Getting There & Away

Buses, minibuses and *sǒrngtǎaou* depart from the **bus terminal** (☎023-511657; Rte 13) about 2km north of town, although if you're coming in from Vientiane you'll most likely be dropped off

BUSES FROM VANG VIENG

DESTINATION	PRICE (K)	DISTANCE (KM)	DURATION (HR)	DEPARTURES
Luang Prabang	110,000	168	6-8	9am, 2pm, 3pm (minibus)
	130,000		6-7	10am, 11am, 12pm, 8pm, 9pm (VIP)
Vientiane	40,000	156	3-4	5.30am, 6.30am, 7am, 12.30pm, 2pm (fan)
	60,000			9am, 10.30am, 1.30pm (minibus)
	80,000			1.30pm, 2pm, 3pm (air-con)

at or near the **bus stop** (Rte 13) near the former runway, a short walk from the centre of town. When leaving Vang Vieng, be aware that, even if you purchased your tickets at the bus station, the more expensive minibuses and air-con buses often cater predominantly to *falang* (Westerners) and will circle town, picking up people at their guesthouses, adding as much as an additional hour to the departure time.

Heading north, buses for Luang Prabang stop at the bus terminal for about five minutes en route from Vientiane about every hour between 11am and 8pm. All the services in the table also stop at Kasi and Phu Khoun (for Phonsavan).

Heading south, there are several bus options to Vientiane (see table, above). Alternatively, *sŏrngtăaou* (30,000K, 3½ to 4½ hours) leave about every 20 minutes from 5.30am until 4.30pm, and as they're often not full the ride can be quite enjoyable.

Getting Around

Vang Vieng is easily negotiated on foot. Renting a bicycle (per day 10,000K) or mountain bike (per day 30,000K) is also popular; they're available almost everywhere. Most of the same places also rent motorcycles for about 50,000K per day (automatics cost 70,000K). For cave sites out of town you can charter *sŏrngtăaou* near the old market site – expect to pay around US$10 per trip up to 20km north or south of town.

Vang Vieng towards Luang Prabang

The road between Vang Vieng and Luang Prabang winds its way up over some stunningly beautiful mountains and back down to the Mekong at Luang Prabang. If you suffer from motion sickness, take precautions before you begin.

Roughly 20km north of Vang Vieng, **Ban Pha Tang** is a pretty riverside village named after Pha Tang, a towering limestone cliff. The town's bridge offers a very photogenic view of its namesake. The only accommodation in the area is the ageing but comfortable **Pha Tang Resort** (☎020-5531 9573; Rte 13; r US$12), about 3km south of the town, literally at the base of Pha Tang. Food is great and the family who runs the place is pleasant.

In the middle of a fertile valley filled with rice fields, **Kasi**, 56km north of Vang Vieng, is a lunch stop for bus passengers and truck drivers travelling on this route. The surrounding area is full of interesting minority villages, and there are allegedly even a few big caves in the area, but few people bother to stop as there isn't much in the way of tourist infrastructure. If you've got trailblazing on your mind, you can base yourself at **Somchit Guesthouse** (☎020-220 8212; Rte 13; r 80,000-170,000K; P ❄ 📶), an expansive and tidy hotel about 1km north of the city. Another option is to book a basic room at **Vanphisith Guest House** (☎023-700084; Rte 13; r 60,000K), conveniently located near the bus stop restaurants and within walking distance of the town's exchange booth.

While Kasi town isn't memorable, the road on towards Luang Prabang certainly is, despite the ravages of slash-and-burn agriculture. For around 50km to Phu Khoun you'll ascend through some of the most spectacular limestone mountains that you'll find anywhere in Laos.

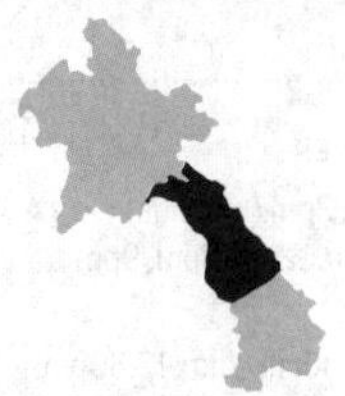

Central Laos

Includes ➡

Best Places to Eat

- Inthira Restaurant (p198)
- Chai Dee (p205)
- Dao Savanh (p206)

Best Places to Stay

- Inthira Hotel (p197)
- Salsavan Guesthouse (p203)
- Thakhek Travel Lodge (p195)

Why Go?

Ever since Tha Khaek opened its French colonial petals to travellers a few years back and the dramatic 7km-long underworld of Tham Kong Lo became a must-see fixture on itineraries, central Laos with its honeycomb of caves and dragon-green jungle, has been enticing you to visit. Immersive treks in Dong Phu Vieng NPA allow you to sleep with the spirits in a Katang village, while caving and kayaking in Khammuan and Bolikhamsai Provinces can be organised in Tha Khaek.

This part of the country claims the most forest cover and the highest concentrations of wildlife, including some species that have disappeared elsewhere in Southeast Asia. With its rugged, intrepid travel, and stylish pockets of comfort in Savannakhet and Tha Khaek, central Laos makes for a great place to combine your inner Indiana Jones with a Bloody Mary.

When to Go

Savannakhet

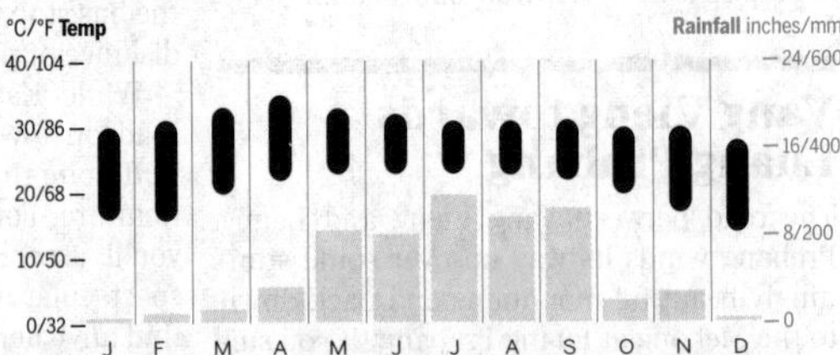

Nov–Feb The best time to visit: temperatures are balmy, paddy fields green and roads passable.

Mar–May Leading up to the monsoon, fields are dry and humidity up. Avoid the oven of the south.

Jun–Nov Pockets of intense rain, but sealed roads are passable, the landscape green and the air cool.

Climate

The Mekong River valley is always pretty warm and from March to May Savannakhet is positively steaming. It gets cooler as you head east towards the Annamite Chain and Lak Sao, and the villages along Rte 8B can be close to freezing during winter nights. The southwestern monsoon brings bucket loads of rain from June to October. Far-eastern areas around the Nakai-Nam Theun NBCA also receive rain from the South China Sea that lasts longer, thus supplying enough water to maintain the thicker vegetation.

National Protected Areas

Central Laos is the most protected part of the country with six national protected areas (NPAs) accounting for vast swathes of the region. Access to Nakai-Nam Theun NBCA, Hin Namno NPA and Se Ban Nuan NPA is limited to those with decent Lao language skills and plenty of time and money, but others are easy to get to.

In Khammuan Province the labyrinth of limestone karsts, caves and rivers in Phu Hin Bun NPA is accessible either on your own or on a community-based or commercial trek. Similar treks lead to the sacred forests and animist villages of Dong Phu Vieng in Savannakhet Province.

Getting There & Around

Rte 13 is sealed and thanks to its vital status as a Chinese trade route, it's particularly well maintained. Other decent roads include Rte 9 from Savannakhet to the Vietnamese border at Lao Bao, Rte 8 between Rte 13 and the Vietnamese border at Nam Phao, Rte 12 between Tha Khaek and the Vietnamese border, and the road to Tham Kong Lo.

BOLIKHAMSAI & KHAMMUAN PROVINCES

Bolikhamsai and Khammuan straddle the narrow, central 'waist' of the country. Physically the land climbs steadily from the Mekong River valley towards the north and east, eventually reaching the Annamite Chain bordering Vietnam, via an area of moderately high but often spectacular mountains. Laid-back Tha Khaek is the logical base.

Lowland Lao, who speak a dialect peculiar to these two provinces, dominate the population and, with smaller groups of tribal Thais, are the people you'll mostly meet. In remoter areas the Mon-Khmer-speaking Makong people (commonly known as Bru) make up more than 10% of the population

TREKKING IN CENTRAL LAOS

Underrated central Laos is a great place to combine a cultural and environmental experience. Most treks in central Laos are run by either the state-run eco-guide units in Tha Khaek and Savannakhet or the private company Green Discovery (p195), and range in cost from approximately US$40 to US$500 per person (prices drop significantly the greater the number of people in the group). Listed below are some particularly recommended trekking destinations in the region:

Phu Hin Bun NPA (p190) From Tha Khaek. For beauty, it's hard to beat these trekking and boating trips through the monolithic limestone karsts. Two- and three-day options are available at Tha Khaek's tourist information centre (p198), and four-day trips with Green Discovery.

Tham Lot Se Bang Fai/Hin Namno NPA (p201) From Tha Khaek. Although trekking here is still in its infancy and mostly revolves around the eponymous Nam Lot cave, it is also possible to combine a homestay with walks in the spectacular Hin Namno NPA. Enquire at Tha Khaek's tourist information centre or with Green Discovery.

Dong Natad (p208) From Savannakhet. One- and two-day trips to the provincial protected area near Savannakhet are cheap and popular for their homestays and explanations of how villagers use the sacred forest. Contact Savannakhet's eco-guide unit (p206) for details.

Dong Phu Vieng NPA (p208) From Savannakhet. This three-day trek (with a fair bit of road time at either end) takes you to two Katang villages where animist beliefs come with a host of taboos. It's a real head-bending cultural experience, but the transport makes prices a bit steep. Organised by Savannakhet's eco-guide unit.

Central Laos Highlights

1. Trek amid the gothic limestone karsts, subterranean caves and the meandering rivers of the **Phu Hin Bun NPA** (p190)
2. Do the **Loop** (p190) and journey through flooded valleys, bad roads, jungle and soaring mountain views
3. Soak up the colonial atmosphere of the historical districts of **Tha Khaek** (p194) and **Savannakhet** (p202)
4. Stay in the remote villages of **Dong Phu Vieng NPA** (p208) and experience life in the spirit forests
5. Go off the beaten track to **Tham Kong Lo** (p192) for a boat trip through this astonishing 7km-long limestone underworld

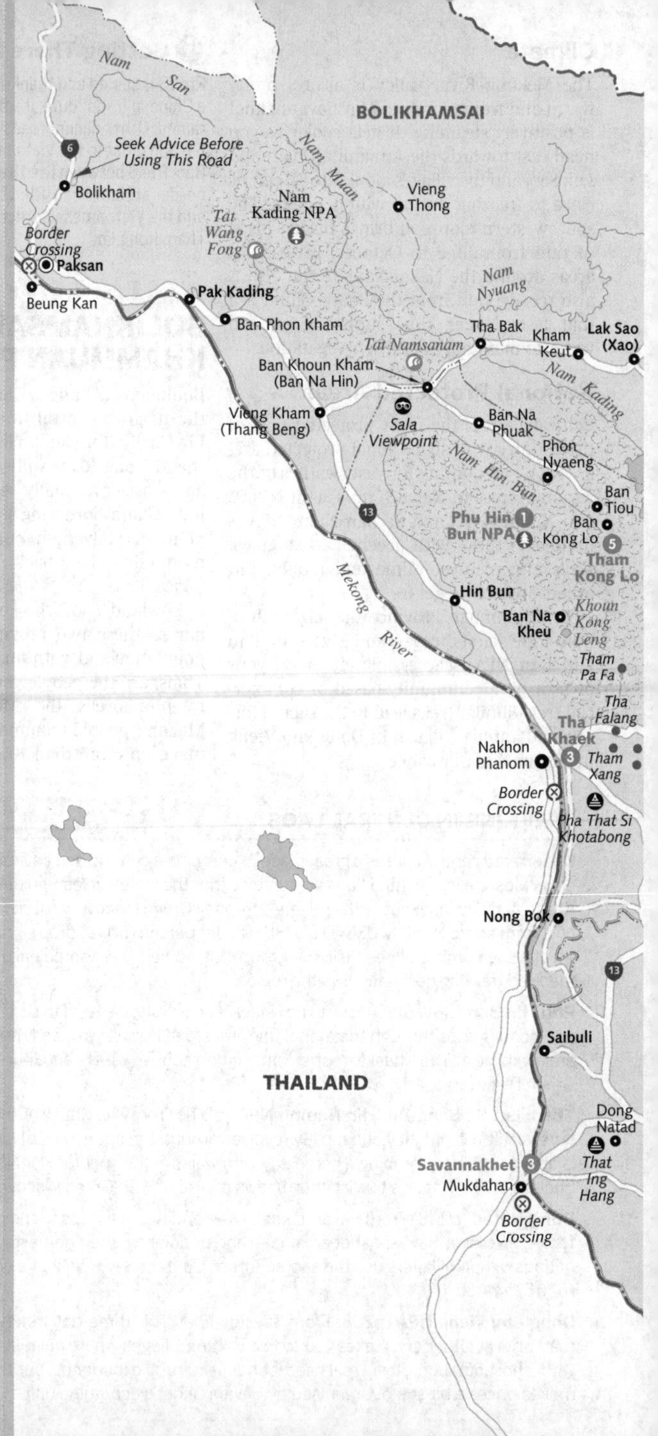

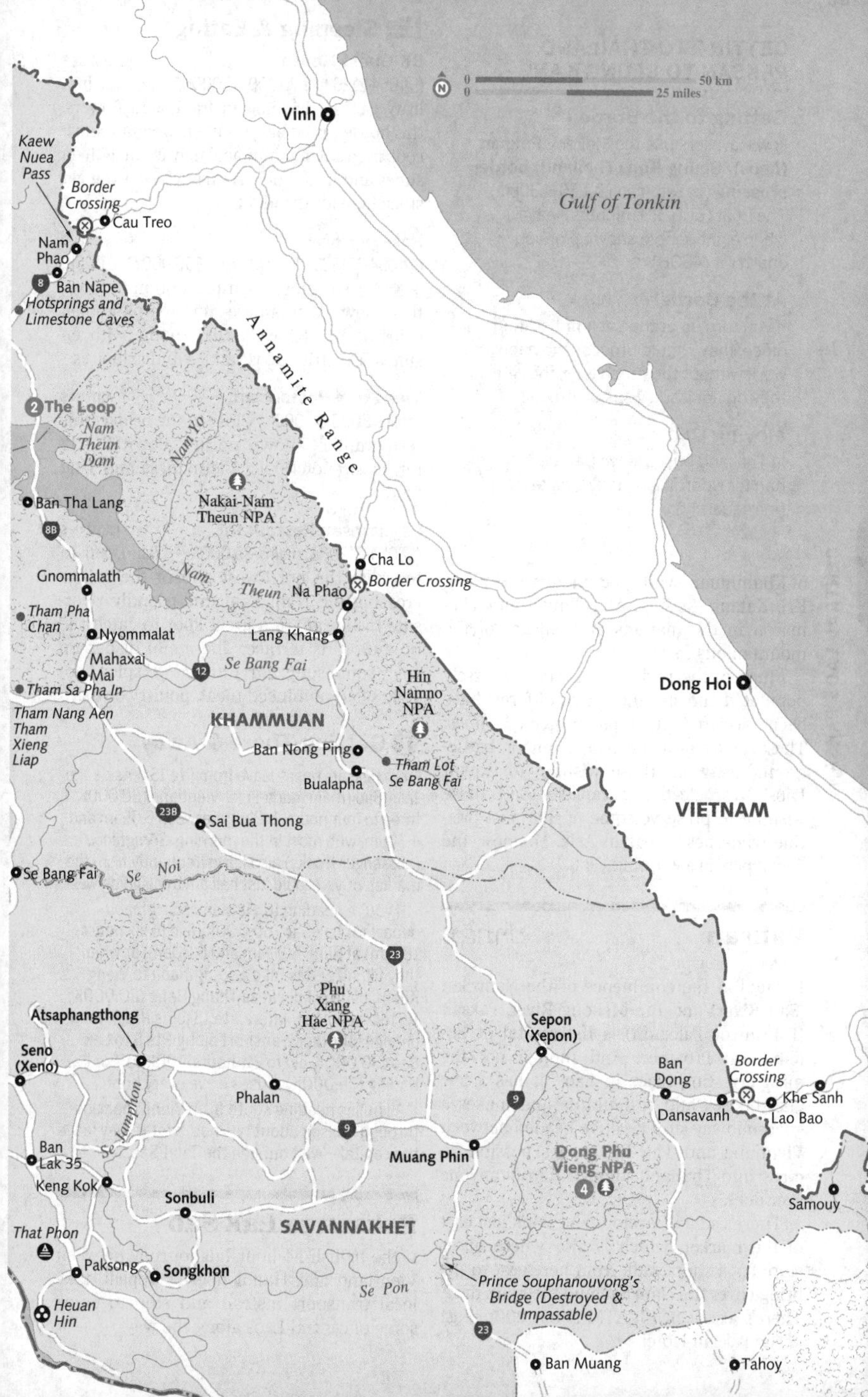

0 50 km
0 25 miles
Vinh
Gulf of Tonkin
Kaew
Nuea
Pass
Border
Crossing
Cau Treo
Nam
Phao
Ban Nape
Hotsprings and
Limestone Caves
Annamite Range
The Loop
Nam
Theun
Dam
Nam Yo
Nakai-Nam
Theun NPA
Ban Tha Lang
Gnommalath
Nam
Theun
Cha Lo
Border Crossing
Na Phao
Tham Pha
Chan
Nyommalat
Lang Khang
Mahaxai
Mai
Se Bang Fai
Tham Sa Pha In
Hin
Namno
NPA
Dong Hoi
Tham Nang Aen
Tham
Xieng
Liap
KHAMMUAN
Ban Nong Ping
Tham Lot
Se Bang Fai
Bualapha
VIETNAM
Sai Bua Thong
Se Bang Fai
Se Noi
Phu
Xang
Hae NPA
Atsaphangthong
Sepon
(Xepon)
Seno
(Xeno)
Ban
Dong
Border
Crossing
Phalan
Dansavanh
Khe Sanh
Lao Bao
Se Lamphon
Ban
Lak 35
Muang Phin
Dong Phu
Vieng NPA
Keng Kok
Sonbuli
Samouy
That Phon
SAVANNAKHET
Paksong
Songkhon
Se Pon
Prince Souphanouvong's
Bridge (Destroyed &
Impassable)
Heuan
Hin
Ban Muang
Tahoy

GETTING TO THAILAND: PAKSAN TO BEUNG KAN

Getting to the Border

Few travellers use the Mekong **Paksan (Laos)/Beung Kan (Thailand) border crossing** (8am-noon & 1.30-4.30pm). The boat (60B, 20 minutes) leaves when eight people show up or you charter it (480B).

At the Border

If you turn up at the Lao immigration office, they should process the paperwork without too much fuss, though they do not issue visas on arrival.

Moving On

In Thailand buses leave Beung Kan for Udon Thani and Bangkok (infrequently).

of Khammuan, while you might see Hmong, Kri, Katang, Maling, Atel, Phuan and Themarou in the markets and villages of the mountainous east.

Much of the region is relatively sparsely populated and six large tracts of forest have been declared national protected areas. These areas have become a major battleground between those wishing to exploit Laos' hydroelectricity capacity and those wishing to preserve some of the most pristine wilderness areas in Asia. For now, the developers are winning.

Paksan ປາກຊັນ

054 / POP 43,700

Located at the confluence of the Nam San (San River) and the Mekong River, Paksan (Pakxan or Pakxanh) is the capital of Bolikhamsai Province. And though not the most arresting place in Laos, it has a few guesthouses and restaurants and makes a good midway stop if you're headed between Vientiane and Tha Khaek. It's possible to cross into Thailand, though hardly anyone ever does.

There's a Lao Development Bank just east of the market, which is also where buses stop. It's a short walk from here east to the bridge over the Nam San and the main drag. There's also a BCEL ATM about 200m east of the Paksan Hotel.

Sleeping & Eating

BK Guest House GUESTHOUSE $

(054-212638; r 70,000-80,000K; P) Set in a leafy garden dripping in frangipani flowers, this house-proud guesthouse has eight rooms: cool, fragrant and immaculately clean with en suites and fresh linen. A great place if you get stuck here for the night.

Paksan Hotel HOTEL $

(054-791333; Rte 13; s/d 100,000/140,000K; P) The most luxurious option in town, this new Vietnamese-run temple-roofed colossus has 32 well-sized rooms with en suites, TVs, fridges, verandas and armoires.

Viengxum Restaurant LAOTIAN $

(mains 8000-30,000K) Close to the bridge, this restaurant is known up and down Rte 13 for its top-notch Lao, Vietnamese and Thai food.

Saynamsan Restaurant LAOTIAN $

(054-212068; mains 35,000K; 7am-11pm) In town, at the northwest end of the bridge crossing the Nam San, this friendly riverside restaurant is a great spot to catch the breeze on its terrace. The menu dishes up spicy squid soup, curry and *làhp* (spicy Lao-style salad of minced meat, poultry or fish).

Getting There & Away

From Paksan, buses leave from Rte 13 outside the Talat Sao (main market) for Vientiane (30,000K, three to four hours, 143km) between 6.05am and 4.30pm, with most in the morning. *Sŏrngtăaou* (passenger trucks) also leave frequently from the market, or you could just hail anything going west.

If you're heading to Vietnam, *sŏrngtăaou* depart for Lak Sao (60,000K, five to six hours, 189km) at 5am, 5.30am and 6.30am, or when they fill. After this take a *sŏrngtăaou* to Vieng Kham, usually known as Thang Beng (20,000K, 1½ to two hours), where Rte 13 joins Rte 8, then change for other transport along Rte 8 to Lak Sao (30,000K, 1½ to 2½ hours, 100km). For Pak Kading (75,000K), buses leave every hour.

All buses heading south from Vientiane pass through Paksan about two hours after they leave the capital – wait outside the Talat Sao.

Paksan to Lak Sao

If the hellish 24-hour bus journey between Vientiane and Hanoi doesn't appeal, take local transport instead and stop to enjoy some of central Laos along the way.

Nam Kading NPA
ປ່າສະຫງວນແຫ່ງຊາດນ້ຳກະດິງ

Heading east along Rte 13 you'll come to the sleepy yet picturesque village of **Pak Kading**, 187km from Vientiane. Pak Kading sits just upstream from the junction of the Mekong River and the **Nam Kading** (Kading River), one of the most pristine rivers in Laos – for now. Flowing through a forested valley surrounded by high hills and menacing-looking limestone formations, this broad, turquoise-tinted river winds its way into the **Nam Kading NPA**. The river is undoubtedly the best way into this wilderness, where confirmed animal rarities include the elephant, giant muntjac, pygmy slow loris, François' langur, douc langur, gibbon, dhole, Asiatic black bear, tiger and many bird species. As usual in Laos, you'll count yourself very lucky to catch anything more than a glimpse of any of these.

Falls or no falls, Pak Kading is a good place to stop for a meal at the **Bounxou Restaurant** (☎055-320046; Rte 13; mains 10,000-25,000K; ⊙8am-9pm), where the fish dishes are famous. If you have to stay there head to **Vilada Guesthouse** (r with fan/air-con 70,000/100,000K; P ❄).

Ban Khoun Kham (Ban Na Hin)
ບ້ານຄູນຄຳ (ບ້ານນາຫີນ)

Ban Khoun Kham's former role as a base from which to visit the extraordinary Tham Kong Lo has been seriously undercut by Ban Kong Lo recently acquitting itself to cater for tourists headed to the nearby cave, and as such there's a little tumbleweed blowing through town. The main local attraction is the impressive twin-cataract of **Tat Namsanam**, 3km north of town (though give it a miss in dry season). The falls are in a striking location surrounded by karst and the upper tier is quite high. Unfortunately, the path and signs leading to the falls aren't entirely clear, and more than one foreign visitor has become lost here. Proceed with caution, or better yet, hire a guide through the excellent **tourist information centre** (☎020-5559 8412; Rte 8; ⊙8am-4pm), just south of the Tat Namsanam entrance, which runs community-based treks from here into the Phu Hin Bun NPA. Ask to speak to Thoum.

As you approach Ban Khoun Kham from Rte 13, there is a *sala* (open-sided shelter) viewpoint between Km 32 and Km 33. Do not, whatever you do, miss the spectacularly dramatic scenery below; somewhere between a dream and a nightmare the landscape rears raggedly with black rock formations.

Sleeping & Eating

Ban Khoun Kham's main strip, which runs parallel to Rte 13, is home to several nearly identical guesthouses, all offering air-con rooms with cable TV and hot water.

Xok Xai Guesthouse GUESTHOUSE $
(☎051-233629; Rte 8; r 80,000K; P ❄) Lovely rooms in a traditional house set back off Rte 8 (or 400m north from the market). Details include spotless varnished floors, thick duvets, TV, air-con, powder-blue curtains and hot-water en suites.

Mi Thuna Restaurant Guesthouse GUESTHOUSE $
(☎020-224 0182; Rte 8; r 60,000K; P ❄) Mi Thuna is about 800m south of the market on Rte 8, past the Shell petrol station, and has pleasant rooms with clean tiled floors, little desks, fan or air-con and rundown en suites. There's a restaurant serving Lao and Western fare – if you can wake the cook up! Ask for a room set back from the road or passing trucks will keep you awake.

Sainamhai Resort RESORT $
(☎020-233 1683; www.sainamhairesort.com; r 130,000K; P ❄ 📶) Sainamhai sits by the Nam Hai (Hai River). There's a handsome longhouse restaurant (mains 25,000K), a fertile garden and 12 well-maintained rattan-walled cabanas with private balconies, en suites and clean linen. One caveat though – noisy cockerel. Bring some earplugs or travel through Tham Kong Lo asleep!

It's 3km east of Rte 8; follow the sign near the junction of Rte 8 and the road that borders the Theun Hin Bun dam housing compound at the east end of town, or via a turn-off a few kilometres down the road that leads to Tham Kong Lo. They'll pick you up for free at the *sŏrngtăaou* station if you call ahead.

Inthapaya Guesthouse GUESTHOUSE $
(☎020-2233 6534; r with fan/air-con 60,000/90,000K; P ⊖ ❄) Fresh-smelling (no smoking) cornflower-blue rooms with tiled floors, clean en suites and optional fan or air-con. There's

also a neat little courtyard cafe. It's northeast of the main street.

Phamarn View GUESTHOUSE $
(☎020-240 3950; r with fan/air-con 60,000/90,000K; P❄📶) Fragrant rooms with peach walls, new beds, TVs, fridges and air-con set around a courtyard. They also have verandahs. You'll find it close to the market and bus station.

Dokkhoun Restaurant LAOTIAN $
(☎020-246 9811; mains 30,000K; ⏰7am-10pm) On the main drag in town, this place very competently turns out fruit juices, fried rice, pork *lâhp* and continental breakfast.

ℹ Getting There & Away

If you're in Tha Khaek there's a daily 8am and 9am departure for Ban Khoun Kham (50,000K, three to four hours). Alternatively, if you're starting your journey in Tha Khaek or Vientiane, another option is to simply hop on any north or southbound bus and get off at Vieng Kham (also known as Thang Beng), at the junction of Rtes 13 and 8, and continue by *sŏrngtăaou* (25,000K, 7am to 7pm, one hour) to Ban Khoun Kham.

All transport along Rte 8 stops in Ban Khoun Kham, including buses for Vientiane (75,000K) and Tha Khaek (75,000K, three hours, 143km), both of which you're more likely to catch in the morning. Later in the day you'll need to take any of the semi-regular *sŏrngtăaou* to Vieng Kham (30,000K, 7am to 5pm) or, if you're bound for the Vietnam border, Lak Sao (25,000K, 7am to 5pm) – both about one hour from Ban Khoun Kham – and change. To Tham Kong Lo, *sŏrngtăaou* leave at 10am, 12.30pm and 3pm (25,000K, one hour).

Phu Hin Bun NPA
ປ່າສະຫງວນແຫ່ງຊາດພູຫີນປູນ

The Phu Hin Bun NPA is a huge (1580 sq km) wilderness area of turquoise streams, monsoon forests and striking karst topography across central Khammuan. It was made a protected area in 1993 and it's no overstatement to say this is some of the most breathtaking country in the region. Passing through on foot or by boat it's hard not to feel awestruck by the very scale of the limestone cliffs that rise almost vertically for hundreds of metres into the sky.

Although much of the NPA is inaccessible by road, local people have reduced the numbers of key forest-dependent species through hunting and logging. Despite this, the area remains home to the endangered

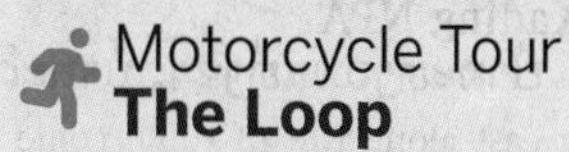

Motorcycle Tour
The Loop

START THA KHAEK
END THA KHAEK
LENGTH 500KM; FOUR DAYS

The Loop, an off-the-beaten-track circuit through some of the more remote parts of Khammuan and Bolikhamsai Provinces, has achieved mythic status with intrepid travellers over the last couple of years. It's possible to make the trip by bicycle, but is best done on a motorbike. And note – we say *motorbike* and not scooter. Thanks to wobbly, narrow wheels and occasionally unreliable brakes, traveller accidents – and, tragically, deaths – on scooters are myriad. Thankfully Mad Monkey Motorbike (p199), a new company renting out quality dirt bikes, has opened in Tha Khaek. Give yourself at least three days, though four is better if you want to see Tham Kong Lo. Fuel is available in most villages along the way.

Begin in ❶ **Tha Khaek** – the tourist information centre can provide advice on the circuit. It's also a good idea to sit down with a cold Beerlao and the ever-expanding travellers' book at Thakhek Travel Lodge before you head off or speak to DC at Mad Monkey.

Spend day one heading east on Rte 12, visiting the caves and swimming spots on the way. The 20km stretch north of ❷ **Mahaxai Mai**, about 40km from Tha Khaek, is where you'll find accommodation options for this leg. Just north of Mahaxai Mai, are two basic guesthouses, **Maniphone** (☎020-215 8699) and **Mahaxai Mai** (☎020-216 4453). The cement bungalows and restaurant at **Linxomphou Resort-Night Club** (☎020-5458 4453), about 15km north of Mahaxai Mai offers another option. Just north of Km 55 is the Rte 12 turn-off to Vietnam and the expansive Nam Theun 2 Main Camp, across from which **Phothavong Guest House** (☎020-5663 5555) is one of the better places to stay along this stretch.

Continuing past Gnommalath, an additional 5km north of the Rte 12 intersection, where there's petrol and basic food, you'll reach Nam Theun 2 Power Station and virtually the last bit of paved road until Lak

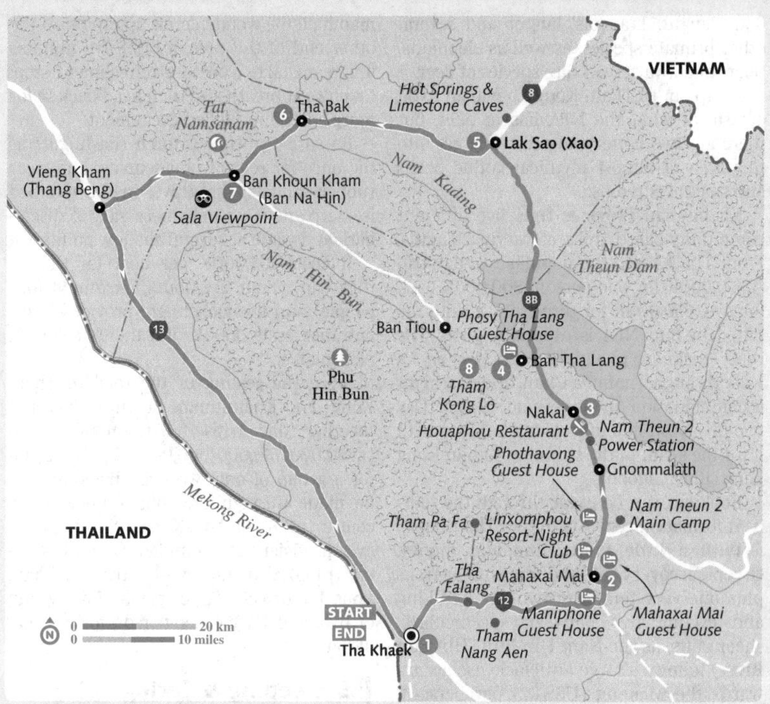

Sao. At the top of the hill the road splits at a busy village called Ban Oudomsouk; keep straight for 3km to 3 **Nakai**, where you can refuel your body at **Houaphou Restaurant** (☎051-620111) and refuel your bike at the petrol station.

The next 23km is a disturbing corridor of pristine jungle on your left and the environmental disaster zone created by the recent flooding of the Nam Theun 2 dam on your right. You'll also start to see *bâan jat sàn*, tidy villages created for those displaced by the flooding. Just before the road crosses the Nam Theun via a new bridge, you'll arrive in tiny 4 **Ban Tha Lang**, where the **Phosy Tha Lang Guesthouse & Restaurant** (☎020-5880 4711) offers respite with clean, basic cabanas with fresh sheets, en suites and balconies. From Mahaxai Mai to Ban Tha Lang took us about two hours.

After crossing the bridge at Ban Tha Long it's about 60km to Lak Sao. This stretch is stunning as you drive through the corridor between the Nakai-Nam Theun NBCA and Phu Hin Bun NPA. But the road can be hellish; a mix of gravelly unsealed surfaces and tight switchbacks. Take it slowly and drink up the view. At times the severely potholed road climbs near vertically through quarries at roadside and past overturned trucks. After 17km keep straight at the junction (the left fork will take you to the Nam Theun 2 dam site). In the dry season this stretch took us about two hours.

When you finally hit the tarmac at the frontier-feel town of 5 **Lak Sao**, you'll be relieved to find available accommodation and food, and it's also a good place if you need bike repairs. Riding the 56km of smooth Rte 8 between Lak Sao and Ban Khoun Kham is like stepping into a video game – the decent, sealed road runs between walls of impregnable karst on one side, into winding hills of deep forest, and crosses the wide Nam Theun at 6 **Tha Bak**, where it's worth stopping for a look at the bomb boats.

7 **Ban Khoun Kham** has a petrol station and heaps of accommodation and is one base for trips into 8 **Tham Kong Lo**, but over the last two years, accommodation has now sprung up in Kong Lo village itself (more convenient for seeing the cave first thing in the morning). From Ban Khoun Kham it's about 145km back to Tha Khaek.

douc langur, François' langur and several other primate species, as well as elephants, tigers and a variety of rare species of deer.

A trip out to Tham Kong Lo will give you a taste of what the NPA has to offer, but there are two better ways to really get into this area of almost mythical gothic peaks and snaking streams.

Khammuan Province runs five different community-based treks of varying lengths. From Tha Khaek, the popular two-day trip (1,350,000K for one person, 800,000K each for two, 650,000K for three to five) into the Phu Hin Bun NPA is especially good. The route includes plenty of karst scenery, a walk through Tham Pa Chan, and overnight accommodation in an ethnic village. Day two involves 15km of trekking but it's worth it for the swim in the stunning Khoun Kong Leng (Blue Lagoon).

Bookings can be made through the tourist information centre (p198) in Tha Khaek.

With a little more time and money, Green Discovery (p195) offers similar treks plus one very tempting two-day kayaking and cycling trip between spectacularly sheer cliffs, as the Nam Hin Bun (Hin Bun River) follows a large anticlockwise arc towards the Mekong (US$453 per person). Additionally there are four-day river trips on the Nam Hin Bun (US$510 per person for a group of two, US$321 per person for a group of four).

Tham Kong Lo ຖ້ຳລອດກອງລໍ

Tham Kong Lo is one of central Laos', if not the country's, most vivid highlights. A journey into this preternatural underworld is like a voyage into darkness itself, with 7km of winding river, scaling small rapids as it passes through the cathedral-high limestone cave. A section of Kong Lo has now been atmospherically lit, allowing you a greater glimpse of this epic spectacle; your longtail docks in a rocky inlet to allow you to explore a stalactite wood of haunting pillars and sprouting stalagmites. Your imagination will be in overdrive as the boat takes you further into the bat-black darkness – you might liken it to Middle Earth (the lights of other boats like Gollum's eyes swallowed in the gloom) or the Greek Underworld of Hades. Either way you won't ever forget it.

Rides take up to an hour each way and in dry season when the river is low you'll have to get out while the boatman and point man haul the wooden craft up rapids. At the other end of the cave, a brief five minutes upstream takes you to a refreshment stop. Catch your breath and then head back in for more adrenalin-fuelled excitement.

Be sure to bring a torch (flashlight) as the ones for rent are inadequate, and wear rubber sandals; the gravel in the riverbed is sharp and it's usually necessary to disembark and wade at several shallow points.

It costs 105,000K per boat for the return trip (about 2½ hours, maximum four people) and life jackets are provided. Cave entrance costs 5000K and there's a 5000K parking fee.

Since the sealing of the road to Tham Kong Lo, Khammuan Province has put together day trips to Tham Kong Lo (1,350,000/750,000/600,000K per person for a group of one/two/five). Bookings can be made through the tourist information centre (p198) in Tha Khaek. Speak to the ever proficient Mr Somkiad. Green Discovery (p195) also run one-day trips to Tham Long Lo for US$141 per person for a group of two, and US$84 per person for a group of four.

Sleeping & Eating

Sala Kong Lor GUESTHOUSE $
(☎020-5564 5111; www.salalao.com; Ban Tiou; bungalows inc breakfast US$6-30; P) Located 1.5km downstream of Tham Kong Lo, these stilted bungalows range from basic to superior and sit by the Nam Hin Bun. En suite rooms are basic but welcoming with brick walls, blue bedspreads, mozzie nets, a few sticks of furniture and private balconies to enjoy the lush river view. There's a clearwater creek nearby to cool off in.

Chantha Guest House GUESTHOUSE $
(☎020-210 0002; Ban Kong Lo; r without/with air-con 60,000/100,000K; P ❄ @ ☎) This Swiss-style accommodation on the main road to Kong Lo and at the beginning of the village, has 15 cool and well-kept rooms with doubles and twins, plus a dorm which sleeps five people (180,000K). There's a DVD lounge and a small cafe, and the owners are friendly. Temperamental wi-fi.

Saylomyen Guest House GUESTHOUSE $
(☎020-7775 5216; Ban Kong Lo; r 40,000-80,000K; P) Stilted Saylomyen is a rattan affair with private balconies out back, colourful bedspreads, fans and en suites. There's also a cafe. At the northern edge of town.

Kong Lo Eco Lodge GUESTHOUSE $
(☎030-906 2772; Ban Kong Lo; r 60,000K; P) This place is set back from the main road and offers 12 spartan rooms without decor. That said, it's clean and cheap. There's a decent cafe too.

Homestay HOMESTAY $
(Ban Kong Lo; per person incl dinner & breakfast 50,000K) Say the word 'homestay' and you'll be hooked up with a family somewhere in the village. Homestay accommodation is also available on the opposite side of the cave, in Ban Na Tan and the prettier Ban Phon Kham. Both villages are within walking distance of the drink stalls where the boats terminate; Ban Na Tan is a 2km walk along the left fork, and Ban Phon Kham is the second village you'll come to after about 1km along the right fork. The drink vendors are more than happy to point you in the right direction.

★ **Auberges Sala Hinboun** GUESTHOUSE $$
(☎041-212445; www.salalao.com; r incl breakfast US$23-29; P) On the banks of the Nam Hin Bun 10km north of Ban Kong Lo, Auberges Sala Hinboun has 12 guacamole-green, homely wood cabanas on stilts. Rooms have gypsy-chic curtains, rattan floors, balconies and comfy beds. The ones facing the river are the largest (US$29), while the smaller ones are decent too (US$25).

The restaurant has a menu of fried fish, roast chicken and Lao salad, and if you're feeling extravagant and there's a few of you, why not try the spit-roasted piglet (450,000K)?

Mithuna Restaurant LAOTIAN $
(Ban Kong Lo; mains 20,000K; ⏰7am-8pm) Close to the entrance to Tham Kong Lo, this semi-alfresco, fan-cooled restaurant serves up noodles, fried rice and pork *láhp*, as well as Western breakfasts.

ℹ Getting There & Away

The 50km road from Ban Khoun Kham to Ban Kong Lo is an easy one-hour motorbike ride or *sŏrngtăaou*. From Ban Kong Lo, *sŏrngtăaou* to Ban Khoun Kham (25,000K) depart at 6.30am, 8am and 11am.

Tha Bak ບ້ານທ່າບັກ

About 18km east of Ban Khoun Kham, Tha Bak sits near the confluence of the Nam Kading and Nam Theun rivers. The town itself is pretty, and pretty quiet; the real reason to stop is to take photos of the river or get out on the incredible **bomb boats**. The name is slightly misleading, as the boats are made out of huge missile-shaped drop tanks that carried fuel for jets operating overhead during the 1960s and '70s. If you fancy a spin in a bomb boat just head down to the riverbank at the east end of the bridge and negotiate a price.

Lak Sao ຫລັກຊາວ

☎054 / POP 31,400

Essentially a dusty two-street affair in the eastern reaches of Bolikhamsai Province near the Vietnam border (32km away), Lak Sao is humming with trucks passing through to nearby Vietnam, and has made its name as a logging town. It's surrounded by beautiful saw-toothed cliffs that come dusk are evocatively etched a burnt charcoal.

There's plenty of uninspiring guesthouses, a maze of a market, a 24-hour ATM, plus a couple of places to eat. Not the prettiest place thanks to the eternal screen of dust that hangs in the air, but useful to stock up on cash, fuel up and catch some Zs if you're on the Loop.

Sleeping & Eating

All the establishments are a short walk to both the market and bus station. Several **small restaurants** (⏰6am-8pm) and *fĕr* (rice-noodle soup) stalls serve Lao and Vietnamese dishes around the market.

Phoutthavong Guest House GUESTHOUSE $
(☎054-341074; Rte 1E; r 80,000K; P❄📶) Sitting back from busy Rte 8, this is a pleasant guesthouse with large rooms, mahogany beds and furniture, basic en suites and TVs. There's a talking myna bird too to keep you company.

Souriya Hotel HOTEL $
(☎054-341111; Rte 1E; r 50,000-80,000K; P❄) All rooms here have fan or air-con (some being smaller than others). The rooms themselves are fresh with hard beds and (for Loop-weary backs) en suites with very hot water. There's a safe place to store your bike. It also has cable TV.

Vongsouda Guest House GUESTHOUSE $
(☎020-210 2020; r 60,000K; ❄) About 300m north of Rte 8 along a dirt road, this family-run place has decent, relatively large rooms and a cosy communal area with a fireplace,

GETTING TO VIETNAM: LAK SAO TO VINH

Getting to the Border

The **Nam Phao (Laos)/Cau Treo (Vietnam) border crossing** (7am-4.30pm) is at the Kaew Neua Pass, 36km from Lak Sao. *Sŏrngtăaou* (20,000K, 45 minutes) leave every hour or so from Lak Sao market and drop passengers at the typically relaxed Lao border post. There is an exchange booth on the Lao side, though the rates aren't generous.

Coming back from Vinh in Vietnam, buses to Tay Song (formerly Trung Tam) leave regularly throughout the day (70,000d, three hours, 70km). From Tay Song, it's another 25km through some richly forested country to the border. It should cost about 50,000d by motorbike or taxi, but drivers will demand several times that. Expect to be ripped off on this route.

At the Border

You'll need to have your Vietnamese visa arranged in advance. Laos issues 30-day visas at the border.

Moving On

Inconveniently, the Vietnam border post is 1km up the road from the Lao border post, and once you pass this you'll be welcomed by an assortment of piranhas masquerading as transport to Vinh. Contrary to their claims, a minibus to Vinh doesn't cost US$30 per person – about US$5 for a seat is more reasonable, though you'll do very well to get that price. A metered taxi costs US$35 to US$40 while a motorbike fare is about 200,000d. Hook up with as many other people as possible to improve your bargaining position.

You can hopefully avoid these guys by taking a bus direct from Lak Sao to Vinh (120,000K, five hours); there are usually four buses leaving between about noon and 2pm. Once in Vinh you can take a bus or a sleeper on the **Reunification Express** (www.vr.com.vn) straight to Hanoi.

though you'll be lucky if anyone else is around.

Only One Restaurant LAOTIAN **$**
(054-341034; Rte 1E; mains 20,000-40,000K; 7am-10pm) This cavernous restaurant has a great terrace out back looking on to the karsts. It's a good place to eat your *láhp*, barbecued pork, stir-fries and fried morning glory.

Information

Lao Development Bank (Rte 1E) Located near the market, this bank changes Thai baht, US dollars, UK pounds and Vietnamese dong.

Post Office (cnr Rte 8 & Rte 1E)

Getting There & Away

Buses leave from east of the market for Vientiane (85,000K, six to eight hours, 334km) daily at 5.30am, 6.30am, 8am and 8pm. These buses stop at Vieng Kham (Thang Beng; 35,000K, 1½ to 2½ hours, 100km), where you can change for regular buses heading south or get off at Paksan (40,000K, five to six hours, 189km). Other buses and *sŏrngtăaou* head along Rte 8 to Vieng Kham/Thang Beng (between 8.30am and 5pm) and one bus goes to Tha Khaek (60,000K, five to six hours, 202km) at 7.30am.

Tha Khaek ທ່າແຂກ

051 / POP 81,000

This ex-Indochinese trading post is a delightful melange of crumbling French villas and warped Chinese merchant's shopfronts, with an easy riverside charm which, despite the new bridge over to nearby Thailand, shows little signs of change. An evocative place to stop for a day and night; you begin the Loop from here, and can also use Tha Khaek as a base from which to make organised day trips to Tham Kong Lo. For the first time direct *sŏrngtăaou* are also now leaving for the latter. There are also loads of caves (some swimmable with lagoons) within a spit of town that can be accessed by scooter or tuk-tuk.

Don't expect Luang Prabang levels of sophistication from Tha Khaek but you will find a historically appealing old town and slice of authentic Lao life. The epicentre (if you can call it that) of the old town is the modest fountain square at the western end of Th Kuvoravong near the river.

History

Tha Khaek traces its present-day roots to French colonial construction in 1911–12. Evidence of this period can be found in the slowly decaying buildings around Fountain Sq. The town served as a port, border post and administrative centre during the French period.

Sights & Activities

Other than wandering the streets and soaking up the atmosphere, there's not a lot to keep you occupied in Tha Khaek, but if you're looking for something (slightly) more active, the town has an abundance of organised *petang* (Lao pétanque) grounds. **Bounthong Petang Field** (020-5561 9331; 4-10.30pm) and **Nang Linly** (020-5522 2021; 4-10.30pm), next door to each other two blocks south of Fountain Sq, let you use their pitches and boules in exchange for the purchase of Beerlao or other drinks. There's also a place off Fountain Sq to take a **massage** (per hr 50,000K; 10am-10pm).

Tours

The tourist information centre runs tours in the area. Trek prices vary depending on group size, so it's worth calling the reliable **Mr Somkiad** (030-5300503, 020-5571 1797; somkiad@yahoo.com) who runs the centre to coordinate with other travellers. As an example, a two-day trek in the Phu Hin Bun NPA for a group of four will cost a reasonable 650,000K per person. These treks typically involve a homestay. Ask him too about the 3km-long newly discovered river cave, Tham Pa Seuam (Fish Cave). Slated to open in late 2013, it's similar in scope to Tham Kong Lo and features staggering stalactites and stalagmites, plus, conveniently, it's only 15km away. Trips with the tourist information centre will eventually cost around 150,000K per person for a group of four.

Green Discovery ADVENTURE TOUR
(051-251390; Inthira Hotel, Th Chao Anou; 8am-9pm) Runs a range of treks and kayaking excursions in the lush Phu Hin Bun NPA, including Tham Kong Lo. Cycling, kayaking and a homestay can also be combined. Has a desk at the Inthira Hotel.

Sleeping

Perhaps surprisingly, given it is the nearest big town to the vast Nam Theun 2 dam site, Tha Khaek has a small range of rooms.

★**Thakhek Travel Lodge** GUESTHOUSE $
(051-212931; thakhektravellodge@gmail.com; Rte 13; dm 30,000K, r 40,000-180,000K; P ❄ @) If only all guesthouses were as calm, inventive and homely as this travellers' oasis. Just five minutes east out of town in a tuk-tuk, it excels with a spectrum of bog-standard patchy rooms to elements of Indo-chic. The lodge's centrepiece is a leafy courtyard with a nightly firepit to swap stories of the Loop.

There's also a natty cafe serving up Lao fare such as *láhp*, Western salads, pork chops and various juices. Just finished when we passed were seven new rooms out back with slate floors, flat-screen TVs and fridges.

DEADWOOD: LAOS' ILLEGAL LOGGING TRADE

Laos has some of the largest remnant tracts of primary rainforest in mainland Southeast Asia. With China, Thailand and Vietnam having implemented stricter regulations to protect their own forests, Laos remains a vulnerable target for foreign companies. The Environmental Investigation Agency (EIA) claims that the furniture industry in Vietnam has grown tenfold since 2000, with Laos facilitating the flow of its timber to enable this. An estimated 500,000 cu metres of logs find their way over the border every year. While an outwardly hard-line approach has been taken against mass logging by the government, it's the self-funded military and local officials in remote areas who can fall prey to bribes.

Forest cover fell from 70% in the 1940s to less than 40% in the early 2000s, with an annual rate of 90,000 ha disappearing every year. NPAs (National Protected Areas), which are supposed to be protected under Lao law, are prey to heavy illegal logging as they contain so much commercially valuable timber. An estimated 30% of forest cover will remain in Laos by 2020.

Tha Khaek

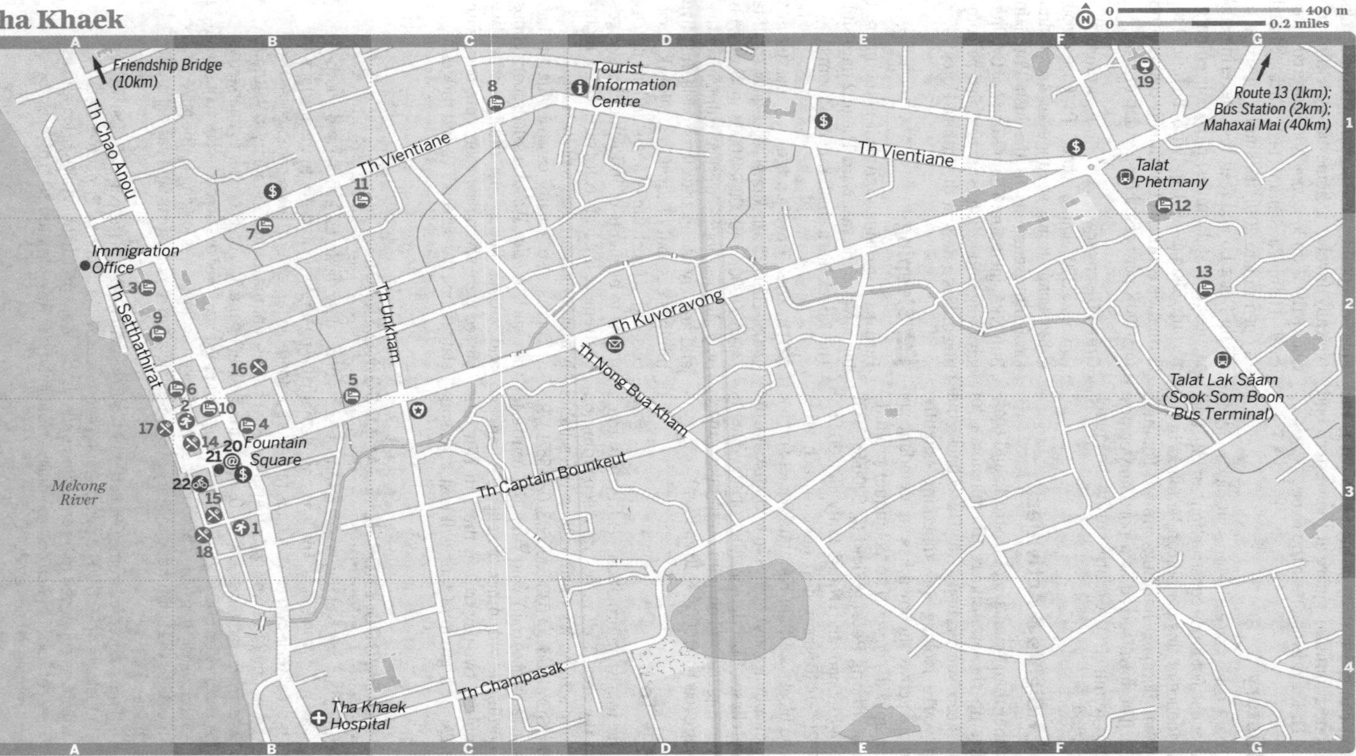
0 400 m
0 0.2 miles
Friendship Bridge (10km)
Tourist Information Centre
Route 13 (1km); Bus Station (2km); Mahaxai Mai (40km)
Th Chao Anou
Th Vientiane
Th Vientiane
Talat Phetmany
Immigration Office
Th Setthathirat
Th Unkham
Th Kuvoravong
Th Nong Bua Kham
Talat Lak Sǎam (Sook Som Boon Bus Terminal)
Fountain Square
Th Captain Bounkeut
Mekong River
Th Champasak
Tha Khaek Hospital
1
2
3
4
5
6
7
8
9
10
11
12
13
14
15
16
17
18
19
20
21
22

Tha Khaek

Activities, Courses & Tours

1 Bounthong Petang Field B3
Green Discovery ....(see 4)
2 Massage B3
Nang Linly ....(see 1)

Sleeping

3 Hotel Riveria A2
4 Inthira Hotel B3
5 Khammuane Inter Guest House B2
6 Mekong Hotel B2
7 Phonepadidh Guesthouse B2
8 Phoukhanna Guesthouse C1
9 Sooksomboon Hotel A2
10 Southida Guest House B3
11 Thakhek Mai B1
12 Thakhek Travel Lodge G1
13 Thipphachanh Guesthouse G2

Eating

14 Duc Restaurant B3
15 Grilled Meat Restaurants B3
Inthira Restaurant ....(see 4)
16 Kesone Restaurant B2
17 Local Food Place A3
18 Smile Barge Restaurant B3

Drinking & Nightlife

19 Phudoi Disco F1

Information

20 Wangwang Internet B3

Transport

21 Mad Monkey Motorbike B3
Mr Ku's Motorbike Rental ....(see 12)
22 Phavilai Restaurant B3
Wangwang Internet ....(see 20)

Phoukhanna Guesthouse GUESTHOUSE $
(051-212092; Th Vientiane; r with fan/air-con & bathroom 65,000/85,000K, r with fan & without bathroom 35,000K;) Set next to its Thai-pop-pulsating restaurant, this guesthouse is pretty noisy. The staff are lacklustre and rooms, though boasting en suites, powder-blue walls and parquet floors, are a tad unloved and a bit dark.

Southida Guest House GUESTHOUSE $
(051-212568; Th Chao Anou; s/d 120,000/150,000K;) Not far from the riverfront and Fountain Sq, the eminently forgettable Southida has clean rooms with cable TV in a modern two-storey building. Most rooms have at least one balcony, but size can vary considerably, so ask to see several. Don't get one close to the road.

Phonepadidh Guesthouse GUESTHOUSE $
(030-777 2826, 020-5672 6111; Th Vientiane; r 100,000K;) This two-storey complex, in a quiet courtyard just off Th Vientiane, offers featureless but white-walled and clean rooms with air-conditioning and hot-water showers.

Mekong Hotel HOTEL $
(051-250777; Th Setthathirat; s/d 130,000/140,000K;) Thanks to a recent repaint, this blue, Soviet-inspired monolith is much improved, with decent rooms enjoying cable TV, air-con and fresh en suites. There's also a restaurant facing the Mekong.

Thipphachanh Guesthouse GUESTHOUSE $
(051-212762; Rte 13; r with fan/air-con 60,000/80,000K;) Despite its dusty location, these digs, based around a courtyard, are fragrantly fresh with white walls, tiled floors, TVs and en suites. There's also clean sheets and blankets for cold nights (do they exist?).

Khammuane Inter Guest House GUESTHOUSE $
(051-212171; Th Kuvoravong; r 50,000-80,000K;) Basic rooms in a large old house. There's wi-fi, desks and fridges, but to be honest we've seen more interesting cheese sandwiches. Also rents scooters (50,000K).

Sooksomboon Hotel GUESTHOUSE $
(051-212225; Th Setthathirat; r 130,000-150,000K;) In a colonial-era police station right on the Mekong. High-ceiling rooms are clean and have TVs, en suites and beds with scrolled mahogany bedsteads. The attached restaurant serves up Korean BBQ, and is enticing by night with Chinese lanterns swinging in the breeze.

Thakhek Mai GUESTHOUSE $
(051-212551; Th Vientiane; r 100,000-120,000K;) With its clean art deco lines, this place could be nice with a bit more love. In its current state it's bland and basic. Rooms have TVs, en suites and a few sticks of cheap furniture.

★ **Inthira Hotel** BOUTIQUE HOTEL $$
(051-251237; www.inthirahotel.com; Th Chao Anou; r incl breakfast US$29-39;) Set in an old French villa, Inthira, with its pretty facade, offers the most romantic, stylish digs in town. Its restaurant fronts the old fountain, and its chic wine-hued rooms are a delight for weary travellers, with exposed brick walls, rain showers, cable TV,

dark-wood furniture, air-con and safety deposit boxes. The best rooms face the street and have balconies.

Hotel Riveria HOTEL **$$**
(051-250000; Th Setthathirat; r US$58-75;) With terrific views of Thailand on one side and even more dramatic vistas of the jagged karsts on the other, this is very much a family/businessman's choice. Large rooms have king-size beds, TVs, fridges, baths and international-style furniture. Downstairs, there's a decent restaurant with a lovely buffet breakfast and egg station. Professional.

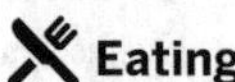

Eating

A minuscule night market unfolds at Fountain Sq every evening, and the adjacent waterfront strip directly south of the night market features several outdoor **grilled meat restaurants** (mains 10,000-20,000K; 11am-11pm) specialising in duck (Ms Noy, Ms Kay and Ms Mo) and goat (Khem Kong).

★**Inthira Restaurant** FUSION **$**
(Th Chao Anou; mains 45,000K; 7am-10pm;) With its industrial-chic exposed cement walls, low-lit ambience, open-range kitchen and handsome bar stocked with brightly glowing spirits, this is the place to stop for breakfast, lunch or dinner. An Asian fusion menu features delicious *steak au poivre*, tom yum soup, copious salads, curries, stir fries and very competent burgers. Recommended.

Local Food Place LAOTIAN **$**
(Th Chao Anou; mains 5000-10,000K; 7am-7pm) Head to the busy local food place, alongside the river, if you fancy tasty Lao favourites such as *pîng kai* (grilled chicken) and sticky rice for next to no money.

Duc Restaurant LAOTIAN **$**
(Th Setthathirat; meals 15,000K; 6am-10pm;) On the riverfront just off Fountain Sq, this fan-cooled, family-run joint is fastidiously clean, has tables inside and out, and with its walls plastered in family photos, looks somewhat like an extension of someone's front room. It serves up delicious *fĕr hàang* (dry rice noodles served in a bowl with various herbs and seasonings but no broth).

Kesone Restaurant FUSION **$**
(051-212563; Th Setthathirat; mains 25,000-35,000K; 9.30am-11.30pm) With dining in the garden or indoors, this is a popular place serving a mix of Thai, Thai-Chinese and Lao dishes. The ice cream is also pretty good.

Smile Barge Restaurant LAOTIAN **$**
(Th Setthathirat; meals 25,000K; noon-11.30pm;) Riverside Smile is atmospheric with antlers and lanterns hung from the walls, and decked verandahs under the shade of trees to coolly work your way thrugh a menu of steak, soup, salad, fried fish and vegie dishes.

Drinking & Nightlife

Phudoi Disco CLUB
(8pm-midnight) Behind the Phudoi Guest House, this place can be a fun Lao night out if you have plenty of energy and fancy getting down to lots of Thai pop, a bit of Lao pop and some cheesy Western classics with the local youth.

Information

There are a couple of places on Th Chao Anou, north of Fountain Sq, that offer decent internet connections. They're open approximately 10am to 10pm and charge 6000K per hour.

BCEL (Th Vientiane) Changes major currencies and travellers cheques, and makes cash advances on Visa. Has three ATMs in town, including one in Fountain Sq, as well as one at the bus station.

Lao Development Bank (Th Vientiane) Cash only – no exchange or visa advance.

Police (cnr Th Kuvoravong & Th Unkham)

Post Office (Th Kuvoravong) Also offers expensive international phone calls.

Tha Khaek Hospital (cnr Th Chao Anou & Th Champasak) Tha Khaek Hospital is fine for minor ailments or commonly seen problems including malaria and dengue. Seek out English-speaking Dr Bounthavi.

Tourist Information Centre (030-530 0503, 020-5571 1797; www.khammuanetourism.com; Th Vientiane; 8.30am-5pm) The excellent tourist information centre has plenty of informative pamphlets and sells maps of the town and province. Also runs tours.

Wangwang Internet (Fountain Sq; per hr 7000K; 7.30am-9.30pm) Offers internet on a few laptops as well as scooter rental (60,000K per day).

Getting There & Away

BUS

Tha Khaek's bus station is about 3.5km from the centre of town and has a sizeable market and basic guesthouses to complement the regular services going north and south. For Vientiane

GETTING TO VIETNAM: THA KHAEK TO DONG HOI

Getting to the Border

Despite the fact that Rte 12 is now fully paved, for *falang* (Westerners) the **Na Phao (Laos)/Cha Lo (Vietnam) border crossing** (⌚7am-4pm) remains one of the least-used and most inconvenient of all Laos' borders. This is partly because transport on both sides is slow and infrequent, though there's a daily *sŏrngtăaou* from Tha Khaek (50,000K, 3½ to four hours, 142km) at 8am bound for Lang Khang, 18km short of the border. If you're determined to cross here, take the early departure as there's no accommodation in the area and you'll almost certainly have to wait a while for transport all the way to the border.

At the Border

Lao 30-day visas can be processed on arrival coming from Vietnam, but it's not possible to obtain a Vietnamese visa on arrival if going the other way.

Moving On

On the Vietnam side the nearest sizeable city is Dong Hoi. A bus does run directly between Tha Khaek and Dong Hoi (90,000K, 10 to 14 hours), leaving Tha Khaek at 7pm on Monday, Wednesday, Friday and Sunday, making this the most logical way to cross this border.

(70,000K, six hours, 332km), buses originate in Tha Khaek at 4am, 5.30am, 7am, 8.30am and 9am, as well as a VIP departure at 9.15am (85,000K) and a sleeper VIP at 1am (85,000K). From 9am to midnight buses stop en route from Pakse and Savannakhet every hour or so. Any bus going north stops at Vieng Kham (Thang Beng; 30,000K, 90 minutes, 102km), Pak Kading (50,000K, three hours, 149km) or Paksan (40,000K, three to four hours, 193km).

Heading south, buses for Savannakhet (30,000K, two to three hours, 125km) depart every half hour, and there's an air-con departure for Pakse (70,000K, six to seven hours, 368km) at 9am and regular local buses every hour during the day (70,000K). There are two daily departures to Attapeu (85,000K, about 10 hours) at 3.30pm and 11pm. Buses originating in Vientiane leave at around 5.30pm for Don Khong (150,000K, about 15 hours, 452km) and around 5.30pm for Nong Khiang (90,000K, about 16 hours, 482km), on the Cambodian border. They stop at Tha Khaek between 5pm and 6pm, but you'd need to be in a hurry.

If you're heading to Vietnam, a bus for Hué (120,000K) leaves every Monday, Tuesday, Wednesday, Saturday and Sunday at 8pm. There are also departures for Danang (120,000K) every Monday and Friday at 8pm, for Dong Hoi (90,000K, 10 to 14 hours) at 7pm on Monday, Wednesday, Friday and Saturday, and for Hanoi (160,000K) at 8pm on Tuesday and Saturday.

SŎRNGTĂAOU

Sŏrngtăaou regularly depart when full from Talat Phetmany to Mahaxai Mai (35,000K, one hour, 50km). One also goes direct to Ban Kong Lo (80,000K, four hours) at 7.30am. Talat Lak Săam (Sook Som Boon Bus Terminal) serves buses into the Khammuan Province interior. *Sŏrngtăaou* leave every hour or so between 7.30am and 9.30am for Gnommalath (45,000K, 1½ to two hours, 63km) and Nakai (45,000K, two hours, 80km). There's a daily departure at 8am for Lang Khang (50,000K), and one at 8pm for Na Phao (80,000K, 3½ hours, 142km), 18km short of the Vietnam border. There are also departures at 7am, 8am and 9am for Bualapha (50,000K, five to six hours).

ℹ Getting Around

It should cost about 20,000K to hire a jumbo (motorised three-wheeled taxi) to the bus terminal, though you'll need to negotiate. From the bus terminal, jumbos don't budge unless they're full or you're willing to fork over 60,000K to charter the entire vehicle. Rides around town can cost around 15,000K per person.

There are now a handful of places around town offering motorbike hire; the tourist information centre carries a comprehensive list. However the one and only place to hire a tough, reliable motocross bike to tackle the Loop and other adventures is **Mad Monkey Motorbike** (☎020-2347 7799, 020-5993 9909; dcn66@hotmail.com; Fountain Sq; 250cc bikes/automatic scooters per day US$38/28; ⌚9am-8pm). Run by DC, a friendly German expat, Mad Monkey has two Honda 250cc dirt bikes, and three automatic, wide-wheeled scooters. If you break down you can phone DC and for a price he'll come and get you and the bike. He can also take you to Tham

GETTING TO THAILAND: THA KHAEK TO NAKHON PHANOM

Getting to the Border

Crossing the Mekong at the **Tha Khaek (Laos)/Nakhon Phanom (Thailand) border** (7am-4pm) is now only possible for locals. Travellers have to catch a tuk-tuk (20,000K) to the Friendship Bridge from the main bus station. Buses run every 30 minutes from 7am to 4.30pm. If crossing after closing time you'll have to pay an overtime fee.

At the Border

In Tha Khaek, Lao immigration issues 30-day tourist visas on arrival and there's a BCEL money exchange service and 24-hour ATM at the immigration office. In Thailand 30-day tourist visas are granted on arrival.

Moving On

Once in Thailand, it's 30B for a share tuk-tuk ride to the bus station, from where buses leave Nakhon Phanom for Udon Thani (regular) and Bangkok (at 7.30am and from 7pm to 8pm).

Kong Lo and back in a day, leaving 8am and returning at 8pm (per person 300,000K for a group of 4 people).

Mr Ku's Motorbike Rental (020-220 6070; per day 100,00K; 7.30am-4.30pm), located at Thakhek Travel Lodge, has 110cc Korean bikes for getting around town or to the closer caves.

Phavilai Restaurant (Fountain Sq; per day 60,000K; 6am-9pm) has a few scooters for hire, as does **Wangwang** (020-5697 8535; Fountain Sq; per day 50,000-60,000K; 8am-9pm) internet shop.

Around Tha Khaek

North & South of Tha Khaek

Pha That Sikhottabong BUDDHIST TEMPLE

(ພະທາດສີໂຄດຕະບອງ) About 6km south of town is the much venerated Pha That Sikhottabong stupa, which stands in the grounds of a 19th-century monastery of the same name. Considered one of the most important *tâht* (stupa) in Laos, Sikhottabong was first renovated by King Setthathirat in the 16th century, when it assumed its current general form. It was again restored in the 1950s and later augmented in the 1970s. It's the site of a major festival each February.

A *wihăhn* (temple hall) on the temple grounds contains a large seated Buddha, constructed by the order of King Anouvong (Chao Anou).

Adjacent to the temple is an interesting open-air museum consisting of nine wooden houses showing the various traditional architectural styles of Khammuan Province.

Tham Pa Fa CAVE

(Buddha Cave; admission 5000K; 8am-noon & 1-4pm) When Mr Bun Nong used a vine to scramble 15m up a sheer 200m-high cliff in April 2004 he discovered a narrow cave mouth and, stepping into the cavern beyond, was greeted by 229 bronze Buddha images. The Buddhas, ranging from 15cm to about 1m tall, were sitting as they had been for centuries facing the entrance of a cave of impressive limestone formations. It's 14km from Tha Khaek and it costs 100,00K to reach by tuk-tuk.

Khoun Kong Leng LAKE

(Evening Gong Lake; admission 5000K) Nestled amid the limestone karsts of the Phu Hin Bun NPA is the stunningly beautiful Evening Gong Lake. The luminescent green waters spring from a subterranean river that filters through the limestone, making the water crystal clear.

You must ask at the village before swimming in the lake. Once you get approval, only swim in the stream that flows from the lake, near the wooden footbridge, and not in the lake itself. Fishing is banned.

Khoun Kong Leng is only about 30km northeast of Tha Khaek. Head north along Rte 13 and turn right (east) at Km 29 onto a dirt road. After 2km, turn right (south) again, and bump up over hills and through villages for 16km until you reach Ban Na Kheu. It's another 1km to the lake.

East on Rte 12

Whether as a day trip or as part of the Loop, the first 22km of Rte 12 east of Tha Khaek is an area with several caves, an abandoned railway line and a couple of swimming spots. This is part of the vast Khammuan Limestone area, which stretches roughly between Rtes 12 and 8 and east towards Rte 8B. There are thousands of caves, sheer cliffs and jagged karst peaks.

All these places can be reached by tuk-tuk, bicycle or hired motorcycle.

Tham Xang CAVE
(ຖ້ຳຊ້າງ, Elephant Cave; admission 5000K) Famous for its stalagmite 'elephant head', which is found along a small passage behind the large golden Buddha; take a torch (flashlight).

Tha Falang CAVE
(ທ່າຝລັ່ງ, French Landing) FREE At Km 11 (about 9km from Rte 13) a rough trail leads 2km north to the water-sculpted rocks at Tha Falang on the scenic Nam Don (Don River). Tha Falang is much more easily accessed than Khoun Kong Leng but is not nearly as attractive, especially in the dry season. In the wet season you'll probably need to hire a small boat from near the Xieng Liap bridge to get there. By tuk-tuk it's 150,000K.

Tham Xieng Liap CAVE
(ຖ້ຳຊຽງລຽບ) FREE Turning off Rte 12 at Km 14 (before a wooden bridge) you'll come across a sign pointing to the cave. Follow the dirt track south for about 400m near the village of Ban Songkhone (about 10.5km from Rte 13), to the stunning limestone cave Tham Xieng Liap, the entrance of which is at the base of a dramatic 300m-high cliff. The cave is about 200m long and, in the dry season, you can walk/wade through and swim in the picturesque valley on the far side. *Paa faa* (soft-shelled turtles) live in the cave, while the cliffs outside are said to be home to the recently discovered *kan yoo* (Laotian rock rat).

Tham Sa Pha In CAVE
(ຖ້ຳສະພານອິນ), Tham Phanya Inh) FREE With high cliffs either side, Rte 12 continues through a narrow pass (about 11.5km from Rte 13) and immediately beyond a track leads north to Tham Sa Pha In. This rarely visited Buddhist holy cave is said to have magical healing powers; swimming is not allowed. There's no sign here; look for the faded brick gateway.

Tham Nang Aen CAVE
(ຖ້ຳນາງແອນ; admission 10,000K; ⏰8am-5pm) The last cave along this stretch of Rte 12 is the touristy Tham Nang Aen, about 18km from Tha Khaek.

The turn-off to the cave is indicated by a clear sign just past a left-hand bend 16km from the junction with Rte 13. The 700m-long track should be passable at all but the wettest times. The pitiful 'zoo' with caged deer and sun bears near the entrance will appeal to people who don't like animals.

Tham Pha Chan CAVE
(ຖ້ຳພະຈັນ) FREE Tham Pha Chan's entrance is 60m high and about 100m wide. A stream runs about 600m through a limestone karst and in the dry season it's possible to walk to the far side. At its western end there is a sandalwood Buddha image in a crevice about 15m above the ground, hence the cave's name, which means Sandalwood Buddha Cave.

Not far from Tham Pha Chan is the **Nam Don Resurgence** (ຂຸນນ້ຳໂດນ), a cave where the Nam Don emerges from the ground. It's quite a physical marvel to see the water coming up and out from the cave, and the lagoon that sits at the bottom of the tall limestone karst is a beautiful swimming spot.

Both are accessed via a rough road that runs 9km north from about 10km east of the junction with Rte 13. Go by motorbike, tuk-tuk or arrange an English-speaking guide through Tha Khaek's tourist information centre.

Tham Lot Se Bang Fai CAVE
(ຖ້ຳລອດເຊບັ້ງໄຟ) The most impressive, and yet least-visited, cave in Khammuan is the amazing Tham Lot Se Bang Fai. Located at the edge of Hin Namno NPA, the cave is the result of Se Bang Fai river plunging 6.5km through a limestone mountain, leaving an underground trail of immense caverns, impressive rock formations, rapids and waterfalls that have been seen by only a handful of foreign visitors.

The cave wasn't professionally mapped until 2006, when the Canadian-American that led the expedition concluded that Tham Lot Se Bang Fai is among the largest river caves in the world. Traversing the entire cave involves eight portages and is only possible during the dry season, from January to March. Local wooden canoes can only go as far as the first portage, about 1km into the cave, making inflatable rafts or kayaks the only practical option for traversing the entire length of the cave.

The base for visiting the cave is Ban Nong Ping, a mixed Lao Loum/Salang village about 2km downstream from the cave entrance. However, homestays are currently unavailable due to recent scams demanding travellers pay exorbitant rates for a goat to be slaughtered to appease the cave's spirits.

With a month's warning you *can* organize a trip here with Green Discovery (p195), but the privilege will cost you a princely US$800. By the end of 2013, assures Tha Khaek's tourist information centre, homestays will resume, as will organised treks out of their office.

SAVANNAKHET PROVINCE

Savannakhet is the country's most populous province and is home to about 15% of all Lao citizens. Stretching between the Mekong and Thailand in the west and the Annamite mountains and Vietnam in the east, it has in recent years become an increasingly important trade corridor between these two bigger neighbours. With the luxuriously smooth tarmac of Rte 9 now complemented by yet another Thai-Lao Friendship Bridge, opened in December 2006, the province is witnessing even more traffic.

The population of approximately 926,000 includes Lowland Lao, Tai Dam, several small Mon-Khmer groups and long-established communities of Vietnamese and Chinese.

There are three NPAs wholly or partly in the province: Dong Phu Vieng to the south of Rte 9, Phu Xang Hae to the north and Se Ban Nuan straddling the border with Salavan Province. Eastern Savannakhet is a good place to see remnants of the Ho Chi Minh Trail, the primary supply route to South Vietnam for the North Vietnamese Army during the Second Indochina War. It is also a major gateway for visitors arriving from Vietnam via Lao Bao.

Savannakhet ສະຫວັນນະເຂດ

☎041 / POP 139,000

Languid, time-trapped and ghostly quiet during the sweltering days that batter the old city's plasterwork, Savannakhet is a beguiling mix of yesteryear coupled with increasingly modern commerce. The best it has to offer is the historic quarter with its staggering – and that might just be the right adjective – display of decaying early 20th-century architecture. Leprous and listing, these grand old villas of Indochina's heyday now lie unwanted like aged dames crying out for a makeover. There's little to do in town but amble the riverfront and plonk yourself down in a local noodle shop or one of a clutch of stylish restaurants and bijou cafes that are steadily growing in number.

That said, there's loads to do nearby and Savannakhet has a dedicated tourist information centre and eco-guide unit who have myriad intrepid trips into the nearby NPAs.

Savannakhet is on a simple north–south grid and although large is pretty easy to navigate on foot.

Sights

Much of the charm of Savannakhet is in wandering through the quiet streets, between the new and old buildings, the laughing children and the slow-moving, *petang*-playing old men. The tourist information centre has put together a brochure called *Savannakhet Downtown*, which features a self-guided tour of the city's most interesting buildings. The centre also offers guided tours of the historic downtown district.

Musee Des Dinosaures MUSEUM
(ຫໍພິພິດທະພັນໄດໂນເສົາ, Dinosaur Museum; ☎041-212597; Th Khanthabuli; admission 5000K; ⏲8am-noon & 1-4pm) In 1930 a major dig in a nearby village unearthed 200-million-year-old dinosaur fossils. This enthusiastically run museum is an interesting place to divert yourself for an hour or so. Savannakhet Province is home to five dinosaur sites.

Wat Sainyaphum BUDDHIST TEMPLE
(ວັດໄຊຍະພູມ; Th Tha He) The oldest and largest monastery in southern Laos. The large grounds include some centuries-old trees and a workshop near the river entrance that's a veritable golden-Buddha production line.

Wat Rattanalangsi BUDDHIST TEMPLE
(ວັດລັດຕະນະລັງສີ; Th Phagnapui) Wat Rattanalangsi was built in 1951 and houses a monks' primary school. The *sĭm* (ordination hall) is unique in that it has glass windows (most windows in Lao temples are unglazed). Other structures include a rather gaudy Brahma shrine, a modern *săhláh lóng tám* (sermon hall) and a shelter containing a 15m reclining Buddha backed by Jataka (stories of the Buddha's past lives) paintings.

Savannakhet Provincial Museum MUSEUM
(ພິພິດທະພັນແຂວງຊະຫວັນນະເຂດ; Th Khanthabuli; admission 5000K; ⏲8-11.30am & 1-4pm Mon-Sat) The Savannakhet Provincial Museum is a good place to see war relics, artillery pieces and inactive examples of the deadly UXO (unexploded ordnance) that has claimed the

lives of more than 12,000 Lao since the end of the Secret War.

Activities

As if it wasn't already hot and humid enough in Savannakhet, there are a couple of places to take part in a Lao-style herbal sauna.

Red Cross MASSAGE
(041-212826; Th Kuvoravong; massage per hr 30,000K, sauna 10,000K; 10am-8pm) The Red Cross offers Lao-style massage plus herbal sauna. It was shut when we passed but is due to reopen in a new building late 2013.

Herbal Sauna SAUNA
(Th Ratsavongseuk; sauna 20,000K; 1-8pm) Sporadically open.

Sleeping

Savannakhet has a reasonable range of budget options but little to excite if you're looking for luxury. Most guesthouses are located within walking distance of the attractive old town.

Souannavong Guest House GUESTHOUSE $
(041-212600; Th Saenna; r without/with air-con 70,000/100,000K;) Unfailingly fresh with clean en suite rooms and an organised reception, this guesthouse down a quiet street abloom in bougainvillea has wi-fi and bikes to rent. A welcoming spot to stay.

Boualuang Hotel HOTEL $
(041-300106; Th Ratsavongseuk; r 150,000K;) A few blocks from Savannakhet's old town, Boualuang has mint-fresh rooms, tasteful bed linen, decent furniture, glacially merciful air-con and TV as standard. The tiled floors are spotless and the bathrooms capacious, but overall the place is lacking a little character.

Leena Guesthouse GUESTHOUSE $
(041-212404; leenaguesthuse@hotmail.com; Th Chaokeen; r 50,000-90,000K;) An oldie but goodie, fairy-lit Leena is something of a motel with kitsch decor in comfortable peach-colored, clean rooms with tiled floors, hot-water showers, TVs and a pleasant breakfast area where you can pick up wi-fi. The air-con rooms are bigger. There's also a cafe.

Nongsoda Guest House GUESTHOUSE $
(041-212522; Th Tha He; r 100,000-150,000K;) About 200m north of Wat Sainyaphum, these quirky old river-facing digs have seen better days but have well-sized rooms with retro furniture and basic en suites. TV and air-con come as standard and there's a little cafe to chill in.

Lelavade Guest House GUESTHOUSE $
(041-212732; Th Chaimeuang; r 60,000-100,000K;) Lacklustre if peaceful compound-style digs a 10-minute walk out of the centre. En suite rooms with TV and fridge smell fresh but look as if people have been freerunning up the wall. That said, they're large, cool and, if you don't mind Soviet-era furniture, they're OK.

Phonevilay Hotel HOTEL $
(041-212284; 172/173 Th Phetsalat; r with fan/air-con 40,000/90,000K;) Phonevilay's air-con rooms with TVs and fridges are decent enough, but the dingy fan rooms with cold water are not. The bed linen seems clean but there's barely a stick of furniture to give you comfort. Overall a bit paint-thirsty.

Savanbanhao Hotel HOTEL $
(041-212202; sbtou@laotel.com; Th Saenna; s/d 70,000/90,000K;) Sitting in a wide, unattractive courtyard, rooms here are pretty basic with semi-tiled walls, a bit of furniture and an ageing beast of an air-con machine that looks like something from a Kafka nightmare. All rooms have hot water and English-language TV.

★ **Salsavan Guesthouse** GUESTHOUSE $$
(041-212371; Th Kuvoravong; s/d incl breakfast US$23/28;) This beautiful French villa, and ex-Thai consulate, has all the makings of a boutique hotel. Rooms are large and atmospherically old-fashioned with wood floors, mozzie nets and deep-coloured walls with shuttered windows and balconies. That said, the en suites are unattractively Soviet and the place feels like it's in need of invigoration. Outside there's a delightful garden terrace.

Nanhai Hotel HOTEL $$
(041-212371; Th Santisouk; r/ste incl breakfast US$25/45;) An elephant-grey Lego brick, this relatively new place exudes blandness and feels as if it were built for a politburo meeting that never happened. Large rooms with TVs, en suites and air-con, but really who cares. As to the broken pool outside – stare at the green water long enough and it might give birth to a *naga* (river serpent)!

Phonepaseud Hotel HOTEL $$
(041-212158; Th Santisouk; r US$25-35 ;) Phonepaseud has a friendly English-speaking owner, a clean lobby and imaginatively tiled,

Savannakhet

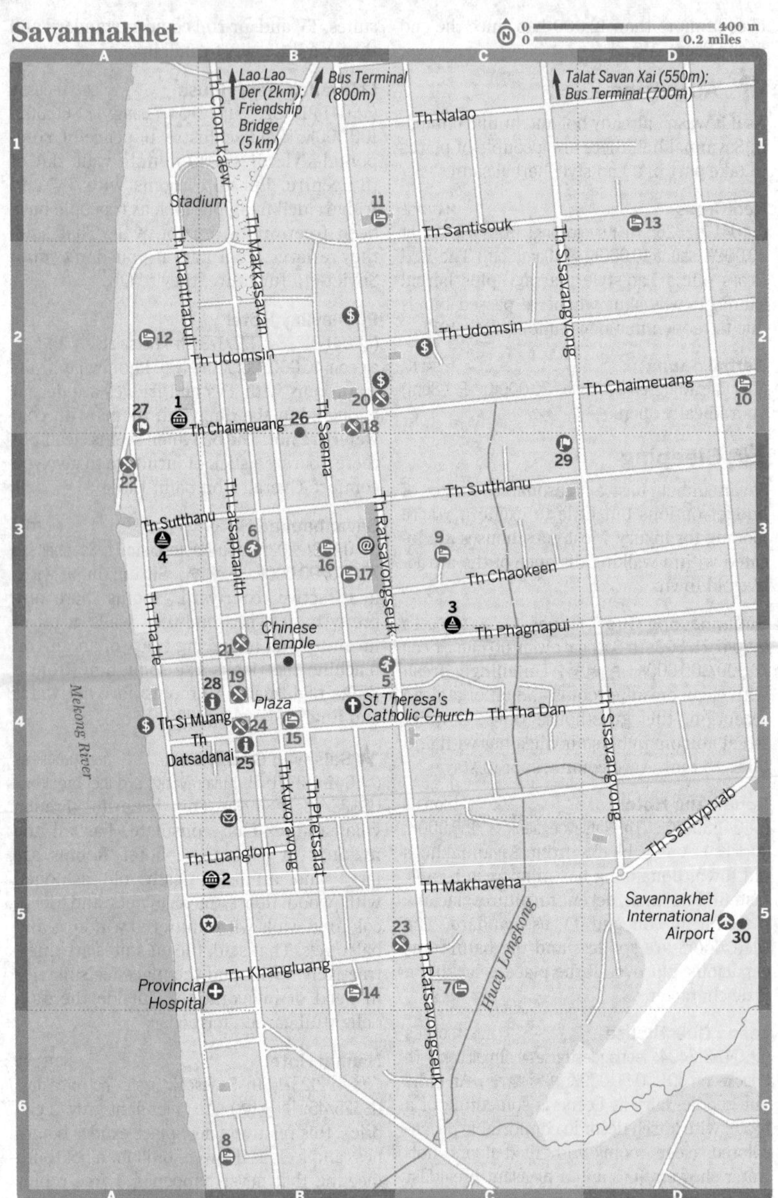

French-wallpapered rooms with air-con, TVs, fridges and en suites. The VIP rooms are much larger. Outside there's a *naga*-guarded fountain, mature trees, plenty of plants and a tennis court. Discounts possible in low season.

Daosavanh Resort & Spa Hotel HOTEL **$$$**
(☎041-212188; Th Tha He; r inc breakfast US$77-90; P ❄ 📶 🏊) Grand, relatively new and Mekong-facing, this hotel is a slice of international comfort and its kidney-shaped pool is a very welcome boon on sweltering days

Savannakhet

Sights

1 Musee Des Dinosaures A2
2 Savannakhet Provincial Museum B5
3 Wat Rattanalangsi C3
4 Wat Sainyaphum A3

Activities, Courses & Tours

5 Herbal Sauna B4
6 Red Cross B3

Sleeping

7 Boualuang Hotel C5
8 Daosavanh Resort & Spa Hotel B6
9 Leena Guesthouse C3
10 Lelavade Guest House D2
11 Nanhai Hotel B1
12 Nongsoda Guest House A2
13 Phonepaseud Hotel D1
14 Phonevilay Hotel B5
15 Salsavan Guesthouse B4
16 Savanbanhao Hotel B3
17 Souannavong Guest House B3

Eating

18 Café Chez Boune B2
Chai Dee .... (see 5)
19 Dao Savanh B4
20 Khao Piak Nang Noy B2
21 Lin's Café B4
22 Riverside Snack & Drink Vendors A3
23 Savan Restaurant C5
24 Xokxay Restaurant B4

Information

25 Eco-Guide Unit B4
Savanbanhao Tourism Co .... (see 16)
26 SK Travel & Tour B2
27 Thai Consulate A2
28 Tourist Information Centre B4
29 Vietnamese Consulate C3

Transport

30 Lao Airlines D5

(most days). There's karaoke, free airport transfers, massage, a gym, and the rooms are large and immaculate.

Eating & Drinking

With new cafes popping up, delicious street food and a scattering of French restaurants to sample, the cuisine on offer is pretty varied. Opposite the Wat Sainyaphum the **riverside snack and drink vendors** (5-10pm) are great for sundowners and, as evening approaches, *seen dàat* (Korean-style barbecue) is also available.

★Chai Dee JAPANESE, INTERNATIONAL $
(020-5988 6767; Th Ratsavongseuk; mains 20,000K; 8.30am-9pm;) Run by friendly Moto, this Japanese cafe is a real traveller magnet. And with good reason: there are rattan mats to lounge on, books to exchange, cool T-shirts for sale and a wide menu of samosas, homemade yoghurt, Thai food and tofu, plus healthy shakes.

★Lin's Café INTERNATIONAL $
(Th Latsaphanith; mains 30,000K; 8am-8pm;) This chic cafe in a former 1930s Chinese merchant's house is on a pretty side street radiating off the old square by St Theresa's Catholic church. Inside it's a mix of antique and modern furniture, easy tunes and coffee with attitude. There are also fruit shakes, stir-fries, vegie dishes, breakfasts, fruit salads and *láhp,* and they even make bacon sandwiches!

Add to this a book exchange, loads of local info brochures and, upstairs, a photo exhibition of all Savannakhet's surviving historic houses.

Xokxay Restaurant LAOTIAN $
(Th Si Muang; mains 15,000K; 9am-9pm;) A great hole in the wall on the square near the Catholic church, Xokxay is clean and popular, and dishes up tasty Laotian food, including noodle dishes, fried rice, salads and crispy fried shrimp.

Khao Piak Nang Noy LAOTIAN $
(020-7774 4248; Th Ratsavongseuk; mains 7000K; 7am-10pm) Nang Noy sells what is probably the most popular, and almost certainly the richest, *kòw pjak sèn* (thick noodles served in a slightly viscous broth with crispy deep-fried pork belly or chicken), in Savannakhet. There's no English-language sign, so look for the busy stall under the purple Tigo sign.

Savan Restaurant KOREAN $
(041-214488; Th Khangluang; mains 20,000-50,000K; 6-11pm;) In an oddly romantic outdoor setting with bamboo stands and private compartments, this place is all about *seen dàat.* It also dishes up breakfast, fruit salads, pad thai and soup.

Lao Lao Der LAOTIAN $$
(041-212270; mains 30,000-70,000K; 10am-11pm) This riverside restaurant, 2km north of the old stadium, is one of the only places in town to offer great Mekong views. The hefty

GETTING TO THAILAND: SAVANNAKHET TO MUKDAHAN

Getting to the Border

Since the construction of the second Thai-Lao Friendship Bridge in 2006, non-Thai and non-Lao citizens are no longer allowed to cross between Mukdahan and Savannakhet by boat.

The Thai-Lao International Bus crosses the **Savannakhet (Laos)/Mukdahan (Thailand) border crossing** (6am-10pm) in both directions. From Savannakhet, the Thai-Lao International Bus (15,000K, 45 minutes) departs approximately every hour from 8am to 7pm. It leaves Mukdahan's bus station (50B, 45 minutes) roughly every hour from 7.30am to 7pm.

At the Border

Crossing into Laos, 30-day visas on arrival are available for US$20 to US$42, depending on your nationality. If you don't have a photo you'll be charged the equivalent of US$2. An additional US$1 'overtime fee' is charged from 6am to 8am and 6pm to 10pm on weekdays, as well as on weekends and holidays. The last obstacle is a US$1/40B 'entry fee'.

Most nationalities do not require a visa to cross into Thailand.

Moving On

Onward from Mukdahan, there are five daily buses bound for Bangkok between 5.30pm and 8.15pm.

menu spans Lao, Thai and Chinese dishes, but Lao Lao Der functions equally well as a bar.

Café Chez Boune FRENCH **$$**

(Th Ratsavongseuk; mains 75,000K; 7am-10pm;) Glacially cool, orange-walled and hung with Parisian oils, Chez Boune has a French-speaking owner and is deservedly popular with expats. Must be something to do with the decent service and tasty steaks, pasta dishes, lasagna, pork chops and filet mignon – all of which are executed with élan.

Dao Savanh FRENCH **$$$**

(Th Si Muang; mains 100,000-150,000K, 3-course cafe lunch 65,000K; 7am-10pm;) With its elegant colonial facade this cool, square-facing restaurant is the city's finest. Fans whir and wine glasses clink as you tuck into a French-accented menu of soups, grilled entrecôte and lamp chop Provençal. The upstairs restaurant is the classy sister (open evenings only) while downstairs the cafe is open all day with salads, sandwiches and croque-monsieur.

Information

There are several internet cafes along the west side of Th Ratsavongseuk between Th Sutthanu and Th Chaokeen; most are open from about 8am to 10pm and charge 6000K per hour.

Tourist information in Savannakhet is plentiful and professional.

BCEL (Th Ratsavongseuk; 8.30am-4pm) ATM, cash exchange and credit-card advances.

Eco-Guide Unit (041-214203; www.savannakhet-trekking.com; Th Latsaphanith; 8am-noon & 1-4.30pm Mon-Fri) The industrious eco-guide unit provides information ranging from bookings for treks to Dong Natad PPA and Dong Phu Vieng NPA, to bus times, accommodation and where to get a decent massage or hire a motorbike (not both at the same time!). Also has free wi-fi.

Lao Development Bank (Th Udomsin; 8.30-11.30am & 1.30-3.30pm) Changes cash and offers credit-card advances. Also has an ATM.

Phongsavanh Bank (041-300888; Th Ratsavongseuk; 8.30am-4pm Mon-Fri, to 11.30am Sat) Limited to cash exchange.

Post Office (041-212205; Th Khanthabuli) For calls, use an internet cafe instead.

Provincial Hospital (041-212717, 020-260 1993; Th Khanthabuli; 8am-12pm & 1-4pm) Ask for English-speaking Dr Outhon.

Savanbanhao Tourism Co (041-212 944; Th Saenna) In the Savanbanhao Hotel, this outfit can arrange tours to Sepon, the Ho Chi Minh Trail and Heuan Hin. It also sells bus tickets to Vietnam.

SK Travel & Tour (041-300177, 041-300176; Th Chaimeuang; 8am-4pm) Can arrange air tickets.

Tourist Information Centre (041-212755; Th Si Muang; 8am-noon & 1-4pm Mon-Fri) The tourist information centre has English-speaking staff who can provide advice on flight info and bus times, as well as a variety of informative pamphlets on everything from local food to self-guided day trips in the area.

Tourist Police (☎041-260 173)

Getting There & Away

AIR

Savannakhet's **airport** (☎041-212140; Th Kaysone Phomvihane) is served solely by Lao Airlines, with domestic connections to Vientiane (895,000K, 55 minutes) at 1.25pm on Monday and at 9.30am and 3pm on Tuesday, Wednesday, Thursday and Friday, and Bangkok (US$145, 80 minutes) on Monday, Wednesday, Thursday and Friday at 10.35am. Tickets can be purchased at the **Lao Airlines office** (☎041-212140; Savannakhet Airport; ⊙6.30am-4.30pm) or travel agents in town.

The airport is at the southeast edge of town and jumbos make the trip downtown for 70,000K.

BUS

Savannakhet's **bus terminal** (☎041-213920; Th Sisavangvong), usually called the *khíw lot*, is near the Talat Savan Xai at the northern edge of town. Buses leave here for Vientiane (75,000K, eight to 11 hours, 457km) roughly every half-hour from 6am to 11.30am. From 1.30pm to 10pm you'll have to hop on a bus passing through from Pakse. They stop at Tha Khaek (30,000K, 2½ to four hours, 125km). There are also hourly *sŏrngtăaou* and minivan departures (30,000K) to Tha Khaek from 8am to 4pm. A VIP sleeper bus (120,000K, six to eight hours) to Vientiane leaves at 9.30pm, or you could try to pick up a seat on one of the VIP buses coming through from Pakse.

Ten buses to Pakse (45,000K, five to six hours, 230km) originate here, the first at 7am and the last one at 10pm. Otherwise jump on one of the regular buses passing through from Vientiane. There's also a daily bus to Don Khong (80,000K, six to eight hours, 367km) at 7pm, and two daily buses to Attapeu (80,000K, eight to 10 hours, 410km) at 9am and 7pm.

Buses leave for the Laos–Vietnam border at Dansavanh (60,000K, four to six hours, 236km) at 7am, 8.30am and 11am, stopping at Sepon (50,000K, four to five hours).

To Vietnam, there's a bus to Dong Ha (80,000K, about seven hours, 350km), departing at 8am on even-numbered dates. For Hué, there's a local bus (90,000K, about 13 hours, 409km) daily at 10pm and a VIP bus (110,000K, about eight hours) at 10.30am from Monday to Friday. There's also a bus to Danang (110,000K, about 10 hours, 508km) on Tuesday, Thursday and Saturday at 10pm; the same bus continues to Hanoi (200,000K, about 24 hours, 650km), but we reckon you'd have to be a masochist to consider this journey.

GETTING TO VIETNAM: SAVANNAKHET TO DONG HA

Getting to the Border

Crossing the **Dansavanh (Laos)/Lao Bao (Vietnam) border** (⊙7am-7.30pm) is a relative pleasure. From Savannakhet, buses leave for Dansavanh (60,000K, four to six hours, 236km) at 7am, 8.30am and 11am. Alternatively, if you're passing this way it's worth breaking the journey for a night in Sepon as a base for seeing the Ho Chi Minh Trail.

The bus station in Dansavanh is about 1km short of the border; Vietnamese teenagers on motorbikes are more than happy to take you the rest of the way for about 10,000K.

At the Border

The Lao border offers 30-day tourist visas on arrival and has an exchange booth. Vietnam visas must be arranged in advance, which can be done at the Vietnam consulate in Savannakhet.

Moving On

Once through, take a motorbike (20,000d) 2km to the Lao Bao bus terminal and transport to Dong Ha (70,000d, two hours, 80km) on Vietnam's main north–south highway and railway. Entering Laos, there are buses to Savannakhet (60,000K, four to five hours) at 7.30am, 9.30am, 10am and noon, as well as regular *sŏrngtăaou* to Sepon (30,000K, one hour) from 7am to 5pm. Simple accommodation is available on both sides of the border.

If you're in a hurry, an alternative is to take one of the various buses from Savannakhet bound for the Vietnamese cities of Dong Ha, Hué and Danang.

Getting Around

Savannakhet is just big enough that you might occasionally need a jumbo – trips around town cost around 15,000K and 20,000K to the bus station, for the whole vehicle.

Motorcycles can be hired at Souannavong Guest House and Nongsoda Guest House for 70,000K to 80,000K per day. The eco-guide unit provides a comprehensive list of places that hire out motorbikes. There are also a few places to rent bicycles, most along Th Ratsavongseuk, charging about 10,000K per day.

Around Savannakhet

Sights

That Ing Hang TEMPLE

(ທາດອີງຮັງ; admission 5000K; ⏲7am-6pm) Thought to have been built in the mid-16th century, this well-proportioned, 9m-high *tâht* is the second-holiest religious edifice in southern Laos after Wat Phu Champasak. The Buddha is believed to have stopped here when he was sick during his wanderings back in ancient times. He rested by leaning *(ing)* on a hang tree (thus the name Ing Hang). A relic of the Buddha's spine is reputed to be kept inside the *tâht.*

Not including the Mon-inspired cubical base, That Ing Hang was substantially rebuilt during the reign of King Setthathirat (1548–71) and now features three terraced bases topped by a traditional Lao stupa and a gold umbrella weighing 40 baht (450g). A hollow chamber in the lower section contains a fairly undistinguished collection of Buddha images; by religious custom, women are not permitted to enter the chamber. The French restored That Ing Hang in 1930.

The **That Ing Hang Festival** is held on the full moon of the first lunar month.

That Ing Hang is about 11.5km northeast of Savannakhet via Rte 9, then 3km east; the turn-off is clearly signed. Any northbound bus can stop here, or you could haggle with a *sakai-làap* (jumbo) driver. You'll do well to knock him down below 100,000K return. Going by hired bicycle or motorbike makes more sense.

Dong Natad WILDLIFE RESERVE

(ດົງນາທາດ) Dong Natad is a semievergreen, sacred forest within a provincial protected area 15km from Savannakhet. It's home to two villages that have been coexisting with the forest for about 400 years, with villagers gathering forest products such as mushrooms (in the rainy season), fruit, oils, honey (from March to May), resins and insects. If you visit, there's a good chance you'll encounter villagers collecting red ants, cicadas or some other critter, depending on the season; all are important parts of their diet and economy.

It's possible to visit Dong Natad on your own, by bicycle, motorbike or in a tuk-tuk from Savannakhet. However, it will be something of a 'forest-lite' experience. It's better to engage one of Savannakhet's English-speaking guides through the eco-guide unit. The unit offers various programs, ranging from multiday homestays to one-day cycling trips, and ranging in price from 1,000,000K to 2,000,000K for one person in a group of two. Prices drop substantially for bigger groups. These community-based treks have had plenty of positive feedback and the combination of English-speaking guide and village guide proves a great source of information about how the local people live. Arrange trips at least a day ahead.

Heuan Hin RUIN

(ເຮືອນຫີນ) On the Mekong River south of Savannakhet, this set of Cham or Khmer ruins, whose name means Stone House, was built between AD 553 and 700. Apart from a few walls, most of the stones of this pre-Angkorian site now lie in piles of laterite rubble. No carvings remain, the only known lintel having been carted off to Paris.

It's a long haul by public transport and you'd need to be a truly dedicated temple enthusiast to make the trip. *Sŏrngtăaou* (30,000K, two to three hours, 78km) leave Talat Savan Xai when full, usually in the mid-morning. With your own transport, head south along Rte 13 and turn west at Ban Nong Nokhian, near Km 490, from where it's a dusty 17km to the site. Guided tours are also available from Savannakhet.

Dong Phu Vieng NPA
ປ່າສະຫງວນແຫ່ງຊາດດົງພູວຽງ

One of the most fascinating treks in Laos is to Dong Phu Vieng NPA, which offers a rare chance to step into a rapidly disappearing world. The park, south of Muang Phin in the centre of Savannakhet Province, is home to a number of Katang villages, where you can stay if you behave yourself.

The trek involves a fair bit of walking through a mix of forests ranging from dense woodlands to bamboo forests and rocky areas with little cover, or paths only accessible during the dry season (November to May). There's a boat trip on the third day. All food is included and eating local forest specialities is a highlight. A village guide leads trekkers through a sacred forest where you'll see *lak la'puep* – clan posts placed in the jungle by village families. Animals regularly seen include the rare silver langur, the leaf monkey and the hornbill.

The three-day trek uses local transport for the 180km to and from the NPA, and it's the long trip that goes some way towards explaining the high price – 1,500,000K per person. Clearly getting a bigger group together makes sense, and if you're interested it pays to go straight to the eco-guide unit and put your name on a list as soon as you arrive in Savannakhet. Better still, call ahead to see when a trip is departing.

Phu Xang Hae NPA

ປ່າສະຫງວນແຫ່ງຊາດຊ້າງແຫ່

Named after Wild Elephant Mountain, Phu Xang Hae NPA is a long expanse of forest stretching east–west across the remote north of Savannakhet Province, and its hills are the source of several smaller rivers. The Phu Thai people who live here, like the Katang of Dong Phu Vieng NPA, observe a series of taboos.

Unfortunately, the diabolical state of the roads means getting into Phu Xang Hae is very difficult. In theory the eco-guide unit in Savannakhet runs a five-day community-based trek staying in villages and in the jungle. However, in 2009 a grand total of three groups did the trek, most likely due to the high cost (US$250 per person; two person minimum).

Sepon (Xepon) & the Ho Chi Minh Trail

ເຊໂປນ/ເສັ້ນທາງໂຮຈິມິນ

041 / POP 40,000

Like so many other towns that needed to be rebuilt following the Second Indochina War, Sepon (often spelt Xepon) today is fairly unremarkable. The main reason for coming here is to see parts of the Ho Chi Minh Trail and what's left of the old district capital, Sepon Kao, 6km to the east.

A trip to **Sepon Kao** (Old Sepon) is a sobering experience. On the banks of the Se Pon, Sepon Kao was bombed almost into the Stone Age during the war. Although a handful of villagers have since moved back, they live among reminders of the war, including the bomb-scarred facade of the wat and a pile of bricks surrounding a safe, which was once the town's bank. If you're on foot or bike, head east from Sepon and turn right just after Km 199; the sign says 'Ban Seponkao'.

Ban Dong, 20km east of Sepon, was on one of the major thoroughfares of the Ho Chi Minh Trail and is the easiest place to see what little materiel is left from the

SLEEPING WITH SPIRITS

The Katang villagers of Dong Phu Vieng NPA believe in the myriad spirits that surround them in the forest. One of the most important is the house spirit, believed to live in the home of every village family. Over the centuries a series of taboos have been developed in an effort to avoid disturbing this spirit and as a visitor in a Katang home it is vitally important you don't break them.

- Never enter the owner's bedroom or touch the spirit place.
- Do not sleep beside a person of the opposite sex, even if that person is your spouse. If you really can't be separated tell the eco-guide unit and they can bring a tent for you.
- Sleep with your head pointed towards the nearest outside wall; never point your feet at the outside wall or, spirits forbid, another person's head.

It goes without saying that these villages are extremely sensitive to outside influence, which is why you can only visit them as part of the organised trek through the eco-guide unit in Savannakhet.

HO CHI MINH TRAIL

The infamous Ho Chi Minh Trail is actually a complex network of dirt paths and gravel roads running parallel to the Laos–Vietnam border from Khammuan Province in the north to Cambodia in the south. The trail's heaviest use occurred between 1966 and 1971 when more than 600,000 North Vietnamese Army (NVA) troops – along with masses of provisions and 500,000 tonnes of trucks, tanks, weapons and ordnance – passed along the route in direct violation of the 1962 Geneva Accords. At any one time around 30,000 NVA troops guarded the trail, which was honeycombed with underground barracks, fuel and vehicle repair depots, hospitals and rest camps, as well as ever more sophisticated anti-aircraft emplacements.

The North Vietnamese denied the existence of the trail throughout most of the war. The USA denied bombing it. In spite of 1.1 million tonnes of saturation bombing (begun in 1965 and reaching up to 900 sorties per day by 1969, including outings by B-52 behemoths), traffic along the route was never interrupted for more than a few days. Like a column of ants parted with a stick, the Vietnamese soldiers and supplies poured southward with only an estimated 15% to 20% of the cargo affected by the bombardment. One estimate says 300 bombs were dropped for every NVA casualty.

Contrary to popular understanding, the trail was neither a single route nor a tiny footpath. Several NVA engineering battalions worked on building roads, bridges and defence installations, and methods to hide the trails from the air were simple but ingenious. Bridges were built just below the water level and branches were tied together to hide what had become wide roads.

Today the most accessible points are at Ban Dong, east of Sepon, and the village of Pa-am in Attapeu Province, which sits almost right on the main thoroughfare. Here you can see a couple of tanks and a surface-to-air missile. Elsewhere you'll need to get way out into the sticks and get locals to guide you. Vientiane-based Don Duvall, otherwise known as the Midnight Mapper (p168), as of late 2013 will run history-infused motorbike trips on the trail.

war. Most of what was previously scattered around the area has been gathered into the gated front lawn of the newly opened **War Museum**. These include two American-built tanks used during Operation Lam Son 719 – a disastrous ARVN (Army of the Republic of Vietnam) assault on the Ho Chi Minh Trail in February 1971. Despite support from US combat aircraft, the ARVN troops retreated across the border at Lao Bao after being routed by seasoned North Vietnamese Army (NVA) troops at Ban Dong. To see the tanks, part of a plane, guns and other scrap, you'll find the museum at the east edge of Ban Dong, bordered by a baby blue and pink fence.

The dirt road that borders the museum was in fact one of the main branches of the **Ho Chi Minh Trail**. It is still used, and if you head another couple of kilometres south you'll come to a swing bridge built by the Vietnamese after the war ended.

In **Muang Phin**, 155km east of Savannakhet and 34km west of Sepon, stands an imposing Vietnamese-built monument to Lao-Vietnamese cooperation during the Indochina wars. Done in the stark Heroes of Socialism style, the monument depicts NVA and PL soldiers waving an AK-47 and Lao flag aloft.

Savannakhet's tourist information centre publishes a map-based guide of the area called *Ho Chi Minh Trail*.

Sleeping & Eating

There are a few places to eat in Sepon, none of which is remarkable, and all of which can be identified by their yellow Beerlao signs. A small night market unfolds every evening at about 5pm near the market/bus stop.

Khamvieng Tienmalay Guesthouse GUESTHOUSE $
(☎020-2246 519; r 80,000-100,000K) There are 10 basic rooms in this new guesthouse just west of the market. Rooms have fans and en suites.

Ki Houng Heuang GUESTHOUSE $
(☎020-2231 1370; Rte 9; r with fan/air-con 50,000/70,000K; ❄) In the centre of Sepon, just past the market on the south side of Rte

9, this hotel offers a handful of comfortable, but forgettable rooms.

Vieng Xay Guesthouse GUESTHOUSE $
(☎ 041-214895; Rte 9; s/d 70,000/80,000K; ❄) Vieng Xay, in the centre of town, is hands-down the town's best digs, and has 30 mostly large rooms with TVs, air-con and hot water. There's also a decent cafe serving Lao fare. A stairway bordered by bomb casings leads to more rooms out the back.

ℹ Getting There & Away

Sŏrngtăaou and the occasional bus leave from outside the market in Sepon for Savannakhet (35,000K, four to six hours, 196km) between about 8am and 3pm, or you can flag down any bus heading west for the same price. There are also relatively frequent *sŏrngtăaou* to Ban Dong (10,000K) and the border at Dansavanh (20,000K, one hour) during the same times, or you could hop on any bus going in that direction – your best bet is in the afternoon.

Southern Laos

Includes ➡

Best Places to Eat

- ➡ Na Dao (p219)
- ➡ King Kong Resort (p257)
- ➡ Four Thousand Sunsets (p258)
- ➡ Little Eden Restaurant (p257)
- ➡ Bolaven Cafe (p218)

Best Places to Stay

- ➡ Kingfisher Eco-Lodge (p231)
- ➡ Residence Sisouk (p217)
- ➡ Inthira Hotel (p225)
- ➡ Hoang Anh Attapeu Hotel (p242)
- ➡ River Garden (p256)

Why Go?

Near the Cambodian border, the Mekong awakes from its slumber, slams into Si Phan Don and disintegrates into a series of churning rapids. Downstream, a dwindling pod of Irrawaddy dolphins seek solace in a peaceful eddy. Upstream, an expanding pod of travellers find their solace in the hammock-strewn bungalows of Don Det and Don Khon.

Kayaking or bicycling around these dreamy islands is the signature southern Laos experience. But don't ignore the rest of this incredibly diverse region, where you'll also find dilapidated Angkorian temples, highland culture on the cool Bolaven Plateau, prime trekking, and raw off-the-beaten-track travel in the eastern provinces. Exploring the area by rented motorbike is a popular and rewarding pastime.

Long a magnet for backpackers, the region now lures higher-end travellers with upscale jungle lodges and boutique hotels on the banks of the Mekong. New highways and dams are changing the landscape forever, so hurry up and get here.

When to Go

Pakse

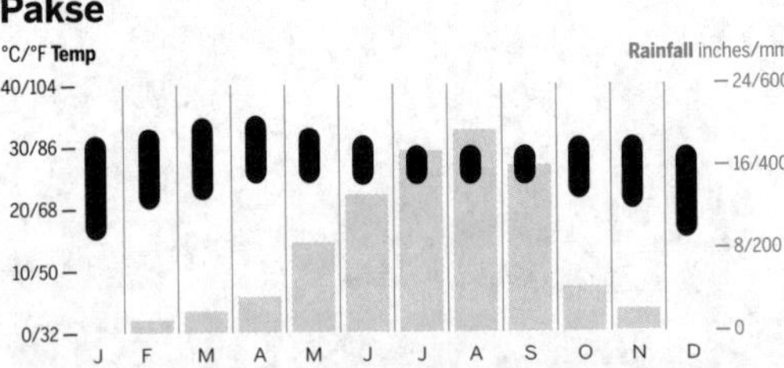

Oct–Nov Ideal time for bike touring, as rains trickle and the dust remains manageable

Dec–Feb Sunny and cooler – make that downright cold – on the Bolaven Plateau

May Pi Mai (New Year) means 10 days of water fights and Beerlao parties, but some resorts close

Southern Laos Highlights

1 Ogle Mekong rapids and spot rare dolphins while touring the **Don Khon** (p222) by bicycle or kayak

2 Watch the sun set over the Mekong from your hammock on **Don Det** (p222), Don Khon's sister island

3 Gaze in awe at 100m-high waterfalls, sip fair-trade coffee and soak in the cool climate at the **Bolaven Plateau** (p232)

4 Wake up early for a dramatic sunrise at the ancient Khmer temple complex at **Wat Phu Champasak** (p228)

5 Waterfall-hop and go hiking around **Tat Lo** (p235), a backpacker magnet with a laid-back vibe

6 Embark on the **Southern Swing** (p240), a bike loop through the Bolaven Plateau and the eastern provinces

7 Climb aboard an elephant to explore **Kiet Ngong** (p230), the region's premier ecotourism area

PAKSE

☎031 / POP 75,000

Pakse (ປາກເຊ), the gateway to southern Laos, sits at the confluence of the Mekong River and the Se Don (Don River). The city retains the sort of Mekong River–town lethargy found in Savannakhet and Tha Khaek further north, though fewer colonial-era buildings remain; look out for the grandiose, Franco-Chinese-style **Chinese Society building** (Th 10) in the centre of town.

Most travellers don't linger long because there is not much to do. The city's main appeal lies in sipping Beerlao on the riverfront, soaking up the laid-back provincial vibe and launching forays to nearby attractions such as the Bolaven Plateau, Tat Lo and Kiet Ngong.

Pakse is the capital of Champasak Province, which was part of the Cambodian Angkor empire between the 10th and 13th centuries. Wat Phu Champasak (p228), near Champasak town, is the most striking relic of that time. Following the decline of Angkor between the 15th and late 17th centuries, this region was absorbed into the nascent Lan Xang kingdom, but broke away to become an independent Lao kingdom between the beginning of the 18th century and the beginning of the 19th century.

Today Champasak Province encompasses Laos' southern Mekong region, including Si Phan Don and the Bolaven Plateau. The province has a population of more than 500,000, including lowland Lao (many of them Phu Thai), Khmers and a host of small Mon-Khmer groups, most of whom inhabit the Bolaven Plateau region.

Sights & Activities

Pakse is much more about being than seeing: its 'sights' are limited.

Champasak Historical Heritage Museum MUSEUM

(ພິພິດທະພັນມໍລະດົກປະຫວັດສາດຈຳປາສັກ; Rte 13; admission 10,000K; ⏲8-11.30am & 1-4pm Mon-Fri) This museum has a few interesting artefacts, including three very old Dong Son bronze drums, a Siam-style sandstone Buddha head dating to the 7th century and striking 7th-century sandstone lintels found at Uo Moung (p230). The simple textile and jewellery collection from the Nyaheun, Suay and Laven groups is also interesting for its large iron ankle bracelets and ivory ear plugs.

Also on display are musical instruments, stelae in Tham script dating from the 15th to 18th centuries, a water jar from the 11th or 12th century, a small lingam (Shiva phallus), a scale model of Wat Phu Champasak, and some American UXOs (unexploded ordnances) and other weaponry.

Wat Luang BUDDHIST TEMPLE

(ວັດຫຼວງ; Th 11) There are about 20 wats in Pakse, among which the 1935 Wat Luang is one of the largest. A monastic school here features ornate concrete pillars, carved wooden doors and murals; the artist's whimsy departs from canonical art without losing the traditional effect. Behind the *sĭm* (ordination hall) is a monks' school in an original wooden building.

Wat Tham Fai BUDDHIST TEMPLE

(ວັດຖ້ຳໄຟ; Rte 13) Founded in 1935, Wat Tham Fai, near the Champasak Palace Hotel, is undistinguished except for its spacious grounds, making it a prime site for temple festivals. It's also known as Wat Pha Bat because there is a small Buddha footprint shrine.

Pakse Golf GOLF

(☎030-534 8280; www.paksegolf.com; Ban Phatana; 18 holes weekday/weekend 405,000/445,000K, club rental 180,000K; ⏲6am-6pm) Duffers can practice their putting here at this technical, long and surprisingly well-maintained course. Head out of town on Th 38, go right at the well signposted turn-off 1km east of the Champasak Grand Hotel and continue for another 3km.

Friendship Bowling BOWLING

(Th 11; bowling incl shoes before/after noon 7000/12,000K, snooker 3000K; ⏲9am-11pm) This is a bargain for those looking for some pin action. There wasn't that much friendship the evening we bowled, as it was basically empty.

Clinic Keo Ou Done MASSAGE

(Traditional Medicine Hospice; ☎020-543 1115, 031-251895; massage 30,000-70,000K, sauna 10,000K; ⏲9am-9pm, sauna 4-9pm) This professional and popular massage centre has an air-con massage room and herbal sauna segregated by gender. To get here, head out of town on Rte 38 and turn right towards Pakse Golf, 1km east of Champasak Grand Hotel. It's on the right-hand side just a couple hundred metres from the Rte 38 turn-off.

Dok Champa Massage MASSAGE

(Th 5; massages from 35,000K, body scrub 200,000K; ⏲9am-10pm) This is the longest-running and still the best massage emporium in the centre of town. Prices are very reasonable for the stylish set-up.

Tours

Many people organise their southern Laos tours and treks out of Pakse. Pretty much all hotels (and many restaurants) advertise day trips to the Bolaven Plateau, Wat Phu Champasak, Tat Lo and Kiet Ngong/Phu Asa. Guides average US$20 to US$50 per day depending on numbers, plus transport.

For adventurous multiday trips, both riverine and terrestrial, you can also try the Provincial Tourism Office (p220).

Green Discovery ADVENTURE TOURS
(031-252908; www.greendiscoverylaos.com; Th 10; 2-day Tree Top Explorer tour 2/4-person group per person US$300/200) Green Discovery's signature tour is the Tree Top Explorer adventure in Dong Hua Sao NPA near Paksong on the Bolaven Plateau. It consists of two or three days of ziplining, canopy walks, jungle trekking and more. Accommodation (included in the price) is in eco-friendly huts set high up above the forest floor. Green Discovery also does rainy-season kayaking trips on the Huay Bang Lieng River near Paksong. There's lots more on offer in the region – check the website.

Xplore-Asia ADVENTURE TOUR
(031-251983; www.xplore-laos.com; Th 14) Xplore-Asia specialises in multi-day adventures, including a variety of options for Mekong River trips to Si Pan Don and on into Cambodia, using boats and/or kayaks. English-speaking guides are US$35 per day. Also sells some interesting books and guidebooks to the region.

Vat Phou BOAT TOUR
(www.vatphou.com; Residence Sisouk, cnr Th 9 & Th 11) Operates luxury cruises between Pakse and Si Phan Don.

Mekong Islands Tours BOAT TOUR
(www.cruisemekong.com) Pricey boat cruises along the Mekong between Pakse and Si Phan Don.

Sleeping

The tourist centre is on Rte 13 between the French Bridge and Th 24. Stay here if you want easy access to travel agencies, motorbike rentals, money changers and touristy restaurants. Around the corner you'll find a few more hotels in the commercial district, which is centred around the Champasak Plaza Shopping Centre (p219). If you are staying anywhere else – such as on the riverfront or in one of the many hotels east of the centre on Rte 13 – you'll probably want to rent a motorbike or bicycle to get around.

★ **Alisa Guesthouse** HOTEL $
(031-251555; www.alisa-guesthouse.com; Rte 13; r 110,000K;) Sleepy service aside, the Alisa is an exceptional deal, offering cleaner and more stylish rooms than anything else in this price range. Rooms have comfy, immaculately made beds, working sat TV, A fridge and good water pressure. There's also a large fleet of motorbikes for hire. It's well-located in the heart of the tourist zone.

Kaesme Guest House GUESTHOUSE $
(020-9948 1616; Se Don riverfront; r 30,000-70,000K;) The quiet location and wood deck over the Se Don are the main draws, but the simple rooms, which come with or without bathrooms and air-con, are a great deal. Towels and soap are a nice bonus.

Fang Sedone Guesthouse GUESTHOUSE $
(031-212158; Th 11; r with fan/air-con 50,000/70,000K;) Rooms here are as basic as it gets, but the riverside setting is quiet compared with budget hotels on the main drag. Air-con rooms include hot water.

Sabaidy 2 Guesthouse GUESTHOUSE $
(031-212992; www.sabaidy2tour.com; Th 24; dm 30,000K, s/d/tr without bathroom 50,000/70,000/114,000K, d with bathroom 85,000-100,000K;) Good reviews of this place are hard to come by, but it's plenty popular by virtue of its reputation as a backpacker magnet. It's often booked out if you walk in so try booking ahead. The en suite rooms out back are good value.

Lankham Hotel HOTEL $
(031-213314; Rte 13; 3-bed dm 40,000K, d with fan/air-con from 60,000/90,000K;) Another popular hotel not known for service, the Lankham nonetheless packs 'em in with its central location and cheap rates. Budget rooms are tiny and loud. Pricier air-con rooms are nicer yet lag behind neighbours Phi Dao and Alisa.

Thaluang Hotel GUESTHOUSE $
(031-251399; Th 21; s/d from 60,000/70,000K;) Thaluang gets the spill-over from popular neighbour Sabaidy 2. Good thing for them, as the musty rooms (some windowless) and ordinary service aren't reason alone

Pakse

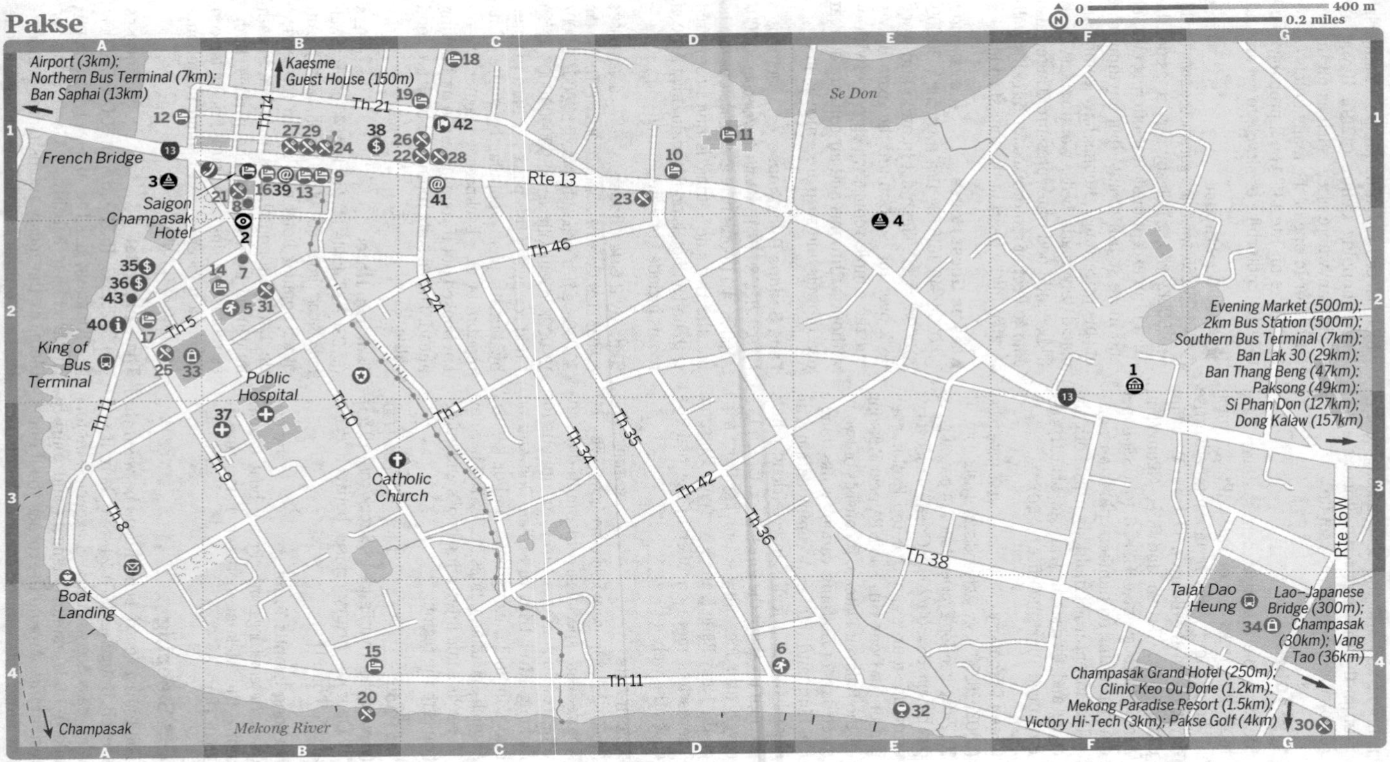

0 400 m
0 0.2 miles

Airport (3km); Northern Bus Terminal (7km); Ban Saphai (13km)
Kaesme Guest House (150m)
French Bridge
Saigon Champasak Hotel
King of Bus Terminal
Public Hospital
Catholic Church
Boat Landing
Champasak
Mekong River
Se Don
Rte 13
Rte 16W
Th 14
Th 21
Th 46
Th 24
Th 5
Th 10
Th 1
Th 9
Th 8
Th 11
Th 34
Th 35
Th 42
Th 36
Th 38
Talat Dao Heung
Lao–Japanese Bridge (300m); Champasak (30km); Vang Tao (36km)
Evening Market (500m); 2km Bus Station (500m); Southern Bus Terminal (7km); Ban Lak 30 (29km); Ban Thang Beng (47km); Paksong (49km); Si Phan Don (127km); Dong Kalaw (157km)
Champasak Grand Hotel (250m); Clinic Keo Ou Done (1.2km); Mekong Paradise Resort (1.5km); Victory Hi-Tech (3km); Pakse Golf (4km)

1 2 3 4 5 6 7 8 9 10 11 12 13 14 15 16 17 18 19 20 21 22 23 24 25 26 27 28 29 30 31 32 33 34 35 36 37 38 39 40 41 42 43

Pakse

to come here. Some of the cheapest air-con rooms in town, however – the best are in the main house. A myna bird hails your arrival.

★ **Residence Sisouk** BOUTIQUE HOTEL **$$**
(031-214716; www.residence-sisouk.com; cnr Th 9 & Th 11; r US$50-100;) This exquisite boutique hotel occupies a lovely 60-year-old colonial house. The rooms enjoy polished hardwood floors, flat-screen TVs, verandahs, Hmong bed runners, lush photography and fresh flowers everywhere. Breakfast is in the penthouse cafe with 360-degree views (it's closed at other times). Paying extra gets you a bigger, brighter room in front; standard rooms are at the back.

Athena Hotel HOTEL **$$**
(031-214888; www.athena-pakse.com; Rte 13; r incl breakfast US$60-90; @) Easily the most modern and slick hotel in Pakse. The beds are marshmallowy delights, and dimming inlaid ceiling lights let you illuminate them in many ways. The three deluxe rooms ratchet up the luxury factor with humongous flat-screen TVs, bathrobes and big bathtubs. The cosy pool is most welcome after a day out on dusty roads. It's about a 10-minute walk from the tourist centre.

Pakse Hotel HOTEL **$$**
(031-212131; www.paksehotel.com; Th 5; s from 200,000K, d incl breakfast 250,000-450,000K; @) This traditional-luxe hotel towering over central Pakse has a gorgeous lobby and breezy corridors festooned with indigenous sculptures and textiles. The economy rooms are dark and the standard rooms cramped, so upgrade to at least a superior, which brings extras like flat-screen TVs, fancy soaps, designer furniture and Mekong views.

Phi Dao Hotel HOTEL **$$**
(031-215588; phidaohotel@gmail.com; Rte 13; s/d/tr from 135,000/155,000/180,000K;)

The service is practically non-existent but you can't argue with the rooms, which are among Pakse's most stylish in lower to midrange. Street-side rooms are loud, however, so request something at the back. Solo travellers should avoid the cramped singles and upgrade to a spacious double.

Pakse Mekong Hotel HOTEL $$
(031-218445; tim_chanthavong@yahoo.com; Th 11; r without/with river view 185,000/210,000K;) Stylish, immaculate rooms with flat-screen TVs, spiffy white bedspreads and huge porcelain sinks distinguish this hotel. The riverfront location is a bonus if you don't mind being slightly removed from the tourist centre. The nondescript, unfurnished balconies and rooftop terrace are curiously wasted.

Champasak Palace Hotel HISTORIC HOTEL $$
(031-212263; www.champasakpalacehotel.com; Rte 13; s/d incl breakfast from US$23/26, ste US$60-200;) You can't miss the vast, wedding-cake-style Champasak Palace. It was originally built as a palace for Chao Boun Oum na Champasak, the last prince of Champasak and the prime minister of the kingdom of Laos between 1960 and 1962. The grounds are faded but the well-kept rooms have comfortable beds and linens, while the graceful restaurant and common areas turn heads with wood columns and French tiles. It is worth investing in a huge VIP suite (US$60), with parquet floors and panoramic views. Cheaper rooms in the newer Sedone building are less inspiring.

Mekong Paradise Resort RESORT $$
(031-254120; mekongparadise@yahoo.com; r incl breakfast US$38-85;) A riverside resort just 3km south of central Pakse is a strange idea, but it actually makes for a wonderful escape from the city. Most rooms have unbeatable Mekong sunset views. The superior rooms ($55) are downright romantic, with sweeping hardwood floors, private balconies and soft lighting. It's quiet out here – sometimes too quiet. Take the turn-off to Pakse Golf off Rte 38 and proceed 500m.

Eating

Chowing down with the locals, especially at breakfast and lunch, is an immersive Lao experience. The **Lankham Noodle Shop** (Rte 13; noodles 15,000-25,000K; 7am-10pm;) under the Lankham Hotel and, just across the road, the **Mengky Noodle Shop** (Rte 13; meals 8000-15,000K; 7am-10pm) are safe and popular places for noodles and soup. Mengky is justly famous for its duck *fěr* breakfasts. Service at the Lankham can be indifferent to the point of being rude, but the soups are worth the struggle.

For a light snack there are **baguette vendors** (Rte 13) and by night the braziers light up with barbecued skewers at the **Evening Market** (Rte 13), 2km east of town on Rte 13. Grab delicious fruit by night from the outdoor **fruit vendors** at the northwest corner of the Champasak Plaza Shopping Centre (p219).

Self-caterers can head to any market or try centrally located **Friendship Minimart** (Rte 13; 8am-8pm).

★**Bolaven Cafe** CAFE $
(www.bolavenfarms.com; Rte 13; mains 20,000-40,000K; 7am-9.30pm Mon-Sat;) Fair-trade organic coffee is all the rage in Pakse and this airy cafe does the best job of roasting it. Take a few bags home (50,000K to 70,000K per bag). Great big coffee-fueled breakfasts and an extensive menu of Laotian and Thai food as well as sandwiches make it worth a stop any time of day. Read about Bolaven Farms' interesting history as you eat.

Xuan Mai Restaurant LAOTIAN, VIETNAMESE $
(Th 5; mains 18,000-30,000K; 6am-11.30pm) Vietnamese-run Xuan Mai serves freshly prepared *fěr* (rice noodles), *năam néuang* (pork balls), *kòw Ƀûn* (white flour noodles with sweet-spicy sauce), fruit shakes and even garlic bread. The house *lâhp* (meat salad) is full of zing.

Champady CAFE $
(mains 15,000-35,000K; 7am-9pm) Set in a French-era building, the Champady has an extensive menu of Thai and Laotian dishes, coffees and desserts such as sweet sticky rice with mango (10,000K).

Sinouk Coffee Shop CAFE $
(cnr Th 9 & Th 11; dishes 25,000-45,000K; 6.30am-8.30pm;) Attached to the terrific Residence Sisouk hotel, this aromatic cafe is a good breakfast or lunch stop, with sandwiches, salads, pasta, pastries, fresh bread and blasting air-con. Rich Arabica coffee from the Bolaven Plateau is sold by the cup and by the bag.

Delta Coffee CAFE $
(Rte 13; mains 25,000-40,000K; 7am-9pm;) Delta does a lot more than 'Coffee' suggests,

including a hearty selection of Italian and Thai dishes. The lasagne, pastas and pizzas are recommended if you've been on a steady diet of sticky rice in the boonies. Owners Alan and Siriporn (he's Chinese, she's Thai) serve coffee from their plantation near Paksong.

Jasmine Restaurant INDIAN $
(Rte 13; mains 20,000-30,000K; ⌚8am-10pm) Delicious curries and Malaysian fare such as nasi goreng with mutton, plus sizzling chicken tikka masala so tasty you'll be wiping the bowl with their pillow-soft naan.

Daolin Restaurant LAOTIAN, INTERNATIONAL $
(Rte 13; mains 15,000-30,000K; ⌚6.30am-10pm) Open-air Daolin owes its immense popularity to its prominent location and a menu with something for everyone. But the best reason to come here is the extravagant ice cream sundaes – we're addicted to the cappuccino parfait (20,000K).

Katuad Café INTERNATIONAL, LAOTIAN $
(Rte 13; mains 15,000-25,000K; ⌚7am-8.30pm; 📶) This simple cafe does a good trade with Western breakfasts, sandwiches, hamburgers and ice cream, as well as stir fries and spicy salads. Great coffee and fruit shakes.

Hasan INDIAN $
(Th 24; ⌚7am-10pm) Another Indian restaurant with Malaysian touches, the owner previously cooked for a high-end Vientiane hotel.

★ **Na Dao** FRENCH $$
(☎255558; cnr Th 38 & Rte 16W; mains 30,000-180,000K; ⌚11am-1.30pm & 6.30-10pm Mon-Sat) Fine French dining has arrived in Pakse. Exiled from Vientiane, the owners migrated south to bring their cultured cuisine to southern Laos. Moorish moments include a salmon and sea bass carpaccio, Paksong goose with olives and a five-course menu degustation (185,000K).

Le Panorama FUSION $$
(Th 5; mains 30,000-70,000K; ⌚4.30-10pm; 📶) The rooftop restaurant of the Pakse Hotel serves up delicious Franco-Asian cuisine and unbeatable 360-degree city views. The menu includes T-bone steak, duck and a succulent *ɓah neung het hŏrm* (stuffed fish).

Banlao Boat Restaurant LAOTIAN $$
(Th 11; mains 40,000-80,000K; ⌚8am-11pm) The best of several floating restaurants on the Mekong, Banlao has a reliable menu of Laotian favourites in addition to worldly offerings like Peking Duck and German pork knuckles, plus exotic fare like ants' eggs for audacious eaters. The main draw is the river setting.

Drinking & Nightlife

Le Panorama (p219) is a required stop for a sunset Beerlao or two. For a more local touch, the Mekong riverfront is lined with open-air BBQs and beer gardens that stare at the sunset. Most are open until about midnight on weekends, but close earlier on weekdays.

Oay BEER GARDEN
(Th 11; 📶) Trendy Oay on the Mekong riverfront has occasional live acoustic music and shows football games on a big flat-screen TV.

Victory Hi-Tech CLUB
(Rte 38) This is the most popular of a handful of youthful nightclubs about 3km south of the Champasak Grand Hotel on the road to Cambodia. It is loud and dark and not exactly Vientiane, but it does stay open until – wait for it – midnight.

Shopping

Coffee from the Bolaven Plateau is the traditional souvenir from the region; pick up a bag at any cafe. Try the markets for sticky-rice baskets and the like. Quality fabrics are sold in the lobby of the Pakse Hotel (p217).

Monument Books BOOKS
(Th 5; ⌚9am-8pm) This upmarket bookshop is your best stop for maps of Southern Laos, other regions of Laos and the entire Mekong region, plus postcards and a superb range of regional historical and cultural books.

Talat Dao Heung MARKET
(Morning Market) This vast market near the Lao–Japanese Bridge is one of the biggest in the country, famous for its selection of fresh produce and coffee from the Bolaven Plateau.

Champasak Plaza Shopping Centre MARKET
The Champasak Plaza Shopping Centre has name-brand bags and clothing, both genuine and knock-off, plus some textiles.

Information

Visit the excellent website www.ecotourismlaos.com for more helpful information.

ATMs are strung out along Rte 13 in the tourist zone, including an ANZ machine outside

Lankham Hotel (p215). The Lankham also has a useful **currency exchange counter** (⌚7am-7pm) that offers decent rates and does cash advances on Visa cards for a small commission.

BCEL (Th 11; ⌚8.30am-3.30pm Mon-Fri) Bank with a dedicated English-speaking counter that changes dollar- and euro-denominated travellers cheques (1% commission) and gives cash advances on Visa and MasterCard (3%). Its exchange office (Th 11; ⌚8.30am-7pm Mon-Fri, to 3pm Sat & Sun) next-door has longer hours, and you'll find BCEL ATMs around the city.

International Hitech Polyclinic (VIP Clinic; ☎031-214712; ihpc_lao@yahoo.com; Th 46; ⌚24hr) Adjacent to the public hospital, with English-speaking staff and much higher standards of care, service and facilities, plus a pharmacy.

Lao Development Bank (Rte 13; ⌚8am-4pm Mon-Fri, to 3pm Sat & Sun) Changes cash and travellers cheques. Also houses a Western Union (money transfers only available weekdays).

Main Post Office (cnr Th 8 & Th 1; ⌚8am-noon & 1-4pm Mon-Fri)

Miss Noy's Internet & Bike Rental (Rte 13; per hour 500K; ⌚7am-8pm) Also rents bicycles and motorbikes.

Police (☎031-212145; Th 10)

Provincial Tourism Office (☎031-212021; Th 11; ⌚8am-noon & 1.30-4pm) The well-organised English-speaking staff can book you onto community-based two- or three-day treks in Se Pian NPA and Phou Xieng Thong NPA, involving kayaking and camping combos; and homestays on Don Kho and Don Daeng. They dole out maps of Pakse and are armed with the latest bus schedules.

SK Internet (Rte 13; per hour 5000K; ⌚7.30am-9pm) Fast connections.

Unitel (Rte 13; ⌚8am-5pm Mon-Fri, to noon Sat) A convenient stop for a local SIM card if you are just arriving in Laos. Staff can set your smart phone up with 3G internet.

Getting There & Away

AIR

Lao Airlines (☎031-212252; Th 11; ⌚8am-noon & 1-5pm Mon-Fri, 8am-noon Sat) has direct flights from **Pakse International Airport** (☎031-251921) to the following cities in Asia:

DESTINATION	PRICE (US$)	FREQUENCY
Vientiane	75-135	2 daily
Savannakhet	35-65	4 weekly
Siem Reap	160	daily
Ho Chi Minh City	170	4 weekly
Bangkok	165	4 weekly

A cheaper way to Bangkok is to travel overland to Ubon Ratchathani and take a budget flight from there.

GETTING TO THAILAND: PAKSE TO UBON RATCHATHANI

Getting to the Border

The **Vang Tao (Laos)/Chong Mek (Thailand) crossing** (⌚5am-6pm) was being reconstructed at the time of research in anticipation of an increase in traffic when new highways to Vietnam are opened.

From Pakse, *sŏrngtăaou* (10,000K, 75 minutes, 37km) run frequently between Talat Dao Heung and Vang Tao until 4pm or so. They leave you at the border and you walk over.

Less stressful is the Thai–Lao International Bus (80,000K, 2½ to three hours, 126km) direct from Pakse's 2km bus terminal to Ubon's main bus station. Departures in both directions are at 8.30am and 3.30pm. Alternatively, you buy a through ticket to Bangkok (from Pakse 235,000K, 14 hours). This may or may not involve a bus change in Ubon. Pakse travel agents also offer a combination bus/sleeper train ticket to the Thai capital (280,000K).

At the Border

Laos issues visas on arrival (around US$35, depending on what passport you hold), while on the Thai side most nationalities are issued 15-day visa waivers free-of-charge. Formalities are straight-forward on both sides.

Moving On

If you're walking over, find a *sŏrngtăaou* on the other side to Phibun Mangsahan (40B, one hour). From the *sŏrngtăaou* stop in Phibun Mangsahan it's a long walk or a short tuk-tuk ride to the bus station, where *sŏrngtăaou* and buses leave to Ubon (40B, one hour, 40km). Alternatively, taxi drivers usually wait outside immigration on the Thai side and want about B900 to B1200 to Ubon Ratchathani (one hour, 82km).

The airport is 3km northwest of town. A *săhm-lór* or tuk-tuk to the airport will cost about 40,000/50,000K.

BOAT

Like so many others, the public boat from Pakse to Champasak and Don Khong has stopped operating. However, a tourist boat motors to Champasak most mornings at 8.30am, provided there are enough punters (one-way per person 70,000K). The return trip from Champasak is at 1.30pm. It's two hours downstream to Champasak, and a bit longer on the return.

BUS & SŎRNGTĂAOU

Pakse, frustratingly, has several bus and *sŏrngtăaou* terminals. The vast majority of tourists simply book bus journeys through their guesthouse or through a travel agency; these usually include free pickup in the centre or a free transfer to the relevant departure point, so you don't really lose any money doing this.

However, on certain routes – especially to Cambodia, Vietnam and Vientiane – you'll want to be careful which service you use: choosing the wrong one could cost you several hours and cause much pain.

There are five main stations:

Southern Bus Terminal (Rte 13) Also known as *khíw lot lák pąet*, or '8km bus terminal'. As the name implies, it's 8km south of town on Rte 13.

Northern Bus Terminal (Rte 13) This is usually called *khíw lot lák jét* (7km bus terminal); it's – you guessed it – 7km north of town. This station is very local and completely lacks scheduling information in English.

Talat Dao Heung (Morning Market) It's mostly *sŏrngtăaou* here, in a big lot at the southern edge of the market.

2km Bus Station (☎031-212428; Rte 13, Km 2) Also known as the Evening Market station, VIP station, or Sengchalean station.

King of Bus Terminal (020-5501 2299; Th 11) Another so-called 'VIP terminal'.

Vientiane & Points North

Most travellers prefer the comfortable night sleeper buses to Vientiane (170,000K, seven to eight hours). You can book these through your guesthouse or head to the King of Bus terminal, from where there are three nightly departures. Other 'VIP' sleeper services depart from the 2-Kilometre station. It's possible to take these buses to Tha Khaek (140,000K, 4½ hours) and Seno (for Savannakhet; 140,000K, three hours).

If you prefer day travel, slow-moving ordinary (non-air-con) buses (110,000K, 16 to 18 hours) and fancier air-con buses (140,000K, 10 to 12 hours) depart throughout the day to Vientiane from the southern bus terminal, stopping at the 2-Kilometre and northern bus terminals on the way out of town. These buses also go to Tha Khaek (ordinary/air-con 60,000/70,000K, eight/six hours) and Seno.

From the northern bus terminal, agonisingly slow ordinary buses rattle north every 40 minutes or so between 6.30am and 4pm to Savannakhet (40,000K, four to five hours, 277km) and Tha Khaek (70,000K, seven hours).

Getting to Ban Saphai (for Don Kho) involves taking a regular *sŏrngtăaou* from Talat Dao Heung (10,000K, 45 minutes).

Bolaven Plateau & Points East

Most transport to the Bolaven Plateau and points east consists of ordinary buses from the southern bus terminal.

Transport to Salavan (25,000K, three to four hours, five daily) can drop you at Tat Lo; the first trip is at 6.45am and the last trip at 4pm. Six loaded buses rumble to Attapeu (45,000K, 5½ hours) between 7.45am and 4pm.

Buses to Attapeu go via Sekong (35,000K, four hours), but this may change when the new Paksong–Attapeu highway is completed. Two additional buses terminate in Sekong. For Paksong (25,000K, 90 minutes) take any Attapeu-bound bus. Air-con buses bound for the Vietnamese border at Bo Y are a more comfortable option to Attapeu/Sekong.

Champasak & Si Phan Don

Regular *sŏrngtăaou* leave Talat Dao Heung for Champasak (20,000K, one to two hours) until noon. Additional morning *sŏrngtăaou* to Champasak leave from the southern bus terminal via the Mekong's eastern bank; these cost the same and include the ferry crossing from Ban Muang.

A fancier bus to Champasak departs from the King of Bus terminal every morning at 8am (45,000K, one hour). There's also a morning tourist bus to Champasak (60,000K, 45 minutes), with a pickup at your hotel, offered by most travel agencies.

For Si Phan Don, tourist buses or minivans, with pickups in town and including boat transfer to Don Khong (60,000K, 2¼ hours), Don Det (70,000K, 2½ hours) and Don Khon (70,000K, 2½ hours), are most popular and convenient. Book these through any guesthouse or travel agent. All departures are in the morning between 7.30am and 8am.

If you want to leave later in the day, take a *sŏrngtăaou* from the southern bus terminal to Ban Nakasang (for Don Det and Don Khon; 40,000K, 3½ hours). These depart when full until 4pm and go via Hat Xai Khun (for Don Khong).

One *sŏrngtăaou* services Kiet Ngong and Ban Phapho (25,000K, two hours or so), leaving around noon.

Vietnam

Transport to Vietnam crosses the border either at Lao Bao (p207) or Bo Y (p244).

Most 'direct' trips to Hue (210,000K to 270,000K, 14 to 16 hours) and Danang (240,000K to 280,000K, 18 to 20 hours) via Lao Bao take a detour into Savannakhet and involve a bus change at the border, plus possible additional bus transfers. You've been warned. Departures are early in the morning from Talat Dao Heung, with a stop at the northern bus terminal on the way out of town. Additional services are operated out of the 2km bus terminal. Most travellers buy tickets from agents in the centre, typically including a free transfer to the departure point.

There's one excruciatingly slow night bus to Hue, but it gets to Lao Bao in the middle of the night and you must wait a few hours for the border to open. Not recommended.

Buses to the border crossing at Bo Y border go via Attapeu and eventually terminate in Kontum or Gia Lai (Pleiku) in Vietnam's Central Highlands. Mai Linh Express operates the most comfortable bus along this route (to Kontum 145,000K, 8½ hours, departure at 5.45am); buy tickets from the Saigon Champasak Hotel in Pakse. Otherwise, packed ordinary buses depart from the southern bus terminal.

Getting Around

Local transport in Pakse is expensive by regional standards. As a foreigner you will need to bargain a bit to avoid being overcharged.

Figure on about 10,000K for a short tuk-tuk or *săhm-lór* trip if you are one person – more if you're in a group. A ride to the northern or southern bus terminals costs 10,000K per person, or 50,000K for a whole tuk-tuk. To the 2km bus terminal it's 20,000/30,000K for a *săhm-lór*/tuk-tuk.

Several shops and guesthouses in the tourist belt along Rte 13 rent bicycles (15,000K per day) and motorbikes (50,000K to 60,000K per day for 100cc bikes, rising to 100,000K for 125cc bikes or an automatic Honda Scoopy). Good bets are Alisa Guesthouse (p215) and Lankham Hotel (p215). The Lankham has 223cc dirt bikes available from 240,000K per day, while a Honda CRF 250L costs from 320,000K.

Europe Car (☎ 031-214946; Th 10; from US$77 per day) rents out 4WD Ford pickup trucks and SUVs.

AROUND PAKSE

Don Kho & Ban Saphai

ດອນໂຄ/ບ້ານສະພາຍ

The Mekong island of **Don Kho** and the nearby village of **Ban Saphai**, about 15km north of Pakse, are famous for their silk weaving. Women can be seen working on large looms underneath their homes, producing distinctive silk and cotton *pàh salóng* (long sarongs for men) and are happy to let you watch.

There are no cars on Don Kho and despite the advent of electricity it's easy to feel like you're stepping back to a more simple time. The 300 or so residents live in villages at either side of the 800m-wide island and farm rice in the centre. Believe it or not, Don Kho was briefly the capital of southern Laos following the French arrival in the 1890s, and it later served as a mooring point for boats steaming between Don Det and Savannakhet. These days, however, the only real sight is **Wat Don Kho**, which has some French-era buildings and an impressive drum tower. In the southeast corner of the grounds is a soaring tree that locals say is 500 years old, though 200 seems more realistic. These trees periodically have fires burned inside the trunks to extract a resin used to seal local boats.

Don Kho is a great place to experience a homestay. Just turn up on the island and say 'homestay' and the villagers will sort you out for 30,000K per bed, with a maximum of two people per house. Meals are taken with the host family and cost 20,000K. In our experience, the food is delicious. Activities offered by locals include Lao-style **fishing trips** and lessons in **silk weaving**.

Don Kho also has a **community guesthouse** at the edge of a **sacred forest** on the far side of the island. There's not much to separate it from a homestay; it's uber-basic and costs the same. The guesthouse is well-signposted from the boat landing (it's about a 700m walk).

The guys in the small **tourist information centre** near the boat pier in Ban Saphai speak some English and can phone ahead to arrange a bed and/or activities. This is part of the Ban Saphai Handicraft Centre, where there are a couple of stalls selling local weaving.

Getting There & Away

Ban Saphai is 17km north of central Pakse; look for a well-marked turn-off on Rte 13 about 13km north of the French Bridge.

Sŏrngtăaou to Ban Saphai (10,000K, 45 minutes) leave fairly regularly from Talat Dao Heung in Pakse. *Săhm-lór* in Pakse ask an outrageous 150,000K round-trip to Ban Saphai, including wait-time, while tuk-tuks ask 250,000K. Try negotiating. One-way trips are only slightly cheaper.

From Ban Saphai to Don Kho, boats cost 20,000K for one to five people. A boat tour around Don Kho costs 70,000K.

Phou Xieng Thong NPA ປ່າສະຫງວນແຫ່ງຊາດພູຊຽງທອງ

Spread over 1200 sq km in Champasak and Salavan provinces, **Phou Xieng Thong NPA** (www.ecotourismlaos.com) is most accessible about 50km upriver from Pakse. The area features scrub, mixed monsoon deciduous forest and exposed sandstone ridges and cave-like outcroppings, some of which contain prehistoric paintings.

Phou Xieng Thong is home to a range of wildlife, including important concentrations of green peafowl. Clouded leopard, banteng, elephant, Asiatic black bear and tiger once roamed here, although it's unclear if any of these remain, and you surely won't see any. If the season is right you're much more likely to see some striking wild orchids.

The best way into the park is on a two- or three-day community-based trek beginning in the Mekong village of **Ban Singsamphan**. The trip involves river transport, a homestay in Ban Singsamphan and, on day two, a four- to five-hour trek over **Phu Khong** (Khong Mountain). The two-day trip sees you return to Pakse by boat down the Mekong late in the afternoon, but we recommend the three-day version, which heads downriver to Don Kho for a homestay there.

To do this tour check with Pakse's provincial tourism office (p220). Limited transport means it is possible but difficult to reach Ban Singsamphan independently – get the low-down from the tourism office.

CHAMPASAK

☎031

It's hard to imagine Champasak (ຈຳປາສັກ) as a seat of royalty, but until only 30 years ago it was just that. These days the town is a somnolent place, the fountain circle in the middle of the main street alluding to a grandeur long since departed with the former royal family. The remaining French colonial-era buildings, including one that once belonged to Chao Boun Oum na Champasak and another to his father Chao Ratsadanai, share space with traditional Lao wooden houses. The few vehicles that venture down the narrow main street share it with buffaloes and cows who seem relaxed even by Lao standards.

With a surprisingly good range of accommodation and several worthwhile attractions in the vicinity – most notably the Angkor-period ruins of Wat Phu Champasak (p228) – it's easy to see why many visitors to the region prefer staying in Champasak over comparatively bustling Pakse.

Just about everything in Champasak is spread along the riverside road, either side of the fountain circle.

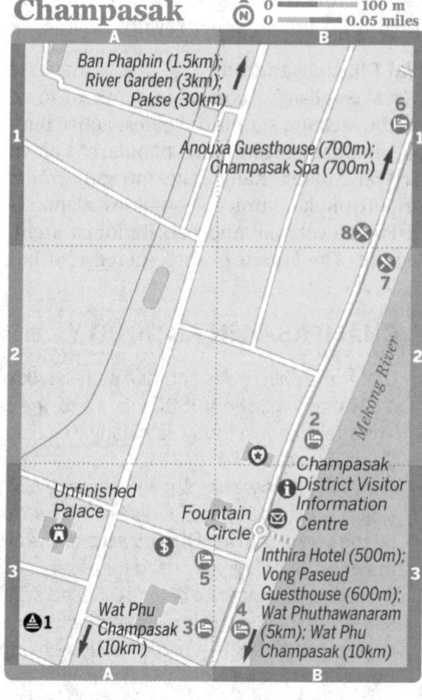

Champasak

Sights

1 Wat Nyutthitham A3

Sleeping

2 Dokchampa Guesthouse and Restaurant B2
3 Khamphouy Guesthouse A3
4 Saythong Guesthouse & Restaurant B3
5 Siamephone Hotel A3
6 Thavisab Guesthouse B1

Eating

7 Champasak With Love B2
8 Frice and Lujane Restaurant B1

Sights & Activities

Champasak has a couple of mildly interesting temples.

Wat Nyutthitham BUDDHIST TEMPLE
(ວັດຍຸດຕິທຳ, Wat Thong) West of the river on the main highway is this late 19th-century temple, more commonly known as Wat Thong. An old *sĭm* features an arched and colonnaded verandah, and has a washed pastel stucco relief on the front. This was the wat used by Champasak's royal family, and the *thâat káduk* here contain the ashes of King Nyutthitham (died 1885), Chao Ratsadanai (died 1946) and Chao Boun Oum (died 1975), among other royalty.

Wat Phuthawanaram BUDDHIST TEMPLE
(Wat Muang Kang) About 5km south of town on the Mekong stands the oldest active temple in Champasak, more popularly known as Wat Muang Kang. The intriguing *hăw tai* (Tripitaka library) combines elements of French-colonial and Lao Buddhist architecture. The *hăw tai*'s three-tiered roof has coloured mosaics at the corners, and a small box with coloured crystal windows at the centre of the top roof ridge, reminiscent of Burmese architecture.

Ostensibly these crystal-sided boxes hold Buddha images, but local legend ascribes a more magical purpose to the one atop the *hăw tai*. Supposedly at a certain moment in the annual lunar calendar (most say it's during the Wat Phu Festival), in the middle of the night, a mystic light beam comes from across the river, bounces through the *kâew* (crystal) and alights atop Sri Lingaparvata, the holy mountain above Wat Phu Champasak.

It's easy enough to reach Wat Muang Kang by bike – head out of town on the riverside road, turn hard left after about 2km when the road takes a big bend to the right, then hug the dirt trail along the Mekong for another 3km or so.

Champasak Spa SPA
(020-5649 9739; www.champasak-spa.com; 10am-noon & 1-7pm) Just when you thought you couldn't get any more relaxed, Champa-

CHAMPASAK IN ANTIQUITY

Under the palm trees and rice paddies 4km south of Champasak town is the remains of a city that was, about 1500 years ago, the capital of the Mon-Khmer Chenla kingdom. The site is known today as Muang Kao (Old City), but scholars believe it was called Shrestapura.

Aerial photographs show the remains of a rectangular city measuring 2.3km by 1.8km, surrounded by double earthen walls on three sides and protected on the east by the Mekong River. Other traces of the old city include small *baray* (a Khmer word meaning 'pond', usually used for ritual purposes), the foundations for circular brick monuments, evidence of an advanced system of irrigation, various Hindu statuary and stone carvings, stone implements and ceramics. The sum of all this is an extremely rare example of an ancient urban settlement in Southeast Asia, one whose design reveals how important religious belief was in the workings of everyday life.

The origin of the city remained a mystery until Southeast Asia's oldest Sanskrit inscription was discovered here. The 5th-century stele stated the city was founded by King Devanika and was called Kuruksetra and also mentions the auspicious Sri Lingaparvata nearby, a clear reference to the mountain near Wat Phu Champasak. 'Honoured since antiquity', the mountain was believed to be the residence or the manifestation of the Hindu god Shiva, and even today local people honour the mountain as the place of Phi Intha (the soul or protecting spirit of the mountain).

By the end of the 5th century the city was thriving. It continued as a major regional centre until at least the 7th century, as showed by two Nandi (Shiva's bull mount) pedestal sculptures discovered in 1994–95 bearing inscriptions by King Citrasena-Mahendravarman, the 'conqueror' who later shifted the kingdom's capital to Sambor Prei Kuk in central Cambodia. Archaeological material suggests the city was inhabited until the 16th century.

Ongoing research by Dr Patrizia Zolese and her team has revealed that a second city was built near Wat Phu after the 9th century. She believes the Ho Nang Sida was at the centre of this city, which was probably Lingapura, a place mentioned in many ancient inscriptions but which has not been categorically identified by modern scholars.

sak Spa offers a perfect sensual antidote to tired muscles in its fragrant oasis overlooking the Mekong River. Treatments include a foot massage (55,000K), traditional Lao body massage (70,000K) and a herbal massage (95,000K), all of which use organic bio products. It's also a good cause as it creates local jobs to allow women to stay in Champasak rather than migrate to the city.

Sleeping

Finding a room in Champasak is straightforward enough except during the Wat Phu Champasak Festival (Magha Puja; usually in February), when you can sleep on the grounds of Wat Phu Champasak. If you do this, ask at one of the food tents for a safe spot. Accommodation, ranging from the basic (homestay) to the luxurious, is also available on nearby Don Daeng.

Anouxa Guesthouse GUESTHOUSE $
(☎031-511006; r with fan 60,000K, with air-con 100,000-200,000K; ❄📶) The pricier air-con rooms here face the river and have balconies to take advantage of those views. Pleasant peach and lime interiors, clean bathrooms and decent linens, along with a tempting riverside restaurant, make it worth the slight splurge. Just don't expect much in the service department.

Vong Paseud Guesthouse GUESTHOUSE $
(☎031-920038; r with fan 30,000-50,000K, with air-con 100,000K; ❄📶) Despite extremely basic rooms, this has long been a popular choice with backpackers thanks to the English- and French-speaking owners and an attractively located riverside restaurant. Excursions booked here cost a bit less than elsewhere.

Saythong Guesthouse & Restaurant GUESTHOUSE $
(☎020-2220 6215; r with fan/air-con 50,000/80,000K; ❄) One of the first guesthouses in town, this place was undergoing renovations when we dropped by, so expect nicer rooms at slightly higher prices. The restaurant occupies a pleasant perch over the Mekong.

Khamphouy Guesthouse GUESTHOUSE $
(☎031-511010; r 30,000-40,000K) The rooms here, while simple, are a step up from the more popular Vong Paseud. Beds and pillows are rock hard, however, and the managers' English is limited, plus it lacks a riverfront location.

Siamephone Hotel HOTEL $
(☎020-5543 1175; r 110,000K; ❄) A step up in comfort and cleanliness from the other budget guesthouses in town, but a step down in atmosphere and service. It is probably Champasak's biggest hotel, in a gaudy concrete structure off the river.

Thavisab Guesthouse GUESTHOUSE $
(☎020-5535 4972; r without/with air-con 50,000/100,000K; ❄) Pleasant rooms with mint-coloured curtains and clean linen in an airy old house set back from the river.

Dokchampa Guesthouse and Restaurant GUESTHOUSE $
(☎020-5535 0910; r with fan/air-con 60,000/100,000K; ❄) Balconies and a well-placed restaurant over the river provide welcome respite from the uninspiring rooms here. The cheap fan rooms at the back are sweltering tinderboxes; upgrade to an air-conditioned room if you can.

★**Inthira Hotel** BOUTIQUE HOTEL $$
(☎031-511011; www.inthira.com; s/d incl breakfast from US$44/49; ❄📶) The belle of the river, Inthira's sumptuous rooms and low-lit Asian fusion restaurant (mains 35,000K) give us yet another reason to stay another day in Champasak. Based in an old Chinese shophouse and in a new complex over the road (facing the river), rooms boast brick floors, high ceilings, ambient lighting, flat-screen TVs, rain showerheads and terrazzo baths. Most rooms are twin setups so get in early if you want a big bed.

River Resort BOUTIQUE HOTEL $$$
(☎020-5685 0198; www.theriverresortlaos.com; garden/riverview villa US$119/139; ❄📶🏊) The 10 duplex villas – seven riverfront and three set back around a garden and pond – are outfitted with gargantuan beds, indigenous wall hangings and runners, sumptuous open-plan bathrooms with dark-wood sinks, and well-furnished balconies that really do justice to the five-star views. They have an infinity pool and a beautiful restaurant, and run upscale excursions by boat and other means. It's 3km north of Champasak but feels miles away from anything.

Eating

Guesthouses tend to have the best food.

Champasak With Love FUSION $
(mains 20,000-40,000K; ⏰8am-10pm) This Thai-owned eatery has a marvellous riverfront

WORTH A TRIP

DON DAENG

Stretched out like an old croc sunning itself in the middle of the Mekong, Don Daeng (ດອນແດງ) is a little like an island that time forgot. It's classic middle Mekong, with eight villages scattered around its edge and rice fields in the middle. The small and mostly shaded track that runs around the edge of the 8km-long island is mercifully free of cars – bicycles, slow-moving motorbikes and the odd *dok dok* (mini tractor) are all the transport that's required. There are plenty of beaches for swimming but remember, this is not Don Det – women are asked to wear sarongs when they bathe, not bikinis.

You can stay in a basic **community guesthouse** (☎020 5527 5277; dm 40,000K) at the northern tip of the island – ask for Mr Khan, who can also arrange homestays (per person 30,000-40,000K). Meals cost 20,000K per person at either.

In a rather different class is **La Folie Lodge** (☎030-534 7603; www.lafolie-laos.com; d incl breakfast low season US$60-90, high season US$110-186;), set on the riverbank facing Wat Phu. Rooms are housed in gorgeous wooden bungalows with lots of attention to detail, including Lao textiles, colonial motifs and polished wood floors. The resort includes an inviting pool with views across to Phu Pasak. The atmospheric poolside restaurant includes a wide selection of Lao and international dishes. La Folie is supporting several community projects on Don Daeng, including renovation of the village hospital.

To get to Don Daeng from Champasak, hire a boat (60,000K to 80,000K return) through your guesthouse or the visitor information centre. From Ban Muang, a boat costs about 40,000/60,000K one-way/return with a certain amount of negotiation. Bring a bicycle from Champasak to explore Don Daeng as it can be hard to find one on the island.

patio made of solid wood – one of the few perches in town that you can be sure won't blow away in the next storm. The food tends toward continental and Thai. Bicycle rental is available and they may soon open a guesthouse.

Frice and Lujane Restaurant ITALIAN $
(mains 40,000-60,000K; 5-9pm) The Italian founder has gone but his legacy, in the form of cuisine inspired by Italy's Friulian alpine region, lives on at this atmospheric restaurant based in a renovated villa. Gnocchi, marinated pork ribs, goulash and homemade sausage grace the menu.

Information

Champasak District Visitor Information Centre (☎020-9920 6710; 8am-4.30pm Mon-Fri) Can arrange boats to Don Daeng and a homestay or a bed in the guesthouse there. Local guides, some of whom speak English, lead day walks around Wat Phu and to Uo Moung. You can also arrange boats to Uo Moung here (450,000K), taking in Don Daeng and Wat Muang Kang.

Internet Cafe (per min 200K; 7am-6pm) About 150m south of the Inthira Hotel.

Lao Development Bank (8.30am-3.30pm Mon-Fri) Has a Visa-only ATM and changes cash and travellers cheques

Getting There & Away

Champasak is 28km from Pakse along a beautiful, almost empty sealed road running along the west bank of the Mekong. All *sŏrngtăaou* along this route to Pakse depart in the early morning, before 8am. There are also tourist buses and boats to/from Pakse.

To/from Pakse you can also travel via Ban Muang on the eastern bank of the Mekong. A small ferry (5000K per person, 20,000K for motorbikes) connects Ban Muang with a boat landing 1.8km north of Champasak in the village of Ban Phaphin. *Sŏrngtăaou* from Ban Muang service Pakse's southern bus terminal until 10am or so.

Going south, guesthouses in Champasak can call ahead to arrange for southbound tourist buses to pick you up at Ban Lak 30 (Km 30), 5km east of Ban Muang on Rte 13. Or just go out to Ban Lak 30 and hail anything going past.

Getting Around

Bicycles (10,000K to 15,000K per day) and motorbikes (80,000K per day) can be rented at the Vong Paseud (p225) and Khamphouy (p225) guesthouses, among others.

AROUND CHAMPASAK

Wat Phu Champasak ວັດພູຈຳປາສັກ

The ancient Khmer religious complex of Wat Phu is one of the highlights of any trip to Laos. Stretching 1400m up to the slopes of Phu Pasak (also known more colloquially as Phu Khuai or Mt Penis), Wat Phu is small compared with the monumental Angkor-era sites near Siem Reap in Cambodia. However, you know the old adage about 'location, location, location' and the tumbledown pavilions, ornate Shiva-lingam sanctuary, enigmatic crocodile stone and tall trees that shroud much of the site in soothing shade add up to give Wat Phu an almost mystical atmosphere. These, and a layout that is unique in Khmer architecture, led to Unesco declaring the Wat Phu complex a World Heritage Site in 2001.

Sanskrit inscriptions and Chinese sources confirm the site has been a place of worship since the mid 5th century. The temple complex was designed as a worldly imitation of heaven and fitted into a larger plan that evolved to include a network of roads, cities, settlement and other temples. What you see today is the product of centuries of building, rebuilding, alteration and addition, with the most recent structures dating from the late-Angkorian period.

At its height, the temple and nearby city formed the most important economic and political centre in the region. But despite its historic importance, the 84-hectare site remains in considerable danger from the elements. Detailed studies reveal that water erosion is pressuring the site and without a systematic water-management plan the buildings will

Around Champasak

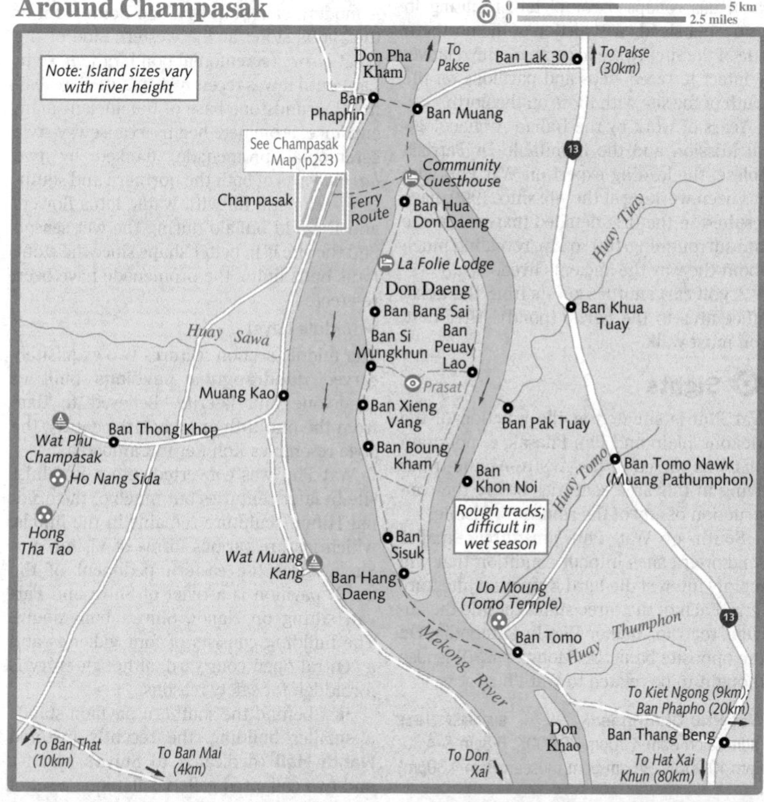

Wat Phu Champasak

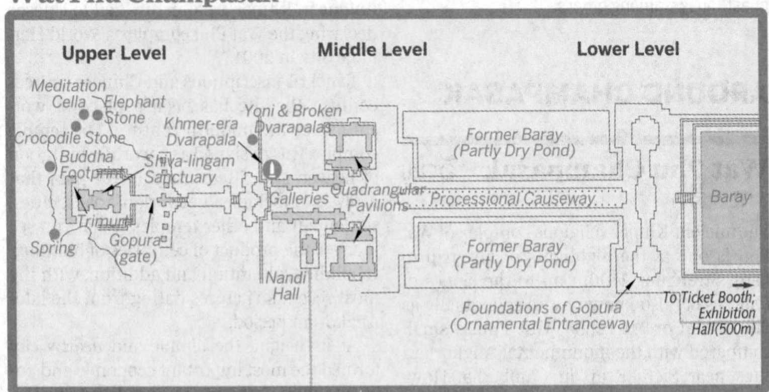

eventually collapse. Italian- and Japanese-funded projects have helped stabilise the southern of two ancient canals built to channel water away from the central structures. However, the equally important northern canal has collapsed completely, resulting in a slow but steady destruction of the northern side of the site. To see it, compare the relatively intact terraced steps and pavilions on the south of the site with those on the north.

Years of work by the Italian Archaeological Mission and the inimitable Dr Patrizia Zolese, the leading expert on Wat Phu who has been working at the site since 1990, have resulted in the first detailed map of the site and surrounding 400 sq km, revealing much about the way the ancients lived.

A golf cart shuttles guests from the ticket office area to the *baray* (pond). After that, you must walk.

Sights

Wat Phu is situated at the junction of the Mekong plain and Phu Phasak, a mountain that was sacred to the Austro-Asiatic tribes living in this area centuries before the construction of any of the ruins now visible.

South of Wat Phu are three smaller Angkor-era sites in poor condition that will mainly interest die-hard Khmer architecture fans. Each of the three stands beside the ancient road to Angkor Wat in Cambodia. On the opposite bank, Uo Moung (p230) is also thought to be related to Wat Phu.

Wat Phu Champasak BUDDHIST TEMPLE
(admission 8am-4.30pm 30,000K, 6-8am & 4.30-6pm 40,000K; 6am-6pm, museum 8am-4.30pm)

The archaeological site itself is divided into six terraces on three main levels joined by a long, stepped promenade flanked by statues of lions and naga.

Lower Level

A modern sala built by Chao Boun Oum in the 1960s stood at the western side of the great *baray* (ceremonial pond; *nǎwng sá* in Lao) until it was recently dismantled, revealing the sandstone base of the ancient main entrance. From here begins a causeway-style ceremonial promenade, flanked by two *baray*. Parts of both the northern and southern *baray* still fill with water, lotus flowers and the odd buffalo during the wet season and the site is in better shape since the stone lotus buds lining the promenade have been re-erected.

Middle Level

The middle section features two exquisitely carved **quadrangular pavilions** built of sandstone and laterite. Believed to date from the mid-10th or early 11th century, the style resembles Koh Ker in Cambodia.

Wat Phu was converted into a Buddhist site in later centuries but much of the original Hindu sculpture remains in the lintels, which feature various forms of Vishnu and Shiva. Over the eastern pediment of the north pavilion is a relief of Shiva and Parvati sitting on Nandi, Shiva's bull mount. The building consists of four galleries and a central open courtyard, although entry is forbidden for safety reasons.

Just behind the southern pavilion stands a smaller building, the recently restored **Nandi Hall** (dedicated to Shiva's mount), and two collapsed galleries flanking a set of laterite steps leading to the next level. From the Nandi Hall an ancient royal road once led south for about 1.3km to Ho Nang Sida, and eventually to Angkor Wat in Cambodia.

At the base of a small stairway leading onward towards the upper level, an impressive **dvarapala** (sentinel figure) stands ramrod straight with sword held at the ready near what was once a *gopura* (ornate entranceway). He was decked out in an orange monk's robe and holding a red umbrella when we visited. If you step down off the walkway and onto the grassy area just north of here you'll come to the remains of a **yoni pedestal**, the cosmic vagina-womb symbol associated with Shaivism. Very near the yoni lie two unusually large, headless and armless **dvarapala statues** half-buried in the grass. These are the largest dvarapala found anywhere in the former Angkorian kingdom.

From the small stairway, a sandstone path ascends to a small terrace where you'll see six ruined brick shrines – only their bases remain. From here a steep naga stairway leads onwards to the upper level and probably dates from the 11th century. It is lined with *dàwk jąmpąa* (plumeria or frangipani), the Lao national tree.

➡ Upper Level

On the uppermost level is the sanctuary itself, which once enclosed a Shiva lingam that was bathed – via a system of sandstone pipes – with waters from the sacred spring that still flows above and behind the complex. The sanctuary now contains a set of unsophisticated-looking Buddha images on an altar. The brick rear section, which might have been built in the 9th century, is a *cella* (cell), where the holy linga was kept.

Sculpted into a large boulder behind the sanctuary is a Khmer-style **Trimurti**, the Hindu holy trinity of Shiva, Vishnu and Brahma. Further back, beyond some terracing, is the cave from which the holy spring flowed into the sanctuary.

Just north of the Shiva linga sanctuary, amid a minefield of rocks and rubble, look around for the **elephant stone** and the hard-to-find **crocodile stone**. Crocodiles were semidivine figures in Khmer culture, but despite much speculation that the stone was used for human sacrifices its function, if there was one, remains unknown. The crocodile is believed to date from the Angkor period, while the elephant is thought to date from the 16th century. Also look out for the remains of stone **meditation cella** and an interesting chunk of a staircase framed by two snakes.

When you've seen everything here, just sitting and soaking up the wide-angle view of the *baray*, the plains and the Mekong is fantastic, especially early in the morning before the crowds arrive.

➡ Exhibition Hall

(admission with Wat Phu ticket; ⌚8am-4.30pm) The Exhibition Hall beside the ticket office showcases dozens of lintels, *naga* (mythical water serpents), Buddhas and other stone work from Wat Phu and its associated sites. Descriptions are in English, plus the building includes clean bathrooms.

Ho Nang Sida BUDDHIST TEMPLE

An easy 1.3km walk to the south of Wat Phu – stick to the trail heading south from the terraced promenade because there may be some UXO (unexploded ordnance) in the area – stands Ho Nang Sida, which probably dates from the early 10th century and might have been the central shrine for a second ancient city.

Hong Tha Tao BUDDHIST TEMPLE

(Lord Turtle Room) Another rubble pile around 2.3km south of Wat Phu.

Prasat BUDDHIST TEMPLE

(ພາສາດ) Close to the village of Ban That south of Wat Phu stand three Khmer *prasat* (square-based brick stupas) reminiscent of similar tripartite monuments in Thailand's Lopburi. No doubt symbolic of the Hindu Trimurti of Shiva, Brahma and Vishnu, the towers are believed to date from the 11th century. Drive here yourself or hire a tuk-tuk.

Festivals

Bun Wat Phu Champasak BUDDHIST

(Wat Phu Champasak Festival) The highlight of the year in Champasak is this three-day festival, held as part of Magha Puja (Makha Busa) during the full moon of the third lunar month, usually in February. The central ceremonies performed are Buddhist, culminating on the full-moon day with an early-morning parade of monks receiving alms from the faithful, followed that evening by a candlelit *wéean téean* (circumambulation) of the lower shrines.

Throughout the three days of the festival Lao visitors climb around the hillside, stopping to pray and leave offerings of flowers and incense. The festival is more commercial than it once was, and for much of the time has an atmosphere somewhere between a kids' carnival and music festival. Events include Thai boxing matches, cockfights, comedy shows and plenty of music and dancing, as bands from as far away as Vientiane arrive. After dark the beer and *lòw-lów* (Lao whisky) flow freely and the atmosphere gets pretty rowdy.

Getting There & Away

Wat Phu Champasak is 46km from Pakse and 10km from Champasak. There might be a morning *sŏrngtăaou* from Champasak but don't count on it. Rent a bicycle or motorbike, or hire a tuk-tuk in Champasak (80,000K to 100,000K return).

Uo Moung (Tomo Temple) ອູໂມງ (ວັດໂຕະໂມະ)

The Khmer temple ruin of **Uo Moung** (Tomo Temple; admission 10,000K; ⏲7.30am-4.30pm) is believed to have been built late in the 9th century during the reign of the Khmer King Yasovarman I. It's about 45km south of Pakse off Rte 13, in a wonderfully shaded forest beside a small tributary of the Mekong. The exact function of the temple is unknown, though its orientation towards the holy mountain Phu Pasak suggests its location was somehow related to Wat Phu.

The ruins include an entranceway bordered by distance markers (often mistaken for lingas) and two crumbling *gopura* (ornate entranceways). The more intact of the *gopura* contains an unusual lingam-style stone post on which two faces have been carved. It's unusual because *mukhalinga* usually have four *mukha* (faces), while most ordinary linga have no face at all. Several sandstone lintels are displayed on rocks beneath towering dipterocarp trees, but the best examples of lintels from this site are in the Champasak Historical Heritage Museum in Pakse. The white building at the heart of the site houses a bronze Sukhothai-style Buddha.

Getting There & Away

To get to Uo Moung on your own, turn west off Rte 13 around Km 42 and continue 5km along a sealed road. Southbound *sŏrngtăaou* from Pakse can drop you at the turn-off, where *săhm-lór* and tuk-tuks wait, but then you face a problem getting back to Pakse. A more sensible plan is to continue on to Champasak by boat, which can be hired in the village of Ban Tomo (the riverbank village about 400m south of the ruins).

You can also visit Uo Moung by boat from Don Daeng or Champasak on the opposite bank of the Mekong. From Champasak, you are looking at about 300,000K return to charter a boat, including waiting time of an hour or so. It's a bit cheaper from Don Daeng, especially if you ride a bicycle to Ban Sisouk at the south end of Don Daeng and take a boat from there (60,000K or so return).

Another excellent option is to rent a bicycle and take a boat first to Don Daeng, then to Uo Moung, then cross the river to Wat Muang Kang, and ride back to Champasak.

Kiet Ngong ບ້ານເຜົາໄພ

The Lao Loum villagers of Kiet Ngong, perched on the edge of Se Pian NPA (p232), have had a centuries-long relationship with elephants. The elephants have traditionally worked moving logs or doing heavy work in the rice fields. Typically each elephant has a different owner and in many cases the relationship between owner and pachyderm has existed for the majority of both lives. But as elephants are expensive to keep and machines now do much of their traditional work, the villagers have turned to tourism to help pay their way.

The result is southern Laos' most successful community-based ecotourism project. Started in the mid-2000s with help from the Asian Development Bank, Kiet Ngong is now functioning on its own. The community-run visitor information centre (p231) organises homestays, trekking, elephant rides, birdwatching and a host of other adventures.

Kiet Ngong sits at the edge of a bird-rich wetland about 10km from Rte 13. Free-ranging elephants and an unusally large herd of buffalo give the wetland a safari feel. It's best to sleep here for at least a night, but it also works as a day trip from Pakse or Champasak.

Visitors heading to Kiet Ngong must pay a 20,000K entry fee for Se Pian NPA.

Activities

Elephant riding is the big draw. Other activities include traditional-canoe rides (wet season only), guided full- and half-day nature walks, and birdwatching by foot or by canoe. Trekking opportunities abound in Se Pian NPA, and guided walks up Phu Asa are also possible. Activities are run out of the Visitor Centre or Kingfisher Eco-Lodge.

Elephant Riding

Almost everyone who comes to Kiet Ngong takes the elephant ride to the summit of a hill called **Phu Asa**, named for a group of 19th-century nationalists who fought against the Siamese. The flat-topped hill is topped by a crumbling and overgrown temple – a few slate-brick columns are about all that's left of it. At the far end a trail leads down to a Buddha footprint.

The site has a Stonehenge feel to it but, contrary to what the locals will tell you, the columns are probably not 1000 years old. From the top you can see across the wetlands and vast swaths of forest, though the 90-minute elephant trek (120,000K per elephant) follows a steep laterite road rather than a forest path.

Elephant rides through the wetlands are another option, and those with iron backsides might opt for a full-day elephant 'safari' (360,000K per elephant).

Kiet Ngong and the neighbouring Suay village of Ban Phapho, 10km to the east, are traditional breeding centres for working elephants. But lately the mahouts of Kiet Ngong and Ban Phapho have been reluctant to let their female elephants mate for fear they will wind up with broken hips (not uncommon, apparently). The owners just can't risk the loss of income.

Now, with support from international conservation groups, the elephants of Kiet Ngong are breeding once again. By the time you read this, the 13 elephants (11 female and 2 male) in Kiet Ngong will hopefully have expanded in number.

Sleeping & Eating

There are two choices in Kiet Ngong: stay at the upscale Kingfisher Eco-Lodge or arrange something through the visitor information centre. Meals are readily available from villagers or through the community guesthouse, and cost 20,000K per meal.

★**Kingfisher Eco-Lodge** LODGE **$$**
(☎020-5572 6315; www.kingfisherecolodge.com; eco/comfort r high season 250,000/720,000K, low season 190,000/600,000K; ⊙closed May-June; ❄@📶) Run by a Lao-Italian family, the Kingfisher Eco-Lodge is set on 7 hectares at the edge of the wetland, about 700m east of Kiet Ngong. It's a beautiful spot. Sitting on your balcony at dawn and watching a herd of buffalo splash their way across the wetland while mahouts ride their elephants towards work is a memorable experience.

The seven comfort rooms ooze Italian panache, with huge wooden countertops in the bathrooms, polished hardwood pillars and floors, lovely beds and – the *coup de grâce* – huge balconies with large rattan hammocks. The four economy (two twin and two queen) rooms have more modest balconies and share a spotless bathroom. Lights and hot water are solar-powered. The two-tiered restaurant and bar could easily be in an East African safari lodge.

Most activities offered by the visitor information centre are also offered here, and there's even a day-long course to learn how to become a mahout (570,000K to 680,000K per person). There are also full-day mountain-bike tours into Se Pian NPA. Kingfisher is extremely transparent about where the benefits of these activities go, including information on village income and lodge profits.

Visitor Information Centre GUESTHOUSE **$**
(per person 40,000K) The visitor information centre offers three types of accommodation. The simplest is a homestay (30,000K per night) with a local family. The second option is a community guesthouse (40,000K per night) about a 15-minute walk from the visitor information centre, with dorm-style sleeping in two big bungalows; the location overlooking the wetland is fantastic. The third option, which had yet to open at the time of research, are more upscale en suite bungalows closer to the village centre; expect these to cost about 80,000K to 100,000K.

Boun Home Guest House GUESTHOUSE **$**
(☎030 534 6293; per bed 30,000K) In Ban Phapho, this place has small, ultrasimple rooms in an authentic wooden house. The bathroom is shared and there's no hot water, but Mr Bounhome and his family are welcoming and speak some English and French. Order meals of *lâhp* (20,000K) and *kòw něeo* in advance. Mr Bounhome can also arrange elephant rides (120,000K) or take you to watch the elephants working (80,000K, in season).

Information

Visitor Information Centre (☎030-991 8155, 020-9699 9793; toui_ps@hotmail.com; ⊙7am-4pm) This community-run facility in the centre of Kiet Ngong can arrange everything you need, including elephant rides, accommodation, transport from Rte 13 and guides. Placards on the walls have useful information on activities, excursions, Se Pian NPA and the ecology and history of the area. Ask for Toui, an English-speaking guide who works at the centre.

Getting There & Away

Kiet Ngong is off the sometimes diabolical Rte 18A that runs east from Ban Thang Beng, 48km south of Pakse on Rte 13, to Attapeu. The turn-off for Kiet Ngong is 7.5km east of Ban Thang Beng along an unsealed road that is easily travelled on a small motorbike; the village is 1.8km south of the turn-off, and Kingfisher Eco-Lodge is another 700m or so along.

One or two *sŏrngtăaou* (30,000K, 1½ to 2½ hours) leave Kiet Ngong for Pakse at about 8am. There's an additional morning *sŏrngtăaou* that leaves Ban Phapho at 8am or 9am. These same *sŏrngtăaou* return from Pakse's southern bus terminal between 3pm and 4pm; Kiet Ngong is often misunderstood so ask instead for 'Phu Asa'. A private *sŏrngtăaou* from Pakse costs 300,000K to 400,000K depending on the number of passengers.

Alternatively, board anything going south on Rte 13, get off at Ban Thang Beng and call the visitor information centre for a pick-up by tuk-tuk (70,000K).

Se Pian NPA
ປ່າສະຫງວນແຫ່ງຊາດເຊປຽນ

Se Pian NPA (www.xepian.org) is one of the most important protected areas in Laos. The 2400 sq km park stretches from Rte 13 in the west into Attapeu Province in the east, and to the Cambodian border in the south. It is fed by three major rivers, the Se Pian, Se Khampho and Se Kong. It boasts small populations of Asiatic black bears, yellow-cheeked crested gibbons and Siamese crocodiles, and is home to many birds, including the rare sarus crane, vultures and hornbills. Banteng, Asian elephants, gaur and tiger once roamed here, but sightings of these creatures have been rare to nonexistent in recent years.

You can get into the park and visit ethnic-minority villages on two- to three-day treks offered by the visitor information centre (p231) in Kiet Ngong and the provincial tourism office (p220) in Pakse. Kingfisher Eco-Lodge in Kiet Ngong also has mountain-bike tours that take you through some villages. Green Discovery (p215) in Pakse has a two-day/one-night camping trip in the park. As of this writing the legendary trek to the Lavae (Brau) village of Ta Ong had been suspended.

Se Pian can also be accessed from Attapeu. Extremely rough Rte 18A between Kiet Ngong and Attapeu has been known to test the most seasoned trail bikers. Don't attempt this on your own without a good bike and plenty of experience. There are several river crossings that require ferry transport most of the year, and the rough road forks frequently.

If you're feeling frisky and adventurous, you can charter a boat down the Sekong from Sanamsay, on Rte 18A about 35km west of Attapeu. This trip toward the Cambodian border gets you deep into a scenic section of Se Pian NPA.

BOLAVEN PLATEAU

Spreading across the northeast of Champasak Province into the southeastern Salavan, Sekong and Attapeu provinces, the fertile Bolaven Plateau (ພູພຽງບໍລະເວນ; known in Lao as Phu Phieng Bolaven) is famous for its cool climate, dramatic waterfalls, fertile soil and high-grade coffee plantations.

The area wasn't farmed intensively until the French started planting coffee, rubber trees and bananas in the early 20th century. Many of the French planters left following independence in the 1950s and the rest followed as US bombardment became unbearable in the late '60s. Controlling the Bolaven Plateau was considered strategically vital to both the Americans and North Vietnamese, as evidenced by the staggering amount of UXO (unexploded ordnance) still lying around.

The slow process of clearing UXO continues, but in areas where it has been cleared, both local farmers and larger organisations are busy cultivating coffee. Other local products include fruit, cardamom and rattan.

The largest ethnic group on the plateau is the Laven (Bolaven means 'home of the Laven'). Several other Mon-Khmer ethnic groups, including the Alak, Katu, Tahoy and Suay, also live on the plateau and its escarpment.

The Bolaven Plateau can be explored by motorbike on a day trip from Pakse, but we recommend taking a few extra days and tackling the 'Southern Swing' (p240).

Paksong & Around ປາກຊອງ

Paksong, Laos' coffee capital, may not be much to look at, most of it having been obliterated in a storm of bombs during the Second Indochina War, but it boasts a temperate climate thanks to its altitude of 1300m. It is an affordable Bolaven base from which to explore the plateau, has a mildly interesting market and is refreshingly cool.

Sights & Activities

Rafting and kayaking trips are possible on Huay Bang Lieng, the river that feeds Tat Fan, during the wet season from July to November. For details speak to Green Discovery (p215) in Pakse.

Numerous breathtaking cascades drop off the Bolaven Plateau within striking distance of Paksong, the most popular of which are Tat Fan and Tat Yuang. Coffee trees of varying sizes blanket the Bolaven Plateau and you can walk through them on the treks from Tat Fan.

Tat Fan WATERFALL
(ຕາດຟານ; Rte 16, Km 38; admission 5,000K) Tat Fan is one of the most spectacular waterfalls in Laos. The twin streams of the Huay Bang Lieng plunge out of dense forest and tumble down more than 120m. The viewing point is at Tad Fane Resort (p234), a jungle lodge that looks down onto the falls from the top of a cliff opposite. This resort and E-TU Resort both run guided treks to the top of the falls, usually in the morning; it takes a couple of hours to get there and back.

The turn-off to Tat Fan is clearly signposted 12km west of Paksong; from the turn-off it's about 800m to the waterfall on an unsealed road. Buses between Pakse and Paksong can drop you at the turn-off.

Tat Yuang WATERFALL
(ຕາດເຍືອງ; Rte 16, Km 40; admission 10,000K; ticket booth 8am-5pm, falls to 6.30pm) Tat Yuang is impressive, with its twin torrents falling about 40m and flowing into lush jungle. It's hugely popular with day-trippers from Pakse and Thailand who like to picnic at the top, so getting there early or lingering until dusk after the crowds have cleared out is a good idea. It's OK to swim at the bottom – women must wear a sarong.

Tat Yuang is well-marked off Rte 16, 10km west of Paksong and 2km east of Tat Fan.

Tat Tha Jet & Tat Kameud WATERFALLS
Those looking for a less touristy waterfall experience can head to Ban Nong Luang, 11km east of Paksong. From this village it's possible to take a local guide and walk to two fairly impressive waterfalls, the seven-tiered Tat Tha Jet and Tat Kameud.

To get to Ban Nong Luang, head east on Rte 16, then take the first right turn after Ban Won coffeeshop.

GAH-FÉH LÁO (LAO COFFEE)

The high, flat ground of the Bolaven Plateau is ideal for growing coffee and the region produces some of the best and most expensive beans on earth. Arabica, Arabica Typica and Robusta are grown, much of it around the 'coffee town' of Paksong.

The French introduced coffee to the Bolaven Plateau in the early 1900s and the Arabica Typica shipped home became known as the 'champagne of coffee'.

After the carpet bombing of the '60s and '70s, business began to pick up in the 1990s and was dominated by a few plantations and companies, the largest being Pakse-based Dao Heung. For the farmers, however, earning less than US$0.50 per kg wasn't really improving their living standards.

These businesses still dominate today but a fair-trade project aimed at empowering small-scale farmers is gathering steam. The **Jhai Coffee Farmer Cooperative** is a 500-member group formed in 2004 with help from the California-based Jhai Foundation and Thanksgiving Coffee in the US. Members come from 12 mainly Laven villages east of Paksong. Machinery has been bought, and cooperative farmers have been trained in modern cultivation methods to maximise the quality of the beans. And with Fairtrade certification the farmers are guaranteed much more money than what they made selling to larger wholesalers.

Those wanting to get close to the action can head to Phuoi, which has become the unofficial headquarters for Jhai co-op. Heading east on Rte 23, take the first right after Bon Won coffeeshop. Phuoi is 4km along.

Tat Etu WATERFALL
(Rt 16, Km 35; admission 7000K) Just below E-TU Resort (p234) 15km west of Paksong, Tat Etu is an easy-to-reach waterfall, although some Thai tour groups find this one too.

Dọng Hua Saọ NPA PARK
(ປ່າສະຫງວນແຫ່ງຊາດດົງຫົວສາວ) Surrounding Paksong and encompassing much of the Bolaven Plateau is the 1100-sq-km Dong Hua Sao NPA, home to large tracts of pristine jungle where you might spot monkeys, large butterflies and rare hornbills. Until recently, wild elephants roamed here but they are gone now according to environmental groups.

Adventure specialist Green Discovery (p215) has its zipline and base of operations in Dong Hua Sao NPA, about 15km south of Paksong. This is the best way to experience the park, but you must arrange these tours in advance at the Green Discovery office in Pakse (apparently you can't just rock up and give the zipline a shot).

The treks and tours run by the Tad Fane and E-TU resorts around Tat Fan also get you into the park.

Tours

Koffie's Tours COFFEE TOUR
(020-2276 0439; koffie@paksong.info; coffee plantation tour per person 50,000K, coffee-roasting workshop per person incl plantation tour 170,000K) For something different, Koffie, a Dutchman associated with Won Coffee (p234), organises coffee plantation tours and coffee-roasting workshops. Ask around for Koffie at Won Coffee or Tad Fane Resort.

Sleeping

There's little need for air-con up here, and indeed most resorts don't even offer it.

Savanna Guesthouse GUESTHOUSE $
(020-5579 0613; r 80,000-100,000K) A friendly spot near a pretty pond. Rooms are modern and bright, including spiffy bathrooms. It's northeast of Paksong's market; heading east on Rte 16, turn left at the Kolau Motorcycle shop and proceed for 900m.

E-TU Resort BOUTIQUE HOTEL $$
(020-2226 7222, 030-955 9144; www.waterfalletupaksong.com; Rte 16, Km 35; dm US$12, d incl breakfast US$30-40; wi-fi) Set on a former coffee and tea plantation 15km west of Paksong, the smart bungalows at this sprawling resort have polished wooden floors, striking Lao textiles, ultrasoft beds and – in the fancier rooms – large balconies within earshot of nearby Tat Etu. The cheaper doubles are twin format.

Sinouk Coffee Resort & Cafe BOUTIQUE HOTEL $$
(www.sinoukcoffeeresort.com; r/ste US$40/80; internet, wi-fi) Set beside a babbling brook on a working coffee plantation 30km west of Paksong on the road to Tha Taeng, this has a hill-station feel. Like its sister resort, Pakse's Residence Sisouk (p217), it's loaded with indigenous textiles, period furniture and framed old-world photos. Groups can rent out one or both of the two stunning chalets on premises. Worth stopping in for a meal if you're passing by.

Tad Fane Resort LODGE $$
(Rte 16, Km 38; r incl breakfast US$27-37; wi-fi) The great location of this jungle lodge overlooking Tat Fan is unfortunately not matched by great management. Hide in your no-frills duplex cottage and enjoy the nightly symphony of forest sounds. During the day crowds arrive to gawk at Tat Fane, so consider escaping on a trek.

Paksong Phuthavada Hotel HOTEL $$
(030-534 8081; r from 1000B; air-con) Visible from all over town, this eerily empty hotel sits atop a hillside overlooking Paksong. Sweep up the grand driveway and into a spacious and sparkling-clean room.

Eating & Drinking

Borlavein Restaurant LAOTIAN $
(020-5583 6326; mains 15,000-40,000K) Set in a thatched house with pretty flowers, this local restaurant specialises in peppery Lao noodle soups. It's at the north end of town on the right as you are heading out.

Won Coffee CAFE
(Rte 16; wi-fi) FREE This is the place to sample fresh coffee (10,000K a cuppa) and green tea fresh from the plateau, including civet-excreted kopi luwak (200,000K per 100g). It's also about the only spot in Paksong proper with wi-fi, and has information on treks in the area.

Information

Information is hard to come by in Paksong. Your best bet is to try the E-TU Resort, or to track down Koffie (p234) through Tad Fane Resort or Won Coffee. Koffie also runs the useful websites www.paksong.info and www.bolaven.com.

Getting There & Away

Buses and *sŏrngtăaou* between Paksong and Pakse's southern (8km) bus terminal leave frequently between about 8am and 4pm (15,000K, 90 minutes).

Tat Lo ຕາດເລາະ

☎034

Tat Lo (pronounced *đàht ló*) is experiencing growing popularity on the backpacker trail thanks to an attractive setting, cheap accommodation and plenty of diversions. Waterfalls are the town's *raison d'être* and they give it a serenity that sees many visitors stay longer than they planned. If you want to explore deeper into the Bolaven Plateau and the southeastern provinces, Tat Lo is by far the best base in the area. The real name of Tat Lo village is Ban Saen Vang, but everybody just calls it Tat Lo.

Sights

There are actually three waterfalls on this stretch of river.

Tat Hang WATERFALL

(ຕາດຮັງ) Tat Hang is the waterfall nearest to town. It can be seen from the bridge and some guesthouses. You can swim here – often along with hordes of locals. Note that during the dry season, dam authorities upstream release water in the evening, more than doubling the waterfall volume. Check out what time the release occurs so you're not standing at the top of the waterfall then – a potentially fatal error.

Tat Lo WATERFALL

(ຕາດເລາະ) Tat Lo, about 700m upriver, is a little bigger than Tat Hang but probably won't knock your socks off. To get there, keep to the path that runs along the west bank of the river from Saise Guest House.

Tat Soung WATERFALL

(ຕາດສູງ) Tat Soung is a 50m drop. Unfortunately a new dam has substantially reduced the flow of this once-spectacular waterfall. If you walk 300m or so upstream from the top of the falls you'll find a delightful swimming hole. You can walk to Tat Soung with a guide, or ride a motorbike or bicycle to the top of the falls – head east out of town, pass Tadlo Lodge and follow the signs. It's about 10km.

Activities

Trekking

For any treks around Tat Lo we advise hiring a guide from the **Tat Lo Guides Association**, operated out of the Tat Lo Tourism Information Centre (p237). This will both enrich your walking experience and prevent you from getting lost.

Most popular are the half- and full-day treks to Tat Soung, taking in Katu, Tahoy and/or Suay minority villages along the way. The half-day trek costs a flat 80,000K per person. Costs for the full-day trek depend on the size of your group.

For something more adventurous, consider the two-day excursion offered by the tourism centre to **Phou Tak Khao Mountain**, with an overnight in an ethnic Suay village. This costs US$60/35 for a group of two/four people.

Elephant Rides

Tadlo Lodge (p237) offers rides on its two female elephants (100,000K per person, 60 minutes). The typical ride plods through

GETTING DOWN WITH THE MINORITIES

Most tour companies in Pakse and Tat Lo include visits to ethnic minority villages in their standard day tours to Tat Lo and around the Bolaven Plateau. Unfortunately, these tours are adversely affecting the most frequently visited villages where, not surprisingly, traditions are being eroded and villagers are fed up with busloads of gawking tourists stopping to snap photos.

Most tour companies head to the same few villages along Rte 20 between Pakse and Tat Lo, and along the road that ascends from Ban Beng to Tha Taeng. Do some due diligence to make sure your tour isn't heading to one of these. If it is, consider skipping the minority component.

Any village near a major road should also be avoided. The more remote the village, the more sustainable and authentic the experience will be. Good places to look are up rough roads like Rte 18A and Rte 23.

The usual rules for visiting ethnic minorities apply (p96).

forest, villages and streams full of slippery rocks you wouldn't dream of crossing on foot. Rides depart from the Tadlo Lodge at set times throughout the day.

Sleeping & Eating

The village is a one-street affair, with most accommodation east of the bridge near the tourist office. If calling ahead, ask your guesthouse about free transfers from the highway (Rte 20).

★Saise Guest House & Restaurant LODGE $
(☎034-211886; r with fan/air-con from 60,000/180,000K, mains 40,000K-60,000K; wi-fi) In lush gardens on the west bank of the river, this place sprawls from Tat Hang to Tat Lo. Rooms range from cheap fan-cooled rooms in the main complex to sophisticated air-conditioned bungalows in an annexe upstream. The restaurant is Tat Lo's best, and includes stir-fries, salads and various fish incarnations. Wi-fi is in the restaurant only.

★Fandee GUESTHOUSE $
(r 50,000-60,000K; wi-fi) Fandee means 'happy' in Lao, and that aptly describes the friendly French hosts here. The four raised wood bungalows are sturdy and more comfortable and airy than anything else in this price range, and feature thatched roofs, private porches and pebble-floor, cold-water bathrooms. A communal vibe reigns in the restaurant, and on Sundays they do picnic excursions to Tat Soung. It's opposite the tourist office.

Palamei Guesthouse GUESTHOUSE $
(☎030-962 0192; r without/with bathroom from 40,000/60,000K; wi-fi) Overlooking a pretty meadow out back, the better rooms have mosquito nets, terraces with tables and, in some cases, fridges and little lean-to kitchens. The owner, Poh, is an excellent cook so it's well worth dropping in for a meal.

Sabai Sabai GUESTHOUSE $
(☎030-962 0200; r 30,000-35,000K) It's billed as a 'homestay' – because all rooms are under one roof we suppose – but it's essentially a guesthouse. The five rooms have mozzie nets, concrete floors and bamboo slats for windows. It's worth paying 5000K extra for the bigger rooms. Motorbikes for rent and crafts for sale. A great deal.

Mama Pap Guesthouse GUESTHOUSE $
(dm 7500-15,000K) It doesn't get cheaper or more basic than this popular backpacker crash pad. Think mattresses with mozzie nets on a floor in a big room. Put two in a bed and pay just 7500K per person. Mama Pap promises 'big food for small kip' at her roadside restaurant.

Tim Guesthouse & Restaurant GUESTHOUSE $
(☎034-211885; soulideth@gmail.com; r 40,000-60,000K; @wi-fi) Tim's has seven red-stained wood bungalows – all of which share a clean bathroom. They are ship-shape but basic, with lumpy mattresses. The cafe is posh by comparison. Wi-fi costs 30,000K per hour.

Siphaseth Guesthouse GUESTHOUSE $
(☎020-9539 1126; r 40,000-70,000K) The location, on the river at the eastern terminus

THE KATU & ALAK BUFFALO SACRIFICE

The Katu and Alak around Tat Lo are well known for an annual water buffalo sacrifice (usually performed on a full moon in March) in homage to the village spirit. The number of buffaloes sacrificed – typically from one to four animals – depends on their availability and the bounty of the previous year's agricultural harvest. During the ceremony, the men of the village don wooden masks, hoist spears and wooden shields, then dance around the buffaloes in the centre of the circle formed by their houses. After a prescribed period of dancing the men converge on the buffaloes and spear them to death. The meat is divided among the villagers and each household places a piece in a basket on a pole in front of their house as a spirit offering.

Other traditions of the Katu and Alak, sometimes shared with the Laven, include face tattoos for women (a custom that is slowly dying out), and arranging their palm-and-thatch houses in a circle. A unique Katu custom is the carving of wooden caskets for each member of the household well in advance of an expected death. The coffins are stored beneath homes or rice sheds until needed – they can occasionally be spotted as your ride around.

of the bridge, is great. The rooms? Not so much. They have hot water but are showing their wear. The simple restaurant (mains 5000K to 25,000K), with stools overlooking the river, is the ideal place for a sundowner Beerlao.

Mr Vieng Organic Homestay HOMESTAY $
(020-9983 7206; per person 20,000K, per meal 15,000K) This is a friendly homestay on a coffee plantation on Rte 20, about 23km west of Tat Lo and 10km west of the village of Lao Ngam. The ethnic Katu couple who run it sell weavings and can organise little excursions in the area.

Tadlo Lodge LODGE $$
(034-211885; www.tadlolodge.com; s/d incl breakfast from US$41/47;) Situated above the falls with an Edenic view of the teal-green river, this is a slice of style just where you need it. The main building is finished in traditional Lao style, with parquet floors and Buddha statuary. Rooms are stylish, with some new bungalows set on the opposite (west) side of the river.

Drinking

Em's Coffee CAFE
(ema.g@gmx.at) Long-time Laos resident Em, an Austrian, slings heavenly organic coffee, sells Katu textiles and offers lessons in wok-roasting coffee beans. He's a pretty good source of info on both the area and the country. It's right next to the tourist centre.

Information

Internet access is available at Tim Guesthouse (p236) for 500K per minute. There are no ATMs in town so come with cash.

Tat Lo Tourism Information Centre (020-5445 5907, 034-211528; kouka222@hotmail.com; 8am-noon & 1-4.30pm) This helpful office runs the Tat Lo Guides Association. It should be your first stop if you need a guide or info on local excursions, or plan to venture deeper into Salavan Province and beyond. They can also help you with public transport options around the Bolaven Plateau and the south-eastern provinces. Maps and brochures on the region are available. Kouka speaks English and is worth contacting in advance to book an English-speaking and/or minority guide.

Getting There & Away

Tat Lo is 86km northeast of Pakse. Just say 'Tat Lo' at Pakse's southern bus terminal and you'll be pointed to one of the five daily buses to Salavan that stop on Rte 20 at Ban Khoua Set (25,000K, two hours), from where it's a 1.5km walk or tuk-tuk ride (10,000K) to Tat Lo.

If you're heading to Paksong, Sekong or Attapeu, you must change buses in Tha Taeng. To get to Tha Taeng, get yourself up to Ban Beng, 5.5km northwest of Ban Khoua Set, where two mid-morning buses from Salavan come through. Otherwise you'll have to negotiate a tuk-tuk or *săhm-lór* for the 21km climb from Ban Beng to Tha Taeng. Additionally, to Paksong there are sporadic direct *sŏrngtăaou* from Ban Beng and occasional minivans from the tourist office in Tat Lo (inquire there).

Salavan ສາລະວັນ

034 / POP 25,000

The capital of Salavan Province is notable more for its remoteness than any traditional tourism draws. Once a Champasak kingdom outpost known as Muang Mam and inhabited mostly by Mon-Khmer minorities, it was renamed Salavan (Sarawan in Thai) by the Siamese in 1828. It was all but destroyed in the Indochina War, when it bounced back and forth between Royal Lao Army and Pathet Lao occupation.

There's talk of a border crossing possibly opening in 2014 or 2015 north of Salavan near Samouy. Until that happens, Salavan is sort of stuck on a road to nowhere and there's not much reason to come here unless you want to explore remote minority villages in the surrounding countryside.

While more than half of the population of Salavan is ethnically Lao (Loum and Soung), none are native to this area. The remainder of the 350,000 inhabitants belong to relatively obscure Mon-Khmer groups, including the Tahoy, Lavai, Katang, Alak, Laven, Ngai, Tong, Pako, Kanay, Katu and Kado.

Just about every major branch of the Ho Chi Minh Trail cuts through Salavan Province at some point and UXO remains a serious problem, so exercise caution if you go out exploring the province on your own. Drop by **UXO Lao** (8am-5pm) on the main road into town to see some of the weapons that clearance teams have collected in the province.

The main attraction is **Nong Bua**, a lake known for its dwindling population of Siamese crocodiles (*khàe* in Lao). There aren't many left (two or three, apparently), and chances of actually seeing the crocs are slim. Instead, look out for 1588m-high Phu Katae nearby. The lake is 15km east of Salavan and can be reached by motorbike or bicycle; in the wet season this will require a couple of ferry crossings.

There are a few places to stay in town. Try the friendly and simple **Thipphaphone Guesthouse** (☎034-211063; r 40,000-70,000K; ❄) if you want cheap and central (it's near the market). If you want something fancier, **Phoufa Hotel** (☎030-537 0799; r 50,000-140,000K; ❄) is on the main road into town, about 3km west of the centre.

Information

The **Provincial Tourism Office**, on the main drag through town one block south of the market, is hit or miss if you plan on heading further into the province. The Tat Lo Tourism Information Centre (p237) is a much better bet for info on Salavan Province, and passes out a useful brochure that highlights the province's main attractions.

There's a BCEL ATM next to the market.

Getting There & Away

Salavan's bus terminal is 2km west of the town centre, where Rte 20 meets Rte 15. There are five daily buses to Pakse (25,000K, 3½ hours), with most continuing on to Savannakhet.

There is an 8.30am bus to Sekong (30,000K, 2½ hours, 94km) via Tha Taeng, a noon *sǒrngtǎaou* to Ta-oy (40,000K, three hours, 84km) and a 1pm bus to Samouy (80,000K, 5½ hours, 148km) via Ta-oy.

Around Salavan

Be careful, the area around Salavan is absolutely riddled with UXO. Stick to established tracks and trails.

Toumlan & Rte 23

About 50km north of Salavan along bumpy Rte 23 is the Katang village of Toumlan. The area is famous for its silk weavings and Lapup festival usually held in late February. The town is very poor but interesting both from a cultural point of view and because of its position on the Ho Chi Minh Trail.

The trip to Toumlan on bumpy Rte 23 takes you via the site of **Prince Souvanaphong's Bridge**, named because it was built by the 'Red Prince' Souphanouvong (who was a trained engineer) in 1942. Unfortunately the bridge was blown up in 1968 and has never been rebuilt.

You can get to Toumlan on your own by motorbike in the dry season (about two hours from Salavan, with at least one ferry crossing), but in the wet season you'll need a serious 4WD truck to ford several rivers en route. From Toumlan you can continue on to Muang Phin on Rte 9.

Ta-oy & the Ho Chi Minh Trail
ເສັ້ນທາງໂຮຈິມິນ

Northeast along Rte 15 is Ta-oy, a centre for the Tahoy ethnic group, who number around 30,000 spread across the eastern areas of Salavan and Sekong Provinces. The Tahoy live in forested mountain valleys at altitudes between 300m and 1000m, often in areas shared with Katu and other Mon-Khmer groups. Like many Mon-Khmer groups in southern Laos, they practise a combination of animism and shamanism; during village ceremonies, the Tahoy put up diamond-patterned bamboo totems to warn outsiders not to enter.

Ta-oy town was an important marker on the Ho Chi Minh Trail and two major branches lead off Rte 15 nearby. The unsealed road from Salavan to Ta-oy has been upgraded and is in decent shape now. You can get there in two hours by motorbike from Salavan, or take daily public transport bound to Ta-oy or Samouy. There are a few guesthouses in Ta-oy as well as places to eat and fuel up.

Sekong (Muang Lamam)
ເຊກອງ (ເມືອງລະມຳ)

☎038 / POP 15,000

Another sleepy backwater that draws few tourists, Sekong may become more relevant once a major new highway from Paksong to the Vietnamese border near Dak Cheung is completed in 2014 or 2015. The highway will shorten the route from Ubon Ratchathani, Thailand, to the Vietnamese port of Danang, as well as facilitate access to gold and other mines on the Dak Cheung Plateau, which rises 1500m above sea level east of Sekong. A new border crossing at Dak Cheung will also be part of the equation.

For now, tourists have little reason to stop in the capital of Sekong Province, unless you want to leave town to explore outlying waterfalls and minority villages. By population Sekong is the smallest of Laos' provinces, but among its 90,000 inhabitants are people from 14 different tribal groups, making it the most ethnically diverse province in the country. About 75% of the province's population are from Mon-Khmer tribes, with the Alak, Katu, Taliang, Yae and Nge the largest groups. Other groups include the Pacoh, Chatong, Suay (Souei), Katang and Tahoy.

These diverse groups are not Buddhists, so you won't see many wats. Rather, their belief systems mix animism and ancestor worship. The Katu and Taliang tend towards monogamy but, unusually in a part of the world so traditionally male dominated, tolerate polyandry (two or more husbands).

The **town market** is mildly interesting, and tribes from outlying areas sometimes arrive early in the morning to trade cloth for Vietnamese goods. War-junk fiends might drop by the **UXO Lao** (8am-5pm) office, behind the Ministry of Finance office, a half-block north of the market.

Sleeping & Eating

Pisaxay Guesthouse HOTEL $
(038-211271; Rte 16; r without/with air-con 60,000/100,000K;) Probably the best all-rounder of a mediocre lot. Simple fan rooms are in a row at the back, while the main building contains mint-green AC rooms – they are nothing special but have alright king-sized beds, ample furniture and high ceilings. It's on the left as you head out of town toward Attapeu.

Thida Hotel HOTEL $
(038-211063; Riverside; r 100,000K;) Located on the Se Kong 2km west of the centre (toward Attapeu), this Thai-run establishment has smallish rooms with sky-blue paint, sparkling white bathrooms and the best beds in Sekong. The riverside restaurant (mains 40,000K to 50,000K) is definitely the most salubrious dining venue in town and stays open until 10pm – much later than most.

Hong Kham Hotel HOTEL $
(038-211777; Rte 16; r 150,000K;) A big hotel on the main highway, the Hong Kham has over-elaborate rooms with a few mod-cons like satellite TV and fridges. The restaurant (mains 40,000K to 60,000K) serves Lao, Chinese and Vietnamese dishes.

Woman Fever Kosmet Centre Guesthouse GUESTHOUSE $
(020-5415 1610; r 40,000K) Next to the Sekong Hotel, this place is grubby but cheap. All rooms share bathrooms. We haven't heard of any guests catching woman fever; proceeds actually go to a malaria education group.

Khamting Restaurant LAOTIAN $
(mains 15,000-40,000K; 7am-8pm) This is one of the few places in the centre of town with both palatable cuisine and a menu in English. If you're hoping to sample flying lemur soup, grilled deer and roast pangolin, don't get your hopes up; while on the menu they are rarely in stock. You'll have better luck with the stir-fries, noodle soups and Thai dishes. It's opposite the Sekong Hotel.

Orientation

Sekong sits on a big westward bend in the Se Kong river, which means that – counterintuitively – you enter the city from the northeast if driving in from Tha Taeng on Rte 16.

The city is set on a basic grid with the main road running roughly east–west through the centre of town. The government buildings and the market are on this main road. The main highway (Rte 16) runs parallel to the north. Another parallel road follows the Se Kong to the south. The Sekong Hotel is on this river road; it isn't much of a hotel, but it's a useful landmark.

The new highway to Vietnam is being built on the opposite bank of the Se Kong river. There's no bridge for now, but you can traverse the river by ferry near the Thida Hotel and pick up the new highway on the other side.

Information

There's a BCEL ATM opposite the market on the main road.

Lao Development Bank (9.30am-4pm Mon-Fri) On the main drag one block west of the tourism office. Can change Thai baht and US dollars

Post Office (8am-noon & 1-5pm Mon-Fri) On the main drag, 200m west of Lao Development Bank.

Sekong Provincial Tourism Office (038-211361; 8am-noon &1-4.30pm Mon-Fri) The tourism office is 100m west of the market on the main drag. Don't expect too much here; they might be able to find you a guide.

Getting There & Away

Sekong's dusty/muddy bus station is on the northeast edge of town off Rte 16. Buses between Pakse and Attapeu pass through here (for now; this may change when the new Paksong–Attapeu Highway is completed). Services to Pakse pass through Paksong. There's a daily bus to Salavan (30,000K, 2½ hours, 94km).

Getting Around

Getting around is difficult without private transport. It's a BYOW (bring your own wheels) situation, as we found no motorbike or bicycle rental in Sekong. A few tuk-tuks hang out at the out-of-the-way bus station. Otherwise, navigate the town by foot.

Around Sekong

South of Sekong, Rte 16 morphs into Rte 11. There are several villages and waterfalls off Rte 11 that could be visited on a day trip or on your way to Attapeu. You can try to find a tuk-tuk or *săhm-lôr* at Sekong's bus station, but don't count on it. Having your own motorbike is infinitely easier, and allows for easy exploration of the dirt roads off Rte 11, many of which lead to Alak, Laven and other minority villages. The new highway to Dak Cheung is also ripe for exploration.

Sights

Tat Faek WATERFALL

(ຕາດແຟກ; admission 5000K) At Km 14.5 on Rte 11 to Attapeu you'll see a turn-off on the left to Tat Faek, a 5m-high waterfall with two pools in which you can swim. Swimmers should use the one above the falls, as a diabolical-sounding puffer fish known as the *pa pao* is believed to lurk in the pool below. Locals report with a sort of gleeful dread how the evil *pa pao* can home in on and sink its razor-sharp teeth into the human penis with uncanny precision. Admittedly, the women are more gleeful about this than the men. The falls are 2.4km from the Rte 11 turnoff. The pools fill up with locals on weekends and holidays.

Tat Hua Khon WATERFALL

(ຕາດຫົວຄົນ; admission 5000K) After about 17.5km along Rte 11, a long bridge crosses the Se Nam Noi and you enter Attapeu Province. Just over of the bridge, at Km 18, a track leads east to Tat Hua Khon. The name translates as 'waterfall of the heads', owing to a WWII episode in which Japanese soldiers decapitated a number of Lao soldiers and tossed their heads into the falls. The falls are about 100m wide and 7m deep.This is a busy place on holidays and weekends. There's a guesthouse here, but we found it empty and somewhat creepy.

Nam Tok Katamtok WATERFALL

(ນ້ຳຕົກກະຕຳຕົກ) Running off the Bolaven Plateau, the Huay Katam drops more than

Motorcycle Tour Southern Swing

START PAKSE
FINISH PAKSONG
LENGTH 430KM; FIVE DAYS

The Southern Swing is a motorbike or bicycle trip starting in Pakse and taking in the Bolaven Plateau and the southern provinces. By motorbike it can take anywhere from three days to as long as you like. The route we've laid out here takes five days but this is only a guide. Distances correspond to the red-and-white 'Km' ('*lák*' in Lao) markers that clearly line all highways. All of the main roads are sealed, and those that are not are in relatively good condition, meaning 110cc bikes are fine.

Head south out of 1 **Pakse** on Rte 13, keeping straight on Rte 16 at the 8km bus terminal. At Km 21, turn left (north) onto Rte 20 (Rte 16 continues straight to Paksong). At this point your GPS will still be working fine, but it's unlikely to last as 3G signals dim as you get further from Pakse.

After 13.5km on Rte 20, you'll see a turn-off to 2 **Utayan Bajiang Champasak** (Phasoume Resort), a Thai-owned ecoresort. The small Tat Pasuam waterfall here is pretty, but busloads of Thai tourists and a cheesy 'museum village' spoil the atmosphere. Still, it makes for an OK lunch stop if you're feeling peckish.

From here it's about 27km to 3 **Mr Vieng Organic Homestay** (p237) – stop in for a coffee at least – and about 50km to Tat Lo. You'll pass a few Katu villages along the way but these are nothing special; we recommend having your minority-village experience elsewhere, preferably well off a major highway. Textile lovers might stop off in the village of Ban Houay Houn, near Mr Vieng's Organic, which is known for its Katu weavers.

It's easy to spend a few nights in 4 **Tat Lo**. When you're ready to leave, head 5.5km up Rte 20 to Ban Beng, turn right, and ascend the Bolaven Plateau via the sealed road to Tha Taeng. Again you'll pass Katu and Alak villages along this route, but the ones along the road have been overrun and arguably spoiled by ogling tour groups visiting from Tat Lo and Pakse.

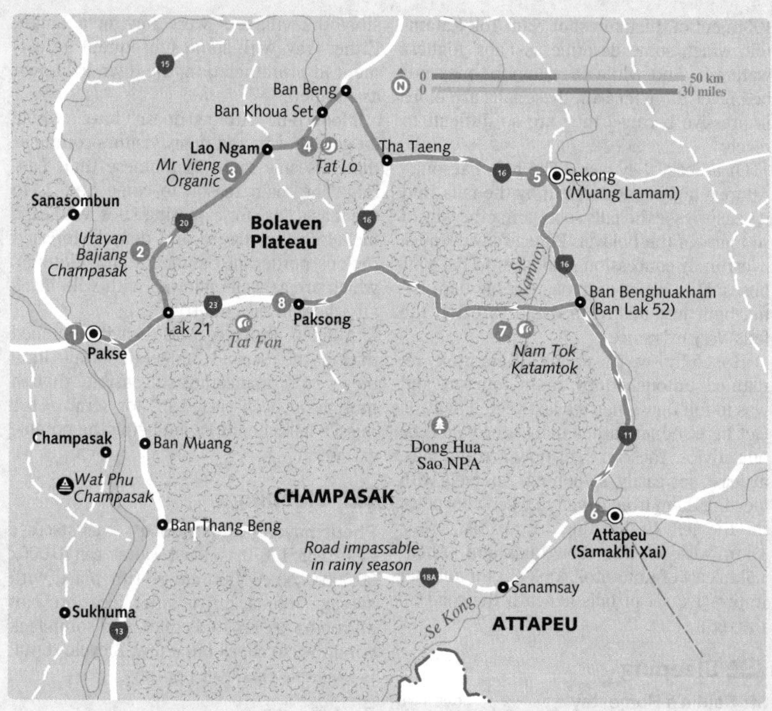

From Tha Taeng, the 'small loop' takes you south along Rte 16 to Paksong (37km) and back to Pakse. The 'big loop' continues due east on Rte 16. It's 47km to 5 **Sekong**, which can be a useful lunch or overnight stop.

The busy 76km road from Sekong to 6 **Attapeu** goes past a couple of smaller waterfalls, though there are plenty of those later on. You could easily spend a few days exploring Attapeu Province.

Next, head towards Paksong. Until recently, this stretch was a rugged ride with little or no traffic that passed isolated waterfalls, pristine jungle and little-visited Laven and other minority communities. Those are still there, but the rutted track has been converted into a four-lane highway. Oh, how the times have changed.

At the time of research, bits of this route were impassable because of construction, but it should be smooth sailing by the time you read this.

The turn-off for the new highway is on Rte 11 at the Km 52 mark (from Attapeu), in the village of Ban Benghuakham (better known simply as Ban Lak 52). From here Paksong is about 75km due west.

The main attraction along this route is the spectacular 7 **Nam Tok Katamtok** (p240). We'll see how it weathers the twin storms of a major highway and a dam being built just upstream.

Once you get to 8 **Paksong**, check out some of the waterfalls, take a trek from Tat Fan and drink some decent coffee. And that's it – you're pretty much back in Pakse.

100m out of thick forest at Nam Tok Katamtok, which some describe as Laos' highest waterfall. And while they may or may not be bigger than Tat Fan, these falls are more impressive because they are so difficult to reach.

Or at least they were. The new Paksong–Attapeu highway cuts right by the falls, and it's easy to see the falls soon going the way of so many of the Bolaven Plateau's waterfalls, overrun by concession stands and Thai tour buses. Even more ominously, a big dam being built just upstream could threaten the falls' very existence.

Hopefully we're wrong. Katamtok remained untouched by mass tourism and was in full flow when we last visited in 2013. Get here sooner rather than later would be our advice. You can't get down to the falls, at least not easily, so content yourself with viewing them from a well-marked viewpoint on the left (if heading toward Paksong), 17km west of Ban Benghuakham. About 1.5km east of Katamtok, look out for another impressive set of falls beneath the road on the right.

Sleeping

Mr Soulin's Homestay HOMESTAY **$**
(☎030-963 2758) This homestay gets rave reviews. Mr Soulin has a few bungalows for rent and can guide you to additional hidden falls in the area. Look for a small sign with waterfalls on it about 12km west of the Nam Tok Katamtok viewpoint.

Attapeu (Samakhi Xai) ອັດຕະປື

☎036 / POP 19,200

The capital of Attapeu Province, set where the mighty Se Kong and the smaller Se Kaman meet, is famed in southern Laos as the 'garden village' for its shady lanes and lush flora.

This reputation is remarkable given that Attapeu actually means 'buffalo shit' in Mon-Khmer dialects. Legend has it that when early Lao Loum people arrived they asked the locals what was the name of their town. In response, the villagers apparently pointed at a nearby pile of buffalo manure, known locally as *itkapu* (*ait krapeau* in contemporary Khmer). Perhaps there was some misunderstanding. Maybe the Lao Loum didn't like the place or possibly the villagers were having a laugh. Either way, with some subsequent adjustment in pronunciation, the town is known as Attapeu.

Modern-day Attapeu doesn't have a whole lot going for it, and many visitors comment that it seems more Vietnamese than Laotian. The main reason to come here is to use it as a base for exploring Laos' wild east, including the rugged and densely forested regions bordering Cambodia and Vietnam, which are as well-endowed with wildlife as anywhere in the country.

Attapeu Province was heavily bombed during the Second Indochina War. Rare pieces of ordnance are still visible, though most have been carted off for scrap – the missile launcher at Pa-am being the notable exception

Sleeping

Phoutthavong Guesthouse GUESTHOUSE **$**
(☎020-5551 7870; r without/with air-con 70,000/90,000K; ❄) A Vietnamese-run place with average rooms, but a quiet location. Not all rooms are created equal, and some lack windows, so check out a few. Bicycle rental is available (15,000K per day).

Souksomphone Guesthouse GUESTHOUSE **$**
(☎036-211046; d without/with air-con 60,000/80,000K; ❄) The place with the mother-of-all hardwood staircases protruding from the front. The fan rooms are small but cosy, if overpriced (they share bathrooms). The air-con twins are en suite and better value. The manager speaks some English.

Dúc Lôc Hotel HOTEL **$**
(☎020-9982 2334; Rte 18A; r 80,0000K; ❄📶) The main reasons to stay here are the wi-fi (rare for Attapeu) and the location, in the centre of things and above the Mai Linh buses to Vietnam. The wood-panelled rooms are functional and quite clean, if susceptible to street noise.

Hoang Anh Attapeu Hotel HOTEL **$$**
(☎036-210035; hoanganhattapeuhotel@gmail.com; s/d incl breakfast from 210,000/300,000K; ❄@📶) The erstwhile Attapeu Palace was rebuilt practically from scratch in advance of a regional economic conference in 2011. You'd be hard-pressed to find rooms this fancy anywhere for this price, although we wonder about construction quality. The service doesn't match up and the breakfast is down-

Attapeu (Samakhi Xai)

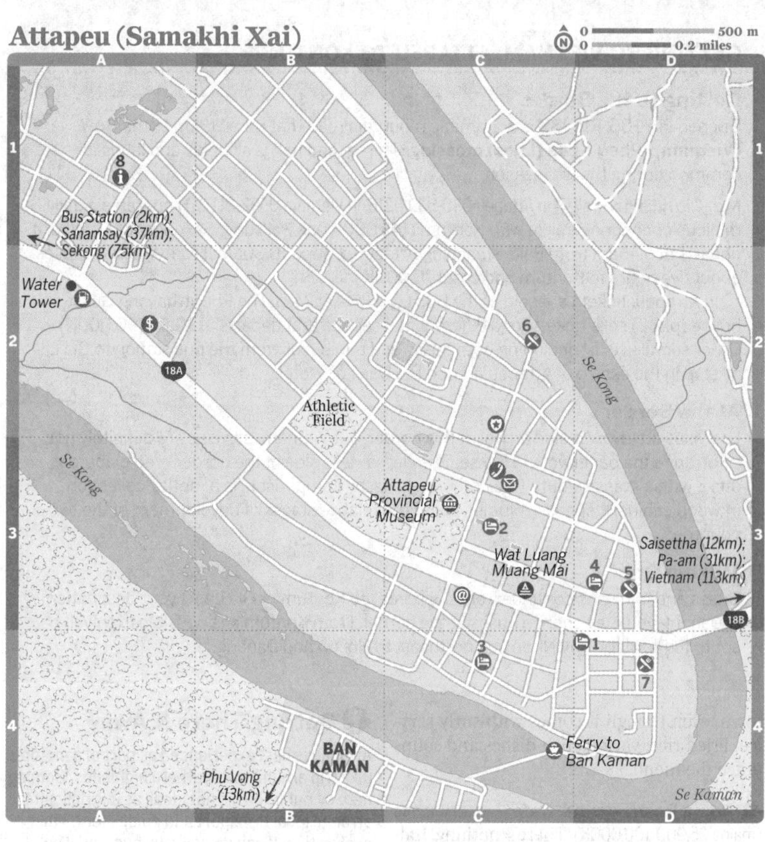

right paltry, but it's nonetheless a great deal for borderline four-star comfort. There's a tennis court but no gym or pool.

Eating

Attapeu is not a culinary destination by any means. Noodle dishes and *fěr* are available during the morning at **Talat Nyai** (Main Market), near the bridge, and other snacks can be had at any time.

The restaurants listed below are among the few in Attapeu with English menus.

Sabaydy Attapeu Restaurant LAOTIAN $
(mains 35,000-50,000K; ⏲8am-8.30pm) It's all about the setting here, in a rustic wooden house with a broad deck overlooking the Se Kong. The menu contains grilled and fried meats galore. We went with the 'fried fish coat flour', which came heaped with papaya salad – delicious combo.

Attapeu (Samakhi Xai)

Sleeping
1 Dúc Lôc Hotel D4
2 Hoang Anh Attapeu Hotel C3
3 Phoutthavong Guesthouse C4
4 Souksomphone Guesthouse D3

Eating
5 Roma Restaurant & Cafe D3
6 Sabaydy Attapeu Restaurant C2
7 Talat Nyai D4
Thi Thi Restaurant ..... (see 1)

Information
8 Attapeu Office of Tourism A1

Transport
Mai Linh Express ..... (see 1)

Thi Thi Restaurant VIETNAMESE $
(Rte 18A; mains 10,000-40,000K; ⏲7am-9pm) The Dúc Lôc Hotel's restaurant is considered some of the best Vietnamese food in

GETTING TO VIETNAM: ATTAPEU TO KONTUM

Getting to the Border

Opened in 2006, Rte 18B is a dramatic mountain road that runs 113km to the **Bo Y (Vietnam)/Phou Keua (Laos) crossing.** The second half is all uphill and landslides are common during the wet season.

Mai Linh Express (☎ in Attapeu 030-539 0216, in Vietnam 0592-211 211) operates a daily minibus connecting Pakse with Kontum (145,000K) via Paksong, Sekong and Attapeu. It departs at 5.45am from Pakse reaching Attapeu around 10.30am. From Attapeu it takes about five hours to Kontum and costs 70,000K.

In Attapeu, tickets are sold at the Dúc Lôc Hotel (p242). The Phoutthavong Guesthouse (p242) sells tickets for a different bus service that departs at 10am (90,000K). Other services exist, including both buses and minibuses from the bus station to Gia Lai; all stop in the centre of Attapeu around the Dúc Lôc Hotel.

At the Border

Lao visas are available on arrival at this border, but Vietnamese visas are definitely not, so arrange the paperwork in Pakse. The Vietnamese side of the border is an elaborate affair, with a massive duty-free complex. Laos, by comparison, is a motley collection of wood cabins. It speaks volumes about the relative stages of development of the two countries.

Moving On

Buses and minivans continue from the border to Kontum or Gia Lai; if your destination is Danang you may change buses at the border. From Kontum it is possible to travel south to Pleiku or Quy Nhon and northeast to Hoi An and Danang.

town, even though it comes with surly service. Fried rice, various fish dishes and soups grace the menu.

★ **Roma Restaurant & Cafe** VIETNAMESE $$
(mains 25,000-100,000K) There's nothing Italian about this place, but a garden dining area shaded by mango trees makes it easily the most pleasant place in the centre for a bite. The menu does not display prices, but if you avoid seafood your wallet should be OK. The adjoining coffeeshop looks Western at first blush (alas, not at second blush).

ℹ Information

Attapeu Office of Tourism (☎ 036-211056) English-speaking guides (200,000K per day) and transport (motorbike or 4WD) are available with some notice, but don't expect to just rock up. The office is 400m northeast of the prominent water tower on Rte 18A.

BCEL (Rte 18A; ⊙8.30am-3.30pm Mon-Fri) Changes US dollars, euros or Thai baht for kip. Also has an ATM.

Internet (Rte 18A; per hour 15,000K; ⊙7am-7pm)

Post Office (⊙8am-noon & 1-4pm Mon-Fri)

ℹ Getting There & Away

Attapeu is best experienced as part of a motorbike trip around the southern highlands. Coming here by public bus is not ideal, as it is difficult to arrange local transport and guides for further exploration. If you do come by bus, you'll be dropped off at the bus terminal, which is 3km northwest of town on Rte 11.

Rte 18A that runs south of the Bolaven Plateau to Champasak Province remains impassable to most traffic, so all transport to or from Pakse goes via Sekong and Paksong. For transport to Vietnam, see p244

ℹ Getting Around

Your best bet for local transport in the centre is the *sŏrngtăaou* stop on Rte 18B just north of the market; you may find a tuk-tuk here. Tuk-tuks also hang out at the out-of-the-way bus station, but this is hardly ideal if you're staying in the centre. A tuk-tuk from the bus station to the centre costs 20,000K.

The only private transport for hire that we found were the bicycles hired out by the Phoutthavong Guesthouse (p242). We were directed to Talat Nyai (p243) for motorbike hire, but struck out. Try querying the tourism office.

Around Attapeu

Saisettha & Around ໄຊເຊດຖາ

Heading east on Rte 18B brings you to Saisettha, a sizable village 12km from Attapeu on the north bank of the Se Kaman. There is an attractive wat in use here and the whole town has a good vibe.

Continue about 3km further east, across the Se Kaman (Kaman River) and take a right 800m beyond the bridge at the 15.2km mark – look for a sign to the village of Phameuang. Proceed 2.3km on a pot-holed road and you get to **Wat Pha Saisettha**, famous because the Lan Xang king Setthathirat is buried here. The stupa in which he is interred is thought to have been built by his son around 1577. Just wandering around the village and wat is an experience.

Pa-am ພະອຳ

A day-trip to Saisettha could happily be combined with a visit to the modest, tree-

GETTING TO CAMBODIA: SOUTHERN LAOS TO STUNG TRENG

Getting to the Border

The remote **Non Nok Khiene (Laos)/Trapaeng Kriel (Cambodia) crossing** (⌚6am-6pm) is a popular crossing point on the Indochina overland circuit. For many years, there was a separate river crossing here, but that's gone now.

Two Cambodian bus companies do the border run daily between Cambodia and Laos. The more reliable is Sorya Phnom Penh Transport, which partners with Pakse-based Lao operator Sengchalean. This bus leaves Pakse at 7.30am from the 2km bus terminal and goes all the way to Phnom Penh (US$27, 12 to 14 hours) via Stung Treng (US$15, 4½ hours) and Kratie (US$20, seven hours) in Cambodia.

The other company, Paramount Angkor, requires a change of buses at the border, a process which often leads to significant delays. Heading south from the border, you may have to switch buses again in Stung Treng and/or Kratie. Tourist agencies in Laos sell tickets for either Sorya or Paramount; they rarely offer both, so seek out a Sorya partner.

Between July and November, **Xplore-Asia** (www.xplore-asia.com; Ban Hua Det, Don Det) can arrange boat or kayak trips over the border to Stung Treng. Near the border kayakers put out and walk through immigration, then put back in on the Cambodian side.

Services from Laos to Siem Reap are also advertised, but until a new bridge over the Mekong in Stung Treng is completed in 2015, we don't recommend these. They take about 17 hours and involve at least one additional bus change (in Skuon, Cambodia). Break up the trip with an overnight in the laid-back riverside town of Kratie. Or ask Xplore-Asia about special trips to Siem Reap taking a short-cut across Northern Cambodia. These reduce travel time to Siem Reap from Si Phan Don to about seven hours.

At the Border

Both Lao and Cambodian visas are available on arrival. In Laos, you'll pay a $2 or 10,000K fee (dubbed either an 'overtime' or a 'processing' fee, depending on when you cross) upon both entry and exit.

Entering Cambodia, they jack up the price of a visa to $25 from the normal $20. The extra US$5 is called 'tea money', as the poor border guards have been stationed at such a remote crossing.

In addition, the Cambodians charge US$2 for a cursory medical inspection upon arrival in the country, and levy a US$2 processing fee upon exit. These fees might be waived if you protest, but don't protest for too long or your bus may leave without you. The bus companies want their cut too, so they charge an extra US$1 to US$2 to handle your paperwork with the border guards. To avoid this fee, insist on doing your own paperwork and go through immigration alone.

Moving On

Aside from the two daily tourist buses, there's virtually zero traffic here. If you're dropped at the border, expect to pay about US$40 for a private taxi heading south to Stung Treng, or 150,000/50,000K for a taxi/*săhm-lór* heading north to Ban Nakasang.

shaded village of Pa-am (San Xai), 31km east of Attapeu on the road to Chaleun Xai, which was once a branch of the Ho Chi Minh Trail. The main attraction is a Russian **surface-to-air missile** (SAM), complete with Russian and Vietnamese stencilling, which was set up by the North Vietnamese to defend against aerial attack. It has survived the scrap hunters and by government order is now on display in the centre of the village, surrounded by a barbed-wire fence and a few cluster bomb casings-cum-planter boxes.

To get to Pa-am, follow the signs to San Xai off Rte 18B – look for the clearly marked turn-off on the left 13.7km from Attapeu. From the turn-off it's 17km along a sealed road to the missile launcher.

North of Pa-am the road quickly turns rocky and continues on to Chaleun Xai, 38km north of Pa-am, then northwest to Sekong. This route has recently been improved somewhat, but it's still rough and recommended for dry-season only.

Phu Vong ພູວົງ

The area southeast of Attapeu was an integral part of the Ho Chi Minh Trail and as such was heavily bombed during the war. The bombers were particularly interested in the village of Phu Vong, 13km southeast of the capital, where two main branches of the trail split – the Sihanouk Trail continuing south into Cambodia and the Ho Chi Minh Trail veering east towards Vietnam. The village is a pleasant diversion for an hour or two. To get there, cross the Se Kong (5000K with motorbike) to Ban Kaman and ride the 13km to Phu Vong.

Dong Amphan NPA ປ່າສະຫງວນແຫ່ງຊາດດົງອຳພານ

The main attraction in this 1975-sq-km protected area in northeast Attapeu Province is fabled **Nong Fa**. This beautiful volcanic lake, similar to but larger than the more heralded Yeak Lom in Cambodia's Ratanakiri Province, was used by the North Vietnamese as an R'n'R for soldiers hurt on the Ho Chi Minh Trail. It is now accessible by road from Attapeu, but it's a long ride involving 100km of surfaced road on Rte 18B and 65km on poor dirt roads. The journey takes almost five hours one way from Attapeu so leave early. We would advise against this in the rainy season.

Dong Amphan NPA was until recently one of the most intact ecosystems in the country. However, timber and wildlife poaching and hydroelectric projects on the Se Kaman and Se Su are threatening the pristine environment.

SI PHAN DON (FOUR THOUSAND ISLANDS)

Si Phan Don (ສີ່ພັນດອນ) is where Laos becomes the land of the lotus eaters, an archipelago of islands where the pendulum of time swings more slowly and life is more laid-back – yes, even by Laos standards. The name literally means 'Four Thousand Islands', and they are so tranquil that you can imagine them just drifting downriver into Cambodia with barely anyone blinking an eyelid. Many a traveller has washed ashore here, succumbed to its charms and stayed longer than expected.

During the rainy season the Mekong around Si Phan Don fills out to a breadth of 14km, the river's widest reach along its 4350km journey from the Tibetan Plateau to the South China Sea. During the dry months the river recedes and leaves behind hundreds (or thousands if you count every sand bar) of islands and islets.

Travellers hone in on three of those islands: Khong, Det and Khon. Don Khong, by far the largest island in Si Phan Don, is sleepiest and sees the fewest tourists. There's much more to do on Don Khon and Don Det, which have become *de rigeur* stops on the Southeast Asia backpacking circuit. Activities include cycling, swimming, tubing, boat cruises, kayaking, and dolphin spotting, although many travellers forsake these and pass the days getting catatonic in a hammock.

The villages of Si Phan Don are often named for their position at the upriver or downriver ends of their respective islands. The upriver end is called *hŭa* (head); the downriver end is called *hăang* (tail). Hence Ban Hua Khong is at the northern end of Don Khong, while Ban Hang Khong is at the southern end.

Don Khong (Khong Island) ດອນໂຂງ

☎031 / POP 13,000

Life moves slowly on Don Khong, like a boat being paddled against the flow on the

Mekong. It's a pleasant place to spend a day or two, wandering past fishing nets drying in the sun, taking a sunset boat ride, pedalling about on a bicycle or just chilling and reading by the river.

Don Khong measures 18km long by 8km at its widest point. Most of the islanders live in and around two villages, Muang Khong on the eastern shore and Muang Saen on the west; an 8km road links the two. Pretty much all of the accommodation is in Muang Khong, where the ferry boats from Hat Xai Khun land.

Khamtay Siphandonethe, the postman who went on to serve as president of Laos from 1998 to 2006, was born in Ban Hua Khong at the north end of Don Khong in 1924.

Sights & Activities

Don Khong is a pretty island with rice fields and low hills in the centre and vegetable gardens around the perimeter, punctuated by small villages, most of which have their own wats. Bicycle (ecofriendly) or motorbike (ecolazy) is the best way to explore it. Two smaller villages at the southern tip of the island worth visiting for old wats are **Ban Huay** and **Ban Hang Khong**.

Muang Khong & Around

Wat Phuang Kaew BUDDHIST TEMPLE

Muang Khong is dominated by Wat Phuang Kaew and its towering modern '*naga* protected' Buddha image facing east.

Wat Jom Thong BUDDHIST TEMPLE

At the northern end of town is Wat Jom Thong, the oldest temple on the island. Dating from the Chao Anou period (1805–28), the main *sǐm* features a unique cruciform floor plan in crumbling brick and stucco with a tile roof. Carved wooden window shutters are a highlight, and an old wooden standing Buddha in one-handed *abhaya mudra* (offering protection) pose is notable.

Muang Khong Market MARKET

The market is fascinating between 4.30am and 6.30am, when people come from all over the islands to buy and sell. Many come by boat and getting yourself down to the small beach at dawn to watch the boats unload their fish, fowl and other fare is a fantastic way to start the day.

Tham Phu Khiaw CAVE

(Green Mountain Cave) A kilometre or so north of Muang Khong, in some hills more or less behind the mayor's office, a trail leads to Tham Phu Khiaw. The cave – actually more of an overhanging ledge – contains some old Buddha images and is the object of local pilgrimages during Lao New Year in April. To find it, head north from Muang Khong for 1.5km and take a track to the left, through a banana plantation. It's only a 15-minute walk (mostly uphill) to the cave entrance, but the track isn't always obvious so it's best to find a local to guide you (15,000K from the tourism office).

Muang Saen & Around

Kompong Sralao VILLAGE

In bustling Muang Saen, boatmen (for a big tip) will take you visa-free across to the Cambodian village of Kompong Sralao on the west bank of the Mekong. There's nothing to see, but you can say that you've been to a part of Cambodia few others have visited and stop to sample an Angkor Beer.

Wat Phu Khao Kaew BUDDHIST TEMPLE

(Glass Hill Monastery) About 5km northeast of Muang Saen, Wat Phu Khao Kaew was built on the site of some Khmer ruins. It is believed to be home to a *naga*, though the entrance to its lair is covered. Look for some boulders leading to a path up to the temple on the eastern side of the hill. You'll have a much easier time finding it with a guide, or take a motorcycle taxi (about 70,000K return from Muang Khong).

Festivals & Events

Bun Suang Heua BOAT RACING

(Bun Nam) A boat-racing festival is held on Don Khong in early December or late November around National Day. Four or five days of carnival-like activity culminate in races opposite Muang Khong, much closer to the shore than in larger towns.

Sleeping & Eating

All of the following are in Muang Khong, on or just back from the riverbank along a 700m-stretch. There are few dedicated restaurants worth tweeting about; guesthouses have the best food, with Pon Arena and Ratana leading the way. Most places serve Don Khong's famous *lòw-lów,* which is often cited as the smoothest in the country.

Si Phan Don

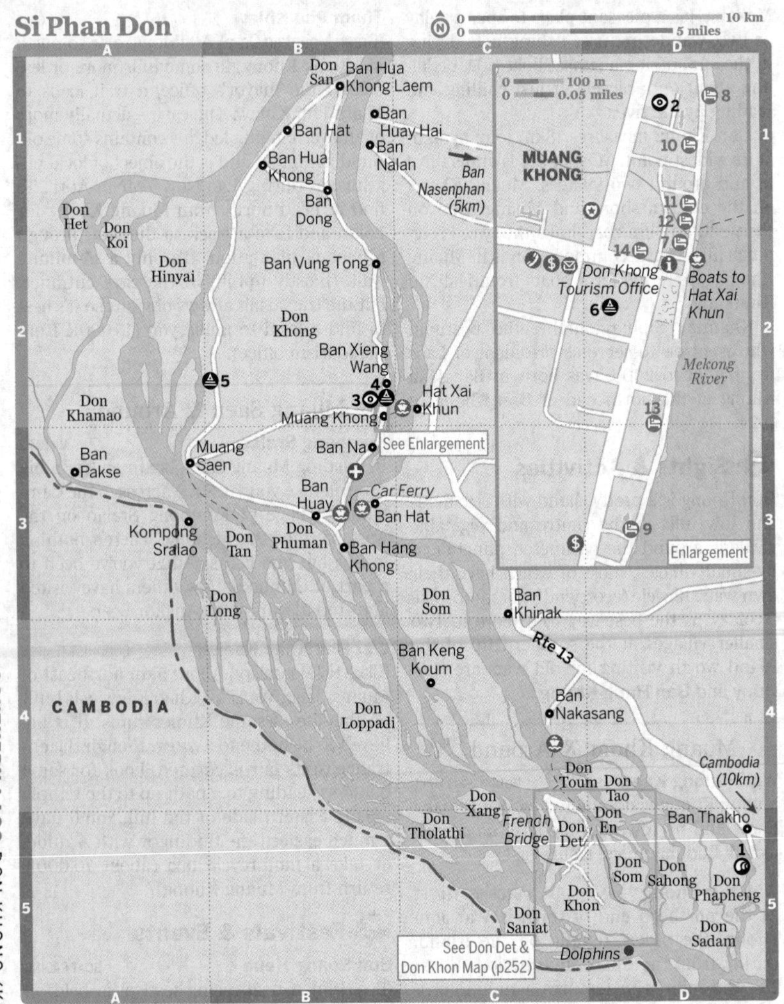

★ Ratana Riverside Guesthouse GUESTHOUSE $
(☎020-2220 1618, 031-213673; vongdonekhong@hotmail.com; r 100,000K, mains 15,000-40,000K; ❄📶) The four comfortable river-facing rooms here enjoy origami-lotus-folded towels, marble floors, balconies, Siberian air-con and handsome furnishings. Ground-floor rooms have enormous windows close to the road – ever felt like a goldfish? – so get one upstairs. The river-deck restaurant has about the best selection of Western food on the island, plus the usual Lao river fare. It also goes by the name Lattana.

Khong View Guesthouse GUESTHOUSE $
(☎020-2244 6449; r with fan/air-con 80,000/100,000K; ❄📶) It's hard to beat the location of this place, where the rooms are set around a breezy wood deck overlooking a big bend in the Mekong. Choose between dark woody riverfront rooms or bright tiled rooms at the back, facing the road. The small rooms have disproportionally large king-sized beds. No restaurant.

Villa Kang Khong GUESTHOUSE $
(☎020-2240 3315; r 50,000-60,000K) The most romantic budget digs in town, this stalwart

Si Phan Don

Sights

1 Khon Phapheng Falls....D5
2 Muang Khong Market....D1
3 Tham Phu Khiaw....B2
4 Wat Jom Thong....B2
5 Wat Phu Khao Kaew....B2
6 Wat Phuang Kaew....D2

Sleeping

7 Done Khong Guesthouse....D2
8 Khong View Guesthouse....D1
9 Mali Guesthouse....D3
10 Pon Arena Hotel....D1
11 Pon's River Guesthouse & Restaurant....D1
12 Ratana Riverside Guesthouse....D1
13 Senesothxeune Hotel....D2
14 Villa Kang Khong....D2

teak house creaks with uneven floors and nostalgic furnishings. Rooms are basic and fan-cooled, and, with their colourful wood interiors, remind us vaguely of Romany gypsy caravans.

Pon's River Guesthouse & Restaurant GUESTHOUSE $
(020-2227 0037; www.ponarenahotel.com; r 60,000-100,000K;) Pon's original guesthouse gets less TLC since he opened the swish Arena Hotel. The basic rooms, which come in fan and air-con flavours, won't knock you over, but that's OK. The sprawling public balcony in view of the river is the place to hang.

Done Khong Guesthouse GUESTHOUSE $
(020-0312 4010; r without/with air-con 70,000/100,00K;) The first place you'll see when you get off the boat, Done Khong has dark rooms with tiled floors, sugar-white linen and homely furnishings in an old house run by a French-speaking lady. Try to bag a river-facing room. The riverside restaurant, with a mostly Lao menu, is a good place to chill.

Mali Guesthouse GUESTHOUSE $
(030-534 6621; athalo@netzero.com; r US$20;) This cosy spot a bit south of the centre lacks the woody charm of some guesthouses, but the clean rooms with green-tile floors and a few mod-cons will appeal to some. Rooms are set around an attractive garden courtyard with a splash pool (empty when we visited in the low season).

★ Pon Arena Hotel BOUTIQUE HOTEL $$
(020-2227 0037, 031-515018; www.ponarenahotel.com; r US$45-85;) This upscale hotel on the river keeps expanding. The most recent addition is a 'Swiss chalet' that sits right on the river and boasts airy rooms with neat wood trim, flat-screen TVs and a community plunge pool in view of the river. The 'Mekong view' rooms sit further back but are, if anything, nicer while even the mountain-view rooms at the back score style points with granite-inlaid bathrooms, fishbowl sinks and soft beds.

Senesothxeune Hotel HOTEL $
(030-526 0577; www.ssx-hotel.com; r incl breakfast US$45-60, ste US$85;) This Thai-style modern hotel has upmarket rooms boasting hardwood floors, TVs, deep baths, milk-white minimalism and a pleasant restaurant with a view of the river through its magnolia-blossoming garden. The pricier rooms have balconies and river views.

Information

For public internet access try the Senesothxeune Hotel (10,000K per hour).

Agricultural Promotion Bank (8.30am-3.30pm Mon-Fri) Offers not terrible rates for US dollars and Thai baht, and cashes US-dollar travellers cheques for a US$4-per-cheque commission. Also has an ATM for Visa and Mastercard holders.

BCEL ATM In front of the Lao Telecom building, next to the Post Office

Don Khong Tourism Office (020-9784 6464; panhjuki@yahoo.com; 8.30am-4pm Mon-Fri) Near the boat landing, this office is manned by helpful Mr Phan. He can set you up with a local guide, and can organise boats to Don Det/Khon through the local boatman's association (about 250,000K per boat). He offers rides on the back of his motorbike to Ban Nakasang, where he lives.

Hospital Mid-way between Muang Khong and Ban Huay. If you have any minor ailments, Dr Bounthavi speaks English and French and is based here.

Police A block back from the river in Muang Khong.

Post Office (8am-noon & 2-4pm Mon-Fri) Just south of the bridge.

Getting There & Away

The vast majority of travellers take a tourist bus or minivan to Hat Xai Khun on the mainland, then squeeze into a small ferry boat for the short hop to Muang Khong (15,000K per head – more if it's after 4pm or if you are one person; bargaining is futile).

With your own motorbike, beeline it to Ban Hat, a few kilometres south of Hat Xai Khun on the mainland, and take the vehicle ferry over (5000K per motorbike, plus 2000K per passenger).

Leaving the island, you have a few choices. For Pakse, it's easiest to take a tourist bus or minivan coming up from Don Det and Don Khon (60,000K including boat transfer, 2½ hours). These arrive in Hat Xai Khun at 11.30am or so. The buses from Cambodia to Pakse come through in the early evening (around 6pm but it varies wildly).

Alternatively, a few slower-moving morning *sŏrngtăaou* plod to Pakse from Hat Xai Khun (40,000K, three hours), and there's an oft-delayed 7.30am bus direct to Pakse from Wat Phuang Kaew on Don Khong (60,000K, three hours).

Heading south, most transport to Don Det/Khon and Cambodia stops in Hat Xai Khun at about 9.30am. After that, head 3km out to Rte 13 and wait for hourly *sŏrngtăaou* from Pakse going south.

Alternatively, the Don Khong boatmen's association runs a boat most days to Don Det/Khon at 8.30am (40,000/60,000K per person one-way/return, minimum six passengers); book this through the tourism office. It's 1½ hours downstream and 2½ hours back.

You can also hire a private boat through your guesthouse or from the local boatmen who hang out under the tree near the boat landing in Muang Khong (40,000K per person, or 250,000K per boat one way).

Getting Around

Bicycles (10,000K per day) and motorbikes (from 60,000K per day) are the way to go and can be hired from many guesthouses or the tourist office. Alternatively, try to find a motorcycle taxi in Muang Khong and haggle away.

Don Det & Don Khon

ດອນເດດ/ດອນຄອນ

The vast majority of travellers to Si Phan Don end up on these twin islands. Don Det in particular has become more popular among younger travellers in recent years, leading some to speculate that it will replace Vang Vieng as the go-to spot in Laos for vice-fuelled excess. That would seem unlikely. There's nothing stronger than grass in the 'happy' snacks sold openly at some bars, and the locals seem to have a genuine desire to keep it that way. Our best guess is that a hippyesque party scene will continue to thrive in Ban Hua Det at the north end of Don Det, but it will never become as depraved as the old Vang Vieng.

Of course, there's much more to these two islands than Scooby snacks. Heading south from Ban Hua Det, the guesthouses thin out and the icons of rural island life – fishermen, rice farmers, weavers, buffalo, sugar palms – are on full display. Chill in a hammock, cycle around the islands or languidly drift downstream in an inner tube in the turquoise arms of the Mekong. Cross the French bridge to Don Khon and pick up trails that lead through forests and rice fields to hidden rapids, beaches and, off the island's extreme southern tip, frolicking Irrawaddy dolphins.

Sights

Most sights are on Don Khon and are best accessed on a bicycle hired from just about any guesthouse for 10,000K per day. When you cross the French bridge to Don Khon, you will be asked to pay 25,000K. This covers the entrance free to Li Phi Falls, so you might as well pay it if you are heading that way. If you aren't, then technically you don't have to pay the toll (good luck trying to convince the ticket collectors of this – they don't speak English). Keep your ticket stub if you'll be crossing the bridge again on subsequent days.

Dolphins POOL

A pod of rare Irrawaddy dolphins hangs out beneath the rapids in a wide pool known as Boong Pa Gooang, off the south tip of Don Khon. Boats are chartered (60,000K, maximum three people) for one-hour trips from the old French landing pier in Ban Hang Khon. Sightings are regular year-round, but the best viewing is from January to May. Try to go early evening or first thing in the morning, when sightings are more regular and the river is at its most scenic.

The Boong Pa Gooang pool lies mostly in Cambodia, which Lao boatmen are reluctant to enter (although kayak tour operators show no such reluctance). You may be able to see them from your boat (as we did), or you may be taken to a small island that looks over the conservation zone in Cambodian waters. Spotting these rare creatures in the wild is a highlight of any trip to southern Laos. On your way back, you can tip the boatman to bring you over to Cambodia for a quick wander around.

PARADISE RETAINED!

The islanders are benefiting from the income tourism brings, but there are a few things you can do on Don Det and Don Khon to keep the smiles genuine and your footprint positive. Having a spliff is part of the backpacker experience and the locals we spoke with seemed to have accepted the arrival of marijuana in Ban Hua Det, but they'd prefer it was an incidental part of a visit rather than the sole reason for coming. If you do partake, be subtle.

Also, the beach on Ban Hua Det has become a cool spot for sunbathing and nightly bonfires, but make sure you pick up your cigarette butts and litter here, even if the locals don't seem to bother. To avoid putting additional strain on the islands' environment, bring a water bottle and pay to refill it – Paradise Bungalows (p256) and Mr Man's (p256) are among several guesthouses that offer this service.

Women should refrain from just wearing a bikini around the islands since the Lao find it culturally insensitive. Be especially mindful of covering up in the wats on Don Khon. Swimming in bikinis is OK.

Tat Somphamit WATERFALL

(Li Phi Falls, ຕາດສົມພາມິດ; admission 25,000K; ⊙ticket booth 8am-5pm) About 1.5km downriver from the French bridge on Don Khon is a raging set of rapids called Tat Somphamit, but referred to by just about everyone as Li Phi Falls. Li Phi means 'spirit trap' and locals believe the falls act as just that – a trap for bad spirits (of deceased people and animals) as they wash down the river. Water churns through the falls at a frenetic pace, even in the dry season.

You may notice local fishermen edging out onto the rocks to clear the enormous bamboo traps. During the early rains, a well-positioned trap can catch half a tonne of fish a day. Some traps here and elsewhere in the area have an intake almost 10m long, funnelling fish into a huge basket at the end. Don't try this stunt yourself – travellers have died slipping off the rocks beyond the barrier.

Continuing west past the falls, a trail descends to sandy Li Phi Beach, where a small eddy forms a potential swimming hole. You'll never see locals swimming at 'Spirit Trap Beach' – mixing with the dead is clearly tempting fate a little too much. You should also think twice about swimming here, as the currents are potentially lethal.

Li Phi Falls are easy to reach – just head southwest from the French bridge, pass a football pitch on your right (feel free to join in if there's a game) and follow the signs. There are plenty of restaurants and concession stands at the falls entrance.

A safer swimming option is a few hundred metres downriver at Long (Tha Sanam) Beach. To get there head back to the Li Phi Falls turnoff, point south and continue to the beach.

Activities

On the Water

Kayaking around the islands is growing in popularity, and for good reason considering the sublime beauty of the Mekong in these parts. Full-day and half-day tours are widely offered. The full-day trips (180,000K per person) take in the dolphin pool and Khon Papaeng Falls; you pick up before the falls off Don Khon and you and your kayaks are transported overland to Ban Hang Khon. **Wonderful Tours** (☎020-5570 5173) is one trustworthy company that offers kayak trips.

Renting a kayak to paddle around on your own costs 50,000K per day, but don't go past the French bridge or you'll hit the fast currents that feed into the lethal falls. The same rule applies to **tubing**, which costs 10,000K (avoid during monsoon when the river runs dangerously quick).

If you prefer less exertion, just about every guesthouse offers some sort of **boat tour**: sunset cruises, full-day island hops, morning birdwatching trips, fishing, Don Khong trips – you name it. Prices vary, but figure on 50,000K to 75,000K per person for a couple-hour excursion provided you have a few people.

On Land

A delightful **Eastern Loop** cycle ride (or long walk) takes you to the waterways at the eastern edge of Don Khon where the French built a series of **concrete channels** used to direct logs. The logs, usually from forests in Sainyabuli Province west of

Don Det & Don Khon

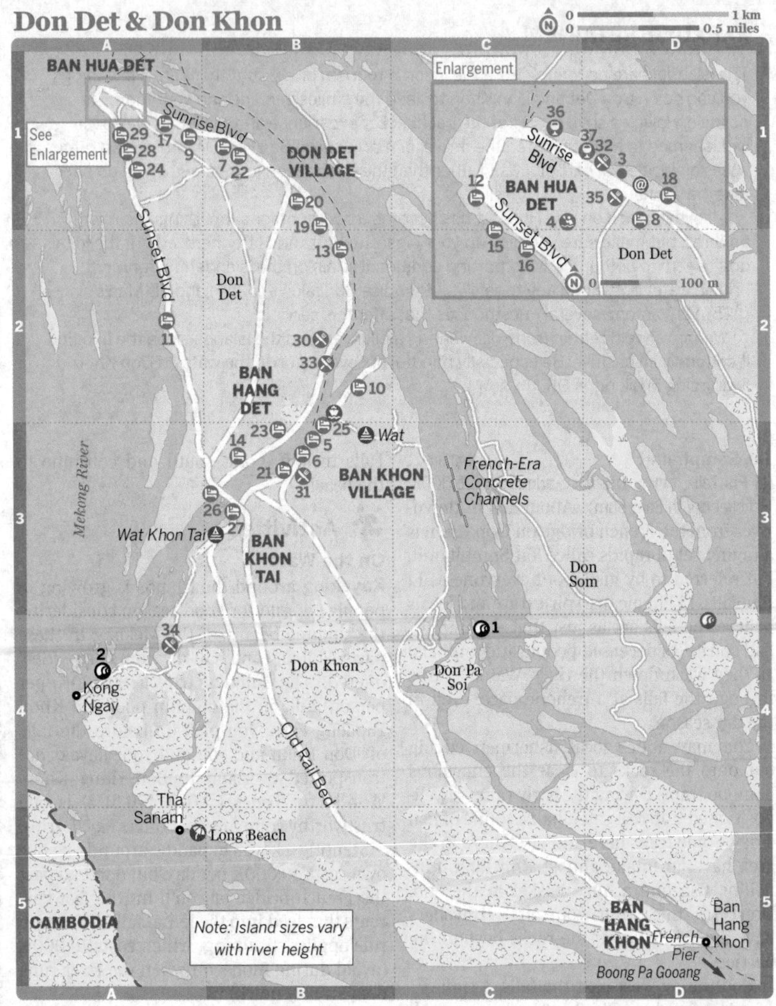

Vientiane, were lashed together into rafts of three. To prevent them going off-course, a Lao 'pilot' would board the raft and steer it through the maze of islands. When they reached the critical area at the north end of Don Khon, the pilots were required to guide the raft onto a reinforced concrete wedge, thus splitting the binds and sending the logs into the channels beyond. The poor 'pilot' would jump for his life moments before impact.

Large portions of the channel walls are clearly visible on your left as you ride or walk along this trail. To access it, head northeast from the French bridge and turn south about 1km along, passing through a wat and following the path through rice fields to the riverbank.

The path continues along the river for awhile before joining a rough road near the small island of **Don Pa Soi**. Signs lead the way to a restaurant overlooking a suspension bridge to the island. Follow the trail on the other side for 100m to **Khon Pa Soi Falls**. They aren't quite Li Phi Falls but they are still pretty impressive and you can find bathing spots, although the water is downright hot in the warmest months.

Don Det & Don Khon

Sights

1 Khon Pa Soi Falls C4
2 Tat Somphamit A4

Activities, Courses & Tours

3 Wonderful Tours D1
4 Xplore-Asia C1

Sleeping

5 Auberge Sala Done Khone B3
6 Bounephan Riverside Guesthouse B3
7 Crazy Gecko B1
8 Dalom Guesthouse D1
9 Don Det Bungalows A1
10 Guesthouse Souksan B2
11 Last Resort A2
12 Little Eden Guesthouse C1
13 Mama Leuah Guesthouse & Restaurant B2
14 Mekong Dream Guesthouse B3
15 Mr B's Sunset View C2
16 Mr Ky's Bungalows C2
17 Mr Man's Bungalows A1
18 Mr Mo's Guesthouse D1
19 Mr Phao's Sunrise Bungalows B1
20 Mr Tho's Bungalows B1
21 Pan's Guesthouse B3
22 Paradise Bungalows B1
23 River Garden B3
24 Sabaidee Don Det A1
25 Sala Phae B3
26 Santiphab Guesthouse B3
27 Seng Ahloune Sunset River Resort B3
28 Sengthavan Guesthouse & Restaurant A1
29 Sunset View A1

Eating

30 Boathouse B2
31 Chanthounma's Restaurant B3
Fleur du Mekong .... (see 27)
Four Thousand Sunsets .... (see 5)
32 Jasmine Restaurant D1
33 King Kong Resort B2
Little Eden Restaurant .... (see 12)
34 Mamadam Restaurant A4
35 Rib Shack D1

Drinking & Nightlife

36 4000 Island Bar C1
37 Reggae Bar D1

Back on the trail, it's a beautiful ride or walk through the forest all the way to the dolphin-watching village of Ban Hang Khon on the southern tip of the island. There are a couple of restaurants and a homestay (30,000K) in Ban Hang Khon.

You can return the way you came or take the main road, which follows the old rail bed 5km through the middle of the island. Rusting **locomotives** sit near either end of the road, including one located about 75m from the south end of the French bridge.

Surrounding the locomotives are placards detailing the history of the islands and the railway, which the French built in the late 1800s as a way of transporting supplies around the impassable falls. The railway has been out of use since WWII, when newly constructed Rte 13 made the railway redundant, and most of the track has long since been carted off.

Sleeping

The general rule of thumb is stay on Don Det if you want to party, and on Don Khon if you want to get away from it all. But that rule is misleading. The party is confined to the north tip of Don Det at Ban Hua Det. The islands' most isolated guesthouses are actually on the quiet southern portion of Don Det. Don Khon has a few upmarket hotels targeting the more discerning traveller. All accommodation on Don Khon is clustered on a 1km strip either side of the French bridge in the village of Ban Khon.

No matter where you stay, it's easy to shuttle between Don Khon and Don Det via the French bridge. Prices fluctuate substantially throughout the year on both islands. Expect a low-season discount of at least 25% off the rates listed here, depending on your haggling skills.

Don Det

It's all about location on Don Det. Extreme penny-pinchers head to the sunset side, where the bungalows are flimsier and packed in a little tighter than on the sunrise side. There's definitely a stoner vibe over here, plus, yeah, those sunsets. The drawback is that late in the day rooms become furnace-like after baking in the afternoon sun.

The sunrise side is more spread out, with a wider range of options, including a few sturdier hotels with air-con in the centre of Ban Hua Det, the busy village where the ferry from Ban Nakasang alights. Further south, toward the tiny village of Don Det

DOLPHINS ENDANGERED

The Irrawaddy dolphin (*Orcaella brevirostris*, called *pąa khaa* in Laos) is one of the Mekong River's most fascinating creatures, and one of its most endangered. The dark blue to grey cetaceans grow to 2.75m long and are recognisable by their bulging foreheads, perpetual grins and small dorsal fins. They are unusually adaptable and can live in freshwater, brackish-water estuaries or semi-enclosed saltwater bodies such as bays.

Among the Lao and Khmer, Irrawaddy dolphins are traditionally considered reincarnated humans and there are many stories of dolphins having saved the lives of fishermen or villagers who have fallen into the river or been attacked by crocodiles. These cultural beliefs mean neither the Lao nor the Khmer intentionally capture dolphins for food or sport.

But gill netting and years of destructive fishing practices such as dynamite fishing in Cambodia have inevitably taken their toll on the dolphins. Education and conservation programs to save the dolphins continue, particularly in Cambodia, but gill netting remains a constant threat – dolphins need to surface and breathe every two to three minutes, and will usually drown before fishermen even know they are in the nets. As if that wasn't bad enough, many juvenile calves have died mysteriously in recent years – illegal electro-fishing and infanticide caused by skewed sex ratios are the two leading suspects.

From the thousands that populated the Mekong and its tributaries in Cambodia and southern Laos as recently as the 1970s, it's now estimated there are fewer than 100 remaining. The surviving few live primarily in several deep-water conservation 'pools' along a 190km stretch of the Mekong between the Lao border and the Cambodian town of Kratie. These areas act as a refuge for the dolphins during the dry season, when river levels drop dangerously low.

In Laos, dolphins used to travel up the Se Kong river, but these days they are largely confined to a 600m-wide, 50m-deep (in the wet season) pool on the Cambodian border known in Laotian as Boong Pa Gooang and in Cambodian as Anlong Cheuteal. It is believed that fewer than 10 dolphins survive in this pool.

proper, guesthouses start to feel more isolated and quieter.

South of Don Det village, along the southeastern edge of the island, it gets downright rural, and the modest party scene of Ban Hua Det feels light years away.

Sunset Strip

★ Sunset View GUESTHOUSE $

(☎020-9788 2978; Sunset Blvd; r 120,000K; P) Slightly higher prices than its immediate neighbours on the sunset strip make this more of a flashpacker option. The bathrooms are shinier, the living quarters roomier and beds thicker than anywhere else in the area. The riverfront rooms are in a wood row house with a common sunset-facing deck that practically hangs over the water. Rates drop by at least half in the low season.

Last Resort RESORT $

(mrwatkinsonlives@googlemail.com; d/tr 50,000/60,000K) Speaking of happy hippy places, it would be hard to match the free-spiritedness of this teepee 'resort' in a field near a friendly village about a 15-minute walk south of the main Sunset Blvd strip. Aussie host Jon grows veggies, bakes bread, loves music consummately and screens movies in the open air. The teepees are utterly unique, and there's a kitchen for self-caterers.

Sengthavan Guesthouse & Restaurant GUESTHOUSE $

(☎020-5613 2696; Sunset Blvd; r 100,000K; wi-fi) Probably the best the sunset side has to offer in the budget range, Sengthavan's en suite rooms are fastidiously clean and enjoy uncluttered balcony views of Cambodia. Its low-key cafe has recliner cushions, checked-tablecloths and a Lao menu.

Mr B's Sunset View GUESTHOUSE $

(☎020-5418 1171; Sunset Blvd; r without/with bathroom from 30,000/50,000K; wi-fi) With English-speaking staff, Mr B's sprawling complex has a wide variety of bungalows, including some with sunset views, for which you pay just a bit extra. All are simple with thin, lumpy mattresses. The restaurant is the bigger draw; the pumpkin burger is the stuff of legend.

Mr Ky's Bungalows GUESTHOUSE $
(r 50,000K) With simple but clean bungalows set around well-manicured grounds, this is a quieter alternative to Mr B's next door. Unfortunately, the sunset views are obstructed by Mr B's.

Sabaidee Don Det GUESTHOUSE $
(bungalow 40,000K, r with fan/air-con 70,000/100,000K;) The menu of the adjoining Happy Bar is certainly happier than the service. Flimsy bungalows right on the water in front and concrete rooms at the back.

★**Little Eden Guesthouse** GUESTHOUSE $$
(030-534 6020; www.littleedenguesthouse-dondet.com; standard/deluxe 250,000/320,000K;) Little Eden is set in lush gardens of sugar palms and betel trees on the northern tip of the island. Fragrant rooms have cool, tiled floors and soft linens. The roomy deluxe rooms, with textile bed runners, white walls, snazzy bathrooms and darkwood trim, are a substantial upgrade on the fairly basic standard rooms, so consider splurging.

Sunrise Strip

★**Crazy Gecko** GUESTHOUSE $
(info@crazygecko.ch; r 150,000K;) In a stilted structure made of solid wood, Crazy Gecko's four rooms surround a balcony that's equal parts funky and functional. Festooned with hammocks, sculptures and random furniture, it's a superior place to relax, even if it's set back from the river. Bathrooms are shared (for now) and rooms are fragrant and simple – just tidy spaces for beds, really. The riverside restaurant across the path is delightful.

Dalom Guesthouse GUESTHOUSE $
(020-5418 8898; Sunrise Blvd; r with fan/air-con 80,000/160,000K;) This is the best option if you want to be near the centre of the action in Ban Hua Det. If comfort is more important than being right on the river, you'll find good-value fan bungalows in the garden and spiffy air-con rooms in a two-storey concrete structure.

Don Det Bungalows GUESTHOUSE $
(030-955 3354; dondet.bungalows@gmail.com; Sunrise Blvd; bungalows from 150,000K;) The bungalows here are a little roomier than most on the island and come with towels and soap, but are a tad overpriced. They are

WORTH A TRIP

KHON PHAPHENG FALLS

South of Don Khon, the Mekong River features a 13km stretch of powerful rapids with several sets of cascades. The largest, and by far the most awesome anywhere along the Mekong, is **Khon Phapheng Falls** (ຕາດຄອນພະເພັງ; admission 30,000K). Khon Phapheng is pure, unrestrained aggression, as millions of litres of water crash over the rocks and into Cambodia every second. This is a spectacular sight, particularly when the Mekong is at full flood, and is one of the most-visited sites in Laos for Thai tourists, who arrive by the busload. Part of the attraction is the spiritual significance the falls hold for both Lao and Thais, who believe Khon Phapheng acts as a spirit trap in the same way as Li Phi Falls near Don Khon.

A pavilion on the Mekong shore affords a good view of the falls. A shaky network of bamboo scaffolds on the rocks next to the falls is used by daring fishermen who are said to have an alliance with the spirits of the cascades.

Khon Phapheng is near the eastern shore of the Mekong, not far from Ban Thakho. From Ban Nakasang it's 3km out to Rte 13, then 8km south to the falls turnoff. To get there from Don Det, take the ferry to Ban Nakasang, then walk 500m to the market and find a *săhm-lór* to take you (about 50,000K return, with some wait time). If heading to Cambodia, a good plan is to get up early, check out the falls and arrange to have your bus pick you up out on Rte 13 around 9.30am or 10am.

The falls are included in many tour itineraries out of Don Det, including the popular kayak and dolphin tours. Since amateurs can't kayak anywhere near these falls, you'll be taken there by vehicle as your kayaks are driven up to Ban Nakasang.

TAKE A STEP BACK

By law, guesthouses on Don Det and Don Khon cannot build en suite bungalows or kitchens within a few metres of a riverbank. This rule has been largely ignored and authorities have turned a blind eye. Now, following in the footsteps of a similar ordinance being enforced in Vang Vieng, there is talk that the same will happen in Don Det and Don Khon, perhaps as early as 2014. The rule may even extend to bungalows that *don't* have bathrooms.

Obviously this would change the guesthouse landscape in Don Det and Don Khon substantially. The majority of guesthouses would have to rebuild their bungalows and/or kitchens behind the riverside path. This would be bad news for those who prefer their bungalows right on the water, and a huge hassle (and cost) for businesses that currently flout this law. On the other hand, perhaps it would be good news for the environment.

set back from the river, so for sunrise hit the restaurant over the way, with mandatory reclining cushions.

Mr Man's Bungalows GUESTHOUSE $
(020-2332 6383; Sunrise Blvd; r without bathroom 50,000K) Mr Man has passed but his legacy lives on at this simple guesthouse where duplex bungalows stare at the water. It's quiet despite being just a short walk from the action in Ban Hua Det. Great value.

Paradise Bungalows GUESTHOUSE
(Sunrise Blvd; bungalows from 60,000K) The seven bungalows are as basic as it gets, but you are right where you want to be: over the Mekong in your hammock. Shared bathrooms with squat toilets are livened up by colourful murals. The cheap restaurant, assisted by an earthy resident American musician couple, serves great crepes. The book exchange benefits a local children's fund.

Mr Mo's Guesthouse GUESTHOUSE $
(020-5575 9252; Sunrise Blvd; r with fan 50,000-120,000K, with air-con 150,000K;) Another substantial cement building in the centre with air-con rooms and hot water. The riverfront location is a plus. Heaps of travel information is available in the restaurant.

Mr Phao's Sunrise Bungalows GUESTHOUSE $
(020-5656 9651; Sunrise Blvd; bungalows 50,000K;) Mr Phao's has a warm family feel, boat trips and utterly basic en suite bungalows set in a pretty riverside garden.

Mr Tho's Bungalows GUESTHOUSE $
(020-5592 8598; Sunrise Blvd; r from 70,000K;) Just south of Don Det village, Mr Tho's has long been popular for the relaxed atmosphere fostered by helpful, English-speaking Mr Tho.

South

★River Garden GUESTHOUSE $
(020-7770 1860; r 60,000-80,000K;) Gay-friendly River Garden brings a whiff of style to the Don Det riverfront that its budget brethren lack. Think carved-wood doors and windows, tidy bathrooms, white-stripey linens and – in the pricier rooms – Lao textiles, bamboo lamps and seductive maroon-stained walls. Twin hammocks outside each room further showcase attention to detail. Hard pillows are our only fuss. Rooms are set back from the river, but opposite them is a shaded riverfront terrace restaurant hung with Buddha paintings.

Mekong Dream Guesthouse GUESTHOUSE $
(020-5527 5728; r 50,000K;) Facing the strip on Don Khon, Mekong Dream is quite stylish. The six rooms, all with private bathrooms and comfortable king-sized beds, are the antidote to claustrophobic rooms elsewhere and share a roomy balcony/hammock lounge to match. Extras like soap and towels are a given.

Mama Leuah Guesthouse & Restaurant GUESTHOUSE $
(020-5907 8792; www.mamaleuah-dondet.com; r without/with bathroom 50,000/60,000K) The rooms are super basic, with squat toilets, but it's super quiet up here and you can hang out at the restaurant, where ambient music plays and excellent Thai cuisine emerges from the kitchen along with Swiss surprises like *Zürcher geschnetzeltes* (pork with cream mushroom sauce).

Santiphab Guesthouse GUESTHOUSE $
(020-5461 4231; r 80,000K;) This old trusty right next to the bridge to Don Khon

Don Khon

★**Four Thousand Sunsets** FUSION $
(mains 30,000-40,000K;) Auberge Sala Done Khone's floating restaurant is a little classier than your average island eatery – think white table cloths, wine glasses and an eclectic menu of European, Thai and other Asian fare. Nothing beats a sunset drink here, watching the light cast its amber net over the Mekong.

Fleur du Mekong LAOTIAN $
(020-5572 1681; mains 15,000-40,000K; 7am-10pm) Run by friendly French-speaking tour guide Mr Noy, Lao dishes here include a delicious duck curry and a steamed fish in banana leaf or *papillote*. It's off the river, roughly opposite Seng Ahloune.

Chanthounma's Restaurant LAOTIAN $
(mains 20,000K) This tumbledown long-timer off the river has been serving 'great food to suit your mood' for years, including spring rolls, papaya salads and veggie options.

Mamadam Restaurant LAOTIAN $
(mains 35,000-50,000K) One of several restaurants at Li Phi Falls, this family-run eatery serves delicious Laotian fare and, for 15,000K extra, will teach you how to prepare what you order.

Drinking & Nightlife

Ban Hua Det is where the action is. There seems to be a semi-official curfew of 11.30pm when the bars wind down and the action moves to the 'beach', where bonfires and midnight dips are not unheard of.

4000 Island Bar BAR
(Sunrise Blvd) Near the boat landing, this was the most happening place in town when we visited, filling up nightly with youthful travellers eager to munch happy snacks and get their freak on. While it officially closes before midnight, it's likely to stay open unofficially until 1am.

Reggae Bar BAR
This is generally more of a warm-up bar for 4000 Island Bar, featuring live bands (not always reggae) or jam sessions most nights.

Information

Paradise Bungalows (p256) has a binder full of useful stuff about the islands, including info on transport, DIY excursions and a good map that you can photograph. Mr Mo's (p256) is another good source of information. Several tour companies have booths on the main strip in Ban Hua Det, but there is little to separate them and they are mainly concerned with selling you tours and tickets.

There are plenty of internet cafes clustered along the main drag in Ban Hua Det, all charging about 400K per minute; try **Mr Khieo Internet** (per min 400K). There are also a handful of places on Don Khon.

There is no bank, so take the ferry over to Ban Nakasang, which has a BCEL with an ATM. Some tours include an ATM stop in Ban Nakasang in the itinerary. Some guesthouses and restaurants will change money at poor rates, and Little Eden Guesthouse (p255) on Don Det will do cash advances on your card for a 5% commission.

Ban Nakasang is also the place to go for medical and postal services.

Getting There & Away

Boat prices to the islands are fixed by a local boat association. Ban Nakasang to Don Det costs 15,000K per person or 30,000K alone. That goes up to 20,000K to 30,000K per person after 4pm and rises further after dark.

A few public boats service Don Khon (25,000K per person or 50,000K alone). If you miss those you are looking at an extortionate price of 200,000K per boat. To save kip, head to Don Det and ride a rented bicycle to Don Khon.

For Pakse, most travellers book through-tickets on the island, including the local boat and a transfer to a bus or minibus (70,000K, three hours). Most departures are at about 11am, with another round of departures in the early evening when the two buses from Cambodia come through. These all stop in Hat Xai Khun (for Don Khong). Slower *sŏrngtăaou* from Ban Nakasang to Pakse leave early morning only, until about 8am (40,000K, 3½ hours).

There are several boat options to Don Khong. You can also charter a private boat to Don Khong from Paradise Bungalows (p256) for 75,000K per person, minimum two people.

Buses to Cambodia originate in Pakse and come through Ban Nakasang at about 9.30am. The Sorya bus is your best bet – see p245.

has seven red-stained stand-alone bungalows with basic interiors, old beds and en suites. The stilted restaurant with views to Don Khon is dreamy late in the day.

Don Khon

Guesthouse Souksan GUESTHOUSE $
(☎020-2233 7722; s/d from 20,000/30,000K; @ ≋) Still the cheapest place on the Don Khon strip, Souksan has rooms set in a bungalow block with a shared riverview terrace, adjacent to a restaurant with cushion seating right over the water. Bathrooms have cold water. Mr Souksan's BBQ boat tours are popular and fun.

Bounephan Riverside Guesthouse GUESTHOUSE $
(☎031-271 0163; r 40,000-60,000K) Choose from basic en suite rooms in a rickety, hammock-strewn wood structure overlooking the river, or slightly spiffier digs across the road in red-painted wood duplexes at 'Mr Boune's'.

Auberge Sala Done Khone BOUTIQUE HOTEL $$
(☎031-260940; www.saladonekhone.salalao.com; r incl breakfast US$50-60; ❄ @ ≋ ≈) In a handsomely renovated French-era hospital, this romantic boutique delights with trompe l'œil floor tiles, four-poster beds and art deco signatured rooms. They're beautiful, if starting to show their age. Outside are spotless A-frame bungalows built in the classic Lao style with ambient-lit, minimalist interiors, while out on the river the **Sala Phae** (r US$60) wing features equally stylish floating cottages with bio-safe toilets.

Pan's Guesthouse GUESTHOUSE $$
(☎020-9797 8222; www.donkhone.com; garden/riverfront d 160,000/200,000K, tr 220,000K; ❄ @ ≋) A range of soporific bungalows finished in solid stained wood with creamy white rattan interiors, immaculate en suites and balconies slung with hammocks. Spring for a riverfront room. Wi-fi is in the restaurant only.

Seng Ahloune Sunset River Resort GUESTHOUSE $$
(☎031-260934; www.sengahloune.com; r incl breakfast US$30-45; ❄ @ ≋) The busy location next to the bridge isn't ideal, but the well-appointed bungalows make up for it, with rattan walls, pink mosquito nets, ornate lamps and wooden bathroom countertops and floors. Its huge riverfront restaurant fills up with tour groups at lunch. Upgrade to a riverfront room.

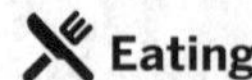

Eating

Many of the best restaurants are on the southeastern shore of Don Det and on Don Khon. Spend a day biking or walking from Ban Hua Det to Don Khon, periodically stopping off for a beer or a bite.

Most guesthouses serve cold Beerlao and a range of Lao and Western favourites.

Don Det

Jasmine Restaurant INDIAN $
(Sunrise Blvd; mains 20,000-35,000K) Sister of the excellent Jasmine in Pakse, this fan-cooled eatery is hugely popular thanks to its central riverside location and excellent Malaysian and Indian grub.

★ **King Kong Resort** INTERNATIONAL $$
(mains 25,000-120,000K) This Brit-run establishment on a peaceful slice of the Mekong in south Don Det is a cut above the competition with an exciting range of pasta, pizzas, burgers, Thai curries, Sunday roasts and – we hear – the tastiest and happiest shakes on the island. Green and yellow trim give it a touch of style. While it does have a few rickety bungalows, this gay-friendly 'resort' is definitely better for dining.

★ **Little Eden Restaurant** LAOTIAN, INTERNATIONAL $$
(mains 35,000-60,000K; ≋) Catching the breeze from the tip of the island, Little Eden is one of the best places to eat upmarket Laotian and Western cuisine. The eclectic menu features tender New Zealand beef steak, spaghetti Bolognese and fish *lâhp*, to name a few. Warm up with a *lòw-lów* mojito.

Boathouse SEAFOOD $$
(☎030-955 5498; mains 25,000-60,000K; ⊙7am-10pm; ≋) Run by a German former fisherman married to a local gal, the emphasis here is on freshly made fish dishes. Try the catfish steamed in banana leaf or the fish BBQ. It's in a sturdy raised structure off the river. Ask about accommodation at adjoining Bountips Guesthouse, as they had plans to upgrade their basic bungalows.

Rib Shack AMERICAN $$
(per rib 10,000K) Lance of Paradise Bungalows fame slings succulent ribs and sides like 'slaw, potato salad and garlic bread from an aptly named shack in the middle of town.

Understand Laos

Laos Today

Much of the change in Laos is relatively recent, following the liberalisation policies of the 1990s. Laos continues to rely on foreign aid, but the traditional donors in the shape of Western governments and NGOs are now overshadowed by private enterprise and the world's newest superdonor, the People's Republic of China. And despite dissatisfaction over a lack of freedoms and rising levels of corruption, the ruling Lao People's Revolutionary Party (LPRP) faces minimal internal challenge to its authority.

Best on Film

The Rocket (2013) The story of a young Lao boy blamed for bringing bad luck to his family. To win back the trust of the family he builds a giant firework to enter the annual Rocket Festival. Set against a backdrop of war, this film has won awards at the Tribeca and Berlin Film Festivals. Shot on location in Laos, it was written and directed by Kim Mordaunt and stars former street kid Sitthiphon Disamoe as Ahlo.

Best in Print

The Coroner's Lunch (Colin Cotterill; 2004) Delve into the delightful world of Dr Siri, full-time national coroner in the 1970s and part-time super sleuth. Try this first instalment and then seek out the other seven titles in the series.

Ant Egg Soup (Natacha Du Pont de Bie; 2004) Subtitled *The Adventures of a Food Tourist in Laos*; the author samples some local delicacies (including some that aren't suitable for a delicate stomach) and includes both recipes and sketches to punctuate the story.

Political System

At first glance the politics of Laos seem simple enough: a one-party system is controlled by ageing revolutionaries who themselves have become a new elite, who have the power to control the exploitation of the country's natural resources, can squash any dissent and cooperate enough with foreign donors to keep the aid dollars coming in. But this generalisation is just that and the reality is more complex.

Laos is indeed a single-party socialist republic, with the only legal political entity being the ruling Lao People's Revolutionary Party (LPRP). Few outside the inner sanctum really understand the political scene, but it's accepted that the LPRP is loosely split between an older, more conservative guard and younger members pushing for limited reform. Cynics will tell you the infighting is mainly for the control of the lucrative kickbacks available to those who command the rights to Laos' rich natural resources. Others say the reformers' primary motivation is to alleviate poverty more quickly by speeding up development. The reality most likely lies somewhere between the two.

Economy

Economically, Laos is in a dynamic period. After the dark days of the Asian financial crisis in the late 1990s, the economy reported 8% growth in 2011, one of the best performances in Asia. However, other numbers don't look so hot. The World Bank rates Laos as one of the least developed countries in East Asia, with more than 75% of people living on less than US$2 a day. More than three-quarters of the population still live as subsistence farmers and gross domestic product was just an estimated US$8.3 billion in 2011.

Major exports are timber products, garments, electricity and coffee, in that order. In recent years tourism has become one of the main generators of foreign income, much of which flows directly into the pockets of those who need it most.

Foreign Aid

Foreign aid remains a constant of the Laos economy, as it has been since the 1800s. First the French established a basic infrastructure, followed by massive wartime investment by the USA. Soviet and Vietnamese assistance helped Laos limp into the 1990s, when the Japanese and Western governments and NGOs started picking up the development tab. Such reliance is unsurprising when you consider there is little effective taxation and the country is only now, for the first time, developing notable export capacity in hydropower.

In recent years China has started spending some of its enormous surplus in Laos. Apart from the obvious investment in infrastructure such as roads, dams and plantations, this has two significant effects. Firstly, Chinese aid comes with few strings attached, meaning that roads, plantations and dams are built by Chinese companies with little or no concern for local people or environments. This is in contrast to the usual carrot-and-stick approach of Western donors, who supply aid in various forms that is dependent on the Lao government improving their systems and getting involved in the development, rather than just sitting back and waiting for the dollars to roll in. Secondly, having China as a major source of funding and as a political role model is unlikely to encourage the Lao government to adopt democratic reforms.

Corruption

Corruption remains a major problem, and laws are flouted because the legal system is under the control of the LPRP. The LPRP is now Marxist-Leninist in nothing but name. Rather, it exercises a single-party dictatorship, whose justification, many argue, is increasingly nationalistic. This may appeal to Lowland Lao, but less to the tribal minorities. Care will be needed to maintain social cohesion. It remains to be seen whether the LPRP has the resourcefulness to meet the challenges ahead.

Increased investment has brought increased exports and increased revenue for the government. Mining royalties are now a significant source of government revenue, as is the giant Nam Theun II hydroelectric dam, completed at the end of 2010. But much of this new wealth finds its way into the pockets of party officials. Transparency International ranks Laos 161 out of 174 countries in its Corruption Perceptions Index 2012, one place below the Democratic Republic of Congo. Indeed, corruption has become widespread at all levels, much to the frustration of the average Laotian, and so the gap between rural and urban living standards continues to widen.

POPULATION: **7 MILLION**

AREA: **236,800 SQ KM**

BORDER COUNTRIES: **CAMBODIA, CHINA, MYANMAR, THAILAND, VIETNAM**

OFFICIAL LANGUAGE: **LAO**

GDP PER CAPITA: **US$2300**

INFLATION: **7.8%**

if Laos were 100 people

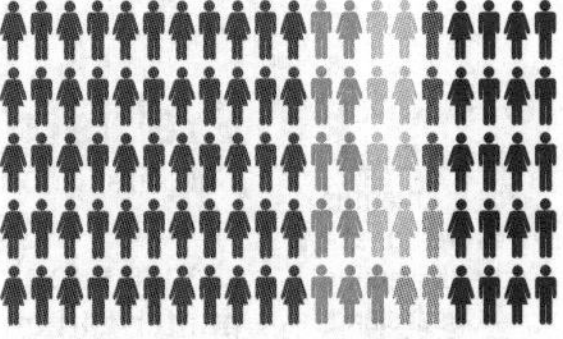

55 would be Lao
11 would be Khmu (Mon-Khmer)
8 would be Hmong
3 would be Chinese
3 would be Vietnamese
20 would be Ethnic Minorities

belief systems

(% of population)

population per sq km

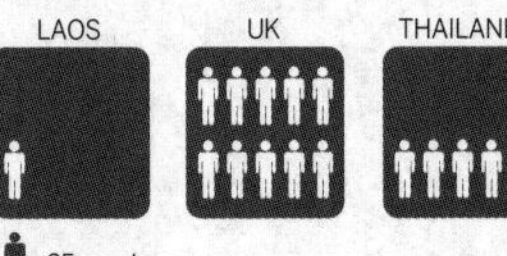

History

Professor Martin Stuart-Fox

Laos first emerged in the region as Lan Xang, or the 'kingdom of a million elephants', in the 14th century. Despite some bursts of independence, the kingdom generally found itself paying tribute to more powerful neighbours, including the Siamese and Vietnamese. Geography ensured Laos was sucked into the Vietnam War and a lengthy civil war culminated in a communist takeover in 1975. After many years of isolation, Laos began to experiment with economic reforms in the 1990s, but political reform remains a distant dream for the average Laos citizen.

Martin Stuart-Fox is Emeritus Professor at the University of Queensland, Australia. He has written seven books and dozens of articles and book chapters on the politics and history of Laos.

Prehistory & Tai-Lao Migration

The first modern humans *(Homo sapiens)* arrived in Southeast Asia around 50,000 years ago. Their stone-age technology remained little changed until a Neolithic culture evolved about 10,000 years ago. These hunter-gatherers spread throughout much of Southeast Asia, including Laos. Their descendants produced the first pottery in the region, and later bronze metallurgy. In time they adopted rice cultivation, introduced down the Mekong River valley from southern China. These people were the ancestors of the present-day upland minorities, collectively known as the Lao Thoeng (Upland Lao), the largest group of which are the Khamu of northern Laos.

The earliest kingdom in southern Laos was identified in Chinese texts as Chenla, dating from the 5th century. One of its capitals was close to Champasak, near the later Khmer temple of Wat Phu. A little later Mon people (speaking another Austro-Asiatic language) established kingdoms on the middle Mekong – Sri Gotapura (Sikhottabong in Lao) with its capital near Tha Khaek, and Chanthaburi in the vicinity of Viang Chan (Vientiane).

Tai peoples probably began migrating out of southern China in about the 8th century. They included the Tai-Lao of Laos, the Tai-Syam and Tai-Yuan of central and northern Thailand, and the Tai-Shan of north-

TIMELINE

500

The early Mon-Khmer Chenla capital of Shrestapura is a thriving city based around the ancient temple of Wat Phu Champasak.

KATIE GARROD/GETTY IMAGES ©

1181

King Jayavarman VII vanquishes the Chams from Angkor and becomes the most powerful ruler of the Khmer empire, extending its boundaries to include most of modern-day Laos.

➡ Wat Phu Champasak (p227)

east Burma. They are called Tai to distinguish them from the citizens (Thai) of modern Thailand, although the word is the same. All spoke closely related Tai languages, practised wet-rice cultivation along river valleys, and organised themselves into small principalities, known as *meuang*, each presided over by a hereditary ruler, or *jow meuang* (lord of the *meuang*). The Tai-Lao, or Lao for short, moved slowly down the rivers of northern Laos, like the Nam Ou and the Nam Khan, running roughly from northeast to southwest, until they arrived at the Mekong, the Great River.

The Kingdom of Lan Xang

The first extended Lao kingdom dates from the mid-14th century. It was established in the context of a century of unprecedented political and social change in mainland Southeast Asia. At the beginning of the 13th century, the great Khmer king Jayavarman VII, who had re-established Cambodian power and built the city of Angkor Thom, sent his armies north to extend the Khmer empire to include all of the middle Mekong region and north-central Thailand. But the empire was overstretched, and by the mid-13th century the Khmer were in retreat. At the same time, the Mongol Yuan dynasty in China abandoned plans for further conquest in Southeast Asia.

This left a political vacuum in central Thailand, into which stepped Ramkhamhaeng, founder of the Tai-Syam kingdom of Sukhothai. To his north, his ally Mangray founded the Tai-Yuan kingdom of Lanna

ALTERNATE ORIGINS

The early Lao text known as the *Nithan (Story of) Khun Borom* recounts the myth of creation of the Lao peoples, their interaction and the establishment of the first Lao kingdom in the vicinity of Luang Prabang. The creation myth tells how two great gourds grew at Meuang Thaeng (Dien Bien Phu, now in Vietnam) from inside which sounds could be heard. Divine rulers, known as *khun*, pierced one of the gourds with a hot poker, and out of the charred hole poured the dark-skinned Lao Thoeng (Upland Lao). The *khun* used a knife to cut a hole in the other gourd, through which escaped the lighter-skinned Tai-Lao (or Lao Loum, Lowland Lao). The gods then sent Khun Borom to rule over both Lao Loum and Lao Thoeng. He had seven sons, whom he sent out to found seven new kingdoms in the regions where Tai peoples settled (in the Tai highlands of Vietnam, the Xishuangbanna of southern China, Shan state in Burma, and in Thailand and Laos). While the youngest son founded the kingdom of Xieng Khuang on the Plain of Jars, the oldest son, Khun Lo, descended the Nam Ou, seized the principality of Meuang Sua from its Lao Thoeng ruler, and named it Xiang Dong Xiang Thong (later renamed Luang Prabang).

1256

Kublai Khan sacks the Tai state of Nan Chao, part of the Xishuangbanna region of modern-day Yunnan in China. This sparks a southern exodus of the Tai people.

1353

Fa Ngum establishes the Lao kingdom of Lan Xang and builds a capital at Xiang Dong Xiang Thong.

1421

King Fa Ngum's son and successor Samsenthai dies and Lan Xang implodes into warring factions for the next century.

1479

The Vietnamese emperor Le Thanh Tong invades Lan Xang, sending a large force including many war elephants.

(meaning 'a million rice fields'), with his capital at Chiang Mai. Other smaller Tai kingdoms were established at Phayao and Xiang Dong Xiang Thong (Luang Prabang). In southern Laos and eastern Thailand, however, the Khmer still held on to power.

The Cambodian court looked around for an ally, and found one in the form of a young Lao prince, Fa Ngum, who was being educated at Angkor. Fa Ngum's princely father had been forced to flee Xiang Dong Xiang Thong after he seduced one of his own father's concubines. So Fa Ngum was in direct line for the throne.

The Khmer gave Fa Ngum a Khmer princess and an army, and sent him north to wrest the middle Mekong from the control of Sukhothai, and so divert and weaken the Tai-Syam kingdom. He was successful and Fa Ngum was pronounced king in Xiang Dong Xiang Thong, before forcibly bringing Viang Chan into his growing empire. He named his new kingdom Lan Xang Hom Khao, which means 'a million elephants and the white parasol'. Fa Ngum built a fine capital at Xiang Dong Xiang Thong and set about organising his court and kingdom.

Fa Ngum performed sacrifices to the *pěe* (traditional spirits) of the kingdom. But he also acquiesced to his wife's request to introduce Khmer Theravada Buddhism to Lan Xang. Here, according to the Lao chronicles, he began to run into problems. The Cambodian king despatched a large contingent of monks and craftsmen up the Mekong, but they only got as far as Viang Chan. There the image they were escorting, the famous Pha Bang, magically refused to move, and had to be left behind. Its reason for refusing to go on to the Lao capital was that it knew that Fa Ngum was not morally worthy. And it seems the Pha Bang was right. Fa Ngum began to seduce the wives and daughters of his court nobles, who decided to replace him. Fa Ngum was sent into exile in Nan (now in Thailand), where he died within five years. His legacy, however, stood the test of time. The kingdom of Lan Xang remained a power in mainland Southeast Asia until early in the 18th century, able to match the power of Siam, Vietnam and Burma.

Fa Ngum was succeeded by his son Un Heuan, who took the throne name Samsenthai, meaning 300,000 Tai, the number of men, his census reported, who could be recruited to serve in the army. He married princesses from the principal Tai kingdoms (Lanna and Ayutthaya, which had replaced Sukhothai), consolidated the kingdom and developed trade. With his wealth he built temples and beautified his capital.

Following Samsenthai's long and stable reign of 42 years, Lan Xang was shaken by succession disputes, a problem faced by all Southeast Asian *mandala* (circles of power). The throne eventually passed to Samsenthai's youngest son, who took the throne name Xainya

WHAT'S IN A NAME?

By naming his kingdom Lan Xang Hom Khao, Fa Ngum was making a statement about power and kingship. Elephants were the battle tanks of Southeast Asian warfare, so to claim to be the kingdom of a million elephants was to issue a warning to surrounding kingdoms: 'Don't mess with the Lao!' A white parasol was the traditional symbol of kingship.

1501
King Visoun comes to the throne and rebuilds the Lao kingdom, marking a cultural renaissance for Lan Xang. He installs the Pha Bang Buddha image in Luang Prabang.

1560
King Setthathirat, grandson of King Visoun, moves the capital to Viang Chan because of the threat from Burma, a rising power in the region.

1638
The great Lao king, Suriya Vongsa, begins a 57-year reign known as the 'Golden Age' of the kingdom of Lan Xang.

1641–42
The first Europeans to write accounts of Lan Xang arrive in Viang Chan providing information about trade and culture, descriptions of King Setthathirat's royal palace and details of the king's power.

Chakkaphat (Universal Ruler). It was an arrogant claim, but he ruled wisely and well.

Tragedy struck at the end of his reign, when Lan Xang suffered its first major invasion. After a bitter battle (recounted at length in the Lao chronicles, which even give the names of the principal war elephants), the Vietnamese captured and sacked Xiang Dong Xiang Thong. Xainya Chakkaphat fled and the Lao mounted a guerrilla campaign. Eventually the Vietnamese were forced to withdraw, their forces decimated by malaria and starvation. So great were their losses that the Vietnamese vowed never to invade Lan Xang again.

Consolidation of the Kingdom

The Lao kingdom recovered under one of its greatest rulers, who came to the throne in 1501. This was King Visoun, who had previously been governor of Viang Chan. There he had been an ardent worshipper of the Pha Bang Buddha image, which he brought with him to Xiang Dong Xiang Thong to become the palladium of the kingdom. For it he built the magnificent temple known as Wat Wisunarat (Wat Visoun), which, though damaged and repaired over the years, still stands in Luang Prabang.

A new power had arisen in mainland Southeast Asia: the kingdom of Burma. It was the threat of Burma that in 1560 convinced King Setthathirat to move his capital to Viang Chan. Before he did so, he built the most beautiful Buddhist temple surviving in Laos, Wat Xieng Thong. He also left behind the Pha Bang, and changed the name of Xiang Dong Xiang Thong to Luang Prabang in its honour. With him he took what he believed to be an even more powerful Buddha image, the Pha Kaew (Emerald Buddha), now in Bangkok.

Setthathirat was the greatest builder in Lao history. Not only did he construct or refurbish several monasteries in Luang Prabang, besides Wat Xieng Thong, but he also did the same in Viang Chan. His most important building projects, apart from a new palace on the banks of the Mekong, were the great That Luang stupa, a temple for the Emerald Buddha (Wat Pha Kaeo) and endowment of a number of royal temples in the vicinity of the palace.

It was more than 60 years before another great Lao king came to the throne, a period of division, succession disputes and intermittent Burmese domination. In 1638 Suriya Vongsa was crowned king. He would rule for 57 years, the longest reign in Lao history and a 'golden age' for the kingdom of Lan Xang. During this time, Lan Xang was a powerful kingdom and Viang Chan was a great centre of Buddhist learning, attracting monks from all over mainland Southeast Asia.

Southeast Asian kingdoms were not states in the modern sense, with fixed frontiers, but varied in extent depending on the power of the centre. Outlying *meuang* (principalities) might transfer their allegiance elsewhere when the centre was weak. That is why scholars prefer the term *mandala,* a Sanskrit word meaning 'circle of power' (in Lao *monthon*).

1694

King Suriya Vongsa dies and Lan Xang once again fractures into competing kingdoms.

1707–13

Lan Xang is divided into three smaller and weaker kingdoms: Viang Chan (Vientiane), Luang Prabang and Champasak.

1769

Burmese armies overrun northern Laos and annex the kingdom of Luang Prabang.

1778

Thai forces invade southern Laos and conquer the kingdom of Champasak.

The Kingdom Divided

King Suriya Vongsa must have been stern and unbending in his old age, because he refused to intervene when his son and heir was found guilty of adultery and condemned to death. As a result, when he died in 1695 another succession dispute wracked the kingdom. This time the result was the division of Lan Xang. First the ruler of Luang Prabang declared independence from Viang Chan, followed a few years later by Champasak in the south.

Paths to Conflagration: Fifty Years of Diplomacy and Warfare in Laos, Thailand and Vietnam, 1778–1828 (1998), by Mayoury Ngaosyvathn and Pheuiphanh Ngaosyvathn, provides the best account of the Lao revolt against Bangkok, from a Lao perspective.

The once great kingdom of Lan Xang was thus fatally weakened. In its place were three (four with Xieng Khuang) weak regional kingdoms, none of which was able to withstand the growing power of the Tai-Syam kingdom of Ayutthaya. The Siamese were distracted, however, over the next half century by renewed threats from Burma. In the end Ayutthaya was sacked by a Burmese army. Chiang Mai was already a tributary to Burma, and Luang Prabang also paid tribute.

However, it did not take the Siamese long to recover. The inspiring leadership of a young military commander called Taksin, son of a Chinese father and a Siamese mother, rallied the Siamese and drove the Burmese out. After organising his kingdom and building a new capital, Taksin sought new fields of conquest. The Lao kingdoms were obvious targets. By 1779 all three had surrendered to Siamese armies and accepted the suzerainty of Siam. The Emerald Buddha was carried off by the Siamese and all Lao kings had to present regular tribute to Bangkok.

When Chao Anou succeeded his two older brothers on the throne of Viang Chan, he determined to assert Lao independence. First he made merit by endowing Buddhist monasteries and building his own temple (Wat Si Saket). Then in 1826 he made his move, sending three armies

FIRST CONTACT

The first European to have left an account of the Lao kingdom arrived in Viang Chan (Vientiane) in 1641. He was a merchant by the name of Gerrit van Wuysthoff, an employee of the Dutch East India Company, who wanted to open a trade route down the Mekong. He and his small party were royally accommodated and entertained during their eight-week stay in the Lao capital. Van Wuysthoff has more to say about the prices of trade goods than about Lao culture or religion, but he was followed a year later by a visitor who can offer us more insight into 17th-century Viang Chan. This was the Jesuit missionary Giovanni-Maria Leria who stayed in Viang Chan for five years. During that time he had singularly little success in converting anyone to Christianity and eventually gave up in disgust. But he liked the Lao people (if not the monks) and has left a wonderful description of the royal palace and the houses of the nobility.

1826–28

Chao Anou succeeds his two older brothers on the throne of Viang Chan and wages war against Siam for Lao independence. He is captured and Viang Chan is sacked by the Siamese armies.

1867

Members of the French Mekong expedition reach Luang Prabang. Over the next 20 years the town is caught up in a struggle which sees the king offered protection by France.

1885

Following centuries of successive invasions by neighbouring powers, the former Lan Xang is broken up into a series of states under Siamese control.

1887

Luang Prabang is looted and burned by a mixed force of Upland Tai and Haw; only Wat Xieng Thong is spared.

down the Mekong and across the Khorat plateau. The Siamese were taken by surprise, but quickly rallied. Siamese armies drove the Lao back and seized Viang Chan. Chao Anou fled, but was captured when he tried to retake the city a year later. This time the Siamese were ruthless. Viang Chan was thoroughly sacked and its population resettled east of the Mekong. Only Wat Si Saket was spared. Chao Anou died a caged prisoner in Bangkok.

For the next 60 years the Lao *meuang*, from Champasak to Luang Prabang, were tributary to Siam. At first these two remaining small kingdoms retained a degree of independence, but increasingly they were brought under closer Siamese supervision. One reason for this was that Siam itself was threatened by a new power in the region and felt it had to consolidate its empire. The new power was France, which had declared a protectorate over most of Cambodia in 1863.

Four years later a French expedition sent to explore and map the Mekong River arrived in Luang Prabang, then the largest settlement upstream from Phnom Penh. In the 1880s the town became caught up in a struggle that pitted Siamese, French and roving bands of Chinese brigands (known as Haw) against each other. In 1887 Luang Prabang was looted and burned by a mixed force of Upland Tai and Haw. Only Wat Xieng Thong was spared. The king escaped downstream. With him was a French explorer named Auguste Pavie, who offered him the protection of France.

French Rule

In the end French rule was imposed through gunboat diplomacy. In 1893 a French warship forced its way up the Chao Phraya River to Bangkok and trained its guns on the palace. Under duress, the Siamese agreed to transfer all territory east of the Mekong to France. So Laos became a French colony, with the kingdom of Luang Prabang as a protectorate and the rest of the country directly administered.

The first Frenchman to arrive in Laos was Henri Mouhot, an explorer and naturalist who died of malaria in 1861 near Luang Prabang (where his tomb can still be seen).

In 1900 Viang Chan (Vientiane) was re-established as the administrative capital of Laos, although real power was exercised from Hanoi, the capital of French Indochina. In 1907 a further treaty was signed with Siam adding two territories west of the Mekong to Laos (Sainyabuli Province and part of Champasak). Siem Reap and Battambang provinces were regained by Cambodia as part of the deal.

Over the next few years the French put into place the apparatus of colonial control, but Laos remained a backwater. Despite French plans for economic exploitation, Laos was always a drain on the budget of Indo-china. Corvée (enforced) labour was introduced, particularly to build roads, and taxes were heavy, but the colony never paid its own way. Some timber was floated down the Mekong, and tin was discovered in central

1893

A French warship reaches Bangkok, guns trained on the palace. This forces the Siamese to give France sovereignty over all Lao territories east of the Mekong.

1904

King Sisavang Vong founds the modern royal family.

1907

The present borders of Laos are established by international treaty. Vientiane (the French spelling of Viang Chan) becomes the administrative capital.

1935

The first two Lao members join the Indochinese Communist Party (ICP), founded by Ho Chi Minh in 1930.

Laos, but returns were meagre. Coffee was grown in southern Laos, and opium in the north, most of it smuggled into China.

In the interwar years the French cast around for ways to make Laos economically productive. One plan was to connect the Lao Mekong towns to coastal Vietnam by constructing a railway across the mountains. The idea was to encourage the migration of industrious Vietnamese peasants into Laos to replace what the French saw as the indolent and easy-going Lao. Eventually Vietnamese would outnumber Lao and produce an economic surplus. The railway was surveyed and construction begun from the Vietnamese side, but the Great Depression intervened, money dried up and the Vietnamisation of Laos never happened.

Nationalism & Independence

The independence movement was slow to develop in Laos. The French justified their colonial rule as protection of the Lao from aggressive neighbours, particularly the Siamese. Most of the small Lao elite, aware of their own weakness, found this interpretation convincing, even though they resented the presence of so many Vietnamese. The Indochinese Communist Party (ICP), founded by Ho Chi Minh in 1930, did not espouse separate independence for Vietnam, Laos and Cambodia. It only managed to recruit its first two Lao members in 1935.

It took the outbreak of war in Europe to weaken the French position in Indochina. A new aggressively nationalist government in Bangkok took advantage of this French weakness to try to regain territory 'lost' 50 years before. It renamed Siam Thailand, and opened hostilities. A Japanese-brokered peace agreement deprived Laos of its territories west of the Mekong, much to Lao anger.

To counter pan-Tai propaganda from Bangkok, the French encouraged Lao nationalism. Under an agreement between Japan and the Vichy French administration in Indochina, French rule continued, although Japanese forces had freedom of movement. The Japanese were in place, therefore, when in early 1945 they began to suspect the French of shifting their allegiance to the allies. On 9 March the Japanese struck in a lightning *coup de force* throughout Indochina, interning all French military and civilian personnel. Only in Laos did a few French soldiers manage to slip into the jungle to maintain some resistance, along with their Lao allies.

Naga Cities of Mekong (2006) by Martin Stuart-Fox provides a narrative account of the founding legends and history of Luang Prabang, Vientiane and Champasak, and a guide to their temples.

The Japanese ruled Laos for just six months before the atomic bombing of Hiroshima and Nagasaki brought WWII to an end. During this time they forced King Sisavang Vong to declare Lao independence, and a nationalist resistance movement took shape, known as the Lao Issara (Free Lao). When the Japanese surrendered on 15 August, the Lao Issara formed an interim government, under the direction of Prince Phetsarat,

1942

As WWII spills over into Asia, the Japanese invade and occupy Laos with the cooperation of pro-Vichy French colonial authorities.

1945

The Japanese occupy Laos then force the king to declare independence; a nationalist resistance movement, the Lao Issara (Free Lao), takes shape and forms an interim government.

1946

The French reoccupy Laos, sending the Lao Issara government into exile.

1949

France grants Laos partial independence within the Indochinese Federation and some of the Lao Issara leaders return to work for complete Lao independence from France.

a cousin of the king. For the first time since the early 18th century, the country was unified. The king, however, thereupon repudiated his declaration of independence in the belief that Laos still needed French protection. The king dismissed Phetsarat as prime minister, so the provisional National Assembly of 45 prominent nationalists passed a motion deposing the king.

Behind these tensions were the French, who were determined to regain their Indochinese empire. In March 1946, while a truce was held in Vietnam between the Viet Minh and the French, French forces struck north to seize control of Laos. The Lao Issara government was forced to flee to exile in Bangkok, leaving the French to sign a modus vivendi with the king reaffirming the unity of Laos and extending the king's rule from Luang Prabang to all of Laos. West Bank territories seized by Thailand in 1940 were returned to Laos.

By 1949 something of a stalemate had developed between the French and the Viet Minh in the main theatre of war in Vietnam. In order to shore up their position in Laos, the French granted the Lao a greater measure of independence. A promise of amnesty for Issara leaders attracted most back to take part in the political process in Laos. Among the returnees was Souvanna Phouma, a younger brother of Phetsarat, who remained in Thailand. Meanwhile Souphanouvong, a half-brother of the two princes, led his followers to join the Viet Minh and keep up the anticolonial struggle.

BAMBOO PALACE

Bamboo Palace: Discovering the Lost Dynasty of Laos (2003) by Christopher Kremmer builds on his personal travelogue told in *Stalking the Elephant Kings* (1997) to try to discover the fate of the Lao royal family.

Rise of the Pathet Lao

The decisions of the three princes to go their separate ways divided the Lao Issara. Those members who returned to Laos continued to work for complete Lao independence from France, but within the legal framework. Those who joined the Viet Minh did so in pursuit of an altogether different political goal – expulsion of the French and formation of a Marxist regime. Their movement became known as the Pathet Lao (Land of the Lao), after the title of the Resistance Government of Pathet Lao, set up with Viet Minh support in August 1950.

The architect of the Lao Issara–Viet Minh alliance was Prince Souphanouvong. In August 1950 Souphanouvong became the public face of the Resistance Government and president of the Free Laos Front (Naeo Lao Issara), successor to the disbanded Lao Issara. Real power lay, however, with two other men, both of whom were members (as Souphanouvong then was not) of the Indochinese Communist Party. They were Kaysone Phomvihane, in charge of defence, and Nouhak Phoumsavan, with the portfolio of economy and finance.

By this time the whole complexion of the First Indochina War had changed with the 1949 victory of communism in China. As Chinese

1950
Lao communists (the Pathet Lao) form a 'Resistance Government'. Souphanouvong becomes the public face of the Resistance Government and president of the Free Laos Front.

1953
The Franco–Lao Treaty of Amity and Association grants full independence to Laos and a Lao delegation attends a conference in Geneva where a regroupment area is set aside for Pathet Lao forces.

1955
Pathet Lao leaders form the Lao People's Party (later the Lao People's Revolutionary Party; :PRP) with a broad political front called the Lao Patriotic Front (LPF).

1957
The First Coalition Government of National Union is formed and collapses after a financial and political crisis.

weapons flowed to the Viet Minh, the war widened and the French were forced onto the defensive. The siege of Dien Bien Phu, close to the Lao border in Northern Vietnam, emerged as the decisive battle of the First Indochina War. The isolated French garrison was surrounded by Viet Minh forces, which pounded the base with artillery hidden in the hills. Supplied only from the air, the French held out for over two months before surrendering on 7 May. The following day a conference opened in Geneva that eventually brought the curtain down on the French colonial period in Indochina.

Division & Unity

Laos had already achieved full independence from France in October 1953, so the Lao delegation attended the conference in Geneva as representatives of a free and independent country. It was agreed to temporarily divide Vietnam into north and south, each with a separate administration, but with the instruction to hold free and fair elections before the end of 1956. Cambodia was left undivided, but in Laos two northeastern provinces (Hua Phan and Phongsali) were set aside as regroupment areas for Pathet Lao forces. There the Pathet Lao consolidated their political and military organisation, while negotiating with the Royal Lao Government (RLG) to reintegrate the two provinces into a unified Lao state.

The first thing Pathet Lao leaders did was to establish a Lao Marxist political party. The Lao People's Party was formed in 1955 and later renamed the Lao People's Revolutionary Party (LPRP) in 1972. Today it remains the ruling party of the Lao PDR (People's Democratic Republic).

The Ravens: Pilots of the Secret War of Laos (1988) by Christopher Robbins tells the story of the American volunteer pilots based in Laos who supplied the 'secret army' and identified targets for US Air Force jets.

In good Marxist fashion, the LPP in 1956 established a broad political front, called the Lao Patriotic Front (LPF). Souphanouvong was president of the front, while Kaysone was secretary-general of the party. Together with other members of the 'team' they led the Lao revolution throughout its '30-year struggle' (1945 to 1975) for power. Over this whole period no factionalism split the movement, which was one of its great strengths compared to the divisions among its opponents.

The first priority for the Royal Lao Government was to reunify the country. This required a political solution to which the Pathet Lao would agree. The tragedy for Laos was that when, after two centuries, an independent Lao state was reborn, it was conceived in the chaos of WWII, nourished during the agony of the First Indochina War and born into the Cold War. From its inception, the Lao state was torn by ideological division, which the Lao tried mightily to overcome, but which was continuously exacerbated by outside interference.

In its remote base areas, the Pathet Lao was entirely dependent for weapons and most other kinds of assistance on the North Vietnamese, whose

1958
The government falls and comes under the control of the right-wing, US-backed Committee for the Defence of National Interests (CDNI).

1960
Guerrilla warfare covers large areas. A neutralist coup d'état is followed by the battle for Vientiane.

1961
Orders given to the CIA to form a 'secret army' in northern Laos with links to the American war in Vietnam.

1962
The Geneva Agreement on Laos establishes the second coalition government that balances Pathet Lao and rightist representation with neutralist voting powers.

THE 'SECRET ARMY' & THE HMONG

After Laos gained independence in 1953, the United States trained and supplied the Royal Lao Army as part of its strategy to combat communism in Southeast Asia. In 1961, CIA agents made contact with the Hmong minority living on and around the Plain of Jars. They spread a simple message – 'Beware of the Vietnamese; they will take your land' – handed out weapons and gave basic training. There were also some vague promises of Hmong autonomy. To protect more vulnerable communities, several thousand Hmong decided to relocate to mountain bases to the south of the plain. Their leader was a young Hmong army officer named Vang Pao.

In October 1961, President John F Kennedy gave the order to recruit a force of 11,000 Hmong under the command of Vang Pao. They were trained by several hundred US and Thai Special Forces advisors and parachuted arms and food supplies by Air America, all under the supervision of the CIA.

With the neutralisation of Laos and formation of the second coalition government in 1962, US military personnel were officially withdrawn. Even as it signed the 1962 Geneva Agreements, however, the US continued its covert operations, in particular the supply and training of the 'secret army' for guerrilla warfare. The CIA's secret headquarters was at Long Cheng, but the largest Hmong settlement, with a population of several thousand, was at Sam Thong.

Over the next 12 years the Hmong 'secret army' fought a continuous guerrilla campaign against heavily armed North Vietnamese regular army troops occupying the Plain of Jars. They were supported throughout by the US, an operation kept secret from the American public until 1970. So while American forces fought in Vietnam, a 'secret war' was also being fought in Laos. The Hmong fought because of their distrust of the communists, and in the hope that the US would support Hmong autonomy.

As the war dragged on, so many Hmong were killed that it became difficult to find recruits. Boys as young as 12 were sent to war. The 'secret army' was bolstered by recruits from other minority groups, including Yao (Mien) and Khamu, and by whole battalions of Thai volunteers. By the early 1970s it had grown to more than 30,000 men, about a third of them Thai.

When a ceasefire was signed in 1973, prior to formation of the third coalition government, the 'secret army' was officially disbanded. Thai volunteers returned home and Hmong units were absorbed into the Royal Lao Army. Hmong casualty figures have been put at 12,000 dead and 30,000 more wounded, but may well have been higher.

Years of warfare had bred deep distrust, however, and as many as 120,000 Hmong out of a population of some 300,000 fled Laos after 1975, rather than live under the Lao communist regime. Most were resettled in the United States. Among the Hmong who sided with the Pathet Lao, several now hold senior positions in the Lao People's Revolutionary Party (LPRP) and in government.

1964

The US begins air war against ground targets in Laos, mostly against communist positions on the Plain of Jars.

JULIET COOMBE/GETTY IMAGES ©

➡ Defused American bomb

1964–73

The Second Indochina War spills over into Laos. Both the North Vietnamese and US presence increases dramatically and bombing extends along the length of Laos.

1968

The Tet Offensive by the Viet Cong in neighbouring Vietnam turns public opinion in the US against the Second Indochina War.

own agenda was the reunification of Vietnam under communist rule. Meanwhile the Royal Lao Government (RLG) became increasingly dependent on the US, which soon took over from France as its principal aid donor. Thus Laos became the cockpit for Cold War enmity.

The Lao politician with the task of finding a way through both ideological differences and foreign interference was Souvanna Phouma. As prime minister of the RLG he negotiated a deal with his half-brother Souphanouvong which saw two Pathet Lao ministers and two deputy ministers included in a coalition government. The Pathet Lao provinces were returned to the royal administration. Elections were held, in which the LPF did surprisingly well. And the US was furious.

Backfire: The CIA's Secret War in Laos and its Link to the War in Vietnam (1995) by Roger Warner provides an informed account of the range of CIA activity in Laos.

Between 1955 and 1958, the US gave Laos US$120 million, or four times what France had provided over the previous eight years. Laos was almost entirely dependent, therefore, on American largesse to survive. When that aid was withheld, as it was in August 1958 in response to the inclusion of Pathet Lao ministers in the government, Laos was plunged into a financial and political crisis. As a result, the first coalition government collapsed after just eight months.

As guerrilla warfare resumed over large areas, moral objections were raised against Lao killing Lao. On 9 August 1960, the diminutive commanding officer of the elite Second Paratroop Batallion of the Royal Lao Army seized power in Vientiane while almost the entire Lao government was in Luang Prabang making arrangements for the funeral of King Sisavang Vong. Captain Kong Le announced to the world that Laos was returning to a policy of neutrality, and demanded that Souvanna Phouma be reinstated as prime minister. King Sisavang Vatthana acquiesced, but General Phoumi refused to take part, and flew to central Laos where he instigated opposition to the new government.

In this, he had the support of the Thai government and the US Central Intelligence Agency (CIA), which supplied him with cash and weapons. The neutralist government still claimed to be the legitimate government of Laos, and as such received arms, via Vietnam, from the Soviet Union. Most of these found their way to the Pathet Lao, however. Throughout the country large areas fell under the control of communist forces. The US sent troops to Thailand, in case communist forces should attempt to cross the Mekong, and it looked for a while as if the major commitment of US troops in Southeast Asia would be to Laos rather than Vietnam.

The Second Indochina War

At this point the new US administration of President John F Kennedy had second thoughts about fighting a war in Laos. In an about-face it decided instead to back Lao neutrality. In May 1961 a new conference on Laos was convened in Geneva. Progress was slow, however, because the

1974
Finally a 1973 ceasefire in Vietnam means an end to fighting in Laos and the formation of the third coalition government.

1975
Communists seize power and declare the Lao People's Democratic Republic (LPDR). This ends 650 years of the Lao monarchy.

1979
Agricultural cooperatives are abandoned and first economic reforms introduced.

1986
The 'New Economic Mechanism' opens the way for a market economy and foreign investment.

three Lao factions could not agree on a political compromise that would allow a second coalition government to be formed.

Delegates of the 14 participating countries reassembled in Geneva in July 1962 to sign the international agreement guaranteeing Lao neutrality and forbidding the presence of all foreign military personnel. In Laos the new coalition government took office buoyed by popular goodwill and hope.

Within months, however, cracks began to appear in the façade of the coalition. The problem was the war in Vietnam. Both the North Vietnamese and the Americans were jockeying for strategic advantage, and neither was going to let Lao neutrality get in the way. Despite the terms of the Geneva Agreements, both continued to provide their respective clients with arms and supplies. But no outside power did the same for the neutralists, who found themselves increasingly squeezed between left and right.

By the end of 1963, as each side denounced the other for violating the Geneva Agreements, the second coalition government had irrevocably broken down. It was in the interests of all powers, however, to preserve the façade of Lao neutrality, and international diplomatic support was brought to bear for Souvanna Phouma to prevent rightist generals from seizing power in coups mounted in 1964 and 1965.

In 1964 the US began its air war over Laos, with strafing and bombing of communist positions on the Plain of Jars. As North Vietnamese infiltration picked up along the Ho Chi Minh Trail, bombing was extended across all of Laos. According to official figures, the US dropped 2,093,100 tons of bombs on 580,944 sorties. The total cost was US$7.2 billion, or US$2 million a day for nine years. No one knows how many people died, but one-third of the population of 2.1 million became internal refugees.

During the 1960s both the North Vietnamese and the US presence increased exponentially. By 1968 an estimated 40,000 North Vietnamese regular army troops were based in Laos to keep the Ho Chi Minh Trail open and support some 35,000 Pathet Lao forces. The Royal Lao Army then numbered 60,000 (entirely paid for and equipped by the US), Vang Pao's forces were half that number (still under the direction of the CIA) and Kong Le's neutralists numbered 10,000. Lao forces on both sides were entirely funded by their foreign backers. For five more years this proxy war dragged on, until the ceasefire of 1973.

The turning point for the war in Vietnam was the 1968 Tet Offensive, which brought home to the American people the realisation that the war was unwinnable by military means, and convinced them of the need for a political solution. The effect in Laos, however, was to intensify both the air war and fighting on the Plain of Jars. When bombing was suspended over North Vietnam, the US Air Force concentrated all its efforts on Laos.

ROADS TO CHINA

During the Second Indochina War, Chinese military engineers built a network of roads into northern Laos. Though these roads assisted the Pathet Lao, they were never bombed by American aircraft, for fear that Chinese troops might join the war in northern Laos.

1987

A three-month border war breaks out between Laos and Thailand, ending in a truce in February 1988.

1991

The constitution of the Lao PDR is proclaimed. General Khamtay Siphandone becomes state president.

1992

Former prime minister and leader of the LPRP, Kaysone Phomvihane, dies at the age of 71.

1995

Luang Prabang is World Heritage–listed. Wat Phu, the ancient Khmer temple near Champasak, is listed shortly after.

The Pathet Lao leadership was forced underground, into the caves of Vieng Xai.

By mid-1972, when serious peace moves were underway, some four-fifths of the country was under communist control. In peace as in war, what happened in Laos depended on what happened in Vietnam. Not until a ceasefire came into effect in Vietnam in January 1973 could the fighting end in Laos. Then the political wrangling began. Not until September was an agreement reached on the composition of the third coalition government and how it would operate.

Revolution & Reform

In April 1975, first Phnom Penh and then Saigon fell to communist forces. Immediately the Pathet Lao brought political pressure to bear on the right in Laos. Escalating street demonstrations forced leading rightist politicians and generals to flee the country. Throughout the country, town after town was peacefully 'liberated' by Pathet Lao forces, culminating with Vientiane in August.

Souvanna Phouma, who could see the writing on the wall, cooperated with the Pathet Lao in order to prevent further bloodshed. Hundreds of senior military officers and civil servants voluntarily flew off to remote camps for 'political re-education', in the belief that they would be there only months at most, but hundreds of these inmates remained in re-education camps for several years.

Kaysone Phomvihane was born in central Laos. As his father was Vietnamese and his mother Lao, he had a Vietnamese surname. He personally adopted the name Phomvihane, which is Lao for Brahmavihara, a series of four divine states – an interesting choice for a committed Marxist.

In November an extraordinary meeting of what was left of the third coalition government bowed to the inevitable and demanded formation of a 'popular democratic regime'. Under pressure, the king agreed to abdicate, and on 2 December a National Congress of People's Representatives assembled by the party proclaimed the end of the 650-year-old Lao monarchy and the establishment of the Lao People's Democratic Republic (Lao PDR). Kaysone Phomvihane, in addition to leading the LPRP, became prime minister in the new Marxist-Leninist government. Souphanouvong was named state president.

The new regime was organised in accordance with Soviet and North Vietnamese models. The government and bureaucracy were under the strict direction of the party and its seven-member politburo. Immediately the party moved to restrict liberal freedoms of speech and assembly, and to nationalise the economy. As inflation soared, price controls were introduced. In response, most members of the Chinese and Vietnamese communities who still remained crossed the Mekong to Thailand. Thousands of Lao did the same. Eventually around 10% of the population, including virtually all the educated class, fled as refugees, setting Lao development back at least a generation.

1997

Laos joins the Association of Southeast Asian Nations (ASEAN).

1998–2000

The Asian economic crisis seriously impacts on the Lao economy. China and Vietnam come to the country's aid with loans and advice.

2000

The economic crisis sparks some political unrest. Anti-government Lao rebels attack a customs post on the Thai border. Five are killed.

2001

A series of small bomb explosions worries the regime, which responds by increasing security.

Though thousands of members of the 'secret army' and their families fled Laos, those who remained still resisted communist control. The Hmong insurgency dragged on for another 30 years. In 1977, fearing the king might escape his virtual house arrest to lead resistance, the authorities arrested him and his family and sent them to Vieng Xai, the old Pathet Lao wartime headquarters. There they were forced to labour in the fields. The king, queen and crown prince all eventually died, probably of malaria and malnutrition, although no official explanation of their deaths has ever been offered.

By 1979 it was clear that policies had to change. Kaysone announced that people could leave cooperatives and farm their own land, and that private enterprise would be permitted. Reforms were insufficient to improve the Lao economy. Over the next few years a struggle took place within the Party about what to do. By the advent of Mikhail Gorbachev in 1985, the Soviet Union was getting tired of propping up the Lao regime, and was embarking on its own momentous reforms. Meanwhile Vietnam had Cambodia to worry about. Eventually Kaysone convinced the Party to follow the Chinese example and open the economy up to market forces while retaining a tight monopoly on political power. The economic reforms were known as the 'new economic mechanism', and were enacted in November 1986.

Economic improvement was slow in coming, partly because relations with Thailand remained strained. In August 1987 the two countries fought a brief border war over disputed territory, which left 1000 people dead. The following year, relations with both Thailand and China were patched up. The first elections for a national assembly were held, and a constitution at last promulgated. Slowly a legal framework was put into place, and by the early 1990s foreign direct investment was picking up and the economy was on the mend.

Post-War Laos: The Politics of Culture, History and Identity (2006) by Vatthana Pholsena expertly examines how ethnicity, history and identity intersect in Laos.

RE-EDUCATION

Re-education camps were all in remote areas. Inmates laboured on road construction, helped local vil lagers and grew their own vegetables. Food was nevertheless scarce, work hard and medical attention inadequate or nonexistent. Except for a couple of high-security camps for top officials and army officers, inmates were allowed some freedom of contact with local villagers. Some even took local girls as partners. Escape was all but impossible, however, because of the remoteness of the camps. Only those showing a contrite attitude to past 'crimes' were released, some to work for the regime, but most to leave the country to join families overseas.

2004

Security is still tight when Laos hosts the 10th Asean summit in Vientiane, the largest gathering of world leaders ever assembled in Laos.

2005

Ten-yearly census is conducted, putting population of Laos at 5,621,982.

2006

The Eighth Congress of the Lao People's Revolutionary Party and National Assembly elections endorse a new political leadership.

2009

Laos hosts the 25th Southeast Asia Games. 4000 Hmong refugees are forcibly repatriated from Thailand.

Modern Laos

In 1992, Kaysone Phomvihane died. He had been the leading figure in Lao communism for more than a quarter of a century. The LPRP managed the transition to a new leadership with smooth efficiency, much to the disappointment of expatriate Lao communities abroad. General Khamtay Siphandone became both president of the LPRP and prime minister. Later he relinquished the latter to become state president. His rise signalled control of the party by the revolutionary generation of military leaders. When Khamtay stepped down in 2006, he was succeeded by his close comrade, General Chummaly Sayasone.

The economic prosperity of the mid-1990s rested on increased investment and foreign aid, on which Laos remained dependent. The Lao PDR enjoyed friendly relations with all its neighbours, particularly Vietnam, and improved relations with China. Relations with Bangkok were bumpy at times, but Thailand was a principal source of foreign investment. In 1997 Laos joined the Association of Southeast Asian Nations (Asean).

The good times came to an end with the Asian economic crisis of the late 1990s. The collapse of the Thai baht led to inflation of the Lao kip, to which it was largely tied through trading relations. The Lao regime took two lessons from this crisis: one was about the dangers of market capitalism; the other was that its real friends were China and Vietnam, both of which came to its aid with loans and advice.

The economic crisis sparked some political unrest. A student demonstration calling for an end to the monopoly of political power by the LPRP was ruthlessly crushed and its leaders given long prison sentences.

In 2003, Western journalists for the first time made contact with Hmong insurgents. Their reports revealed an insurgency on the point of collapse. Renewed military pressure forced some Hmong to surrender, while others made their way to refuge in Thailand. However, the Thai classified the Hmong as illegal immigrants; negotiations for resettlement in third countries stalled, and in December 2009, some 4000 Hmong were forcibly repatriated to Laos.

In the decade to 2010, China greatly increased investment in Laos. Japan remained the largest aid donor. However, Chinese companies invested in major projects in mining, hydropower and plantation agriculture and timber. Meanwhile, cross-border trade grew apace. Increased economic power brought political influence at the expense of Vietnam, though Lao-Vietnamese relations remained close. Senior Lao party cadres still take courses in Marxism-Leninism in Vietnam, although their economic inspiration is more likely from the mighty northern neighbour, China.

POLITICAL CULTURE

The Politics of Ritual and Remembrance: Laos Since 1975 (1998) by Grant Evans provides a penetrating study of Lao political culture, including attitudes to Buddhism and the 'cult' of communist leader Kaysone.

2010

The Nam Theun II hydropower dam, the largest in mainland Southeast Asia, begins production.

2011

Laos wins gold medals in the petanque events at the Southeast Asian games, but it's not yet slated to be included as an Olympic sport.

2012

Laos plays host to the 9th ASEM (Asia-Europe Meeting) in Vientiane in November.

2013

Work begins on the Xayaboury Dam, the first dam to be built on the Mekong River in Laos. Cambodia and Vietnam raise objections.

People & Culture

It's hard to think of any other country with a population as laid-back as Laos. *Bor ben nyăng* ('no problem') could be the national motto. On the surface at least, nothing seems to faze the Lao. Of course, it's not as simple as 'people just smiling all the time because they're happy', as we heard one traveller describe it. The Lao national character is a complex combination of culture, environment and religion.

To a large degree 'Lao-ness' is defined by Buddhism, specifically Theravada Buddhism, which emphasises the cooling of human passions. Thus, strong emotions are a taboo in Lao society. *Kamma* (karma), more than devotion, prayer or hard work, is believed to determine one's lot in life, so the Lao tend not to get too worked up over the future. It's a trait often perceived by outsiders as a lack of ambition.

Laos: Culture and Society (2000), by Grant Evans (ed), brings together a dozen essays on Lao culture, among them a profile of a self-exiled Lao family that eventually returned to Laos, and two well-researched studies of the modernisation and politicalisation of the Lao language.

Lao commonly express the notion that 'too much work is bad for your brain' and they often say they feel sorry for people who 'think too much'. Education in general isn't highly valued, although this attitude is changing with modernisation and greater access to opportunities beyond the country's borders. Avoiding any undue psychological stress, however, remains a cultural norm. From the typical Lao perspective, unless an activity – whether work or play – contains an element of *móoan* (fun), it will probably lead to stress.

The contrast between the Lao and the Vietnamese is an example of how the Annamite Chain has served as a cultural fault line dividing Indo-Asia and Sino-Asia, as well as a geographic divide. The French summed it up as: 'The Vietnamese plant the rice, the Cambodians tend the rice and the Lao listen to it grow.' And while this saying wasn't meant as a compliment, a good number of French colonialists found the Lao way too seductive to resist, and stayed on.

The Lao have always been quite receptive to outside assistance and foreign investment, since it promotes a certain degree of economic development without demanding a corresponding increase in productivity. The Lao government wants all the trappings of modern technology – the skyscrapers seen on socialist propaganda billboards – without having to give up Lao traditions, including the *móoan* philosophy. The challenge for Laos is to find a balance between cultural preservation and the development of new attitudes that will lead the country towards a measure of self-sufficiency.

Lifestyle

Maybe it's because everything closes early, even in the capital, that just about everyone in Laos gets up before 6am. Their day might begin with a quick breakfast, at home or from a local noodle seller, before work. In Lao Loum (Lowland Lao) and other Buddhist areas, the morning also sees monks collecting alms, usually from women who hand out rice and vegetables outside their homes in return for a blessing.

School-age children will walk to a packed classroom housed in a basic building with one or two teachers. Secondary students often board during the week because there are fewer secondary schools and it can be too far to commute. Almost any family who can afford it pays for their kids to learn English, which is seen as a near-guarantee of future employment.

Two slim books of *Lao Folktales*, collected by Steve Epstein, retell some of Laos' better-known folklore. They're great for kids and offer an interesting insight into Lao humour and values.

Given that most Lao people live in rural communities, work is usually some form of manual labour. Depending on the season, and the person's location and gender (women and men have clearly defined tasks when it comes to farming), work might be planting or harvesting rice or other crops. Unlike neighbouring Vietnam, the Lao usually only harvest one crop of rice each year, meaning there are a couple of busy periods followed by plenty of time when life can seem very laid-back.

During these quiet periods, men will fish, hunt and repair the house, while women might gather flora and fauna from the forest, weave fabrics and collect firewood. At these times there's something wonderfully social and uncorrupted about arriving in a village mid-afternoon, sitting in the front of the local 'store' and sharing a *lòw-lów* (whisky) or two with the locals, without feeling like you're stealing their time.

Where vices are concerned, *lòw-lów* is the drug of choice for most Lao, particularly in rural areas where average incomes are so low that Beerlao is beyond most budgets. Opium is the most high-profile of the other drugs traditionally used – and tolerated – in Laos, though recent crop-clearing has made it less available. In cities, *yaba* (methamphetamine), in particular, is becoming popular among young people.

Because incomes are rock-bottom in Laos (US$100 per month could be considered middle-class) the Lao typically socialise as families, pooling their resources to enjoy a *bun wat* (temple festival) or picnic at the local waterfall together. The Lao tend to live in extended families, with three or more generations sharing one house or compound, and dine together sitting on mats on the floor with rice and dishes shared by all.

Most Lao don some portion of the traditional garb during ceremonies and celebrations: the men a *pàh bẹeang* (shoulder sash), the women a similar sash, tight-fitting blouse and *pàh nung* (sarong). In everyday life men wear neat but unremarkable shirt-and-trousers combinations. However, it's still normal for women to wear the *pàh nung* or *sin* (wraparound skirt or sarong). Other ethnicities living in Laos, particularly Chinese and Vietnamese women, will wear the *pàh nung* when they visit a government office, or risk having any civic requests denied.

Ethnic Groups of Laos, Vols 1-3 (2003) by Joachim Schliesinger is a well-respected modern ethnography of Laos. Schliesinger's scheme enumerates and describes 94 ethnicities in detail.

Population

Laos has one of the lowest population densities in Asia, but the number of people has more than doubled in the last 30 years, and continues to grow quickly. One-third of the country's seven million inhabitants live in cities in the Mekong River valley, chiefly Vientiane, Luang Prabang, Savannakhet and Pakse. Another third live along other major rivers.

This rapid population growth comes despite the fact that about 10% of the population fled the country after the 1975 communist takeover. Vientiane and Luang Prabang lost the most inhabitants, with approximately a quarter of the population of Luang Prabang going abroad. During the last couple of decades this emigration trend has been reversed so that the influx of immigrants (mostly repatriated Lao, but also Chinese, Vietnamese and other nationalities) now exceeds the number of émigrés.

Most expatriate Westerners living in Laos are temporary employees of multilateral and bilateral aid organisations. A smaller number are employed by foreign companies involved in mining, petroleum, hydropower and tourism industries.

Ethnic Groups

Laos is often described as less a nation state than a conglomeration of tribes and languages. And depending on who you talk with, that conglomeration consists of between 49 and 134 different ethnic groups. The lower figure is officially used by the government.

While the tribal groups are many and varied, the Lao traditionally divide themselves into four categories: Lao Loum, Lao Tai, Lao Thoeng and Lao Soung. These classifications loosely reflect the altitudes at which the groups live, and, by implication (it's not always accurate), their cultural proclivities. To address some of these inaccuracies, the Lao government recently reclassified ethnic groups into three major language families: Austro-Tai, Austro-Asiatic and Sino-Tibetan. However, many people do not know which language family they come from, so we'll stick here with the more commonly understood breakdown.

Foreign ethnographers who have carried out field research in Laos have identified anywhere from 49 to 134 different ethnic groups.

Just over half the population are ethnic Lao or Lao Loum (Lowland Lao), and these are clearly the most dominant group. Of the rest, 10% to 20% are tribal Tai; 20% to 30% are Lao Thoeng (Upland Lao or lower-mountain dwellers, mostly of proto-Malay or Mon-Khmer descent); and 10% to 20% are Lao Soung (Highland Lao, mainly Hmong or Mien tribes who live higher up).

The Lao government has an alternative three-way split, in which the Lao Tai are condensed into the Lao Loum group. This triumvirate is represented on the back of every 1000 kip bill, in national costume, from left to right: Lao Soung, Lao Loum and Lao Thoeng.

Small Tibeto-Burman hill-tribe groups in Laos include the Lisu, Lahu, Lolo, Akha and Phu Noi. They are sometimes classified as Lao Thoeng, but like the Lao Soung they live in the mountains of northern Laos.

Lao Loum

The dominant ethnic group is the Lao Loum (Lowland Lao), who live in the fertile plains of the Mekong River valley or lower tributaries of the Mekong. Through superior numbers and living conditions, they have dominated the smaller ethnic groups for centuries. Their language is the national language; their religion, Buddhism, is the national religion; and many of their customs, including the eating of sticky rice and the *bąasìi* ceremony, are interpreted as those of the Lao nation, even though they play no part in the lives of many other ethnic groups.

Lao Loum culture has traditionally consisted of a sedentary, subsistence lifestyle based on wet-rice cultivation. The people live in raised homes and, like most Austro-Tais, are Theravada Buddhists who retain strong elements of animist spirit worship.

The distinction between 'Lao' and 'Thai' is a rather recent historical phenomenon, especially considering that 80% of all those who speak a language recognised as 'Lao' reside in northeastern Thailand. Even Lao living in Laos refer idiomatically to different Lao Loum groups as 'Tai' or 'Thai', such as Thai Luang Phabang (Lao from Luang Prabang).

Due to Laos' ethnic diversity, 'Lao culture' only exists among the Lao Loum (Lowland Lao), who represent about half the population. Lao Loum culture predominates in the cities, towns and villages of the Mekong River valley.

Lao Tai

Although they're closely related to the Lao, these Tai (or sometimes Thai) subgroups have resisted absorption into mainstream Lao culture and tend to subdivide themselves according to smaller tribal distinctions. Like the Lao Loum, they live along river valleys, but the Lao Tai have chosen to reside in upland valleys rather than in the lowlands of the Mekong floodplains.

Depending on their location, they cultivate dry (mountain) rice as well as wet (irrigated) rice. The Lao Tai also mix Theravada Buddhism and animism, but tend to place more importance on spirit worship than do the Lao Loum.

Generally speaking, the various Lao Tai groups are distinguished from one another by the predominant colour of their clothing, or by the general area of habitation; for example, Tai Dam (Black Tai), Tai Khao (White Tai), Tai Pa (Forest Tai), Tai Neua (Northern Tai) and so on.

Lao Thoeng

The Lao Thoeng (Upland Lao) are a loose affiliation of mostly Austro-Asiatic peoples who live on mid-altitude mountain slopes in northern and southern Laos. The largest group is the Khamu, followed by the Htin, Lamet and smaller numbers of Laven, Katu, Katang, Alak and some other Mon-Khmer groups in the south. The Lao Thoeng are also known by the pejorative term *khàa,* which means 'slave' or 'servant'. This is because they were used as indentured labour by migrating Austro-Tai peoples in earlier centuries and more recently by the Lao monarchy. They still often work as labourers for the Lao Soung.

The Lao Thoeng have a much lower standard of living than any of the three other groups. Most trade between the Lao Thoeng and other Lao is carried out by barter.

The Htin (also called Lawa) and Khamu languages are closely related, and both groups are thought to have been in Laos long before the arrival of the Loum Lao, tribal Tai or Lao Soung. During the Lao New Year celebrations in Luang Prabang the Loum Lao offer a symbolic tribute to the Khamu as their historical predecessors and as 'guardians of the land'.

TABOO

Traditional Khamu houses often have the skulls of domestic animals hanging on a wall with an altar beneath. The skulls are from animals the family has sacrificed to their ancestors, and it is strictly taboo to touch them.

Lao Soung

The Lao Soung (Highland Lao) include the hill tribes who live at the highest altitudes. Of all the peoples of Laos, they are the most recent immigrants, having come from Myanmar, southern China and Tibet within the last 150 years.

The largest group is the Hmong, also called Miao or Meo, who number more than 300,000 in four main subgroups, the White Hmong, Striped Hmong, Red Hmong and Black Hmong. The colours refer to certain clothing details and these groups are found in the nine provinces of the north, plus Bolikhamsai in central Laos.

The agricultural staples of the Hmong are dry rice and corn raised by the slash-and-burn method. The Hmong also breed cattle, pigs, water buffaloes and chickens, traditionally for barter rather than sale. For years their only cash crop was opium and they grew and manufactured more than any other group in Laos. However, an aggressive eradication program run by the government, with support from the US, has eliminated most of the crop. The resulting loss of a tradeable commodity has hit many Hmong communities very hard. The Hmong are most numerous in Hua Phan, Xieng Khuang, Luang Prabang and northern Vientiane provinces.

The second-largest group are the Mien (also called Iu Mien, Yao and Man), who live mainly in Luang Nam Tha, Luang Prabang, Bokeo, Udomxai and Phongsali. The Mien, like the Hmong, have traditionally cultivated opium poppies. Replacement crops, including coffee, are taking time to bed in and generate income.

The Mien and Hmong have many ethnic and linguistic similarities, and both groups are predominantly animist. The Hmong are considered more aggressive and warlike than the Mien, however, and as such were perfect for the CIA-trained special Royal Lao Government forces in the 1960s and early 1970s. Large numbers of Hmong–Mien left Laos and fled abroad after 1975.

Other Asians

As elsewhere in Southeast Asia, the Chinese have been migrating to Laos for centuries to work as merchants and traders. Most come directly from Yunnan but more recently many have also arrived from Vietnam. Estimates of their numbers vary from 2% to 5% of the total population. At least half of all permanent Chinese residents in Laos are said to live in Vientiane and Savannakhet. There are also thousands of Chinese migrant workers in the far north.

Substantial numbers of Vietnamese live in all the provinces bordering Vietnam and in the cities of Vientiane, Savannakhet and Pakse. For the most part, Vietnamese residents in Laos work as traders and own small businesses, although there continues to be a small Vietnamese military presence in Xieng Khuang and Hua Phan Provinces. Small numbers of Cambodians live in southern Laos.

The Laos Cultural Profile (www.culturalprofiles.net/Laos) is established by Visiting Arts and the Ministry of Information and Culture of Laos covering a broad range of cultural aspects, from architecture to music. It's an easy entry point to Lao culture.

Religion

Buddhism

About 60% of the people of Laos are Theravada Buddhists, the majority being Loum Lao, with a sprinkling of tribal Tais. Theravada Buddhism was apparently introduced to Luang Prabang (then known as Muang Sawa) in the late 13th or early 14th centuries, although there may have been contact with Mahayana Buddhism during the 8th to 10th centuries and with Tantric Buddhism even earlier.

King Visoun, a successor of the first monarch of Lan Xang, King Fa Ngum, declared Buddhism the state religion after accepting the Pha Bang Buddha image from his Khmer sponsors. Today the Pha Bang is kept at Royal Palace Museum in Luang Prabang. Buddhism was fairly slow to spread throughout Laos, even among the lowland peoples, who were reluctant to accept the faith instead of, or even alongside, *pěe* (earth spirit) worship.

Theravada Buddhism is an earlier and, according to its followers, less corrupted school of Buddhism than the Mahayana schools found in east Asia and the Himalayas. It's sometimes referred to as the 'southern' school since it took the southern route from India through Sri Lanka and Southeast Asia.

Theravada doctrine stresses the three principal aspects of existence: *dukkha* (suffering, unsatisfactoriness, disease), *anicca* (impermanence, transience of all things) and *anatta* (nonsubstantiality or nonessentiality of reality; no permanent 'soul'). Comprehension of *anicca* reveals that no experience, no state of mind, no physical object lasts. Trying to hold onto experience, states of mind and objects that are constantly changing creates *dukkha*. *Anatta* is the understanding that there is no part of the changing world we can point to and say 'This is me' or 'This is God' or 'This is the soul'.

The Lao believe most *nahk* (snake deities) have been converted to become serpent protectors of Buddhism, called *naga* (in Lao *nak*). They still require propitiation, however, and annual boat races are held for their amusement. Many Buddhist wats have protective *naga* balustrades.

The ultimate goal of Theravada Buddhism is *nibbana* (nirvana in Sanskrit), which literally means the 'blowing-out' or 'extinction' of all causes of *dukkha*. Effectively it means an end to all corporeal or even heavenly existence, which is forever subject to suffering and which is conditioned from moment to moment by *kamma* (karma, intentional action). In reality, most Lao Buddhists aim for rebirth in a 'better' existence rather than the goal of *nibbana*. By feeding monks, giving donations to temples and performing regular worship at the local wat (temple), Lao Buddhists acquire enough 'merit' (Pali *puñña;* Lao *bun*) for their future lives. And it's in the pursuit of merit that you're most likely to see Lao Buddhism 'in action'. Watching monks walking through their neighbourhoods at dawn to collect offerings of food from people who are kneeling in front of their homes is a memorable experience.

Lao Buddhists visit the wat on no set day. Most often they'll visit on *wán pa* (literally 'excellent days'), which occur with every full, new and quarter moon, ie roughly every seven days. On such a visit, typical activities include the offering of lotus buds, incense and candles at various altars and bone reliquaries, offering food to the monks, meditating, and attending a *táirt* (*dhamma* talk) by the abbot.

Monks & Nuns

Unlike other religions in which priests or nuns make a lifelong commitment to their religious vocation, being a Buddhist monk or nun can be a much more transient experience. Socially, every Lao Buddhist male is expected to become a *kóo-bąh* (monk) for at least a short period in his life, optimally between the time he finishes school and starts a career or marries. Men or boys under 20 years of age may enter the Sangha (monastic order) as *náirn* (novices) and this is not unusual since a family earns merit when one of its sons takes robe and bowl. Traditionally the length of time spent in the wat is three months, during the *pansăh* (Buddhist lent), which coincides with the rainy season. However, nowadays men may spend as little as a week or 15 days to accrue merit as monks or novices. There are, of course, some monks who do devote all or most of their lives to the wat.

POST-REVOLUTION BUDDHISM

During the 1964–73 war years, both sides sought to use Buddhism to legitimise their cause. By the early 1970s, the Lao Patriotic Front (LPF) was winning this propaganda war as more and more monks threw their support behind the communists.

Despite this, major changes were in store for the Sangha (monastic order) following the 1975 takeover. Initially, Buddhism was banned as a primary-school subject and people were forbidden to make merit by giving food to monks. Monks were also forced to till the land and raise animals in direct violation of their monastic vows.

Mass dissatisfaction among the faithful prompted the government to rescind the ban on the feeding of monks in 1976. By the end of that year, the government was not only allowing traditional giving of alms, it was offering a daily ration of rice directly to the Sangha.

In 1992, in what was perhaps its biggest endorsement of Buddhism since the Revolution, the government replaced the hammer-and-sickle emblem that crowned Laos' national seal with a drawing of Pha That Luang, the country's holiest Buddhist symbol.

Today the Department of Religious Affairs (DRA) controls the Sangha and ensures that Buddhism is taught in accordance with Marxist principles. All monks must undergo political indoctrination as part of their monastic training, and all canonical and extra-canonical Buddhist texts have been subject to 'editing' by the DRA. Monks are also forbidden to promote *pěe* (earth spirit) worship, which has been officially banned in Laos along with *săinyasąht* (magic). The cult of *kwăn* (the 32 guardian spirits attached to mental/physical functions), however, has not been tampered with.

One major change in Lao Buddhism was the abolition of the Thammayut sect. Formerly, the Sangha in Laos was divided into two sects, the Mahanikai and the Thammayut (as in Thailand). The Thammayut is a minority sect that was begun by Thailand's King Mongkut. The Pathet Lao saw it as a tool of the Thai monarchy (and hence US imperialism) for infiltrating Lao political culture.

For several years all Buddhist literature written in Thai was also banned, severely curtailing the teaching of Buddhism in Laos. This ban has since been lifted and Lao monks are even allowed to study at Buddhist universities throughout Thailand. However, the Thammayut ban remains and has resulted in a much weaker emphasis on meditation, considered the spiritual heart of Buddhist practice in most Theravada countries. Overall, monastic discipline in Laos is far more relaxed than it was before 1975.

There is no similar hermetic order for nuns, but women may reside in temples as *náhng sée* (lay nuns), with shaved heads and white robes.

Spirit Cults

No matter where you are in Laos the practice of *pěe* (spirit) worship, sometimes called animism, won't be far away. *Pěe* worship predates Buddhism and despite being officially banned it remains the dominant non-Buddhist belief system. But for most Lao it is not a matter of Buddhism *or* spirit worship. Instead, established Buddhist beliefs coexist peacefully with respect for the *pěe* that are believed to inhabit natural objects.

An obvious example of this coexistence is the 'spirit house', which are found in or outside almost every home. Spirit houses are often ornately decorated miniature temples, built as a home for the local spirit. Residents must share their space with the spirit and go to great lengths to keep it happy, offering enough incense and food that the spirit won't make trouble for them.

In Vientiane, Buddhism and spirit worship flourish side by side at Wat Si Muang. The central image at the temple is not a Buddha figure but the *lák méuang* (city pillar from the time of the Khmer empire), in which the guardian spirit for the city is believed to reside. Many local residents make daily offerings before the pillar, while at the same time praying to a Buddha figure. A form of *pěe* worship visitors can partake in is the *bąasǐi* ceremony (p284).

Outside the Mekong River valley, the *pěe* cult is particularly strong among the tribal Tai, especially the Tai Dam, who pay special attention to a class of *pěe* called *then*. The *then* are earth spirits that preside not only over the plants and soil, but over entire districts as well. The Tai Dam also believe in the 32 *khwǎn* (guardian spirits). *Mǒr* (master/shaman), who are specially trained in the propitiation and exorcism of spirits, preside at important Tai Dam festivals and ceremonies. It is possible to see some of the spiritual beliefs and taboos in action by staying in a Katang village during a trek into the forests of Dong Phu Vieng NPA.

The Hmong–Mien tribes also practise animism, plus ancestral worship. Some Hmong groups recognise a pre-eminent spirit that presides over all earth spirits; others do not. The Akha, Lisu and other Tibeto-Burman groups mix animism and ancestor cults.

Article 9 of the current Lao constitution forbids all religious proselytising, and the distribution of religious materials outside churches, temples or mosques is illegal. Foreigners caught distributing religious materials may be arrested and expelled from the country.

Other Religions

A small number of Lao, mostly those of the remaining French-educated elite, are Christians. An even smaller number of Muslims live in Vientiane, mostly Arab and Indian merchants whose ancestry as Laos residents dates as far back as the 17th century. Vientiane also harbours a small community of Chams, Cambodian Muslims who fled Pol Pot's Kampuchea in the 1970s. In northern Laos there are pockets of Muslim Yunnanese, known among the Lao as *jęen hór*.

Women in Laos

For the women of Laos, roles and status vary significantly depending on their ethnicity, but it's fair to say that whatever group they come from they are seen as secondary to men. As you travel around Laos the evidence is overwhelming. While men's work is undoubtedly hard, women always seem to be working harder, for longer and with far less time for relaxing and socialising.

Lao Loum women gain limited benefits from bilateral inheritance patterns, whereby both women and men can inherit land and business ownership. This derives from a matrilocal tradition, where a husband joins the wife's family on marriage. Often the youngest daughter and her husband will live with and care for her parents until they die, when they

Festivals of Laos (2010) by Martin Stuart-Fox and Somsanouk Mixay covers the full annual cycle of Lao festivals, from New Year to That Luang, with the added bonus of Steve Northup's stunning photographs.

inherit at least some of their land and business. However, even if a Lao Loum woman inherits her father's farmland, she will have only limited control over how it is used. Instead, her husband will have the final say on most major decisions, while she will be responsible for saving enough money to see the family through any crisis.

This fits with the cultural beliefs associated with Lao Buddhism, which commonly teaches that women must be reborn as men before they can attain nirvana, hence a woman's spiritual status is generally less than that of a man. Still, Lao Loum women enjoy a higher status than women from other ethnic groups, who become part of their husband's clan on marriage and rarely inherit anything.

Women in Laos face several other hurdles: fewer girls go to school than boys; women are relatively poorly represented in government and other senior positions; and although they make up more than half the workforce, their pay is often lower than male equivalents. If a Lao woman divorces, no matter how fair her reasons, it's very difficult for her to find another husband unless he is older or foreign.

In the cities, however, things are changing as fast as wealth, education and exposure to foreign ideas allows, and in general women in cities are more confident and willing to engage with foreigners than their rural counterparts. Women are pushing into more responsible positions, particularly in foreign-controlled companies.

Arts

The focus of most traditional art in Lao culture has been religious, specifically Buddhist. Yet unlike the visual arts of Thailand, Myanmar and Cambodia, Lao art never encompassed a broad range of styles and periods, mainly because Laos has a much more modest history in terms of power and because it has only existed as a political entity for a short

BĄASĬÍ (BACI)

The *bąasĭi* ceremony is a peculiarly Lao ritual in which guardian spirits are bound to the guest of honour by white or orange strings tied around the wrists. Among Lao it's more commonly called *su khwăn,* meaning 'calling of the soul'.

Lao believe everyone has 32 spirits, known as *khwăn,* each of which acts as a guardian over a specific organ or faculty, both mental and physical. *Khwăn* occasionally wander away from their owner, which is really only a problem when that person is about to embark on a new project or journey away from home, or when they're very ill. Then it's best to perform the *bąasĭi* to ensure that all the *khwăn* are present, thus restoring the equilibrium. In practice, *bąasĭi* are also performed at festivals, weddings, and when special guests arrive – hence villagers often hold a *bąasĭi* when trekkers arrive during a community-based trek.

The *bąasĭi* ceremony is performed seated around a *pàh kwăn,* a conical shaped arrangement of banana leaves, flowers and fruit from which hang cotton threads. A village elder, known as the *mŏr porn,* calls in the wandering *kwăn* during a long Buddhist mantra while he, and the honoured guests, lean in to touch the *pa kwăn.* When the chanting is finished, villagers take the thread from the *pa kwăn* and begin tying it around the wrists of the guests.

At this point the ceremony becomes a lot of fun. Villagers move around the room, stopping in front of guests to tie thread around their wrists. They'll often start by waving the thread across your hand, three times outwards accompanied by 'out with the bad, out with the bad, out with the bad', or something similar, and three times in with 'in with the good'. As they tie they'll also wish you a safe journey and good health.

After the ceremony everyone shares a meal. You're supposed to keep the threads on your wrists for three days and then untie, not cut, them.

time. Furthermore, since Laos was intermittently dominated by its neighbours, much of the art that was produced was either destroyed or, as in the case of the Emerald Buddha, carted off by conquering armies.

Laos' relatively small and poor population, combined with a turbulent recent history, also goes some way toward explaining the absence of any strong tradition of contemporary art. This is slowly changing, and in Vientiane and Luang Prabang modern art in a variety of media is finding its way into galleries and stores.

Weaving is the one art form that is found almost everywhere and has distinct styles that vary by place and tribal group. It's also the single most accessible art the traveller can buy, often directly from the artist.

Literature & Film

Of all classical Lao literature, *Pha Lak Pha Lam,* the Lao version of the Indian epic the Ramayana, is the most pervasive and influential in the culture. The Indian source first came to Laos with the Hindu Khmer as stone reliefs at Wat Phu Champasak and other Angkor-period temples. Oral and written versions may also have been available; later the Lao developed their own version of the epic, which differs greatly both from the original and from Cambodia's *Reamker.*

Of the 547 Jataka tales in the *Pali Tipitaka,* each chronicling a different past life of the Buddha, most appear in Laos almost word for word as they were first inscribed in Sri Lanka. A group of 50 'extra' or apocryphal stories, based on Lao-Thai folk tales of the time, were added by Pali scholars in Luang Prabang between 300 and 400 years ago.

Contemporary literature has been hampered by decades of war and communist rule. The first Lao-language novel was printed in 1944, and only in 1999 was the first collection of contemporary Lao fiction, Ounthine Bounyavong's *Mother's Beloved: Stories from Laos,* published in a bilingual Lao and English edition. Since then, a growing number of Lao novels and short stories have been translated into Thai, but very few have seen English-language translations. One of the most popular was 2009's *When the Sky Turns Upside Down: Memories of Laos,* a translation of short stories, some of which date back 60 years, by prominent Lao authors Dara Viravongs Kanlaya and Douangdeuane Bounyavong.

Not surprisingly, Laos also has one of the quietest film industries in Southeast Asia, and 2008's *Good Morning, Luang Prabang* is only one of a handful of feature films produced in the country since 1975. Starring Lao-Australian heartthrob Ananda Everingham and led by Thai director Sakchai Deenan, the film features a predictably 'safe' love-based plot that nonetheless required the close attention of the Lao authorities during filming.

The Betrayal (Nerakhoon; 2008) is a documentary directed by American Ellen Kuras, with the help of the film's main subject, Thavisouk Phrasavath. Shot over a 23-year period, the film documents the Phrasavath family's experience emigrating from Laos to New York City after the communist revolution.

In 2013, *The Rocket,* the story of a young Lao boy who builds a rocket to regain his family's trust, was released.

LAO FILM

Feature-film making resumed in Laos in 1997 with the release of *Than Heng Phongphai* (The Charming Forest), directed by Vithoun Sundara. This was followed in 2001 by *Falang Phon* (Clear Skies After Rain), and in 2004 by *Leum Teua* (Wrongfulness), also directed by Sundara.

Music & Dance

Lao classical music was originally developed as court music for royal ceremonies and classical dance-drama during the 19th-century reign of Vientiane's Chao Anou, who had been educated in the Siamese court in Bangkok. The standard ensemble for this genre is the *sep nyai,* which consists of *kôrng wóng* (a set of tuned gongs), the *ranyâht* (a xylophone-like instrument), the *kooi* (bamboo flute) and the *ƃee* (a double-reed wind instrument similar to the oboe).

The practice of classical Lao music and drama has been in decline for some time, as 40 years of intermittent war and revolution has simply made this kind of entertainment a low priority among most Lao. Generally, the only time you'll hear this type of music is during the occasional public performance of the *Pha Lak Pha Lam,* a dance-drama based on the Hindu Ramayana epic.

North Illinois University has pages of information on Lao culture, language, history, folklore and music at www.seasite.niu.edu/lao, including recordings of the *káan*.

Not so with Lao folk and pop, which have always stayed close to the people. The principal instrument in folk, and to a lesser extent in pop, is the *káan* (common French spelling: *khene*), a wind instrument made of a double row of bamboo-like reeds fitted into a hardwood soundbox and made airtight with beeswax. The rows can be as few as four or as many as eight courses (for a total of 16 pipes), and the instrument can vary in length from around 80cm to about 2m. An adept player can produce a churning, calliope-like dance music.

When the *káan* is playing locals dance the *lám wóng* (circle performance), easily the most popular folk dance in Laos. Put simply, in the *lám wóng* couples dance circles around one another until there are three circles in all: a circle danced by the individual, a circle danced by the couple, and one danced by the whole crowd.

Mŏr Lám

The Lao folk idiom also has its own musical theatre, based on the *mŏr lám* tradition. *Mŏr lám* is difficult to translate but roughly means 'master of verse'. Led by one or more vocalists, performances always feature a witty, topical combination of talking and singing that ranges across themes as diverse as politics and sex. Very colloquial, even bawdy, language is employed. This is one art form that has always bypassed government censors and it continues to provide an important outlet for grass-roots expression.

There are several different types of *mŏr lám,* depending on the number of singers and the region the style hails from. *Mŏr lám koo* (couple *mŏr lám*) features a man and woman who engage in flirtation and verbal repartee. *Mŏr lám jót* (duelling *mŏr lám*) has two performers of the same gender who 'duel' by answering questions or finishing an incomplete story issued as a challenge, similar to free-style rap.

Traditional Music of the Lao (1985), by Terry Miller, although mainly focused on northeast Thailand, is the only book-length work yet to appear on Lao music, and is very informative.

Northern Lao *káan*-based folk music is usually referred to as *káp* rather than *lám.* Authentic live *mŏr lám* can be heard at temple fairs and on Lao radio. Born-and-bred American artist Jonny Olsen (also known as Jonny Khaen) has become a celebrity in Laos for his *káan*-based music.

Lao Pop

Up until 2003, performing 'modern' music was virtually outlawed in Laos. The government had decided it just wasn't the Lao thing, and bands such as local heavy-metal outfit Sapphire, who chose to play anyway, were effectively shut down. Instead the youth listened to pirated Thai and Western music, while Lao-language pop was limited to the *look tûng,* syrupy arrangements combining cha-cha and bolero rhythms with Lao-Thai melodies.

Then the government decided that if Lao youth were going to listen to modern pop, it might as well be home-grown. The first 'star' was Thidavanh Bounxouay, a Lao-Bulgarian singer more popularly known as Alexandra. Her brand of pop wasn't exactly radical, but it was decidedly upbeat compared with what went before. In the last couple of years other groups have followed including girl band Princess and pop-rock group Awake.

In recent years, slightly edgier rock bands such as Crocodile and Leprozy have emerged, the latter of which have even played relatively high-profile gigs in Thailand. The hard-rock band Cells is another example of a Lao band for whom success has been much more rewarding in Thailand, where they've played big and relatively lucrative gigs in Bangkok.

There's also a tiny but burgeoning school of Lao-language hip hop that until recently was almost exclusively associated with Los Angeles and that city's Lao diaspora. However, in recent years a domestic scene has developed around homegrown acts such as Hip Hop Ban Na and L.O.G., the latter of which scored a chart-topping hit in Thailand.

In Vientiane, recordings by many if not all of the artists mentioned above are available at the open-air market near Pha That Luang and at Talat Sao mall. Some artists can also be caught live at venues in Vientiane, though you're more likely to see them at outdoor gigs to celebrate major holidays.

Architecture

As with all other artistic endeavour, for centuries the best architects in the land have focused their attention on Buddhist temples. The results are most impressive in Luang Prabang.

However, it's not only in temples that Laos has its own peculiar architectural traditions. The *tâht* (stupas) found in Laos are different to those found anywhere else in the Buddhist world. Stupas are essentially monuments built on top of a reliquary which itself was built to hold a relic of the Buddha, commonly a hair or fragment of bone. Across Asia they come in varying shapes and sizes, ranging from the multilevel tapered pagodas found in Vietnam to the buxom brick monoliths of Sri Lanka. Laos has its own unique style combining hard edges and comely

TEMPLE ARCHITECTURE: A TALE OF THREE CITIES

The *uposatha* (Lao *sǐm;* ordination hall) is always the most important structure in any Theravada Buddhist wat. The high-peaked roofs are layered to represent several levels (usually three, five, seven or occasionally nine), which correspond to various Buddhist doctrines. The edges of the roofs almost always feature a repeated flame motif, with long, fingerlike hooks at the corners called *chôr fâh* (sky clusters). Umbrella-like spires along the central roof-ridge of a *sǐm,* called *nyôrt chôr fâh* (topmost *chôr fâh)* sometimes bear small pavilions (*nagas* – mythical water serpents) in a double-stepped arrangement representating Mt Meru, the mythical centre of the Hindu-Buddhist cosmos.

There are basically three architectural styles for such buildings: the Vientiane, Luang Prabang and Xieng Khuang styles.

The front of a *sǐm* in the Vientiane style usually features a large verandah with heavy columns supporting an ornamented overhanging roof. Some will also have a less-ornamented rear verandah, while those that have a surrounding terrace are Bangkok-influenced.

In Luang Prabang, the temple style is akin to that of the northern Siamese (Lanna) style, hardly surprising as for several centuries Laos and northern Thailand were part of the same kingdoms. Luang Prabang temple roofs sweep very low, almost reaching the ground in some instances. The overall effect is quite dramatic, as if the *sǐm* were about to take flight. The Lao are fond of saying that the roof line resembles the wings of a mother hen guarding her chicks.

Little remains of the Xieng Khuang style of *sǐm* architecture because the province was so heavily bombed during the Second Indochina War. Pretty much the only surviving examples are in Luang Prabang and to look at them you see aspects of both Vientiane and Luang Prabang styles. The *sǐm* raised on a multilevel platform is reminiscent of Vientiane temples, while wide sweeping roofs that reach especially low are similar to the Luang Prabang style, though they're not usually tiered. Cantilevered roof supports play a much more prominent role in the building's overall aesthetic, giving the *sǐm's* front profile a pentagonal shape.

curves. The most famous of all Lao stupas is the golden Pha That Luang in Vientiane, which doubles as the national symbol.

Lao Textiles and Traditions (1997), by Mary F Connors, is useful to visitors interested in Lao weaving; it's the best overall introduction to the subject.

Traditional housing in Laos, whether in the river valleys or in the mountains, consists of simple wooden or bamboo-thatch structures with leaf or grass roofing. Among Lowland Lao, houses are raised on stilts to avoid flooding during the monsoons and allow room to store rice underneath, while the highlanders typically build directly on the ground. The most attractive Lowland Lao houses often have a starburst pattern in the architraves, though these are increasingly difficult to find.

Colonial architecture in urban Laos combined the classic French provincial style – thick-walled buildings with shuttered windows and pitched tile roofs – with balconies and ventilation to promote air circulation in the stifling Southeast Asian climate. Although many of these structures were torn down or allowed to decay following independence from France, today they are much in demand, especially by foreigners. Luang Prabang and Vientiane both boast several lovingly restored buildings from this era. By contrast, in the Mekong River towns of Tha Khaek, Savannakhet and Pakse, French-era buildings are decaying at a disturbing rate.

Buildings erected in post-Revolution Laos followed the socialist realism school that was enforced in the Soviet Union, Vietnam and China. Straight lines, sharp angles and an almost total lack of ornamentation were the norm. More recently, a trend towards integrating classic Lao architectural motifs with modern functions has taken hold. Prime examples of this include Vientiane's National Assembly and the Luang Prabang airport, both of which were designed by Havana- and Moscow-trained architect Hongkad Souvannavong. Other design characteristics, such as those represented by the Siam Commercial Bank on Th Lan Xang in Vientiane, seek to gracefully reincorporate French colonial features ignored for the last half-century.

Sculpture

Of all the traditional Lao arts, perhaps most impressive is the Buddhist sculpture of the period from the 16th to 18th centuries, the heyday of the kingdom of Lan Xang. Sculptural media usually included bronze, stone or wood and the subject was invariably the Lord Buddha or figures associated with the Jataka (*sáh-dók;* stories of the Buddha's past lives). Like other Buddhist sculptors, the Lao artisans emphasised the features thought to be peculiar to the historical Buddha, including a beak-like nose, extended earlobes and tightly curled hair.

LAO BUDDHA

Lao Buddha: The Image & Its History (2000), by Somkiart Lopetcharat, is a large coffee-table book containing a wealth of information on the Lao interpretation of the Buddha figure.

Two types of standing Buddha image are distinctive to Laos. The first is the 'Calling for Rain' posture, which depicts the Buddha standing with hands held rigidly at his side, fingers pointing towards the ground. This posture is rarely seen in other Southeast Asian Buddhist art traditions. The slightly rounded, 'boneless' look of the image recalls Thailand's Sukhothai style, and the way the lower robe is sculpted over the hips looks vaguely Khmer. But the flat, slablike earlobes, arched eyebrows and aquiline nose are uniquely Lao. The bottom of the figure's robe curls upward on both sides in a perfectly symmetrical fashion that is also unique and innovative.

The other original Lao image type is the 'Contemplating the Bodhi Tree' Buddha. The Bodhi tree ('Tree of Enlightenment'), refers to the large banyan tree that the historical Buddha was purportedly sitting beneath when he attained enlightenment in Bodhgaya, India, in the 6th century BC. In this image the Buddha is standing in much the same way as in the 'Calling for Rain' pose, except that his hands are crossed at the wrists in front of his body.

The finest examples of Lao sculpture are found in Vientiane's Haw Pha Kaeo and Wat Si Saket, and in Luang Prabang's Royal Palace Museum.

Handicrafts

Mats and baskets woven of various kinds of straw, rattan and reed are common and are becoming a small but important export. Minority groups still wear these baskets, affirming that until recently most Lao handicrafts were useful as well as ornamental. In villages it's possible to buy direct from the weaver. Among the best baskets and mats are those woven by the Htin (Lao Thoeng).

TEXTILES

Silk and cotton fabrics are woven in many different styles according to the geographic provenance and ethnicity of the weavers. Although Lao textiles do have similarities with other Southeast Asian textiles, Lao weaving techniques are unique in both loom design and weaving styles, generating fabrics that are very recognisably Lao.

Southern weavers, who often use foot looms rather than frame looms, are known for the best silk weaving and for intricate *mat-mii* (ikat or tie-dye) designs that include Khmer-influenced temple and elephant motifs. The result is a soft, spotted pattern similar to Indonesian ikat. *Mat-mii* cloth can be used for different types of clothing or wall-hangings. In Sekong and Attapeu Provinces some fabrics mix beadwork with weaving and embroidery. One-piece *pàh nung* (sarongs) are more common than those sewn from separate pieces.

In central Laos, typical weavings include indigo-dyed cotton *mat-mii* and minimal weft brocade (*jók* and *kit*), along with mixed techniques brought by migrants to Vientiane.

Generally speaking, the fabrics of the north feature a mix of solid colours with complex geometric patterns – stripes, diamonds, zigzags, animal and plant shapes – usually in the form of a *pàh nung* or *sin* (women's wrap-around skirt). Sometimes gold or silver thread is woven in along the borders. Another form the cloth takes is the *pàh bẹeang*, a narrow Lao-Thai shawl that men and women wear singly or in pairs over the shoulders during weddings and festivals.

Gold and silver brocade is typical of traditional Luang Prabang patterns, along with intricate patterns and imported Tai Lü designs. Northerners generally use frame looms; the waist, body and narrow *sín* (bottom border) of a *pàh nung* are often sewn together from separately woven pieces.

In northeastern Laos, tribal Tai produce *yìap ko* (weft brocade) using raw silk, cotton yarn and natural dyes, sometimes with the addition of *mat-mii* techniques. Large diamond patterns are common.

Among the Hmong and Mien tribes, square pieces of cloth are embroidered and quilted to produce strikingly colourful fabrics in apparently abstract patterns that contain ritual meanings. In Hmong these are called *pandau* (flowercloth). Some larger quilts feature scenes that represent village life, including both animal and human figures.

Many tribes among the Lao Soung and Lao Thoeng groups produce woven shoulderbags in the Austro-Tai and Tibetan-Burmese traditions, like those seen all across the mountains of South Asia and Southeast Asia. In Laos, these are called *nyahm*. Among the most popular *nyahm* nowadays are those made with older pieces of fabric from 'antique' *pàh nung* or from pieces of hill-tribe clothing. Vientiane's Talat Sao is one of the best places to shop for this kind of accessory.

Natural sources for Lao dyes include ebony (both seeds and wood), tamarind (seeds and wood), red lacquer extracted from the *Coccus iacca* (a tree-boring insect), turmeric (from a root) and indigo. A basic palette of five natural colours – black, orange, red, yellow and blue – can be combined to create an endless variety of colours. Other unblended, but more subtle, hues include khaki (from the bark of the Indian trumpet tree), pink (sappanwood) and gold (jackfruit and breadfruit woods).

Among the Hmong and Mien hill tribes, silversmithing plays an important role in 'portable wealth' and inheritances. In years past, the main source of silver was French coins, which were either melted down or fitted straight into the jewellery of choice. In northern villages it's not unusual to see newer coins worn in elaborate head dresses.

The Lowland Lao also have a long tradition of silversmithing and goldsmithing. While these arts have been in decline for quite a while now, there are still plenty of jewellers working over flames in markets around the country.

Paper handcrafted from *săh* (the bark of a mulberry tree) is common in northwestern Laos, and is available in Vientiane and Luang Prabang. Environmentally friendly *săh* is a renewable paper resource that needs little processing compared with wood pulp.

Sport

Laos has a few traditional sports that are as often as much an excuse for betting as they are a means of exercise. *Gá-đôr* (a Lao ball game)and *móoay láo* (Lao boxing) certainly do involve exercise, and these are taken increasingly seriously as international competition raises their profiles.

Cockfighting, however, does not involve exercise. Cockfights follow the usual rules, except that in Laos the cocks are not fitted with blades so they often survive the bout.

In ethnic Tai areas you might find the more off-beat 'sport' of beetle fighting. These bouts involve notoriously fractious rhinoceros beetles squaring off while a crowd, usually more vociferous after liberal helpings of *lòw-lów,* bets on the result. The beetles hiss and attack, lifting each other with their horns, until one decides it no longer wants to be part of this 'entertainment' and runs. If you bet on the runner, you lose. Beetle bouts are limited to the wet season.

Kids in Laos are likely to be seen chasing around a football. Opportunities for pursuing football professionally are few, limited by an almost complete lack of quality coaching, pitches and youth leagues where players can get experience of proper competition. Interprovincial matches at the National Stadium in Vientiane or in modest stadia in provincial capitals draw relatively large crowds.

Gá-đôr

Gá-đôr, a contest in which a woven rattan or plastic ball about 12cm in diameter is kicked around, is almost as popular in Laos as it is in Thailand and Malaysia.

Traditional *gá-đôr* involved players standing in a circle (the size of the circle depending on the number of players) and trying to keep the ball airborne by kicking it football-style. Points were scored for style, difficulty and variety of kicking manoeuvres.

A modern variation on *gá-đôr,* the one used in local or international competitions, is played with a volleyball net, using all the same rules as in volleyball except that only the feet and head are permitted to touch the

PETANG

While you'll see plenty of *gá-đôr* and football, the sport you'll most likely be able to actually play is *petang*. Introduced by the French, *petang* is a local corruption of pétanque. All over Laos you'll see small courts made of packed dirt or gravel.

While it's been around for decades, Lao involvement in international competition has sparked a renewed interest in the game. In the 2005 Southeast Asian Games, Laos won gold in the men's singles and silver in the men's doubles, and in subsequent competitions the country has bagged plenty more medals.

ball. It's amazing to see the players perform aerial pirouettes, spiking the ball over the net with their feet.

Móoay Láo (Lao Boxing)

The Lao seem to have an almost insatiable appetite for televised kick-boxing, whether the pictures are coming from Thailand (*móoay thái*) or from a local fight, known as *móoay láo*. *Móoay láo* is not nearly as developed a sport in Laos as its counterpart in Thailand, and is mostly confined to amateur fights at upcountry festivals, but on most weekends you'll see the bigger fights broadcast on TV.

All surfaces of the body are considered fair targets and any part of the body except the head may be used to strike an opponent. Common blows include high kicks to the neck, elbow thrusts to the face and head, knee hooks to the ribs and low crescent kicks to the calf. A contestant may even grasp an opponent's head between his hands and pull it down to meet an upward knee thrust. Ouch!

International boxing *(móoay săhgọn)* is gaining popularity in Laos and is encouraged by the government in spite of the obvious Lao preference for the bang-up Southeast Asian version.

Environment

Laos' environment has long benefited from the country's small population which, until recently, exerted relatively little pressure on the ecosystem. But with a growing population, for whom wildlife equals protein and forests mean potential fields, the environment is increasingly under strain. Add to that the ongoing problems of legal and illegal logging and increased mining and agriculture. Yet tourism is increasingly being recognised as a lucrative natural resource, and may be the key to preserving Laos' remaining natural areas.

The Land

The Mekong River is known as Lancang Jiang (Turbulent River) in China; Mae Nam Khong in Thailand, Myanmar and Laos; Tonle Thom (Great Water) in Cambodia and Cuu Long (Nine Dragons) in Vietnam.

Covering an area slightly larger than Great Britain, landlocked Laos shares borders with China, Myanmar, Thailand, Cambodia and Vietnam. Rivers and mountains dominate, folding the country into a series of often-spectacular ridges and valleys, rivers and mountain passes, extending westward from the Laos–Vietnam border.

Mountains and plateaus cover more than 70% of the country. Running about half the length of Laos, parallel to the course of the Mekong River, is the Annamite Chain, a rugged mountain range with peaks averaging between 1500m and 2500m in height. Roughly in the centre of the range is the Khammuan Plateau, a world of dramatic limestone grottoes and gorges where vertical walls rise hundreds of metres from jungle-clad valleys. At the southern end of the Annamite Chain, covering 10,000 sq km, the Bolaven Plateau is an important area for the cultivation of high-yield mountain rice, coffee, tea and other crops that flourish in the cooler climes found at these higher altitudes.

The larger, northern half of Laos is made up almost entirely of mountain ranges. The highest mountains are found in Xieng Khuang Province, including Phu Bia, the country's highest peak at 2820m, though this remains off-limits to travellers for now. Just north of Phu Bia stands the Xieng Khuang plateau, the country's largest mountain plateau, which rises 1200m above sea level. The most famous part of the plateau is the Plain of Jars, an area somewhat reminiscent of the rolling hills of Ireland, except for the thousands of bomb craters. It's named for the huge prehistoric stone jars that dot the area, as if the local giants have pub-crawled across this neighbourhood and left their empty beer mugs behind.

Much of the rest of Laos is covered by forest, most of which is mixed deciduous forest. This forest enjoys a complex relationship with the Mekong and its tributaries, acting as a sponge for the monsoon rains and then slowly releasing the water into both streams and the atmosphere during the long dry season.

Around 85% of Laos is mountainous terrain and less than 4% is considered arable.

The Mekong & Other Rivers

Springing forth nearly 5000km from the sea, high up on the Tibetan Plateau, the Mekong River so dominates Lao topography that, to a large extent, the entire country parallels its course. Although half of the Mekong's length runs through China, more of the river's volume courses through Laos than through any other Southeast Asian country. At its widest, near Si Phan Don in the south, the river can expand to 14km across during the rainy season, spreading around thousands of islands and islets on its inevitable course south.

The Mekong's middle reach is navigable year-round, from Heuan Hin (north of the Khemmarat Rapids in Savannakhet Province) to Kok Phong in Luang Prabang. However, these rapids and the brutal falls at Khon Phapheng in Si Phan Don, have prevented the Mekong from becoming the sort of regional highway other great rivers have.

The fertile Mekong River flood plain, running from Sainyabuli to Champasak, forms the flattest and most tropical part of Laos. Virtually all of the domestic rice consumed in Laos is grown here, and if our experience seeing rice packaged up as 'Produce of Thailand' is any indication, then a fair bit is exported via Thailand, too. Most other large-scale farming takes place here as well. The Mekong and, just as importantly, its tributaries are also an important source of fish, a vital part of the diet for most people living in Laos. The Mekong valley is at its largest around Vientiane and Savannakhet, which, not surprisingly, are two of the major population centres.

The Mekong: Turbulent Past, Uncertain Future (2000), by Milton Osborne, is a fascinating cultural history of the Mekong that spans 2000 years of exploration, mapping and war.

Major tributaries of the great river include the Nam Ou (Ou River) and the Nam Tha (Tha River), both of which flow through deep, narrow limestone valleys from the north, and the Nam Ngum (Ngum River), which flows into the Mekong across a broad plain in Vientiane Province. The Nam Ngum is the site of one of Laos' oldest hydroelectric plants, which provides power for Vientiane-area towns and Thailand. The Se Kong (Kong River) flows through much of southern Laos before eventually reaching the Mekong in Cambodia, and the rivers Nam Kading (Kading River) and Nam Theun (Theun River) are equally important in central Laos.

All the rivers and tributaries west of the Annamite Chain drain into the Mekong, while waterways east of the Annamites (in Hua Phan and Xieng Khuang Provinces only) flow into the Gulf of Tonkin off the coast of Vietnam.

Wildlife

Laos boasts one of the least disturbed ecosystems in Asia due to its overall lack of development and its low population density. Least disturbed, however, does not mean undisturbed, and for many species the future remains uncertain.

Marco Polo was probably the first European to cross the Mekong, in the 13th century, and was followed by a group of Portuguese emissaries in the 16th century. Dutch merchant Gerrit van Wuysthoff arrived by boat in the 17th century. In 1893 the French and Siamese signed the Treaty of Bangkok, designating the Mekong as the border between Siam and French Indochina.

Animals

The mountains, forests and river networks of Laos are home to a range of animals both endemic to the country and shared with its Southeast Asian neighbours. Nearly half of the animal species native to Thailand are shared by Laos, with the higher forest cover and fewer hunters meaning that numbers are often greater in Laos. However, almost all wild animals are threatened to some extent by hunting and habitat loss.

In spite of this Laos has seen several new species discovered in recent years, while others thought to be extinct have turned up in remote forests. Given their rarity, these newly discovered species are on the endangered list.

As in Cambodia, Vietnam, Myanmar and much of Thailand, most of the fauna in Laos belong to the Indochinese zoogeographic realm (as opposed to the Sundaic domain found south of the Isthmus of Kra in southern Thailand or the Palaearctic to the north in China).

Notable mammals endemic to Laos include the lesser panda, raccoon dog, Lao marmoset rat, Owston's civet and the pygmy slow loris. Other important exotic species found elsewhere in the region include the Malayan and Chinese pangolins, 10 species of civet, marbled cat, Javan and crab-eating mongoose, the serow (sometimes called Asian mountain goat) and goral (another type of goat-antelope), and cat species including the leopard cat and Asian golden cat.

Among the most notable of Laos' wildlife are the primates. Several smaller species are known, including Phayre's leaf monkey, François' langur, the Douc langur and several macaques. Two other primates that are endemic to Laos are the concolour gibbon and snub-nosed langur. It's the five species of gibbon that attract most attention. Sadly, the black-cheeked crested gibbon is endangered, being hunted both for its meat and to be sold as pets in Thailand. Several projects are underway to educate local communities to set aside safe areas for the gibbons, including the celebrated Gibbon Experience (p116).

Wildlife Trade in Laos: The End of the Game (2001), by Hanneke Nooren & Gordon Claridge, is a frightening description of animal poaching in Laos.

Elephants

Laos might once have been known as the land of a million elephants, but these days only about 1000 remain. For an animal as threatened as the Asiatic elephant, this population is one of the largest in the region. Exact figures are hard to come by, but it's generally believed that there are about 800 wild elephants, roaming in open-canopy forest areas predominantly in Sainyabuli Province west of Vientiane, Bolikhamsai Province in the Phu Khao Khuay NPA, and along the Nakai Plateau in central eastern Laos.

RESPONSIBLE TRAVEL & WILDLIFE

Throughout your travels in Laos the opportunity to buy or consume wildlife is likely to come about. In the interests of wildlife conservation, the Wildlife Conservation Society, Lao PDR strongly urges you not to partake in the wildlife trade. While subsistence hunting is permitted by the Government of Lao PDR for local rural villagers, the sale and purchase of *any* wildlife is illegal in Laos. The wildlife trade is damaging to biodiversity and to local livelihoods.

While strolling through rural and city markets you'll come across wild animals for sale as meat or live pets. In a misguided attempt to do the right thing travellers have been known to buy these live animals in order to release them. While it might feel like this is a positive step towards thwarting the wildlife trade it actually has the opposite effect as vendors, unaware of the buyer's motivation, interpret the sale as increased demand.

Be prepared for some bizarre and disturbing items on restaurant menus and in food markets in Laos. While it may be tempting to experience the unusual, it's strongly recommended that the following animals be avoided: soft shelled turtles, rat snakes, mouse deer, sambar deer, squirrel, bamboo rat, muntjac deer and pangolins. Many of these species are endangered or are a source of prey for endangered species.

Thinking of purchasing a stuffed wild animal? A bag or wallet made from animal skin? Or perhaps an insect in a framed box? Think again. The money made in the sale of these peculiar trinkets goes directly towards supporting the illegal wildlife trade. Also to be avoided are the rings and necklaces made from animal teeth (sellers may tell you that this is buffalo bone, but it's just as likely that it's bear or wild pig bone) and the bottles of alcohol with snakes, birds, or insects inside. Though widely sold, this trade is illegal in Laos, and you'll most likely find your new libido-enhancing snake oil confiscated by customs in your home country anyway. Keep an eye out for products with a CITES-certified label. These are legal to buy in Laos and take home.

For many species of wildlife in Laos, populations are at critically low levels. The WCS Lao PDR program (www.wcs.org/international/Asia/laos) is collaborating with the Vientiane Capital City government to monitor and control wildlife trade.

By the Wildlife Conservation Society, Lao PDR (www.wcs.org/international/asia/laos)

Hunting and habitat loss are their main threats. In areas such as the Nakai Plateau, Vietnamese poachers kill elephants for their meat and hides, while the Nam Theun 2 hydropower project in Khammuan Province has swallowed up a large chunk of habitat. The Wildlife Conservation Society (WCS) has an ongoing project in this area, with a long-term aim of establishing a 'demonstration site that will serve as a model for reducing human-elephant conflict nationwide'.

Working or domesticated elephants are also found in most provinces, totalling between 1100 and 1350 countrywide. They have traditionally been used for the heavy labour involved in logging and agriculture, but modern machinery is rapidly putting them out of work. As a result, the mahouts (elephant keepers and/or drivers) in some elephant villages are working with NGOs like **Elefantasia** (www.elefantasia.org) to find alternative income through tourism. Projects such as the impressive Elephant Conservation Center (p126) near Sainyabuli offer an immersive elephant experience for visitors, and the yearly elephant festival held here is growing in popularity as a tourist event. Working elephants are most visible in Sainyabuli, Udomxai, Champasak and Attapeu provinces.

Despite these problems, Laos is in the rare position of having the raw materials – both the elephant numbers and the habitat – to ensure the jumbos have a long and healthy future. What is missing is money and, perhaps, sufficient political will.

Endangered Species

To a certain extent, all wild animals in Laos are endangered due to widespread hunting and gradual but persistent habitat loss. Laos ratified the UN Convention on International Trade in Endangered Species of Wild Flora and Fauna (CITES) in 2004, which, combined with other legal measures, has made it easier to prosecute people trading species endangered as a direct result of international trade. But in reality you won't need 20/20 vision to pick out the endangered species, both dead and alive, on sale in markets around the country. Border markets, in particular, tend to attract the most valuable species, with Thais buying species such as gibbons as pets, and Chinese and Vietnamese shopping for exotic food and medicines.

Of the hundreds of species of mammals known in Laos, several dozen are endangered according to the **IUCN Red List** (www.iucnredlist.org). These range from bears, including the Asiatic black bear and Malayan sun bear, through the less glamorous wild cattle such as the gaur and banteng, to high-profile cats like the tiger, leopard and clouded leopard. Exactly how endangered they are is difficult to say. Camera-trapping projects (setting up cameras in the forest to take photos of anything that wanders past) are being carried out by various NGOs and, in the the Nakai-Nam Theun NPA, by the Nam Theun 2 dam operators themselves.

The Nakai-Nam Theun research is part of a deal brokered by the World Bank that ensures US$1 million a year is set aside for environmental study and protection in the dam's catchment area. Results of camera trapping in the Nakai-Nam Theun NPA have been both encouraging and depressing. The cameras returned photos of limited numbers of several species, but also a hunter posing proudly with his kill – not quite the shots they were hoping for.

The WCS is focusing its conservation activities on species including the Asian elephant, Siamese crocodile, tiger, western black-crested gibbon and Eld's deer. For more details, see www.wcs.org.

Some endangered species are so rare they were unknown until very recently. Among these is the spindlehorn (*Pseudoryx nghethingensis;* known as the *saola* in Vietnam, *nyang* in Laos), a horned mammal

CATFISH

The giant Mekong catfish may grow up to 3m long and weigh as much as 300kg. Due to Chinese blasting of shoals in the Upper Mekong, it now faces extinction in the wild.

found in the Annamite Chain along the Laos–Vietnam border in 1992. The spindlehorn, which was described in 14th-century Chinese journals, was long thought not to exist, and when discovered it became one of only three land mammals to earn its own genus in the 20th century. Unfortunately, horns taken from spindlehorn are a favoured trophy among certain groups on both sides of the border.

In 2005 WCS scientists visiting a local market in Khammuan Province discovered a 'Laotian rock rat' laid out for sale. But what was being sold as meat turned out to be a genetically distinct species named the *Laonastes aenigmamus*. Further research revealed it to be the sole survivor of a prehistoric group of rodents that died out about 11 million years ago. If you're very lucky you might see one on the cliffs near the caves off Rte 12 in Khammuan Province.

Among the most seriously endangered of all mammals is the Irrawaddy dolphin found in increasingly small pockets of the Mekong River near the Cambodian border.

Birds

Those new to Laos often ask: 'Why don't I see more birds?' The short answer is 'cheap protein'. If you can get far enough away from people, you'll find the forests and mountains of Laos do in fact harbour a rich selection of resident and migrating bird species. Surveys carried out by a British team of ornithologists in the 1990s recorded 437 species, including eight globally threatened and 21 globally near-threatened species. Some other counts rise as high as 650 species.

Notable among these are the Siamese fireback pheasant, green peafowl, red-collared woodpecker, brown hornbill, tawny fish-owl, Sarus crane, giant ibis and the Asian golden weaver. Hunting keeps urban bird populations noticeably thin. In 2008, scientists from the WCS and the University of Melbourne conducting research in central Laos discovered a new bird species, the bare-faced bulbul, the first bald songbird to be spotted in mainland Asia, and the first new bulbul to have been discovered in the last century.

The World Conservation Union believes wildlife in Laos has a much better chance of surviving than in neighbouring Vietnam. Lending weight to this is the Vietnam warty pig *(Sus bucclentus)*, a species found in Laos but last recorded in Vietnam in 1892 and until recently considered extinct.

Up until a few years ago, it wasn't uncommon to see men pointing long-barrelled muskets at upper tree branches in cities as large as Savannakhet and Vientiane. Those days are now gone, but around almost every village you'll hear hunters doing their business most afternoons.

Plants

According to the UN Food and Agriculture Organization, in 2005 forest covered more than 69% of Laos. Current figures vary from 45% to 60% depending on the sources. Of these woodlands, about 11% can be classified as primary forest.

Most indigenous vegetation in Laos is associated with monsoon forests, a common trait in areas of tropical mainland Southeast Asia that experience dry seasons lasting three months or longer. In such mixed deciduous forests many trees shed their leaves during the dry season to conserve water. Rainforests, which are typically evergreen, don't exist in Laos, although nonindigenous rainforest species such as the coconut palm are commonly seen in the lower Mekong River valley. There are undoubtedly some big trees in Laos, but don't expect the sort of towering forests found in some other parts of Southeast Asia. The conditions do not, and never have, allowed these sorts of giants to grow here.

Instead the monsoon forests of Laos typically grow in three canopies. Dipterocarps – tall, pale-barked, single-trunked trees that can grow beyond 30m high – dominate the top canopy of the forest, while a middle canopy consists of an ever-dwindling population of prized hardwoods, including teak, padauk (sometimes called 'Asian rosewood') and mahogany. Underneath there's a variety of smaller trees, shrubs, grasses and, along river habitats, bamboo. In certain plateau areas of the south, there are dry dipterocarp forests in which the forest canopies are more open, with less of a middle layer and more of a grass-and-bamboo undergrowth. Parts of the Annamite Chain that receive rain from both the southwestern monsoon as well as the South China Sea are covered by tropical montane evergreen forest, while tropical pine forests can be found on the Nakai Plateau and Sekong area to the south.

In addition to the glamour hardwoods, the country's flora includes a toothsome array of fruit trees, bamboo (more species than any country outside Thailand and China) and an abundance of flowering species such as the orchid. However, in some parts of the country orchids are being stripped out of forests (often in protected areas) for sale to Thai tourists; look for the markets near the waterfalls of the Bolaven Plateau to see them. In the high plateaus of the Annamite Chain, extensive grasslands or savannahs are common.

For more detailed descriptions of all Laos' National Protected Areas, see the comprehensive website www.ecotourism-laos.com.

National Protected Areas (NPAs)

Laos boasts one of the youngest and most comprehensive protected-area systems in the world. In 1993 the government set up 18 National Biodiversity Conservation Areas, comprising a total of 24,600 sq km, or just over 10% of the country's land mass. Most significantly, it did this following sound scientific consultation rather than creating areas on an ad hoc basis (as most other countries have done). Two more were added in 1995, for a total of 20 protected areas covering 14% of Laos. A further 4% of Laos is reserved as Provincial Protected Areas, making Laos one of the most protected countries on earth.

The areas were renamed National Protected Areas (NPAs) a few years ago. And while the naming semantics might seem trivial, they do reflect some important differences. The main one is that an NPA has local communities living within its boundaries, unlike a national park, where only rangers and those working in the park are allowed to live and where traditional activities such as hunting and logging are banned. Indeed, forests in NPAs are divided into production forests for timber, protection forests for watershed and conservation forests for pure conservation.

The largest protected areas are in southern Laos, which, contrary to popular myth, bears a higher percentage of natural forest cover than the north. The largest of the NPAs, Nakai-Nam Theun, covers 3710 sq km and is home to the recently discovered spindlehorn, as well as several other species unknown to the scientific world a decade ago.

While several NPAs remain difficult to access without mounting a full-scale expedition, several others have become much easier to reach in recent years. The best way in is usually by foot.

The wildlife in these areas, from rare birds to wild elephants, is relatively abundant. The best time to view wildlife in most of the country is just after the monsoon in November. However, even at these times you'll be lucky to see very much. There are several reasons for this, the most important of which is that ongoing hunting means numbers of wild animals are reduced and those living are instinctively scared of humans. It's also difficult to see animals in forest cover at the best of times, and many animals are nocturnal.

Environmental Issues

Flying over Laos it's easy to think that much of the country is blanketed with untouched wilderness. But first impressions can be deceiving. What that lumpy carpet of green conceals is an environment facing several interrelated threats.

For the most part they're issues of the bottom line. Hunting endangers all sorts of creatures of the forest but it persists because the hunters can't afford to buy meat from the market. Forests are logged at unsustainable rates because the timber found in Laos is valuable and loggers see more profit in cutting than not. And hydropower projects affect river systems and their dependent ecologies, including the forests, because Laos needs the money hydroelectricity can bring and it's relatively cheap and easy for energy companies to develop in Laos.

Laws do exist to protect wildlife and, as mentioned, plenty of Laos is protected as NPAs. But most Laotians are completely unaware of global conservation issues and there is little will and less money to pay for conservation projects, such as organised park rangers, or to prosecute

ECOTOURISM IN LAOS

With forests covering about half of the country, 20 National Protected Areas (NPAs), 49 ethnic groups, over 650 bird species and hundreds of mammals, it's no mystery why Laos is known as having some of Southeast Asia's healthiest ecosystems and is a haven for travellers looking to get off the beaten path. Nowadays there are many tour companies and local tour guides offering forest trekking, cave exploration, village homestays and special river journeys to where the roads don't go. These types of activities are very popular in Laos and their availability has exploded over the past decade. Following the success of the Nam Ha Ecotourism Project in Luang Namtha Province, which began in 1999, the ecotourism industry has grown from the bottom up and today the Lao government is actively promoting ecotourism as one way to help reduce poverty and support the protection of the environment and local culture. It is estimated that culture- and nature-based tourism generates more than half of the country's annual tourism revenue.

The Lao National Tourism Administration defines ecotourism as 'tourism activity in rural and protected areas that minimizes negative impacts and is directed towards the conservation of natural and cultural resources, rural socio-economic development and visitor understanding of, and appreciation for, the places they are visiting.' A few Lao tour operators and guesthouses have taken this definition to heart and operate their businesses in a way that upholds the principles of Lao ecotourism.

Unfortunately, some unscrupulous companies label everything as 'ecotourism', so it is important to determine who is actually upholding the principles of ecotourism, and who is simply greening their pockets. Some questions to ask to ensure you are on the right track include:

- Does my trip benefit local people financially, help to protect biodiversity and support the continuation of traditional culture? How?
- What will I learn on this trip, and what opportunities will local people have to learn from me?
- Are facilities designed in local style, do they use local, natural construction materials, and conserve energy and water? Is there local food on the menu?
- Will I be led by a local guide who is from the area?
- Is there a permit, entrance fee or other fee included in the price of the trip that is directed towards conservation activities?
- Are there sensible limits in place concerning group size and frequency of departures to minimize negative environmental impacts?

Supporting businesses that can give clear, positive and believable answers to these questions will most likely result in an enjoyable, educational experience, where you'll make more than a few local friends along the way. It also raises the profile of sustainable business operators, hopefully encouraging others to follow their example. See www.ecotourismlaos.com for further information on environmentally sustainable tourism in Laos.

By Steven Schipani, Ecotourism Expert

offenders. Lack of communication between national and local governments and poor definitions of authority in conservation areas just add to the issues.

One of the biggest obstacles facing environmental protection in Laos is corruption among those in charge of enforcing conservation regulations. Illegal timber felling, poaching and the smuggling of exotic wildlife species would decrease sharply if corruption among officials was properly tackled.

However, there is some good news. With the support of several dedicated individuals and NGOs, ecotourism is growing to the point where some local communities are beginning to understand – and buying into – the idea that an intact environment can be worth money. Added to that, the government has generally avoided giving contracts to companies wanting to develop large-scale resorts, although the same can't be said for many non-tourism projects. Air pollution and carbon emissions are about as low as you'll find anywhere in the region because most Lao still live at or just above a subsistence level and there is little heavy industry. Laos has one of the lowest per capita energy-consumption rates in the world.

One long-standing environmental problem has been the unexploded ordnance (UXO) contaminating parts of eastern Laos where the Ho Chi Minh Trail ran during the Second Indochina War. Bombs are being found and defused at a painstakingly slow rate, but progress is being made.

Thus the major challenges facing Laos' environment are the internal pressures of economic growth and external pressures from the country's more populated and affluent neighbours, particularly China, Vietnam and Thailand, who would like to exploit Laos' abundant resources as much as possible.

Odd-shaped rocks are venerated across Laos. Even in what appears to be the middle of nowhere, you'll see saffron robes draped over rocks that look vaguely like turtles, fishing baskets, stupas and more. Local legends explain how the rocks came to be or what they were used for, and some are famous around the country.

Hydropower Projects

At the time of writing the electricity industry lobby in Laos was reporting on its website (www.poweringprogress.org) that 14 hydroelectric dams are currently in operation and construction is proceeding on five more. In addition to this, the Lao government is planning another 20 hydropower projects, several of which would dam the Mekong itself.

Hydropower is a relatively clean source of energy and to a certain extent dams in Laos are inevitable. But the high number of new projects has the potential to seriously impact on the ecology of almost every major river system in the country.

Aside from displacing tens of thousands of people, dam projects inundate large swaths of forest (rarely agricultural land), permanently change the water flows, block or change fish migrations – thus affecting the fisheries local people have been relying on for centuries – and alter the ecosystems that support forests and the species that live in them. These forests are also the source of myriad nontimber products that contribute to local livelihoods, and the effects on these are often severe.

NGOs in Laos

- *ElefantAsia* (p122)
- *Traffic East Asia* (www.traffic.org)
- *Wildlife Conservation Society* (www.wcs.org)
- *World Conservation Union* (IUCN; www.iucn.org/lao/)
- *World Wildlife Fund* (www.panda.org)

Habitat Loss

Deforestation is another major environmental issue in Laos. Although the official export of timber is tightly controlled, no one really knows how much teak and other hardwoods are being smuggled into Vietnam, Thailand and especially China. The policy in northern Laos has been to allow the Chinese to take as much timber as they want in return for building roads. The Lao army is still removing huge chunks of forest in Khammuan Province and from remote areas in the country's far south, near the Se Pian and Dong Hua Sao NPAs, much of it going to Vietnam. The national electricity-generating company also profits from the timber sales each time it links a Lao town or village with the national power

DEVELOPING THE MEKONG: RELIEVING POVERTY OR DAM CRAZY?

For millennia the Mekong River has been the lifeblood of Laos and the wider Mekong region. This is the region's primary artery, and about 60 million people depend on the rich fisheries and other resources provided by the river and its tributaries. The Mekong is the world's 12th-longest river and 10th-largest in terms of volume. But unlike other major rivers, a series of rapids have prevented it from developing into a major transport and cargo thoroughfare, or as a base for large industrial cities.

Except in China, the Mekong's mainstream is not dammed, but this is all set to change with the construction of the Xayaboury dam, the first dam on the actual Mekong River in Laos. The greater river system has long been seen as a potentially lucrative source of hydroelectricity. With regional demand for power rising rapidly, plans to turn Laos into the 'battery of Southeast Asia' have been revived after almost two decades of stagnation and the Asian financial crisis.

For a country as poor as Laos there are definite benefits. Selling electricity to its neighbours will bring much-needed foreign exchange to the economy. In theory, this windfall can be spent on developing the country while at the same time reducing its reliance on foreign aid and loans. It's an attractive proposition, and one that the Laos government and several international agencies seem happy to pursue.

The first, and biggest, dam was the Nam Theun 2 dam in Khammuan Province, finished in 2010. This controversial hydropower project was more than a decade in the planning, and as such is probably one of the most studied dam projects in history. Dozens of research projects were carried out because the dam needed World Bank approval before investors would commit, and the World Bank was under sustained pressure to reduce the negative impacts as much as possible. Some organisations questioned whether the environmental impacts could be adequately reduced at all.

However, not all projects are as big or get as much publicity as Nam Theun 2. When the World Bank finally approved the project in 2005, it was the equivalent of opening hydropower's Pandora's box. In the ensuing period a flurry of agreements have been signed between the Laos government and private developers, all looking for a slice of the hydropower pie. The many dams proposed for the Mekong River's mainstream have proved especially controversial. More than 30 hydropower projects are currently under construction or in the advanced stages of planning in Laos, raising the question of whether the government has gone 'dam' crazy.

For critics, including the rivers watchdog International Rivers, the answer is a resounding yes. They claim that these lower-profile dams have potentially far greater environmental and social impacts because there is no transparency and they are much harder to monitor. Although the government requires full environmental impact assessments for all hydropower schemes, if they have been carried out, few have been released to the public.

The negative impacts associated with dams include both the obvious and more difficult to see. Obvious effects include displacement of local communities, loss of livelihood, flooding upstream areas, reduced sediment flows and increased erosion downstream with resulting issues for fish stocks and the fisherfolk who work the rivers. Less immediately visible, but with a potentially much greater influence in the long term, are the changes these dams will have on the Mekong's flood pulse, especially the Tonlé Sap Lake in Cambodia, which is critical to the fish spawning cycle, and thus the food source of millions of people.

All up, this is a hugely complex issue. More information can be found around the web.

Asian Development Bank (www.adb.org)

International Rivers (www.internationalrivers.org)

Laos Energy Lobby (www.poweringprogress.org)

Mekong River Commission (www.mrcmekong.org)

Save the Mekong Coalition (www.savethemekong.org)

WWF (www.panda.org)

grid, clear-cutting a wider-than-necessary swathe along Lao highways. Increasingly large-scale plantations and mining, also largely funded by Laos' neighbours, are also leading to significant habitat loss.

Essentially, the Lao authorities express a seemingly sincere desire to conserve the nation's forests, but not at the cost of rural livelihoods. However, in most rural areas 70% of non-rice foods come from the forest. Thus forest destruction, whether as a result of logging or dam-building, can lead to increased poverty and reduced local livelihoods.

Other pressures on the forest cover come from swidden (slash-and-burn) methods of cultivation, in which small plots of forest are cleared, burnt for nitrogenation of the soil and farmed intensively for two or three years, after which they are infertile and unfarmable for between eight and 10 years. Considering the sparse population, swidden cultivation is probably not as great an environmental threat as logging. But neither is it an efficient use of resources.

Forestry is not all bad and effective management could maintain Laos' forests as a source of income for a long time to come. Creating NPAs has been a good start, but examples of forest regeneration and even planting high-value trees for future harvest are rare. All too often the name of the game is short-term gain.

Hunting & Overfishing

The majority of Lao citizens derive most of their protein from food culled from nature, not from farms or ranches. How threatening traditional hunting habits are to species survival in Laos is debatable given the nation's extremely sparse population. But, combined with habitat loss, hunting for food is placing increasing pressure on wildlife numbers.

The cross-border trade in wildlife is also potentially serious. Much of the poaching that takes place in Laos' NPAs is allegedly carried out by Vietnamese hunters who have crossed into central Laos illegally to round up species such as pangolins, civets, barking deer, goral and raccoon dogs to sell back home. These animals are highly valued for both food and medicinal purposes in Vietnam, Thailand and China, and as the demand in those countries grows in line with increasing wealth, so too do the prices buyers are prepared to pay.

Foreign NGOs run grass-roots education campaigns across Laos in an effort to raise awareness of endangered species and the effects of hunting on local ecosystems. But, as usual, money is the key to breaking the cycle. And while hunters remain dirt poor, the problem seems here to stay.

In more densely populated areas such as Savannakhet and Champasak Provinces, the overfishing of lakes and rivers poses a danger to certain fish species. Projects to educate fishermen about exactly where their catch comes from, and how to protect that source, have been successful in changing some unsustainable practices. One area given particular attention is fishing using explosives. This practice, whereby fishermen throw explosives into the water and wait for the dead fish to float to the surface, is incredibly destructive. Most fishermen don't realise that for every dead fish they collect from the surface, another two or three lie dead on the riverbed. The practice is illegal in Laos, and anecdotal evidence suggests education and the law have reduced the problem.

OPIUM

While opium has been cultivated and used in Laos for centuries, the country didn't become a major producer until the passing of the 1971 Anti-Narcotics Law, a move that helped drive up regional prices steeply.

Survival Guide

Directory A–Z

Accommodation

The range and quality of accommodation in Laos is rapidly improving. However, off the beaten track the options are more modest.

Homestays

Staying in a village home is becoming increasingly popular. Homestays are invariably in rural areas, are cheap (about US$5 to US$10 for bed, dinner and breakfast) and provide a chance for travellers to experience local life, Lao style.

Villages are small, dusty/muddy depending on the season, and full of kids. You'll be billeted with a family, usually with a maximum of two travellers per family. Toilets will be the squat variety, with scoop flush, in a dark hut at the corner of the block. You'll bathe before dinner, either in a nearby stream or river, or by using a scoop to pour water over yourself from a well, 44-gallon drum or concrete reservoir in your family's yard. Bathing is usually a public event – don't forget a sarong. Don't expect a mirror.

Food will be simple fare, usually two dishes and sticky rice. In our experience it's almost always been delicious, but prepare yourself for a sticky rice extravaganza – it's not uncommon to encounter the starch at every single meal. Even if the food doesn't appeal, you should eat something or your host will lose face. Dinner is usually served on mats on the floor, so prepare to sit lotus-style or with legs tucked under. Don't sit on pillows as that's bad form, and always take off your shoes before entering the house.

Your meal will most likely be followed by a communal drinking session. If you're lucky this will mean cold bottles of Beerlao, but more likely it will revolve around homemade rice alcohol served from a communal cup. The stuff can be pretty harsh, but if you can stomach it, it's a great icebreaker, and some of our best nights in Laos have been spent this way.

Sleeping will probably be under a mosquito net on a mattress on the floor, and might change to 'waking' once the cocks start crowing outside your window.

It might not be luxurious but homestay is very much the 'real Laos' and is a thoroughly worthwhile experience. Just remember that for most villagers, dealing with *falang* tourists is pretty new and they are sensitive to your reactions. Their enthusiasm will remain as long

SLEEPING PRICE RANGES

Accommodation prices listed are high-season prices for double rooms with attached bathrooms unless otherwise stated. An icon is included to indicate if air-con is available; otherwise, assume that a fan will be provided.

$ less than US$25 (200,000K)

$$ US$25–75 (200,000–600,000K)

$$$ more than US$75 (600,000K)

Paying in the requested currency is usually cheaper than letting the hotel or guesthouse convert the price into another currency. If the price is quoted in kip, pay in kip; if priced in dollars, pay in dollars.

It's worth remembering that rates are pretty reasonable by international standards before trying to bargain the price down, particularly at the budget end where competition is fierce and margins are small. Generally speaking, the Lao are happy to bargain a little, but they are not keen on protracted negotiations or arguments over price.

Room rates may go up as inflation and cost of living are real issues for the everyday Lao population.

as their guests engage with them and accept them and their lifestyle without undue criticism. To get the most out of it take a phrasebook and photos of your family, and a torch, flip-flops, a sarong and toilet paper.

Guesthouses

The distinction between 'guesthouse', 'hotel' and 'resort' often exists in name only, but legally speaking a guesthouse in Laos has fewer than 16 rooms. In places such as Don Det in southern Laos or Muang Ngoi Neua in northern Laos there are guesthouses consisting of simple bamboo-thatch huts with shared facilities, costing just US$3 a night.

Facilities are improving across the country, but the most inexpensive places might still have cold-water showers or simple Lao-style bathing. Hot water is hardly a necessity in lowland Laos, but is very welcome in the mountains.

The price of simple rooms in most towns averages between US$5 and US$10 a night with shared bathrooms. For an attached bathroom and hot shower expect to pay about US$10 to US$20; anything above this will usually have air-conditioning and a TV, with some English-language channels. Some guesthouses, especially in Luang Prabang, have stepped up the style and offer upscale rooms from US$20 to US$50.

Hotels

Hotel rooms in Vientiane, Luang Prabang, Vang Vieng, Savannakhet and Pakse offer private bathrooms and fans as standard features for between about US$10 and US$20 per night.

Small and medium-size hotels oriented towards Asian business and leisure travellers and tour groups exist in the larger cities. Prices at these hotels run from about US$40 to US$100 for rooms with air-con, hot water, TVs and refrigerators.

Then there are the few top-end hotels with better decor, more facilities and personalised service. These typically cost between US$80 and US$200, occasionally more in Luang Prabang.

While the price is undoubtedly right, the trade-off, however, is in the service. Few hotels in Laos have managed to hone their service to Western standards, and English levels are often quite weak, even in more expensive hotels.

Resorts

The term 'resort' in the Lao context may be used for any accommodation situated outside towns or cities. It does not imply, as it usually does in many other countries, the availability of sports activities, a spa and other similar features.

Lao resorts typically cost about the same as a midrange hotel, from about US$25 to US$75 a night. A few, such as those outside Luang Prabang, come closer to the international idea of a resort, with prices to match.

Children

Like many places in Southeast Asia, travelling with children in Laos can be a lot of fun as long as you come prepared with the right attitude. Lonely Planet's *Travel with Children* contains useful advice on how to cope with kids on the road and what to bring along to help things go more smoothly.

Practicalities

Child-friendly amenities such as high chairs in restaurants, car seats, and changing facilities in public restrooms are virtually unknown in Laos. Parents have to be extra resourceful in seeking out substitutes or follow the example of Lao families, which means holding smaller children on their laps much of the time.

The Lao adore children and in many instances will shower attention on your offspring, who will readily find playmates among their Lao peers and a temporary nanny service at practically every stop.

Baby formula and nappies (diapers) are available at minimarkets in larger towns and cities, but bring a sufficient supply to rural areas.

For the most part parents needn't worry too much about health concerns, although it pays to lay down a few ground rules – such as regular hand-washing or using hand-cleansing gel. All the usual health precautions apply. Children should especially be warned not to play with animals encountered along the way as rabies is disturbingly common in Laos.

Do not let children stray from the path in remote areas of Laos that were heavily bombed during the Second Indochina War. Bombies remain an everyday threat in some regions and children are the most common victims, as the bombies resemble tennis balls.

Sights & Activities

Younger children usually don't find the historic temples as inspiring as their parents do, but travelling with children does offer a different perspective on things. The chicken's-eye view of a three-year-old, for example, means they tend to notice all sorts

BOOK YOUR STAY ONLINE

For more accommodation reviews by Lonely Planet authors, check out http://lonelyplanet.com/hotels/. You'll find independent reviews, as well as recommendations on the best places to stay. Best of all, you can book online.

of things at ground level their parents often miss. As long as they don't try to put any of them in their mouths, this is usually no problem.

If boredom does set in, the best cure in Laos is always the outdoors. In Luang Prabang the waterfalls at Tat Sae and Tat Kuang Si are a big draw. Boat trips are usually well-received too.

Most children also take to the unique Hindu-Buddhist sculpture garden of Xieng Khuan outside Vientiane. The capital also has a few more mainstream activities, such as swimming pools and ten-pin bowling alleys.

Climate

The annual monsoon cycles that affect all of mainland Southeast Asia produce a 'dry and wet monsoon climate' with three basic seasons for most of Laos. The southwest monsoon arrives in Laos between May and July and lasts into November.

The monsoon is followed by a dry period (from November to May), beginning with lower relative temperatures and cool breezes created by Asia's northeast monsoon and lasting until mid-February. Exceptions to this general pattern include Xieng Khuang, Hua Phan and Phongsali Provinces, which may receive rainfall coming from Vietnam and China during the months of April and May.

Temperatures also vary according to altitude. In the humid, low-lying Mekong River valley, temperatures range from 15°C to 38°C, while in the mountains of the far north they can drop to 0°C at night.

Courses

Cooking

Lao cooking courses are available to tourists in Luang Prabang, Vientiane and Udomxai.

Language

At the time of research, regular courses in spoken and written Lao were only available at one institute. **Summer Study Abroad in Laos** (SAIL; www.laostudies.org/sail) offers an intensive eight-week language study program at a variety of levels hosted by the Lao-American College in Vientiane.

Meditation

If you can speak Lao or Thai, or can arrange an interpreter, you may be able to study *vipassana* (insight meditation) at Wat Sok Pa Luang in Vientiane.

Customs Regulations

Customs inspections at ports of entry are lax as long as you're not bringing in more than a moderate amount of luggage. You're not supposed to enter the country with more than 500 cigarettes or 1L of distilled spirits. All the usual prohibitions on drugs, weapons and pornography apply.

Electricity

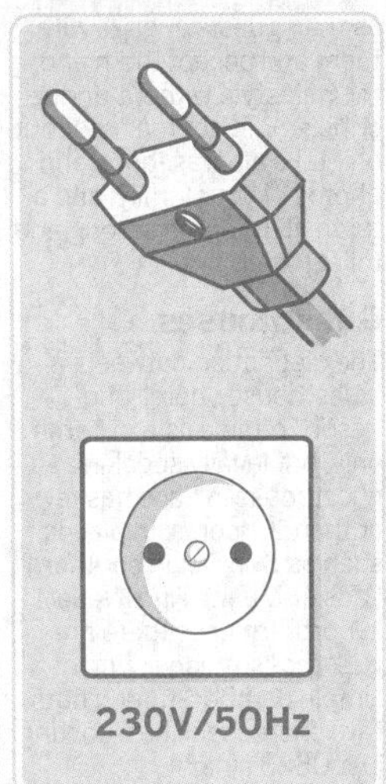

Embassies & Consulates

There are about 25 embassies and consulates in Vientiane. Many nationalities are served by their embassies in Bangkok, Hanoi or Beijing.

Australian Embassy (Map p138; ☎021-353800; www.laos.embassy.gov.au; Th Tha Deua, Ban Wat Nak, Vientiane; ⌚8:30am-5pm Mon-Fri) Also represents nationals of Canada and New Zealand.

Cambodian Embassy (Map p138; ☎021-314952; Th Tha Deua, Km 3, Ban That Khao, Vientiane) Issues visas for US$20.

Chinese Embassy (Map p138; ☎021-315105; http://la.china-embassy.org/eng; Th Wat Nak Nyai, Ban Wat Nak, Vientiane; ⌚8-11.30am Mon-Fri) Issues visas in four working days.

French Embassy (Map p142; ☎021-215258; www.ambafrance-laos.org; Th Setthathirat, Ban Si Saket, Vientiane; ⌚9am-12.30pm & 2-5.30pm Mon-Fri)

German Embassy (Map p138; ☎021-312110; www.vientiane.diplo.de; Th Sok Pa Luang, Vientiane; ⌚9am-noon Mon-Fri)

Myanmar Embassy (Map p138; ☎021-314910; Th Sok Pa Luang, Vientiane) Issues tourist visas in three days for US$20.

Thai Embassy (Map p138; ☎021-214581; www.thaiembassy.org/vientiane; Th Kaysone Pomvihane, Vientiane; ⏰8.30am-noon & 1-3.30pm Mon-Fri) Head to the Vientiane consulate (Map p138; ☎021-214581; 15 Th Bourichane, Vientiane; ⏰8am-noon & 1-4.30pm) for visa renewals and extensions. Thailand also has a consulate in Savannakhet (Map p204; ☎041-212373; cnr Th Tha He & Th Chaimeuang, Savannakhet), which issues same-day tourist and non-immigrant visas (1000B).

UK Embassy (☎030-770 0000; www.gov.uk; Th J Nehru, Ban Saysettha, Vientiane; ⏰8.30am-11.30am Mon-Fri)

US Embassy (Map p142; ☎021-267000; http://laos.usembassy.gov; Th Bartholomie, Vientiane)

Vietnamese Embassy (Map p138; ☎021-413400; www.mofa.gov.vn/vnemb.la; Th That Luang, Vientiane; ⏰8.30am-5.30pm Mon-Fri) Issues tourist visas in three working days for US$45, or in one day for US$60. The Luang Prabang consulate (Map p36; Th Naviengkham, Luang Prabang) issues tourist visas for US$60 in a few minutes or US$45 if you wait a few days. At the consulates in Pakse (Map p216; ☎031-214199; www.vietnamconsulate-pakse.org; Th 21, Pakse; ⏰7.30-11.30am & 2-4.30pm Mon-Fri) and Savannakhet (Map p204; ☎041-212418; Th Sisavangvong, Savannakhet), visas cost US$60.

Food

Lao cuisine lacks the incredible variety of Thai food, but there are some distinctive dishes to sample. The standard Lao breakfast is *fěr* (rice noodles), usually served floating in a broth with vegetables and a meat of your choice. The trick is in the seasoning, and Lao people will stir in some fish sauce, lime juice, dried chillies, mint leaves, basil, or one of the wonderful speciality hot chilli sauces that many noodle shops make, testing it along the way.

Láhp is the most distinctively Lao dish, a delicious spicy salad made from minced beef, pork, duck, fish or chicken, mixed with fish sauce, small shallots, mint leaves, lime juice, roasted ground rice and lots and lots of chillies. Another famous Lao speciality is *đạm màhk hung* (known as *som tam* in Thailand), a salad of shredded green papaya mixed with garlic, lime juice, fish sauce, sometimes tomatoes, palm sugar, land crab or dried shrimp and, of course, chillies by the handful.

In lowland Lao areas almost every dish is eaten with *kòw něeo* (sticky rice), which is served in a small basket. Take a small amount of rice and, using one hand, work it into a walnut-sized ball before dipping it into the food.

In main centres, delicious French baguettes are a popular breakfast food. Sometimes they're eaten with condensed milk, or with *kai* (eggs) in a sandwich that also contains Lao-style pâté and vegetables.

Almost all Lao dishes contain some sort of animal product, be it fish sauce, shrimp paste or lard. There are very few dedicated vegetarian or vegan restaurants in Laos, but traveller-oriented restaurants and cafes usually have some vegetarian dishes available. It is important to learn some basic food vocabulary in remote areas. The best all-round phrase to learn is 'I only eat vegetables' or '*kòy gin đaa pak*' in Lao.

On the drinks front, Beerlao remains a firm favourite with 90% of the nation, while officially illegal *lòw-lów* (Lao liquor or rice whisky) is a popular drink among lowland Lao. It's usually taken neat and offered in villages as a welcoming gesture.

Water purified for drinking purposes is simply called *nâm deum* (drinking water), whether it's boiled or filtered. All water offered to customers in restaurants or hotels will be purified, and purified water is sold everywhere. Check that the ice in any drink originated from purified water.

Juice bars proliferate around Vientiane and Luang Prabang, and smoothies are usually on the menu in most Western-leaning cafes. Lao coffee is usually served strong and sweet. Thankfully, lattes and cappuccinos are springing up across the country with pasteurised milk coming from Thailand.

Chinese-style green tea is the usual ingredient in *nâm sáh* or *sáh lôw*, the weak, refreshing tea traditionally served free in restaurants. For Lipton-style tea, ask for *sáh hôrn* (hot tea).

Gay & Lesbian Travellers

For the most part Lao culture is very tolerant of homosexuality, although lesbianism is often either denied completely or misunderstood. The gay and lesbian scene is not nearly as prominent

EATING PRICE RANGES

Virtually all restaurants in Laos are inexpensive by international standards. The following price ranges refer to a main course.

$ less than US$5 (40,000K)

$$ US$5–15 (40,000–120,000K)

$$$ more than US$15 (120,0000K)

PRACTICALITIES

- The **Vientiane Times** (www.vientianetimes.org.la), published Monday to Saturday, is the country's only English-language newspaper and follows the party line.
- Francophones can read **Le Rénovateur** (www.lerenovateur.org.la), a government mouthpiece similar to the *Vientiane Times*.
- **Lao National Radio** (LNR; www.lnr.org.la) broadcasts sanitised English-language news twice daily.
- Short-wave radios can pick up BBC, VOA, Radio Australia and Radio France International.
- **Lao National TV** is so limited that most people watch Thai TV and/or karaoke videos.
- The metric system is used for measurements. Gold and silver are sometimes weighed in baht (15g).

as in neighbouring Thailand. Strictly speaking, homosexuality is illegal, though we haven't heard of police busting anyone in recent years. In any case, public displays of affection, whether heterosexual or homosexual, are frowned upon.

Sticky Rice (www.stickyrice.ws) Gay travel guide covering Laos and Asia.

Utopia (www.utopia-asia.com) Gay travel information and contacts, including some local gay terminology.

Insurance

As always, a good travel-insurance policy is a wise idea. Laos is generally considered a high-risk area, and with limited medical services it's vital to have a policy that covers being evacuated (medivaced), by air if necessary, to a hospital in Thailand. Read the small print in any policy to see if hazardous activities are covered; rock climbing, rafting and motorcycling often are not.

If you undergo medical treatment in Laos or Thailand, be sure to collect all receipts and copies of the medical report, in English if possible, for insurance purposes.

Worldwide travel insurance is available at www.lonelyplanet.com/travel_services. You can buy, extend and claim online anytime – even if you're already on the road.

Internet Access

Internet cafes are pretty common, and it is possible to get online in most provincial capitals. Free wi-fi is also now pretty standard and available in many guesthouses, hotels and cafes in the main tourist destinations around Laos. Prices range from 5000K per hour in popular centres to as much as 20,000K per hour in provincial backwaters.

Computers in most internet cafes have instant-messaging software such as MSN Messenger and Skype, although headsets are not always available.

Legal Matters

Although Laos guarantees certain rights, the reality is that you can be fined, detained or deported for any reason, as has been demonstrated repeatedly in cases involving foreigners.

If you stay away from anything you know to be illegal, you should be fine. If not, things might get messy and expensive. Drug possession and using prostitutes are the most common crimes for which travellers are caught, often with the dealer or consort being the one to inform the authorities. Sexual relationships between foreigners and Lao citizens who are not married are illegal. Penalties for failing to register a relationship range from fines of US$500 to US$5000, and possibly imprisonment or deportation.

If you are detained, ask to call your embassy or consulate in Laos, if there is one. A meeting or phone call between Lao officers and someone from your embassy/consulate may result in quicker adjudication and release.

Police sometimes ask for bribes for traffic violations and other petty offences.

Maps

The best all-purpose country map that's generally available is GT-Rider.com's *Laos*, with a scale of 1:1,650,000. It's available at bookshops in Thailand and at many guesthouses in Laos, as well as online at www.gt-rider.com.

Chiang Mai–based **Hobo Maps** (www.hobomaps.com; 25,000K) has produced a series of good maps of Vientiane, Luang Prabang and Vang Vieng. The Lao National Tourism Administration (LNTA) has also produced a few city maps in recent years, available at the tourist information centre in Vientiane.

Money

The official national currency in Laos is the Lao kip (K). Although only kip is legally negotiable in everyday transactions, in reality three currencies are used for commerce: kip, Thai baht (B) and US dollars (US$).

Laos relies heavily on the Thai baht and the US dollar for the domestic cash economy. An estimated one-third of all cash circulating in Vientiane, in fact, bears the portrait of the Thai king, while another third celebrates US presidents. Kip is usually preferred for small purchases, while more expensive items and services may be quoted in kip, baht or dollars. Anything costing the equivalent of US$100 or more is likely to be quoted in US dollars.

However, the majority of transactions will be carried out in kip, so it's always worth having a wad in your pocket. Notes come in denominations of 500, 1000, 2000, 5000, 10,000, 20,000, 50,000 and 100,000 kip. Small vendors, especially in rural areas, will struggle to change 100,000K notes. For larger transactions the dollar and the baht are favoured.

ATMs

ATMs are now found all over Laos. But before you get too excited, ATMs dispense a maximum of 700,000K to 2 million K (about US$85 to US$250) per transaction, depending on the bank, not to mention a variable withdrawal fee. If you also have to pay extortionate charges to your home bank on each overseas withdrawal, this can quickly add up.

Credit Cards

A growing number of hotels, upmarket restaurants and gift shops in Vientiane and Luang Prabang accept Visa and MasterCard, and, to a much lesser extent, Amex and JCB. Outside of these main towns, credit cards are virtually useless.

Banque pour le Commerce Extérieur Lao (BCEL) branches in most major towns offer cash advances/withdrawals on MasterCard and Visa credit/debit cards for a 3% transaction fee. Other banks may have slightly different charges, so it might be worth shopping around in Vientiane.

Moneychangers

After years of volatility the kip has in recent times remained fairly stable at about 8000K to the US dollar. Don't, however, count on this remaining the same.

Exchange rates are usually virtually the same whether you're changing at a bank or a moneychanger. Both are also likely to offer a marginally better rate for larger bills (US$50 and US$100) than smaller bills (US$20 and less). Banks in Vientiane and Luang Prabang can generally change UK pounds, euros, Canadian, US and Australian dollars, Thai baht and Japanese yen. Elsewhere most provincial banks usually change only US dollars or baht.

Licensed moneychangers maintain booths around Vientiane (including at Talat Sao) and at some border crossings. Their rates are similar to the banks, but they stay open longer.

There is no real black market in Laos and unless there's an economic crash that's unlikely to change.

For the latest rates from BCEL, check www.bcellaos.com.

Tipping

Tipping is not customary in Laos except in tourist-oriented restaurants, where 10% of the bill is appreciated, but only if a service charge hasn't already been added.

Travellers Cheques

Travellers cheques can be cashed at most banks in Laos, but normally only in exchange for kip. Cheques in US dollars are the most readily acceptable. Very few merchants accept travellers cheques.

Opening Hours

Government offices are typically open from 8am to 11.30am or noon and from 1pm to 5pm Monday to Friday.

Shops and private businesses open and close a bit later and usually stay open during lunch. On Saturday some businesses are open all day, others only half a day. Most businesses, except restaurants, are closed on Sunday.

BARGAINING 101

Bargaining is a tradition introduced by early Arab and Indian traders, however, in most places in Laos it's not nearly as aggressive as in other parts of Southeast Asia. Good bargaining, which takes practice, is one way to cut costs. Lao-style bargaining is generally a friendly transaction where two people try to agree on a price that is fair to both of them.

Most things bought in a market can be bargained for, but in shops prices are mostly fixed these days. The first rule to bargaining is to have a general idea of the price. Ask around at a few vendors to get a ballpark figure. Once ready to buy, it's generally a good strategy to start at 50% of the asking price and work up from there. In general, keeping a friendly, flexible demeanour throughout the transaction will almost always work in your favour. Don't get angry or upset over a few thousand kip. The locals, who invariably have less money than foreign visitors, never do this.

Business hours for restaurants vary according to their clientele and the food they serve.

➡ Shops selling noodles and/or rice soup are typically open from 7am to 1pm.

➡ Lao restaurants with a larger menu of dishes served with rice are often open from 10am to 10pm.

➡ International restaurants offering both Lao and *falang* (Western) food, and open for breakfast, lunch and dinner, usually open their doors around 7am and serve till 10pm.

➡ Tourist restaurants that don't open for breakfast generally serve from 11am to 11pm.

Photography

Digital photography has taken off in Laos and, particularly in popular tourist centres such as Vientiane, Luang Prabang, Vang Vieng and Pakse, the usual range of batteries, memory cards and even a limited range of cameras is available.

Most internet cafes have card readers and can write photos to either CD or DVD for about US$1 or US$2.

Lao officials are sensitive about photography of airports and military installations.

Post

Sending post from Laos is not all that expensive and is fairly reliable, but people still tend to wait until they get to Thailand to send parcels. Heading to Cambodia, it's probably smarter to post any parcels from Laos.

When posting any package leave it open for inspection by a postal officer. Incoming parcels might also need to be opened for inspection; there may be a small charge for this mandatory 'service'.

The main post office in Vientiane has a poste restante service.

Public Holidays

Schools and government offices are closed on these official holidays, and the organs of state move pretty slowly, if at all, during festivals.

International New Year (1 January)

Army Day (20 January)

International Women's Day (8 March)

Lao New Year (14–16 April)

International Labour Day (1 May)

International Children's Day (1 June)

Lao National Day (2 December)

Safe Travel

Over the last couple of decades Laos has earned a reputation among visitors as a remarkably safe place to travel, with little crime reported and few of the scams so often found in more touristed places such as Vietnam, Cambodia and Thailand. And while the vast majority of Laotians remain honest and welcoming, things aren't quite as idyllic as they once were. The main change has been in the rise of petty crimes, such as theft and low-level scams, which are more annoying than dangerous.

Accidents

Better roads, better vehicles and fewer insurgents mean road travel in Laos is quite safe, if not always comfortable. However, while the scarcity of traffic in Laos means there are far fewer accidents than in neighbouring countries, accidents are still the main risk for travellers.

As motorbikes become increasingly popular among travellers, so the number of accidents is rising. Even more likely is the chance of earning yourself a Lao version of the 'Thai tattoo' – that scar on the calf caused by a burn from a hot exhaust pipe.

The speedboats that careen along the Mekong in northern Laos are as dangerous as they are fast. We recommend avoiding all speedboat travel unless absolutely necessary.

Armed attack

With the Hmong insurgency virtually finished, travel along Rtes 7 and 13, particularly in the vicinity of Phu Khoun and Kasi, is as safe as it has been for decades. There have been no reported attacks on traffic since 2004. If you're concerned, ask around in Vientiane or Luang Prabang to make sure the situation remains secure before travelling along Rte 7 to Phonsavan or Rte 13 between Vang Vieng and Luang Prabang. Rte 1 from Paksan to Phonsavan is still considered a risk due to occasional banditry.

Queues

The Lao follow the usual Southeast Asian method of queuing for services, which is to say they don't form a line at all but simply push en masse towards the counter or doorway. The system is 'first seen, first served'. Learn to play the game the Lao way, by pushing your money, passport, letters or whatever to the front of the crowd as best you can.

Theft

While Lao are generally trustworthy people and theft is much less common than elsewhere in Southeast Asia, it has been on the rise in recent years. Most of the reports we've heard involve opportunistic acts that are fairly easily avoided.

Money or items going missing from hotel rooms is becoming more common, so don't leave cash or other tempting belongings on show. When riding a crowded bus, watch the luggage and don't keep money in loose trouser pockets. When riding a bicycle or motorcycle in Vientiane, don't place anything of value in the basket, as thieving duos on motorbikes may ride by and snatch a bag.

UXO

Large areas of eastern Laos are contaminated by unexploded ordnance (UXO). According to surveys by the Lao National UXO Programme (UXO Lao) and other non-government UXO clearance organisations, the provinces of Salavan, Savannakhet and Xieng Khuang are the most severely affected provinces, followed by Champasak, Hua Phan, Khammuan, Luang Prabang, Attapeu and Sekong.

Statistically speaking, the UXO risk for the average foreign visitor is low, but travellers should exercise caution when considering off-road wilderness travel in the aforementioned provinces. Stick only to marked paths. Never touch an object that may be UXO, no matter how old and defunct it may appear.

Shopping

Shopping in Laos is improving fast. The growth in tourist numbers has been matched, if not exceeded, by the number of stores flogging fabrics, handicrafts and regional favourites from Vietnam and Thailand. Vientiane and Luang Prabang are the main shopping centres and in these cities it's easiest to compare quality and price. It is, however, always nice to buy direct from the producer, and in many villages that's possible.

There is a *total* ban on the export of antiques and Buddha images from Laos, though the enforcement of this ban is lax.

Antiques

Vientiane and Luang Prabang each have a sprinkling of antique shops. Anything that looks old could be up for sale in these shops, including Asian pottery (especially porcelain from the Ming dynasty of China), old jewellery, clothes, carved wood, musical instruments, coins and bronze statuettes.

Carvings

The Lao produce well-crafted carvings in wood, bone and stone. Subjects include anything from Hindu or Buddhist mythology to themes from everyday life. Authentic opium pipes can be found, especially in the north, and sometimes have intricately carved bone or bamboo shafts.

To shop for carvings, look in antique or handicraft stores. Don't buy anything made from ivory.

Jewellery

Gold and silver jewellery are good buys in Laos, although you must search hard for well-made pieces. Some of the best silverwork is done by the hill tribes.

Textiles

Textiles are among the most beautiful, most recognisable and easiest items to buy while travelling in Laos. Unlike many handicrafts that are ubiquitous throughout Indochina, these are unmistakably Lao.

The best place to buy fabric is in the weaving villages themselves, where you can watch how it's made and get 'wholesale' prices. Failing this, you can find a decent selection and reasonable prices at open markets in provincial towns, including Vientiane's Talat Sao. Tailor shops and handicraft stores generally charge more and quality is variable.

Solo Travellers

Travelling alone in Laos is very common among both men and women. Lone women should exercise the usual caution when in remote areas or out late at night.

Telephone

The introduction of mobile phones has revolutionised communication in Laos.

International calls can be made from Lao Telecom offices or the local post office in most provincial capitals. Hours typically run from about 7.30am to 9.30pm.

International calls are also charged on a per-minute basis, with a minimum charge of three minutes. Calls to most countries cost about 2000K to 4000K per minute. Nowadays it's almost always cheaper to use Skype via an internet cafe.

Mobile Phones

Lao Telecom and several private companies offer mobile phone services on the GSM and 3G systems. Competition is fierce and you can buy a local SIM card for as little as 10,000K from almost anywhere. Calls are cheap and recharge cards are widely

GOVERNMENT TRAVEL ADVICE

Most governments have travel advisory services detailing potential pitfalls and areas to avoid.

Australian Department of Foreign Affairs (www.smartraveller.gov.au)

British Foreign Office (www.fco.gov.uk)

Canadian Government (www.voyage.gc.ca)

New Zealand Ministry of Foreign Affairs (www.safetravel.govt.nz)

US State Department (www.travel.state.gov)

available. Network coverage varies depending on the company and the region.

Phone Codes

Until a few years ago most cities in Laos could only be reached through a Vientiane operator. These days you can direct-dial across the country.

The country code for calling Laos is ☎856. For long-distance calls within the country, dial 0 first, then the area code and number. For international calls dial ☎00 first, then the country code, area code and number.

All mobile phones have a ☎020 code at the beginning of the number. Similar to this are WIN satellite phones, which begin with ☎030.

Time

Laos is seven hours ahead of GMT/UTC. Thus, noon in Vientiane is 10pm the previous day in San Francisco, 1am in New York, 5am in London and 3pm in Sydney. There is no daylight saving time.

Toilets

While Western-style 'thrones' are now found in most midrange and top-end accommodation, budget travellers should expect the rather-less-royal squat toilet to be the norm.

Even in places where sitdown toilets are installed, the plumbing may not be designed to take toilet paper. In such cases there will usually be a rubbish bin for the used paper.

Public toilets are uncommon outside hotel lobbies and airports. While on the road between towns and villages it's perfectly acceptable to go behind a tree or use the roadside. Lao tour guides use the euphemism "shooting rabbits" for men and "picking flowers" for women in case you wonder what on earth they are talking about.

Tourist Information

The Lao National Tourism Administration (LNTA) has tourist offices all around Laos, with the ones in Vientiane and Luang Prabang particularly worth visiting.

Many offices are well-stocked with brochures and maps, and have English-speaking staff to answer your questions. Offices in Tha Khaek, Savannakhet, Pakse, Luang Namtha, Sainyabuli, Phongsali and Sam Neua are all pretty good, with staff trained to promote treks and other activities in their provinces and able to hand out brochures and first-hand knowledge about them. They should also be able to help with local transport options and bookings.

If you find the local LNTA officials to be unhelpful, you can usually get up-to-date information from a popular guesthouse.

The LNTA also runs three very good websites that offer valuable pre-departure information.

Central Laos Trekking (www.trekkingcentrallaos.com)

Lao Ecotourism (www.ecotourismlaos.com)

Lao National Tourism Administration (www.tourismlaos.org)

Travellers with Disabilities

With its lack of paved roads or footpaths (sidewalks), Laos presents many physical obstacles for people with mobility impairments. Rarely do public buildings feature ramps or other access points for wheelchairs, nor do most hotels make efforts to provide access for the physically disabled, the few exceptions being at the top end. Public transport is particularly crowded and difficult, even for the fully ambulatory.

For wheelchair users, any trip to Laos will require a good deal of advance planning. Fortunately a growing network of information sources can put you in touch with those who may have wheeled through Laos before.

Access-Able Travel Source (www.access-able.com)

Mobility International USA (www.miusa.org)

Society for Accessible Travel & Hospitality (www.sath.org)

Visas

Getting into Laos is easier than ever and travellers from many countries can get 30-day tourist visas at nearly all border points.

Tourist Visa on Arrival

The Lao government issues 30-day tourist visas on arrival at all international airports and most international border crossings.

The whole process is very straightforward. You need between US$20 and US$42 cash, one passport-size photo and the name of a hotel or guesthouse. Those without a photo will have to pay an additional fee of about US$2. Arriving on a weekend or holiday, or outside of office hours, there is also an 'overtime fee' of US$1 or US$2.

The visa fee varies depending on the passport of origin, with Canadians having to fork out the most (US$42) and most other nationalities paying between US$30 and US$35. Pay in US dollars as a flat rate of 1500B (around US$50) is applicable in Thai baht. No other foreign currencies are accepted.

Tourist Visa

For those not eligible for a visa on arrival, Lao embassies and consulates abroad offer 30-day tourist visas. The process involves roughly

the same cost and documentation as described above and generally takes three working days. In Bangkok you can get your visa on the same day for an additional 200B express fee.

Business Visas

Business visas, valid for 30 days, are relatively easy to obtain as long as you have a sponsoring agency in Laos. A business visa can be extended up to a year.

Visa Extensions

The 30-day tourist visa is extendable an additional 90 days at a cost of US$2 per day, although this can only be done in Vientiane and Luang Prabang.

Overstaying Your Visa

Overstaying a visa is not a major crime, but it is expensive. It costs US$10 for each day overstayed, paid at the immigration checkpoint on departure.

Volunteering

Volunteers have been working in Laos for years, usually on one- or two-year contracts that include a minimal monthly allowance. Volunteers are often placed with a government agency and attempt to 'build capacity'. These sort of jobs can lead to non-volunteer work within the non-government organisation (NGO) community.

The alternative approach to volunteering, where you actually pay to be placed in a 'volunteer' role for a few weeks or months, has yet to arrive in Laos in any great capacity. A couple of groups in Luang Prabang need volunteers occasionally, and there are also local projects in places as diverse as Huay Xai, Muang Khua and Sainyabuli. The website **Stay Another Day** (www.stayanotherday.org) is a good resource for unpaid volunteer opportunities.

Australian Volunteers International (www.australianvolunteers.com) Places qualified Australian residents on one- to two-year contracts.

Global Volunteers (www.globalvolunteers.org) Coordinates teams of volunteers on short-term humanitarian and economic development projects.

Voluntary Service Overseas (VSO; www.vsointernational.org) Places qualified and experienced volunteers for up to two years.

Women Travellers

Laos is an easy country for women travellers, although it is necessary to be more culturally aware or sensitive than in many parts of neighbouring Thailand. Laos is very safe and violence against women travellers is extremely rare. Everyday incidents of sexual harassment may be more common than they were a few years ago, but they're still much less frequent than in virtually any other Asian country.

The relative lack of prostitution in Laos, as compared with Thailand, has benefits for women travellers. While a Thai woman who wants to preserve a 'proper' image often won't associate with foreign males for fear of being perceived as a prostitute, in Laos this is not the case. Hence a foreign woman seen drinking in a cafe or restaurant is not usually perceived as being 'loose' or available as she might be in Thailand. This in turn means that there are generally fewer problems with uninvited male solicitations.

The best way to avoid unwanted attention is to avoid overly revealing clothes. It's highly unusual for most Lao women to wear singlet tops or very short skirts or shorts. So when travellers do, people tend to stare.

Lao people will almost never confront you about what you're wearing, but that doesn't mean they don't care. As one woman in Vang Vieng told us: 'I wouldn't say anything, but I'd prefer it if they put on a sarong when they get out of the river. It's not our way to dress like that [a bikini only] and it's embarrassing to see it.' If you're planning on bathing in a village or river, a sarong is essential.

Traditionally women didn't sit on the roofs of riverboats, because this was believed to bring bad luck. These days most captains aren't so concerned, but if you are asked to get off the roof while men are not, this is why.

Work

With a large number of aid organisations and a fast-growing international business community, especially in energy and mining, the number of jobs available to foreigners is increasing, but still relatively small. The greatest number of positions are in Vientiane.

Possibilities include teaching English privately or at one of the handful of language centres in Vientiane, work which pays about US$5 to US$10 an hour. Certificates or degrees in English teaching aren't absolutely necessary, but they do help.

If you have technical expertise or international volunteer experience, you might be able to find work with a UN-related program or an NGO providing foreign aid or technical assistance to Laos. These jobs are difficult to find; your best bet is to visit the Vientiane offices of each organisation and inquire about personnel needs and vacancies, then start seeking out potential employers socially and buying them lots of Beerlao. For a list of NGOs operating in Laos, see the excellent www.directoryofngos.org.

Transport

GETTING THERE & AWAY

Many travellers enter or exit Laos via the country's numerous land and river borders. Flying into Laos is a relatively easy option as there is only a small number of airlines serving Laos and prices don't vary much. Flights and tours can be booked online at www.lonelyplanet.com/travel_services.

Air

Airports & Airlines

There are four international airports in Laos: **Wattay International Airport** (Map p138; ☎021-512165) in Vientiane, **Luang Prabang International Airport** (☎071-212173), **Savannakhet International Airport** (Map p204; ☎041-212140; Th Kaysone Phomvihane) and **Pakse International Airport** (☎031-251921).

The following airlines operate international flights to/from Laos although Lao Airlines is the national carrier and monopolises the majority of flights in and out of the country:

Air Asia (www.airasia.com) Vientiane to Kuala Lumpur several times per week.

Bangkok Airways (www.bangkokair.com) Connects Luang Prabang, Vientiane and Pakse to Bangkok, plus Luang Prabang to Chiang Mai.

China Eastern Airlines (www.ce-air.com) Flies daily to Kunming and Nanning from Vientiane.

Lao Airlines (www.laoairlines.com) National carrier. The extensive international flight network includes Vientiane to Bangkok, Chiang Mai, Danan, Guangzhou, Hanoi, Ho Chi Minh City, Kunming, Phnom Penh, Siem Reap and Singapore; Luang Prabang to Bangkok, Chiang Mai, Hanoi and Siem Reap; Pakse to Bangkok, Danang, Ho Chi Minh City and Siem Reap; and Savannakhet to Bangkok and Danang.

Thai Airways International (www.thaiairways.com) Vientiane to Bangkok connections twice daily.

Vietnam Airlines (www.vietnamairlines.com) Connects Vientiane with Ho Chi Minh City, Hanoi and Phnom Penh, plus Luang Prabang with Hanoi and Siem Reap.

Tickets

The most convenient international gateway to Laos is Bangkok. Luckily there are plenty of flights to the Thai capital. Generally, it is cheaper to take an indirect flight to Bangkok with a stop on the way. Once in Bangkok, there are trains, planes and buses heading to Laos.

Buying direct from the airline is usually more expensive, unless the airline has a special promotion or you are flying with a budget carrier offering online deals. The time of year has a major

CLIMATE CHANGE & TRAVEL

Every form of transport that relies on carbon-based fuel generates CO_2, the main cause of human-induced climate change. Modern travel is dependent on aeroplanes, which might use less fuel per kilometre per person than most cars but travel much greater distances. The altitude at which aircraft emit gases (including CO_2) and particles also contributes to their climate change impact. Many websites offer 'carbon calculators' that allow people to estimate the carbon emissions generated by their journey and, for those who wish to do so, to offset the impact of the greenhouse gases emitted with contributions to portfolios of climate-friendly initiatives throughout the world. Lonely Planet offsets the carbon footprint of all staff and author travel.

Laos Air Fares

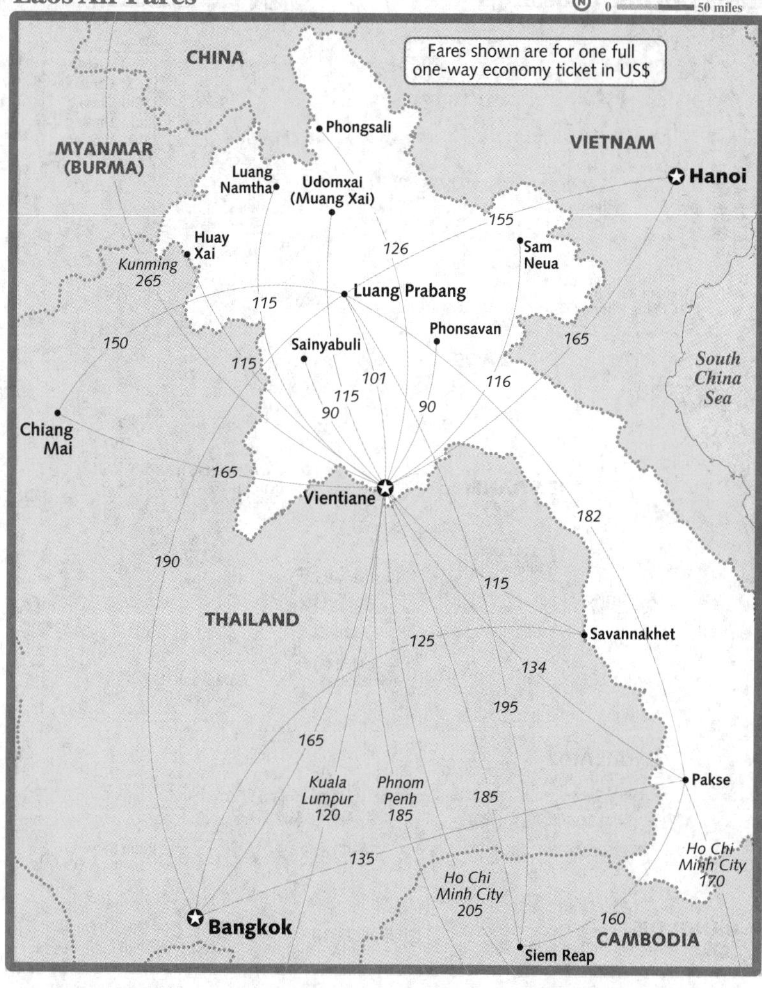

impact on flight prices. Starting out from Europe, North America or Australia, figure on prices rising dramatically over Christmas and during July and August, and dropping significantly during lax periods of business like February, June and October.

Land

Laos shares land and/or river borders with Thailand, Myanmar, Cambodia, China and Vietnam. We cover all the border crossings currently open to foreigners. Border-crossing details change regularly, so ask around and check the **Thorntree** (lonelyplanet.com/thorntree) before setting off.

It's possible to bring a vehicle into Laos from Cambodia and Thailand with the right paperwork and Lao customs don't object to visitors bringing bicycles into the country.

Cambodia

There are daily buses and minibuses connecting Pakse with Stung Treng (four hours), Kratie (six hours) and Phnom Penh (11 hours). These also call at Ban Nakasang and Ban Hat Xai in both directions for travellers planning to relax in Si Phan Don. It's best to take one of these through-buses, as it's pretty tough to arrange transport at the Dong Kiaw (Laos)/Trapaeng Kriel (Cambodia) border.

Laos Border Crossings

China

Handy through-buses link major towns in Yunnan to northern Laos. Routes include Luang Namtha–Jinghong (six hours), Udomxai–Mengla (five hours) and Kunming–Luang Prabang (around 24 hours on a Chinese sleeper bus). It's also perfectly feasible to make the journey in hops via Boten, the only China–Lao border crossing currently open to foreigners. From Móhān on the Chinese side it's around a two-hour minibus ride to Mengla, the nearest large town.

Myanmar

It is effectively not possible to cross by land between Laos and Myanmar at this time. The easiest option is to transit through Thailand, via Chiang Khong and Mae Sai to the Burmese town of Tachilek.

Thailand

There are eight crossings to Thailand open to foreigners. Some involve taking a boat across the Mekong, or crossing the river on one of the Friendship Bridges.

THAILAND TO VIENTIANE

Through-buses run regularly between Vientiane and the Thai towns of Khon Kaen (four hours), Nakhon Ratchasima (seven hours), Nong Khai (1½ hours) and Udon Thani (2½ hours) via the Friendship Bridge. There are also several daily trains (www.railway.co.th/english)

from Bangkok to Nong Khai (about 12 hours), as well as daily departures between Nong Khai and Vientiane's Dongphasy Station. From Udon Thani there are budget flights to Bangkok and other domestic destinations in Thailand.

THAILAND TO NORTHERN LAOS

The majority of visitors are heading to or from Luang Prabang. There are three main options but no route allows you to make the trip in a single journey. The Chiang Rai–Huay Xai–Luang Prabang route is by far the most tourist-friendly and potentially the quickest route (around 24 hours using buses, two days by bus-boat combination).

Travel this way is via Chiang Khong/Huay Xai. Departing from Chiang Rai on the first bus of the day it is possible to connect with the slowboat from Huay Xai to Luang Prabang, arriving the following evening. Or leave Chiang Rai at lunchtime and connect with the 5pm overnight bus (faster but not really recommended), arriving in Luang Prabang late next morning. Through-tickets from Chiang Mai or Chiang Rai agencies are generally overpriced.

Other possibilities are perfectly feasible but see almost no foreign tourists so you'll need to be comfortable with local languages or gesticulations. These routes can also take several days due to limited transport and poor roads. Choose from the Nan–Muang Ngeun–Luang Prabang route or the even more remote Loei–Pak Lai–Sainyabuli option.

THAILAND TO CENTRAL LAOS

Although relatively few tourists use them, the border crossings that straddle the Mekong between northeastern Thailand and central Laos are almost universally convenient and straightforward.

The river crossing between Nakhon Phanom and Tha Khaek is a breeze and there are several daily buses between Bangkok and Nakhon Phanom (12 hours).

The bridge between Mukdahan and Savannakhet is the southernmost Mekong River crossing open to non-Thai and non-Lao nationals. Several buses link Bangkok and Mukdahan (about 10 hours), and the Thai-Lao International Bus runs between the latter and Savannakhet's bus station (45 minutes).

The river crossing between Beung Kan and Paksan is the weak link with a dearth of regular transport on the Thai side.

THAILAND TO SOUTHERN LAOS

International buses connect Pakse with Ubon Ratchathani (four hours including crossing) via the Vang Tao (Laos) and Chong Mek (Thailand) border twice daily, plus there is one through service a day to Bangkok. Combination bus and train tickets can also be purchased in Pakse.

Vietnam

At the time of writing, foreigners can cross between Laos and Vietnam at seven different border posts. Laos issues 30-day tourist visas at all of these, but Vietnamese visas must be arranged in advance in Luang Prabang, Vientiane, Savannakhet or Pakse. In every case we recommend using a through-bus rather than trying to make the trip in hops, as it can be very difficult to arrange onward transport from the remote border posts.

VIETNAM TO NORTHERN LAOS

An increasingly popular alternative to the hellish 24-hour buses between Hanoi and Vientiane is to start from northwestern Vietnam and use the daily Dien Bien Phu–Muang Khua bus, crossing the border at Tay Trang, before arriving in fascinating Phongsali province. Reaching Luang Prabang from Dien Bien Phu is possible in two days (one night in Muang Khua). Better is to take it slowly using the Nam Ou riverboats with a stop in Nong Khiaw.

Other decent alternatives start from the Vietnamese towns of Thanh Hoa and Vinh. Thanh Hoa–Sam Neua buses (daily), which pass through the border at Nam Soi, take a beautiful route and are ideal for visiting the memorable Vieng Xai Caves on a long overland trip to Luang Prabang.

Buses on the Vinh–Phonsavan route, which pass the border at lonely Nam Can, allow a visit to the enigmatic Plain of Jars but don't run daily.

VIETNAM TO CENTRAL LAOS

There are direct buses from both Hanoi and Ho Chi Minh City to Vientiane, but a more interesting alternative is to break up the trip in beautiful but seldom visited central Laos.

Starting out in central Vietnam, there are a few different options. The border at Lao Bao, easily accessed from Dong Ha, is the largest and easiest of all crossings to/from Vietnam. Once in Laos, break the journey with stays in Sepon, visiting what's left of the Ho Chi Minh Trail, or in Savannakhet. Moving north, there's a crossing at Cha Lo, but virtually the only traffic is the buses that run between Dong Hoi and Tha Khaek. The most popular crossing is at Cau Treo, which is easily accessed via Vinh, and which is also the route that the direct buses between Vientiane and Hanoi use. Punctuate the journey with a visit to the spectacular underground river at Tham Kong Lo.

VIETNAM TO SOUTHERN LAOS

There is a daily bus service (in both directions) between

LAOS BORDER CROSSINGS

Cambodia

BORDER CROSSING	CONNECTING TOWNS	VISA AVAILABLE ON ARRIVAL	MORE INFORMATION
Non Nok Khiene (L), Trapeang Kriel (C)	Si Phan Don (L), Stung Treng (C)	Yes	p245

China

BORDER CROSSING	CONNECTING TOWNS	VISA AVAILABLE ON ARRIVAL	MORE INFORMATION
Boten (L), Móhān (C)	Luang Nam Tha (L), Mengla (C)	Laos only	p103

Thailand

BORDER CROSSING	CONNECTING TOWNS	VISA AVAILABLE ON ARRIVAL	MORE INFORMATION
Nong Khai (T), Tha Na Leng (L)	Nong Khai (T), Vientiane (L)	Yes	p166
Paksan (L), Beung Kan (T)	Paksan (L), Beung Kan (T)	No	p188
Huay Xai(L), Chiang Khong (T)	Huay Xai (L), Chiang Rai (T)	Yes	p118
Tha Khaek(L), Nakhon Phanom(T)	Tha Khaek (L), Nakhon Phanom (T)	Yes	p200
Savannakhet (L), Mukdahan (T)	Savannakhet (L), Mukdahan (T)	Yes	p206
Vang Tao (L), Chong Mek (T)	Pakse (L), Ubon Ratchathani (T)	Yes	p220
Muang Ngeun (L), Huay Kon (T)	Hongsa (L), Phrae (T)	Yes	p123
Kaen Thao (L), Tha Li (T)	Pak Li (L), Loei (T)	Yes	p127

Vietnam

BORDER CROSSING	CONNECTING TOWNS	VISA AVAILABLE ON ARRIVAL	MORE INFORMATION
Dansavanh (L), Lao Bao (V)	Savannakhet (L), Dong Ha (V)	Laos only	p207
Phou Keua (L), Bo Y (V)	Attapeu (L), Kontum (V)	Laos only	p244
Na Phao (L), Cha Lo (V)	Tha Khaek (L), Dong Hoi (L)	Laos only	p199
Nong Haet (L), Nam Can (V)	Phonsavan (L), Vinh (V)	Laos only	p74
Nam Phao (L), Cau Treo (V)	Tha Khaek (L), Vinh (V)	Laos only	p194
Na Meo (L), Nam Soi (V)	Sam Neua (L), Thanh Hoa (V)	Laos only	p80
Pang Hok (L), Tay Trang (V)	Muang Khua (L), Dien Bien Phu (V)	Laos only	p92

Pakse and Kontum, passing through both Sekong and Attapeu, as well as the Phou Keua (Laos)/Bo Y (Vietnam) border. It takes about eight to nine hours to complete the entire journey or about half that between Attapeu and Kontum.

GETTING AROUND

Getting around Laos can be pretty slow going. Although a growing number of main roads are sealed, and there are more domestic flights than ever, domestic transport is still infrequent, unreliable and time-consuming.

Air

Lao Airlines (www.laoairlines.com) is the main airline in Laos. Smaller destinations are handled by **Lao Air** (www.lao-air.com) using smaller planes. For domestic flights, Vientiane is the main hub. For the latest fares check Lao Airlines' website.

With the exception of Lao Airlines' offices in Vientiane and Luang Prabang, where credit cards are accepted for both international and domestic tickets, it is necessary to pay cash in US dollars.

Domestic flights with Lao Air to smaller airports like Boun Neua (Phongsali) or Nathong (Sam Neua) suffer fairly frequent cancellations due to fog and, in March, due to heavy smoke during the forest-burning season. During the holiday season it's best to book ahead as flights can fill fast. At other times, when flights are more likely to be cancelled, confirm the flight is still departing a day or two before.

Bicycle

The stunning roads and light, relatively slow traffic in most towns and on most highways make Laos arguably the best country for cycling in Southeast Asia. For more on cycling in Laos, see p27.

Boat

More than 4600km of navigable rivers are the highways and byways of traditional Laos, the main thoroughfares being the Mekong, Nam Ou, Nam Khan, Nam Tha, Nam Ngum and Se Kong. The Mekong is the longest and most important route and is navigable year-round between Luang Prabang in the north and Savannakhet in the south. Smaller rivers accommodate a range of smaller boats, from dugout canoes to 'bomb boats' made from war detritus.

Whether it's on a tourist boat from Huay Xai to Luang Prabang or on a local boat you've rustled up in some remote corner of the country, it's still worth doing at least one river excursion while in Laos.

River Ferries (Slow Boats) & River Taxis

The most popular river trip in Laos, the slow boat between Huay Xai and Luang Prabang, is still a daily event and relatively cheap at about 200,000K or US$25 per person for the two-day journey. From Huay Xai, these basic boats are often packed, while travelling in the other direction from Luang Prabang there seems to be more room. Passengers sit, eat and sleep on the wooden decks. The toilet (if there is one) is an enclosed hole in the deck at the back of the boat.

For shorter river trips, such as Luang Prabang to the Pak Ou Caves, it's usually best to hire a river taxi. The *héua hang nyáo* (longtail boats) are the most common and cost around US$10 an hour.

Along the upper Mekong River between Huay Xai and Vientiane, Thai-built *héua wái* (speedboats) are common. They can cover a distance in six hours that might take a ferry two days or more. Charters cost at least US$30 per hour, but some ply regular routes so the cost can be shared among passengers. They are, however, rather dangerous.

Tours

With public boat routes becoming increasingly hard to find, tour companies are

KNOW YOUR BOAT

Following are some of the *héua* (boats) that you may encounter in your adventures along Laos' many waterways:

Héua sáh (double-deck slow boats) Big, old boats; almost extinct.

Héua dooan (express boat) Roofed cargo boats, common on the Huay Xai–Luang Prabang route. Still slow, but faster than double-deck boats.

Héua wái (speedboat) These resemble a surfboard with a car engine strapped to the back: very fast, exhilarating, deafeningly loud, uncomfortable and rather dangerous.

Héua hăhng nyáo (longtail boat) Boats with the engine gimbal-mounted on the stern; found all over Laos.

Héua pái (rowboat) Essentially a dugout, common in Si Phan Don.

offering kayaking and rafting trips on some of the more scenic stretches of river. The best places to organise these are Luang Namtha, Luang Prabang, Nong Khiaw, Vang Vieng, Tha Khaek and Pakse.

For something a bit more luxurious, **Mekong Cruises** (www.mekong-cruises.com) and **Mekong River Cruises** (www.cruisemekong.com) both offer multiday cruises along the Mekong on refurbished river barges.

Bus, Sŏrngtăaou & Lot Doi Saan

Long-distance public transport in Laos is either by bus or *sŏrngtăaou* (literally 'two rows'), which are converted pick-ups or trucks with benches down either side. Private operators have established VIP buses on some busier routes, offering faster and more luxurious air-con services that cost a little more than normal buses. Many guesthouses can book tickets for a small fee.

Sŏrngtăaou usually service shorter routes within a given province. Most decent-sized villages have at least one *sŏrngtăaou*, which will run to the provincial capital and back most days.

Car & Motorcycle

Driving in Laos is easier than it looks. Sure, the road infrastructure is pretty basic, but outside of the large centres there are so few vehicles that it's a doddle compared to Vietnam, China or Thailand.

Motorcyclists planning to ride through Laos should check out the wealth of information at **Golden Triangle Rider** (www.gt-rider.com). Doing some sort of motorbike loop out of Vientiane is becoming increasingly popular among travellers.

Bringing your own Vehicle

Bringing a vehicle into Laos is easy enough if you have proof of ownership and a *carnet de passage*. Simply get the *carnet* stamped at any international border and there is no extra charge or permit required.

Coming from Thailand, which doesn't recognise the *carnet* system, an International Transport Permit, known in Thailand as the *lêm sĕe môoang* (purple book) is required. This is available at Nong Khai's **Land Transport Office** (☎042-411591, ext 103; ⏰8.30am-4.30pm). You'll need your vehicle's official registration book and tax receipts, your passport and an international driving permit or Thai driver's licence.

On the Lao side you'll need all the documents mentioned above and will also need to arrange Lao vehicle insurance (about 300B for a week).

ROAD DISTANCES (KM)

	Attapeu	Luang Namtha	Luang Prabang	Muang Khong	Nong Haet	Pakse	Phongsali	Phonsavan	Sam Neua	Savannakhet	Tha Khaek	Udomxai	Vang Vieng
Luang Namtha	1400												
Luang Prabang	1130	270											
Muang Khong	190	1380	1110										
Nong Haet	1280	580	350	1260									
Pakse	210	1250	980	120	1130								
Phongsali	1550	360	410	1520	720	1390							
Phonsavan	1170	470	250	1150	110	1020	620						
Sam Neua	1350	450	460	1320	300	1190	590	180					
Savannakhet	410	1050	780	390	930	250	1190	820	990				
Tha Khaek	480	920	650	460	800	370	1070	690	870	130			
Udomxai	1290	110	180	1270	470	1140	250	360	440	940	820		
Vang Vieng	970	440	170	940	320	810	580	220	480	650	490	350	
Vientiane	810	680	390	790	470	660	810	380	620	500	330	580	150

MOTORCYCLE DIARIES

There are few more liberating travel experiences than renting a motorbike and setting off; stopping where you want, when you want. The lack of traffic and stunningly beautiful roads make Laos one of the best places in the region to do it. There are, however, a few things worth knowing before you hand over your passport as collateral to rent a bike.

The bike Price and availability mean that the vast majority of travellers rent Chinese 110cc bikes. No 110cc bike was designed to be used like a dirt bike, but Japanese bikes deal with it better and are worth the extra few dollars a day.

The odometer Given that many roads have no kilometre stones and turn-offs are often unmarked, it's worth getting a bike with a working odometer. Most bike shops can fix an odometer in about 10 minutes for a few dollars. Money well spent, as long as you remember to note the distance when you start.

The gear Don't leave home without sunscreen, a hat, a plastic raincoat or poncho, a bandanna and sunglasses. Even the sealed roads in Laos get annoyingly dusty, so these last two are vital. A helmet is essential (ask for one if they don't offer), as is wearing pants and shoes, lest you wind up with the ubiquitous leg burn.

The problems Unless you're very lucky, something will go wrong. Budget some time for it.

The responsibility In general, you can ride a motorbike in Laos without a licence, a helmet or any safety gear whatsoever, but for all this freedom you must take all the responsibility. If you have a crash, there won't be an ambulance to pick you up, and when you get to the hospital, facilities will be basic. Carrying a basic medical kit and phone numbers for hospitals in Thailand and your travel insurance provider is a good idea. The same goes for the bike. If it really dies you can't just call the company and get a replacement. You'll need to load it onto the next pick-up or *sŏrngtăaou* and take it somewhere they can fix it. Do not abandon it by the road, or you'll have to pay for another one.

Exiting into Thailand or Cambodia is fairly hassle-free if your papers are in order. Vietnam is a different story and it is probably best not to even consider a crossing. Heading to China it's virtually impossible to drive a vehicle larger than a bicycle across the border.

Driving Licences

Officially at least, to drive in Laos a valid international driving permit is required. If you're only renting motorbikes you'll never be asked for any sort of licence.

Fuel & Spare Parts

At the time of research fuel cost about US$1.20 a litre for petrol, slightly less for diesel. Fuel for motorcycles is available from drums or Beerlao bottles in villages across the country, although prices are almost always higher than at service stations. Diesel is available in most towns.

It's best to fuel up in bigger towns at big-brand service stations because the quality of fuel can be poor in remote areas.

Spare parts for four-wheeled vehicles are expensive and difficult to find, even in Vientiane.

Hire

Chinese- and Japanese-made 100 and 110cc step-through motorbikes can be hired for approximately 40,000K to 100,000K per day in most large centres and some smaller towns, although the state of the bikes can vary greatly. No licence is required. Try to get a Japanese bike if travelling any distance out of town. In Vientiane and Luang Prabang, 250cc dirt bikes are available for about US$25 per day.

It's possible to hire a self-drive vehicle, but when you consider that a driver usually costs no more, takes responsibility for damage and knows where he's going, it seems pointless. Costs run from US$40 to US$100 per day, depending on the route.

Vientiane-based **Europcar** (Map p142; ☎021-223867; www.europcarlaos.com; Th Setthathirath; ⏰8.30am-6.30pm Mon-Fri, 8.30am-1pm Sat & Sun) and **Jules' Classic Rental** (Map p142; ☎020-9728 2636; www.bike-rental-laos.com; Th Setthathirath; per day US$35, minimum rental 1 week) have good reputations.

Insurance

Car-hire companies will provide insurance, but be sure to check exactly what is covered. Note that most travel-insurance policies don't cover use of motorcycles.

Road Conditions

While the overall condition of roads is poor, work over the last decade has made most of the main roads quite comfortable.

Elsewhere, unsurfaced roads are the rule. Laos has about 23,000km of classified roads and less than a quarter are sealed. Unsurfaced roads are particularly tricky in the wet season when many routes are impassable to all but 4WD vehicles and motorbikes, while in the dry season the clouds of dust kicked up by passing traffic make travel highly uncomfortable, especially in a *sŏrngtăaou* or by motorbike. Bring a facemask. Wet or dry, Laos is so mountainous that relatively short road trips can take forever.

Road Hazards

Try to avoid driving at dusk and after dark: cows, buffaloes, chickens and dogs, not to mention thousands of people, head for home on the unlit roads, turning them into a dangerous obstacle course.

Road Rules

The single most important rule to driving in Laos is to expect the unexpected. Driving is on the right side, but it's not unusual to see Lao drivers go the wrong way down the left lane before crossing over to the right, a potentially dangerous situation if you're not ready for it. At intersections it's normal to turn right without looking left.

Local Transport

Although most town centres are small enough to walk around, even relatively small settlements often place their bus stations several kilometres out of town.

Bus

Vientiane is the only city with a network of local buses, though they're not much use to travellers.

Jumbo, Săhm-Lór, Sakai-Làap & Tuk-Tuk

The various three-wheeled taxis found in Vientiane and provincial capitals have different names depending on where you are. Larger ones are called *jąmbǫh* (jumbo) and can hold four to six passengers on two facing seats. In Vientiane they are sometimes called tuk-tuks as in Thailand (though traditionally in Laos this refers to a slightly larger vehicle than the jumbo). These three-wheeled conveyances are also labelled simply *taak-see* (taxi) or, usually for motorcycle sidecar-style vehicles, *săhm-lór* (three-wheels). The old-style bicycle *săhm-lór* (pedicab), known as a *cyclo* elsewhere in Indochina, is an endangered species in Laos.

Taxi

Vientiane has a handful of taxis that are used by foreign business people and the occasional tourist, though in other cities a taxi of sorts can be arranged. They can be hired by the trip, by the hour or by the day. Typical all-day hire within a town or city costs between US$35 and US$45 subject to negotiations.

Tours

A growing number of tour operators run trips in Laos and it's cheaper to book directly with them rather than through a foreign-based agency. Tailor-made itineraries are available and more specialised tours are growing in popularity, with cycling, boat tours, motorcycling and photographic tours all available.

Adventure Tours

Exotissimo (www.exotissimo.com) Large company with a mix of pure sightseeing and adventure tours.

Stray (www.straytravel.asia) Budget bus tours throughout Laos, including short hops from place to place and longer adventure tours upcountry.

Xplore-Asia (www.xplore-asia.com) Popular with backpackers for its cheap adventure tours, especially from Pakse, Si Phan Don and Vang Vieng.

Cycling Tours

Several tour agencies and guesthouses offer mountain-biking tours, ranging in duration from a few hours to several weeks.

Green Discovery (www.greendiscoverylaos.com) The original Laos-based adventure company offers a range of two-wheeled tours.

Grasshopper Tours (www.grasshopperadventures.com) This bicycle-touring outfit also offers elephant-centric photo tours of Laos.

Laosabaidee Travel (www.laosabaidee.com) Family-run outfit that specialises in bicycle tours of Laos.

Spice Roads (www.spiceroads.com) Specialises in cycling tours.

Motorcycle Tours

A handful of companies offer motorcycle tours of Laos. Guided tours are all-inclusive, and in addition to accommodation, food and petrol, typically include rental of a 250cc dirt bike and protective gear.

Explore Indochina (www.exploreindochina.com) Guided tours of the Ho Chi Minh Trail on vintage Soviet motorcycles.

Remote Asia (www.remote-asia.com/motorbike.html) Self-guided motorcycle tours of Laos ranging in duration from four to 12 days are on offer here. Motorcycle and equipment rental are also available.

Siam Enduro (www.siamenduro.com) This Thailand-based outfit has brought together its two decades of experience in the region to put together a two-week tour of northern Laos.

Health

Dr Trish Batchelor

Health issues and the quality of medical facilities vary enormously depending on where and how you travel in Laos. Travellers tend to worry about contracting infectious diseases when in the tropics, but infections are a rare cause of serious illness or death in travellers. Pre-existing medical conditions such as heart disease and accidental injury account for most of the life-threatening problems. Falling ill in some way, however, is relatively common. Fortunately, most common illnesses can either be prevented with common-sense behaviour or be treated easily with a well-stocked traveller's medical kit.

The following advice is a general guide only and does not replace the advice of a doctor trained in travel medicine.

BEFORE YOU GO

Pack medications in their original, clearly labelled, containers. A signed and dated letter from your physician describing your medical conditions and medications, including generic names, is also a good idea. If carrying syringes or needles, be sure to have a physician's letter documenting their medical necessity.

If you happen to take any regular medication, bring double your needs in case of loss or theft. In Laos it can be difficult to find some newer drugs, particularly the latest antidepressant drugs, blood-pressure medications and contraceptive pills.

Insurance

Even if you are fit and healthy, don't travel without health insurance, as accidents can happen. Declare any existing medical conditions you have: the insurance company *will* check if your problem is pre-existing and will not cover you if it is undeclared. You may require extra cover for adventure activities such as rock climbing. If your health insurance doesn't cover you for medical expenses abroad, consider getting extra insurance: check www.lonelyplanet.com/travel_services for more information. If you're uninsured, emergency evacuation is extremely expensive.

Find out in advance if your insurance plan will make payments directly to providers or reimburse you later for overseas health expenditures. In Laos, most doctors expect payment in cash. If you have to claim later, keep all the documentation.

Recommended Vaccinations

The only vaccine required by international regulations is yellow fever. Proof of vaccination will only be required if you have visited a country in the yellow-fever zone within the six days prior to entering Southeast Asia.

Specialised travel-medicine clinics are the best source of information on vaccines and will be able to give tailored recommendations.

Most vaccines don't produce immunity until at least two weeks after they're given, so visit a doctor four to eight weeks before departure. Ask the doctor for an International Certificate of Vaccination (otherwise known as the yellow booklet), which will list all the vaccinations received.

Medical Checklist

The following are some recommended items for a personal medical kit:

- antifungal cream, eg Clotrimazole
- antibacterial cream, eg Muciprocin
- antibiotics for diarrhoea, eg Norfloxacin or Ciprofloxacin; Azithromycin for bacterial diarrhoea; and Tinidazole for giardiasis or amoebic dysentery
- antihistamines for allergies, eg Cetrizine for daytime and Promethazine for night
- anti-inflammatories, eg Ibuprofen
- antinausea medication, eg Prochlorperazine

RECOMMENDED & REQUIRED VACCINATIONS

Short-Term Travellers

The World Health Organization (WHO) recommends the following vaccinations for travellers to Southeast Asia, although some do have side effects:

Adult diphtheria and tetanus Single booster recommended if you've had none in the previous 10 years.

Hepatitis A Provides almost 100% protection for up to a year; a booster after 12 months provides at least another 20 years' protection.

Hepatitis B Now considered routine for most travellers. Given as three shots over six months. A rapid schedule is also available, as is a combined vaccination with Hepatitis A. Lifetime protection occurs in 95% of people.

Measles, mumps and rubella Two doses of MMR required unless you have had the diseases. Many young adults require a booster.

Polio Since 2006, India, Indonesia, Nepal and Bangladesh are the only countries in Asia to have reported cases of polio. Only one booster is required as an adult for lifetime protection.

Typhoid Recommended unless the trip is less than a week and only to developed cities. The vaccine offers around 70% protection, lasts for two to three years and comes as a single shot.

Long-Term Travellers

These vaccinations are recommended for people travelling for more than one month, or those at special risk:

Japanese B Encephalitis Three injections in all. Booster recommended after two years.

Meningitis Single injection. There are two types of vaccination: the quadrivalent vaccine gives two to three years protection; meningitis group C vaccine gives around 10 years protection. Recommended for long-term backpackers aged under 25.

Rabies Three injections in all. A booster after one year will provide 10 years protection.

Tuberculosis Adult long-term travellers are usually recommended to have a TB skin test before and after travel, rather than vaccination. Only one vaccine is given in a lifetime.

- antiseptic for cuts and scrapes, eg Betadine
- antispasmodic for stomach cramps, eg Buscopan
- contraceptives
- decongestant for colds and flus, eg Pseudoephedrine
- DEET-based insect repellent
- diarrhoea 'stopper', eg Loperamide
- first-aid items such as scissors, plasters (Band Aids), bandages, gauze, thermometer (electronic, not mercury), sterile needles and syringes, and tweezers
- indigestion medication, eg Quick Eze or Mylanta
- iodine tablets to purify water
- oral-rehydration solution for diarrhoea, eg Gastrolyte
- paracetamol for pain
- permethrin (to impregnate clothing and mosquito nets) for repelling insects
- sunscreen and hat
- throat lozenges
- thrush (vaginal yeast infection) treatment, eg Clotrimazole pessaries or Diflucan tablet

Websites

There is a wealth of travel health advice on the internet.

World Health Organization (WHO; www.who.int/ith) Publishes a superb book called *International Travel & Health*, which is revised annually and is available online at no cost.

MD Travel Health (www.mdtravelhealth.com) Provides complete travel-health recommendations for every country and is updated daily.

Centers for Disease Control and Prevention (CDC; www.cdc.gov) Good general information.

IN LAOS

Availability & Cost of Healthcare

Laos has no facilities for major medical emergencies. The state-run hospitals and clinics are among the most basic in Southeast Asia in terms of the standards of hygiene, staff training, supplies and equipment.

For minor to moderate conditions, including malaria, **Mahasot Hospital's International Clinic** (☎021-214022, 021-214021; Th Fa Ngoum; ⏲24hr) in Vientiane has a decent reputation. Some foreign embassies in Vientiane also maintain small but professional medical centres, including the **Australian Embassy Clinic** (☎021-353840; ⏲8.30am-5pm Mon-Fri) and the **French Embassy Medical Center** (☎021-214 150).

For any serious conditions, Thailand is the destination of choice. If a medical problem can wait until Bangkok, then all the better, as there are excellent hospitals there.

For medical emergencies that must be treated before reaching Bangkok, ambulances can be arranged from nearby Nong Khai or Udon Thani in Thailand. **Nong Khai Wattana General Hospital** (☎042-465201) in Nong Khai is the closest. The better **Aek Udon Hospital** (☎042-342555) in Udon Thani is an hour further from the border by road.

Buying medication over the counter is not recommended, as fake medications and poorly stored or out-of-date drugs are common in Laos.

Infectious Diseases

Dengue Fever

This mosquito-borne disease is becomingly increasingly problematic throughout Laos, especially in the cities. As there is no vaccine it can only be prevented by avoiding mosquito bites. The mosquito that carries dengue bites day and night, so use insect avoidance measures at all times. Symptoms include high fever, severe headache and body ache (dengue was once known as 'breakbone fever'). Some people develop a rash and diarrhoea. There's no specific treatment, just rest and paracetamol. Do not take aspirin as it increases the likelihood of haemorrhaging. See a doctor to be diagnosed and monitored.

Hepatitis A

A problem throughout the region, this food- and water-borne virus infects the liver, causing jaundice (yellow skin and eyes), nausea and lethargy. There is no specific treatment for hepatitis A, you just need to allow time for the liver to heal. All travellers to Southeast Asia should be vaccinated against hepatitis A.

Hepatitis B

The only sexually transmitted disease that can be prevented by vaccination, hepatitis B is spread by body fluids, including sexual contact. In some parts of Southeast Asia, up to 20% of the population are carriers of hepatitis B, and usually are unaware of this. The long-term consequences can include liver cancer and cirrhosis.

Hepatitis E

Hepatitis E is transmitted through contaminated food and water and has similar symptoms to hepatitis A, but is far less common. It is a severe problem in pregnant women and can result in the death of both mother and baby. There is currently no vaccine; prevention is by following safe eating and drinking guidelines.

HIV

According to Unaids and WHO, Laos remains a 'low HIV prevalence country'. However, it's estimated that only about one fifth of all HIV cases in Laos are actually reported. Heterosexual sex is the main method of transmission in Laos. The use of condoms greatly decreases but does not eliminate the risk of HIV infection.

Malaria

Many parts of Laos, particularly populated areas, have minimal to no risk of malaria, and the risk of side effects from the antimalaria medication may outweigh the risk of getting the disease. For some rural areas, however, the risk of contracting the disease far outweighs the risk of any tablet side effects. Remember that malaria can be fatal.

Malaria is caused by a parasite transmitted by the bite of an infected mosquito. The most important symptom of malaria is fever, but general symptoms such as headache, diarrhoea, cough or chills may also occur. Diagnosis can only be made by taking a blood sample.

Two strategies should be combined to prevent malaria:

HEALTH ADVISORIES

It's usually a good idea to consult your government's travel-health website before departure, if one is available.

Australia Health Advisory (www.smartraveller.gov.au/tips/travelwell.html)

Canada Health Advisory (www.travelhealth.gc.ca)

New Zealand Health Advisory (www.safetravel.govt.nz)

UK Health Advisory (www.fco.gov.uk/en/travel-and-living-abroad/staying-safe)

US Health Advisory (www.cdc.gov/travel)

mosquito avoidance and antimalarial medications. Most people who catch malaria are taking inadequate or no antimalarial medication.

Travellers are advised to prevent mosquito bites by taking these steps:

- Choose accommodation with screens and fans.
- Impregnate clothing with Permethrin in high-risk areas.
- Sleep under a mosquito net impregnated with Permethrin.
- Spray your room with insect repellent before going out for your evening meal.
- Use an insect repellent containing DEET on exposed skin.
- Wear long sleeves and trousers in light colours.

MALARIA MEDICATION

There are a variety of medications available. Lariam (Mefloquine) has received much bad press, some of it justified, some not. This weekly tablet suits many people. Serious side effects are rare but include depression, anxiety, psychosis and seizures. Anyone with a history of depression, anxiety, other psychological disorders or epilepsy should not take Lariam. It is around 90% effective in most parts of Southeast Asia, but there is significant resistance in parts of northern Thailand, Laos and Cambodia. Tablets must be taken for four weeks after leaving the risk area.

Doxycycline, taken daily, is a broad-spectrum antibiotic that has the added benefit of helping to prevent a variety of tropical diseases. The potential side effects include photosensitivity (a tendency to sunburn), thrush in women, indigestion, heartburn, nausea and interference with the contraceptive pill. More serious side effects include ulceration of the oesophagus – you can help prevent this by taking your tablet with a meal and a large glass of water, and never lying down within half an hour of taking it. It must be taken for four weeks after leaving the risk area.

Malarone is a new drug combining Atovaquone and Proguanil. Side effects are uncommon and mild – most commonly nausea and headaches. It is the best tablet for those on short trips to high-risk areas. It must be taken for one week after leaving the risk area.

A final option is to take no preventive medication but to have a supply of emergency medication should you develop the symptoms of malaria. This is less than ideal, and you'll need to get to a good medical facility within 24 hours of developing a fever. If you choose this option the most effective and safest treatment is Malarone (four tablets once daily for three days).

Opisthorchiasis (Liver Flukes)

These are tiny worms that are occasionally present in freshwater fish in Laos. The main risk comes from eating raw or undercooked fish. Travellers should in particular avoid eating uncooked *ƀąh dàak* (an unpasteurised fermented fish used as an accompaniment for many Lao foods) when travelling in rural Laos.

A rarer way to contract liver flukes is by swimming in the Mekong River or its tributaries around Don Khong in the far south of Laos.

At low levels, there are virtually no symptoms at all; at higher levels, an overall fatigue, low-grade fever and swollen or tender liver (or general abdominal pain) are the usual symptoms, along with worms or worm eggs in the faeces. Opisthorchiasis is easily treated with medication.

Rabies

This uniformly fatal disease is spread by the bite or lick of an infected animal, most commonly a dog or monkey. You should seek medical advice immediately after any animal bite and commence post-exposure treatment. Having a pretravel vaccination means the postbite treatment is greatly simplified. If an animal bites you, gently wash the wound with soap and water, and apply iodine based antiseptic. If you are not vaccinated you will need to receive rabies immunoglobulin as soon as possible.

STDs

Sexually transmitted diseases most common in Laos include herpes, warts, syphilis, gonorrhoea and chlamydia. People carrying these diseases often have no signs of infection. Condoms will prevent gonorrhoea and chlamydia but not warts or herpes. If after a sexual encounter you develop any rash, lumps, discharge or pain when passing urine seek immediate medical attention. If you have been sexually active during your travels have an STD check on your return home.

Tuberculosis

Tuberculosis (TB) is very rare in short-term travellers. Medical and aid workers, and long-term travellers who have significant contact with the local population, should take precautions, however. Vaccination is usually only given to children under the age of five, but adults at risk are advised to get pre- and post-travel TB testing. The main symptoms are fever, cough, weight loss, night sweats and tiredness.

Typhoid

This serious bacterial infection is also spread via food and water. It gives a high, slowly progressive fever and headache, and may be accompanied by a dry cough and stomach pain. It is diagnosed by blood tests and treated with antibiotics. Vaccination is recommended for all travellers spending more than a week in Southeast Asia, or travelling outside of the major cities.

Traveller's Diarrhoea

Traveller's diarrhoea is by far the most common problem affecting travellers. Somewhere between 30% and 50% of people will suffer from it within two weeks of starting their trip.

Traveller's diarrhoea is defined as the passage of more than three watery bowel actions within 24 hours, plus at least one other symptom such as fever, cramps, nausea, vomiting or feeling generally unwell.

Treatment consists of staying well hydrated. Rehydration solutions like Gastrolyte are the best for this. Antibiotics such as Norfloxacin, Ciprofloxacin or Azithromycin will kill the bacteria quickly.

Loperamide is just a 'stopper' and doesn't get to the cause of the problem, but can be helpful when taking a long bus ride. Don't take Loperamide if you have a fever, or blood in your stools. Seek medical attention quickly if you do not respond to an appropriate antibiotic.

AMOEBIC DYSENTERY

Amoebic dysentery is very rare in travellers but is often misdiagnosed by poor-quality labs in Southeast Asia. Symptoms are similar to bacterial diarrhoea, ie fever, bloody diarrhoea and generally feeling unwell. You should always seek reliable medical care if you have blood in your diarrhoea. Treatment involves two drugs: Tinidazole or Metronidazole to kill the parasite in your gut and then a second drug to kill the cysts. If left untreated complications such as liver or gut abscesses can occur.

GIARDIASIS

Giardia lamblia is a parasite that is relatively common in travellers. Symptoms include nausea, bloating, excess gas, fatigue and intermittent diarrhoea. The parasite will eventually go away if left untreated but this can take months. The treatment of choice is Tinidazole, with Metronidazole being a second-line option.

Environmental Hazards

Food

Eating in restaurants is the biggest risk factor for contracting traveller's diarrhoea. Ways to avoid it include eating only freshly cooked food, and avoiding shellfish and food that has been sitting around in buffets. Peel all fruit and cook all vegetables. Eat in busy restaurants with a high turnover of customers.

Heat

Many parts of Southeast Asia are hot and humid throughout the year and it takes time to adapt to the climate. Swelling of the feet and ankles is common, as are muscle cramps caused by excessive sweating. Prevent these by avoiding dehydration and excessive activity.

Dehydration is the main contributor to heat exhaustion. Symptoms include feeling weak, headache, irritability, nausea or vomiting, sweaty skin, a fast, weak pulse and a normal or slightly elevated body temperature. Treatment involves getting out of the heat and/or sun, fanning the victim and applying cool wet cloths to the skin and rehydrating with water containing a quarter of a teaspoon of salt per litre. Recovery is usually rapid, though it is common to feel weak for some days afterwards.

Heatstroke is a serious medical emergency. Symptoms come on suddenly and include weakness, nausea, a hot dry body with a body temperature of over 41°C, dizziness, confusion, loss of coordination, seizures and eventually collapse and loss of consciousness. Seek medical help and commence cooling by getting the person out of the heat, removing their clothes, fanning them and applying cool wet cloths or ice to their body, especially to the groin and armpits.

Prickly heat is a common skin rash in the tropics, caused by sweat being trapped under the skin. The result is an itchy rash of tiny lumps. Treat by moving out of the heat and into an air-conditioned area for a few hours and by having cool showers. Locally bought prickly heat powder can be helpful.

Insect Bites & Stings

Bedbugs don't carry disease but their bites are very itchy. They live in the cracks of furniture and walls and then migrate to the bed at night to

DRINKING WATER

- Never drink tap water.
- Bottled water is generally safe, but do check the seal is intact at purchase.
- Boiling water is the most efficient method of purifying it.
- The best chemical purifier is iodine. It should not be used by pregnant women or people who suffer with thyroid problems.
- Water filters should protect against viruses. Ensure your filter has a chemical barrier such as iodine and a small pore size.

feed on you. You can treat the itch with an antihistamine.

Ticks are contracted during walks in rural areas. They are commonly found behind the ears, on the belly and in armpits. If you have had a tick bite and experience symptoms such as a rash, fever or muscle aches, then see a doctor. Doxycycline prevents tick-borne diseases.

Leeches are found in humid forest areas. They do not transmit any disease but their bites are often intensely itchy for weeks afterwards and can easily become infected. Apply an iodine-based antiseptic to any leech bite to help prevent infection.

Bee and wasp stings mainly cause problems for people who are allergic to them. Anyone with a serious bee or wasp allergy should carry an injection of adrenaline for emergency treatment.

Skin Problems

Fungal rashes are common in humid climates. The problem starts as a red patch that slowly spreads and is usually itchy. Treatment involves keeping the skin dry, avoiding chafing and using an antifungal cream such as Clotrimazole or Lamisil.

Cuts and scratches become easily infected in humid climates. Take meticulous care of any cuts and scratches to prevent complications such as abscesses. Immediately wash all wounds and apply antiseptic.

Snakes

Southeast Asia is home to many species of both poisonous and harmless snakes. Assume all snakes are poisonous and never try to catch one. Always wear boots and long pants if walking in an area that may have snakes. First aid in the event of a snakebite involves pressure immobilisation via an elastic bandage firmly wrapped around the affected limb, starting at the bite site and working up towards the chest. The bandage should not be so tight that the circulation is cut off, and the fingers or toes should be kept free so the circulation can be checked. Do not use tourniquets or try to suck the venom out.

Sunburn

Even on a cloudy day, sunburn can occur rapidly. Always use a strong sunscreen, making sure to reapply after a swim, and always wear a wide-brimmed hat and sunglasses outdoors. Avoid lying in the sun during the hottest part of the day. If you are sunburnt stay out of the sun until you have recovered.

Women's Health

In the urban areas of Southeast Asia, supplies of sanitary products are readily available. Birth control options may be limited though so bring adequate supplies. Heat, humidity and antibiotics can all contribute to thrush. Treatment is with antifungal creams and pessaries such as Clotrimazole. A practical alternative is a single tablet of Fluconazole (Diflucan).

Pregnant women should receive specialised advice before travelling. The ideal time to travel is in the second trimester (between 16 and 28 weeks), when the risk of pregnancy-related problems are lowest. Always carry a list of quality medical facilities available at your destination and ensure you continue your standard antenatal care at these facilities. Most of all, ensure travel insurance covers all pregnancy-related possibilities, including premature labour.

Malaria is a high-risk disease during pregnancy.

Traditional Medicine

Throughout Southeast Asia, traditional medical systems are widely practised. There is a big difference between these traditional healing systems and 'folk' medicine. Folk remedies should be avoided, as they often involve rather dubious procedures with potential complications. In comparison, traditional healing systems such as traditional Chinese medicine are well respected, and aspects of them are being increasingly used by Western medical practitioners.

All traditional Asian medical systems identify a vital life force, and see blockage or imbalance as causing disease. Techniques such as herbal medicines, massage, and acupuncture are utilised to bring this vital force back into balance, or to maintain balance. These therapies are best used for treating chronic disease such as chronic fatigue, arthritis, irritable bowel syndrome and some chronic skin conditions. Traditional medicines should be avoided for treating serious acute infections such as malaria.

Language

The official language of Laos is the dialect spoken and written in Vientiane. As an official language, it has successfully become the lingua franca between all Lao and non-Lao ethnic groups in the country.

In Lao, many identical syllables are differentiated by their tone only. Vientiane Lao has six tones. Three of the tones are level (low, mid and high) while three follow pitch inclines (rising, high falling and low falling). All six variations in pitch are relative to the speaker's natural vocal range, ie one person's low tone is not necessarily the same pitch as another person's.

- **low tone** – Produced at the relative bottom of your conversational tonal range – usually flat level, eg dẹe (good).
- **mid tone** – Flat like the low tone, but spoken at the relative middle of your vocal range. No tone mark is used, eg het (do).
- **high tone** – Flat again, this time at the relative top of your vocal range, eg héu·a (boat).
- **rising tone** – Begins a bit below the mid tone and rises to just at or above the high tone, eg săhm (three).
- **high falling tone** – Begins at or above the high tone and falls to the mid level, eg sôw (morning).
- **low falling tone** – Begins at about the mid level and falls to the level of the low tone, eg kòw (rice).

> **WANT MORE?**
>
> For in-depth language information and handy phrases, check out Lonely Planet's *Lao Phrasebook*. You'll find it at **shop.lonelyplanet.com**, or you can buy Lonely Planet's iPhone phrasebooks at the Apple App Store.

There is no official method of transliterating the Lao language, though the public and private sectors in Laos are gradually moving towards a more internationally recognisable system along the lines of Royal Thai General Transcription (RTGS), since Thai and Lao have very similar writing and sound systems. This book uses a custom system of transliteration.

In our coloured pronunciation guides, the hyphens indicate syllable breaks within words, eg àng-gít (English). Some syllables are further divided with a dot to help you pronounce compound vowels, eg kĕe·an (write).

The pronunciation of vowels goes like this: i as in 'it'; ee as in 'feet'; ai as in 'aisle'; ah as the 'a' in 'father'; a as the short 'a' in 'about'; aa as in 'bad'; air as in 'air'; er as in 'fur'; eu as in 'sir'; u as in 'put'; oo as in 'food'; ow as in 'now'; or as in 'jaw'; o as in 'phone'; oh as in 'toe'; ee·a as in 'Ian'; oo·a as in 'tour'; ew as in 'yew'; and oy as in 'boy'.

Most consonants correspond to their English counterparts. The exceptions are đ (a hard 't' sound, a bit like 'dt') and ƀ (a hard 'p' sound, a bit like 'bp').

BASICS

Hello.	ສະບາຍດີ	sábạ̀i-dĕe
Goodbye.	ສະບາຍດີ	sábạ̀i-dĕe
Excuse me.	ຂໍໂທດ	kŏr tôht
Sorry.	ຂໍໂທດ	kŏr tôht
Please.	ກະລຸນາ	ga-lú-náh
Thank you.	ຂອບໃຈ	kòrp jại
Yes./No.	ແມນ/ບໍ່	maan/bor

How are you?
ສະບາຍດີບໍ່ — sábại-dĕe bor

I'm fine, and you?
ສະບາຍດີ ເຈົ້າເດ — sábại-dĕe jôw dâir

What's your name?
ເຈົ້າຊື່ຫຍັງ jôw seu nyǎng

My name is ...
ຂ້ອຍຊື່ ... kòy seu ...

Do you speak English?
ເຈົ້າປາກ jôw ɓàhk
ພາສາອັງກິດໄດ້ບໍ່ páh-sǎh ąng·kít dâi bor

I don't understand.
ບໍ່ເຂົ້າໃຈ bor kòw jąi

ACCOMMODATION

hotel	ໂຮງແຮມ	hóhng háam
guesthouse	ຫໍຮັບແຂກ	hŏr hap káak

Do you have a room?
ມີຫ້ອງບໍ່ mée hòrng bor

single room
ຫ້ອງນອນຕຽງດຽວ hòrng nórn đěe·ang dee·o

double room
ຫ້ອງນອນຕຽງຄູ່ hòrng nórn đěe·ang koo

How much ...?	... ເທົ່າໃດ	... tow dąi
per night	ຄືນລະ	kéun-la
per week	ອາທິດລະ	ąh-tit-la

air-con	ແອເຢັນ	ąa yen
bathroom	ຫ້ອງນ້ຳ	hòrng nâm
fan	ພັດລົມ	pat lóm
hot water	ນ້ຳຮ້ອນ	nâm hôrn

DIRECTIONS

Where is the ...?
... ຢູ່ໃສ ... yòo sǎi

Which (street) is this?
ບອນນີ້ (ຖະໜົນ) ຫຍັງ born nêe (ta-nŏn) nyǎng

How far?
ໄກເທົ່າໃດ kąi tow dąi

Turn left/right.
ລ້ຽວຊ້າຍ/ຂວາ lêe·o sâi/kwǎh

straight ahead
ໄປຊື່ໆ ɓąi seu-seu

EATING & DRINKING

What do you have that's special?
ມີຫຍັງພິເສດບໍ່ mée nyǎng pi-sèt bor

I'd like to try that.
ຂ້ອຍຢາກລອງກິນເບິ່ງ kòy yàhk lórng gın berng

I eat only vegetables.
ຂ້ອຍກິນແຕ່ຜັກ kòy gın đaa pák

I (don't) like it hot and spicy.
(ບໍ່) ມັກເຜັດ (bor) mak pét

I didn't order this.
ຂ້ອຍບໍ່ໄດ້ສັ່ງແນວນີ້ kòy bor dâi sang náa·ou nêe

Please bring the bill.
ຂໍແຊັກແດ້ kŏr saak daa

Key Words

bottle	ແກ້ວ	kâa·ou
bowl	ຖ້ວຍ	tòo·ay
chopsticks	ໄມ້ທູ່	mâi too
fork	ສ້ອມ	sôrm
glass	ຈອກ	jòrk
knife	ມີດ	mêet
menu	ລາຍການ ອາຫານ	lái-gąhn ąh-hǎhn
plate	ຈານ	jąhn
spoon	ບ່ວງ	boo·ang

Meat & Fish

beef	ຊີ້ນງົວ	sèen ngóo·a
chicken	ໄກ່	kai
crab	ປູ	ɓọo
fish	ປາ	ɓąh
pork	ຊີ້ນໝູ	sèen mŏo
seafood	ອາຫານທະເລ	ąh-hǎhn ta-láir
shrimp/prawn	ກຸ້ງ	gûng

Fruit & Vegetables

banana	ໝາກກ້ວຍ	màhk gôo·ay
bean sprouts	ຖົ່ວງອກ	too·a ngôrk
beans	ຖົ່ວ	too·a
cabbage	ກະລຳປີ	gá-lam ɓẹe
cauliflower	ກະລຳປີດອກ	gá-lam ɓẹe dòrk
coconut	ໝາກພ້າວ	màhk pôw
cucumber	ໝາກແຕງ	màhk đạang
eggplant	ໝາກເຂືອ	màhk kěua
garlic	ຫົວຜັກທຽມ	hŏo·a pák tée·am

green beans	ຖົ່ວຍາວ	too·a nyów
guava	ໝາກສີດາ	màhk sěe-dạh
jackfruit	ໝາກມີ້	màhk mêe
lettuce	ຜັກສະລັດ	pák sá-lat
lime	ໝາກນາວ	màhk nów
longan	ໝາກຍຳໄຍ	màhk nyám nyái
lychee	ໝາກລິ້ນຈີ່	màhk lîn-jee
mandarin	ໝາກກ້ຽງ	màhk gêe·ang
mango	ໝາກມ່ວງ	màhk moo·ang
onion (bulb)	ຫົວຜັກບົວ	hŏoa pák boo·a
onion (green)	ຕົ້ນຜັກບົວ	đôn pák boo·a
papaya	ໝາກຫຸ່ງ	màhk hung
peanuts	ໝາກຖົ່ວດິນ	màhk too·a dịn
pineapple	ໝາກນັດ	màhk nat
potato	ມັນຝລັ່ງ	mán fa-lang
rambutan	ໝາກເງາະ	màhk ngo
sugarcane	ອ້ອຍ	ôy
tomato	ໝາກເລັ່ນ	màhk len
vegetables	ຜັກ	pak
watermelon	ໝາກໂມ	màhk móh

Other

bread (plain)	ເຂົ້າຈີ່	kòw jẹe
butter	ເບີ	bẹr
chilli	ໝາກເຜັດ	màhk pét
egg	ໄຂ່	kai
fish sauce	ນ້ຳປາ	nâm ɓạh
ice	ນ້ຳກ້ອນ	nâm gôrn
rice	ເຂົ້າ	kòw
salt	ເກືອ	gẹua
soy sauce	ນ້ຳສະອີ້ວ	nâm sá-éw
sugar	ນ້ຳຕານ	nâm-đạhn

Drinks

beer	ເບຍ	bẹe·a
coffee	ກາແຟ	gạh-fáir
draught beer	ເບຍສດ	bẹe·a sót
drinking water	ນ້ຳດື່ມ	nâm deum
milk (plain)	ນ້ຳນມ	nâm nóm
orange juice	ນ້ຳໝາກກ້ຽງ	nâm màhk gêe·ang
rice whisky	ເຫຼົ້າລາວ	lòw-lów
soda water	ນ້ຳໂສດາ	nâm sŏh-dạh
tea	ຊາ	sáh
yoghurt	ນມສົ້ມ	nóm sòm

EMERGENCIES

Help!	ຊ່ວຍແດ່	soo·ay daa
Go away!	ໄປເດີ້	ɓại dêr

Call a doctor!
ຊ່ວຍຕາມຫາໝໍ ໃຫ້ແດ່ — soo·ay đạhm hăh mŏr hài daa

Call the police!
ຊ່ວຍເອີ້ນຕຳລວດແດ່ — soo·ay êrn đam-lòo·at daa

Where are the toilets?
ຫ້ອງນ້ຳຢູ່ໃສ — hòrng nâm yoo săi

I'm lost.
ຂ້ອຍຫລົງທາງ — kòy lŏng táhng

I'm not well.
ຂ້ອຍບໍ່ສະບາຍ — kòy bor sá-bại

SHOPPING & SERVICES

I'm looking for ...
ຂ້ອຍຊອກຫາ ... — kòy sòrk hăh ...

How much (for) ...?
... ເທົ່າໃດ — ... tow dại

The price is very high.
ລາຄາແພງຫລາຍ — láh-káh páang lăi

I want to change money.
ຂ້ອຍຢາກປ່ຽນເງິນ — kòy yàhk ɓee·an ngérn

bank	ທະນາຄານ	ta-náh-káhn
bookshop	ຮ້ານຂາຍປຶ້ມ	hâhn kăi ɓeum
pharmacy	ຮ້ານຂາຍຢາ	hâhn kăi yạh
post office	ໄປສະນີ (ໂຮງສາຍ)	ɓại-sá-née (hóhng săi)

TIME & DATES

What time is it?
ເວລາຈັກໂມງ — wáir-láh ják móhng

this morning	ເຊົ້ານີ້	sôw nêe
this afternoon	ບ່າຍນີ້	bai nêe
tonight	ຄືນນີ້	kéun nêe

yesterday	ມື້ວານນີ້	mêu wáhn nêe
today	ມື້ນີ້	mêu nêe
tomorrow	ມື້ອື່ນ	mêu eun

Monday	ວັນຈັນ	wán jạn
Tuesday	ວັນອັງຄານ	wán ạng-káhn
Wednesday	ວັນພຸດ	wán put
Thursday	ວັນພະຫັດ	wán pa-hát
Friday	ວັນສຸກ	wán súk
Saturday	ວັນເສົາ	wán sŏw
Sunday	ວັນອາທິດ	wán ạh-tit

TRANSPORT

boat	ເຮືອ	héu·a
bus	ລົດເມ	lot máir
minivan	ລົດຕູ້	lot đôo
plane	ເຮືອບິນ	héu·a bĭn

airport
ສະໜາມບິນ — sá-năhm bĭn

bus station
ສະຖານີລົດປະຈຳທາງ — sa-tăh-nee lot ɓá-jạm táhng

bus stop
ບ່ອນຈອດລົດປະຈຳທາງ — born jòrt lot ɓá-jạm táhng

taxi stand
ບ່ອນຈອດລົດແທກຊີ — born jòrt lot taak-sêe

I want to go to ...
ຂ້ອຍຢາກໄປ ... — kòy yàhk ɓại ...

I'd like a ticket.
ຂ້ອຍຢາກໄດ້ປີ້ — kòy yàhk dâi ɓêe

Where do we get on the boat?
ລົງເຮືອຢູ່ໃສ — lóng héu·a yoo săi

What time will the ... leave?
... ຈະອອກຈັກໂມງ — ... já òrk ják móhng

What time does it arrive there?
ຈະໄປຮອດພຸ້ນຈັກໂມງ — já ɓai hôrt pûn ják móhng

Can I sit here?
ນັ່ງບ່ອນນີ້ໄດ້ບໍ່ — nang born nêe dâi bor

Please tell me when we arrive in ...
ເວລາຮອດ ... ບອກຂ້ອຍແດ່ — wáir-láh hôrt ... bòrk kòy daa

Stop here.
ຈອດຢູ່ນີ້ — jòrt yoo nêe

Numbers

1	ໜຶ່ງ	neung
2	ສອງ	sŏrng
3	ສາມ	săhm
4	ສີ່	see
5	ຫ້າ	hàh
6	ຫກ	hók
7	ເຈັດ	jét
8	ແປດ	ɓàat
9	ເກົ້າ	gôw
10	ສິບ	síp
11	ສິບເອັດ	síp-ét
12	ສິບສອງ	síp-sŏrng
20	ຊາວ	sów
21	ຊາວເອັດ	sów-ét
22	ຊາວສອງ	sów-sŏrng
30	ສາມສິບ	săhm-síp
40	ສີ່ສິບ	see-síp
50	ຫ້າສິບ	hàh-síp
60	ຫກສິບ	hók-síp
70	ເຈັດສິບ	jét-síp
80	ແປດສິບ	ɓàat-síp
90	ເກົ້າສິບ	gôw-síp
100	ຮ້ອຍ	hôy
200	ສອງຮ້ອຍ	sŏrng hôy
1000	ພັນ	pán
10,000	ໝື່ນ(ສິບພັນ)	meun (síp-pán)
100,000	ແສນ(ຮ້ອຍພັນ)	săan (hôy pán)
1,000,000	ລ້ານ	lâhn

I'd like to hire a ...
ຂ້ອຍຢາກເຊົ່າ ... — kòy yàhk sôw ...

bicycle	ລົດຖີບ	lot tèep
car	ລົດ(ໂອໂຕ)	lot (ŏh-đŏh)
motorcycle	ລົດຈັກ	lot ják
passenger truck	ສອງແຖວ	sŏrng-tăa·ou
pedicab	ສາມລໍ້	săhm-lôr
taxi	ລົດແທກຊີ	lot tâak-sée
tuk-tuk	ຕຸ໊ກ ຕຸ໊ກ	đúk-đúk

GLOSSARY

ąahaan – food

anatta – Buddhist concept of nonsubstantiality or nonessentiality of reality, ie no permanent 'soul'

anicca – Buddhist concept of impermanence, the transience of all things

Asean – Association of South East Asian Nations

bâhn – the general Lao word for house or village; written Ban on maps

bąhsĕe – sometimes spelt basi or *baci;* a ceremony in which the 32 *kwăn* (guardian spirits) are symbolically bound to the participant for health and safety

baht – *(bàht)* Thai unit of currency, commonly negotiable in Laos; also a Lao unit of measure equal to 15g

BCEL – Banque pour le Commerce Extérieur Lao; in English, Lao Foreign Trade Bank

bęea – beer; *bęea sót* is draught beer

bun – pronounced *bųn,* often spelt boun; a festival; also spiritual 'merit' earned through good actions or religious practices

corvée – enforced, unpaid labour

đàht –waterfall; also *nâm tók;* written Tat on maps

đalàht – market; *talàat sâo* is the morning market; *talàat mèut* is the free, or 'black', market; written Talat on maps

Don – pronounced *dąwn;* island

dukkha – Buddhist concept of suffering, unsatisfactoriness, disease

falang – from the Lao *falang-sèht* or 'French'; Western, a Westerner

fĕr – rice noodles, one of the most common dishes in Laos

hăi – jar

héua – boat

héua hăhng nyáo – longtail boat

héua pái – row boat

héua wái – speedboat

hŏr đąi – monastery building dedicated to the storage of the Tripitaka (Buddhist scriptures)

hùay – stream; written Huay on maps

Jataka – (Pali-Sanskrit) mythological stories of the Buddha's past lives; *sáa-dók* in Lao

jęen hór – Lao name for the Muslim Yunnanese who live in Northern Laos

jęhdii – a Buddhist stupa; also written Chedi

jumbo – a motorised three-wheeled taxi, sometimes called tuk-tuk

káan – a wind instrument devised of a double row of bamboo-like reeds fitted into a hardwood soundbox and made air-tight with beeswax

kanŏm – pastry or sweet

kip – pronounced gèep; Lao unit of currency

kòw – rice

kòw jee – bread

kòw nĕeo – sticky rice, the Lao staple food

kóo-bąh – Lao Buddhist monk

kwăn – guardian spirits

láhp – a spicy Lao-style salad of minced meat, poultry or fish

lák méuang – city pillar

lám wóng – 'circle dance', the traditional folk dance of Laos, as common at discos as at festivals

Lao Issara – Lao resistance movement against the French in the 1940s

lòw-lów – distilled rice liquor

Lao Loum – 'lowland Lao', ethnic groups belonging to the Lao–Thai Diaspora

Lao Soung – 'highland Lao', hill tribes who make their residence at higher altitudes, such as Hmong, Mien; also spelt Lao Sung

Lao Thoeng – 'upland Lao', a loose affiliation of mostly Mon-Khmer peoples who live on midaltitude mountain slopes

lingam – a pillar or phallus symbolic of Shiva, common in Khmer-built temples

LNTA – Lao National Tourism Administration

LPDR – Lao People's Democratic Republic

LPRP – Lao People's Revolutionary Party

maa nâm – literally, water mother; river; usually shortened to *nâm* with river names, as in Nam Khong (Mekong River)

meuang – pronounced *méuang;* district or town; in ancient times a city state; often written Muang on maps

moo bâhn – village

móoan – fun, which the Lao believe should be present in all activities

mŏr lám – Lao folk musical theatre tradition; roughly translates as 'master of verse'

Muang – see *meuang*

naga – *nâa-kha* in Lao; mythical water serpent common to Lao–Thai legends and art

náhng sée – Buddhist nuns

náirn – Buddhist novice monk; also referred to as *samanera*

nâm – water; can also mean 'river', 'juice', 'sauce': anything of a watery nature

NGO – nongovernmental organisation, typically involved in the foreign-aid industry

nibbana – 'cooling', the extinction of mental defilements; the ultimate goal of Theravada Buddhism

NPA – National Protected Area, a classification assigned to 20 wildlife areas throughout Laos

NVA – North Vietnamese Army

ƀąh – fish

ƀąh dàak – fermented fish sauce, a common accompaniment to Lao food

pa – holy image, usually referring to a Buddha; venerable

pàh – cloth

pàh bẹeang – shoulder sash worn by men

pàh nung – sarong, worn by almost all Lao women

pàh salóng – sarong, worn by Lao men

Pathet Lao – literally, Country of Laos; both a general term for the country and a common journalistic reference to the military arm of the early Patriotic Lao Front (a cover for the Lao People's Party); often abbreviated to PL

Pha Lak Pha Lam – the Lao version of the Indian epic, the Ramayana

phúu – hill or mountain; also spelt phu

săhláh lóng tám – a *sala* (hall) where monks and lay people listen to Buddhist teachings

săhm-lór – a three-wheeled pedicab

sakai-làap – alternative name for jumbo in southern Laos due to the perceived resemblance to a space capsule (Skylab)

sala – pronounced *săa-láa;* an open-sided shelter; a hall

samana – pronounced *săamanáa;* 'seminar'; euphemism for labour and re-education camps established after the 1975 Revolution

samanera – Buddhist novice monk; also referred to as náirn

se – also spelt *xe;* Southern Laos term for river; hence Se Don means Don River and Pakse means *pàak* (mouth) of the river

sĕe – sacred; also spelt *si*

shophouse – two-storey building designed to have a shop on the ground floor and a residence above

sĭm – ordination hall in a Lao Buddhist monastery; named after the *sima,* (pronounced *siimáa*) or sacred stone tablets, which mark off the grounds dedicated for this purpose

soi – lane

sŏrngtăaou – literally two-rows; a passenger truck

taak-sée – taxi

tanŏn – street/road; often spelt Thanon on maps; shortened to 'Th' as street is to 'St'

tâht – Buddhist stupa or reliquary; written That on maps

tuk-tuk – see jumbo

UXO – unexploded ordnance

Viet Minh – the Vietnamese forces who fought for Indochina's independence from the French

vipassana – insight meditation

wat – Lao Buddhist monastery

wihăhn – (Pali-Sanskrit vihara) a temple hall

Behind the Scenes

SEND US YOUR FEEDBACK

Things change – prices go up, schedules change, good places go bad and bad places go bankrupt. So if you find things better or worse, recently opened or long since closed, or you just want to tell us what you loved or loathed about this book, please get in touch and help make the next edition even more accurate and useful. We love to hear from readers – your comments keep us on our toes and our well-travelled team reads every word. Although we can't reply individually to postal submissions, we always guarantee that your feedback goes straight to the appropriate authors, in time for the next edition. Each person who sends us information is thanked in the next edition – the most useful submissions are rewarded with a selection of digital PDF chapters.

Visit **lonelyplanet.com/contact** to submit your updates and suggestions or to ask for help. Our award-winning website also features inspirational travel stories, news and discussions.

Note: We may edit, reproduce and incorporate your comments in Lonely Planet products such as guidebooks, websites and digital products, so let us know if you don't want your comments reproduced or your name acknowledged. For a copy of our privacy policy visit lonelyplanet.com/privacy.

OUR READERS

Many thanks to the travellers who used the last edition and wrote to us with helpful hints, useful advice and interesting anecdotes:

A Manuela Arigoni, Núria Arnau, Victor Ashe **B** Chris Backe, Susanne Böhme, Amelia Borofsky, Werner Bruyninx **C** Christian Cantos, Raphaèle Caubel, Jean-Daniel Champod, Dona Chilcoat, Michael Chow, **D** T. de Ruijter, Renaud Delaplace, Toon Dewerchin, Emile Du Moulin, Pavel Dudek, Uwe Düffert **F** Eric Feigenbaum, Kennet Fischer, Orly Flax, Keith Forward, Oscar Fowelin, Ann Fransen **G** Nani Gadd, John Garcia, **H** Martin Hellwagner, Morgan Herrick, Wendy Hodge, Dennis Hoffart, Uli Holzmueller **I** Neal Irvine **J** Joris Jan Voermans **K** John Key, Laura Kingdon, Matthias Kläy, Christoph Knop, Patrick Kooijman **L** David Lempert, Rhonda Lerner, Ron Lister, Peter Lloyd, Jean Lobert **M** Massimo Mera, Christian Mogeltoft, Natalie Moyen, David Murphy **N** Anita Newton, Elisabeth Nielsen **O** David Owens **P** Elizabeth Purdy **R** Torben Retboll, Kenta Richard Nakama, Paul Roth, Beth Roughsedge **S** Tini Samel, Karin Schaechtele, Erin Schneider, Sebastian Schuster, Damian Seagar, Stephanie Sievers, Kate Simer, Dirk Slootmans, Brian Smith, Sam Staelens, Debbie Sturgess, Annette Suter, Teoh Sze Soong **T** Jerry Taylor, Eline Thijssen **O** Arie van Oosterwijk **V** Michael & Yvonne Vintiner **W** Jon Weis, Kate Woolf.

AUTHOR THANKS

Nick Ray

A huge and heartfelt thanks to the people of Laos, whose warmth, humour, stoicism and spirit make it a happy yet humbling place to be. Biggest thanks are reserved for my wife Kulikar Sotho, as without her support and encouragement the adventures would not be possible. And to our children Julian and Belle for enlivening our lives immeasurably.

Thanks to fellow travellers and residents, friends and contacts in Laos who have helped shape my knowledge. Thanks also to my co-authors and friends Rich Waters and Greg Bloom for going the extra mile to ensure this is a worthy new edition.

Finally, thanks to the Lonely Planet team who have worked on this title.

Greg Bloom

The biggest thank you goes out to Lucy, my observant wing-woman on the Southern Swing ride from Pakse to Attapeu and back. On the road, tips were provided by Renaud in Pakse, while Lance and Donna in Don Det provided both on-the-ground and remote assistance. A special shout-out to diligent tourist officers Toui of Kiet Ngong (Toui) and Kouka of Tat Lo – the *only* tourist information centres in southern Laos that were open over Pi Mai!

Richard Waters

Special thanks go to Alex for his zeal and generosity, as well as to Vianney for his much-needed wisdom, Elizabeth for her fiery Bloody Marys at the inspiring Icon, Mr Somkiad for his patience, DC for fixing my bike, Thierry for the sturdy Baja, Lao Heritage Hotel, Scandi Bakery for keeping me round, Don Duvall for his excellent help, Welshman Tom, Adri Berger, and as ever to the Lao people who make me wonder why the rest of the planet can't possess a little more of their gentle essence.

ACKNOWLEDGMENTS

Climate map data adapted from Peel MC, Finlayson BL & McMahon TA (2007) 'Updated World Map of the Köppen-Geiger Climate Classification', Hydrology and Earth System Sciences, 11, 163344

Cover Photograph: Monks at Tat Kuang Si, Luang Prabang, Laos; Na Gen Imaging/Getty Images.

THIS BOOK

This guidebook was commissioned in Lonely Planet's Melbourne office, and produced by the following:

Commissioning Editor Ilaria Walker

Coordinating Editors Elin Berglund, Paul Harding

Senior Cartographers Corey Hutchison, Diana Von Holdt

Coordinating Layout Designer Katherine Marsh

Managing Editors Sasha Baskett, Bruce Evans

Senior Editor Karyn Noble

Managing Layout Designer Jane Hart

Assisting Editors Laura Gibb, Helen Koehne, Gabrielle Stefanos

Assisting Cartographers Julie Dodkins, Jennifer Johnston

Cover Research Naomi Parker

Internal Image Research Kylie McLaughlin

Language Content Branislava Vladisavljevic

Thanks to Anita Banh, Ryan Evans, Larissa Frost, Chris Girdler, Genesys India, Jouve India, Trent Paton, Dianne Schallmeiner, Kerrianne Southway, Gerard Walker

Index

Map Pages **000**
Photo Pages **000**

L

M

N

O

P

R

Map Pages **000**
Photo Pages **000**

Map Legend

Sights
- Beach
- Bird Sanctuary
- Buddhist
- Castle/Palace
- Christian
- Confucian
- Hindu
- Islamic
- Jain
- Jewish
- Monument
- Museum/Gallery/Historic Building
- Ruin
- Sento Hot Baths/Onsen
- Shinto
- Sikh
- Taoist
- Winery/Vineyard
- Zoo/Wildlife Sanctuary
- Other Sight

Activities, Courses & Tours
- Bodysurfing
- Diving
- Canoeing/Kayaking
- Course/Tour
- Skiing
- Snorkelling
- Surfing
- Swimming/Pool
- Walking
- Windsurfing
- Other Activity

Sleeping
- Sleeping
- Camping

Eating
- Eating

Drinking & Nightlife
- Drinking & Nightlife
- Cafe

Entertainment
- Entertainment

Shopping
- Shopping

Information
- Bank
- Embassy/Consulate
- Hospital/Medical
- Internet
- Police
- Post Office
- Telephone
- Toilet
- Tourist Information
- Other Information

Geographic
- Beach
- Hut/Shelter
- Lighthouse
- Lookout
- Mountain/Volcano
- Oasis
- Park
- Pass
- Picnic Area
- Waterfall

Population
- Capital (National)
- Capital (State/Province)
- City/Large Town
- Town/Village

Transport
- Airport
- Border crossing
- Bus
- Cable car/Funicular
- Cycling
- Ferry
- Metro station
- Monorail
- Parking
- Petrol station
- Subway station
- Taxi
- Train station/Railway
- Tram
- Underground station
- Other Transport

Note: Not all symbols displayed above appear on the maps in this book

Routes
- Tollway
- Freeway
- Primary
- Secondary
- Tertiary
- Lane
- Unsealed road
- Road under construction
- Plaza/Mall
- Steps
- Tunnel
- Pedestrian overpass
- Walking Tour
- Walking Tour detour
- Path/Walking Trail

Boundaries
- International
- State/Province
- Disputed
- Regional/Suburb
- Marine Park
- Cliff
- Wall

Hydrography
- River, Creek
- Intermittent River
- Canal
- Water
- Dry/Salt/Intermittent Lake
- Reef

Areas
- Airport/Runway
- Beach/Desert
- Cemetery (Christian)
- Cemetery (Other)
- Glacier
- Mudflat
- Park/Forest
- Sight (Building)
- Sportsground
- Swamp/Mangrove

OUR STORY

A beat-up old car, a few dollars in the pocket and a sense of adventure. In 1972 that's all Tony and Maureen Wheeler needed for the trip of a lifetime – across Europe and Asia overland to Australia. It took several months, and at the end – broke but inspired – they sat at their kitchen table writing and stapling together their first travel guide, *Across Asia on the Cheap*. Within a week they'd sold 1500 copies. Lonely Planet was born.

Today, Lonely Planet has offices in Melbourne, London, Oakland and Delhi, with more than 600 staff and writers. We share Tony's belief that 'a great guidebook should do three things: inform, educate and amuse'.

OUR WRITERS

Nick Ray

Coordinating Author, Luang Prabang & Around, Northern Laos A Londoner of sorts, Nick comes from Watford, the sort of town that makes you want to travel. He currently lives in Phnom Penh and has written for countless guidebooks on the Mekong region, including Lonely Planet's *Cambodia* and *Vietnam*, as well as *Southeast Asia on a Shoestring*. When not writing, he is often out exploring the remote parts of the region as a location scout or line producer for the world of television and film, including anything from *Top Gear Vietnam* to *Tomb Raider*. Luang Prabang is one of his favourite places on earth and he was thrilled to finally explore the fabled Vieng Xai Caves that once sheltered the Pathet Lao.

Greg Bloom

Southern Laos Greg first visited Laos as a backpacker in 1997, journeying from Vientiane to Muang Sing via the lonely backwaters of Vang Vieng and Luang Prabang. Finally returning 15 years later he is happy to report that, while thoroughly discovered, the country has lost none of its indolent charm. These days Greg lives in Cambodia. He has written close to 20 books for Lonely Planet, mostly about Southeast Asia and the former Soviet Union. Read about his trips at www.mytripjournal.com/bloomblogs.

Read more about Greg at:
lonelyplanet.com/members/gbloom4

Richard Waters

Vientiane & Around, Central Laos Richard is an award-winning journalist and photographer and regularly works for The Independent, Sunday Times, Wanderlust and National Geographic Traveller. He lives with his fiancée and two kids in the Cotswolds. He has just published his Lao-set travel thriller Black Buddha on Kindle.

CONTRIBUTING AUTHORS

Professor Martin Stuart-Fox wrote the History chapter. He is Emeritus Professor at University of Queensland and has written extensively about Laos' history and politics.

Published by Lonely Planet Publications Pty Ltd
ABN 36 005 607 983
8th edition – February 2014
ISBN 978 1 74179 954 5

10 9 8 7 6 5 4 3 2 1
Printed in China